WOMEN IN LITERATURE
Life Stages Through Stories, Poems, and Plays

Sandra Eagleton, Ph.D.

PRENTICE HALL
Englewood Cliffs, New Jersey 07632

Library of Congress Cataloging-in-Publication Data

Eagleton, Sandra (date)
  Women in literature.

  Includes index.
  1. Women—Literary collections.   2. American literature—Women authors.   3. English literature—Women
authors.   I. Title.
PS509.W6E24   1987   808.8´0352042   87-13932
ISBN 0-13-962283-7

Cover painting: Mary Cassatt, *Portrait of an Elderly Lady,* c.1887, National Gallery of
Art, Washington, D.C., Chester Dale Collection.

Editorial/production supervision and interior design: Laura Cleveland
Cover design: Allen Moore & Associates
Manufacturing buyer: Ray Keating

© 1988 by Prentice-Hall, Inc.
A division of Simon & Schuster
Englewood Cliffs, New Jersey 07632

Printed in the United States of America

10   9   8   7   6   5   4   3   2   1

ISBN 0-13-962283-7

Prentice-Hall International (UK) Limited, *London*
Prentice-Hall of Australia Pty. Limited, *Sydney*
Prentice-Hall Canada Inc., *Toronto*
Prentice-Hall Hispanoamericana, S.A., *Mexico*
Prentice-Hall of India Private Limited, *New Delhi*
Prentice-Hall of Japan, Inc., *Tokyo*
Simon & Schuster Asia Pte. Ltd., *Singapore*
Editora Prentice-Hall do Brasil, Ltda., *Rio de Janeiro*

CONTENTS

v

PREFACE

Throughout the ages literature by and about women has contributed significantly to the development of the genres of fiction, poetry, and drama. Yet, a student once remarking on my collection of women's literature responded, "So many books . . . and nothing to read." Paradoxically, this anthology responds to that complaint, while it denies its validity: great literature is not dull, especially when it is not presented as simply a list of famous names and titles to be mastered as an academic exercise. Certain archetypal themes and images that transcend all times and all cultures are discernible in the most abstruse as well as the most accessible works of art.

The genesis of this collection is the premise that the desire to read literature is rooted in the desire to know oneself—the crucial parts of oneself strengthened by the central experiences of childhood, adolescence, adulthood, old age, and death. To ignore the full range of these life stages is to forget that women and men are composites of their pasts, presents, and futures.

Thus, a unique feature of this text is its organization according to life stages, a popular topic in both academic and general readership. A related feature is that it deals with childhood and adolescence, areas often ignored by other texts that deal largely with adult experiences. Discussing women's literature from the perspective of aging allows us to say something new about old familiar stories, and to provide a natural way of introducing unfamiliar works by less well-known women authors. An important quality of this anthology is its connectedness; seemingly disparate works are drawn together in a coherent framework less arbitrary than, for example, chronological organization or arrangement by genre or nationality alone.

Class-tested in manuscript form, the book contains 31 short stories, 49 poems, 2 novel excerpts, and 4 plays chronicling each stage of women's lives, with sections on childhood, adolescence, adulthood (work, family, society), old age, and death. There are works from many time periods and cultures, with representative literature from women writing about alternative life styles.

The interrelationships and diversities among the works are discussed in the introductions to each life stage and each section of fiction, poetry, and drama. Additional apparatus includes discussion questions at the end of each section, a selected bibliography at the end of the book, and an index of authors and titles. Further, each individual story is preceded by a brief comment to stimulate interest, and is followed by a series of questions "For Further Exploration" (referring to at least one other work on a similar theme). The questions are intended to suggest further connections among the works, and can be used by the instructor for discussion, or by the student for essay topics.

In addition to women-in-literature courses, courses for which this text might be helpful are women's studies, sociology, or psychology, as well as special topics such as adolescence, gerontology, or death studies. Although the text was designed for a college audience, it is also appropriate for use on the high-school level because of the many selections on different levels from which to choose, and the strong apparatus for student help.

My impulse in creating this collection was to stimulate readers and to let them know that literature by and about women exists and is worth reading not only for its literary value, but also for its particular insights into women's lives. During speaking engagements, I have been constantly surprised to learn how few women authors audiences can name, and yet how eager both men and women are to discover literature written by and about women in various life stages.

This anthology asserts that women everywhere have been and will continue writing about subjects of universal importance, deserving both popular and critical attention. The "For Further Exploration" references to extended reading possibilities promote the integral assumption of this book: we are all searching for great works that may be lying on library shelves but appear at first glance to have little to do with our own lives or our previous reading.

The impulse we all hope to engender is similar to Eudora Welty's experience revealed in "A Sweet Devouring," in which she describes weekly childhood trips to the library on her bicycle to find writers with multiple volumes to satisfy her voracious appetite for literature. The great joy when she discovers an author with many volumes and fascinating stories (Mark Twain) is the joy we hope that students will discover in reading Welty's own wide-ranging works, and the numerous works by the over 80 other authors represented here.

In preparing this anthology, I am especially grateful to a few individuals for their many contributions: Carl Van Buskirk, who edited each draft of the manuscript and provided unfailing support, and the following reviewers, who provided excellent assistance in determining selections and focus: Lisa Albrecht, University of Minnesota; Joseph Boles, Northern Arizona University; Gwen Constant, West Valley Community College; Ruth V. Elcan, Holyoke Community College; Joanne H. McCarthy, Tacoma Community College; Nan Nowik, Denison University; Jo Ann Pevoto, College of the Mainland; Susan Squier, State University of New York at Stony Brook; and Barbara F. Waxman, University of North Carolina—Wilmington.

Helpful advice on research and concepts in life-stage psychology was provided by Nancy Lane Palés, Maxine E. Lentz, Albert Petitpas, Phyllis Barrett, Judith Waldron, and Rhoda Spiro; thanks are also due to Henry Dutcher, Bethany Nichols, John Blake, and Richard Kelly for their help in researching and preparing biographies and bibliographies; and to Beth Van Buskirk, Kim Osborne, and Kim Wolcott for help in obtaining permissions. I am also grateful to my parents Martha and Arthur Eagleton, to my sister Martha Eagleton Begalla, and to James Begalla for their continued support; and to Philip Miller at Prentice-Hall for his editorial expertise and unflagging enthusiasm for the project.

Sandra Eagleton

INTRODUCTION

WOMEN IN LITERATURE

What roles have women played as authors and as characters in literature throughout the ages? What effect has literary criticism had on the reception of women writers in the past and present? Are the subjects or styles of women's writings in any sense different from writing by men?

To begin a study of stories, poems, and plays by and about women, it is necessary to explore these critical issues that arise again and again in discussions of women's literature. In considering these questions and analyzing the works that follow, we should keep in mind that literature is a reflection of life and, historically, literature has been written largely by men; also, literature has been written primarily about men. Perhaps even more important in the long run, literature has been analyzed by men. Literature by women has been less frequently published and less accepted by critics than has work by male writers.

To see the effects of the long history of predominantly male authors, male characters, and male critics, consider the comments made in 1852 by George Henry Lewes about "The Lady Novelists," reprinted in *Women's Liberation and Literature:*

> Of all the departments of literature, Fiction is the one to which, by nature and by circumstance, women are best adapted. Exceptional women will of course be found competent to the highest success in other departments; but speaking generally, novels are their forte. The domestic experiences which form the bulk of woman's knowledge finds an appropriate form in novels; while the very nature of fiction calls for the predominance of Sentiment which we have already attributed to the feminine mind.

While Lewes was more generous in acknowledging women authors than were many nineteenth-century critics, his condescending tone and compartmentalizing of "women's themes" is highly offensive to most modern readers. Regrettably, even some recent literary criticism by men and women echoes Lewes' sentiments.

Further, female characters in literature have seldom been main characters, and when women have been central figures, they most often have been viewed in relation to men rather than as themselves. Almost every female character in literature is classified according to her biological, physical, or "female role" before any other: we find out immediately if she is married or

1

single, a mother or childless, attractive or unappealing. On the other hand, male characters might be stereotyped in restricted sex roles (the "macho" image or "studious type" are two examples), but they are not as often one-dimensional figures. Men are more often portrayed as complex individuals concerned with issues such as politics, professions, religion, ethics, art, or war.

As part of the differences in character descriptions, women frequently are cast into inferior roles revolving around men, and have stereotypical personality traits ascribed to them (emotionality, passivity, etc.) that are considered inferior. Both women characters and women authors are sex stereotyped. In fact, even in male characters, "feminine" qualities are considered inferior: emotion is presented as inferior to logic, passive to active, home to outside world.

These assertions about women's roles throughout literature leave us with a discouragingly bleak view. No doubt one could argue that times have changed, that now more women are writing, are being published, are writing about women, are being criticized by female critics, and are being accepted into the mainstream of "good literature." While some of these changes have occurred, almost all of the same issues about women's acceptance in literature still exist, albeit to a lesser degree. The study of women in literature remains largely a separate field from the study of "mainstream" literature, with only a small number of "token" women authors known to general readers. This situation keeps the spotlight on a few literary "stars" while casting a shadow over less known women writers.

Recognizing the historically sexist bias in how women's literature has been received, we must find ways to rise above and beyond these limitations. In studying works by women or men about women, we may tend to fall into the trap characterized by antifeminists as scholarly attention only to the "ravages of patriarchy" in literature. In truth, there is much more to say about women characters and authors than whether the portrayal or criticism of them is sexist. As Adrienne Rich aptly noted in her introduction to *Working It Out,* a study of creative achieving women, women's commonality is not based solely on the fact of having been oppressed as a group. Instead, we must recognize other sources of commonality.

LIFE STAGES

One common world women share is the life cycle itself. At each stage there are many dimensions of woman's selfhood to consider, with both positive and negative ramifications to explore from childhood through adolescence, adulthood, old age, and death.

Literature by and about women reveals the differences between men and women's life stage development and shows the similarities among women as described in literature throughout the ages. Just as there are recurrent issues related to the discussion of women's literature, there are also a number of issues in life stage research that are directly related to the same subject. For example, what effect do childhood experiences and the impact of society have on a woman's development from childhood to adulthood, and are there differences between men and women's development? What qualities are women expected to have in each life stage? Are affiliation and caretaking primary characteristics or stereotypes of being a woman, and to what extent are expectations for women based on their physical attributes and bodily changes throughout the life cycle? Do women develop autonomy as individuals, and do they transcend to new levels of enlightenment upon reaching maturity and old age? How do women deal with physical, mental, and emotional change, and with the ultimate transformation, death?

These and other issues will be discussed in connection with stories, poems, and plays about each life stage; however, it is helpful first to review the psychosocial underpinnings of the topic of life stages.

Life stages, life cycle, life span, and *life course* are terms often used synonymously. To describe stages within the life cycle, researchers use analogies such as "seasons," "passages," and life "maps." Life cycle psychologists began mainly with studies of men's lives, or with research that supposedly did not differentiate between the sexes—an approach challenged by later researchers. More recently, studies have been designed and conducted specifically about women.

Freud's studies of the psychological effects of childhood on later life, and Jung's extension of Freud's theories to include the impact of society on adult development paved the way for Erik Erikson's contribution of an eight-stage paradigm from infancy to old age. Daniel Levinson's *Seasons of a Man's Life* incorporates some of Erikson's model, and delineates four eras of about twenty years each: childhood and adolescence, early adulthood, middle adulthood, and late adulthood.

In *Passages*, Gail Sheehy includes many of the same topics as Levinson, and both use case studies to answer the basic question "Is there life after youth?" But Sheehy challenges Erikson's idea of midlife "generativity" (other-directed energy) as a stage of life; she points out that for women, the altruistic, caretaking role occurs throughout life, rather than being reserved for late adulthood. Carol Gilligan's *In a Different Voice* also asserts women's important role of affiliation, in contrast to men's individuation.

Penelope Washbourn's *Becoming Woman* builds on the concept of life crises that need to be negotiated in order to reach a higher stage. She bases her discussion of women's life crises on physical changes of a woman, such as menstruation, sex, pregnancy, and menopause. Like Gilligan, Washbourn emphasizes what makes women different from men, although Washbourn starts with the premise of biological identity.

The question of whether anatomy is destiny relates to Madonna Kolbenschlag's claim in *Kiss Sleeping Beauty Goodbye* that male models are inappropriate to describe women's lives. Applying life stage study to the realm of literature, Kolbenschlag argues that unlike men, women in literature do not move to a new level of insight. More often, in myths and other fiction, women remain static, go mad, or die.

The same controversy emerges in death stage research such as Robert Jay Lifton's comments on death encounters and Elisabeth Kübler-Ross's important work on stages of death. While Kübler-Ross's stages—denial, anger, bargaining, depression, and acceptance—are reflected to a certain extent in literary accounts of women dying, the final stage (acceptance) is often not reached by women in fiction and drama. There is the same lack of transcendence into a new self noted in women's versus men's literature.

At the heart of the many controversies about female versus male life stages is the whole notion of change. Maurice Shroder in "The Novel as a Genre" indicates that a change in the main character is so often the major subject of fiction that it in fact can serve as the definition of a novel. But how many women are truly transformed in literature?

In literature, many examples about death show that women are seldom transformed to reach the final stage of acceptance—creating inner peace. Even in studies of real life, we have already noted Sheehy's claim that women do not have a separate stage that represents a change to nurturing and caretaking. Perhaps, as Jung suggested, the progress of the individual psyche parallels the development of a society; thus, women might not be reaching peace and acceptance individually because women as a group have not been able to do so in society. In contrast, we can hope with Penelope Washbourn that women can slough off old selves to make way for transformations.

LITERATURE AND LIFE

In this anthology, literary works are brought together to represent each stage of a woman's life, from childhood to death. Instead of drawing conclusions about what happens in each life stage by recording real-life behavior, this study presents a creative record of women's behavior as it appears in stories, poems, and plays.

For simplicity and accessibility, the stories, poems, and plays are organized into five major stages—childhood, adolescence, adulthood, old age, and death. Because only literature intended to be read by adults is included, "children's literature" and "adolescent literature" are not represented here. Within the adulthood stage there are three sections—work, family, and society—which are thematic rather than sequential (that is, there is no implication that a woman first works, then has a family, then becomes a part of society).

In identifying the life stages and subcategories, there is a deliberate attempt to avoid defining a woman's life in terms of her physical and biological roles. While some researchers have been able to focus successfully on the crises in a woman's life directly related to her physical changes (menstruation, pregnancy, motherhood, etc.), there is more to a woman's life than being a biological "other," and too often the categorizing of women by what makes them different from men results in stereotyping.

We are our genes, but we are not only our genes. Women in literature and in life are not only married or single, childbearing or childless, menopausal or premenopausal (although topics such as these appear and are discussed throughout the life cycle literature); women are involved in politics, work, religion, art, and ethics, just as are multidimensional men in life and in literature.

Childhood

Female children in literature are described as confronting a wide world of natural and material objects, people, and ideas. Common themes one might expect to see, such as dealing with parents and siblings, learning the often restrictive mores of society, and expanding communication with others do indeed appear. In addition, several motifs emerge in childhood which might at first seem surprising, such as the notions of coming to terms with death, having an adult woman friend, and enjoying a private place in nature.

Typical childhood topics having to do with living in a family group include learning to give and to share, developing a feeling of security, experiencing the exchange of love and the extreme domination of parents. However, much of the unconscious concern in childhood has to do with a child learning a sex role—the process of socialization that teaches girls to be more docile, less aggressive, than boys. Female children develop a desire to acquiesce and to please that stays with them much of their lives, culminating in the modern adult phenomenon of women trying to learn to express their anger, while men are trying to repress their aggression.

Young girls do not restrain potential aggression only because "boys are bigger," but also because they learn to seek male approval in all areas. With less emphasis on competitive games and team sports for girls, women later find themselves more likely to compete with members of the same sex (for male attention in areas such as jobs, husbands, recognition) than to see women as members of the same team. In addition, from infancy, codes of proper behavior—such as not being unruly, boisterous—are reinforced by the wearing of restrictive clothing meant to be kept neat, clean, and pretty. This pristine image of the "ideal" girl in life is evident in much of the literature about women's childhood stage, and is subtly satirized by several of the authors.

Adolescence

Of course a girl does not wake up suddenly at thirteen as an adolescent; nor is the onset of menstruation always a sudden turning point in women's lives. As a transition period between childhood and adulthood, adolescence is gradual and could be divided into many substages, according to each individual's development.

In almost every work of literature or research about adolescence, several common characteristics of the female adolescent emerge. In addition to the extreme passivity noted in many studies of adolescents—the young woman waiting for some other person to give her an identity—there is an enormous preoccupation with physical appearance. Linked to the desire to please and attract young men, the desire for glamorous good looks is a predominant attribute of teenage girls. Often unfortunate victims of peer scorn are those young women who either do not like men or have an unconventional interest in intellectual pursuits or "nonfemale" hobbies.

Even in families expecting academic achievement for their female children, it is rare when it is not assumed that the young woman will also marry and have children. Further, in late childhood and early adolescence women begin to develop a dislike or fear of male-dominated areas such as science and math, pursuing instead "female" subjects that will eventually lead most of them to "women's work" in adulthood—childrearing, domestic and clerical work, or teaching. The enculturation process teaches young women to be helpmates in the home or at work, or at best executive assistants or middle managers, but not top decision makers in life.

As some poems and stories about adolescence show, ideally this period could be the start of a woman's best time of life. If young women could maintain the exuberance and questioning mentality of childhood, without succumbing to parental and societal pressures, they could perhaps achieve the personal autonomy most authors advocate. Some of the teenagers in literature show real promise, leading readers to wonder what external and internal forces have in store for each young woman as adulthood approaches.

Adulthood

Women and Work   The topic of women and work is discussed first in the adulthood stage, not because it is a woman's most important role, but because work considerations have had such a powerful influence on women's family lives and places in society. Issues of child care, division of labor in the home, self-image and status in society, even infidelity and divorce are influenced by the work situations in which women find themselves.

Many people have noted that an unfortunate byproduct of the women's movement is that the old unrealistic dream of all women finding total happiness in the home has been replaced with a new unrealistic dream of all women finding total fulfillment at work. At the same time that women are expected to be high achievers in paid positions, studies such as Matina Horner's on fear of success show that the feelings of inferiority women develop in childhood and adolescence are not easily cast off in adulthood.

Statistics on women working show that women do feel the pressure to succeed in a career, but that the majority of working women are also expected to perform a second job in the home. According to *The Sociology of Housework*, "housewives" spend about seventy-seven hours per week doing housework, with a working woman spending forty-five hours at the same tasks. Other research shows that modern men agree that they should do housework, but spend few hours a week at domestic chores. As hard as writers have struggled to kill the image of women working slavishly at home and work, and as much as each woman fights against it in her mind, the image of the Superwoman has not died, and the image of the Superman has yet to change character.

However, times have changed in terms of the number of women in the work force, and the impact is evident in every aspect of women's adult lives. Women now hold almost half of the jobs in the United States. Most, though, are engaged in "women's work," and a third of the women working have clerical jobs with steadily decreasing pay. And women continue to earn less money for the same jobs held by men. The "bottom line" is that women are paid less to do more, both at home and at work.

Fiction and poetry about women working supports the notion that hard work—at home and/or an outside place of employment—is the lot of women. As typists, waitresses, or business managers, women in the stories and poems do not find an easy road to success. Further, while women are working so hard and long, few are reaching top positions, a fact reflected in the paucity of high quality stories, poems, and plays about women executives. At the decision-making level, the number of women in management positions is increasing, but there are few women at the very top of major corporations.

The "old boy network" continues to act as a pernicious barrier for women, called the "glass ceiling" by the *Wall Street Journal*, and described in this collection by the "Cinderella" poem about women's token status in the workplace. Poems about women and work often show the frustration unappreciated women experience in paid and unpaid jobs. Narratives and plays, on the other hand, more often show that women's work need not be considered inferior or trivial, as it often is in life.

Women and Family As Cinderella is the fairy tale model for women at work, Goldilocks is the model for women at home. With "affiliation" as her primary characteristic, Goldilocks is forever looking for the perfect family. However, the definition of "family" has changed so radically that if Goldilocks wandered into a household today she would have only an eleven percent chance of finding papa bear, mama bear, and two baby bears.

Although ninety percent of American youth expect to marry and want it to last, the Census Bureau predicts that almost half of today's marriages will end in divorce. The fairy tale of the "normal" family is challenged also by the two million unmarried couples living together, and the rapidly increasing number of homosexual family units.

As a result of these changes, there is a wide diversity of descriptions of family life in literature. Stories, poems, and plays show not only women living with husbands and children, but also single mothers, women living with women, alone, with men, or with parents. Stories and plays about mother-daughter relationships are of great interest and frequency—a virtually unexplored subject for literature until recently.

The major factor in changing the nature of family (and consequently, literature about women and family) has been women working. The fact that there is a high correlation between women's achievement at work and the divorce rate, however, is inaccurately attributed to the stereotype that "bad mothers go to work and break up the family"; instead, divorce rates have been affected by the new financial independence women have experienced as workers. Economic power enables women to escape from what otherwise might have been a permanent trap, and the realization of the equation "money equals power" in turn prods women to pursue careers with tenacity.

Numerous contemporary stories deal with divorced women or single women looking for life partners, bearing out the statistic that more than one-fifth of the heads of American households are single or divorced women. Some of these women would prefer to live in a conventional marriage, and some deliberately have chosen a solitary lifestyle. A controversial study indicating that a woman's chance of marrying after forty is smaller than her chance of being killed by a terrorist, while insulting in its implication that all women are looking for men to marry, is all too true for some women and many modern literary characters searching in vain for a permanent male partner.

Many women also feel victimized by the "biological clock" that forces them to decide about childbearing before they are forty. It is true, as is pointed out in *Sooner or Later: The Timing of Parenthood in Adult Lives*, that with the lengthening of the human life cycle has come the shortening of the time required for child raising. However, it is also true that women often have to decide between career advancement and having children, a choice men do not have to make. Poems and stories about motherhood or the decision not to be a mother raise issues about women juggling the many roles they now play in society.

Women and Society Women's roles in society incorporate many issues already mentioned, such as politics, religion, etc. But the primary questions to which most researchers return are "What is women's status in the social order?" and "What is seen as a woman's purpose, or mission, or reason for being in society?"

About the question of status, *Toward a New Psychology of Women* answers that there are two kinds of inequality: temporary inequality (social rankings, such as bosses and workers, parents and children), and permanent inequality (by birth, such as minorities and women). "Superiors" or "dominants" give tasks to "inferiors" or "subordinates." In the power structure, helping others is the lesser task given to women. It is their contribution to society—their mission. Inspirational and satirical literature throughout the ages supports this concept; for example, in the nineteenth century Catharine Esther Beecher told the Christian Women of America that women's mission was to train ignorant people to obey the word of God, and Maria Weston Chapman exhorted women to end slavery by telling men that slavery is wrong (uncomfortably similar to women's current crusades for peace). The power structure here is clear; women embrace their secondary status even while denouncing slavery or war, by attempting to influence the real decision makers—men.

The controversy about women as helpers, the altruists of society, comes up many times in research and literature. Paradoxically, woman's best quality is also her worst quality, for kindness and caretaking often give way to passive acquiescence to the status quo. For example, it is still more likely for a woman to be active in religion (although still not in the number-one position) than to be active in politics. Unfortunately, in much of the literature about women, politics and other societal realms of interest often considered "male," such as sports and war, do indeed get short shrift. This continuation of the sex role messages of childhood and adolescence is evident in the popular phenomenon of cadres of women working for peace or against drunk driving. Only in these limited spheres are women's voices expected to rise above a whisper or a prayer.

Old Age

In old age one would expect to see women "coming into their own," especially since they usually outlive men, and often are not confronted with men's shock of having to create a home life after retirement. For some women, old age is a peaceful, secure time, or a time for personal growth after years of giving to others. A large determinant of happiness or dissatisfaction in old age is the woman's life circumstance—physical health, financial security, living arrangement, degree of independence, and so forth.

Declining physical health is difficult for any woman or man to deal with at any age, but added to the burden is the societally enforced dictate that a woman should try not to lose her physical attractiveness as she ages. Journalist Ellen Goodman has written a clever diatribe against the "cult of mid-life beauty" that extends into a woman's old age: if we did not look like Raquel Welch or Jane Fonda at twenty, says Goodman, we cannot expect to look like them at forty or fifty. Yet women fight the onset of wrinkling and graying to a greater extent than do men growing old.

A further burden for older women is that they are the most economically disadvantaged segment of the population, which accounts for the dominant theme of money, or lack of it, in the stories and plays about aging women. "Genteel poverty" is the badge of elderly women, a phrase seldom used about men. With more women developing financial security in adulthood, eventually the label may disappear and literary accounts will change accordingly.

In addition to economic conditions, a woman's living arrangement clearly has an impact on her adaptability to old age. Contradicting the maxim that a woman should marry so that someone can take care of her in her declining years, in fact unmarried women are better adapted to old age, because they have learned self-reliance and or have developed support systems outside of the family unit. Probably the most extreme example of satisfied "spinsterhood" in literature is Emily Dickinson, and one of the first stage directions in *The Belle of Amherst,* a play about her life, is that Dickinson's age of fifty-three is not really relevant.

Nevertheless, isolation and loneliness remain severe problems among elderly women, who often do not have financial independence or the opportunities to remarry or to live with their children. Even in middle age, mothers often experience the "empty nest" syndrome, and how they deal with the abandonment by children to a certain extent predicts how they will deal with the death or abandonment of a spouse.

As described in famous literature such as Tillie Olsen's *Tell Me A Riddle* and Margaret Laurence's *Stone Angel,* women more often than men resist going to a nursing home, having well established their domestic lives and being unwilling to give up home as a primary part of personal identity. It also is difficult for the older women to accept the fact of having to be taken care of, after a lifetime of taking care of others.

In art and in life, the aging process is difficult to accept as a potentially meaningful change, another step in self-knowledge. Stories about old age show that women who accept aging best are those who see it as an opportunity to shun hypocrisy and cultivate meaningful human interactions, despite earlier adulthood's power struggles or mutual dependencies.

Death

The act of death and the process of dying have come to mean almost the same thing, for the awareness of the existence of death is the recognition that all of life is part of moving toward dying. This realization leads women either to affirmation or to denial—of both life and death. Death is indeed an opportunity for growth, and is a continual process, not just occurring at the physical end of life.

However, fear and denial of death (like fear and denial of aging) still greatly overshadow women's potential to accept death; and even Kübler-Ross in describing the final stage of death—acceptance—does not show it to be a happy period, but a time devoid of feeling. When death is accompanied by pain and suffering, it is even more difficult for an individual to accept.

Perhaps the most difficult role a woman plays in dying, apart from her own death, is to care for and attend any family member, friend, or even acquaintance who is dying. Women are in charge of old age and dying: they are expected to visit the elderly, minister to the sick, comfort the dying, and take casseroles to the bereaved. Women do these things because they are "strong," whereas men "just cannot deal with hospitals and sickness and death." Again women's strength is in stereotypical altruism, while men are supposedly "strong" enough to lead, to make decisions, perhaps to kill—but not to be around death.

In the literature about women dealing with death, many of the stereotypes and motifs become polarized struggles. The house versus the outside world becomes a struggle unto death; logic versus emotionality remains an important dichotomy; and the dream self versus the "real" self is dramatically exaggerated. Misguided power struggles between men and women even take the form of physical assault in one of the death stories in this collection, and the images of repression versus freedom that began with hats in childhood and dresses in adolescence culminate in physical restrictions such as bed-straps in old age and death.

The women in literature, like women in real life, die as they have lived. Each life stage is a form of death in the sense that coming to terms with the aging process is part of coming to terms with life, especially for a woman.

CHILDHOOD

Initiation; exploring the personal universe; developing expectations; relating to the family; establishing rituals; moving from fantasy to reality

Childhood in these stories and poems is depicted as a matter of "coming to terms"—with the family, peers, the emerging self, and the many realities of life and death. Throughout the childhood period, young girls struggle to create meaning out of the fragments of information and experience presented by daily life. This struggle is represented in fiction and poetry by a myriad of visual and auditory images. The young girls demonstrate a number of conflicting feelings toward the people and objects they encounter, but all display a sense of wonder as their personal universes expand.

The highly charged emotional states of childhood described in stories such as "A Child's Day" are accompanied by physiological effects such as tightening of the throat, a pain in the head from thinking, and a pronounced heartbeat. The young girls cry, laugh, sigh, and scream; yet these emotional expressions seem unfamiliar to the children, who are surprised by the suddenness of their own bodies' responses to strong feelings. A mark of the age group is that the characters themselves often do not realize that they are growing and changing. Not only is there a notable lack of the self-awareness that develops with age, but there is often a rejection of confusing feelings and responses.

Learning to cope with strong feelings is a dominant theme, with growing, expanding, and opening up as recurrent images. The process of increasing awareness is depicted as both painful and exhilarating. But the overwhelming feeling so beautifully reproduced in these stories is childhood's sense of waiting—waiting for "something wonderful" to happen, for some relief from the boredom of living without purpose, some "secret phrase" or "magic sentence" to clarify the meaning of life.

The waiting for a magic answer can be discomfiting as well, because of the powerlessness of children—parents seem either not to listen, or to be overly intrusive, or to answer in riddles. Children in the stories question, wait to be told, and are generally at the mercy of adult whims. The process of growing up seems to be a gradual shift in the balance of power, with independence increasing until adulthood is reached, then diminishing when the individual self is again in danger of becoming relatively dependent in old age.

In response to the feeling of powerlessness, the children often select an adult as supporter or confidante. The young girls depicted here often form a bond with an older woman (usually not the mother), for connecting and affirming life outside of the family. In "My Goddaughter," for example, a girl claims that her mother discourages her, while her godmother understands her. In other words, girls seem to be looking for external judgments on the seemingly repressive codes of the family.

While other adults provide an outlet for the children's frustrations, parents often serve as societal "enforcers" in the stories. Images of repression and restriction are prevalent, and are usually associated with maternal concern for the young girl's personal appearance and social appearances. The mother or grandmother is often seen as the conveyer of society's message of conformity; it is not until the stories of later life that women begin to look back on their relationships with their mothers through an enlightened perspective.

One might expect older female children to serve as mentors for young girls, but the main characters in these stories reject or are rejected by older children going through changes of their own. Also interesting to note is the paradoxical attitude of the girls to communication with others: they want to share feelings with a special friend, but at the same time they seek out and savor time alone. The children find hiding places under staircases, behind doors, or outside in natural enclosures (as in the poem "Lisa"). Unlike the women in stories about old age, the young girls find solace in self-imposed solitude.

Another paradox of childhood is that while the girls in the stories are trying to be exactly like everyone else, they also want to be special and different. Although they have not yet developed a firm sense of personal identity (and are constantly readjusting their perceptions and actions to fit the views of others), the concept of "self" is so strong that they would be surprised to learn that others felt as unique as they. The intrinsic "rightness" of self is asserted by characters such as Shirley in "The Loudest Voice," even when there are hard lessons to be learned.

Each girl tries to balance the enjoyment and pain of being alone or together, alike or different. Despite the conflicting desires of childhood, both the states of solitude and of camaraderie often culminate in epiphany in these stories, boldly represented by elemental images of flames, sky, and water. Cynthia in "The Fire" stands by flames with her adult confidante, "inarticulate, full of a strange, excited, shouting hope. . . . "

Nowhere does the added exhilaration of nature seem so strong as in these stories and poems of childhood; the world of animals, flowers, sunshine, and rain inebriates the growing girls. Beautiful natural sites promote dreaming, and it begins to seem as if half of childhood is spent in the hypnagogic state. The young girls seem lost at times in trancelike states, mesmerised by nature or by the voices of others.

Dreams contrast with the realities each child must face, including dilemmas about money, work, social status, race, and class. Each story raises real questions of childhood such as those in "The Lesson," in which a girl who has inadvertently fallen into a "trance" makes an effort to look clearly at reality: Why must everyone be concerned with petty details of chores to be done and bills to be paid? How much do things in the "real world" cost, and why can't everyone have them? Why is there such a difference between rich and poor, black and white? Why doesn't everyone get along? Why isn't life as exciting as in books and dreams?

The many lessons of childhood, with the resulting conflicts and emotional highs and lows, are well described by the women writing these stories and poems. Childhood is presented as the period in which the self is bombarded with all of the complexity of life's impressions and realities, despite the desire to dream alone or to commune with a special friend. Young girls strive to preserve their own uniqueness, while at the same time they begin to conform to the standards of society passed along by family and peers. The wonder and joy of discovering the natural world, and the perplexity of making sense of the many "lessons" of the real world contribute to the tone of bemusement often evident in these representations of childhood.

Fiction About Childhood

Stories and novels of girls growing up are often regarded with pleasant surprise by readers who rediscover the naturalness of childhood depicted by these authors and others. It is refreshing to see females as vigorous and forthright children devoid of pretense, or at least relatively unhampered by the restrictive codes that too often become a source of conflict later in life. While it is true that society's force is already a palpable presence in the stories, social codes are not yet as blatantly internalized as in many accounts of later life stages.

Indeed, the children shout and quarrel and question in these stories, demonstrating that they are truly alive and engaged in each new world they encounter—nature, family, school, and friends. They seek knowledge and identity for themselves, rather than for or through others as many women begin to do in adolescence and beyond: they are self-ish in the best sense of the term, neither docile nor domineering.

The "lessons" these young women begin to learn vary widely in the stories from meaningful experience to didactic guidelines as to how to become socially acceptable. In some cases, parents themselves present models of behavior that suggest lifetimes of sex-stereotyped behavior, with little opportunity for the individual expression these young women obviously seek. The final question raised by many of these stories is whether the girls can remain visible and real, or will become near-invisible shadows of their former selves as children.

Jessamyn West

1907–1984

Minta, the young girl in this story, portrays what is perhaps the most important vision of childhood—the belief that one is special, destined for greatness, and different from the rest of the family. Can she preserve the joy and inspiration of her "child's day"?

A CHILD'S DAY

"I Minta," the child said, "in the October day, in the dying October day." She walked over to the fireplace and stood so that the slanting sunlight fell onto her bare shoulder with a red wine stain. The ashes, so light and dry, smelled raw, rain-wet. Or perhaps it's the water on the chrysanthemums, she thought, or perhaps the bitter, autumn-flavored chrysanthemums themselves.

She listened for her second heartbeat, the three-day tap of the loosened shingle. But it was dead, it beat no more. For three days the Santa Ana had buffeted the house, but now at evening it had died down, had blown itself out. It was blown out, but it left its signs: the piled sand by the east door sills, the tumble weeds caught in the angle of the corral, the sign board by the electric tracks, face down; the eucalyptus upright, but with torn limb dangling.

"The Sabbath evening," said the girl, "the autumn Sabbath evening." And bright and warm against the day's sober death, the year's sad end, burned her own bright living.

She walked to her own room, across her fallen nightgown, past her unmade bed, and opened the casement window and leaned out toward the west. There the sun was near to setting, red in the dust, and the lights in the distant well riggings already blazed. She watched the sun drop until the black tracery of a derrick crossed its face.

"The day dies," murmured the girl; "its burnished wrack burns in yon western sky."

Then she was quiet so that no single word should fall to ripple the clear surface of her joy. The pepper tree rustled; there was a little stir in the leaves of the bougainvillaea. From the ocean, twenty miles away, the sea air was beginning to move back across the land. "It is as good against the dry face as water." She pushed her crackling hair away from her cheeks. "I won't have a wind break as thin even as one hair against my face."

She arched her bony chest under the tightly wrapped lace scarf, so that she could project as much of herself as possible into the evening's beauty. "Now the sun is down and the day's long dream ended. Now I must make the air whistle about my ears."

She came out of the long black lace scarf like an ivory crucifix—with a body no wider than her arms. Bloomers, slip, green rep dress on, and there she was—thirteen again, and the supper to get, and the house to clean. She had the supper in mind: a fitting meal for Sunday evening. Oyster soup. Oysters that actresses ate, floating in a golden sea of milk, and marble cup-cakes veined like old temples.

She had supper ready when the Duro turned into the driveway bringing her family home from their drive—the cakes out of the oven, the milk just on for the soup.

"Well," said her father when he entered the room, "this is pretty nice." He walked over and held his hands to the fire. "Wood box full, too."

Her mother ran her finger over the top of the bookcase while she unwound her veil. "Minta, you'll burn us out dusting with kerosene."

Clenmie said, sniffing the air, "Did you bake me a little cake, Mintie?"

Minta watched the scarlet accordion pleating in the opening of her mother's slit skirt fan out as she held her foot toward the fire.

Father took off Clenmie's coat. "You should have gone with us, Minta. The wind's done a lot of damage over in Riverside County. Lost count of the roofs off and trees down."

"Is supper ready?" Mother asked.

"Soon as the milk heats, and I put the oysters in."

"Oyster soup!" exclaimed Father. "The perfect dish for a Sunday October evening. Did you get your studying done?" he asked curiously.

Minta nodded. Studying. Well, it was studying. There were her books and papers.

Father had said that morning before they left, "You're a bright girl, Minta. No need your spending a whole day studying. Do you more good to go for a ride with us."

"No, Father, I'm way behind." She could hardly wait until they left.

Finally at ten they got into the car, Mother on the front seat close to Father, Clenmie behind. Father backed out of the driveway and a dusty swirl of wind caught Mother's scarlet veil. They waved her a sad good-by.

She had watched the red Duro out of sight, then turned and claimed the empty house for herself. She was as happy as a snail that expels the last grain of sand which has separated its sensitive fluid from its shell. Now she flowed back against the walls of her house in pure contentment. She stood stock still and shut her eyes and listened to the house sounds: first the dry, gusty breathing of the wind and the shingle's tap, then the lessening hiss of the tea kettle as the breakfast fire died, and the soft, animal pad of the rug as a slackening air current let it fall.

She opened her eyes. In the dining room the curtains lifted and fell with a summer movement in the autumn wind. She felt this to be perfect happiness: to stand in one room and watch in another the rise and fall of curtains. The egg-rimmed dishes still stood on the uncleared breakfast table. She regarded the disorder happily. "Oh," she whispered, "it's like being the only survivor on an abandoned ship."

Stealthily she ran to lower all the blinds so that the room was left in yellow, dusty twilight. Then she made herself a fire of the petroleum soaked refuse from the oil fields that they used for wood. When the oil began to bubble and seethe, and the flames darted up, black and red, she started her work.

She cleaned the fumed-oak library table and ranged her books and papers precisely before her. Now her day began. Now she inhabited two worlds at once, and slid amphibian-like from one to the other, and had in each the best. She moved in Shelley's world of luminous mist, and emerged to hold her hand to the fire and to listen to the bone-dry sound of the wind in the palm trees.

She laid her hand across her open book feeling that the words there

CHILDHOOD

were so strong and beautiful that they would enter her veins through her palms and so flow to her heart. She listened to the wind and saw all the objects that bent before it: she saw the stately movement of dark tree tops, the long ripple of bleached, hair-like grass, the sprayed sea water, the blown manes of horses in open pasture, the lonely sway of electric signs along dusty main streets. "Far across the steppes," she said, "and the prairie lands, the high mesas and the grass-covered pampas." She watched the oil bubble stickily out of the wood and wondered how it seemed to feel again after these thousands of years the touch of the wind.

But this was dreaming, not doing her work. She opened her notebook to a half-filled page headed, "Beautiful, Lilting Phrases from Shelley." The list slid across her tongue like honey: "Rainbow locks, bright shadows, riven waves, spangled sky, aery rocks, sanguine sunrise, upward sky, viewless gale." She felt the texture of the words on her fingers as she copied them. The shingle tapped, the wind blew grittily across the pane, the fire seethed.

She finished Shelley and started on her own word list. She was through with the o's, ready to begin on the p's. She opened her old red dictionary. What words would she find here? Beautiful, strange ones? She looked ahead: pamero: a cold wind that sweeps over the pampas; parsalene: a mock moon; panada: bread crumbs boiled in milk; picaroon: a rogue, pilgarlic: a baldheaded man; plangent: resounding like a wave. Her eyes narrowed and her cheek bones ached regarding this rich store.

She rolled her black, ribbed, gartered stocking back and forth across her knee and copied words and definitions. When she finished the q's she put her word notebook away and took out one called "The Poems of Aminta Eilertsen, Volume III." Each Sunday she copied one poem from her week's output into her poem book. Her poems were nothing like Shelley's. Shelley was beautiful, but he was not a modern. Minta was a modern, and when she wrote poetry she scorned the pretty and euphonious. This week's poem was called "You Do Not Have to Wipe the Noses of Your Dreams," and Minta thought it as stark and brutal as anything she had ever done. Slowly she copied it:

I was lithe and had dreams;
Now I am fat and have children.
Dreams are efflorescent,
Dreams fade.
Children do not.
But then you do not have to
Wipe the noses of your dreams.

"Yes," she said to her father, having remembered the poems, hers and Shelley's, the long list of words, "I finished my studying all right."
"Did anyone come while we were gone?" Mother asked.
"Mrs. Beal knocked, but she left before I got to the door."

She had scarcely moved from her table all morning. Now her back was stiff; she was cold and hungry. She put another petroleum-soaked timber on the fire and sat on the hassock warming her knees and eating her lunch: a mixture of cocoa, sugar, and condensed milk as thick and brown as mud. She spooned it from gravy bowl to mouth and watched the murky flames and listened to the block of wood which was burning as noisily as a martyr. The oil seethed and bubbled like blood. She crouched on the hearth and heard behind the drawn curtains the hiss of sand against the windows. A current of air like a cold finger touched her cheek.

"What do I here," she wondered, "alone, abandoned, hiding?"

She pressed herself closely against the bricks and listened intently. She took a bite and let the sweet, brown paste slide down her throat so that no sound of swallowing should mask the approaching footfall, the heavy, guarded breathing. The room was filled with a noiseless activity. Well, she had known this would be her end. Soon or late they would come, search her out. In some such sordid, dirty, ill-lit hole as this she had been destined to make her end.

"In solitude and from this broken crockery, then, this last meal," she mused, and looked scornfully at the cracked bowl. "And those for whom the deed was done eat from crystal, on linen napery, and talk with light voices."

The wind had died down. But the curtains moved stealthily and the door into the hallway trembled a little in its frame. From somewhere in the house came the light click, click of metal on metal. Light, but continuous. She had not heard it before. She shifted her weight cautiously on the hassock so that she faced the room.

The wind came up again with a long, low, sick whistle; the shingle beat feverishly. She put down her bowl and started the search she knew must be made. She stepped out of her shoes and noiselessly opened the door into the hall. Cold, dark, and windowless it stretched the length of the house. Three bedroom doors opened off it, two to the west, one to the east. She searched the bedrooms carefully, though her heartbeat jarred her cheeks. She lunged against the long, hanging garments that might have concealed a hidden figure. She threw back the covers of the unmade beds. She watched the mirrors to see if from their silver depths a burning, red-rimmed eye might look into hers.

In Clenmie's room she finished her search. The loose shingle tapped like the heart of a ghost. Then she heard it: the sound she had been born to hear, the footstep her ears had been made to echo. Furtive footsteps: now fast, now slow, now pausing altogether. She leaned against the side of Clenmie's crib and waited for the steps to turn toward the house.

"But how could they know this was the house. What sign did I leave? What clew not destroy?"

The footsteps came on inexorably, turned out of the road onto the graveled walk, then proceeded quickly and resolutely to the front door. First there was a light, insistent knock, then the latched screen door was heavily shaken.

"He must have a force with him," Minta thought, "he is so bold," and waited for the crash of splintering boards, and braced her body for the thrust of cold steel that would follow. She thought fleetingly of Clenmie, and of her father and mother, and wondered if any sudden coldness about their hearts warned them of her plight.

The screen door shook again, and a woman's voice, old and quiet, called out, "Is there anyone there? I say, is there anyone home?" and ceased.

Slowly, cautiously Minta crept to the living room, lifted the side of the green blind. Old Mrs. Beal, her Sunday black billowing in the wind, was homeward bound from dinner with her daughter.

"I saw it was old Mrs. Beal on her way home from her daughter's," she told her father, giving him as much truth as she thought he could handle.

"Minta, you can get to the door fast enough when some of your friends are calling."

"I was busy," replied Minta with dignity. Her father looked at her doubtfully, but said no more.

Her mother combed out Clenmie's soft, white hair with her rhinestone back comb. "Did you forget to feed Brownie?" she asked.

"Of course I fed Brownie. I'll never forget her. She's my dearest friend."

Against the warm reality of Mrs. Beal's broad, homeward-bound back, the world that had been cold and full of danger dissolved. The dear room; her books, her papers; Clenmie's toys; Mother's tissue cream on top of the piano; the fire sending its lazy red tongue up the chimney's black throat.

She stood warming herself, happy and bemused, like a prisoner unexpectedly pardoned. Then she heard again the click, click she had not recognized. Brownie at the back door!

"O poor Brownie, I forgot you. Poor kitty, are you hungry?" There was Brownie sitting on the back step, with fur blown and dusty, patiently waiting to be let in and fed. She was a young cat, who had never had a kit of her own, but she looked like a grandmother. She looked as if she should have a gingham apron tied around her waist, and spectacles on her nose, and now out of her grandmother's eyes she gave Minta a look of tolerance. Minta snatched the cat up and held her close to her face, and rubbed her nose in the soft, cool fur. When she got out the can of condensed milk she put Brownie by the fire and poured the milk into the bowl from which she had eaten her own lunch. Brownie lapped the yellow arc as it fell from can to bowl.

Minta crouched on the hearth with her eyes almost on a level with Brownie's. It was blissful, almost mesmeric to watch the quick, deft dart of the red tongue into the yellow milk. Her own body seemed to participate in that darting, rhythmic movement and was lulled and happy. "It is almost as if she rocked me, back and forth, back and forth, with her tongue," mused Minta.

When Brownie finished eating, Minta took her in her arms, felt the soft little body beneath the shaggy envelope of cinnamon fur. She lay on the floor close to the fire and cradled Brownie drowsily. Suddenly she kissed her. "My darling, my darling," she said, and caressed the cat the length of its long, soft body. Her hand tingled a little as it passed over the little pin-point nipples.

Some day her mother would tell her the secret phrase, the magic sentence—something the other girls already knew. Then the boys would notice her. Then he would come. Ellen and Margaret and Phyllis already had notes from boys, and candy hearts on Valentine's day, and a piece of mistletoe at Christmas time. The boys rode them on their handle bars and showed them wrestling holds, and treated them to sodas. "But no one," she mourned, "ever looks at me." She pressed her apricot-colored hair close to the cat's cinnamon fur. "It's because mother hasn't told me yet. Something the other girls know. Sometime she'll tell me—some beautiful word I've been waiting a long time to hear. Then I'll be like a lamp lighted, a flower bloomed. Maybe she'll tell me tomorrow—and when I walk into school everyone will see the change, know I know. How will they know? My lips, my eyes, a walk, a gesture, the movement of my arms. But there's not a boy here I'd have, but someone far away, no boy. He will come and we will walk out along the streets hand in hand and everyone will see us and say, 'They were made for each other.' His hair will be like fur, soft and sooty black, and on his thin brown cheek will be a long, cruel scar. He will say, 'Kiss it, Minta, and I will bless the man who did it.' Ah, we shall walk together like sword and flower. All eyes will follow us and the people will say, 'This is Minta. Why did we never see her before?'"

Fire and wind were dying. Brownie slept on her arm. "He will come, he will come." Minta lifted Brownie high overhead, then brought her down sharply and closely to her breast.

"He will come, he will come." She kissed Brownie fiercely and put her on the floor, and ran to her mother's room, undressing as she went. She stepped out of her serge skirt and threw her Norfolk jacket across the room and sent her bloomers in a flying arc. She knew what she wanted. She had used it before—mother's long, black lace fascinator. She wound it tightly about herself from armpits to thighs. She unbraided her hair and let it hang across her shoulders. Then she turned to the mirror. "I have a beautiful body," she breathed, "a beautiful, beautiful body."

And because she regarded herself, thinking of him, him who was yet to come, it was as if he too saw her. She loaned him her eyes so that he might see her, and to her flesh she gave this gift of his seeing. She raised her arms and slowly turned and her flesh was warm with his seeing. Somberly and quietly she turned and swayed and gravely touched now thigh, now breast, now cheek, and looked and looked with the eyes she had given him.

She moved through the gray dust-filled room weaving an ivory pattern. Not any of the dust or disorder of her mother's room fazed her, not its ugliness or funny smell. Hair bubbled out of the hair receiver, the stopper was out of the Hoyt's cologne bottle, the mirror was spattered with liquid powder. She made, in her mind, a heap of all that was ugly and disordered. She made a dunghill of them and from its top she crowed.

"The curtains, green as vomit, and hanging crooked, the gray neckband on the white flannel nightgown, the dust on the patent leather shoes, I hate them and dance them down. Nothing can touch me. I am Minta. Or I can dance with them," and she clasped the sour-smelling nightgown to her and leaped and bent. "This is evil, to be naked, to like the feel of gritty dust under my feet, the bad smell, the dim light."

She regarded her face more closely in the spattered mirror. "There is something wanton and evil there," she thought, "something not good. Perhaps I shall be faithless," and she trembled with pity for that dark one who loved her so dearly. She shook back her hair and pressed her cool hands to her burning cheeks and danced so that the dust motes in the slanting shaft of light shot meteor-like, up and down.

"I can dance the word," she whispered, "but I cannot say it." So she danced it, wrapped in the black fascinator, with the dust motes dancing about her. She danced it until she trembled and leaning on bent elbows looked deep into the mirror and said, "There is nothing I will not touch. I am Minta. I will know everything."

All at once she was tired. She turned and walked slowly to the living room. Brownie lay by the dead fire. "I, Minta," she had said, "in the October day, in the dying October day," and turned to do the evening work.

"If the milk boils your soup will be spoiled," Mother said. "We've been here long enough for it to heat."

"Yes, Sister, let's eat," said Father, "it's been a long day."

"Yes, let's eat," cried Minta. "It's been a long, beautiful day," and she ran to the kitchen to put the oysters in the milk.

[1940]

For Discussion

1. In what ways is Minta different from her family? Do they see her as different?

2. What are Minta's dreams for her future? What suggestions can you find to support the idea that she will be special and perhaps famous? to support the idea that she will repeat her mother's life style?

3. Who does Minta think is at the door, and why is she afraid? Why is she later disappointed that it is just a neighbor?

4. List the range of emotions Minta expresses. Describe how and where each state of mind in the story shifts into the next.

5. Why is it so important for her to be alone? What role does privacy play in the story?

6. What symbols and images suggest Minta's emerging sexuality? What does she expect in a mate?

7. Does the scene with the cat have overtones of sensuality, maternalism, or camaradarie?

8. What does Minta's poem "You Do Not Have to Wipe the Noses of Your Dreams" have to do with the story?

9. What is the tone of the end of the story? Is there the final expectation that Minta's dreams will come true, or that she will be disillusioned in later life?

For Further Exploration

1. Two Australian women have written semi-autobiographical novels about the lives of young girls growing up in the country and yearning to be educated for careers as writers. Read Miles Franklin's *My Brilliant Career* or Henry H. Richardson's *The Getting of Wisdom* (both filmed) and relate the account to Minta's dream and struggles in "A Child's Day."

2. Compare "A Child's Day" with Alice Munro's story "Boys and Girls," about sex stereotyping of children growing up in a rural community. What does the young woman in Munro's story have in common with Minta?

Colette

1873–1954

In this variation on the dramatic monologue form, French author Colette conveys the joys and sorrows of childhood through a child's comments to her godmother. As in many stories of childhood, the presence of an adult who listens provides an outlet for expressing the mixed feelings of a young girl growing up.

MY GODDAUGHTER

"Is it you who's calling me, Godmother? I'm here, under the stairs."

". . .?"

"No, Godmother, I'm not sulking."

". . .?"

"No, Godmother, I'm not crying anymore. I'm done now. But I'm very discouraged."

". . .?"

"Oh, it's always the same thing, for a change. I'm mad at Mama. And she's mad at me, too."

". . .!"

"Why 'naturally'? No, not 'naturally' at all! There are times when she's mad without me being mad back—it depends on if she's right."

". . .!"

"Oh, please, Godmother, not today! You can tell this to me another day. There are plenty of days when I'm in a good mood and when you can make me lay back my ears. . ."

". . ."

"No, not lay *down*, lay *back!* When you scold the dog, what does he do? he lays back his ears. Me too, I've laid my ears back since lunch. So, I'll start over; you can lay back my ears about my parents, and the fairness of parents, and how a child shouldn't judge his parents, and this and that. . . But it's no use today."

". . .?"

"What's the matter? The matter is that Mama discourages me. Come here, so I can tell you about it. You're still the one I tell the most, because you don't have any children. You understand better."

". . .!"

Yes, it does make sense! You don't have any children, you still have a mama, you get scolded, you storm, you rage, and you have the reputation of being unreasonable: Mama shrugs her shoulders when she talks about you, like with me. . . . That pleases me. That gives me confidence."

". . ."

"There's no need to apologize, I don't do it on purpose. . . Come on, we'll go sit by the fire: I've had enough of sitting under these stairs, too! There, now, Mama discourages me. I can't seem to make her understand certain things."

". . .?"

"Serious things, things about life. Can you believe she just bought me a hat to go to school in! . . . Oh, yes, it's true, you don't know, you're not from the country. . . In Montigny, the girls in the public school *never* wear hats, except in the summer for the sun, and I'm only telling you this under the ceiling of secrecy. . . "

". . . !"

"The *ceiling,* I'm telling you! The proof is that you don't say it in another room. . . So, I'm telling you under the ceiling of secrecy that we go 'Boo!' in the street at the students of the nuns, because they wear hats to school. No repeating?"

". . . !"

"Good. So then Mama buys me a hat. And so I make a face at the hat! Naturally, Mama starts a two-hour lecture, which has nothing to do with the point: that I'm more than ten years old, and that I'm almost a young lady, and that I should set the example of an irreproachable appearance. . . She finally ended up upsetting me. I lost my patience, I told her that it didn't concern her, that my life at school was a special life which parents don't understand anything about, et cetera. . . 'Tell me, Mama,' I said to her, 'do you tell Papa what he should do at his office? It's the same thing with me at school. I have a very noticeable position at school, a very delicate position, because I have personality, as Mademoiselle says. To hear you, Mama, I should only concern myself with my family! You send me to school, I spend half my life there. Well, that counts, half of my life. . . School's like another world, you don't talk about it the same: what's appropriate here isn't at school, and if I tell you I shouldn't go to class in the winter with a hat, it's because I shouldn't wear a hat! You see, Mama, there are things you sense, there are nuances!' I spelled this all out to her very calmly, all at once, so that she didn't have the time to get a word in edgewise, because you know how mamas are, don't you? They fly off the handle, and besides, they don't have a sense of proportion."

". . . ?"

"I mean, they rant and rave over everything, as much for a broken glass as for something very, very bad. Mine especially. She's easily affected. Afterward, she was looking at me as if I fell from the moon, and she said in a soft voice, 'My God, this child . . . this child. . . ' She looked so unhappy and so astonished, you would have thought I was the one who had scolded her. So much so that I put my arm around her like this and I rocked her up against me, saying, 'There . . . there . . . my little darling, there! . . . ' It ended very happy."

". . . ?"

"Yes, we are! we *are* angry, but for a different reason. The story of the hat is from yesterday. Today . . . here, look at my finger."

". . . !"

"Yes, a cut, a big one, and the nail is split. It has hydrogen peroxide and I don't know what else on it. And here, on my cheek, you can see a red burn; it stings. And my hair, can't you see, on my forehead? Smell it: It must still smell a little like when they singe the pig in the square. These are all today's ordeals, which got Mama and me angry with each other. . . I wanted curly bangs on my forehead; so, so I cut a few hairs—big deal! I know you always go further than you want with scissors. . . And I burned my cheek trying to turn the curling iron, to cool it down, like the hairdresser, you know: it makes it so pretty. . . "

". . . ?"

"The cut, that was the scissors. A little farther and I would have poked out my eye. . . . So, here I am, right, with my hand covered with blood, my hair singed and cut like a staircase, my cheek burned. . . And naturally, right when Mama comes back! Boy, did I ever catch it!"

". . .!"

"Yes, I was in the wrong, but she scolded me in a way that wasn't the way she usually does. I'm sure it wasn't a question of what's appropriate, or of dress, or of children who get into everything and are punished for it! It wasn't even a question of me—or barely!"

". . .?"

"Wait, I'm about to remember. . . She was like a fury. She said that I had ruined *her* daughter for her! She said, 'What have you done with *my* beautiful hair which I tended so patiently? You had no right to touch it! And that cheek, who gave you permission to spoil it! And this little hand? . . . How? . . . I've taken years, I've spent my days and my nights trembling over this masterpiece and all it takes is one of your exploits, you destructive little demon, to ruin the adorable result of so many pains! What you've done to it is cowardly, it's shameful! Your beauty is mine, you don't have the right to take away what I entrust to you!' What do you think of that, Godmother?"

". . ."

"Me either, I couldn't think of anything to say. But it shook me up. I went under the stairs without saying a word. And I felt as sorry for myself as I could. I felt my hands, my legs, my head. 'Poor little things,' I said to myself, 'your hands, your legs, your head aren't even yours! You're like a slave, then! A lot of good it did for your mother to give you birth, since she's taken back all the rest! You wouldn't dare even lose a single baby tooth or break a nail, for fear that your mother will claim it back from you. . . .' Well, you know how you talk to yourself when you want to make yourself cry. . . Oh, I have a mother who torments me so much, Godmother!"

". . ."

"You think I do the same to her! It's possible. So, if she's nice to me at dinner, I can forgive her, too?"

". . ."

"I really want to. It's true, she did call me a destructive demon, but . . . "

". . .?"

"But she also called me an 'adorable result,' and I like that."

[about 1922]

For Discussion

1. What is the godmother saying in the ellipses (". . . ?" etc.)? What is the godmother's role in the interchange, and why does Colette leave out her responses?

2. Describe the event which precipitated the goddaughter's tears—why is she "mad at Mamma"?

3. The young girl creates her own lively language to describe feelings and situations. Find highly figurative phrases (such as "lay back my ears") and identify the significance of each phrase for the goddaughter and for youth in general.

4. What similarity does the goddaughter see between herself and her god-mother? How do they differ from "Mamma"?

5. How are the roles temporarily reversed between the daughter and the mother?

6. What does "Mama's" reaction to her child's "destructiveness" show about the type of mother she represents?

7. What is the daughter's argument about informal school codes? How many different worlds are described in the story, and which are in conflict?

8. How strong is the concern with a young girl's appearance in this story? Who is concerned, and why?

9. Why is the daughter so offended by her mother's comments, and why is she also pleased? What paradoxes of the mother-daughter relationship are presented?

For Further Exploration

1. Read Tillie Olsen's "I Stand Here Ironing" (Women and Family section), a dramatic monologue from a mother's point of view. What feelings are expressed by the mother that we don't get a chance to hear in the child's monologue in "My Goddaughter"? Are any of the same concerns expressed?

2. Read a story about male children, such as Frank O'Connor's "First Confession" or "The Drunkard," or stories from James Joyce's *Dubliners* collection, such as "Eveline" or "Araby." How are portrayals of boys growing up similar or different from this story of a young girl?

Toni Cade Bambara

1939–

The lessons of childhood are not learned just through the family, but through other adult teachers as well. In this story, a bright young girl is confronted with lessons to learn about society, and must eventually choose whether to accept a passive or active approach to life.

THE LESSON

Back in the days when everyone was old and stupid or young and foolish and me and Sugar were the only ones just right, this lady moved on our block with nappy hair and proper speech and no makeup. And quite naturally we laughed at her, laughed the way we did at the junk man who went about his business like he was some big-time president and his sorry-ass horse his secretary. And we kinda hated her too, hated the way we did the winos who cluttered up our parks and pissed on our handball walls and stank up our hallways and stairs so you couldn't halfway play hide-and-seek without a goddamn gas mask. Miss Moore was her name. The only woman on the block with no first name. And she was black as hell, cept for her feet, which were fish-white and spooky. And she was always planning these boring-ass things for us to do, us being my cousin, mostly, who lived on the block cause we all moved North the same time and to the same apartment then spread out gradual to breathe. And our parents would yank our heads into some kinda shape and crisp up our clothes so we'd be presentable for travel with Miss Moore, who always looked like she was going to church, though she never did. Which is just one of the things the grownups talked about when they talked behind her back like a dog. But when she came calling with some sachet she'd sewed up or some gingerbread she'd made or some book, why then they'd all be too embarrassed to turn her down and we'd get handed over all spruced up. She'd been to college and said it was only right that she should take responsibility for the young ones' education, and she not even related by marriage or blood. So they'd go for it. Specially Aunt Gretchen. She was the main gofer in the family. You got some ole dumb shit foolishness you want somebody to go for, you send for Aunt Gretchen. She been screwed into the go-along for so long, it's a blood-deep natural thing with her. Which is how she got saddled with me and Sugar and Junior in the first place while our mothers were in a la-de-da apartment up the block having a good ole time.

So this one day Miss Moore rounds us all up at the mailbox and it's puredee hot and she's knockin herself out about arithmetic. And school suppose to let up in summer I heard, but she don't never let up. And the starch in my pinafore scratching the shit outta me and I'm really hating this nappy-head bitch and her goddamn college degree. I'd much rather go to the pool or to the show where it's cool. So me and Sugar leaning on the mailbox being surly, which is a Miss Moore word. And Flyboy checking out what everybody brought for lunch. And Fat Butt already wasting his peanut-butter-and-jelly sandwich like the pig he is. And Junebug punchin on Q.T.'s arm for potato chips. And Rosie Giraffe shifting from one hip to the other waiting for somebody to step on her foot or ask her if she from Georgia so she can kick ass, preferably Mercedes'. And Miss Moore asking us do we know what money is, like we a bunch of retards. I mean real money, she say, like it's only poker chips or monopoly papers we lay on the grocer. So right away I'm tired of this and say so. And would much rather snatch Sugar and go to the Sunset and terrorize the West Indian kids and take their hair ribbons and their money too. And Miss Moore files that remark away for next week's lesson on brotherhood, I can tell. And finally I say we oughta get to the subway cause it's cooler and besides we might meet some cute boys. Sugar done swiped her mama's lipstick, so we ready.

So we heading down the street and she's boring us silly about what things cost and what our parents make and how much goes for rent and how money ain't divided up right in this country. And then she gets to the part about we all poor and live in the slums, which I don't feature. And I'm ready to speak on that, but she steps out in the street and hails two cabs just like that. Then she hustles half the crew in with her and hands me a five-dollar bill and tells me to calculate 10 percent tip for the driver. And we're off. Me and Sugar and Junebug and Flyboy hangin out the window and hollering to everybody, putting lipstick on each other cause Flyboy a faggot anyway, and making farts with our sweaty armpits. But I'm mostly trying to figure how to spend this money. But they all fascinated with the meter ticking and Junebug starts laying bets as to how much it'll read when Flyboy can't hold his breath no more. Then Sugar lays bets as to how much it'll be when we get there. So I'm stuck. Don't nobody want to go for my plan, which is to jump out at the next light and run off to the first bar-b-que we can find. Then the driver tells us to get the hell out cause we there already. And the meter reads eighty-five cents. And I'm stalling to figure out the tip and Sugar say give him a dime. And I decide he don't need it bad as I do, so later for him. But then he tries to take off with Junebug foot still in the door so we talk about his mama something ferocious. Then we check out that we on Fifth Avenue and everybody dressed up in stockings. One lady in a fur coat, hot as it is. White folks crazy.

"This is the place," Miss Moore say, presenting it to us in the voice she uses at the museum. "Let's look in the windows before we go in."

"Can we steal?" Sugar asks very serious like she's getting the ground rules squared away before she plays. "I beg your pardon," say Miss Moore, and we fall out. So she leads us around the windows of the toy store and me and Sugar screamin, "This is mine, that's mine, I gotta have that, that was made for me, I was born for that," till Big Butt drowns us out.

"Hey, I'm goin to buy that there."

"That there? You don't even know what it is, stupid."

"I do so," he say punchin on Rosie Giraffe. "It's a microscope."

"Whatcha gonna do with a microscope, fool?"

"Look at things."

"Like what, Ronald?" ask Miss Moore. And Big Butt ain't got the first notion. So here go Miss Moore gabbing about the thousands of bacteria in a drop of water and the somethinorother in a speck of blood and the million and one living things in the air around us is invisible to the naked eye. And what she say that for? Junebug go to town on that "naked" and we rolling. Then Miss Moore ask what it cost. So we all jam into the window smudgin it up and the price tag say $300. So then she ask how long'd take for Big Butt and Junebug to save up their allowances. "Too long," I say. "Yeh," adds Sugar, "outgrown it by that time." And Miss Moore say no, you never outgrow learning instruments. "Why, even medical students and interns and," blah, blah, blah. And we ready to choke Big Butt for bringing it up in the first damn place.

"This here costs four hundred eighty dollars," say Rosie Giraffe. So we pile up all over her to see what she pointin out. My eyes tell me it's a chunk of glass cracked with something heavy, and different-color inks dripped into the splits, then the whole thing put into a oven or something. But for $480 it don't make sense.

"That's a paperweight made of semi-precious stones fused together under tremendous pressure," she explains slowly, with her hands doing the mining and all the factory work.

"So what's a paperweight?" asks Rosie Giraffe.

"To weigh paper with; dumbbell," say Flyboy, the wise man from the East.

"Not exactly," say Miss Moore, which is what she say when you warm or way off too. "It's to weigh paper down so it won't scatter and make your desk untidy." So right away me and Sugar curtsy to each other and then to Mercedes who is more the tidy type.

"We don't keep paper on top of the desk in my class," say Junebug, figuring Miss Moore crazy or lyin one.

"At home, then," she say. "Don't you have a calendar and a pencil case and a blotter and a letter-opener on your desk at home where you do your homework?" And she know damn well what our homes look like cause she nosys around in them every chance she gets.

"I don't even have a desk," say Junebug. "Do we?"

"No. And I don't get no homework neither," says Big Butt.

"And I don't even have a home," say Flyboy like he do at school to keep the white folks off his back and sorry for him. Send this poor kid to camp posters, is his specialty.

"I do," says Mercedes. "I have a box of stationery on my desk and a picture of my cat. My godmother bought the stationery and the desk. There's a big rose on each sheet and the envelopes smell like roses."

"Who wants to know about your smelly-ass stationery," say Rosie Giraffe fore I can get my two cents in.

"It's important to have a work area all your own so that . . ."

"Will you look at this sailboat, please," say Flyboy, cuttin her off and pointin to the thing like it was his. So once again we tumble all over each other to gaze at this magnificent thing in the toy store which is just big enough to maybe sail two kittens across the pond if you strap them to the posts tight. We all start reciting the price tag like we in assembly. "Hand-crafted sailboat of fiberglass at one thousand one hundred ninety-five dollars."

"Unbelievable," I hear myself say and am really stunned. I read it again for myself just in case the group recitation put me in a trance. Same thing. For some reason this pisses me off. We look at Miss Moore and she lookin at us, waiting for I dunno what.

"Who'd pay all that when you can buy a sailboat set for a quarter at Pop's, a tube of glue for a dime, and a ball of string for eight cents? It must have a motor and a whole lot else besides," I say. "My sailboat cost me about fifty cents."

"But will it take water?" say Mercedes with her smart ass.

"Took mine to Alley Pond Park once," say Flyboy. "String broke. Lost it. Pity."

"Sailed mine in Central Park and it keeled over and sank. Had to ask my father for another dollar."

"And you got the strap," laugh Big Butt. "The jerk didn't even have a string on it. My old man wailed on his behind."

Little Q.T. was staring hard at the sailboat and you could see he wanted it bad. But he too little and somebody'd just take it from him. So what the hell. "This boat for kids, Miss Moore?"

"Parents silly to buy something like that just to get all broke up," say Rosie Giraffe.

"That much money it should last forever," I figure.

"My father'd buy it for me if I wanted it."

"Your father, my ass," say Rosie Giraffe getting a chance to finally push Mercedes.

"Much be rich people shop here," say Q.T.

"You are a very bright boy," say Flyboy. "What was your first clue?" And he rap him on the head with the back of his knuckles, since Q.T. the only one he could get away with. Though Q.T. liable to come up behind you years later and get his licks in when you half expect it.

"What I want to know is," I says to Miss Moore though I never talk to her, I wouldn't give the bitch that satisfaction, "is how much a real boat costs? I figure a thousand'd get you a yacht any day."

"Why don't you check that out," she says, "and report back to the group?" Which really pains my ass. If you gonna mess up a perfectly good swim day least you could do is have some answers. "Let's go in," she say like she got something up her sleeve. Only she don't lead the way. So me and Sugar turn the corner to where the entrance is, but when we get there I kinda hang back. Not that I'm scared, what's there to be afraid of, just a toy store. But I feel funny, shame. But what I got to be shamed about? Got as much right to go in as anybody. But somehow I can't seem to get hold of the door, so I step away for Sugar to lead. But she hangs back too. And I look at her and she looks at me and this is ridiculous. I mean, damn, I have never ever been shy about doing nothing or going nowhere. But then Mercedes steps up and then Rosie Giraffe and Big Butt crowd in behind and shove, and next thing we all stuffed into the doorway with only Mercedes squeezing past us, smoothing out her jumper and walking right down the aisle. Then the rest of us tumble in like a glued-together jigsaw done all wrong. And people lookin at us. And it's like the time me and Sugar crashed into the Catholic church on a dare. But once we got in there and everything so hushed and holy and the candles and the bowin and the handkerchiefs on all the drooping heads, I just couldn't go through with the plan. Which was for me to run up to the altar and do a tap dance while Sugar played the nose flute and messed around in the holy water. And Sugar kept givin me the elbow. Then later teased me so bad I tied her up in the shower and turned it on and locked her in. And she'd be there till this day if Aunt Gretchen hadn't finally figured I was lyin about the boarder takin a shower.

Same thing in the store. We all walkin on tiptoe and hardly touchin the games and puzzles and things. And I watched Miss Moore who is steady watchin us like she waitin for a sign. Like Mama Drewery watches the sky and sniffs the air and takes note of just how much slant is in the bird formation. Then me and Sugar bump smack into each other, so busy gazing at the toys, 'specially the sailboat. But we don't laugh and go into our fat-lady bump-stomach routine. We just stare at that price tag. Then Sugar run a finger over the whole boat. And I'm jealous and want to hit her. Maybe not her, but I sure want to punch somebody in the mouth.

"Watcha bring us here for, Miss Moore?"

"You sound angry, Sylvia. Are you mad about something?" Givin me one of them grins like she tellin a grown-up joke that never turns out to be funny. And she's lookin very closely at me like maybe she plannin to do my portrait from memory. I'm mad, but I won't give her that satisfaction. So I slouch around the store bein very bored and say, "Let's go."

Me and Sugar at the back of the train watchin the tracks whizzin by large then small then gettin gobbled up in the dark. I'm thinkin about this tricky toy I saw in the store. A clown that somersaults on a bar then does chin-ups just cause you yank lightly at his leg. Cost $35. I could see me askin my mother for a $35 birthday clown. "You wanna who that costs what?" she'd say, cocking her head to the side to get a better view of the hole in my head. Thirty-five dollars could buy new bunk beds for Junior and Gretchen's boy. Thirty-five dollars and the whole household could go visit Granddaddy Nelson in the country. Thirty-five dollars would pay for the rent and the piano bill too. Who are these people that spend that much for performing clowns and $1000 for toy sailboats? What kinda work they do and how they live and how come we ain't in on it? Where we are is who we are, Miss Moore always pointin out. But it don't necessarily have to be that way, she always adds then waits for somebody to say that poor people have to wake up and demand their share of the pie and don't none of us know what kind of pie she talkin about in the first damn place. But she ain't so smart cause I still got her four dollars from the taxi and she sure ain't gettin it. Messin up my day with this shit. Sugar nudges me in my pocket and winks.

Miss Moore lines us up in front of the mailbox where we started from, seem like years ago, and I got a headache for thinkin so hard. And we lean all over each other so we can hold up under the draggy-ass lecture she always finishes us off with at the end before we thank her for borin us to tears. But she just looks at us like she readin tea leaves. Finally she say, "Well, what did you think of F. A. O. Schwarz?"

Rosie Giraffe mumbles, "White folks crazy."

"I'd like to go there again when I get my birthday money," says Mercedes, and we shove her out the pack so she has to lean on the mailbox by herself.

"I'd like a shower. Tiring day," say Flyboy.

Then Sugar surprises me by sayin, "You know, Miss Moore, I don't think all of us here put together eat in a year what that sailboat costs." And Miss Moore lights up like somebody goosed her. "And?" she say, urging Sugar on. Only I'm standin on her foot so she don't continue.

"Imagine for a minute what kind of society it is in which some people can spend on a toy what it would cost to feed a family of six or seven. What do you think?"

"I think," say Sugar pushing me off her feet like she never done before, cause I whip her ass in a minute, "that this is not much of a democracy if you ask me. Equal chance to pursue happiness means an equal crack at the dough, don't it?" Miss Moore is besides herself and I am disgusted with Sugar's treachery. So I stand on her foot one more time to see if she'll shove me. She shuts up, and Miss Moore looks at me, sorrowfully I'm thinkin. And somethin weird is goin on, I can feel it in my chest.

"Anybody else learn anything today?" lookin dead at me. I walk away and Sugar has to run to catch up and don't even seem to notice when I shrug her arm off my shoulder.

"Well, we got four dollars anyway," she says.

"Uh hunh."

"We could go to Hascombs and get half a chocolate layer and then go to the Sunset and still have plenty money for potato chips and ice cream sodas."

"Uh hunh."

"Race you to Hascombs," she say.

We start down the block and she gets ahead which is O.K. by me cause I'm going to the West End and then over to the Drive to think this day through. She can run if she want to and even run faster. But ain't nobody gonna beat me at nuthin.

[1972]

For Discussion

1. Why do the narrator and her cousin "kinda hate" Miss Moore? List characteristics they dislike, and explain why they go along with Miss Moore anyway.

2. What are the messages of Miss Moore's lessons? What is she looking for from the children?

3. On the trip to Fifth Avenue, what opposite lessons are implied by the discussions of the microscope and the paperweight? How do the children's reactions reflect attitudes different types of people adopt later in life?

4. Describe the narrator's tone throughout. What kinds of jokes does she make? How does her colorful language (such as "tumble in like a glued together jigsaw done all wrong") fit each situation?

5. What are the young narrator's concerns and interests in life? How do they fit with Miss Moore's ideas, and why does Miss Moore keep staring at Sylvia?

6. How is the Catholic Church incident repeated in the toy store, and what do the incidents show about the children's states of mind?

7. Explain what is meant by "Where we are is who we are."

8. What emotional stages does the narrator go through? How are each of the narrator's conflicting feelings mirrored by the final comments of the other characters?

9. What might the narrator's headaches suggest in the story? Do Miss Moore's lessons have any effect? Explain the irony of the last line.

For Further Exploration

1. Jean Stafford's story "Bad Characters" shows the humor and creativity a supposedly "bad" child can exhibit. What is similar and different about the "misbehavior" and "unacceptable attitudes" of Bambara's and Stafford's characters?

2. The dividing lines between rich and poor, black and white are explored in other stories and novels such as Toni Morrison's *The Bluest Eye*. Read Morrison's novel and examine the impact of wealth, race, and social status on young girls growing up.

Helen Rose Hull

1888–1971

In "The Fire," the relationship between a young girl and her older mentor is questioned by the girl's family, highlighting the differences between two lifestyles. Cynthia's divided loyalties become part of the process of growing up, and the image of fire serves as a beginning as well as an end.

THE FIRE

Cynthia blotted the entry in the old ledger and scowled across the empty office at the door. Mrs. Moriety had left it ajar when she departed with her receipt for the weekly fifty cents on her "lot." If you supplied the missing gilt letters, you could read the sign on the glass of the upper half: "H. P. Bates. Real Estate. Notary Public." Through the door at Cynthia's elbow came the rumbling voice of old Fleming, the lawyer down the hall; he had come in for his Saturday night game of chess with her father.

Cynthia pushed the ledger away from her, and with her elbows on the spotted, green felt of the desk, her fingers burrowing into her cheeks, waited for two minutes by the nickel clock; then, with a quick, awkward movement, she pushed back her chair and plunged to the doorway, her young face twisted in a sort of fluttering resolution.

"Father—"

Her father jerked his head toward her, his fingers poised over a pawn. Old Fleming did not look up.

"Father, I don't think anybody else will be in."

"Well, go on home, then." Her father bent again over the squares, the light shining strongly on the thin places about his temples.

"Father, please,"—Cynthia spoke hurriedly,—"you aren't going for a while? I want to go down to Miss Egert's for a minute."

"Eh? What's that?" He leaned back in his chair now, and Mr. Fleming lifted his severe, black beard to look at this intruder. "What for? You can't take any more painting lessons. Your mother doesn't want you going there any more."

"I just want to get some things I left there. I can get back to go home with you."

"But your mother said she didn't like your hanging around down there in an empty house with an old maid. What did she tell you about it?"

"Couldn't I just get my sketches, Father, and tell Miss Egert I'm not coming any more? She would think it was awfully funny if I didn't. I won't stay. But she—she's been good to me—"

"What set your mother against her, then? What you been doing down there?"

Cynthia twisted her hands together, her eyes running from Fleming's amused stare to her father's indecision. Only an accumulated determination could have carried her on into speech.

"I've just gone down once a week for a lesson. I want to get my things. If I'm not going, I ought to tell her."

"Why didn't you tell her that last week?"

"I kept hoping I could go on."

"Um." Her father's glance wavered toward his game. "Isn't it too late?"

"Just eight, Father." She stepped near her father, color flooding her cheeks. "If you'll give me ten cents, I can take the car—"

"Well—" He dug into his pocket, nodding at Fleming's grunt, "The women always want cash, eh, Bates?"

Then Cynthia, the dime pressed into her palm, tiptoed across to the nail where her hat and sweater hung, seized them, and still on tiptoe, lest she disturb the game again, ran out to the head of the stairs.

She was trembling as she pulled on her sweater; as she ran down the dark steps to the street the tremble changed to a quiver of excitement. Suppose her father had known just what her mother *had* said! That she could not see Miss Egert again; could never go hurrying down to the cluttered room they called the studio for more of those strange hours of eagerness and pain when she bent over the drawing-board, struggling with the mysteries of color. That last sketch—the little, purpling mint-leaves from the garden— Miss Egert had liked that. And they thought she could leave those sketches there! Leave Miss Egert, too, wondering why she never came again! She hurried to the corner, past the bright store-windows. In thought she could see Miss Egert setting out the jar of brushes, the dishes of water, pushing back the litter of magazines and books to make room for the drawing-board, waiting for her to come. Oh, she had to go once more, black as her disobedience was!

The half-past-eight car was just swinging round the curve. She settled herself behind two German housewives, shawls over their heads, market-baskets beside them. They lived out at the end of the street; one of them sometimes came to the office with payments on her son's lot. Cynthia pressed against the dirty window, fearful lest she miss the corner. There it was, the new street light shining on the sedate old house! She ran to the platform, pushing against the arm the conductor extended.

"Wait a minute, there!" He released her as the car stopped, and she fled across the street.

In front of the house she could not see a light, up-stairs or down, except staring reflections in the windows from the white arc light. She walked past the dark line of box which led to the front door. At the side of the old square dwelling jutted a new, low wing; and there in two windows were soft slits of light along the curtain-edges. Cynthia walked along a little dirt path to a door at the side of the wing. Standing on the door-step, she felt in the shadow for the knocker. As she let it fall, from the garden behind her came a voice:

"I'm out here. Who is it?" There was a noise of feet hurrying through dead leaves, and as Cynthia turned to answer, out of the shadow moved a blur of face and white blouse.

"Cynthia! How nice!" The woman touched Cynthia's shoulder as she pushed open the door. "There, come in."

The candles on the table bent their flames in the draft; Cynthia followed Miss Egert into the room.

"You're busy?" Miss Egert had stood up by the door an old wooden-toothed rake. "I don't want to bother you." Cynthia's solemn, young eyes implored the woman and turned hastily away. The intensity of defiance which had brought her at such an hour left her confused.

"Bother? I was afraid I had to have my grand bonfire alone. Now we can have it a party. You'd like to?"

Miss Egert darted across to straighten one of the candles. The light caught in the folds of her crumpled blouse, in the soft, drab hair blown out around her face.

"I can't stay very long." Cynthia stared about the room, struggling to hide her turmoil under ordinary casualness. "You had the carpenter fix the bookshelves, didn't you?"

"Isn't it nice now! All white and gray and restful—just a spark of life in that mad rug. A good place to sit in and grow old."

Cynthia looked at the rug, a bit of scarlet Indian weaving. She wouldn't see it again! The thought poked a derisive finger into her heart.

"Shall we sit down just a minute and then go have the fire?"

Cynthia dropped into the wicker chair, wrenching her fingers through one another.

"My brother came in to-night, his last attempt to make me see reason," said Miss Egert.

Cynthia lifted her eyes. Miss Egert wasn't wondering why she had come; she could stay without trying to explain.

Miss Egert wound her arms about her knees as she went on talking. Her slight body was wrenched a little out of symmetry, as though from straining always for something uncaptured; there was the same lack of symmetry in her face, in her eyebrows, in the line of her mobile lips. But her eyes had nothing fugitive, nothing pursuing in their soft, gray depth. Their warm, steady eagerness shone out in her voice, too, in its swift inflections.

"I tried to show him it wasn't a bit disgraceful for me to live here in a wing of my own instead of being a sort of nurse-maid adjunct in his house." She laughed, a soft, throaty sound. "It's my house. It's all I have left to keep me a person, you see. I won't get out and be respectable in his eyes."

"He didn't mind your staying here and taking care of—them!" cried Cynthia.

"It's respectable, dear, for an old maid to care for her father and mother; but when they die she ought to be useful to some one else instead of renting her house and living on an edge of it."

"Oh,"—Cynthia leaned forward,—"I should think you'd hate him! I think families are—terrible!"

"Hate him?" Miss Egert smiled. "He's nice. He just doesn't agree with me. As long as he lets the children come over—I told him I meant to have a beautiful time with them, with my real friends—with you."

Cynthia shrank into her chair, her eyes tragic again.

"Come, let's have our bonfire!" Miss Egert, with a quick movement, stood in front of Cynthia, one hand extended.

Cynthia crouched away from the hand.

"Miss Egert,"—her voice came out in a desperate little gasp,—"I can't come down any more. I can't take any more painting lessons." She stopped. Miss Egert waited, her head tipped to one side. "Mother doesn't think I better. I came down—after my things."

"They're all in the workroom." Miss Egert spoke quietly. "Do you want them now?"

"Yes." Cynthia pressed her knuckles against her lips. Over her hand her eyes cried out. "Yes, I better get them," she said heavily.

Miss Egert, turning slowly, lifted a candle from the table.

"We'll have to take this. The wiring isn't done." She crossed the room, her thin fingers, not quite steady, bending around the flame.

Cynthia followed through a narrow passage. Miss Egert pushed open a door, and the musty odor of the store-room floated out into a queer chord with the fresh plaster of the hall.

"Be careful of that box!" Miss Egert set the candle on a pile of trunks. "I've had to move all the truck from the attic and studio in here. Your sketches are in the portfolio, and that's—somewhere!"

Cynthia stood in the doorway, watching Miss Egert bend over a pile of canvases, throwing up a grotesque, rounded shadow on the wall. Round the girl's throat closed a ring of iron.

"Here they are, piled up—"

Cynthia edged between the boxes. Miss Egert was dragging the black portfolio from beneath a pile of books.

"And here's the book I wanted you to see." The pile slipped crashing to the floor as Miss Egert pulled out a magazine. "Never mind those. See here." She dropped into the chair from which she had knocked the books, the portfolio under one arm, the free hand running through the pages of an old art magazine. The chair swung slightly; Cynthia, peering down between the boxes, gave a startled "Oh!"

"What is it?" Miss Egert followed Cynthia's finger. "The chair?" She was silent a moment. "Do you think I keep my mother prisoner here in a wheel-chair now that she is free?" She ran her hand along the worn arm. "I tried to give it to an old ladies' home, but it was too used up. They wanted more style."

"But doesn't it remind you—" Cynthia hesitated.

"It isn't fair to remember the years she had to sit here waiting to die. You didn't know her. I've been going back to the real years—" Miss Egert smiled at Cynthia's bewildered eyes. "Here, let's look at these." She turned another page. "See, Cynthia. Aren't they swift and glad? That's what I was trying to tell you the other day. See that arm, and the drapery there! Just a line—" The girl bent over the page, frowning at the details the quick finger pointed out. "Don't they catch you along with them?" She held the book out at arm's-length, squinting at the figures. "Take it along. There are several more." She tucked the book into the portfolio and rose. "Come on; we'll have our fire."

"But, Miss Egert,"—Cynthia's voice hardened as she was swept back into her own misery,—"I can't take it. I can't come any more."

"To return a book?" Miss Egert lowered her eyelids as if she were again sizing up a composition. "You needn't come just for lessons."

Cynthia shook her head.

"Mother thinks—" She fell into silence. She couldn't say what her mother thought—dreadful things. If she could only swallow the hot pressure in her throat!

"Oh. I hadn't understood." Miss Egert's fingers paused for a swift touch on Cynthia's arm, and then reached for the candle. "You can go on working by yourself."

"It isn't that—" Cynthia struggled an instant, and dropped into silence again. She couldn't say out loud any of the things she was feeling. There were too many walls between feeling and speech: loyalty to her mother, embarrassment that feelings should come so near words, a fear of hurting Miss Egert.

"Don't mind so much, Cynthia." Miss Egert led the way back to the living-room. "You can stay for the bonfire? That will be better than sitting here. Run into the kitchen and bring the matches and marshmallows—in a dish in the cupboard."

Cynthia, in the doorway, stared at Miss Egert. Didn't she care at all! Then the dumb ache in her throat stopped throbbing as Miss Egert's gray eyes held her steadily a moment. She did care! She did! She was just helping her. Cynthia took the candle and went back through the passageway to the kitchen, down at the very end.

She made a place on the table in the litter of dishes and milk-bottles for the candle. The matches had been spilled on the shelf of the stove and into the sink. Cynthia gathered a handful of the driest. Shiftlessness was one of her mother's counts against Miss Egert. Cynthia flushed as she recalled her stumbling defense: Miss Egert had more important things to do; dishes were kept in their proper place; and her mother's: "Important! Mooning about!"

"Find them, Cynthia?" The clear, low voice came down the hall, and Cynthia hurried back.

Out in the garden it was quite black. As they came to the far end, the old stone wall made a dark bank against the sky, with a sharp star over its edge. Miss Egert knelt; almost with the scratch of the match the garden leaped into yellow, with fantastic moving shadows from the trees and in the corner of the wall. She raked leaves over the blaze, pulled the great mound into firmer shape, and then drew Cynthia back under the wall to watch. The light ran over her face; the delighted gestures of her hands were like quick shadows.

"See the old apple-tree dance! He's too old to move fast."

Cynthia crouched by the wall, brushing away from her face the scratchy leaves of the dead hollyhocks. Excitement tingled through her; she felt the red and yellow flames seizing her, burning out the heavy rebellion, the choking weight. Miss Egert leaned back against the wall, her hands spread so that her thin fingers were fire-edged.

"See the smoke curl up through those branches! Isn't it lovely, Cynthia?" She darted around the pile to push more leaves into the flames.

Cynthia strained forward, hugging her arms to her body. Never had there been such a fire! It burned through her awkwardness, her self-consciousness. It ate into the thick, murky veils which hung always between her and the things she struggled to find out. She took a long breath, and the crisp scent of smoke from the dead leaves tingled down through her body.

Miss Egert was at her side again. Cynthia looked up; the slight, asymmetrical figure was like the apple-tree, still, yet dancing!

"Why don't you paint it?" demanded Cynthia, abruptly, and then was frightened as Miss Egert's body stiffened, lost its suggestion of motion.

"I can't." The woman dropped to the ground beside Cynthia, crumpling a handful of leaves. "It's too late." She looked straight at the fire. "I must be content to see it." She blew the pieces of leaves from the palm of her hand and smiled at Cynthia. "Perhaps some day you'll paint it—or write it."

"I can't paint." Cynthia's voice quivered. "I want to do something. I can't even see things except what you point out. And now—"

Miss Egert laid one hand over Cynthia's clenched fingers. The girl trembled at the cold touch.

"You must go on looking." The glow, as the flames died lower, flushed her face. "Cynthia, you're just beginning. You mustn't stop just because you aren't to come here any more. I don't know whether you can say things with your brush; but you must find them out. You mustn't shut your eyes again."

"It's hard alone."

"That doesn't matter."

Cynthia's fingers unclasped, and one hand closed desperately around Miss Egert's. Her heart fluttered in her temples, her throat, her breast. She clung to the fingers, pulling herself slowly up from an inarticulate abyss.

"Miss Egert,"—she stumbled into words,—"I can't bear it, not coming here! Nobody else cares except about sensible things. You do, beautiful, wonderful things."

"You'd have to find them for yourself, Cynthia." Miss Egert's fingers moved under the girl's grasp. Then she bent toward Cynthia, and kissed her with soft, pale lips that trembled against the girl's mouth. "Cynthia, don't let any one stop you! Keep searching!" She drew back, poised for a moment in the shadow before she rose. Through Cynthia ran the swift feet of white ecstasy. She was pledging herself to some tremendous mystery, which trembled all about her.

"Come, Cynthia, we're wasting our coals."

Miss Egert held out her hands. Cynthia, laying hers in them, was drawn to her feet. As she stood there, inarticulate, full of a strange, excited, shouting hope, behind them the path crunched. Miss Egert turned, and Cynthia shrank back.

Her mother stood in the path, making no response to Miss Egert's "Good evening, Mrs. Bates."

The fire had burned too low to lift the shadow from the mother's face. Cynthia could see the hem of her skirt swaying where it dipped up in front. Above that two rigid hands in gray cotton gloves; above that the suggestion of a white, strained face.

Cynthia took a little step toward her.

"I came to get my sketches," she implored her. Her throat was dry. What if her mother began to say cruel things—the things she had already said at home.

"I hope I haven't kept Cynthia too late," Miss Egert said. "We were going to toast marshmallows. Won't you have one, Mrs. Bates?" She pushed the glowing leaf-ashes together. The little spurt of flame showed Cynthia her mother's eyes, hard, angry, resting an instant on Miss Egert and then assailing her.

"Cynthia knows she should not be here. She is not permitted to run about the streets alone at night."

"Oh, I'm sorry." Miss Egert made a deprecating little gesture. "But no harm has come to her."

"She has disobeyed me."

At the tone of her mother's voice Cynthia felt something within her breast curl up like a leaf caught in flame.

"I'll get the things I came for." She started toward the house, running past her mother. She must hurry, before her mother said anything to hurt Miss Egert.

She stumbled on the door-step, and flung herself against the door. The portfolio was across the room, on the little, old piano. The candle beside it had guttered down over the cover. Cynthia pressed out the wobbly flame, and, hugging the portfolio, ran back across the room. On the threshold she turned for a last glimpse. The row of Botticelli details over the bookcases were blurred into gray in the light of the one remaining candle; the Indian rug had a wavering glow. Then she heard Miss Egert just outside.

"I'm sorry Cynthia isn't to come any more," she was saying.

Cynthia stepped forward. The two women stood in the dim light, her mother's thickened, settled body stiff and hostile, Miss Egert's slight figure swaying toward her gently.

"Cynthia has a good deal to do," her mother answered. "We can't afford to give her painting lessons, especially—" Cynthia moved down between the women—"especially," her mother continued, "as she doesn't seem to get much of anywhere. You'd think she'd have some pictures to show after so many lessons."

"Perhaps I'm not a good teacher. Of course she's just beginning."

"She'd better put her time on her studies."

"I'll miss her. We've had some pleasant times together."

Cynthia held out her hand toward Miss Egert, with a fearful little glance at her mother.

"Good-by, Miss Egert."

Miss Egert's cold fingers pressed it an instant.

"Good night, Cynthia," she said slowly.

Then Cynthia followed her mother's silent figure along the path; she turned her head as they reached the sidewalk. Back in the garden winked the red eye of the fire.

They waited under the arc light for the car, Cynthia stealing fleeting glances at her mother's averted face. On the car she drooped against the window-edge, away from her mother's heavy silence. She was frightened now, a panicky child caught in disobedience. Once, as the car turned at the corner below her father's office, she spoke:

"Father will expect me—"

"He knows I went after you," was her mother's grim answer.

Cynthia followed her mother into the house. Her small brother was in the sitting-room, reading. He looked up from his book with wide, knowing eyes. Rebellious humiliation washed over Cynthia; setting her lips against their quivering, she pulled off her sweater.

"Go on to bed, Robert," called her mother from the entry, where she was hanging her coat. "You've sat up too late as it is."

He yawned, and dragged his feet with provoking slowness past Cynthia.

"Was she down there, Mama?" He stopped on the bottom step to grin at his sister.

"Go on, Robert. Start your bath. Mother'll be up in a minute."

"Aw, it's too late for a bath." He leaned over the rail.

"It's Saturday. I couldn't get back sooner."

Cynthia swung away from the round, grinning face. Her mother went past her into the dining-room. Robert shuffled upstairs; she heard the water splashing into the tub.

Her mother was very angry with her. Presently she would come back, would begin to speak. Cynthia shivered. The familiar room seemed full of hostile, accusing silence, like that of her mother. If only she had come straight home from the office, she would be sitting by the table in the old Morris chair, reading, with her mother across from her sewing, or glancing through the evening paper. She gazed about the room at the neat scrolls of the brown wall-paper, at a picture above the couch, cows by a stream. The dull, ordinary comfort of life there hung about her, a reproaching shadow, within which she felt the heavy, silent discomfort her transgression dragged after it. It would be much easier to go on just as she was expected to do. Easier. The girl straightened her drooping body. That things were hard didn't matter. Miss Egert had insisted upon that. She was forgetting the pledge she had given. The humiliation slipped away, and a cold exaltation trembled through her, a remote echo of the hope that had shouted within her back there in the garden. Here it was difficult to know what she had promised, to

CHILDHOOD

what she had pledged herself—something that the familiar, comfortable room had no part in.

She glanced toward the dining-room, and her breath quickened. Between the faded green portières stood her mother, watching her with hard, bright eyes. Cynthia's glance faltered; she looked desperately about the room as if hurrying her thoughts to some shelter. Beside her on the couch lay the portfolio. She took a little step toward it, stopping at her mother's voice.

"Well, Cynthia, have you anything to say?"

Cynthia lifted her eyes.

"Don't you think I have trouble enough with your brothers? You, a grown girl, defying me! I can't understand it."

"I went down for this." Cynthia touched the black case.

"Put that down! I don't want to see it!" The mother's voice rose, breaking down the terrifying silences. "You disobeyed me. I told you you weren't to go there again. And then I telephoned your father to ask you to do an errand for me, and find you there—with that woman!"

"I'm not going again." Cynthia twisted her hands together. "I had to go a last time. She was a friend. I could not tell her I wasn't coming—"

"A friend! A sentimental old maid, older than your mother! Is that a friend for a young girl? What were you doing when I found you? Holding hands! Is that the right thing for you? She's turned your head. You aren't the same Cynthia, running off to her, complaining of your mother."

"Oh, no!" Cynthia flung out her hand. "We were just talking." Her misery confused her.

"Talking? About what?"

"About—" The recollection rushed through Cynthia—"about beauty." She winced, a flush sweeping up to the edge of her fair hair, at her mother's laugh.

"Beauty! You disobey your mother, hurt her, to talk about beauty at night with an old maid!"

There was a hot beating in Cynthia's throat; she drew back against the couch.

"Pretending to be an artist," her mother drove on, "to get young girls who are foolish enough to listen to her sentimentalizing."

"She was an artist," pleaded Cynthia. "She gave it up to take care of her father and mother. I told you all about that—"

"Talking about beauty doesn't make artists."

Cynthia stared at her mother. She had stepped near the table, and the light through the green shade of the reading-lamp made queer pools of color about her eyes, in the waves of her dark hair. She didn't look real. Cynthia threw one hand up against her lips. She was sucked down and down in an eddy of despair. Her mother's voice dragged her again to the surface.

"We let you go there because you wanted to paint, and you maunder and say things you'd be ashamed to have your mother hear. I've spent my life working for you, planning for you, and you go running off—" Her voice broke into a new note, a trembling, grieved tone. "I've always trusted you, depended on you: now I can't even trust you."

"I won't go there again. I had to explain."

"I can't believe you. You don't care how you make me feel."

Cynthia was whirled again down the sides of the eddy.

"I can't believe you care anything for me, your own mother."

Cynthia plucked at the braid on her cuff.

"I didn't do it to make you sorry," she whispered. "I—it was—" The eddy closed about her, and with a little gasp she dropped down on the couch, burying her head in the sharp angle of her elbows.

The mother took another step toward the girl; her hand hovered above the bent head and then dropped.

"You know mother wants just what is best for you, don't you? I can't let you drift away from us, your head full of silly notions."

Cynthia's shoulders jerked. From the head of the stairs came Robert's shout:

"Mama, tub's full!"

"Yes; I'm coming."

Cynthia looked up. She was not crying. About her eyes and nostrils strained the white intensity of hunger.

"You don't think—" She stopped, struggling with her habit of inarticulateness. "There might be things—not silly—you might not see what—"

"Cynthia!" The softness snapped out of the mother's voice.

Cynthia stumbled up to her feet; she was as tall as her mother. For an instant they faced each other, and then the mother turned away, her eyes tear-brightened. Cynthia put out an awkward hand.

"Mother," she said piteously, "I'd like to tell you—I'm sorry—"

"You'll have to show me you are by what you do." The woman started wearily up the stairs. "Go to bed. It's late."

Cynthia waited until the bath-room door closed upon Robert's splashings. She climbed the stairs slowly, and shut herself into her room. She laid the portfolio in the bottom drawer of her white bureau; then she stood by her window. Outside, the big elm-tree, in fine, leafless dignity, showed dimly against the sky, a few stars caught in the arch of its branches.

A swift, tearing current of rebellion swept away her unhappiness, her confused misery; they were bits of refuse in this new flood. She saw, with a fierce, young finality that she was pledged to a conflict as well as to a search. As she knelt by the window and pressed her cheek on the cool glass, she felt the house about her, with its pressure of useful, homely things, as a very prison. No more journeyings down to Miss Egert's for glimpses of escape. She must find her own ways. Keep searching! At the phrase, excitement again glowed within her; she saw the last red wink of the fire in the garden.

[1917]

For Discussion

1. What attitude towards the girl and towards Miss Egert do the father and Fleming exhibit at the beginning of the story?

2. What is different about Miss Egert, and why does Cynthia want to see her again?

3. Describe Miss Egert's interests, and contrast them with Cynthia's family's topics of conversation. What worlds are in opposition here?

4. What does Miss Egert's brother's point of view represent in the story? Why does Cynthia "think families are—terrible!"?

5. Why are Miss Egert's "real friends" children? Explain what she means by referring to "real years," "real friends." Why does she say that her mother is now "free"?

6. List the mother's complaints about Miss Egert, then list Cynthia's reasons for liking the older woman. Can we tell what the author's attitude is?

7. How do you interpret Miss Egert's kissing Cynthia?

8. What creates the epiphany (moment of insight and exhilaration) Cynthia experiences at the fire?

9. What principles are in opposition in the final scene, and what do they suggest about Cynthia's maturation process?

For Further Exploration

1. Gail Godwin's best-selling novel *The Finishing School* is extremely similar to this story about the relationship between an older woman and a young girl. After reading Godwin's novel, explain what the young girls gain by associating with an older woman not part of the family.

2. Discuss a number of possible interpretations of the title of the story, as it relates to the fire at the end and to the overall motifs. How does Hull build to the final scene, and why is fire appropriate as an image to connect the different levels of meaning of the story?

Grace Paley

1922–

*Shirley Abramowitz rises to the top of her world with grace and humor.
Despite the attempted restrictions of a confining society, a few helpmates
challenge the child with the loudest voice and the strongest heart to grow
and to enlarge the worlds of others.*

THE LOUDEST VOICE

There is a certain place where dumb-waiters boom, doors slam, dishes crash;
every window is a mother's mouth bidding the street shut up, go skate
somewhere else, come home. My voice is the loudest.

There, my own mother is still as full of breathing as me and the grocer
stands up to speak to her. "Mrs. Abramowitz," he says, "people should not
be afraid of their children."

"Ah, Mr. Bialik," my mother replies, "if you say to her or her father
'Ssh,' they say, 'In the grave it will be quiet.' "

"From Coney Island to the cemetery," says my papa. "It's the same
subway; it's the same fare."

I am right next to the pickle barrel. My pinky is making tiny whirlpools
in the brine. I stop a moment to announce: "Campbell's Tomato Soup.
Campbell's Vegetable Beef Soup. Campbell's S-c-otch Broth . . ."

"Be quiet," the grocer says, "the labels are coming off."

"Please, Shirley, be a little quiet," my mother begs me.

In that place the whole street groans: Be quiet! Be quiet! but steals from
the happy chorus of my inside self not a tittle or a jot.

There, too, but just around the corner, is a red brick building that has
been old for many years. Every morning the children stand before it in double lines which must be straight. They are not insulted. They are waiting
anyway.

I am usually among them. I am, in fact, the first, since I begin with "A."

One cold morning the monitor tapped me on the shoulder. "Go to Room
409, Shirley Abramowitz," he said. I did as I was told. I went in a hurry up a
down staircase to Room 409, which contained sixth-graders. I had to wait at
the desk without wiggling until Mr. Hilton, their teacher, had time to speak.

After five minutes he said, "Shirley?"

"What?" I whispered.

He said, "My! My! Shirley Abramowitz! They told me you had a particularly loud, clear voice and read with lots of expression. Could that be true?"

"Oh yes," I whispered.

"In that case, don't be silly; I might very well be your teacher someday.
Speak up, speak up."

"Yes," I shouted.

"More like it," he said. "Now, Shirley, can you put a ribbon in your hair
or a bobby pin? It's too messy."

"Yes!" I bawled.

"Now, now, calm down." He turned to the class. "Children, not a
sound. Open at page 39. Read till 52. When you finish, start again." He

looked me over once more. "Now, Shirley, you know, I suppose, that Christmas is coming. We are preparing a beautiful play. Most of the parts have been given out. But I still need a child with a strong voice, lots of stamina. Do you know what stamina is? You do? Smart kid. You know, I heard you read 'The Lord is my shepherd' in Assembly yesterday. I was very impressed. Wonderful delivery. Mrs. Jordan, your teacher, speaks highly of you. Now listen to me, Shirley Abramowitz, if you want to take the part and be in the play repeat after me, 'I swear to work harder than I ever did before.' "

I looked to heaven and said at once, "Oh, I swear." I kissed my pinky and looked at God.

"That is an actor's life, my dear," he explained. "Like a soldier's, never tardy or disobedient to his general, the director. Everything," he said, "absolutely everything will depend on you."

That afternoon, all over the building, children scraped and scrubbed the turkeys and the sheaves of corn off the schoolroom windows. Goodbye Thanksgiving. The next morning a monitor brought red paper and green paper from the office. We made new shapes and hung them on the walls and glued them to the doors.

The teachers became happier and happier. Their heads were ringing like the bells of childhood. My best friend Evie was prone to evil, but she did not get a single demerit for whispering. We learned "Holy Night" without an error. "How wonderful!" said Miss Glacé, the student teacher. "To think that some of you don't even speak the language!" We learned "Deck the Halls" and "Hark! The Herald Angels". . . . They weren't ashamed and we weren't embarrassed.

Oh, but when my mother heard about it all, she said to my father: "Misha, you don't know what's going on there. Cramer is the head of the Tickets Committee."

"Who?" asked my father. "Cramer? Oh yes, an active woman."

"Active? Active has to have a reason. Listen," she said sadly, "I'm surprised to see my neighbors making tra-la-la for Christmas."

My father couldn't think of what to say to that. Then he decided: "You're in America! Clara, you wanted to come here. In Palestine the Arabs would be eating you alive. Europe you had pogroms. Argentina is full of Indians. Here you got Christmas. . . . Some joke, ha?"

"Very funny, Misha. What is becoming of you? If we came to a new country a long time ago to run away from tyrants, and instead we fall into a creeping pogrom, that our children learn a lot of lies, so what's the joke? Ach, Misha, your idealism is going away."

"So is your sense of humor."

"That I never had, but idealism you had a lot of."

"I'm the same Misha Abramovitch, I didn't change an iota. Ask anyone."

"Only ask me," says my mama, may she rest in peace. "I got the answer."

Meanwhile the neighbors had to think of what to say too.

Marty's father said: "You know, he has a very important part, my boy."

"Mine also," said Mr. Sauerfeld.

"Not my boy!" said Mrs. Klieg. "I said to him no. The answer is no. When I say no! I mean no!"

The rabbi's wife said, "It's disgusting!" But no one listened to her. Under the narrow sky of God's great wisdom she wore a strawberry-blond wig.

Every day was noisy and full of experience. I was Right-hand Man. Mr.

Hilton said: "How could I get along without you, Shirley?"

He said: "Your mother and father ought to get down on their knees every night and thank God for giving them a child like you."

He also said: "You're absolutely a pleasure to work with, my dear, dear child."

Sometimes he said: "For God's sakes, what did I do with the script? Shirley! Shirley! Find it."

Then I answered quietly: "Here it is, Mr. Hilton."

Once in a while, when he was very tired, he would cry out: "Shirley, I'm just tired of screaming at those kids. Will you tell Ira Pushkov not to come in till Lester points to that star the second time?"

Then I roared: "Ira Pushkov, what's the matter with you? Dope! Mr. Hilton told you five times already, don't come in till Lester points to that star the second time."

"Ach, Clara," my father asked, "what does she do there till six o'clock she can't even put the plates on the table?"

"Christmas," said my mother coldly.

"Ho! Ho!" my father said. "Christmas. What's the harm? After all, history teaches everyone. We learn from reading this is a holiday from pagan times also, candles, lights, even Chanukah. So we learn it's not altogether Christian. So if they think it's a private holiday, they're only ignorant, not patriotic. What belongs to history, belongs to all men. You want to go back to the Middle Ages? Is it better to shave your head with a secondhand razor? Does it hurt Shirley to learn to speak up? It does not. So maybe someday she won't live between the kitchen and the shop. She's not a fool."

I thank you, Papa, for your kindness. It is true about me to this day. I am foolish but I am not a fool.

That night my father kissed me and said with great interest in my career, "Shirley, tomorrow's your big day. Congrats."

"Save it," my mother said. Then she shut all the windows in order to prevent tonsillitis.

In the morning it snowed. On the street corner a tree had been decorated for us by a kind city administration. In order to miss its chilly shadow our neighbors walked three blocks east to buy a loaf of bread. The butcher pulled down black window shades to keep the colored lights from shining on his chickens. Oh, not me. On the way to school, with both my hands I tossed it a kiss of tolerance. Poor thing, it was a stranger in Egypt.

I walked straight into the auditorium past the staring children. "Go ahead, Shirley!" said the monitors. Four boys, big for their age, had already started work as propmen and stagehands.

Mr. Hilton was very nervous. He was not even happy. Whatever he started to say ended in a sideward look of sadness. He sat slumped in the middle of the first row and asked me to help Miss Glacé. I did this, although she thought my voice too resonant and said, "Showoff!"

Parents began to arrive long before we were ready. They wanted to make a good impression. From among the yards of drapes I peeked out at the audience. I saw my embarrassed mother.

Ira, Lester, and Meyer were pasted to their beards by Miss Glacé. She almost forgot to thread the star on its wire, but I reminded her. I coughed a few times to clear my throat. Miss Glacé looked around and saw that everyone was in costume and on line waiting to play his part. She whispered, "All right . . ." Then:

Jackie Sauerfeld, the prettiest boy in first grade, parted the curtains with his skinny elbow and in a high voice sang out:

"Parents dear
We are here
To make a Christmas play in time.
It we give
In narrative
And illustrate with pantomime."

He disappeared.

My voice burst immediately from the wings to the great shock of Ira, Lester, and Meyer, who were waiting for it but were surprised all the same.

"I remember, I remember, the house where I was born . . ."

Miss Glacé yanked the curtain open and there it was, the house—an old hayloft, where Celia Kornbluh lay in the straw with Cindy Lou, her favorite doll. Ira, Lester, and Meyer moved slowly from the wings toward her, sometimes pointing to a moving star and sometimes ahead to Cindy Lou.

It was a long story and it was a sad story. I carefully pronounced all the words about my lonesome childhood, while little Eddie Braunstein wandered upstage and down with his shepherd's stick, looking for sheep. I brought up lonesomeness again, and not being understood at all except by some women everybody hated. Eddie was too small for that and Marty Groff took his place, wearing his father's prayer shawl. I announced twelve friends, and half the boys in the fourth grade gathered round Marty, who stood on an orange crate while my voice harangued. Sorrowful and loud, I declaimed about love and God and Man, but because of the terrible deceit of Abie Stock we came suddenly to a famous moment. Marty, whose remembering tongue I was, waited at the foot of the cross. He stared desperately at the audience. I groaned, "My God, my God why hast thou forsaken me?" The soldiers who were sheiks grabbed poor Marty to pin him up to die, but he wrenched free, turned again to the audience, and spread his arms aloft to show despair and the end. I murmured at the top of my voice, "The rest is silence, but as everyone in this room, in this city—in this world—now knows, I shall have life eternal."

That night Mrs. Kornbluh visited our kitchen for a glass of tea.

"How's the virgin?" asked my father with a look of concern.

"For a man with a daughter, you got a fresh mouth, Abramovitch."

"Here," said my father kindly, "have some lemon, it'll sweeten your disposition."

They debated a little in Yiddish, then fell in a puddle of Russian and Polish. What I understood next was my father, who said, "Still and all, it was certainly a beautiful affair, you have to admit, introducing us to the beliefs of a different culture."

"Well, yes," said Mrs. Kornbluh. "The only thing . . . you know Charlie Turner—that cute boy in Celia's class—a couple others? They got very small parts or no part at all. In very bad taste, it seemed to me. After all, it's their religion."

"Ach," explained my mother, "what could Mr. Hilton do? They got very small voices; after all, why should they holler? The English language they know from the beginning by heart. They're blond like angels. You think it's so important they should get in the play? Christmas . . . the whole piece of goods . . . they own it."

I listened and listened until I couldn't listen any more. Too sleepy, I climbed out of bed and kneeled. I made a little church of my hands and said, "Hear, O Israel . . ." Then I called out in Yiddish, "Please, good night, good night. Ssh." My father said, "Ssh yourself," and slammed the kitchen door.

I was happy. I fell asleep at once. I had prayed for everybody: my talking family, cousins far away, passersby, and all the lonesome Christians. I expected to be heard. My voice was certainly the loudest.

[1956]

For Discussion

1. Reread the first two sentences personifying the "certain place" inhabited by the main character. What is this place, and how is the personification of place continued?

2. What does the grocer think of Shirley's voice? What is her mother's attitude? her father's? Mr. Hilton, the teacher's?

3. Why do some people object to Shirley's loud voice, or to her part in the Christmas play? Explain the relationship between this story and larger issues in society.

4. What does Mr. Hilton want in an actor? What "lessons for success" does his advice contain?

5. What does Shirley do as "Right-hand Man"? How is she "foolish but not a fool"?

6. Explain the significance of the Christmas tree incident and Shirley's "kiss of tolerance."

7. What role does Shirley have in the play, and what parts are played by Marty Groff and Abie Stock? How does the narrator's version of the "long . . . sad story" give new meaning to the Christmas story, which Shirley's father says is "not altogether Christian" and "belongs to history, belongs to all men"?

8. Discuss the meaning of the adults' interchange Shirley overhears. How does the line "the whole piece of goods . . . they own it" relate to this story and others about childhood?

9. Explain what Shirley's prayers and her goodnights show about her attitudes to the people who would have denied her part in the play. What does she as a person have in common with the part she played?

10. Discuss Shirley's possible future, given her attitude in the last two sentences.

For Further Exploration

1. Read another story in which religion and growing up are intertwined as themes, such as "A Temple of the Holy Ghost," by Flannery O'Connor, or "The Conversion of the Jews," by Philip Roth. In what ways is the ironic interplay between religious lessons and coming to adulthood evident in these stories? Explore ways in which the lessons learned have an impact on the lives in O'Connor or Roth's story and the girl's life in Paley's story,

in an attempt to determine the effects that sex roles and religious teaching have on children.

2. Examine the author's use of language, style, and tone. What makes this quite short story at once funny, sad, and touching? What keeps the use of Jewish dialect from being offensively stereotyped, and how does the author create gentle humor, rather than bitter satire?

Poetry About Childhood

The views of childhood presented by these poets show a range of emotions also evident in the fiction—from happiness and exhilaration to sadness, despair, and even outrage. There are "happy birthdays and very good Christmasses," as well as deprivation and loneliness. Despite the international character and disparate time periods of the poems, the mixed emotions of childhood emerge as universal.

As in fiction about childhood, in poems the senses are bombarded with images of color, sights, sounds, and smells, whether leading to bitterness or to joy for the young girls. The natural world and the world of people are alive to the senses of the child growing up, and the same paradoxical desires to be alone and to be with others are evident. Extending this dichotomy, the poets explore the meaning of loneliness in childhood, and each has a different attitude towards what it means to be "quiet" as a female child.

Constance Carrier

1908–

LISA

Under the great down-curving lilac branches,
a dome of coolness and a cave of bloom,
Lisa, vague-eyed, chin-propped, cross-legged, is sitting
within a leaf-walled room.

Beyond the curtaining green, her brothers wrangle,
cars pass, a huckster shouts, a bicycle bell
is brisk, is brief, dogs bark. She does not hear them.
She is netted in silence, she is lost in a spell.

She has chosen to come here, but she is not hiding,
nor in disgrace, nor sulky. She is alone
of her free will—alone and yet not lonely:
this quarter hour her own.

She could not tell you herself what she is thinking,
or what she makes of this kingdom she has found.
Presently she will go and join the others:
her voice will sound

with theirs. But now the candid light, come sifting
thro leaves, illuminates another view.
O leaf and light, that can divide thus cleanly
the world in two

and give the halves to a child, so to acquaint her
with the mind's need of quietude for growth,
yet interpose no barrier between them,
that she may move in both.

[1955]

Anne Sexton
1928–1974

YOUNG

A thousand doors ago
when I was a lonely kid
in a big house with four
garages and it was summer
as long as I could remember,
I lay on the lawn at night,
clover wrinkling under me,
the wise stars bedding over me,
my mother's window a funnel
of yellow heat running out,
my father's window, half shut,
an eye where sleepers pass,
and the boards of the house
were smooth and white as wax
and probably a million leaves
sailed on their strange stalks
as the crickets ticked together
and I, in my brand new body,
which was not a woman's yet,
told the stars my questions
and thought God could really see
the heat and the painted light,
elbows, knees, dreams, goodnight.

[1962]

Tahereh Saffarzadeh

1939–

BIRTHPLACE

I have never seen the place where I was born

the place my mother
laid down beneath a ceiling
her womb's cumbrous load—

The first tick-tockings of my small heart
still live in the chimney fittings
and in the crannies of the old bricks
and there still visible on the door and walls
is that look of shame,
my mother's look
at my father
and my grandfather

A choked voice murmured
"It's a girl"
The midwife trembled
unsure of her birthing fee
—and goodbye to the circumcision feast

The first visit I make to my birthplace
I'll peel from the walls
that shamed look of my mother
and there where the bold rhythm of my pulse began
I'll make confession:
my clear hands
bear no urge to clench and strike
Brawling drunk isn't my language
I take no pride in killing
Male supremacy
never fattened me at its table

[about 1973]

Translated from the Farsi by Deirdre Lashgari

Nikki Giovanni

1943–

NIKKI–ROSA

childhood remembrances are always a drag
if you're Black
you always remember things like living in Woodlawn
with no inside toilet
and if you become famous or something
they never talk about how happy you were to have
your mother
all to yourself and
how good the water felt when you got your bath
from one of those
big tubs that folk in chicago barbecue in
and somehow when you talk about home
it never gets across how much you
understood their feelings
as the whole family attended meetings about Hollydale
and even though you remember
your biographers never understand
your father's pain as he sells his stock
and another dream goes
And though you're poor it isn't poverty that
concerns you
and though they fought a lot
it isn't your father's drinking that makes any difference
but only that everybody is together and you
and your sister have happy birthdays and very good
Christmasses
and I really hope no white person ever has cause
to write about me
because they never understand
Black love is Black wealth and they'll
probably talk about my hard childhood
and never understand that
all the while I was quite happy

[1973]

May Swenson

1914–

THE CENTAUR

The summer that I was ten—
Can it be there was only one
summer that I was ten? It must

have been a long one then—
each day I'd go out to choose
a fresh horse from my stable

which was a willow grove
down by the old canal.
I'd go on my two bare feet.

But when, with my brother's jack-knife,
I had cut me a long limber horse
with a good thick knob for a head,

and peeled him slick and clean
except a few leaves for the tail,
and cinched my brother's belt

around his head for a rein,
I'd straddle and canter him fast
up the grass bank to the path,

trot along in the lovely dust
that talcumed over his hoofs,
hiding my toes, and turning

his feet to swift half-moons.
The willow knob with the strap
jouncing between my thighs

was the pommel and yet the poll
of my nickering pony's head.
My head and my neck were mine,

yet they were shaped like a horse.
My hair flopped to the side
like the mane of a horse in the wind.

My forelock swung in my eyes,
my neck arched and I snorted.
I shied and skittered and reared,

stopped and raised my knees,
pawed at the ground and quivered.
My teeth bared as we wheeled

and swished through the dust again.
I was the horse and the rider,
and the leather I slapped to his rump

spanked my own behind.
Doubled, my two hoofs beat
a gallop along the bank,

the wind twanged in my mane,
my mouth squared to the bit.
And yet I sat on my steed

quiet, negligent riding,
my toes standing the stirrups,
my thighs hugging his ribs.

At a walk we drew up to the porch.
I tethered him to a paling.
Dismounting, I smoothed my skirt

and entered the dusky hall.
My feet on the clean linoleum
left ghostly toes in the hall.

Where have you been? said my mother.
Been riding, I said from the sink,
and filled me a glass of water.

What's that in your pocket? she said.
Just my knife. It weighted my pocket
and stretched my dress awry.

Go tie back your hair, said my mother,
and *Why is your mouth all green?*
*Rob Roy, he pulled some clover
as we crossed the field,* I told her.

[1956]

George Eliot

1819–1880

BROTHER AND SISTER

I

I cannot choose but think upon the time
When our two lives grew like two buds that kiss
At lightest thrill from the bee's swinging chime,
Because the one so near the other is.

He was the elder and a little man
Of forty inches, bound to show no dread,
And I the girl that puppy-like now ran,
Now lagged behind my brother's larger tread.

I held him wise, and when he talked to me
Of snakes and birds, and which God loved the best,
I thought his knowledge marked the boundary
Where men grew blind, though angels knew the rest.

> If he said "Hush!" I tried to hold my breath;
> Wherever he said "Come!" I stepped in faith.

II

Long years have left their writing on my brow,
But yet the freshness and the dew-fed beam
Of those young mornings are about me now,
When we two wandered toward the far-off stream

With rod and line. Our basket held a store
Baked for us only, and I thought with joy
That I should have my share, though he had more,
Because he was the elder and a boy.

The firmaments of daisies since to me
Have had those mornings in their opening eyes,
The bunched cowslip's pale transparency
Carries that sunshine of sweet memories,

> And wild-rose branches take their finest scent
> From those blest hours of infantine content.

III

Our mother bade us keep the trodden ways,
Stroked down my tippet,[1] set my brother's frill,
Then with the benediction of her gaze
Clung to us lessening, and pursued us still

[1] Cape.

Across the homestead to the rookery[2] elms,
Whose tall old trunks had each a grassy mound,
So rich for us, we counted them as realms
With varied products: here were earth-nuts found,

And here the Lady-fingers in deep shade;
Here sloping toward the Moat the rushes grew,
The large to split for pith,[3] the small to braid:
While over all the dark rooks cawing flew,

And made a happy strange solemnity,
A deep-toned chant from life unknown to me.

IV

Our meadow-path had memorable spots:
One where it bridged a tiny rivulet,
Deep hid by tangled blue Forget-me-nots;
And all along the waving grasses met

My little palm, or nodded to my cheek,
When flowers with upturned faces gazing drew
My wonder downward, seeming all to speak
With eyes of souls that dumbly heard and knew.

Then came the copse,[4] where wild things rushed unseen,
And black-scathed grass betrayed the past abode
Of mystic gypsies, who still lurked between
Me and each hidden distance of the road.

A gypsy once had startled me at play,
Blotting with her dark smile my sunny day

V

Thus rambling we were schooled in deepest lore,
And learned the meanings that give words a soul,
The fear, the love, the primal passionate store,
Whose shaping impulses make manhood whole.

Those hours were seed to all my after good;
My infant gladness, through eye, ear, and touch,
Took easily as warmth a various food
To nourish the sweet skill of loving much.

For who in age shall roam the earth and find
Reasons for loving that will strike out love
With sudden rod from the hard year-pressed mind?
Were reasons sown as thick as stars above,

[2] Rook or raven's nest.
[3] Plant stems.
[4] Wooded area.

'Tis love must see them, as the eye sees light:
Day is but Number[5] to the darkened sight.

VI

Our brown canal was endless to my thought;
And on its banks I sat in dreamy peace,
Unknowing how the good I loved was wrought,
Untroubled by the fear that it would cease.

Slowly the barges floated into view
Rounding a grassy hill to me sublime
With some Unknown beyond it, whither flew
The parting cuckoo toward a fresh spring time.

The wide-arched bridge, the scented elder-flowers,
The wondrous watery rings that died too soon,
The echoes of the quarry, the still hours
With white robe sweeping on the shadeless noon,

Were but my growing self, are part of me,
My present Past, my root of piety.

VII

Those long days measured by my little feet
Had chronicles which yield me many a text;
Where irony still finds an image meet
Of full-grown judgments in this world perplext.

One day my brother left me in high charge,
To mind the rod, while he went seeking bait,
And bade me, when I saw a nearing barge,
Snatch out the line, lest he should come too late.

Proud of the task, I watched with all my might
For one whole minute, till my eyes grew wide,
Till sky and earth took on a strange new light
And seemed a dream-world floating on some tide—

A fair pavilioned boat for me alone
Bearing me onward through the vast unknown.

VIII

But sudden came the barge's pitch-black prow,
Nearer and angrier came my brother's cry,
And all my soul was quivering fear, when lo!
Upon the imperilled line, suspended high,

A silver perch! My guilt that won the prey,
Now turned to merit, had a guerdon[6] rich

[5] Disembodied idea.
[6] Reward.

Of hugs and praises, and made merry play,
Until my triumph reached its highest pitch

When all at home were told the wondrous feat,
And how the little sister had fished well.
In secret, though my fortune tasted sweet,
I wondered why this happiness befell.

> "The little lass had luck," the gardener said:
> And so I learned, luck was with glory wed.

IX

We had the self-same world enlarged for each
By loving difference of girl and boy:
The fruit that hung on high beyond my reach
He plucked for me, and oft he must employ

A measuring glance to guide my tiny shoe
Where lay firm stepping-stones, or call to mind
"This thing I like my sister may not do
For she is little, and I must be kind."

Thus boyish Will the nobler mastery learned
Where inward vision over impulse reigns,
Widening its life with separate life discerned,
A Like unlike, a Self that self restrains.

> His years with others must the sweeter be
> For those brief days he spent in loving me.

X

His sorrow was my sorrow, and his joy
Sent little leaps and laughs through all my frame;
My doll seemed lifeless and no girlish toy
Had any reason when my brother came.

I knelt with him at marbles, marked his fling
Cut the ringed stem and make the apple drop,
Or watched him winding close the spiral string
That looped the orbits of the humming top.

Grasped by such fellowship my vagrant thought
Ceased with dream-fruit dream-wishes to fulfil;
My aëry-picturing fantasy was taught
Subjection to the harder, truer skill

> That seeks with deeds to grave[7] a thought-tracked line,
> And by "What is," "What will be" to define.

---

[7] Engrave.

XI

School parted us; we never found again
That childish world where our two spirits mingled
Like scents from varying roses that remain
One sweetness, nor can evermore be singled.

Yet the twin habit of that early time
Lingered for long about the heart and tongue:
We had been natives of one happy clime,
And its dear accents to our utterance clung.

Till the dire years whose awful name is Change
Had grasped our souls still yearning in divorce.[8]
And pitiless shaped them in two forms that range
Two elements which sever their life's course.

But were another childhood-world my share,
I would be born a little sister there.

[1874]

For Discussion

1. How is Lisa in the poem by Constance Carrier "between two worlds"? What are the worlds she inhabits, and how do they relate to the paradoxes of childhood evident in the stories?

2. In Sexton's poem, "Young," why is there so much hyperbole (exaggeration) and figurative language such as "clover wrinkling under me," "wise stars," etc.? What does each figure of speech have to do with childhood?

3. What is the tone of "Birthplace," and what point does it make about women's place in society?

4. What are the two opposite impressions of childhood Giovanni describes in "Nikki-Rosa"? What is her interpretation of the impact of environment on childhood?

5. What is the significance of the dialog between the mother and daughter at the end of Swenson's "The Centaur"?

6. How do George Eliot's "Brother and Sister" differ from the brother and sister in "The Centaur"?

For Further Exploration

1. Anne Sexton also has written a poem called "Houses" which suggests that young women and their mothers *are* houses, which become "another kind of skin" from which men move in and out. Examine the poems in this section for "house images" and relate them to the girls' and women's roles in each.

---

[8] Separation.

2. Select another image or symbol—trees, or animals, or sunlight, or parts of the body, or elder relatives—and examine its use in the poems. Why is each image selected appropriate to the poet's theme? What does each image provide that another image might not?

For Discussion or Writing About This Section

1. How might the theme of "lessons" be applied to each of the stories in this section? What lessons are learned by children? by female children? Are there any lessons learned later, or are all of the major topics of life introduced in childhood?

2. Explore the language of childhood, finding creative uses of words and phrases by the various characters in the stories. How does language reflect each child's world view?

3. What roles do fine arts such as painting and poetry play in the girls' lives? What form does self-expression take in each story?

4. Stories and poems about childhood often combine humor and pathos. Find examples and explain how the two modes function together.

5. Explore the significance of girls' clothing in the stories. What do hats, veils, or hair ribbons suggest as symbols for young girls?

6. Examine the roles of the parents depicted, determining the child's impressions of them in each case. Why are there so many absent parents in the stories, and so many other adult women and relatives with an impact on the children's lives?

7. What creates the joys of childhood in each story or poem? What creates the sadness or resentment? Are these provocations for smiles and tears the same as those in later life?

8. Imagine each of these girls in later life. Which stories and poems end with the child's confidence in her future? What clues does each author give about the main character's likelihood of success?

ADOLESCENCE

The search for identity; extending the horizons; moving from innocence to experience; relating to peers; experiencing disillusionment; completing enculturation; moving on

Adolescence does not happen abruptly; nor is it a surprise to see many of the same motifs of childhood repeated in these stories. But the strength with which society's force engages young women in traditional sex-related patterns is astonishing when one looks at a group of stories and poems about adolescence. The primary characteristic of adolescent females in life stage research and in literature is the act of waiting for another person to give meaning and direction to their lives.

Childhood's hint of the existence of a mysterious secret to life is strengthened to a full-fledged belief that the answer lies in the arrival of another person—the prince of one's dreams. And so these adolescent females dream on, "being" rather than "doing," becoming increasingly passive and dependent. Even the teenagers portrayed in these stories and poems as struggling to develop a talent or to be independent find themselves wondering about their own capabilities and hoping for some kind of deliverance from the responsibilities of their dreams. At the same time, in stories such as "Wunderkind," the young women's struggles are contrasted sharply with the experiences of male characters of the same age.

Out of this morass of dependency, several of the adolescents described here find the answer in a semblance of power, the "secret" of the female sex to gain ascendancy by passivity, or dominance through the pretense of giving in. The hidden weapon is sex itself, made more powerful by physical beauty, which is then cultivated according to prevailing social norms. The literary image for this passage of the "secret"—that women can control men by having men desire them—is THE DRESS, the prom gown or party dress often selected by an older member of the family and initially uncomfortable to the adolescent herself. Judy in the story "Debut" is a good example of an adolescent who must wear the dress and learn the secret. Whether or not the young woman reconciles herself to THE DRESS is often a clue to her later success in using "the secret."

The role of parents in this enculturation process is strong, and many more stories of adolescence have visible parents than do the stories of childhood. A young woman's mother (or substitute mother) in the stories is often seen as "what she should become" if all goes well, and shows the values of the families, including what constitutes success for women later in life. Mind-dulling, ordinary jobs for teenage girls reinforce the image of escape through another person, rather than success through individual advancement.

Moral dilemmas abound in these stories—not simply in terms of sexual coming of age, but also in terms of what kind of person to be. In many cases, decisions about how to deal with the consequences of male interest (to resist, to succumb, or to take advantage) reflect what the young woman's personal character will be in the future. To show alternative value systems and ways of life, the authors use character pairs (the young women and their sisters or other adolescents) again and again. These adolescents continually compare their appearances and performances with others', just as in the childhood stories the girls compare their parents' reality with the experiences of other adults they encounter.

Related to choices of how to "be" with others and how to "act" within and outside of the home is the question of whether to stay the same (childish, dependent, secure, and loved) or whether to change (which often entails a physical removal from the home itself). While the movement "out" or "away" on one level is presented as a natural and healthy change, it is also depicted as menacing if precipitated by the wrong impulses. Whether the impetus is from adults or from the adolescent herself, there are potential dangers in forcing growth too fast; several authors warn not to prod a child to become an adult too soon (or to become a star musician or debutante).

The "public" versus "private" selves of these young women become more polarized than in childhood, and the ability to be loved and accepted in both inner and outer circles becomes increasingly difficult. The young woman of fiction and poetry may be literally going out and coming back in, walking along a road (as is the young woman at the end of "By the Sea"), or pausing on a threshold as she decides to stay or to leave (a decision often depicted as a "lady or the tiger" choice in which the doors to stagnation or to growth are unmarked). The fact that several of the stories end with the adolescent going out of a door (usually reluctantly, but drawn by other influences) reinforces the sleeping beauty image of self-induced paralysis.

The trancelike atmosphere surrounding the women in these stories differs from the emotional ups and downs of childhood: life is a walking dream, an altered state so profound that few except the "deliverer" (who may or may not arrive) can penetrate. For teenagers such as Connie in "Where Are You Going, Where Have You Been?" the prince who arrives may not be exactly as welcome as he was in her dreams.

Music and reading, escape mechanisms for many women in these stories and in life, reinforce the passivity of the female characters, rather than challenging it. Adolescent females in the stories change their reading habits from literature to popular magazines and advertisements, further indicating that they avoid serious issues and questions unrelated to the self. Gone are the crisp pages of dictionary definitions and poems of "A Child's Day," in favor of words and phrases as placebos; the magazines one teenager reads make her "almost happy, for that limited time, like a drug."

Meanwhile, these authors make readers fear that the teenagers will remain shallow and superficial forever, and make us wonder what will become of some of them. No real "answers" are given about proper values or codes of behavior, and not one viable philosophy is available to emulate. The women in one poem give the nebulous advice, "put Xmas in your eyes" to a teenager looking for direction. As a result, the parents and the teenagers seem at times to be equally deplorable and pitiable.

Underlying this sense of ineffectuality, however, is often a serious tone of admonition. Several of even the most modern stories warn against the dangers of adolescent turpitude. Young women in the poems are also warned that men will try to victimize them, and even nature is threatening in the poem "The Young Girl and the Beach." According to these poets and story tellers, inimical forces seem to lie in wait for an adolescent. There is the sense that all is not well in the modern world young women must confront, and that the old training for old roles leaves teenagers unwary of real temptation and ultimately empty of real values.

Fiction About Adolescence

While stories about the childhoods of women differ in several ways from fiction about young boys (there is more concern with personal appearance and restrictive behavior for girls, for example), portrayals of female versus male adolescence reveal a single dramatic difference that forms the core of later distinctions between characters in literature and people in life: while young boys are shown to be active and adventuresome, young women seem to simply stop growing and being themselves, waiting instead for a magical male answer to their personal identities. The teenage girls display a conspicuous lack of conscious thought in many of these stories.

The adage of "fight or flee" in response to conflict takes on an added dimension in stories about young women confronting the many problems of adolescence. The impulse to "flee" into a dream world is not resisted by these women, and the images of escape take on a variety of forms. The majority of the young protagonists finally walk off into a world lacking even the pretense of being real—hence the question posed by one story title, "Where Are You Going, Where Have You Been?" There is only a hollow echo of the question in these stories, with little hope of response.

It is also evident in these stories that adults are unsure of the response they would hope for if asked. Expectations are unclear; should the young women remain children or become adults? Should they be dependent or independent, active or idle, sexually aware or naive? The disconcerting message these authors convey is that the teens are eventually expected to take their places as women indistinguishable from others of their gender, rather than as strong representatives of individuality and personal achievement.

Carson McCullers

1917–1967

Adolescence is not an easy time, even for this young woman who had been considered a child prodigy. The transition to adult feelings and mature performance is shown here to be more difficult for Frances than for her male counterpart.

WUNDERKIND

She came into the living room, her music satchel plopping against her winter-stockinged legs and her other arm weighted down with schoolbooks, and stood for a moment listening to the sounds from the studio. A soft procession of piano chords and the tuning of a violin. Then Mister Bilderbach called out to her in his chunky, guttural tones:

"That you, Bienchen?"

As she jerked off her mittens she saw that her fingers were twitching to the motions of the fugue she had practiced that morning. "Yes," she answered. "It's me."

"I," the voice corrected. "Just a moment."

She could hear Mister Lafkowitz talking—his words spun out in a silky, unintelligible hum. A voice almost like a woman's, she thought, compared to Mister Bilderbach's. Restlessness scattered her attention. She fumbled with her geometry book and *Le Voyage de Monsieur Perrichon* before putting them on the table. She sat down on the sofa and began to take her music from the satchel. Again she saw her hands—the quivering tendons that stretched down from her knuckles, the sore finger tip capped with curled, dingy tape. The sight sharpened the fear that had begun to torment her for the past few months.

Noiselessly she mumbled a few phrases of encouragement to herself. A good lesson—a good lesson—like it used to be—Her lips closed as she heard the stolid sound of Mister Bilderbach's footsteps across the floor of the studio and the creaking of the door as it slid open.

For a moment she had the peculiar feeling that during most of the fifteen years of her life she had been looking at the face and shoulders that jutted from behind the door, in a silence disturbed only by the muted, blank plucking of a violin string. Mister Bilderbach. Her teacher, Mister Bilderbach. The quick eyes behind the horn-rimmed glasses; the light, thin hair and the narrow face beneath; the lips full and loose shut and the lower one pink and shining from the bites of his teeth; the forked veins in his temples throbbing plainly enough to be observed across the room.

"Aren't you a little early?" he asked, glancing at the clock on the mantelpiece that had pointed to five minutes of twelve for a month. "Jósef's in here. We're running over a little sonatina by someone he knows."

"Good," she said, trying to smile. "I'll listen." She could see her fingers sinking powerless into a blur of piano keys. She felt tired—felt that if he looked at her much longer her hands might tremble.

He stood uncertain, halfway in the room. Sharply his teeth pushed down on his bright, swollen lip. "Hungry, Bienchen?" he asked. "There's some apple cake Anna made, and milk."

"I'll wait till afterward," she said. "Thanks."

"After you finish with a very fine lesson—eh?" His smile seemed to crumble at the corners.

There was a sound from behind him in the studio and Mister Lafkowitz pushed at the other panel of the door and stood beside him.

"Frances?" he said, smiling. "And how is the work coming now?"

Without meaning to, Mister Lafkowitz always made her feel clumsy and overgrown. He was such a small man himself, with a weary look when he was not holding his violin. His eyebrows curved high above his sallow, Jewish face as though asking a question, but the lids of his eyes drowsed languorous and indifferent. Today he seemed distracted. She watched him come into the room for no apparent purpose, holding his pearl-tipped bow in his still fingers, slowly gliding the white horsehair through a chalky piece of rosin. His eyes were sharp bright slits today and the linen handkerchief that flowed down from his collar darkened the shadows beneath them.

"I gather you're doing a lot now," smiled Mister Lafkowitz, although she had not yet answered the question.

She looked at Mister Bilderbach. He turned away. His heavy shoulders pushed the door open wide so that the late afternoon sun came through the window of the studio and shafted yellow over the dusty living room. Behind her teacher she could see the squat long piano, the window, and the bust of Brahms.

"No," she said to Mister Lafkowitz, "I'm doing terribly." Her thin fingers flipped at the pages of her music. "I don't know what's the matter," she said, looking at Mister Bilderbach's stooped muscular back that stood tense and listening.

Mister Lafkowitz smiled. "There are times, I suppose, when one—"

A harsh chord sounded from the piano. "Don't you think we'd better get on with this?" asked Mister Bilderbach.

"Immediately," said Mister Lafkowitz, giving the bow one more scrape before starting toward the door. She could see him pick up his violin from the top of the piano. He caught her eye and lowered the instrument. "You've seen the picture of Heime?"

Her fingers curled tight over the sharp corner of the satchel. "What picture?"

"One of Heime in the *Musical Courier* there on the table. Inside the top cover."

The sonatina began. Discordant yet somehow simple. Empty but with a sharp-cut style of its own. She reached for the magazine and opened it.

There Heime was—in the left-hand corner. Holding his violin with his fingers hooked down over the strings for a pizzicato. With his dark serge knickers strapped neatly beneath his knees, a sweater and rolled collar. It was a bad picture. Although it was snapped in profile his eyes were cut around toward the photographer and his finger looked as though it would pluck the wrong string. He seemed suffering to turn around toward the picture-taking apparatus. He was thinner—his stomach did not poke out now— but he hadn't changed much in six months.

Heime Israelsky, talented young violinist, snapped while at work in his teacher's studio on Riverside Drive. Young Master Israelsky, who will soon celebrate his fifteenth birthday, has been invited to play the Beethoven concerta with—

That morning, after she had practiced from six until eight, her dad had made her sit down at the table with the family for breakfast. She hated breakfast; it gave her a sick feeling afterward. She would rather wait and get four chocolate bars with her twenty cents lunch money and munch them during school—bringing up little morsels from her pocket under cover of her handkerchief, stopping dead when the silver paper rattled. But this morning her dad had put a fried egg on her plate and she had known that if it burst—so that the slimy yellow oozed over the white—she would cry. And that had happened. The same feeling was upon her now. Gingerly she laid the magazine back on the table and closed her eyes.

The music in the studio seemed to be urging violently and clumsily for something that was not to be had. After a moment her thoughts drew back from Heime and the concerta and the picture—and hovered around the lesson once more. She slid over on the sofa until she could see plainly into the studio—the two of them playing, peering at the notations on the piano, lustfully drawing out all that was there.

She could not forget the memory of Mister Bilderbach's face as he had stared at her a moment ago. Her hands, still twitching unconsciously to the motions of the fugue, closed over her bony knees. Tired, she was. And with a circling, sinking-away feeling like the one that often came to her just before she dropped off to sleep on the nights when she had over-practiced. Like those weary half-dreams that buzzed and carried her out into their own whirling space.

A *Wunderkind*—a *Wunderkind*—a *Wunderkind*. The syllables would come out rolling in the deep German way, roar against her ears and then fall to a murmur. Along with the faces circling, swelling out in distortion, diminishing to pale blobs—Mister Bilderbach, Mrs. Bilderbach, Heime, Mister Lafkowitz. Around and around in a circle revolving to the guttural *Wunderkind*. Mister Bilderbach looming large in the middle of the circle, his face urging—with the others around him.

Phrases of music seesawing crazily. Notes she had been practicing falling over each other like a handful of marbles dropped downstairs. Bach, Debussy, Prokofieff, Brahms—timed grotesquely to the far-off throb of her tired body and the buzzing circle.

Sometimes—when she had not worked more than three hours or had stayed out from high school—the dreams were not so confused. The music soared clearly in her mind and quick, precise little memories would come back—clear as the sissy "Age of Innocence" picture Heime had given her after their joint concert was over.

A *Wunderkind*—a *Wunderkind*. That was what Mister Bilderbach had called her when, at twelve, she first came to him. Older pupils had repeated the word.

Not that he had ever said the word to her. "Bienchen—" (She had a plain American name but he never used it except when her mistakes were enormous.) "Bienchen," he would say, "I know it must be terrible. Carrying around all the time a head that thick. Poor Bienchen—"

Mister Bilderbach's father had been a Dutch violinist. His mother was from Prague. He had been born in this country and had spent his youth in Germany. So many times she wished she had not been born and brought up in just Cincinnati. How do you say *cheese* in German? Mister Bilderbach, what is Dutch for *I don't understand you?*

The first day she came to the studio. After she played the whole Second Hungarian Rhapsody from memory. The room graying with twilight. His face as he leaned over the piano.

"Now we begin all over," he said that first day. "It—playing music—is more than cleverness. If a twelve-year-old girl's fingers cover so many keys to a second—that means nothing."

He tapped his broad chest and his forehead with his stubby hand. "Here and here. You are old enough to understand that." He lighted a cigarette and gently blew the first exhalation above her head. "And work—work—work— We will start now with these Bach inventions and these little Schumann pieces." His hands moved again—this time to jerk the cord of the lamp behind her and point to the music. "I will show you how I wish this practiced. Listen carefully now."

She had been at the piano for almost three hours and was very tired. His deep voice sounded as though it had been straying inside her for a long time. She wanted to reach out and touch his muscle-flexed finger that pointed out the phrases, wanted to feel the gleaming gold band ring and the strong hairy back of his hand.

She had lessons Tuesday after school and on Saturday afternoons. Often she stayed, when the Saturday lesson was finished, for dinner, and then spent the night and took the streetcar home the next morning. Mrs. Bilderbach liked her in her calm, almost dumb way. She was much different from her husband. She was quiet and fat and slow. When she wasn't in the kitchen, cooking the rich dishes that both of them loved, she seemed to spend all her time in their bed upstairs, reading magazines or just looking with a half-smile at nothing. When they had married in Germany she had been a *lieder* singer. She didn't sing anymore (she said it was her throat). When he would call her in from the kitchen to listen to a pupil she would always smile and say that it was *gut, very gut.*

When Frances was thirteen it came to her one day that the Bilderbachs had no children. It seemed strange. Once she had been back in the kitchen with Mrs. Bilderbach when he had come striding in from the studio, tense with anger at some pupil who had annoyed him. His wife stood stirring the thick soup until his hand groped out and rested on her shoulder. Then she turned—stood placid—while he folded his arms about her and buried his sharp face in the white, nerveless flesh of her neck. They stood that way without moving. And then his face jerked back suddenly, the anger diminished to a quiet inexpressiveness, and he had returned to the studio.

After she had started with Mister Bilderbach and didn't have time to see anything of the people at high school, Heime had been the only friend of her own age. He was Mister Lafkowitz's pupil and would come with him to Mister Bilderbach's on evenings when she would be there. They would listen to their teachers' playing. And often they themselves went over chamber music together—Mozart sonatas or Bloch.

A *Wunderkind*—a *Wunderkind.*

Heime was a *Wunderkind.* He and she, then.

Heime had been playing the violin since he was four. He didn't have to go to school; Mister Lafkowitz's brother, who was crippled, used to teach him geometry and European history and French verbs in the afternoon. When he was thirteen he had as fine a technique as any violinist in Cincinnati—everyone said so. But playing the violin must be easier than the piano. She knew it must be.

Heime always seemed to smell of corduroy pants and the food he had eaten and rosin. Half the time, too, his hands were dirty around the knuckles and the cuffs of his shirts peeped out dingily from the sleeves of his sweater. She always watched his hands when he played—thin only at the joints with the hard little blobs of flesh bulging over the short-cut nails and the babyish-looking crease that showed so plainly in his bowing wrist.

In the dreams, as when she was awake, she could remember the concert only in a blur. She had not known it was unsuccessful for her until months after. True, the papers had praised Heime more than her. But he was much shorter than she. When they stood together on the stage he came only to her shoulders. And that made a difference with people, she knew. Also, there was the matter of the sonata they played together. The Bloch.

"No, no—I don't think that would be appropriate," Mister Bilderbach had said when the Bloch was suggested to end the programme. "Now that John Powell thing—the Sonate Virginianesque."

She hadn't understood then; she wanted it to be the Bloch as much as Mister Lafkowitz and Heime.

Mister Bilderbach had given in. Later, after the reviews had said she lacked the temperament for that type of music, after they called her playing thin and lacking in feeling, she felt cheated.

"That oie oie stuff," said Mister Bilderbach, crackling the newspapers at her. "Not for you, Bienchen. Leave all that to the Heimes and vitses and skys."

A *Wunderkind*. No matter what the papers said, that was what he had called her.

Why was it Heime had done so much better at the concert than she? At school sometimes, when she was supposed to be watching someone do a geometry problem on the blackboard, the question would twist knife-like inside her. She would worry about it in bed, and even sometimes when she was supposed to be concentrating at the piano. It wasn't just the Bloch and her not being Jewish—not entirely. It wasn't that Heime didn't have to go to school and had begun his training so early, either. It was—?

Once she thought she knew.

"Play the Fantasia and Fugue," Mister Bilderbach had demanded one evening a year ago—after he and Mister Lafkowitz had finished reading some music together.

The Bach, as she played, seemed to her well done. From the tail of her eye she could see the calm, pleased expression on Mister Bilderbach's face, see his hands rise climactically from the chair arms and then sink down loose and satisfied when the high points of the phrases had been passed successfully. She stood up from the piano when it was over, swallowing to loosen the bands that the music seemed to have drawn around her throat and chest. But—

"Frances—" Mister Lafkowitz had said then, suddenly, looking at her with his thin mouth curved and his eyes almost covered by their delicate lids. "Do you know how many children Bach had?"

She turned to him, puzzled. "A good many. Twenty some odd."

"Well then—" The corners of his smile etched themselves gently in his pale face. "He could not have been so cold—then."

Mister Bilderbach was not pleased; his guttural effulgence of German words had *Kind* in it somewhere. Mister Lafkowitz raised his eyebrows. She had caught the point easily enough, but she felt no deception in keeping her face blank and immature because that was the way Mister Bilderbach wanted her to look.

Yet such things had nothing to do with it. Nothing very much, at least, for she would grow older. Mister Bilderbach understood that, and even Mister Lafkowitz had not meant just what he said.

In the dreams Mister Bilderbach's face loomed out and contracted in the center of the whirling circle. The lips surging softly, the veins in his temples insisting.

But sometimes, before she slept, there were such clear memories; as when she pulled a hole in the heel of her stocking down, so that her shoe would hide it. "Bienchen, Bienchen!" And bringing Mrs. Bilderbach's work basket in and showing her how it should be darned and not gathered together in a lumpy heap.

And the time she graduated from Junior High.

"What you wear?" asked Mrs. Bilderbach the Sunday morning at breakfast when she told them about how they had practiced to march into the auditorium.

"An evening dress my cousin had last year."

"Ah—Bienchen!" he said, circling his warm coffee cup with his heavy hands, looking up at her with wrinkles around his laughing eyes. "I bet I know what Bienchen wants—"

He insisted. He would not believe her when she explained that she honestly didn't care at all.

"Like this, Anna," he said, pushing his napkin across the table and mincing to the other side of the room, swishing his hips, rolling up his eyes behind his horn-rimmed glasses.

The next Saturday afternoon, after her lessons, he took her to the department stores downtown. His thick fingers smoothed over the filmy nets and crackling taffetas that the saleswomen unwound from their bolts. He held colors to her face, cocking his head to one side, and selected pink. Shoes, he remembered too. He liked best some white kid pumps. They seemed a little like old ladies' shoes to her and the Red Cross label in the instep had a charity look. But it really didn't matter at all. When Mrs. Bilderbach began to cut out the dress and fit it to her with pins, he interrupted his lessons to stand by and suggest ruffles around the hips and neck and a fancy rosette on the shoulder. The music was coming along nicely then. Dresses and commencement and such made no difference.

Nothing mattered much except playing the music as it must be played, bringing out the thing that must be in her, practicing, practicing, playing so that Mister Bilderbach's face lost some of its urging look. Putting the thing into her music that Myra Hess had, and Yehudi Menuhin—even Heime!

What had begun to happen to her four months ago? The notes began springing out with a glib, dead intonation. Adolescence, she thought. Some kids played with promise—and worked and worked until, like her, the least little thing would start them crying, and worn out with trying to get the thing across—the longing thing they felt—something queer began to happen— But not she! She was like Heime. She had to be. She—

Once it was there for sure. And you didn't lose things like that. A *Wunderkind*. . . . A *Wunderkind*. . . . Of her he said it, rolling the words in the sure, deep German way. And in the dreams even deeper, more certain than ever. With his face looming out at her, and the longing phrases of music mixed in with the zooming, circling round, round, round— A *Wunderkind*. A *Wunderkind*. . . .

This afternoon Mister Bilderbach did not show Mister Lafkowitz to the front door, as he usually did. He stayed at the piano, softly pressing a solitary note. Listening, Frances watched the violinist wind his scarf about his pale throat.

"A good picture of Heime," she said, picking up her music. "I got a letter from him a couple of months ago—telling about hearing Schnabel and Huberman and about Carnegie Hall and things to eat at the Russian Tea Room."

To put off going into the studio a moment longer she waited until Mister Lafkowitz was ready to leave and then stood behind him as he opened the door. The frosty cold outside cut into the room. It was growing late and the air was seeped with the pale yellow of winter twilight. When the door swung to on its hinges, the house seemed darker and more silent than ever before she had known it to be.

As she went into the studio Mister Bilderbach got up from the piano and silently watched her settle herself at the keyboard.

"Well, Bienchen," he said, "this afternoon we are going to begin all over. Start from scratch. Forget the last few months."

He looked as though he were trying to act a part in a movie. His solid body swayed from toe to heel, he rubbed his hands together, and even smiled in a satisfied, movie way. Then suddenly he thrust this manner brusquely aside. His heavy shoulders slouched and he began to run through the stack of music she had brought in. "The Bach—no, not yet," he murmured. "The Beethoven? Yes. The Variation Sonata. Opus 26."

The keys of the piano hemmed her in—stiff and white and dead-seeming.

"Wait a minute," he said. He stood in the curve of the piano, elbows propped, and looked at her. "Today I expect something from you. Now this sonata—it's the first Beethoven sonata you ever worked on. Every note is under control—technically—you have nothing to cope with but the music. Only music now. That's all you think about."

He rustled through the pages of her volume until he found the place. Then he pulled his teaching chair halfway across the room, turned it around and seated himself, straddling the back with his legs.

For some reason, she knew, this position of his usually had a good effect on her performance. But today she felt that she would notice him from the corner of her eye and be disturbed. His back was stiffly tilted, his legs looked tense. The heavy volume before him seemed to balance dangerously on the chair back. "Now we begin," he said with a peremptory dart of his eyes in her direction.

Her hands rounded over the keys and then sank down. The first notes were too loud, the other phrases followed dryly.

Arrestingly his hand rose up from the score. "Wait! Think a minute what you're playing. How is this beginning marked?"

"An-andante."

"All right. Don't drag it into an *adagio* then. And play deeply into the keys. Don't snatch it off shallowly that way. A graceful, deep-toned *andante*—"

She tried again. Her hands seemed separate from the music that was in her.

"Listen," he interrupted. "Which of these variations dominates the whole?"

"The dirge," she answered.

"Then prepare for that. This is an *andante*—but it's not salon stuff as you just played it. Start out softly, *piano*, and make it swell out just before the arpeggio. Make it warm and dramatic. And down here—where it's marked *dolce* make the counter melody sing out. You know all that. We've gone over all that side of it before. Now play it. Feel it as Beethoven wrote it down. Feel that tragedy and restraint."

She could not stop looking at his hands. They seemed to rest tentatively on the music, ready to fly up as a stop signal as soon as she would begin, the gleaming flash of his ring calling her to halt. "Mister Bilderbach—maybe if I—if you let me play on through the first variation without stopping I could do better."

"I won't interrupt," he said.

Her pale face leaned over too close to the keys. She played through the first part, and, obeying a nod from him, began the second. There were no flaws that jarred on her, but the phrases shaped from her fingers before she had put into them the meaning that she felt.

When she had finished he looked up from the music and began to speak with dull bluntness: "I hardly heard those harmonic fillings in the right hand. And incidentally, this part was supposed to take on intensity, develop the foreshadowings that were supposed to be inherent in the first part. Go on with the next one, though."

She wanted to start it with subdued viciousness and progress to a feeling of deep, swollen sorrow. Her mind told her that. But her hands seemed to gum in the keys like limp macaroni and she could not imagine the music as it should be.

When the last note had stopped vibrating, he closed the book and deliberately got up from the chair. He was moving his lower jaw from side to side—and between his open lips she could glimpse the pink healthy lane to his throat and his strong, smoke-yellowed teeth. He laid the Beethoven gingerly on top of the rest of her music and propped his elbows on the smooth, black piano top once more. "No," he said simply, looking at her.

Her mouth began to quiver. "I can't help it. I—"

Suddenly he strained his lips into a smile. "Listen, Bienchen," he began in a new, forced voice. "You still play the Harmonious Blacksmith, don't you? I told you not to drop it from your repertoire."

"Yes," she said. "I practice it now and then."

His voice was the one he used for children. "It was among the first things we worked on together—remember. So strongly you used to play it—like a real blacksmith's daughter. You see, Bienchen, I know you so well—as if you were my own girl. I know what you have—I've heard you play so many things beautifully. You used to—"

He stopped in confusion and inhaled from his pulpy stub of cigarette. The smoke drowsed out from his pink lips and clung in a gray mist around her lank hair and childish forehead.

"Make it happy and simple," he said, switching on the lamp behind her and stepping back from the piano.

For a moment he stood just inside the bright circle the light made. Then impulsively he squatted down to the floor. "Vigorous," he said.

She could not stop looking at him, sitting on one heel with the other foot resting squarely before him for balance, the muscles of his strong thighs straining under the cloth of his trousers, his back straight, his elbows staunchly propped on his knees. "Simply now," he repeated with a gesture of his fleshy hands. "Think of the blacksmith—working out in the sunshine all day. Working easily and undisturbed."

She could not look down at the piano. The light brightened the hairs on the backs of his outspread hands, made the lenses of his glasses glitter.

"All of it," he urged. "Now!"

She felt that the marrows of her bones were hollow and there was no blood left in her. Her heart that had been springing against her chest all afternoon felt suddenly dead. She saw it gray and limp and shriveled at the edges like an oyster.

His face seemed to throb out in space before her, come closer with the lurching motion in the veins of his temples. In retreat, she looked down at the piano. Her lips shook like jelly and a surge of noiseless tears made the white keys blur in a watery line. "I can't," she whispered. "I don't know why, but I just can't—can't any more."

His tense body slackened and, holding his hand to his side, he pulled himself up. She clutched her music and hurried past him.

Her coat. The mittens and galoshes. The schoolbooks and the satchel he had given her on her birthday. All from the silent room that was hers. Quickly—before he would have to speak.

As she passed through the vestibule she could not help but see his hands—held out from his body that leaned against the studio door, relaxed and purposeless. The door shut to firmly. Dragging her books and satchel she stumbled down the stone steps, turned in the wrong direction, and hurried down the street that had become confused with noise and bicycles and the games of other children.

[1936]

For Discussion

1. Describe the teacher-pupil relationship between Mr. Bilderbach and Frances. What do we know of the relationship between Mr. Lafkowitz and Heime? In what ways might the pairs function differently?

2. What does the title "Wunderkind" mean, and what other epithets does Mr. Bilderbach use to refer to Frances? Explain what these nicknames suggest about Mr. Bilderbach's attitude.

3. Why does the picture of Heime make Frances want to cry, and why was Heime more successful in the concert than she?

4. Analyze the issue of "overpracticing" that leads to strange dreams. How much of Frances' problem with music can be attributed to the "adolescent" stage, how much to Mr. Bilderbach's methods, and how much to Frances' ability?

5. Examine the many physical details Frances notices about Mr. Bilderbach. Which details in the description and in Mr. Bilderbach's behavior could be interpreted as sexually symbolic?

6. Reread the scene in which Mr. Bilderbach selects Frances' dress. How are the expectations expressed in this episode related to Frances' problems with music?

7. What is Mrs. Bilderbach's role in the story? What might cause Frances to become another Mrs. Bilderbach?

8. Find the references to the "head" versus the "heart." What does this dichotomy have to do with adolescence and growing up?

9. What other impulses are in conflict in the final scene? Explain what the "Harmonious Blacksmith" and the last line have to do with the themes of the story.

For Further Exploration

1. Carson McCullers has written many stories about adolescents, including *The Member of the Wedding* and *The Heart is a Lonely Hunter* (both filmed). Compare the adolescent state of mind in one of McCullers' other works with Frances' turmoil in this story.

2. Probably the most well-known fictional account of an adolescent boy is J. D. Salinger's *Catcher in the Rye*. Holden Caulfield cannot decide whether to grow up or to remain a child, and resists the pressure of family and teachers to live up to adult standards. Compare Holden's problems with those of Frances as a female adolescent.

Kristin Hunter

1931–

As in "Wunderkind," the young woman here is expected to fulfill the expectations of others. In this story, however, Judy seems to find a magic answer which gives her confidence and a sense of power over men and even over her family.

DEBUT

"Hold *still*, Judy," Mrs. Simmons said around the spray of pins that protruded dangerously from her mouth. She gave the thirtieth tug to the tight sash at the waist of the dress. "Now walk over there and turn around slowly."

The dress, Judy's first long one, was white organdy over taffeta, with spaghetti straps that bared her round brown shoulders and a floating skirt and a wide sash that cascaded in a butterfly effect behind. It was a dream, but Judy was sick and tired of the endless fittings she had endured so that she might wear it at the Debutantes' Ball. Her thoughts leaped ahead to the Ball itself . . .

"*Slowly*, I said!" Mrs. Simmons' dark, angular face was always grim, but now it was screwed into an expression resembling a prune. Judy, starting nervously, began to revolve by moving her feet an inch at a time.

Her mother watched her critically. "No, it's still not right. I'll just have to rip out that waistline seam again."

"Oh, Mother!" Judy's impatience slipped out at last. "Nobody's going to notice all those little details."

"They will too. They'll be watching you every minute, hoping to see something wrong. You've got to be the *best*. Can't you get that through your head?" Mrs. Simmons gave a sigh of despair. "You better start noticin' 'all those little details' yourself. I can't do it for you all your life. Now turn around and stand up straight."

"Oh, Mother," Judy said, close to tears from being made to turn and pose while her feet itched to be dancing, "I can't stand it any more!"

"You can't stand it, huh? How do you think *I* feel?" Mrs. Simmons said in her harshest tone.

Judy was immediately ashamed, remembering the weeks her mother had spent at the sewing machine, pricking her already tattered fingers with needles and pins, and the great weight of sacrifice that had been borne on Mrs. Simmons' shoulders for the past two years so that Judy might bare hers at the Ball.

"All right, take it off," her mother said. "I'm going to take it up the street to Mrs. Luby and let her help me. It's got to be right or I won't let you leave the house."

"Can't we just leave it the way it is, Mother?" Judy pleaded without hope of success. "I think it's perfect."

"You would," Mrs. Simmons said tartly as she folded the dress and prepared to bear it out of the room. "Sometimes I think I'll never get it through your head. You got to look just right and act just right. That Rose Griffin and those other girls can afford to be careless, maybe, but you can't. You're gonna be the darkest, poorest one there.''

Judy shivered in her new lace strapless bra and her old, childish knit snuggies. "You make it sound like a battle I'm going to instead of just a dance."

"It is a battle," her mother said firmly. "It starts tonight and it goes on for the rest of your life. The battle to hold your head up and get someplace and be somebody. We've done all we can for you, your father and I. Now you've got to start fighting some on your own." She gave Judy a slight smile; her voice softened a little. "You'll do all right, don't worry. Try and get some rest this afternoon. Just don't mess up your hair."

"All right, Mother," Judy said listlessly.

She did not really think her father had much to do with anything that happened to her. It was her mother who had ingratiated her way into the Gay Charmers two years ago, taking all sorts of humiliation from the better-dressed, better-off, lighter-skinned women, humbly making and mending their dresses, fixing food for their meetings, addressing more mail and selling more tickets than anyone else. The club had put it off as long as they could, but finally they had to admit Mrs. Simmons to membership because she worked so hard. And that meant, of course, that Judy would be on the list for this year's Ball.

Her father, a quiet carpenter who had given up any other ambitions years ago, did not think much of Negro society or his wife's fierce determination to launch Judy into it. "Just keep clean and be decent," he would say. "That's all anybody has to do."

Her mother always answered, "If that's all I did we'd still be on relief," and he would shut up with shame over the years when he had been laid off repeatedly and her days' work and sewing had kept them going. Now he had steady work but she refused to quit, as if she expected it to end at any moment. The intense energy that burned in Mrs. Simmons' large dark eyes had scorched her features into permanent irony. She worked day and night and spent her spare time scheming and planning. Whatever her personal ambitions had been, Judy knew she blamed Mr. Simmons for their failure; now all her schemes revolved around their only child.

Judy went to her mother's window and watched her stride down the street with the dress until she was hidden by the high brick wall that went around two sides of their house. Then she returned to her own room. She did not get dressed because she was afraid of pulling a sweater over her hair—her mother would notice the difference even if it looked all right to Judy—and because she was afraid that doing anything, even getting dressed, might precipitate her into the battle. She drew a stool up to her window and looked out. She had no real view, but she liked her room. The wall hid the crowded tenement houses beyond the alley, and from its cracks and bumps and depressions she could construct any imaginary landscape she chose. It was how she had spent most of the free hours of her dreamy adolescence.

"Hey, can I go?"

It was the voice of an invisible boy in the alley. As another boy chuckled, Judy recognized the familiar ritual; if you said yes, they said, "Can I go with you?" It had been tried on her dozens of times. She always walked past, head in the air, as if she had not heard. Her mother said that was the only thing to do; if they knew she was a lady, they wouldn't dare bother her. But this time a girl's voice, cool and assured, answered.

"If you think you're big enough," it said.

It was Lucy Mae Watkins; Judy could picture her standing there in a tight dress with bright, brazen eyes.

"I'm big enough to give you a baby," the boy answered.

Judy would die if a boy ever spoke to her like that, but she knew Lucy Mae could handle it. Lucy Mae could handle all the boys, even if they ganged up on her, because she had been born knowing something other girls had to learn.

"Aw, you ain't big enough to give me a shoe-shine," she told him.

"Come here and I'll show you how big I am," the boy said.

"Yeah, Lucy Mae, what's happenin'?" another boy said. "Come here and tell us."

Lucy Mae laughed. "What I'm puttin' down is too strong for little boys like you."

"Come here a minute, baby," the first boy said. "I got a cigarette for you."

"Aw, I ain't studyin' your cigarettes," Lucy Mae answered. But her voice was closer, directly below Judy. There were the sounds of a scuffle and Lucy Mae's muffled laughter. When she spoke her voice sounded raw and cross. "Come on now, boy. Cut it out and give me the damn cigarette." There was more scuffling, and the sharp crack of a slap, and then Lucy Mae said, "Cut it out, I said. Just for that I'm gonna take 'em all." The clack of high heels rang down the sidewalk with a boy's clumsy shoes in pursuit.

Judy realized that there were three of them down there. "Let her go, Buster," one said. "You can't catch her now."

"Aw, hell, man, she took the whole damn pack," the one called Buster complained.

"That'll learn you!" Lucy Mae's voice mocked from down the street. "Don't mess with nothin' you can't handle."

"Hey, Lucy Mae. Hey, I heard Rudy Grant already gave you a baby," a second boy called out.

"Yeah. Is that true, Lucy Mae?" the youngest one yelled.

There was no answer. She must be a block away by now.

For a moment the hidden boys were silent; then one of them guffawed directly below Judy, and the other two joined in the secret male laughter that was oddly high-pitched and feminine.

"Aw man, I don't know what you all laughin' about," Buster finally grumbled. "That girl took all my cigarettes. You got some, Leroy?"

"Naw," the second boy said.

"Me neither," the third one said.

"What we gonna do? I ain't got but fifteen cent. Hell, man, I want more than a feel for a pack of cigarettes." There was an unpleasant whine in Buster's voice. "Hell, for a pack of cigarettes I want a bitch to come across."

"She will next time, man," the boy called Leroy said.

"She better," Buster said. "You know she better. If she pass by here again, we gonna jump her, you hear?"

"Sure, man," Leroy said. "The three of us can grab her easy."

"Then we can all three of us have some fun. Oh, *yeah*, man," the youngest boy said. He sounded as if he might be about fourteen.

Leroy said, "We oughta get Roland and J.T. too. For a whole pack of cigarettes she oughta treat all five of us."

"Aw, man, why tell Roland and J.T.?" the youngest voice whined.

"They ain't in it. Them was *our* cigarettes."

"They was *my* cigarettes, you mean," Buster said with authority. "You guys better quit it before I decide to cut you out."

"Oh, man, don't do that. We with you, you know that."

"Sure, Buster, we your aces, man."

"All right, that's better." There was a minute of silence.

Then, "What we gonna do with the girl, Buster?" the youngest one wanted to know.

"When she come back we gonna jump the bitch, man. We gonna jump her and grab her. Then we gonna turn her every way but loose." He went on, spinning a crude fantasy that got wilder each time he retold it, until it became so secretive that their voices dropped to a low indistinct murmur punctuated by guffaws. Now and then Judy could distinguish the word "girl" or the other word they used for it; these words always produced the loudest guffaws of all. She shook off her fear with the thought that Lucy Mae was too smart to pass there again today. She had heard them at their dirty talk in the alley before and had always been successful in ignoring it; it had nothing to do with her, the wall protected her from their kind. All the ugliness was on their side of it, and this side was hers to fill with beauty.

She turned on her radio to shut them out completely and began to weave her tapestry to its music. More for practice than anything else, she started by picturing the maps of the places to which she intended to travel, then went on to the faces of her friends. Rose Griffin's sharp, Indian profile appeared on the wall. Her coloring was like an Indian's too and her hair was straight and black and glossy. Judy's hair, naturally none of these things, had been "done" four days ago so that tonight it would be "old" enough to have a gloss as natural-looking as Rose's. But Rose, despite her handsome looks, was silly; her voice broke constantly into high-pitched giggles and she became even sillier and more nervous around boys.

Judy was not sure that she knew how to act around boys either. The sisters kept boys and girls apart at the Catholic high school where her parents sent her to keep her away from low-class kids. But she felt that she knew a secret: tonight, in that dress, with her hair in a sophisticated upsweep, she would be transformed into a poised princess. Tonight all the college boys her mother described so eagerly would rush to dance with her, and then from somewhere *the boy* would appear. She did not know his name; she neither knew nor cared whether he went to college, but she imagined that he would be as dark as she was, and that there would be awe and diffidence in his manner as he bent to kiss her hand. . . .

A waltz swelled from the radio; the wall, turning blue in deepening twilight, came alive with whirling figures. Judy rose and began to go through the steps she had rehearsed for so many weeks. She swirled with a practiced smile on her face, holding an imaginary skirt at her side; turned, dipped, and flicked on her bedside lamp without missing a fraction of the beat. Faster and faster she danced with her imaginary partner, to an inner music that was better than the sounds on the radio. She was "coming out," and tonight the world would discover what it had been waiting for all these years.

"Aw git it, baby." She ignored it as she would ignore the crowds that lined the streets to watch her pass on her way to the Ball.

"Aw, do your number." She waltzed on, safe and secure on her side of the wall.

"Can I come up there and do it with you?"

At this she stopped, paralyzed. Somehow they had come over the wall or around it and into her room.

"Man, I sure like the view from here," the youngest boy said. "How come we never tried this view before?"

She came to life, ran quickly to the lamp and turned it off, but not before Buster said, "Yeah, and the back view is fine, too."

"Aw, she turned off the light," a voice complained.

"Put it on again, baby, we don't mean no harm."

"Let us see you dance some more. I bet you can really do it."

"Yeah, I bet she can shimmy on down."

"You know it, man."

"Come on down here, baby," Buster's voice urged softly, dangerously. "I got a cigarette for you."

"Yeah, and he got something else for you, too."

Judy, flattened against her closet door, gradually lost her urge to scream. She realized that she was shivering in her underwear. Taking a deep breath, she opened the closet door and found her robe. She thought of going to the window and yelling down, "You don't have anything I want. Do you understand?" But she had more important things to do.

Wrapping her hair in a protective plastic, she ran a full steaming tub and dumped in half a bottle of her mother's favorite cologne. At first she scrubbed herself furiously, irritating her skin. But finally she stopped, knowing she would never be able to get cleaner than this again. She could not wash away the thing they considered dirty, the thing that made them pronounce "girl" in the same way as the other four-letter words they wrote on the wall in the alley; it was part of her, just as it was part of her mother and Rose Griffin and Lucy Mae. She relaxed then because it was true that the boys in the alley did not have a thing she wanted. She had what they wanted, and the knowledge replaced her shame with a strange, calm feeling of power.

After her bath she splashed on more cologne and spent forty minutes on her makeup, erasing and retracing her eyebrows six times until she was satisfied. She went to her mother's room then and found the dress; finished and freshly pressed, on its hanger.

When Mrs. Simmons came upstairs to help her daughter she found her sitting on the bench before the vanity mirror as if it were a throne. She looked young and arrogant and beautiful and perfect and cold.

"Why, you're dressed already," Mrs. Simmons said in surprise. While she stared, Judy rose with perfect, icy grace and glided to the center of the room. She stood there motionless as a mannequin.

"I want you to fix the hem, Mother," she directed. "It's still uneven in back."

Her mother went down obediently on her knees muttering, "It looks all right to me." She put in a couple of pins. "That better?"

"Yes," Judy said with a brief glance at the mirror. "You'll have to sew it on me, Mother. I can't take it off now. I'd ruin my hair."

Mrs. Simmons went to fetch her sewing things, returned and surveyed her daughter. "You sure did a good job on yourself, I must say," she admitted grudgingly. "Can't find a thing to complain about. You'll look as good as anybody there."

"Of course, Mother," Judy said as Mrs. Simmons knelt and sewed. "I don't know what you were so worried about." Her secret feeling of confidence had returned, stronger than ever, but the evening ahead was no longer a vague girlish fantasy she had pictured on the wall; it had hard, clear outlines leading up to a definite goal. She would be the belle of the Ball because she knew more than Rose Griffin and her silly friends; more than her mother, more, even than Lucy Mae, because she knew better than to settle for a mere pack of cigarettes.

"There," her mother said, breaking the thread. She got up. "I never expected to get you ready this early. Ernest Lee won't be here for another hour."

"That silly Ernest Lee," Judy said, with a new contempt in her young voice. Until tonight she had been pleased by the thought of going to the dance with Ernest Lee; he was nice, she felt comfortable with him, and he might even be the awe-struck boy of her dream. He was a dark, serious neighborhood boy who could not afford to go to college; Mrs. Simmons had reluctantly selected him to take Judy to the dance because all the Gay Charmers' sons were spoken for. Now, with an undertone of excitement, Judy said, "I'm going to ditch him after the first dance, Mother. You'll see. I'm going to come home with one of the college boys."

"It's very nice, Ernest Lee," she told him an hour later when he handed her the white orchid, "but it's rather small. I'm going to wear it on my wrist, if you don't mind." And then, dazzling him with a smile of sweetest cruelty, she stepped back and waited while he fumbled with the door.

"You know, Edward, I'm not worried about her any more," Mrs. Simmons said to her husband after the children were gone. Her voice became harsh and grating. "Put down that paper and listen to me! Aren't you interested in your child?—That's better," she said as he complied meekly. "I was saying, I do believe she's learned what I've been trying to teach her, after all."

[1968]

For Discussion

1. What is Judy's original attitude toward the dress fittings? How do her feelings resemble those of girls in the childhood section?

2. Describe Mrs. Simmons' attitude towards her daughter and the dance. Explain the significance of her comment that Judy will be the "darkest, poorest one there." What motifs are suggested by the comment that are repeated throughout the story?

3. Analyze the few references to the father in the story. What role does he play that might resemble the role of future men in Judy's life?

4. What does the overheard incident between Lucy Mae and the boys outside have to do with Judy's situation? Discuss Hunter's use of character pairs and its effect on the theme of choices available for adolescent women.

5. What is the meaning of Judy's thought that the boys use "girl" as another four-letter word?

6. After Judy's initial shock at being watched by the boys, why does she discover a "calm feeling of power"?

7. How does Judy treat people after her discovery that she "know[s] more than" her mother and friends?

8. Has Judy learned what her mother was "trying to teach her, after all"? What lesson has Judy learned?

9. What does Judy want out of life, and how does she intend to get it? What type of a person will she be, and how will she be the same or different from her mother?

For Further Exploration

1. Richard Wright's *Black Boy* tells a story of a young black male growing up in poverty and struggling for personal power. Compare Wright's narrative to this account of a young black female: which factors seem stronger in creating power or powerlessness for an adolescent—race, sex, age, or other factors?

2. In Madonna Kolbenschlag's *Kiss Sleeping Beauty Goodbye*, how can the following criticism of Marabel Morgan's *Total Woman* be applied to the lesson Judy learns in "Debut"?

   The objective of much of the advice in *Total Woman* seems to be to stroke the male ego enough to reduce him to a slobbering, adoring fool. In effect, the goal is adulation and creating the craving for it—not on relationship and communication (as between two autonomous persons), but on manipulation and dissimulation.

Joyce Carol Oates

1938–

Connie, the teenager in this story, leads two lives—one at home and one with her peers. But when she wants to return to the security of the home and family she has been trying to escape, she learns that "you can't go home again."

WHERE ARE YOU GOING, WHERE HAVE YOU BEEN?

Her name was Connie. She was fifteen and she had a quick nervous giggling habit of craning her neck to glance into mirrors, or checking other people's faces to make sure her own was all right. Her mother, who noticed everything and knew everything and who hadn't much reason any longer to look at her own face, always scolded Connie about it. "Stop gawking at yourself, who are you? You think you're so pretty?" she would say. Connie would raise her eyebrows at these familiar complaints and look right through her mother, into a shadowy vision of herself as she was right at that moment: she knew she was pretty and that was everything. Her mother had been pretty once too, if you could believe those old snapshots in the album, but now her looks were gone and that was why she was always after Connie.

"Why don't you keep your room clean like your sister? How've you got your hair fixed—what the hell stinks? Hair spray? You don't see your sister using that junk."

Her sister June was twenty-four and still lived at home. She was a secretary in the high school Connie attended, and if that wasn't bad enough—with her in the same building—she was so plain and chunky and steady that Connie had to hear her praised all the time by her mother and her mother's sisters. June did this, June did that, she saved money and helped clean the house and cooked and Connie couldn't do a thing, her mind was all filled with trashy daydreams. Their father was away at work most of the time and when he came home he wanted supper and he read the newspaper at supper and after supper he went to bed. He didn't bother talking much to them, but around his bent head Connie's mother kept picking at her until Connie wished her mother was dead and she herself was dead and it was all over. "She makes me want to throw up sometimes," she complained to her friends. She had a high, breathless, amused voice which made everything she said sound a little forced, whether it was sincere or not.

There was one good thing: June went places with girl friends of hers, girls who were just as plain and steady as she, and so when Connie wanted to do that her mother had no objections. The father of Connie's best girl friend drove the girls the three miles to town and left them off at a shopping plaza, so that they could walk through the stores or go to a movie, and when he came to pick them up again at eleven he never bothered to ask what they had done.

They must have been familiar sights, walking around that shopping plaza in their shorts and flat ballerina slippers that always scuffed the sidewalk, with charm bracelets jingling on their thin wrists; they would lean together to whisper and laugh secretly if someone passed by who amused or interested them. Connie had long dark blond hair that drew anyone's eye to it, and she wore part of it pulled up on her head and puffed out and the rest of it she let fall down her back. She wore a pullover jersey blouse that looked one way when she was at home and another way when she was away from home. Everything about her had two sides to it, one for home and one for anywhere that was not home: her walk that could be childlike and bobbing, or languid enough to make anyone think she was hearing music in her head, her mouth which was pale and smirking most of the time, but bright and pink on these evenings out, her laugh which was cynical and drawling at home—"Ha, ha, very funny"—but high-pitched and nervous anywhere else, like the jingling of the charms on her bracelet.

Sometimes they did go shopping or to a movie, but sometimes they went across the highway, ducking fast across the busy road, to a drive-in restaurant where older kids hung out. The restaurant was shaped like a big bottle, though squatter than a real bottle, and on its cap was a revolving figure of a grinning boy who held a hamburger aloft. One night in mid-summer they ran across, breathless with daring, and right away someone leaned out a car window and invited them over, but it was just a boy from high school they didn't like. It made them feel good to be able to ignore him. They went up through the maze of parked and cruising cars to the bright-lit, fly-infested restaurant, their faces pleased and expectant as if they were entering a sacred building that loomed out of the night to give them what haven and what blessing they yearned for. They sat at the counter and crossed their legs at the ankles, their thin shoulders rigid with excitement, and listened to the music that made everything so good: the music was always in the background like music at a church service, it was something to depend upon.

A boy named Eddie came in to talk with them. He sat backwards on his stool, turning himself jerkily around in semi-circles and then stopping and turning again, and after a while he asked Connie if she would like something to eat. She said she did and so she tapped her friend's arm on her way out— her friend pulled her face up into a brave droll look—and Connie said she would meet her at eleven, across the way. "I just hate to leave her like that," Connie said earnestly, but the boy said that she wouldn't be alone for long. So they went out to his car and on the way Connie couldn't help but let her eyes wander over the windshields and faces all around her, her face gleaming with a joy that had nothing to do with Eddie or even this place; it might have been the music. She drew her shoulders up and sucked in her breath with the pure pleasure of being alive, and just at that moment she happened to glance at a face just a few feet from hers. It was a boy with shaggy black hair, in a convertible jalopy painted gold. He stared at her and then his lips widened into a grin. Connie slit her eyes at him and turned away, but she couldn't help glancing back and there he was still watching her. He wagged a finger and laughed and said, "Gonna get you, baby," and Connie turned away again without Eddie noticing anything.

She spent three hours with him, at the restaurant where they ate hamburgers and drank Cokes in wax cups that were always sweating, and then down an alley a mile or so away, and when he left her off at five to eleven only the movie house was still open at the plaza. Her girl friend was there, talking with a boy. When Connie came up the two girls smiled at each other and Connie said, "How was the movie?" and the girl said, "*You* should know." They rode off with the girl's father, sleepy and pleased, and Connie couldn't help but look at the darkened shopping plaza with its big empty parking lot and its signs that were faded and ghostly now, and over at the drive-in restaurant where cars were still circling tirelessly. She couldn't hear the music at this distance.

Next morning June asked her how the movie was and Connie said, "Soso."

She and that girl and occasionally another girl went out several times a week that way, and the rest of the time Connie spent around the house—it was summer vacation—getting in her mother's way and thinking, dreaming, about the boys she met. But all the boys fell back and dissolved into a single face that was not even a face, but an idea, a feeling, mixed up with the urgent insistent pounding of the music and the humid night air of July. Connie's mother kept dragging her back to the daylight by finding things for her to do or saying, suddenly, "What's this about the Pettinger girl?"

And Connie would say nervously, "Oh, her. That dope." She always drew thick clear lines between herself and such girls, and her mother was simple and kindly enough to believe her. Her mother was so simple, Connie thought, that it was maybe cruel to fool her so much. Her mother went scuffling around the house in old bedroom slippers and complained over the telephone to one sister about the other, then the other called up and the two of them complained about the third one. If June's name was mentioned her mother's tone was approving, and if Connie's name was mentioned it was disapproving. This did not really mean she disliked Connie and actually Connie thought that her mother preferred her to June because she was prettier, but the two of them kept up a pretense of exasperation, a sense that they were tugging and struggling over something of little value to either of them. Sometimes, over coffee, they were almost friends, but something would come up—some vexation that was like a fly buzzing suddenly around their heads—and their faces went hard with contempt.

One Sunday Connie got up at eleven—none of them bothered with church—and washed her hair so that it could dry all day long, in the sun. Her parents and sister were going to a barbecue at an aunt's house and Connie said no, she wasn't interested, rolling her eyes to let mother know just what she thought of it. "Stay home alone then," her mother said sharply. Connie sat out back in a lawn chair and watched them drive away, her father quiet and bald, hunched around so that he could back the car out, her mother with a look that was still angry and not at all softened through the windshield, and in the back seat poor old June all dressed up as if she didn't know what a barbecue was, with all the running yelling kids and the flies. Connie sat with her eyes closed in the sun, dreaming and dazed with the warmth about her as if this were a kind of love, the caresses of love, and her mind slipped over onto thoughts of the boy she had been with the night before and how nice he had been, how sweet it always was, not the way someone like June would suppose but sweet, gentle, the way it was in movies and promised in songs; and when she opened her eyes she hardly knew where she was, the back yard ran off into weeds and a fence-line of trees and behind it the sky was perfectly blue and still. The asbestos "ranch house" that was now three years old startled her—it looked small. She shook her head as if to get awake.

It was too hot. She went inside the house and turned on the radio to drown out the quiet. She sat on the edge of her bed, barefoot, and listened for an hour and a half to a program called XYZ Sunday Jamboree, record after record of hard, fast, shrieking songs she sang along with, interspersed by exclamations from "Bobby King": "An' look here you girls at Napoleon's—Son and Charley want you to pay real close attention to this song coming up!"

And Connie paid close attention herself, bathed in a glow of slow-pulsed joy that seemed to rise mysteriously out of the music itself and lay languidly about the airless little room, breathed in and breathed out with each gentle rise and fall of her chest.

After a while she heard a car coming up the drive. She sat up at once, startled, because it couldn't be her father so soon. The gravel kept crunching all the way in from the road—the driveway was long—and Connie ran to the window. It was a car she didn't know. It was an open jalopy, painted a bright gold that caught the sunlight opaquely. Her heart began to pound and her fingers snatched at her hair, checking it, and she whispered "Christ. Christ," wondering how bad she looked. The car came to a stop at the side door and the horn sounded four short taps as if this were a signal Connie knew.

She went into the kitchen and approached the door slowly, then hung out the screen door, her bare toes curling down off the step. There were two boys in the car and now she recognized the driver: he had shaggy, shabby black hair that looked crazy as a wig and he was grinning at her.

"I ain't late, am I?" he said.

"Who the hell do you think you are?" Connie said.

"Toldja I'd be out, didn't I?"

"I don't even know who you are."

She spoke sullenly, careful to show no interest or pleasure, and he spoke in a fast bright monotone. Connie looked past him to the other boy, taking her time. He had fair brown hair, with a lock that fell onto his forehead. His sideburns gave him a fierce, embarrassed look, but so far he hadn't even bothered to glance at her. Both boys wore sunglasses. The driver's glasses were metallic and mirrored everything in miniature.

"You wanta come for a ride?" he said.

Connie smirked and let her hair fall loose over one shoulder.

"Don'tcha like my car? New paint job," he said. "Hey."

"What?"

"You're cute."

She pretended to fidget, chasing flies away from the door.

"Don'tcha believe me, or what?" he said.

"Look, I don't even know who you are," Connie said in disgust.

"Hey, Ellie's got a radio, see. Mine's broke down." He lifted his friend's arm and showed her the little transistor the boy was holding, and now Connie began to hear the music. It was the same program that was playing inside the house.

"Bobby King?" she said.

"I listen to him all the time. I think he's great."

"He's kind of great," Connie said reluctantly.

"Listen, that guy's *great*. He knows where the action is."

Connie blushed a little, because the glasses made it impossible for her to see just what this boy was looking at. She couldn't decide if she liked him or if he was just a jerk, and so she dawdled in the doorway and wouldn't come down or go back inside. She said, "What's all that stuff painted on your car?"

"Can'tcha read it?" He opened the door very carefully, as if he was afraid it might fall off. He slid out just as carefully, planting his feet firmly on the ground, the tiny metallic world in his glasses slowing down like gelatin hardening and in the midst of it Connie's bright green blouse. "This here is my name, to begin with," he said. ARNOLD FRIEND was written in tar-like black letters on the side, with a drawing of a round grinning face that reminded Connie of a pumpkin, except it wore sunglasses. "I wanta introduce myself,

I'm Arnold Friend and that's my real name and I'm gonna be your friend, honey, and inside the car's Ellie Oscar, he's kinda shy.'' Ellie brought his transistor radio up to his shoulder and balanced it there. "Now these numbers are a secret code, honey," Arnold Friend explained. He read off the numbers 33, 19, 17 and raised his eyebrows at her to see what she thought of that, but she didn't think much of it. The left rear fender had been smashed and around it was written, on the gleaming gold background: DONE BY CRAZY WOMAN DRIVER. Connie had to laugh at that. Arnold Friend was pleased at her laughter and looked up at her. "Around the other side's a lot more—you wanta come and see them?"

"No."

"Why not?"

"Why should I?"

"Don'tcha wanta see what's on the car? Don'tcha wanta go for a ride?"

"I don't know."

"Why not?"

"I got things to do."

"Like what?"

"Things."

He laughed as if she had said something funny. He slapped his thighs. He was standing in a strange way, leaning back against the car as if he were balancing himself. He wasn't tall, only an inch or so taller than she would be if she came down to him. Connie liked the way he was dressed, which was the way all of them dressed: tight faded jeans stuffed into black, scuffed boots, a belt that pulled his waist in and showed how lean he was, and a white pull-over shirt that was a little soiled and showed the hard small muscles of his arms and shoulders. He looked as if he probably did hard work, lifting and carrying things. Even his neck looked muscular. And his face was a familiar face, somehow: the jaw and chin and cheeks slightly darkened, because he hadn't shaved for a day or two, and the nose long and hawk-like, sniffing as if she were a treat he was going to gobble up and it was all a joke.

"Connie, you ain't telling the truth. This is your day set aside for a ride with me and you know it," he said, still laughing. The way he straightened and recovered from his fit of laughing showed that it had been all fake.

"How do you know what my name is?" she said suspiciously.

"It's Connie."

"Maybe and maybe not."

"I know my Connie," he said, wagging his finger. Now she remembered him even better, back at the restaurant, and her cheeks warmed at the thought of how she sucked in her breath just at the moment she passed him—how she must have looked to him. And he had remembered her. "Ellie and I come out here especially for you," he said. "Ellie can sit in back. How about it?"

"Where?"

"Where what?"

"Where're we going?"

He looked at her. He took off the sunglasses and she saw how pale the skin around his eyes was, like holes that were not in shadow but instead in light. His eyes were like chips of broken glass that catch the light in an amiable way. He smiled. It was as if the idea of going for a ride somewhere, to some place, was a new idea to him.

"Just for a ride, Connie sweetheart."

"I never said my name was Connie," she said.

"But I know what it is. I know your name and all about you, lots of things," Arnold Friend said. He had not moved yet but stood still leaning back against the side of his jalopy. "I took a special interest in you, such a pretty girl, and found out all about you like I know your parents and sister are gone somewheres and I know where and how long they're going to be gone, and I know who you were with last night, and your best girl friend's name is Betty. Right?"

He spoke in a simple lilting voice, exactly as if he were reciting the words to a song. His smile assured her that everything was fine. In the car Ellie turned up the volume on his radio and did not bother to look around at them.

"Ellie can sit in the back seat," Arnold Friend said. He indicated his friend with a casual jerk of his chin, as if Ellie did not count and she should not bother with him.

"How'd you find out all that stuff?" Connie said.

"Listen: Betty Schultz and Tony Fitch and Jimmy Pettinger and Nancy Pettinger," he said, in a chant. "Raymond Stanley and Bob Hutter—"

"Do you know all those kids?"

"I know everybody."

"Look, you're kidding. You're not from around here."

"Sure."

"But—how come we never saw you before?"

"Sure you saw me before," he said. He looked down at his boots, as if he were a little offended. "You just don't remember."

"I guess I'd remember you," Connie said.

"Yeah?" He looked up at this, beaming. He was pleased. He began to mark time with the music from Ellie's radio, tapping his fists lightly together. Connie looked away from his smile to the car, which was painted so bright it almost hurt her eyes to look at it. She looked at that name, ARNOLD FRIEND. And up at the front fender was an expression that was familiar—MAN THE FLYING SAUCERS. It was an expression kids had used the year before, but didn't use this year. She looked at it for a while as if the words meant something to her that she did not yet know.

"What're you thinking about? Huh?" Arnold Friend demanded. "Not worried about your hair blowing around in the car, are you?"

"No."

"Think I maybe can't drive good?"

"How do I know?"

"You're a hard girl to handle. How come?" he said. "Don't you know I'm your friend? Didn't you see me put my sign in the air when you walked by?"

"What sign?"

"My sign." And he drew an X in the air, leaning out toward her. They were maybe ten feet apart. After his hand fell back to his side the X was still in the air, almost visible. Connie let the screen door close and stood perfectly still inside it, listening to the music from her radio and the boy's blend together. She stared at Arnold Friend. He stood there so stiffly relaxed, pretending to be relaxed, with one hand idly on the door handle as if he were keeping himself up that way and had no intention of ever moving again. She recognized most things about him, the tight jeans that showed his thighs and buttocks and the greasy leather boots and the tight shirt, and even that slippery friendly smile of his, that sleepy dreamy smile that all the boys used to get across ideas they didn't want to put into words. She recognized all this and also the singsong way he talked, slightly mocking, kidding, but serious and a little melancholy, and she recognized the way he tapped one fist against the other in homage to the perpetual music behind him. But all these things did not come together.

She said suddenly, "Hey, how old are you?"

His smile faded. She could see then that he wasn't a kid, he was much older—thirty, maybe more. At this knowledge her heart began to pound faster.

"That's a crazy thing to ask. Can'tcha see I'm your own age?"

"Like hell you are."

"Or maybe a coupla years older, I'm eighteen."

"Eighteen?" she said doubtfully.

He grinned to reassure her and lines appeared at the corners of his mouth. His teeth were big and white. He grinned so broadly his eyes became slits and she saw how thick the lashes were, thick and black as if painted with a black tar-like material. Then he seemed to become embarrassed, abruptly, and looked over his shoulder at Ellie. "*Him*, he's crazy," he said. "Ain't he a riot, he's a nut, a real character." Ellie was still listening to the music. His sunglasses told nothing about what he was thinking. He wore a bright orange shirt unbuttoned halfway to show his chest, which was a pale, bluish chest and not muscular like Arnold Friend's. His shirt collar was turned up all around and the very tips of the collar pointed out past his chin as if they were protecting him. He was pressing the transistor radio up against his ear and sat there in a kind of daze, right in the sun.

"He's kinda strange," Connie said.

"Hey, she says you're kinda strange! Kinda strange!" Arnold Friend cried. He pounded on the car to get Ellie's attention. Ellie turned for the first time and Connie saw with shock that he wasn't a kid either—he had a fair, hairless face, cheeks reddened slightly as if the veins grew too close to the surface of his skin, the face of a forty-year-old baby. Connie felt a wave of dizziness rise in her at this sight and she stared at him as if waiting for something to change the shock of the moment, make it all right again. Ellie's lips kept shaping words, mumbling along with the words blasting in his ear.

"Maybe you two better go away," Connie said faintly.

"What? How come?" Arnold Friend cried. "We come out here to take you for a ride. It's Sunday." He had the voice of the man on the radio now. It was the same voice, Connie thought. "Don'tcha know it's Sunday all day and honey, no matter who you were with last night today you're with Arnold Friend and don't you forget it!—Maybe you better step out here," He said, and this last was in a different voice. It was a little flatter, as if the heat was finally getting to him.

"No. I got things to do."

"Hey."

"You two better leave."

"We ain't leaving until you come with us."

"Like hell I am—"

"Connie, don't fool around with me. I mean, I mean, don't fool *around*," he said, shaking his head. He laughed incredulously. He placed his sunglasses on top of his head, carefully, as if he were indeed wearing a wig, and brought the stems down behind his ears. Connie stared at him, another wave of dizziness and fear rising in her so that for a moment he wasn't even in focus but was just a blur, standing there against his gold car, and she had the idea that he had driven up the driveway all right but had come from no-where before that and belonged nowhere and that everything about him and even about the music that was so familiar to her was only half real.

"If my father comes and sees you—"

"He ain't coming. He's at a barbecue."

"How do you know that?"

"Aunt Tillie's. Right now they're—uh—they're drinking. Sitting around," he said vaguely, squinting as if he were staring all the way to town and over to Aunt Tillie's back yard. Then the vision seemed to get clear and he nodded energetically. "Yeah. Sitting around. There's your sister in a blue dress, huh? And high heels, the poor sad bitch—nothing like you, sweet-heart! And your mother's helping some fat woman with the corn, they're cleaning the corn—husking the corn—"

"What fat woman?" Connie cried.

"How do I know what fat woman. I don't know every goddam fat woman in the world!" Arnold Friend laughed.

"Oh, that's Mrs. Hornby. . . . Who invited her?" Connie said. She felt a little light-headed. Her breath was coming quickly.

"She's too fat. I don't like them fat. I like them the way you are, honey," he said, smiling sleepily at her. They stared at each other for a while, through the screen door. He said softly, "Now what you're going to do is this: you're going to come out that door. You're going to sit up front with me and Ellie's going to sit in the back, the hell with Ellie, right? This isn't Ellie's date. You're my date. I'm your lover, honey."

"What? You're crazy—"

"Yes, I'm your lover. You don't know what that is but you will," he said. "I know that too. I know all about you. But look: it's real nice and you couldn't ask for nobody better than me, or more polite. I always keep my word. I'll tell you how it is, I'm always nice at first, the first time. I'll hold you so tight you won't think you have to try to get away or pretend anything be-cause you'll know you can't. And I'll come inside you where it's all secret and you'll give in to me and you'll love me—"

"Shut up! You're crazy!" Connie said. She backed away from the door. She put her hands against her ears as if she'd heard something terrible, something not meant for her. "People don't talk like that, you're crazy," she muttered. Her heart was almost too big now for her chest and its pumping made sweat break out all over her. She looked out to see Arnold Friend pause and then take a step toward the porch lurching. He almost fell. But, like a clever drunken man, he managed to catch his balance. He wobbled in his high boots and grabbed hold of one of the porch posts.

"Honey?" he said. "You still listening?"

"Get the hell out of here!"

"Be nice, honey. Listen."

"I'm going to call the police—"

He wobbled again and out of the side of his mouth came a fast spat curse, an aside not meant for her to hear. But even this "Christ!" sounded forced. Then he began to smile again. She watched this smile come, awk-ward as if he were smiling from inside a mask. His whole face was a mask, she thought wildly, tanned down onto his throat but then running out as if he had plastered make-up on his face but had forgotten about his throat.

"Honey—? Listen, here's how it is. I always tell the truth and I promise you this: I ain't coming in that house after you."

"You better not! I'm going to call the police if you—if you don't—"

"Honey," he said, talking right through her voice, "honey, I'm not coming in there but you are coming out here. You know why?"

She was panting. The kitchen looked like a place she had never seen before, some room she had run inside but which wasn't good enough, wasn't going to help her. The kitchen window had never had a curtain, after three years, and there were dishes in the sink for her to do—probably—and if you ran your hand across the table you'd probably feel something sticky there.

"You listening, honey? Hey?"

"—going to call the police—"

"Soon as you touch the phone I don't need to keep my promise and can come inside. You won't want that."

She rushed forward and tried to lock the door. Her fingers were shaking. "But why lock it," Arnold Friend said gently, talking right into her face. "It's just a screen door. It's just nothing." One of his boots was at a strange angle, as if his foot wasn't in it. It pointed out to the left, bent at the ankle. "I mean, anybody can break through a screen door and glass and wood and iron or anything else if he needs to, anybody at all and specially Arnold Friend. If the place got lit up with a fire honey you'd come running out into my arms, right into my arms and safe at home—like you knew I was your lover and'd stopped fooling around. I don't mind a nice shy girl but I don't like no fooling around." Part of those words were spoken with a slight rhythmic lilt, and Connie somehow recognized them—the echo of a song from last year, about a girl rushing into her boy friend's arms and coming home again—

Connie stood barefoot on the linoleum floor, staring at him. "What do you want?" she whispered.

"I want you," he said.

"What?"

"Seen you that night and thought, that's the one, yes sir. I never needed to look any more."

"But my father's coming back. He's coming to get me. I had to wash my hair first—" She spoke in a dry, rapid voice, hardly raising it for him to hear.

"No, your daddy is not coming and yes, you had to wash your hair and you washed it for me. It's nice and shining and all for me, I thank you, sweetheart," he said, with a mock bow, but again he almost lost his balance. He had to bend and adjust his boots. Evidently his feet did not go all the way down; the boots must have been stuffed with something so that he would seem taller. Connie stared out at him and behind him Ellie in the car, who seemed to be looking off toward Connie's right, into nothing. This Ellie said, pulling the words out of the air one after another as if he were just discovering them, "You want me to pull out the phone?"

"Shut your mouth and keep it shut," Arnold Friend said, his face red from bending over or maybe from embarrassment because Connie had seen his boots. "This ain't none of your business."

"What—what are you doing? What do you want?" Connie said. "If I call the police they'll get you, they'll arrest you—"

"Promise was not to come in unless you touch that phone, and I'll keep that promise," he said. He resumed his erect position and tried to force his shoulders back. He sounded like a hero in a movie, declaring something important. He spoke too loudly and it was as if he were speaking to someone behind Connie. "I ain't made plans for coming in that house where I don't belong but just for you to come out to me, the way you should. Don't you know who I am?"

"You're crazy," she whispered. She backed away from the door but did not want to go into another part of the house, as if this would give him permission to come through the door. "What do you. . . . You're crazy, you . . ."

"Huh? What're you saying, honey?"

Her eyes darted everywhere in the kitchen. She could not remember what it was, this room.

"This is how it is, honey: you come out and we'll drive away, have a nice ride. But if you don't come out we're gonna wait till your people come home and then they're all going to get it."

"You want that telephone pulled out?" Ellie said. He held the radio away from his ear and grimaced, as if without the radio the air was too much for him.

"I toldja shut up, Ellie," Arnold Friend said, "you're deaf, get a hearing aid, right? Fix yourself up. This little girl's no trouble and's gonna be nice to me, so Ellie keep to yourself, this ain't your date—right? Don't hem in on me. Don't hog. Don't crush. Don't bird dog. Don't trail me," he said in a rapid meaningless voice, as if he were running through all the expressions he'd learned but was no longer sure which one of them was in style, then rushing on to new ones, making them up with his eyes closed, "Don't crawl under my fence, don't squeeze in my chipmunk hole, don't sniff my glue, suck my popsicle, keep your own greasy fingers on yourself!" He shaded his eyes and peered in at Connie, who was backed against the kitchen table. "Don't mind him honey he's just a creep. He's a dope. Right? I'm the boy for you and like I said you come out here nice like a lady and give me your hand, and nobody else gets hurt, I mean, your nice old bald-headed daddy and your mummy and your sister in her high heels. Because listen: why bring them in this?"

"Leave me alone," Connie whispered.

"Hey, you know that old woman down the road, the one with the chickens and stuff—you know her?"

"She's dead!"

"Dead? What? You know her?" Arnold Friend said.

"She's dead—"

"Don't you like her?"

"She's dead—she's—she isn't here any more—"

"But don't you like her, I mean, you got something against her? Some grudge or something?" Then his voice dipped as if he were conscious of a rudeness. He touched the sunglasses perched on top of his head as if to make sure they were still there. "Now you be a good girl."

"What are you going to do?"

"Just two things, or maybe three," Arnold Friend said. "But I promise it won't last long and you'll like me that way you get to like people you're close to. You will. It's all over for you here, so come on out. You don't want your people in any trouble, do you?"

She turned and bumped against a chair or something, hurting her leg, but she ran into the back room and picked up the telephone. Something roared in her ear, a tiny roaring, and she was so sick with fear that she could do nothing but listen to it—the telephone was clammy and very heavy and her fingers groped down to the dial but were too weak to touch it. She began to scream into the phone, into the roaring. She cried out, she cried for her mother, she felt her breath start jerking back and forth in her lungs as if it were something Arnold Friend were stabbing her with again and again with no tenderness. A noisy sorrowful wailing rose all about her and she was locked inside it the way she was locked inside this house.

After a while she could hear again. She was sitting on the floor with her wet back against the wall.

Arnold Friend was saying from the door, "That's a good girl. Put the phone back."

She kicked the phone away from her.

"No, honey. Pick it up. Put it back right."

She picked it up and put it back. The dial tone stopped.

"That's a good girl. Now you come outside."

She was hollow with what had been fear, but what was now just an emptiness. All that screaming had blasted it out of her. She sat, one leg cramped under her, and deep inside her brain was something like a pinpoint of light that kept going and would not let her relax. She thought, I'm not going to see my mother again. She thought, I'm not going to sleep in my bed again. Her bright green blouse was all wet.

Arnold Friend said, in a gentle-loud voice that was like a stage voice, "The place where you came from ain't there any more, and where you had in mind to go is cancelled out. This place you are now—inside your daddy's house—is nothing but a cardboard box I can knock down any time. You know that and always did know it. You hear me?"

She thought, I have got to think. I have to know what to do.

"We'll go out to a nice field, out in the country here where it smells so nice and it's sunny," Arnold Friend said. "I'll have my arms tight around you so you won't need to try to get away and I'll show you what love is like, what it does. The hell with this house! It looks solid all right," he said. He ran a fingernail down the screen and the noise did not make Connie shiver, as it would have the day before. "Now put your hand on your heart, honey. Feel that? That feels solid too but we know better, be nice to me, be sweet like you can because what else is there for a girl like you but to be sweet and pretty and give in?—and get away before her people come back?"

She felt her pounding heart. Her hand seemed to enclose it. She thought for the first time in her life that it was nothing that was hers, that belonged to her, but just a pounding, living thing inside this body that wasn't really hers either.

"You don't want them to get hurt," Arnold Friend went on. "Now get up, honey. Get up all by yourself."

She stood.

"Now turn this way. That's right. Come over here to me—Ellie, put that away, didn't I tell you? You dope. You miserable creepy dope," Arnold Friend said. His words were not angry but only part of an incantation. The incantation was kindly. "Now come out through the kitchen to me honey and let's see a smile, try it, you're a brave sweet little girl and now they're eating corn and hotdogs cooked to bursting over an outdoor fire, and they don't know one thing about you and never did and honey you're better than them because not a one of them would have done this for you."

Connie felt the linoleum under her feet; it was cool. She brushed her hair back out of her eyes. Arnold Friend let go of the post tentatively and opened his arms for her, his elbows pointing in toward each other and his wrists limp, to show that this was an embarrassed embrace and a little mocking, he didn't want to make her self-conscious.

She put out her hand against the screen. She watched herself push the door slowly open as if she were safe back somewhere in the other doorway, watching this body and this head of long hair moving out into the sunlight where Arnold Friend waited.

"My sweet little blue-eyed girl," he said, in a half-sung sigh that had nothing to do with her brown eyes but was taken up just the same by the vast sunlit reaches of the land behind him and on all sides of him, so much land that Connie had never seen before and did not recognize except to know that she was going to it.

[1965]

For Discussion

1. Contrast Connie's appearance and behavior with that of her sister June. What effect does this character contrast have on the story?

2. Describe Connie's two selves, "home" and "not-home."

3. Identify each time that music is mentioned in the story. What function does music play for Connie?

4. Describe Connie's "altered state" in the back yard. How do the references to mirrors throughout the story relate to Connie's state of mind?

5. Describe Connie's first meeting with the "boy with shaggy black hair, in a convertible jalopy." What might be suggested by these remarks Connie makes to him later: "Christ. Christ. . . . Who the hell do you think you are?" "Like hell you are. . . . Like hell I am"?

6. Why does his hair look like a wig, and face like a mask? What else is "fake" about his appearance?

7. Why does Arnold Friend's face seem familiar? In what sense might he be An Old Friend (or An Old Fiend?), and what might the other names in the story signify?

8. How does Arnold know Connie's name, her friends' names, and what her family is doing at the barbecue? How does he know a dead woman, and what might the X in the air suggest? What could explain the fact that his feet do "not go all the way down," and that his boots are stuffed?

9. What might the problems with the telephone symbolize in the story? Also, explain what the house suggests as a symbol, and why Arnold won't go in, but expects Connie to come out.

10. What does Arnold mean by "I'm your lover"? Explain the line, "The place where you came from ain't there any more, and where you had in mind to go is cancelled out." How does it relate to the last line of the story?

For Further Exploration

1. See *Smooth Talk*, the film based on this story, and compare the two versions, especially the endings. In what sense is Oates's story a didactic

warning to teenagers? What problems does she suggest are associated with growing up in the modern world?

2. Two similar stories by Joyce Carol Oates are "The Girl" and "Boy and Girl." Find out the meaning of the "Faustian theme" in literature (start by looking up "Faust" in the dictionary), and determine which of Oates' stories associate the theme with adolescence.

Alice Adams

1926–

Approaching adulthood, young Dylan wants to be rescued from a mind-dulling teenage existence and dead-end job. Unwilling to seek the adult forms of escapism her mother uses to cope with men and the world, Dylan dreams of an ideal savior who will provide her escape.

BY THE SEA

Because she looked older than she was, eighteen, and was very pretty, her two slightly crooked front teeth more than offset by wheat-blond hair and green eyes, Dylan Ballentyne was allowed to be a waitress at the Cypress Lodge without having been a bus girl first. She hated the work—loathed, despised it—but it was literally the only job in town, town being a cluster of houses and a couple of stores on the northern California coast. Dylan also hated the town and the wild, dramatically desolate landscape of the area, to which she and her mother had moved at the beginning of the summer, coming down from San Francisco, where Dylan had been happy in the sunny Mission District, out of sight of the sea.

Now she moved drearily through days of trays and dishes, spilled coffee and gelatinous ash-strewn food, fat cross guests or hyper-friendly ones. She was sustained by her small paycheck and somewhat more generous tips, and by her own large fantasies of ultimate rescue, or escape.

The Lodge, an ornately Victorian structure with pinnacles and turrets, was on a high bluff two miles south of town, surrounded by sharply sloping meadows which were edged with dark-green cypresses and pines, overlooking the turbulent, shark-infested, almost inaccessible sea. (One more disappointment: talking up the move, Dylan's mother, self-named Flower, had invented long beach days and picnics; they would both learn to surf, she had said.)

Breakfast was served at the Lodge from eight till ten-thirty, lunch from eleven-thirty until two, in a long glassed-in porch, the dining room. Supposedly between those two meals the help got a break, half an hour for a sandwich or a cigarette, but more often than not it was about five minutes, what with lingering breakfasters and early, eager lunchers. Dinner was at six, set up at five-thirty, and thus there really was a free hour or sometimes two, in the mid to late afternoon. Dylan usually spent this time in the "library" of the Lodge, a dim, musty room, paneled in fake mahogany. Too tired for books, although her reading habits had delighted English teachers in high school, she leafed through old *House Beautifuls, Gourmets* or *Vogues*, avidly drinking in all those ads for the accoutrements of rich and leisurely exotic lives.

Curiously, what she saw and read made her almost happy, for that limited time, like a drug. She could nearly believe that she saw herself in *Vogue*, in a Rolls-Royce ad: a tall thin blond woman (she was thin, if not very tall) in silk and careless fur, one jeweled hand on the fender of a silver car, and in the background a handsome man, dark, wearing a tuxedo.

Then there was dinner. Drinks. Wines. Specifics as to the doneness of steaks or roasts. Complaints. I ordered *medium* rare. Is this crab really *fresh*? And heavy trays. The woman who managed the restaurant saw to it that waitresses and bus girls "shared" that labor, possibly out of some vaguely egalitarian sense that the trays were too heavy for any single group. By eight-thirty or so, Dylan and all the girls would be slow-witted with exhaustion, smiles stiffening on their very young faces, perspiration drying under their arms and down their backs. Then there would come the stentorian voice of the manageress: "*Dylan*, are you awake? You look a thousand miles away."

Actually, in her dreams, Dylan was less than two hundred miles away, in San Francisco.

One fantasy of rescue which Dylan recognized as childish, and unlikely, probably, was that a nice older couple (in their fifties, anyway: Flower was only thirty-eight) would adopt her. At the end of their stay at the Lodge, after several weeks, they would say, "Well, Dylan, we just don't see how we're going to get along without you. Do you think you could possibly . . . ?" There had in fact been several couples who could have filled that bill—older people from San Francisco, or even L.A., San Diego, Scottsdale—who stayed for a few weeks at the Lodge, who liked Dylan and tipped her generously. But so far none of them had been unable to leave without her; they didn't even send her postcards.

Another fantasy, a little more plausible, more grown up, involved a man who would come to the Lodge alone and would fall in love with Dylan and take her away. The man was as indistinct as the one in the Rolls-Royce ads, as vaguely handsome, dark and rich.

In the meantime, the local boys who came around to see the other waitresses tried to talk to Dylan; their hair was too long and their faces splotchily sunburned from cycling and surfing, which were the only two things they did, besides drinking beer. Dylan ignored them, and went on dreaming.

The usual group of guests at the Lodge didn't offer much material for fantasy: youngish, well-off couples who arrived in big new station wagons with several children, new summer clothes and new sports equipment. Apart from these stylish parents, there were always two or three very young couples, perhaps just married or perhaps not, all with the look of not quite being able to afford where they were.

And always some very old people.

There was, actually, one unmarried man (almost divorced) among the guests, and although he was very nice, intelligent, about twenty-eight, he did not look rich, or, for that matter, handsome and dark. Whitney Iverson was a stocky red-blond man with a strawberry birthmark on one side of his neck. Deep-set blue eyes were his best feature. Probably he was not the one to fall in love and rescue Dylan, although he seemed to like her very much. Mr. Iverson, too, spent his late afternoons in the Lodge's library.

Exactly what Mr. Iverson did for a living was not clear; he mentioned the Peace Corps and VISTA, and then he said that he was writing; not novels— articles. His wife was divorcing him and she was making a lot of trouble about money, he said: a blow, he hadn't thought she was like that. (But how could he have enough money for anyone to make trouble about, Dylan wondered.) He had brought down a carload of books. When he wasn't reading in his room, or working on whatever he was writing, he took long, long walks, every day, miles over the meadows, back and forth to what there was of a town. Glimpsing him through a window as she set up tables, Dylan noted his stride, his strong shoulders. Sometimes he climbed down the steep perilous banks to the edge of the sea, to the narrow strip of coarse gray sand that passed for a beach. Perfectly safe, he said, if you checked the tides. Unlike Dylan, he was crazy about this landscape; he found the sea and the stretching hills of grass and rock, the acres of sky, all marvelous; even the billowing fog that threatened all summer he saw as lovely, something amazing.

Sometimes Dylan tried to see the local scenery with Whitney Iverson's eyes, and sometimes, remarkably, this worked. She was able to imagine herself a sojourner in this area, as he was, and then she could succumb to the sharp blue beauty of that wild Pacific, the dark-green, wind-bent feathery cypresses, and the sheer cliffs going down to the water, with their crevices of moss and tiny brilliant wild flowers.

But usually she just looked around in a dull, hating way. Usually she was miserably bored and hopelessly despondent.

They had moved down here to the seaside, to this tiny nothing town, Dylan and Flower, so that Flower could concentrate on making jewelry, which was her profession. Actually, the move was the idea of Zachery, Flower's boyfriend. Flower would make the jewelry and Zach would take it up to San Francisco to sell; someday he might even try L.A. And Zach would bring back new materials for Flower to use—gold and silver and pearls. Flower, who was several months behind in her rent, had agreed to this plan. Also, as Dylan saw it, Flower was totally dominated by Zach, who was big and dark and roughly handsome, and sometimes mean. Dylan further suspected that Zach wanted them out of town, wanted to see less of Flower, and the summer had borne out her theory: instead of his living with them and making occasional forays to the city, as Flower had imagined, it was just the other way around. Zach made occasional visits to them, and the rest of the time, when she wasn't working or trying to work on some earrings or a necklace, Flower sat sipping the harsh, local red wine and reading the used paperbacks that Zach brought down in big cartons along with the jewelry materials—"to keep you out of mischief," he had said.

Flower wore her graying blond hair long, in the non-style of her whole adult life, and she was putting on weight. When she wanted to work she took an upper, another commodity supplied by Zach, but this didn't do much to keep her weight down, just kept her "wired," as she sometimes said. Dylan alternated between impatience and the most tender sympathy for her mother, who was in some ways more like a friend; it was often clear to Dylan that actually she had to be the stronger person, the one in charge. But Flower was so nice, really, a wonderful cook and generous to her friends, and she could be funny. Some of the jewelry she made was beautiful—recently, a necklace of silver and stones that Zach said were real opals. Flower had talent, originality. If she could just dump Zach for good, Dylan thought, and then not replace him with someone worse, as she usually did. Always some mean jerk. If she could just not drink, not take speed.

From the start Flower had been genuinely sympathetic about Dylan's awful job. "Honey, I can hardly stand to think about it," she would say, and her eyes would fill. She had been a waitress several times herself. "You and those heavy trays, and the mess. Look, why don't you just quit? Honestly, we'll get by like we always have. I'll just tell Zach he's got to bring more stuff down, and sell more, too. And you can help me."

This seemed a dangerous plan to Dylan, possibly because it relied on Zach, who Dylan was sure would end up in jail, or worse. She stubbornly stuck with her job, and on her two days off (Mondays and Tuesdays, of all useless days) she stayed in bed a lot, and read, and allowed her mother to "spoil" her, with breakfast trays ("Well, after all, who deserves her own tray more than you do, baby?") and her favorite salads for lunch, with every available fresh vegetable and sometimes shrimp.

When she wasn't talking to her mother or helping out with household chores, Dylan was reading a book that Mr. Iverson had lent her—*The Eustace Diamonds*, by Trollope. This had come about because one afternoon, meeting him in the library, Dylan had explained the old *Vogues*, the *House Beautifuls* scattered near her lap, saying that she was too tired just then to read, and that she missed television. The winter before, she had loved *The Pallisers*, she said, and, before that, *Upstairs, Downstairs*. Mr. Iverson had recommended *The Eustace Diamonds*. "It's really my favorite of the Palliser novels," he said, and he went to get it for her—running all the way up to his room and back, apparently; he was out of breath as he handed her the book.

But why was he so eager to please her? She knew that she was pretty, but she wasn't all that pretty, in her own estimation; she was highly conscious of the two crooked front teeth, although she had perfected a radiant, slightly false smile that almost hid them.

"I wonder if he could be one of *the* Iversons," Flower mused, informed by Dylan one Monday of the source of her book.

"The Iversons?" In Flower's voice it had sounded like the Pallisers.

"One of the really terrific, old San Francisco families. You know, Huntingtons, Floods, Crockers, Iversons. What does he look like, your Mr. Iverson?"

Dylan found this hard to answer, although usually with Flower she spoke very easily, they were so used to each other. "Well." She hesitated. "He's sort of blond, with nice blue eyes and a small nose. He has this birthmark on his neck, but it's not really noticeable."

Flower laughed. "In that case, he's not a real Iverson. They've all got dark hair and the most aristocratic beaky noses. And none of them could possibly have a birthmark—they'd drown it at birth."

Dylan laughed, too, although she felt an obscure disloyalty to Mr. Iverson.

And, looking at Flower, Dylan thought, as she had before, that Flower *could* change her life, take charge of herself. She was basically strong. But in the next moment Dylan decided, as she also had before, more frequently, that probably Flower wouldn't change; in her brief experience people didn't, or not much. Zach would go to jail and Flower would find somebody worse, and get grayer and fatter. And she, Dylan, had better forget about anything as childish as being adopted by rich old people; she must concentrate on marrying someone who really had *money*. Resolution made her feel suddenly adult.

"Honey," asked Flower, "are you sure you won't have a glass of wine?"

"My mother wonders if you're a real Iverson." Dylan had not quite meant to say this; the sentence spoke itself, leaving her slightly embarrassed, as she sat with Whitney Iverson on a small sofa in the library. It was her afternoon break; she was tired, and she told herself that she didn't know what she was saying.

Mr. Iverson, whose intense blue eyes had been staring into hers, now turned away, so that Dylan was more aware of the mark on his neck than she had been before. Or could it have deepened to a darker mulberry stain?

He said, "Well, I am and I'm not, actually. I think of them as my parents and I grew up with them, in the Atherton house, but actually I'm adopted."

"Really?" Two girls Dylan knew at Mission High had got pregnant and had given up their babies to be adopted. His real mother, then, could have been an ordinary highschool girl? The idea made her uncomfortable, as though he had suddenly moved closer to her.

"I believe they were very aware of it, my not being really theirs," Whitney Iverson said, again looking away from her. "Especially when I messed up in some way, like choosing Reed, instead of Stanford. Then graduate school . . ."

As he talked on, seeming to search for new words for the feelings engendered in him by his adoptive parents, Dylan felt herself involuntarily retreat. No one had ever talked to her in quite that way, and she was uneasy. She looked through the long leaded windows to the wavering sunlight beyond; she stared at the dust-moted shafts of light in the dingy room where they were.

In fact, for Dylan, Whitney's very niceness was somehow against him; his kindness, his willingness to talk, ran against the rather austere grain of her fantasies.

Apparently sensing what she felt, or some of it, Whitney stopped short, and he laughed in a self-conscious way. "Well, there you have the poor-adopted-kid self-pity trip of the month," he said. " 'Poor,' Christ, they've drowned me in money."

Feeling that this last was not really addressed to her (and thinking of Flower's phrase about the birthmark, "drowned at birth"), Dylan said nothing. She stared at his hands, which were strong and brown, long-fingered, and she suddenly, sharply, wished that he would touch her. Touch, instead of all this awkward talk.

Later, considering that conversation, Dylan found herself moved, in spite of herself. How terrible to feel not only that you did not really belong with your parents but that they were disappointed in you. Whitney Iverson hadn't said anything about it, of course, but they must have minded about the birthmark, along with college and graduate school.

She and Flower were so clearly mother and daughter—obviously, irrevocably so; her green eyes were Flower's, even her crooked front teeth. Also, Flower had always thought she was wonderful. "My daughter Dylan," she would say, in her strongest, proudest voice.

But what had he possibly meant about "drowned in money"? Was he really rich, or had that been a joke? His car was an old VW convertible, and his button-down shirts were frayed, his baggy jackets shabby. Would a rich person drive a car like that, or wear those clothes? Probably not, thought Dylan; on the other hand, he did not seem a man to say that he was rich if he was not.

In any case, Dylan decided that she was giving him too much thought, since she had no real reason to think that he cared about her. Maybe he was an Iverson, and a snob, and did not want anything to do with a waitress. If he had wanted to see her, he could have suggested dinner, a movie or driving down to Santa Cruz on one of her days off. Probably she would have said yes, and on the way home, maybe on a bluff overlooking the sea, he could have parked the car, have turned to her.

So far, Dylan had had little experience of ambiguity; its emerging presence made her both impatient and confused. She did not know what to do or how to think about the contradictions in Whitney Iverson.

Although over the summer Dylan and Whitney had met almost every day in the library, this was never a stated arrangement, and if either of them missed a day, as they each sometimes did, nothing was said. This calculated diffidence seemed to suit them; they were like children who could not quite admit to seeking each other out.

One day, when Dylan had already decided that he would not come, and not caring really—she was too tired to care, what with extra guests and heavier trays—after she had been in the library for almost half an hour, she heard running steps, his, and then Whitney Iverson burst in, quite out of breath. "Oh . . . I'm glad you're still here," he got out, and he sat down heavily beside her. "I had some terrific news." But then on the verge of telling her, he stopped, and laughed, and said, "But I'm afraid it won't sound all that terrific to you."

Unhelpfully she looked at him.

"The *Yale Review*," he said. "They've taken an article I sent them. I'm really pleased."

He had been right, in that the *Yale Review* was meaningless to Dylan, but his sense of triumph was real and visible to her. She *felt* his success, and she thought just then that he looked wonderful.

September, once Labor Day was past, was much clearer and warmer, the sea a more brilliant blue, than during the summer. Under a light, fleece-clouded sky the water shimmered, all diamonds and gold, and the rocky cliffs in full sunlight were as pale as ivory. Even Dylan admitted to herself that it was beautiful; sometimes she felt herself penetrated by that scenery, her consciousness filled with it.

Whitney Iverson was leaving on the fifteenth; he had told Dylan so, naming the day as they sat together in the library. And then he said, "Would it be okay if I called you at home, sometime?"

The truth was, they didn't have a phone. Flower had been in so much trouble with the phone company that she didn't want to get into all that again. And so now Dylan blushed, and lied. "Well, maybe not. My mother's really strict."

He blushed, too, the birthmark darkening. "Well, I'll have to come back to see you," he said. "But will you still be here?"

How could she know, especially since he didn't even name a time when he would come? With a careless lack of tact she answered, "I hope not," and then she laughed.

Very seriously he asked, "Well, could we at least go for a walk or something before I go? I could show you the beach." He gave a small laugh, indicating that the beach was really nothing much to see, and then he said, "Dylan, I've wanted so much to see you, I *care* so much for you—but here, there would have been . . . implications . . . you know . . . ."

She didn't know; she refused to understand what he meant, unless he was confirming her old suspicion of snobbery: his not wanting to be seen with a waitress. She frowned slightly, and said, "Of course," and thought that she would not, after all, see him again. So much for Whitney Iverson.

But the next afternoon, during her break, in the brilliant September weather the library looked to her unbearably dingy, and all those magazines were so old. She stepped outside through the door at the end of the porch, and there was Mr. Iverson, just coming out through another door.

He smiled widely, said, "Perfect! We can just make it before the tide."

Wanting to say that she hadn't meant to go for a walk with him—she was just getting some air, and her shoes were wrong, canvas sandals—Dylan said neither of those things, but followed along, across the yellowing grass, toward the bluff.

He led her to a place that she hadn't known was there, a dip in the headland, from which the beach was only a few yards down, by a not steep, narrow path. Whitney went ahead, first turning back to reach for her hand, which she gave him. Making her way just behind, Dylan was more aware of his touch, of their firmly joined warm hands, than of anything else in the day: the sunlight, the sea, her poorly shod feet.

But as they reached the narrow strip of land, instead of turning to embrace her, although he still held her hand, Whitney cried out, "See? Isn't it fantastic?"

A small wave hit Dylan's left foot, soaking the fabric of her sandal. Unkissed, she stared at the back of his shirt collar, which was more frayed even than his usual shirts, below his slightly too long red-blond hair.

Then he turned to her; he picked up her other hand from her side, gazing intently down into her face. But it was somehow too late. Something within her had turned against him, whether from her wet foot or his worn-out collar, or sheer faulty timing, so that when he said, "You're so lovely, you make me shy," instead of being moved, as she might have been, Dylan thought he sounded silly (a grown man, shy?) and she stepped back a little, away from him.

He could still have kissed her, easily (she later thought), but he did not. Instead, he reached into one of the pockets of his jeans, fishing about, as he said, ". . . for something I wanted you to have."

Had he brought her a present, some small valuable keepsake? Prepared to relent, Dylan then saw that he had not; what he was handing her was a cardboard square, a card, on which were printed his name and telephone number. He said, "I just got these. My mother sent them. She's big on engraving." He grimaced as Dylan thought, Oh, your mother really is an Iverson. "The number's my new bachelor pad," he told her. "It's unlisted. Look, I really wish you'd call me. Any time. Collect. I'll be there." He looked away from her, for a moment out to sea, then down to the sand, where for the first time he seemed to notice her wet foot. "Oh Lord!" he exclaimed. "Will you have to change? I could run you home. . . ."

Not liking the fuss, and not at all liking the attention paid to those particular shoes (cheap, flimsy), somewhat coldly Dylan said no; the guests had thinned out and she was going home anyway as soon as the tables had been set up.

"Then I won't see you?"

She gave him her widest, most falsely shining smile, and turned and started up the path ahead of him. At the top she smiled again, and was about to turn away when Whitney grasped her wrist and said, with a startling, unfamiliar scowl, "*Call* me, you hear? I don't want to lose you."

What Dylan had said about being able to leave after setting up the tables was true; she had been told that she could then go home, which she did. The only problem, of course, was that she would earn less money; it could be a very lean, cold winter. Thinking about money, and, less clearly, about Whitney Iverson, Dylan was not quite ready for the wild-eyed Flower, who greeted her at the door: "We're celebrating. Congratulate me! I've dumped Zach."

But Dylan had heard this before, and she knew the shape of the evening that her mother's announcement presaged: strong triumphant statements along with a festive dinner, more and more wine, then tears. Sinkingly she listened as her mother described that afternoon's visit from Zach, how terrible he was and how firm she, Flower, had been, how final. "And we're celebrating with a really great fish soup," finished Flower, leading Dylan into the kitchen.

The evening did go more or less as Dylan had feared and imagined that it would. Ladling out the rich fish soup, Flower told Dylan how just plain fed up she was with men, and she repeated a line that she had recently heard and liked: "A woman without a man is like a mushroom without a bicycle."

Dylan did not find this as terrifically funny as Flower did, but she dutifully laughed.

A little later, sopping French bread into the liquid, Flower said, "But maybe it's just the guys I pick? I really seem to have some kind of instinct."

Flower had said that before, and Dylan always, if silently, agreed with her: it was too obvious to repeat. And then, maybe there really weren't any nice men around anymore, at her mother's age? Maybe they all got mean and terrible, the way a lot of women got fat? Dylan thought then of Whitney Iverson, who was only about ten years younger than Flower was; would he, too, eventually become impossible, cruel and unfaithful?

In a way that would have seemed alarmingly telepathic if Dylan had not been used to having her thoughts read by her mother, Flower asked, "What ever happened to your new friend, Mr. Iverson? Was he really one of *them?*"

"I don't know. I guess so," Dylan muttered, wishing that she had never mentioned Whitney to her mother.

Over salad, Flower announced that she was going on a diet. "Tomorrow. First thing. Don't worry, I'll still have the stuff you like around for you, but from now on no more carbohydrates for me."

At least, this time, she didn't cry.

At some hour in the middle of the night, or early morning, Dylan woke up—a thing she rarely did. Her ears and her mind were full of the distant sound of the sea, and she could see it as it had been in the afternoon, vastly glittering, when she had been preoccupied with her wet shoe, with Whitney's not kissing her. And she felt a sudden closeness to him; suddenly she understood what he had not quite said. By "implications" he had meant that the time and place were wrong for them. He was shy and just then not especially happy, what with his divorce and all, but he truly cared about her. If he had felt less he probably would have kissed her, in the careless, meaningless way of a man on vacation kissing a pretty waitress and then going back to his own real life. Whitney was that rarity her mother despaired of finding: a truly nice man. On her way back to sleep Dylan imagined calling him. She could go up to see him on the bus, or he could come down, and they could go out together, nothing to do with the Lodge. Could talk, be alone.

However, Dylan woke up the next morning in quite another mood. She felt wonderful, her own person, needing no one, certainly not a man who had not bothered, really, to claim her. Looking in the mirror, she saw herself as more than pretty, as almost beautiful; it was one of her very good days.

Flower, too, at breakfast seemed cheerful, not hung over. Maybe there was something in the air? Passing buttered English muffins to Dylan, Flower took none, although she loved them. "Tomato juice and eggs and black coffee, from here on in," she said. She did not take any pills.

Later, walking toward the Lodge, Dylan felt lighthearted, energetic. And how beautiful everything was! (Whitney Iverson had been right.) The sloping meadows, the pale clear sky, the chalky cliffs, the diamond-shining sea were all marvelous. She had a strong presentiment of luck; some good fortune would come to her at last.

At the sound of a car behind her she moved out of the way, turning then to look. She had had for a moment the crazy thought that it could be Whitney coming back for her, but of course it was not. It was a new gray Porsche, going slowly, looking for something. Walking a little faster, Dylan began to adjust her smile.

[1976]

For Discussion

1. Explain the relationship of the opening line to the themes of growing up in the other stories in this section.

2. Describe Dylan's fantasies of rescue from her situation. What forms of escape does she use at the lodge?

3. Characterize Whitney Iverson. Why is his view of the landscape so different from Dylan's? Why doesn't he fit her fantasy picture?

4. Describe Flower's work, and her forms of escape. What parallels are there between Dylan and Whitney, and what is different about them?

5. Why is Dylan uncomfortable with Whitney's life story talk? Compare and contrast Dylan and Whitney's family situations.

6. How would you describe the types of men represented by Zach versus Whitney?

7. Analyze each character's work in the story, and his/her attitude towards it.

8. Explain the ending: what is Dylan looking for in life?

9. What are the ironies of the story in terms of Dylan's dreams, her mother's dreams, and the realities and opportunities available to them?

For Further Exploration

1. "Roses, Rhododendron," also by Alice Adams, contrasts the lives of two young girls and their families. How do the girls' dreams suggest the same themes evident in this story? Determine what constitutes "success" for Adams's characters, in terms of family, love, and work.

2. Read another story or novel about the internal and external pressures on teenagers, such as "Louisa, Please Come Home," by Shirley Jackson; "Paul's Case," by Willa Cather; or A Slipping Down Life, by Anne Tyler. Which pressures and conflicts are related to each character's gender?

Poetry About Adolescence

Growing up is both a threat and a promise in these poems about teenagers. The world for these young women is divided into two parts—the "haves" and the "have nots," according to physical beauty. Will they be lithe and graceful, attractive? Should they avoid chocolates and smile with their mouths closed, as recommended by well-wishing elders? And if they do blossom into beauty, will they be able to resist the advances of the men they have enticed?

These artificial and arbitrary social codes are ironically portrayed against a background of natural images of sand and sea, leaves, and flower petals. Legs are the body parts most often described, and dancing is as much a part of adolescent poetry as the dance dress is the symbol of adolescent fiction. But there is the sense that some of the dances these young women dance are set to pernicious music, and that if they want to be free they might instead choose the "screaming, flying, and laughing" of the final poem.

Sophia de Mello Breyner
1919–

THE YOUNG GIRL AND THE BEACH

A young girl moves like an ear of grain
Slender legs the color of sand
Eyes blue-green and gray

A young girl moves like an ear of grain
Carnal and kernel, intact, curled tight
But the wind sinks its blade in the girl

And the wind scatters all with its hands

[1977]

Translated from the Portuguese by Alexis Levitin.

Kimiko Hahn

1955–

DANCE INSTRUCTIONS FOR A YOUNG GIRL[1]

Stand: knees slightly
bent, toes in *posed*
you watch the hawk over the river
curve, until his voice, shoulders back
gently *overcome by Seiji's mouth*
against yours, the white breath, and elbows
close to your side. *The silk cords*
and sash crush your lungs you are
young — beautiful, and almost
elegant. The layers of cloth pastel,
bright red, and moist
twist around. Follow his flow
of steps, a shallow stream between rocks
the carp. Seiji draws your hand
toward him or a stroke.
Before you look back turn your chin
in a figure eight, tilt, balance
then kneel quickly *the relief of cloth*
pulled off. Bow to him and the audience.
When you straighten, his black and red lines
against the white powder
are drawn, as his gesture
and step, perfectly. More perfectly *the weight*
of his chest than your own, although his
belong to you, a woman.

[1978]

[1]Geisha were often told to imitate the female impersonator Kabuki actors.

Kathleen Fraser

1937–

POEM IN WHICH MY LEGS ARE ACCEPTED

Legs!
How we have suffered each other,
never meeting the standards of magazines
     or official measurements.

I have hung you from trapezes,
  sat you on wooden rollers,
  pulled and pushed you
      with the anxiety of taffy,
and still, you are yourselves!

Most obvious imperfection, blight on my fantasy life,
strong,
plump,
never to be skinny
or even hinting of the svelte beauties in history books
      or Sears catalogues.
Here you are—solid, fleshy and
white as when I first noticed you, sitting on the toilet,
      spread softly over the wooden seat,
having been with me only twelve years,
      yet
as obvious as the legs of my thirty-year-old gym teacher.

Legs!
O that was the year we did acrobatics in the annual gym show.
How you split for me!
    One-handed cartwheels
    from this end of the gymnasium to the other,
    ending in double splits,
legs you flashed in blue rayon slacks my mother bought for the
  occasion
and tho you were confidently swinging along,
the rest of me blushed at the sound of clapping.

Legs!
How I have worried about you, not able to hide you,
embarrassed at beaches, in highschool
    when the cheerleaders' slim brown legs
      spread all over
      the sand
      with the perfection
      of bamboo.

I hated you, and still you have never given out on me.

With you
I have risen to the top of blue waves,
with you
I have carried food home as a loving gift
                              when my arms began
                              unjelling like madrilene.
Legs, you are a pillow,
white and plentiful with feathers for his wild head.
You are the endless scenery
behind the tense sinewy elegance of his two dark legs.
You welcome him joyfully
and dance.
And you will be the locks in a new canal between continents.
                    The ship of life will push out of you
                    and rejoice
                        in the whiteness,

                    in the first floating and rising of water.

                                                    [1966]

Colleen J. McElroy

1935–

DEFINING IT FOR VANESSA

She is too young to eat
chocolates
they blossom on her black face
like peppercorns
she is 16 and dreams
of the alphabet stitched
to the winter wool
of teenage gladiators
in single capital letters
she leans across the table
and asks us older ladies
about love and the future
but we cannot see past
a few days at any time
we are pregnant
with memories
and move slowly
like Egyptian geese grazing

we tell her put Xmas
in your eyes
and keep your voice low
knowing this answer
as insane as any
will soothe her
while she dreams
wrapped like a mummy
inside her flowered sheets
she thinks we hold secrets
and watches us closely
as we shop for dried flowers
lovely center pieces
for the best china
we tell her smiling

later when we describe
our little aches and pains
she turns away
puzzled by the antidotes
of blues reds and greens
we tell her how the reds
stick like anger
or clock the tides of the moon
we tell her how she'll guard
her lovely eyes

how only in her blackness
will she grow
large as the moon
we tell her how women
with whiskey voices
will try to stop her
how men will strip her clean
of secrets
how the flesh hurts
how the world does not end
with the body
but the longing for it

[1979]

Bettie Sellers

1926–

IN THE COUNSELOR'S WAITING ROOM

The terra cotta girl
with the big flat farm feet
traces furrows in the rug
with her toes,
reads an existentialist paperback
from psychology class,
finds no ease there
from the guilt of loving
the quiet girl down the hall.
Their home soil has seen to this visit,
their Baptist mothers,
who weep for the waste of sturdy hips
ripe for grandchildren.

[1981]

Pauli Murray

1910–1985

RUTH

Brown girl chanting Te Deums on Sunday
Rust-colored peasant with strength of granite,
Bronze girl welding ship hulls on Monday,
Let nothing smirch you, let no one crush you.

Queen of ghetto, sturdy hill-climber,
Walk with the lilt of ballet dancer,
Walk like a strong down-East wind blowing,
Walk with the majesty of the First Woman.

Gallant challenger, millioned-hope bearer,
The stars are your beacons, earth your inheritance,
Meet blaze and cannon with your own heart's passion,
Surrender to none the fire of your soul.

[1970]

Jean Tepperman

1945–

WITCH

They told me
I smile prettier with my mouth closed.
They said—
better cut your hair—
long, it's all frizzy,
looks Jewish.
They hushed me in restaurants
looking around them
while the mirrors above the table
jeered infinite reflections
of a raw, square face.
They questioned me
when I sang in the street.
They stood taller at tea
smoothly explaining
my eyes on the saucers,
trying to hide the hand grenade
in my pants pocket,
or crouched behind the piano.
They mocked me with magazines
full of breasts and lace,
published their triumph
when the doctor's oldest son
married a nice sweet girl.
They told me tweed-suit stories
of various careers of ladies.
I woke up at night
afraid of dying.
They built screens and room dividers
to hide unsightly desire
sixteen years old
raw and hopeless
they buttoned me into dresses
covered with pink flowers.
They waited for me to finish
then continued the conversation.
I have been invisible,
weird and supernatural.
I want my black dress.
I want my hair
curling wild around me.
I want my broomstick
from the closet where I hid it.
Tonight I meet my sisters
in the graveyard.

Around midnight
if you stop at a red light
in the wet city traffic,
watch for us against the moon.
We are screaming,
we are flying,
laughing, and won't stop.

[1969]

For Discussion

1. What effect does the personification of the wind have on the vision of adolescence in "The Young Girl and the Beach"?
2. Read separately and explain the meanings of the "two poems in one" in "Dance Instructions for a Young Girl." What do the dance instructions have to do with the narrative in italics?
3. Analyze each bit of condemnation or praise for the narrator's legs in Fraser's "Poem in Which My Legs Are Accepted." In what ways are legs appropriate symbols for the poem's themes?
4. What is the "longing" of the sixteen-year-old and of the "older ladies" who are "Defining It for Vanessa"? Are their dreams the same, or different?
5. How do the images of "home soil" versus college life reinforce the theme in Sellers' "In the Counselor's Waiting Room"?
6. How do images of color and symbols of the elements (earth, fire, etc.) relate to each other in the poem "Ruth"?
7. Discuss the dichotomy between repression and freedom in the poem "Witch." How does the tone differ from that of the other poems?

For Further Exploration

1. Compare these poems with Janis Ian's song beginning "I knew the truth at seventeen, that love was meant for beauty queens." Which poem(s) does the message of Ian's song most closely resemble, and why?
2. Review the poems, listing pluses and minuses of adolescence: in what way might the worst parts of being a teenager (such as dreaming) also have the potential for being the best parts? Explain.

For Discussion and Writing About This Section

1. Which of these young women make the transition well between childhood and adulthood, and which don't? What makes the difference—internal, or external factors?

2. Divide female role models for these teenagers into categories according to the types of futures they suggest for the young women.

3. Find incidents in which young women *act*, rather than sleep, wait, or dream. Explore the consequences of their actions—happy, sad, violent, etc.

4. What are the fathers' and other men's roles in these stories and poems of adolescents growing up?

5. Analyze the images of leaving, staying, or coming back; connect these images with the theme of the divided self (for example, Connie's "home" versus "not home" selves).

6. Explore the themes of temptation, giving in, and resisting. Identify several types of behavior the authors warn against. What decisions do each of the women make about moral dilemmas?

7. Examine the houses as symbols in the stories and poems. What different definitions of "home" are presented?

8. Find instances in which the adolescents compare themselves or their performances with others'—is this practice seen as healthy, or stifling?

9. So many of the stories and poems include dancing or the dance dress as the first sign of transition to adulthood. If these symbols are uniquely female, what do they mean?

10. Examine the hypnagogic or "waking dream" states in these poems and stories. If these young women are between two worlds, what are they?

ADULTHOOD
Women and Work

Searching for satisfying work; work within and outside the home; dealing with competition; male and female peers; success and failure; struggling for equity

Has "women working" replaced "women's work"? Or, do the old stereotypes of women working solely in the home still apply? What do writers of fiction and poetry have to say that confirms or contradicts the following concerns: that many working women have two jobs—one paid, the other unpaid; that women are paid less to do more; that jobs and careers remain largely sex-segregated; that women's talents are underutilized and underappreciated, whether women work within or outside of the home.

In these stories and poems, we see women doing domestic work, both paid and unpaid, and being secretaries, waitresses, factory workers, business managers, and set designers. And these portrayals do what essays and data analyses cannot be expected to do—present women's feelings about their roles as workers, while they depict the resulting delicate web of relationships with coworkers and bosses, family and friends.

Women's traditional role as responsible for housework is presented with mixed feelings in poems such as "Housewife's Letter: To Mary" and "I Sit and Sew." Women want to be of use, but do not want to be used or used up in meaningless, repetitive tasks. Interestingly, the same complaints are evident in works about women in office and business settings; no single role seems to arise as the universal answer to job satisfaction.

While women's frustrations in the workplace are shown by these authors in tell-tale incidents, women's triumphs are described as well. The woman in "One Off the Short List" is the most notable example of someone happy in her work and part of a viable team of coworkers, and in fact, all of the women in the stories are determined to work well. Motivated by the desire for self-worth in addition to the basic need to survive, even overburdened women workers still seem to keep trying to be considered of value by their overseers.

In the face of male opposition to women at work, several of the women in these stories and poems strive for "a triumphant indifference" or maintain a "cool distance." Others are constantly striving to please or are looking for symbols of approval. However, no matter what attitude the women take, the path to success and job satisfaction is not easy. Even the most successful of the women have to make compromises and deal with opposition at home or in society. A man who initially seems to enjoy the reversal of traditional roles in the story "Tom's Husband" says that he wouldn't mind if his wife failed in business. More dramatically, another woman's excellence at work only stimulates a man's desire to "have" her sexually.

In many of these narratives, the more successful and self-confident the women become, the more the men feel like failures. And no statistics could reveal the senses of fear and threat as vividly as fiction and poetry: the fear that women will come out "on top" in a covertly sexual battle, the fear that women will be more powerful or more successful than their male counterparts, and the threat that women will be unfaithful in word or deed or will make men literally or symbolically impotent.

As always, the subtlety of language is a powerful vehicle for expressing these undercurrents of feelings and attitudes. Themes intertwined with the work motif—sex, fidelity and infidelity, power, aggression—are exemplified in words the characters use to describe each other. Diminutives and epithets such as "my dear little girl" and "problem child" reveal condescending attitudes unmitigated by the tone of pretended affection. Recurrent images of women as subservient animals further contribute to the negative part of the picture of women at work.

The theme of competition between women in the workplace is almost as strong as that of dominance of men over women. There is an unfortunate struggle among women to gain approval and recognition. Even in the most flattering portrait of women at work, the female worker is forced into passing the male loyalty test of implicitly denigrating another woman's work.

Seldom do the women in these stories support another's work and, although women in literature are beginning to be depicted as friends (see other sections), there are few stories and poems about female friendships in the workplace. More often, situations are described such as in the poem "Cinderella," with only one token woman in high places, forced to deprecate her "ugly" stepsisters.

Personal appearance is once again a major factor in women's acceptance, although both good looks and bad interfere more than help with success in these stories. Fine clothing and makeup are seen as sex symbols, while ordinary clothes make the woman nondescript. One male character spends an inordinate amount of time assessing the woman's outward appearance, saying that she looks drab without makeup, but "armoured . . . no longer defenceless" with it.

In the same sense that women are "damned if they do and damned if they don't" in terms of good or poor looks in the workplace, neither passive nor aggressive behavior seems to be the answer in these stories, reflecting male executives' complaints that tough women at work aren't "feminine," but "womanly women" can't do the job. In both literature and life, the choice between being liked and being respected is difficult for women wanting just to be themselves.

Before confronting these myriad problems, women seem to carry the adolescent dream of being "special but accepted" with them to the workplace. Some seem surprised by the opposition to the dream, but become resigned to the lack of individuality allowed. Others try to ignore or to rise above situations, and some become aggressive as Delia in "Sweat" who is forced to defend her work with an upraised frying pan.

Yet the women continue to dream of being satisfied and accepted, seeing themselves as characters in the Bible, novels, or television. The various forms of escapism in the stories show that the women find ways of coping with their situations, even when work becomes drudgery. Women here, as in the stories in other sections, demonstrate a powerful societally reinforced capacity for accepting suffering. Most either smile or pretend to smile, continuing to strive for daily survival with a hope of eventual success.

The American dream that anyone willing to work hard can not only find meaningful work, but can "make it to the top" as well is brought to our renewed attention in the story "America and I," an immigrant's initial view of work in America. In this story and others, authors ask, is there a place in the American dream for women, immigrants, and other minority workers to rise above the secondary roles that society has given them? As the play *Trifles* makes clear, women's contributions are not as trifling as they may appear to be to the world of working men.

Fiction About
Women and Work

The constantly engaging quality of stories of women working is that they remind us of the great potential of women to relate to many different kinds of worlds—domestic, business, artistic, and so forth. When women forge any strong bond with the outside world, they begin to gain a sense of status which unfortunately is often lacking in the unpaid nurturing and caretaking activities at home. Each story demonstrates the identity of a woman as related to her home work or outside job, and each vivifies the qualities women bring to the workplace which may have been ignored elsewhere.

For women, paid work outside of the home adds social status as well as the ability to develop a sense of camaraderie with other women and men. Ideally, relationships formed through the common bond of employment should transcend gender, whereas in many of these stories the reverse is true. Themes of competition emerge in several stories, and few of the women characters seem to get along on personal qualifications alone; other factors are often evident, such as the willingness to accommodate men as often as deemed necessary. An interesting quality about the work depicted here, however, is that it appears to have been selected more by choice and the desire for individual achievement than by pure necessity—even though in real life paid work has become necessary for many women. Perhaps the most accurate description of the subject of these stories is work for both the monetary and personal rewards produced: every woman working in these stories likes her work, and resents the efforts of men or other women in society to deny her the privilege of earning her own living. Whether work is appreciated or unappreciated, in the home or outside, women portrayed here enjoy participating in meaningful employment.

Zora Neale Hurston

1903–1960

The tenacity of one woman making a living at what has traditionally been considered "women's work" is demonstrated dramatically in this story. In the face of powerful physical and psychological opposition, Delia maintains her home, work, faith, and sense of personal identity.

SWEAT

It was eleven o'clock of a Spring night in Florida. It was Sunday. Any other night, Delia Jones would have been in bed for two hours by this time. But she was a washwoman, and Monday morning meant a great deal to her. So she collected the soiled clothes on Saturday when she returned the clean things. Sunday night after church, she sorted them and put the white things to soak. It saved her almost a half day's start. A great hamper in the bedroom held the clothes that she brought home. It was so much neater than a number of bundles lying around.

She squatted in the kitchen floor beside the great pile of clothes, sorting them into small heaps according to color, and humming a song in a mournful key, but wondering through it all where Sykes, her husband, had gone with her horse and buckboard.

Just then something long, round, limp and black fell upon her shoulders and slithered to the floor beside her. A great terror took hold of her. It softened her knees and dried her mouth so that it was a full minute before she could cry out or move. Then she saw that it was the big bull whip her husband liked to carry when he drove.

She lifted her eyes to the door and saw him standing there bent over with laughter at her fright. She screamed at him.

"Sykes, what you throw dat whip on me like dat? You know it would skeer me—looks just like a snake, an' you knows how skeered Ah is of snakes."

"Course Ah knowed it! That's how come Ah done it." He slapped his leg with his hand and almost rolled on the ground in his mirth. "If you such a big fool dat you got to have a fit over a earth worm or a string, Ah don't keer how bad Ah skeer you."

"You aint got no business doing it. Gawd knows it's a sin. Some day Ah'm gointuh drop dead from some of yo' foolishness. 'Nother thing, where you been wid mah rig? Ah feeds dat pony. He aint fuh you to be drivin' wid no bull whip."

"You sho is one aggravatin' nigger woman!" he declared and stepped into the room. She resumed her work and did not answer him at once. "Ah done tole you time and again to keep them white folks' clothes outa dis house."

He picked up the whip and glared down at her. Delia went on with her work. She went out into the yard and returned with a galvanized tub and set it on the washbench. She saw that Sykes had kicked all of the clothes together again, and now stood in her way truculently, his whole manner hoping, *praying,* for an argument. But she walked calmly around him and commenced to re-sort the things.

"Next time, Ah'm gointer kick 'em outdoors," he threatened as he struck a match along the leg of his corduroy breeches.

Delia never looked up from her work, and her thin, stooped shoulders sagged further.

"Ah aint for no fuss t'night, Sykes. Ah just come from taking sacrament at the church house."

He snorted scornfully. "Yeah, you just come from de church house on a Sunday night, but heah you is gone to work on them clothes. You ain't nothing but a hypocrite. One of them amen-corner Christians—sing, whoop, and shout, then come home and wash white folks' clothes on the Sabbath."

He stepped roughly upon the whitest pile of things, kicking them helter-skelter as he crossed the room. His wife gave a little scream of dismay, and quickly gathered them together again.

"Sykes, you quit grindin' dirt into these clothes! How can Ah git through by Sat'day if Ah don't start on Sunday?"

"Ah don't keer if you never git through. Anyhow, Ah done promised Gawd and a couple of other men, Ah aint gointer have it in mah house. Don't gimme no lip neither, else Ah'll throw 'em out and put mah fist up side yo' head to boot."

Delia's habitual meekness seemed to slip from her shoulders like a blown scarf. She was on her feet; her poor little body, her bare knuckly hands bravely defying the strapping hulk before her.

"Looka heah, Sykes, you done gone too fur. Ah been married to you fur fifteen years, and Ah been takin' in washin' fur fifteen years. Sweat, sweat, sweat! Work and sweat, cry and sweat, pray and sweat!"

"What's that got to do with me?" he asked brutally.

"What's it got to do with you, Sykes? Mah tub of suds is filled yo' belly with vittles more times than yo' hands is filled it. Mah sweat is done paid for this house and Ah reckon Ah kin keep on sweatin' in it."

She seized the iron skillet from the stove and struck a defensive pose, which act surprised him greatly, coming from her. It cowed him and he did not strike her as he usually did.

"Naw you won't," she panted, "that ole snaggle-toothed black woman you runnin' with aint comin' heah to pile up on *mah* sweat and blood. You aint paid for nothin' on this place, and Ah'm gointer stay right heah till Ah'm toted out foot foremost."

"Well, you better quit gittin' me riled up, else they'll be totin' you out sooner than you expect. Ah'm so tired of you Ah don't know whut to do. Gawd! how Ah hates skinny wimmen!"

A little awed by this new Delia, he sidled out of the door and slammed the back gate after him. He did not say where he had gone, but she knew too well. She knew very well that he would not return until nearly daybreak also. Her work over, she went on to bed but not to sleep at once. Things had come to a pretty pass!

She lay awake, gazing upon the debris that cluttered their matrimonial trail. Not an image left standing along the way. Anything like flowers had long ago been drowned in the salty stream that had been pressed from her heart. Her tears, her sweat, her blood. She had brought love to the union and he had brought a longing after the flesh. Two months after the wedding, he had given her the first brutal beating. She had the memory of his numerous trips to Orlando with all of his wages when he had returned to her penniless, even before the first year had passed. She was young and soft then, but now she thought of her knotty, muscled limbs, her harsh knuckly hands, and drew herself up into an unhappy little ball in the middle of the big feather bed. Too late now to hope for love, even if it were not Bertha it would be someone else. This case differed from the others only in that she was bolder than the others. Too late for everything except her little home. She had built it for her old days, and planted one by one the trees and flowers there. It was lovely to her, lovely.

Somehow, before sleep came, she found herself saying aloud: "Oh well, whatever goes over the Devil's back, is got to come under his belly. Sometime or ruther, Sykes, like everybody else, is gointer reap his sowing." After that she was able to build a spiritual earthworks against her husband. His shells could no longer reach her. *Amen.* She went to sleep and slept until he announced his presence in bed by kicking her feet and rudely snatching the covers away.

"Gimme some kivah heah, an' git yo' damn foots over on yo' own side! Ah oughter mash you in yo' mouf fuh drawing dat skillet on me."

Delia went clear to the rail without answering him. A triumphant indifference to all that he was or did.

The week was as full of work for Delia as all other weeks, and Saturday found her behind her little pony, collecting and delivering clothes.

It was a hot, hot day near the end of July. The village men on Joe Clarke's porch even chewed cane listlessly. They did not hurl the caneknots as usual. They let them dribble over the edge of the porch. Even conversation had collapsed under the heat.

"Heah come Delia Jones," Jim Merchant said, as the shaggy pony came 'round the bend of the road toward them. The rusty buckboard was heaped with baskets of crisp, clean laundry.

"Yep," Joe Lindsay agreed. "Hot or col', rain or shine, jes ez reg'lar ez de weeks roll 'roun' Delia carries 'em an' fetches 'em on Sat'day."

"She better if she wanter eat," said Moss. "Syke Jones aint wuth de shot an' powder hit would tek tuh kill 'em. Not to *huh* he aint."

"He sho' aint," Walter Thomas chimed in. "It's too bad, too, cause she wuz a right pritty lil trick when he got huh. Ah'd uh mah'ied huh mahseff if he hadnter beat me to it."

Delia nodded briefly at the men as she drove past.

"Too much knockin' will ruin *any* 'oman. He done beat huh 'nough tuh kill three women, let 'lone change they looks," said Elijah Moseley. "How Syke kin stommuck dat big black greasy Mogul he's layin' roun' wid, gits me. Ah swear dat eight-rock couldn't kiss a sardine can Ah done thowed out de back do' 'way las' yeah."

"Aw, she's fat, thass how come. He's allus been crazy 'bout fat women," put in Merchant. "He'd a' been tied up wid one long time ago if he could a' found one tuh have him. Did Ah tell yuh 'bout him come sidlin' roun' *mah* wife—bringin' her a basket uh peecans outa his yard fuh a present? Yessir, mah wife! She tol' him tuh take em right straight back home, cause Delia works so hard ovah dat wash tub she reckon everything on de place taste lak sweat an' soapsuds. Ah jus' wisht Ah'd a caught 'im 'roun' dere! Ah'd a' made his hips ketch on fiah down dat shell road."

"Ah know he done it, too. Ah sees 'im grinnin' at every 'oman dat passes," Walter Thomas said. "But even so, he useter eat some mighty big hunks uh humble pie tuh git dat lil' 'oman he got. She wuz ez pritty ez a speckled pup! Dat wuz fifteen yeahs ago. He useter be so skeered uh losin' huh, she could make him do some parts of a husband's duty. Dey never wuz de same in de mind."

"There oughter be a law about him," said Lindsay. "He aint fit tuh carry guts tuh a bear."

Clarke spoke for the first time. "Taint no law on earth dat kin make a man be decent if it aint in 'im. There's plenty men dat takes a wife lak dey do a joint uh sugar-cane. It's round, juicy an' sweet when dey gits it. But dey squeeze an' grind, squeeze an' grind an' wring tell dey wring every drop uh pleasure dat's in 'em out. When dey's satisfied dat dey is wrung dry, dey treats 'em jes lak dey do a cane-chew. Dey throws 'em away. Dey knows whut dey is doin' while dey is at it, an' hates theirselves fuh it but they keeps on hangin' after huh tell she's empty. Den dey hates huh fuh bein' a cane-chew an' in de way."

"We oughter take Syke an' dat stray 'oman uh his'n down in Lake Howell swamp an' lay on de rawhide till they cain't say Lawd a' mussy.' He allus wuz uh ovahbearin' niggah, but since dat white 'oman from up north done teached 'im how to run a automobile, he done got too biggety to live— an' we oughter kill 'im," Old Man Anderson advised.

A grunt of approval went around the porch. But the heat was melting their civic virtue and Elijah Moseley began to bait Joe Clarke.

"Come on, Joe, git a melon outa dere an' slice it up for yo' customers. We'se all sufferin' wid de heat. De bear's done got *me!*"

Thass right, Joe, a watermelon is jes' whut Ah needs tuh cure de eppizudicks,"[1] Walter Thomas joined forces with Moseley. "Come on dere, Joe. We all is steady customers an' you aint set us up in a long time. Ah chooses dat long, bowlegged Floridy favorite."

"A god, an' be dough. You all gimme twenty cents and slice way," Clarke retorted. "Ah needs a col' slice m'self. Heah, everybody chip in. Ah'll lend y'll mah meat knife."

The money was quickly subscribed and the huge melon brought forth. At that moment, Sykes and Bertha arrived. A determined silence fell on the porch and the melon was put away again.

Merchant snapped down the blade of his jackknife and moved toward the store door.

"Come on in, Joe, an' gimme a slab uh sow belly an' uh pound uh coffee—almost fuhgot 'twas Sat'day. Got to git on home." Most of the men left also.

Just then Delia drove past on her way home, as Sykes was ordering magnificently for Bertha. It pleased him for Delia to see.

"Git whutsoever yo' heart desires, Honey. Wait a minute, Joe. Give huh two bottles uh strawberry soda-water, uh quart uh parched ground-peas, an' a block uh chewin' gum."

With all this they left the store, with Sykes reminding Bertha that this was his town and she could have it if she wanted it.

The men returned soon after they left, and held their watermelon feast.

"Where did Syke Jones git da 'oman from nohow?" Lindsay asked.

"Ovah Apopka. Guess dey musta been cleanin' out de town when she lef'. She don't look lak a thing but a hunk uh liver wid hair on it."

---

[1]"Epizootic," or disease attacking many animals at the same time.

"Well, she sho' kin squall," Dave Carter contributed. "When she gits ready tuh laff, she jes' opens huh mouf an' latches it back tuh de las' notch. No ole grandpa alligator down in Lake Bell ain't got nothin' on huh."

Bertha had been in town three months now. Sykes was still paying her room rent at Della Lewis'—the only house in town that would have taken her in. Sykes took her frequently to Winter Park to "stomps." He still assured her that he was the swellest man in the state.

"Sho' you kin have dat lil' ole house soon's Ah kin git dat 'oman outa dere. Everything b'longs tuh me an' you sho' kin have it. Ah sho' 'bominates uh skinny 'oman. Lawdy, you sho' is got one portly shape on you! You kin git *anything* you wants. Dis is *mah* town an' you sho' kin have it."

Delia's work-worn knees crawled over the earth in Gethsemane and up the rocks of Calvary many, many times during these months. She avoided the villagers and meeting places in her efforts to be blind and deaf. But Bertha nullified this to a degree, by coming to Delia's house to call Sykes out to her at the gate.

Delia and Sykes fought all the time now with no peaceful interludes. They slept and ate in silence. Two or three times Delia had attempted a timid friendliness, but she was repulsed each time. It was plain that the breaches must remain agape.

The sun had burned July to August. The heat streamed down like a million hot arrows, smiting all things living upon the earth. Grass withered, leaves browned, snakes went blind in shedding and men and dogs went mad. Dog days!

Delia came home one day and found Sykes there before her. She wondered, but started to go on into the house without speaking, even though he was standing in the kitchen door and she must either stoop under his arm or ask him to move. He made no room for her. She noticed a soap box beside the steps, but paid no particular attention to it, knowing that he must have brought it there. As she was stooping to pass under his outstretched arm, he suddenly pushed her backward, laughingly.

"Look in de box dere Delia, Ah done brung yuh somethin'!"

She nearly fell upon the box in her stumbling, and when she saw what it held, she all but fainted outright.

"Syke! Syke, mah Gawd! You take dat rattlesnake 'way from heah! You *gottuh.* Oh, Jesus, have mussy!"

"Ah aint gut tuh do nuthin' uh de kin'—fact is Ah aint got tuh do nothin' but die. Taint no use uh you puttin' on airs makin' out lak you skeered uh dat snake—he's gointer stay right heah tell he die. He wouldn't bite me cause Ah knows how tuh handle 'im. Nohow he wouldn't risk breakin' out his fangs 'gin yo' skinny laigs."

"Naw, now Syke, don't keep dat thing 'roun' heah tuh skeer me tuh death. You knows Ah'm even feared uh earth worms. Thass de biggest snake Ah evah did see. Kill 'im Syke, please."

"Doan ast me tuh do nothin' fuh yuh. Goin' 'roun' tryin' tuh be so damn asterperious. Naw, Ah aint gonna kill it. Ah think uh damn sight mo' uh him dan you! Dat's a nice snake an' anybody doan lak 'im kin jes' hit de grit."

The village soon heard that Sykes had the snake, and came to see and ask questions.

"How de hen-fire did you ketch dat six-foot rattler, Syke?" Thomas asked.

"He's full uh frogs so he caint hardly move, thass how Ah eased up on 'im. But Ah'm a snake charmer an' knows how tuh handle 'em. Shux, dat aint nothin'. Ah could ketch one eve'y day if Ah so wanted tuh."

"Whut he needs is a heavy hick'ry club leaned real heavy on his head. Dat's de bes' way tuh charm a rattlesnake."

"Naw, Walt, y'll jes' don't understand dese diamon' backs lak Ah do," said Sykes in a superior tone of voice.

The village agreed with Walter, but the snake stayed on. His box remained by the kitchen door with its screen wire covering. Two or three days later it had digested its meal of frogs and literally came to life. It rattled at every movement in the kitchen or the yard. One day as Delia came down the kitchen steps she saw his chalky-white fangs curved like scimitars hung in the wire meshes. This time she did not run away with averted eyes as usual. She stood for a long time in the doorway in a red fury that grew bloodier for every second that she regarded the creature that was her torment.

That night she broached the subject as soon as Sykes sat down to the table.

"Syke, Ah wants you tuh take dat snake 'way fum heah. You done starved me an' Ah put up widcher, you done beat me an Ah took dat, but you done kilt all mah insides bringin' dat varmint heah."

Sykes poured out a saucer full of coffee and drank it deliberately before he answered her.

"A whole lot Ah keer 'bout how you feels inside uh out. Dat snake aint goin' no damn wheah till Ah gits ready fuh 'im tuh go. So fur as beatin' is concerned, yuh aint took near all dat you gointer take ef yuh stay 'roun' *me*."

Delia pushed back her plate and got up from the table. "Ah hates you, Sykes," she said calmly. "Ah hates you tuh de same degree dat Ah useter love yuh. Ah done took an' took till mah belly is full up tuh mah neck. Dat's de reason Ah got mah letter fum de church an' moved mah membership tuh Woodbridge—so Ah don't haftuh take no sacrament wid yuh. Ah don't wantuh see yuh 'roun' me atall. Lay 'roun' wid dat 'oman all yuh wants tuh, but gwan 'way fum me an' mah house. Ah hates yuh lak uh suck-egg dog."

Sykes almost let the huge wad of corn bread and collard greens he was chewing fall out of his mouth in amazement. He had a hard time whipping himself up to the proper fury to try to answer Delia.

"Well, Ah'm glad you does hate me. Ah'm sho' tiahed uh you hangin' ontuh me. Ah don't want yuh. Look at yuh stringey ole neck! Yo' rawbony laigs an' arms is enough tuh cut uh man tuh death. You looks jes' lak de devvul's doll-baby tuh *me*. You cain't hate me no worse dan Ah hates you. Ah been hatin' *you* fuh years."

"Yo' ole black hide don't look lak nothin' tuh me, but uh passle uh wrinkled up rubber, wid yo' big ole yeahs flappin' on each side lak uh paih uh buzzard wings. Don't think Ah'm gointuh be run 'way fum mah house neither. Ah'm goin' tuh de white folks bout *you*, mah young man, de very nex' time you lay yo' han's on me. Mah cup is done run ovah."

Delia said this with no signs of fear and Sykes departed from the house, threatening her, but made not the slightest move to carry out any of them.

That night he did not return at all, and the next day being Sunday, Delia was glad she did not have to quarrel before she hitched up her pony and drove the four miles to Woodbridge.

She stayed to the night service—"love feast"—which was very warm and full of spirit. In the emotional winds her domestic trials were borne far and wide so that she sang as she drove homeward,

"Jurden water, black an' col'
Chills de body, not de soul
An' Ah wantah cross Jurden in uh calm time."

She came from the barn to the kitchen door and stopped.

"Whut's de mattah, ol' satan, you aint kickin' up yo' racket?" She addressed the snake's box. Complete silence. She went on into the house with a new hope in its birth struggles. Perhaps her threat to go to the white folks had frightened Sykes! Perhaps he was sorry! Fifteen years of misery and suppression had brought Delia to the place where she would hope *anything* that looked towards a way over or through her wall of inhibitions.

She felt in the match safe behind the stove at once for a match. There was only one there.

"Dat niggah wouldn't fetch nothin' heah tuh save his rotten neck, but he kin run thew whut Ah brings quick enough. Now he done toted off nigh on tuh haff uh box uh matches. He done had dat 'oman heah in mah house too."

Nobody but a woman could tell how she knew this even before she struck the match. But she did and it put her into a new fury.

Presently she brought in the tubs to put the white things to soak. This time she decided she need not bring the hamper out of the bedroom: she would go in there and do the sorting. She picked up the pot-bellied lamp and went in. The room was small and the hamper stood hard by the foot of the white iron bed. She could sit and reach through the bedposts—resting as she worked.

"Ah wantah cross Jurden in uh calm time." She was singing again. The mood of the "love feast" had returned. She threw back the lid of the basket almost gaily. Then, moved by both horror and terror, she sprang back toward the door. *There lay the snake in the basket!* He moved sluggishly at first, but even as she turned round and round, jumped up and down in an insanity of fear, he began to stir vigorously. She saw him pouring his awful beauty from the basket upon the bed, then she seized the lamp and ran as fast as she could to the kitchen. The wind from the open door blew out the light and the darkness added to her terror. She sped to the darkness of the yard, slamming the door after her before she thought to set down the lamp. She did not feel safe even on the ground, so she climbed up in the hay barn.

There for an hour or more she lay sprawled upon the hay a gibbering wreck.

Finally she grew quiet, and after that, coherent thought. With this, stalked through her a cold, bloody rage. Hours of this. A period of introspection, a space of retrospection, then a mixture of both. Out of this an awful calm.

"Well, Ah done de bes' Ah could. If things aint right, Gawd knows taint mah fault."

She went to sleep—a twitch sleep—and woke up to a faint gray sky. There was a loud hollow sound below. She peered out. Sykes was at the wood-pile, demolishing a wire-covered box.

He hurried to the kitchen door, but hung outside there some minutes before he entered, and stood some minutes more inside before he closed it after him.

The gray in the sky was spreading. Delia descended without fear now, and crouched beneath the low bedroom window. The drawn shade shut out the dawn, shut in the night. But the thin walls held back no sound.

"Dat ol' scratch is woke up now!" She mused at the tremendous whirr inside, which every woodsman knows, is one of the sound illusions. The rattler is a ventriloquist. His whirr sounds to the right, to the left, straight ahead, behind, close under foot—everywhere but where it is. Woe to him who gueses wrong unless he is prepared to hold up his end of the argument! Sometimes he strikes without rattling at all.

Inside, Sykes heard nothing until he knocked a pot lid off the stove while trying to reach the match safe in the dark. He had emptied his pockets at Bertha's.

The snake seemed to wake up under the stove and Sykes made a quick leap into the bedroom. In spite of the gin he had had, his head was clearing now.

"Mah Gawd!" he chattered, "ef Ah could on'y strack uh light!"

The rattling ceased for a moment as he stood paralyzed. He waited. It seemed that the snake waited also.

"Oh, fuh de light! Ah thought he'd be too sick"—Sykes was muttering to himself when the whirr began again, closer, right underfoot this time. Long before this, Sykes' ability to think had been flattened down to primitive instinct and he leaped—onto the bed.

Outside Delia heard a cry that might have come from a maddened chimpanzee, a stricken gorilla. All the terror, all the horror, all the rage that man possibly could express, without a recognizable human sound.

A tremendous stir inside there, another series of animal screams, the intermittent whirr of the reptile. The shade torn violently down from the window, letting in the red dawn, a huge brown hand seizing the window stick, great dull blows upon the wooden floor punctuating the gibberish of sound long after the rattle of the snake had abruptly subsided. All this Delia could see and hear from her place beneath the window, and it made her ill. She crept over to the four-o'clocks[2] and stretched herself on the cool earth to recover.

She lay there. "Delia, Delia!" She could hear Sykes calling in a most despairing tone as one who expected no answer. The sun crept on up, and he called. Delia could not move—her legs were gone flabby. She never moved, he called, and the sun kept rising.

"Mah Gawd!" She heard him moan, "Mah Gawd fum Heben!" She heard him stumbling about and got up from her flower-bed. The sun was growing warm. As she approached the door she heard him call out hopefully, "Delia, is dat you Ah heah?"

She saw him on his hands and knees as soon as she reached the door. He crept an inch or two toward her—all that he was able, and she saw his horribly swollen neck and his one open eye shining with hope. A surge of pity too strong to support bore her away from that eye that must, could not, fail to see the tubs. He would see the lamp. Orlando with its doctors was too far. She could scarcely reach the Chinaberry tree, where she waited in the growing heat while inside she knew the cold river was creeping up and up to extinguish that eye which must know by now that she knew.

[1926]

---

[2]Flowering plant.

For Discussion

1. Compare the symbols of whip and snake associated with Sykes with the "tears, sweat, and blood" associated with Delia.

2. Why does Sykes claim that he doesn't want Delia to wash clothes for a living, and what might be some underlying reasons?

3. When Delia changes from meekness to aggression, what is she protecting? Explain.

4. Consider the function of the "other woman" in the story, and the role of the other men in the town. What does the men's conversation about Bertha, Sykes, and Delia reveal about the major forces in conflict in the story?

5. What is meant by the comment about Delia that "After that she was able to build a spiritual earthworks against her husband"? How is this attitude carried through to the end of the story?

6. What evidence is there to support the claim that religion helps to keep oppressed people in their places? In contrast, how would you argue the benefits of religion for Delia? The term "meek" is used several times; do the meek inherit the earth in this story?

7. Explain the final scenes—how the snake got out of the box, and what Sykes and Delia each did or did not do.

8. How does the author foreshadow the ending of the story? Look for telling lines and hints leading to the end.

9. Do you interpret the final scene as triumph or tragedy?

For Further Exploration

1. Alice Walker, author of *The Color Purple* (novel made into a film) and many other works, acknowledges the strong influence of Zora Neale Hurston's writing. Reading either *The Color Purple* or Walker's story "Everyday Use" (section on Women and Family) compare the types of women depicted. Or, compare Walker's depiction of husbands in *The Color Purple* with Zora Neale Hurston's depiction of Sykes in this story.

2. Explore the nature of "women's work" and "women working" in this story, examining each character's attitude; for example, why does Delia work, and why does she do the kind of work she does? Why doesn't Bertha work, and why does Delia indirectly support her?

Sarah Orne Jewett

1849–1909

*In this nineteenth century story, Jewett describes a marriage in which
the expected roles of husband and wife are reversed—a situation not so
unusual now, but still subject to the potential problems Jewett describes.
Unlike the story "Sweat," this story takes place in the most conducive of
atmospheres, a loving home in which each partner knows her or his
skills and interests.*

TOM'S HUSBAND

I shall not dwell long upon the circumstances that led to the marriage of my
hero and heroine; though their courtship was to them, the only one that has
ever noticeably approached the ideal, it had many aspects in which it was
entirely commonplace in other people's eyes. While the world in general
smiles at lovers with kindly approval and sympathy, it refuses to be aware of
the unprecedented delight which is amazing to the lovers themselves.

But, as has been true in many other cases, when they were at last married, the most ideal of situations was found to have been changed to the most
practical. Instead of having shared their original duties, and, as school-boys
would say, going halves, they discovered that the cares of life had been doubled. This led to some distressing moments for both our friends; they understood suddenly that instead of dwelling in heaven they were still upon earth,
and had made themselves slaves to new laws and limitations. Instead of being freer and happier than ever before, they had assumed new responsibilities; they had established a new household, and must fulfill in some way or
another the obligations of it. They looked back with affection to their engage-
ment; they had been longing to have each other to themselves, apart from
the world, but it seemed that they never felt so keenly that they were still
units in modern society. Since Adam and Eve were in Paradise, before the
devil joined them, nobody has had a chance to imitate that unlucky couple.
In some respects they told the truth when, twenty times a day, they said that
life had never been so pleasant before; but there were mental reservations on
either side which might have subjected them to the accusation of lying.
Somehow, there was a little feeling of disappointment, and they caught
themselves wondering—though they would have died sooner than confess
it—whether they were quite so happy as they had expected. The truth was,
they were much happier than people usually are, for they had an uncommon
capacity for enjoyment. For a little while they were like a sail-boat that is
beating and has to drift a few minutes before it can catch the wind and start
off on the other tack. And they had the same feeling, too, that any one is
likely to have who has been long pursuing some object of his ambition or
desire. Whether it is a coin, or a picture, or a stray volume of some old edition
of Shakespeare, or whether it is an office under government or a lover, when
fairly in one's grasp there is a loss of the eagerness that was felt in pursuit.
Satisfaction, even after one has dined well, is not so interesting and eager a
feeling as hunger.

My hero and heroine were reasonably well established to begin with: they each had some money, though Mr. Wilson had most. His father had at one time been a rich man, but with the decline, a few years before, of manufacturing interests, he had become, mostly through the fault of others, somewhat involved; and at the time of his death his affairs were in such a condition that it was still a question whether a very large sum or a moderately large one would represent his estate. Mrs. Wilson, Tom's step-mother, was somewhat of an invalid; she suffered severely at times with asthma, but she was almost entirely relieved by living in another part of the country. While her husband lived, she had accepted her illness as inevitable, and rarely left home; but during the last few years she had lived in Philadelphia with her own people, making short and wheezing visits only from time to time, and had not undergone a voluntary period of suffering since the occasion of Tom's marriage, which she had entirely approved. She had a sufficient property of her own, and she and Tom were independent of each other in that way. Her only other step-child was a daughter, who had married a navy officer, and had at this time gone out to spend three years (or less) with her husband, who had been ordered to Japan.

It is not unfrequently noticed that in many marriages one of the persons who choose each other as partners for life is said to have thrown himself or herself away, and the relatives and friends look on with dismal forebodings and ill-concealed submission. In this case it was the wife who might have done so much better, according to public opinion. She did not think so herself, luckily, either before marriage or afterward, and I do not think it occurred to her to picture to herself the sort of career which would have been her alternative. She had been an only child, and had usually taken her own way. Some one once said that it was a great pity that she had not been obliged to work for her living, for she had inherited a most uncommon business talent, and, without being disreputably keen at a bargain, her insight into the practical working of affairs was very clear and far-reaching. Her father, who had also been a manufacturer, like Tom's, had often said it had been a mistake that she was a girl instead of a boy. Such executive ability as hers is often wasted in the more contracted sphere of women, and is apt to be more a disadvantage than a help. She was too independent and self-reliant for a wife; it would seem at first thought that she needed a wife herself more than she did a husband. Most men like best the women whose natures cling and appeal to theirs for protection. But Tom Wilson, while he did not wish to be protected himself, liked these very qualities in his wife which would have displeased some other men; to tell the truth, he was very much in love with his wife just as she was. He was a successful collector of almost everything but money, and during a great part of his life he had been an invalid, and he had grown, as he laughingly confessed, very old-womanish. He had been badly lamed, when a boy, by being caught in some machinery in his father's mill, near which he was idling one afternoon, and though he had almost entirely outgrown the effect of his injury, it had not been until after many years. He had been in college, but his eyes had given out there, and he had been obliged to leave in the middle of his junior year, though he had kept up a pleasant intercourse with the members of his class, with whom he had been a great favorite. He was a good deal of an idler in the world. I do not think his ambition, except in the case of securing Mary Dunn for his wife, had ever been distinct; he seemed to make the most he could of each day as it came, without making all his days' works tend toward some grand result, and go toward the upbuilding of some grand plan and purpose. He consequently gave no promise of being either distinguished or great. When his eyes would allow, he was an indefatigable reader; and although he would have said that he read only for amusement, yet he amused himself with books that were well worth the time he spent over them.

The house where he lived nominally belonged to his step-mother, but she had taken for granted that Tom would bring his wife home to it, and assured him that it should be to all intents and purposes his. Tom was deeply attached to the old place, which was altogether the pleasantest in town. He had kept bachelor's hall there most of the time since his father's death, and he had taken great pleasure, before his marriage, in refitting it to some extent, though it was already comfortable and furnished in remarkably good taste. People said of him that if it had not been for his illnesses, and if he had been a poor boy, he probably would have made something of himself. As it was, he was not very well known by the townspeople, being somewhat reserved, and not taking much interest in their every-day subjects of conversation. Nobody liked him so well as they liked his wife, yet there was no reason why he should be disliked enough to have much said about him.

After our friends had been married for some time, and had outlived the first strangeness of the new order of things, and had done their duty to their neighbors with so much apparent willingness and generosity that even Tom himself was liked a great deal better than he ever had been before, they were sitting together one stormy evening in the library, before the fire. Mrs. Wilson had been reading Tom the letters which had come to him by the night's mail. There was a long one from his sister in Nagasaki, which had been written with a good deal of ill-disguised reproach. She complained of the smallness of the income of her share in her father's estate, and said that she had been assured by American friends that the smaller mills were starting up everywhere, and beginning to do well again. Since so much of their money was invested in the factory, she had been surprised and sorry to find by Tom's last letters that he had seemed to have no idea of putting in a proper person as superintendent, and going to work again. Four per cent on her other property, which she had been told she must soon expect instead of eight, would make a great difference to her. A navy captain in a foreign port was obliged to entertain a great deal, and Tom must know that it cost them much more to live than it did him, and ought to think of their interests. She hoped he would talk over what was best to be done with their mother (who had been made executor, with Tom, of his father's will).

Tom laughed a little, but looked disturbed. His wife had said something to the same effect, and his mother had spoken once or twice in her letters of the prospect of starting the mill again. He was not a bit of a business man, and he did not feel certain, with the theories which he had arrived at of the state of the country, that it was safe yet to spend the money which would have to be spent in putting the mill in order. "They think that the minute it is going again we shall be making money hand over hand, just as father did when we were children," he said. "It is going to cost us no end of money before we can make anything. Before father died he meant to put in a good deal of new machinery, I remember. I don't know anything about the business myself, and I would have sold out long ago if I had had an offer that came anywhere near the value. The larger mills are the only ones that are good for anything now, and we should have to bring a crowd of French Canadians here; the day is past for the people who live in this part of the country to go into the factory again. Even the Irish all go West when they come into the country, and don't come to places like this any more."

ADULTHOOD, Women and Work

"But there are a good many of the old work-people down in the village," said Mrs. Wilson. "Jack Towne asked me the other day if you weren't going to start up in the spring."

Tom moved uneasily in his chair, "I'll put you in for superintendent, if you like," he said, half angrily, whereupon Mary threw the newspaper at him; but by the time he had thrown it back he was in good humor again.

"Do you know, Tom," she said, with amazing seriousness, "that I believe I should like nothing in the world so much as to be the head of a large business? I hate keeping house,—I always did; and I never did so much of it in all my life put together as I have since I have been married. I suppose it isn't womanly to say so, but if I could escape from the whole thing I believe I should be perfectly happy. If you get rich when the mill is going again, I shall beg for a housekeeper, and shirk everything. I give you fair warning. I don't believe I keep this house half so well as you did before I came here."

Tom's eyes twinkled. "I am going to have that glory,—I don't think you do, Polly; but you can't say that I have not been forbearing. I certainly have not told you more than twice how we used to have things cooked. I'm not going to be your kitchen-colonel."

"Of course it seemed the proper thing to do," said his wife, meditatively; "but I think we should have been even happier than we have if I had been spared it. I have had some days of wretchedness that I shudder to think of. I never know what to have for breakfast; and I ought not to say it, but I don't mind the sight of dust. I look upon housekeeping as my life's great discipline"; and at this pathetic confession they both laughed heartily.

"I've a great mind to take it off your hands," said Tom. "I always rather liked it, to tell the truth, and I ought to be a better housekeeper,—I have been at it for five years; though housekeeping for one is different from what it is for two, and one of them a woman. You see you have brought a different element into my family. Luckily, the servants are pretty well drilled. I do think you upset them a good deal at first!"

Mary Wilson smiled as if she only half heard what he was saying. She drummed with her foot on the floor and looked intently at the fire, and presently gave it a vigorous poking. "Well?" said Tom, after he had waited patiently as long as he could.

"Tom! I'm going to propose something to you. I wish you would really do as you said, and take all the home affairs under your care, and let me start the mill. I am certain I could manage it. Of course I should get people who understood the thing to teach me. I believe I was made for it; I should like it above all things. And this is what I will do: I will bear the cost of starting it, myself,—I think I have money enough, or can get it; and if I have not put affairs in the right trim at the end of a year I will stop, and you may make some other arrangement. If I have, you and your mother and sister can pay me back."

"So I am going to be the wife, and you the husband," said Tom, a little indignantly; "at least, that is what people will say. It's a regular Darby and Joan affair, and you think you can do more work in a day than I can do in three. Do you know that you must go to town to buy cotton? And do you know there are a thousand things about it that you don't know?"

"And never will?" said Mary, with perfect good humor. "Why, Tom, I can learn as well as you, and a good deal better, for I like business, and you don't. You forget that I was always father's right-hand man after I was a dozen years old, and that you have let me invest my money and some of your own, and I haven't made a blunder yet."

Tom thought that his wife had never looked so handsome or so happy. "I don't care, I should rather like the fun of knowing what people will say. It is a new departure, at any rate. Women think they can do everything better than men in these days, but I'm the first man, apparently, who has wished he were a woman."

"Of course people will laugh," said Mary, "but they will say that it's just like me, and think I am fortunate to have married a man who will let me do as I choose. I don't see why it isn't sensible: you will be living exactly as you were before you married, as to home affairs; and since it was a good thing for you to know something about housekeeping then, I can't imagine why you shouldn't go on with it now, since it makes me miserable, and I am wasting a fine business talent while I do it. What do we care for people's talking about it?"

"It seems to me that it is something like women's smoking: it isn't wicked, but it isn't the custom of the country. And I don't like the idea of your going among business men. Of course I should be above going with you, and having people think I must be an idiot; they would say that you married a manufacturing interest, and I was thrown in. I can foresee that my pride is going to be humbled to the dust in every way," Tom declared in mournful tones, and began to shake with laughter. "It is one of your lovely castles in the air, dear Polly, but an old brick mill needs a better foundation than the clouds. No, I'll look around, and get an honest, experienced man for agent. I suppose it's the best thing we can do, for the machinery ought not to lie still any longer; but I mean to sell the factory as soon as I can. I devoutly wish it would take fire, for the insurance would be the best price we are likely to get. That is a famous letter from Alice! I am afraid the captain has been growling over his pay, or they have been giving too many little dinners on board ship. If we were rid of the mill, you and I might go out there this winter. It would be capital fun."

Mary smiled again in an absent-minded way. Tom had an uneasy feeling that he had not heard the end of it yet, but nothing more was said for a day or two. When Mrs. Tom Wilson announced, with no apparent thought of being contradicted, that she had entirely made up her mind, and she meant to see those men who had been overseers of the different departments, who still lived in the village, and have the mill put in order at once, Tom looked disturbed, but made no opposition; and soon after breakfast his wife formally presented him with a handful of keys, and told him there was some lamb in the house for dinner; and presently he heard the wheels of her little phaeton rattling off down the road. I should be untruthful if I tried to persuade any one that he was not provoked; he thought she would at least have waited for his formal permission, and at first he meant to take another horse, and chase her, and bring her back in disgrace, and put a stop to the whole thing. But something assured him that she knew what she was about, and he determined to let her have her own way. If she failed, it might do no harm, and this was the only ungallant thought he gave her. He was sure that she would do nothing unladylike, or be unmindful of his dignity; and he believed it would be looked upon as one of her odd, independent freaks, which always had won respect in the end, however much they had been laughed at in the beginning. "Susan," said he, as that estimable person went by the door with the dustpan, "you may tell Catherine to come to me for orders about the house, and you may do so yourself. I am going to take charge again, as I did before I was married. It is no trouble to me, and Mrs. Wilson dislikes it. Besides, she is going into business, and will have a great deal else to think of."

"Yes, sir; very well, sir," said Susan, who was suddenly moved to ask so many questions that she was utterly silent. But her master looked very happy; there was evidently no disapproval of his wife; and she went on up the stairs, and began to sweep them down, knocking the dust-brush about excitedly, as if she were trying to kill a descending colony of insects.

Tom went out to the stable and mounted his horse, which had been waiting for him to take his customary after-breakfast ride to the post-office, and he galloped down the road in quest of the phaeton. He saw Mary talking with Jack Towne, who had been an overseer and a valued workman of his father's. He was looking much surprised and pleased.

"I wasn't caring so much about getting work, myself," he explained; "I've got what will carry me and my wife through; but it'll be better for the young folks about here to work near home. My nephews are wanting something to do; they were going to Lynn next week. I don't say but I should like to be to work in the old place again. I've sort of missed it, since we shut down."

"I'm sorry I was so long in overtaking you," said Tom, politely, to his wife. "Well, Jack, did Mrs. Wilson tell you she's going to start the mill? You must give her all the help you can."

" 'Deed I will," said Mr. Towne, gallantly, without a bit of astonishment.

"I don't know much about the business yet," said Mrs. Wilson, who had been a little overcome at Jack Towne's lingo of the different rooms and machinery, and who felt an overpowering sense of having a great deal before her in the next few weeks. "By the time the mill is ready, I will be ready, too," she said, taking heart a little; and Tom, who was quick to understand her moods, could not help laughing, as he rode alongside. "We want a new barrel of flour, Tom, dear," she said, by way of punishment for his untimely mirth.

If she lost courage in the long delay, or was disheartened at the steady call for funds, she made no sign; and after a while the mill started up, and her cares were lightened, so that she told Tom that before next pay day she would like to go to Boston for a few days, and go to the theatre, and have a frolic and a rest. She really looked pale and thin, and she said she never worked so hard in all her life; but nobody knew how happy she was, and she was so glad she had married Tom, for some men would have laughed at it.

"I laughed at it," said Tom, meekly. "All is, if I don't cry by and by, because I am a beggar, I shall be lucky." But Mary looked fearlessly serene, and said that there was no danger at present.

It would have been ridiculous to expect a dividend the first year, though the Nagasaki people were pacified with difficulty. All the business letters came to Tom's address, and everybody who was not directly concerned thought that he was the motive power of the reawakened enterprise. Sometimes business people came to the mill, and were amazed at having to confer with Mrs. Wilson, but they soon had to respect her talents and her success. She was helped by the old clerk, who had been promptly recalled and reinstated, and she certainly did capitally well. She was laughed at, as she had expected to be, and people said they should think Tom would be ashamed of himself; but it soon appeared that he was not to blame, and what reproach was offered was on the score of his wife's oddity. There was nothing about the mill that she did not understand before very long, and at the end of the second year she declared a small dividend with great pride and triumph. And she was congratulated on her success, and every one thought of her project in a different way from the way they had thought of it in the beginning. She had singularly good fortune: at the end of the third year she was making money for herself and her friends faster than most people were, and approving letters began to come from Nagasaki. The Ashtons had been ordered to stay in that region, and it was evident that they were continually being obliged to entertain more instead of less. Their children were growing fast, too, and constantly becoming more expensive. The captain and his wife had already begun to congratulate themselves secretly that their two sons would in all probability come into possession, one day, of their uncle Tom's handsome property.

For a good while Tom enjoyed life, and went on his quiet way serenely. He was anxious at first, for he thought that Mary was going to make ducks and drakes of his money and her own. And then he did not exactly like the looks of the thing, either; he feared that his wife was growing successful as a business person at the risk of losing her womanliness. But as time went on, and he found there was no fear of that, he accepted the situation philosophically. He gave up his collection of engravings, having become more interested in one of coins and medals, which took up most of his leisure time. He often went to the city in pursuit of such treasures, and gained much renown in certain quarters as a numismatologist of great skill and experience. But at last his house (which had almost kept itself, and had given him little to do beside ordering the dinners, while faithful old Catherine and her niece Susan were his aids) suddenly became a great care to him. Catherine, who had been the main-stay of the family for many years, died after a short illness, and Susan must needs choose that time, of all others, for being married to one of the second hands in the mill. There followed a long and dismal season of experimenting, and for a time there was a procession of incapable creatures going in at one kitchen door and out of the other. His wife would not have liked to say so, but it seemed to her that Tom was growing fussy about the house affairs, and took more notice of those minor details than he used. She wished more than once, when she was tired, that he would not talk so much about the housekeeping; he seemed sometimes to have no other thought.

In the early days of Mrs. Wilson's business life, she had made it a rule to consult her husband on every subject of importance; but it had speedily proved to be a formality. Tom tried manfully to show a deep interest which he did not feel, and his wife gave up, little by little, telling him much about her affairs. She said that she liked to drop business when she came home in the evening; and at last she fell into the habit of taking a nap on the library sofa, while Tom, who could not use his eyes much by lamp-light, sat smoking or in utter idleness before the fire. When they were first married his wife had made it a rule that she should always read him the evening papers, and afterward they had always gone on with some book of history or philosophy, in which they were both interested. These evenings of their early married life had been charming to both of them, and from time to time one would say to the other that they ought to take up again the habit of reading together. Mary was so unaffectedly tired in the evening that Tom never liked to propose a walk; for, though he was not a man of peculiarly social nature, he had always been accustomed to pay an occasional evening visit to his neighbors in the village. And though he had little interest in the business world, and still less knowledge of it, after a while he wished that his wife would have more to say about what she was planning and doing, or how things were getting on. He thought that her chief aid, old Mr. Jackson, was far more in her thoughts than he. She was forever quoting Jackson's opinions. He did not like to find that she took it for granted that he was not interested in the welfare of his own property; it made him feel like a sort of pensioner and dependent,

ADULTHOOD, Women and Work

though, when they had guests at the house, which was by no means seldom, there was nothing in her manner that would imply that she thought herself in any way the head of the family. It was hard work to find fault with his wife in any way, though, to give him his due, he rarely tried.

But, this being a wholly unnatural state of things, the reader must expect to hear of its change at last, and the first blow from the enemy was dealt by an old woman, who lived nearby, and who called to Tom one morning, as he was driving down to the village in a great hurry (to post a letter, which ordered his agent to secure a long-wished-for ancient copper coin, at any price), to ask him if they had made yeast that week, and if she could borrow a cupful, as her own had met with some misfortune. Tom was instantly in a rage, and he mentally condemned her to some undeserved fate, but told her aloud to go and see the cook. This slight delay, besides being killing to his dignity, caused him to lose the mail, and in the end his much-desired copper coin. It was a hard day for him, altogether; it was Wednesday, and the first days of the week having been stormy the washing was very late. And Mary came home to dinner provokingly good-natured. She had met an old schoolmate and her husband driving home from the mountains, and had first taken them over her factory, to their great amusement and delight, and then had brought them home to dinner. Tom greeted them cordially, and manifested his usual graceful hospitality; but the minute he saw his wife alone he said in a plaintive tone of rebuke, "I should think you might have remembered that the servants are unusually busy to-day. I do wish you would take a little interest in things at home. The women have been washing, and I'm sure I don't know what sort of a dinner we can give your friends. I wish you had thought to bring home some steak. I have been busy myself, and couldn't go down to the village. I thought we would only have a lunch."

Mary was hungry, but she said nothing, except that it would be all right,—she didn't mind; and perhaps they could have some canned soup.

She often went to town to buy or look at cotton, or to see some improvement in machinery, and she brought home beautiful bits of furniture and new pictures for the house, and showed a touching thoughtfulness in remembering Tom's fancies; but somehow he had an uneasy suspicion that she could get along pretty well without him when it came to the deeper wishes and hopes of her life, and that her most important concerns were all matters in which he had no share. He seemed to himself to have merged his life in his wife's; he lost his interest in things outside the house and grounds; he felt himself fast growing rusty and behind the times, and to have somehow missed a good deal in life; he had a suspicion that he was a failure. One day the thought rushed over him that his had been almost exactly the experience of most women, and he wondered if it really was any more disappointing and ignominious to him than it was to women themselves. "Some of them may be contented with it," he said to himself, soberly. "People think women are designed for such careers by nature, but I don't know why I ever made such a fool of myself."

Having once seen his situation in life from such a standpoint, he felt it day by day to be more degrading, and he wondered what he should do about it; and once, drawn by a new, strange sympathy, he went to the little family burying-ground. It was one of the mild, dim days that come sometimes in early November, when the pale sunlight is like the pathetic smile of a sad face, and he sat for a long time on the limp, frost-bitten grass beside his mother's grave.

But when he went home in the twilight his step-mother, who just then was making them a little visit, mentioned that she had been looking through some boxes of hers that had been packed long before and stowed away in the garret. "Everything looks very nice up there," she said, in her wheezing voice (which, worse than usual that day, always made him nervous), and added, without any intentional slight to his feelings, "I do think you have always been a most excellent housekeeper."

"I'm tired of such nonsense!" he exclaimed, with surprising indignation. "Mary, I wish you to arrange your affairs so that you can leave them for six months at least. I am going to spend this winter in Europe."

"Why, Tom, dear!" said his wife, appealingly. "I couldn't leave my business any way in the"—

But she caught sight of a look on his usually placid countenance that was something more than decision, and refrained from saying anything more.

And three weeks from that day they sailed.

[1884]

For Discussion

1. What effect does the use of the observer-narrator point of view have on the tone and substance of the story? At what points does the narrator intrude on the story to make comments?

2. Near the beginning, the narrator comments on the difference between the romantic and practical sides of marriage. Give examples of how this theme of ideal vs. real is carried throughout the rest of the story.

3. Listing the characteristics of Tom and of Mary described by the author, explain how the issue of sex stereotypes is handled, and what tone is adopted about stereotyping.

4. Why does Tom decide to hire a male manager?

5. What do we know about how Mary and Tom's unconventional arrangement is accepted in their community?

6. Identify each state in the gradual reversal of traditional roles of husband and wife. At what points are power struggles evident?

7. Why does Tom become less acquiescent towards the end of the story, and how is Jewett using his dissatisfaction to comment on "women's work"?

8. What does the final scene suggest about Mary and Tom's present and future relationship?

For Further Exploration

1. Read another story about a woman working instead of the husband, such as Helen Reimensnyder Martin's "A Poet Though Married" or Eugene O'Neill's one-act play *Before Breakfast*. What different attitudes are exhibited about these reversals of traditional roles?

2. In the recent study, *The Female Hero,* Pearson and Pope argue that there are many examples in literature to belie the usual image of women staying at home while male heroes explore the world outside. Examine the list of examples in the second chapter of *The Female Hero,* or create your own list from stories, novels, plays, or poems to support or deny Pearson and Pope's thesis.

Doris Lessing

1919–

The many possible attitudes men can take towards successful working women are evident in this story, calling to our attention the multiple levels on which battles between the sexes can be waged. The overtly sexual battle here reveals the hidden threat of women's success and self-esteem.

ONE OFF THE SHORT LIST

When he had first seen Barbara Coles, some years before, he only noticed her because someone said: "That's Johnson's new girl." He certainly had not used of her the private erotic formula: *Yes, that one.* He even wondered what Johnson saw in her. "She won't last long," he remembered thinking, as he watched Johnson, a handsome man, but rather flushed with drink, flirting with some unknown girl while Barbara stood by a wall looking on. He thought she had a sullen expression.

She was a pale girl, not slim, for her frame was generous, but her figure could pass as good. Her straight yellow hair was parted on one side in a way that struck him as gauche. He did not notice what she wore. But her eyes were all right, he remembered: large, and solidly green, square-looking because of some trick of the flesh at their corners. Emeraldlike eyes in the face of a schoolgirl, or young schoolmistress who was watching her lover flirt and would later sulk about it.

Her name sometimes cropped up in the papers. She was a stage decorator, a designer, something on those lines.

Then a Sunday newspaper had a competition for stage design and she won it. Barbara Coles was one of the "names" in the theatre, and her photograph was seen about. It was always serious. He remembered having thought her sullen.

One night he saw her across the room at a party. She was talking with a well-known actor. Her yellow hair was still done on one side, but now it looked sophisticated. She wore an emerald ring on her right hand that seemed deliberately to invite comparison with her eyes. He walked over and said: "We have met before, Graham Spence." He noted, with discomfort, that he sounded abrupt. "I'm sorry, I don't remember, but how do you do?" she said, smiling. And continued her conversation.

He hung around a bit, but soon she went off with a group of people she was inviting to her home for a drink. She did not invite Graham. There was about her an assurance, a carelessness, that he recognised as the signature of success. It was then, watching her laugh as she went off with her friends, that he used the formula: *"Yes, that one."* And he went home to his wife with enjoyable expectation, as if his date with Barbara Coles were already arranged.

His marriage was twenty years old. At first it had been stormy, painful, tragic—full of partings, betrayals and sweet reconciliations. It had taken him at least a decade to realise that there was nothing remarkable about this marriage that he had lived through with such surprise of the mind and the senses. On the contrary, the marriages of most of the people he knew, whether they were first, second or third attempts, were just the same. His had run true to form even to the serious love affair with the young girl for whose sake he had *almost* divorced his wife—yet at the last moment had changed his mind, letting the girl down so that he must have her for always (not unpleasurably) on his conscience. It was with humiliation that he had understood that this drama was not at all the unique thing he had imagined. It was nothing more than the experience of everyone in his circle. And presumably in everybody else's circle too?

Anyway, round about the tenth year of his marriage he had seen a good many things clearly, a certain kind of emotional adventure went from his life, and the marriage itself changed.

His wife had married a poor youth with a great future as a writer. Sacrifices had been made, chiefly by her, for that future. He was neither unaware of them, nor ungrateful; in fact he felt permanently guilty about it. He at last published a decently successful book, then a second which now, thank God, no one remembered. He had drifted into radio, television, book reviewing.

He understood he was not going to make it; that he had become—not a hack, no one could call him that—but a member of that army of people who live by their wits on the fringes of the arts. The moment of realisation was when he was in a pub one lunchtime near the B.B.C. where he often dropped in to meet others like himself: he understood that was why he went there—they *were* like him. Just as that melodramatic marriage had turned out to be like everyone else's—except that it had been shared with one woman instead of with two or three—so it had turned out that his unique talent, his struggles as a writer had led him here, to this pub and the half dozen pubs like it, where all the men in sight had the same history. They all had their novel, their play, their book of poems, a moment of fame, to their credit. Yet here they were, running television programmes about which they were cynical (to each other or to their wives) or writing reviews about other people's books. Yes, that's what he had become, an impresario of other people's talent. These two moments of clarity, about his marriage and about his talent, had roughly coincided: and (perhaps not by chance) had coincided with his wife's decision to leave him for a man younger than himself who had a future, she said, as a playwright. Well, he had talked her out of it. For her part she had to understand he was not going to be the T. S. Eliot or Graham Greene of our time—but after all, how many were? She must finally understand this, for he could no longer bear her awful bitterness. For his part he must stop coming home drunk at five in the morning, and starting a new romantic affair every six months which he took so seriously that he made her miserable because of her implied deficiencies. In short he was to be a good husband. (He had always been a dutiful father.) And she a good wife. And so it was: the marriage became stable, as they say.

The formula: *Yes, that one* no longer implied a necessarily sexual relationship. In its more mature form, it was far from being something he was ashamed of. On the contrary, it expressed a humorous respect for what he was, for his real talents and flair, which had turned out to be not artistic after all, but to do with emotional life, hard-earned experience. It expressed an ironical dignity, a proving to himself not only: I can be honest about myself, but also: I have earned the best in *that* field whenever I want it.

He watched the field for the women who were well known in the arts, or in politics; looked out for photographs, listened for bits of gossip. He made a point of going to see them act, or dance, or orate. He built up a not unshrewd picture of them. He would either quietly pull strings to meet her or—more often, for there was a gambler's pleasure in waiting—bide his time until he met her in the natural course of events, which was bound to happen sooner or later. He would be seen out with her a few times in public, which was in order, since his work meant he had to entertain well-known people, male and female. His wife always knew, he told her. He might have a brief affair with this woman, but more often than not it was the appearance of an affair. Not that he didn't get pleasure from other people envying him—he would make a point, for instance, of taking this woman into the pubs where his male colleagues went. It was that his real pleasure came when he saw her surprise at how well she was understood by him. He enjoyed the atmosphere he was able to set up between an intelligent woman and himself: a humorous complicity which had in it much that was unspoken, and which almost made sex irrelevant.

Onto the list of women with whom he planned to have this relationship went Barbara Coles. There was no hurry. Next week, next month, next year, they would meet at a party. The world of well-known people in London is a small one. Big and little fishes, they drift around, nose each other, flirt their fins, wriggle off again. When he bumped into Barbara Coles, it would be time to decide whether or not to sleep with her.

Meanwhile he listened. But he didn't discover much. She had a husband and children, but the husband seemed to be in the background. The children were charming and well brought up, like everyone else's children. She had affairs, they said; but while several men he met sounded familiar with her, it was hard to determine whether they had slept with her, because none directly boasted of her. She was spoken of in terms of her friends, her work, her house, a party she had given, a job she had found someone. She was liked, she was respected, and Graham Spence's self-esteem was flattered because he had chosen her. He looked forward to saying in just the same tone: "Barbara Coles asked me what I thought about the set and I told her quite frankly. . . ."

Then by chance he met a young man who did boast about Barbara Coles; he claimed to have had the great love affair with her, and recently at that; and he spoke of it as something generally known. Graham realised how much he had already become involved with her in his imagination because of how perturbed he was now, on account of the character of this youth, Jack Kennaway. He had recently become successful as a magazine editor—one of those young men who, not as rare as one might suppose in the big cities, are successful from sheer impertinence, effrontery. Without much talent or taste, yet he had the charm of his effrontery. "Yes, I'm going to succeed, because I've decided to; yes, I may be stupid, but not so stupid that I don't know my deficiencies. Yes, I'm going to be successful because you people with integrity, etc., etc., simply don't believe in the possibility of people like me. You are too cowardly to stop me. Yes, I've taken your measure and I'm going to succeed because I've got the courage, not only to be unscrupulous, but to be quite frank about it. And besides, you admire me, you must, or otherwise you'd stop me. . . ." Well, that was young Jack Kennaway, and he shocked Graham. He was a tall, languishing young man, handsome in a dark melting way, and, it was quite clear, he was either asexual or homosexual. And this youth boasted of the favours of Barbara Coles; boasted, indeed, of her love. Either she was a raving neurotic with a taste for neurotics; or Jack Kennaway was a most accomplished liar; or she slept with anyone. Graham was intrigued. He took Jack Kennaway out to dinner in order to hear him talk about Barbara Coles. There was no doubt the two were pretty close—all those dinners, theatres, weekends in the country—Graham Spence felt he had put his finger on the secret pulse of Barbara Coles; and it was intolerable that he must wait to meet her; he decided to arrange it.

It became unnecessary. She was in the news again, with a run of luck. She had done a successful historical play, and immediately afterwards a modern play, and then a hit musical. In all three, the sets were remarked on. Graham saw some interviews in newspapers and on television. These all centered around the theme of her being able to deal easily with so many different styles of theatre; but the real point was, of course, that she was a woman, which naturally added piquancy to the thing. And now Graham Spence was asked to do a half-hour radio interview with her. He planned the questions he would ask her with care, drawing on what people had said of her, but above all on his instinct and experience with women. The interview was to be at nine-thirty at night; he was to pick her up at six from the theatre where she was currently at work, so that there would be time, as the letter from the B.B.C. had put it, "for you and Miss Coles to get to know each other."

At six he was at the stage door, but a message from Miss Coles said she was not quite ready, could he wait a little. He hung about, then went to the pub opposite for a quick one, but still no Miss Coles. So he made his way backstage, directed by voices, hammering, laughter. It was badly lit, and the group of people at work did not see him. The director, James Poynter, had his arm around Barbara's shoulders. He was newly well-known, a carelessly good-looking young man reputed to be intelligent. Barbara Coles wore a dark blue overall, and her flat hair fell over her face so that she kept pushing it back with the hand that had the emerald on it. These two stood close, side by side. Three young men, stagehands, were on the other side of a trestle which had sketches and drawings on it. They were studying some sketches. Barbara said, in a voice warm with energy: "Well, so I thought if we did *this*—do you see, James? What do you think, Steven?" "Well, love," said the young man she called Steven, "I see your idea, but I wonder if . . ." "I think you're right, Babs," said the director. "Look," said Barbara, holding one of the sketches toward Steven, "look, let me show you." They all leaned forward, the five of them, absorbed in the business.

Suddenly Graham couldn't stand it. He understood he was shaken to his depths. He went off stage, and stood with his back against a wall in the dingy passage that led to the dressing rooms. His eyes were filled with tears. He was seeing what a long way he had come from the crude, uncompromising, admirable young egomaniac he had been when he was twenty. That group of people there—working, joking, arguing, yes, that's what he hadn't known for years. What bound them was the democracy of respect for each other's work, a confidence in themselves and in each other. They looked like people banded together against a world which they—no, not despised, but which they measured, understood, would fight to the death, out of respect for what *they* stood for, for what *it* stood for. It was a long time since he felt part of that balance. And he understood that he had seen Barbara Coles when she was most herself, at ease with a group of people she worked with. It was then, with the tears drying on his eyelids, which felt old and ironic, that he decided he would sleep with Barbara Coles. It was a necessity for him. He went back through the door onto the stage, burning with this single determination.

The five were still together. Barbara had a length of blue gleaming stuff which she was draping over the shoulder of Steven, the stagehand. He was showing it off, and the others watched. "What do you think, James?" she asked the director. "We've got that sort of dirty green, and I thought . . ." "Well," said James, not sure at all, "well, Babs, well . . ."

Now Graham went forward so that he stood beside Barbara, and said: "I'm Graham Spence, we've met before." For the second time she smiled socially and said: "Oh I'm sorry, I don't remember." Graham nodded at James, whom he had known, or at least had met off and on, for years. But it was obvious James didn't remember him either.

"From the B.B.C.," said Graham to Barbara, again sounding abrupt, against his will. "Oh I'm sorry, I'm so sorry, I forgot all about it. I've got to be interviewed," she said to the group. "Mr. Spence is a journalist." Graham allowed himself a small smile ironical of the word journalist, but she was not looking at him. She was going on with her work. "We should decide tonight," she said. "Steven's right." "Yes, I am right," said the stagehand. "She's right, James, we need that blue with that sludge-green everywhere." "James," said Barbara, "James, what's wrong with it? You haven't said." She moved forward to James, passing Graham. Remembering him again, she became contrite. "I'm sorry," she said, "we can none of us agree. Well, look"—she turned to Graham—"you advise us, we've got so involved with it that . . ." At which James laughed, and so did the stagehands. "No, Babs," said James, "of course Mr. Spence can't advise. He's just this moment come in. We've got to decide. Well I'll give you till tomorrow morning. Time to go home, it must be six by now."

"It's nearly seven," said Graham, taking command.

"It isn't!" said Barbara, dramatic. "My God, how terrible, how appalling, how could I have done such a thing. . . ." She was laughing at herself. "Well, you'll have to forgive me, Mr. Spence, because you haven't got any alternative."

They began laughing again: this was clearly a group joke. And now Graham took his chance. He said firmly, as if he were her director, in fact copying James Poynter's manner with her: "No, Miss Coles, I won't forgive you, I've been kicking my heels for nearly an hour." She grimaced, then laughed and accepted it. James said: "There, Babs, that's how you ought to be treated. We spoil you." He kissed her on the cheek, she kissed him on both his, the stagehands moved off. "Have a good evening, Babs," said James, going, and nodding to Graham, who stood concealing his pleasure with difficulty. He knew, because he had had the courage to be firm, indeed, peremptory, with Barbara, that he had saved himself hours of maneuvering. Several drinks, a dinner—perhaps two or three evenings of drinks and dinners—had been saved because he was now on this footing with Barbara Coles, a man who could say: "No, I won't forgive you, you've kept me waiting."

She said: "I've just got to . . ." and went ahead of him. In the passage she hung her overall on a peg. She was thinking, it seemed, of something else, but seeing him watching her, she smiled at him, companionably: he realised with triumph it was the sort of smile she would offer one of the stagehands, or even James. She said again: "Just one second . . ." and went to the stage-door office. She and the stage doorman conferred. There was some problem. Graham said, taking another chance: "What's the trouble, can I help?"—as if he could help, as if he expected to be able to. "Well . . ." she said, frowning. Then, to the man: "No, it'll be all right. Goodnight." She came to Graham. "We've got ourselves into a bit of a fuss because half the set's in Liverpool and half's here and—but it will sort itself out." She stood, at ease, chatting to him, one colleague to another. All this was admirable, he felt; but there would be a bad moment when they emerged from the special atmosphere of the theatre into the street. He took another decision, grasped her arm firmly, and said: "We're going to have a drink before we do anything at all, it's a terrible evening out." Her arm felt resistant, but remained within his. It was raining outside, luckily. He directed her, authoritative: "No, not that pub, there's a nicer one around the corner." "Oh, but I like this pub," said Barbara, "we always use it."

"Of course you do," he said to himself. But in that pub there would be the stagehands, and probably James, and he'd lose contact with her. He'd become a *journalist* again. He took her firmly out of danger around two corners, into a pub he picked at random. A quick look around—no, they weren't there. At least, if there were people from the theatre, she showed no sign. She asked for a beer. He ordered her a double Scotch, which she accepted. Then, having won a dozen preliminary rounds already, he took time to think. Something was bothering him—what? Yes, it was what he had observed backstage, Barbara and James Poynter. Was she having an affair with him? Because if so, it would all be much more difficult. He made himself see the two of them together, and thought with a jealousy surprisingly strong: *Yes, that's it.* Meantime he sat looking at her, seeing himself look at her, *a man gazing in calm appreciation at a woman:* waiting for her to feel it and respond. She was examining the pub. Her white woollen suit was belted, and had a not unprovocative suggestion of being a uniform. Her flat yellow hair, hastily pushed back after work, was untidy. Her clear white skin, without any colour, made her look tired. Not very exciting, at the moment, thought Graham, but maintaining his appreciative pose for when she would turn and see it. He knew what she would see: he was relying not only on the "warm kindly" beam of his gaze, for this was merely a reinforcement of the impression he knew he made. He had black hair, a little greyed. His clothes were loose and bulky—masculine. His eyes were humorous and appreciative. He was not, never had been, concerned to lessen the impression of being settled, dependable: the husband and father. On the contrary, he knew women found it reassuring.

When she at last turned she said, almost apologetic: "Would you mind if we sat down? I've been lugging great things around all day." She had spotted two empty chairs in a corner. So had he, but rejected them, because there were other people at the table. "But my dear, of course!" They took the chairs, and then Barbara said, "If you'll excuse me a moment." She had remembered she needed make-up. He watched her go off, annoyed with himself. She was tired; and he could have understood, protected, sheltered. He realised that in the other pub, with the people she had worked with all day, she would not have thought: "I must make myself up, I must be on show." That was for outsiders. She had not, until now, considered Graham an outsider, because of his taking his chance to seem one of the working group in the theatre; but now he had thrown his opportunity away. She returned armoured. Her hair was sleek, no longer defenceless. And she had made up her eyes. Her eyebrows were untouched, pale gold streaks above the brilliant green eyes whose lashes were blackened. Rather good, he thought, the contrast. Yes, but the moment had gone when he could say: Did you know you had a smudge on your cheek? Or—my dear girl!—pushing her hair back with the edge of a brotherly hand. In fact, unless he was careful, he'd be back at starting point.

He remarked: "That emerald is very cunning"—smiling into her eyes.

She smiled politely, and said: "It's not cunning, it's an accident, it was my grandmother's." She flirted her hand lightly by her face, though, smiling. But that was something she had done before, to a compliment she had had before, and often. It was all social, she had become social entirely. She remarked: "Didn't you say it was half past nine we had to record?"

"My dear Barbara, we've got two hours. We'll have another drink or two, then I'll ask you a couple of questions, then we'll drop down to the studio and get it over, and then we'll have a comfortable supper."

"I'd rather eat now, if you don't mind. I had no lunch, and I'm really hungry."

"But my dear, of course." He was angry. Just as he had been surprised by his real jealousy over James, so now he was thrown off balance by his anger: he had been counting on the long quiet dinner afterwards to establish intimacy. "Finish your drink and I'll take you to Nott's." Nott's was expensive. He glanced at her assessingly as he mentioned it. She said: "I wonder if you know Butler's? It's good and it's rather close." Butler's was good, and it was cheap, and he gave her a good mark for liking it. But Nott's it was going to be. "My dear, we'll get into a taxi and be at Nott's in a moment, don't worry."

She obediently got to her feet: the way she did it made him understand how badly he had slipped. She was saying to herself: Very well, he's like that, then all right, I'll do what he wants and get it over with. . . .

Swallowing his own drink he followed her, and took her arm in the pub doorway. It was polite within his. Outside it drizzled. No taxi. He was having bad luck now. They walked in silence to the end of the street. There Barbara glanced into a side street where a sign said: BUTLER'S. Not to remind him of it, on the contrary, she concealed the glance. And here she was, entirely at his disposal, they might never have shared the comradely moment in the theatre.

They walked half a mile to Nott's. No taxis. She made conversation: this was, he saw, to cover any embarrassment he might feel because of a half-mile walk through rain when she was tired. She was talking about some theory to do with the theatre, with designs for theatre building. He heard himself saying, and repeatedly: Yes, yes, yes. He thought about Nott's, how to get things right when they reached Nott's. There he took the headwaiter aside, gave him a pound, and instructions. They were put in a corner. Large Scotches appeared. The menus were spread. "And now, my dear," he said, "I apologise for dragging you here, but I hope you'll think it's worth it."

"Oh, it's charming, I've always liked it. It's just that . . ." She stopped herself saying: it's such a long way. She smiled at him, raising her glass, and said: "It's one of my very favourite places, and I'm glad you dragged me here." Her voice was flat with tiredness. All this was appalling; he knew it; and he sat thinking how to retrieve his position. Meanwhile she fingered the menu. The headwaiter took the order, but Graham made a gesture which said: Wait a moment. He wanted the Scotch to take effect before she ate. But she saw his silent order; and, without annoyance or reproach, leaned forward to say, sounding patient: "Graham, please, I've got to eat, you don't want me drunk when you interview me, do you?"

"They are bringing it as fast as they can," he said, making it sound as if she were greedy. He looked neither at the headwaiter nor at Barbara. He noted in himself, as he slipped further and further away from contact with her, a cold determination growing in him; one apart from, apparently, any conscious act of will, that come what may, if it took all night, he'd be in her bed before morning. And now, seeing the small pale face, with the enormous green eyes, it was for the first time that he imagined her in his arms. Although he had said: *Yes, that one,* weeks ago, it was only now that he imagined her as a sensual experience. Now he did, so strongly that he could only glance at her, and then away towards the waiters who were bringing food.

"Thank the Lord," said Barbara, and all at once her voice was gay and intimate. "Thank heavens. Thank every power that is. . . ." She was making fun of her own exaggeration; and, as he saw, because she wanted to put him at his ease after his boorishness over delaying the food. (She hadn't been taken in, he saw, humiliated, disliking her.) "Thank all the gods of Nott's," she went on, "because if I hadn't eaten inside five minutes I'd have died, I tell you." With which she picked up her knife and fork and began on her steak. He poured wine, smiling with her, thinking that *this* moment of closeness he would not throw away. He watched her frank hunger as she ate, and thought: Sensual—it's strange I hadn't wondered whether she would be or not.

"Now," she said, sitting back, having taken the edge off her hunger: "Let's get to work."

He said: "I've thought it over very carefully—how to present you. The first thing seems to me, we must get away from that old chestnut: Miss Coles, how extraordinary for a woman to be so versatile in her work . . . I hope you agree?" This was his trump card. He had noted, when he had seen her on television, her polite smile when this note was struck. (The smile he had seen so often tonight.) This smile said: All right, if you *have* to be stupid, what can I do?

Now she laughed and said: "What a relief. I was afraid you were going to do the same thing."

"Good, now you eat and I'll talk."

In his carefully prepared monologue he spoke of the different styles of theatre she had shown herself mistress of, but not directly: he was flattering her on the breadth of her experience; the complexity of her character, as shown in her work. She ate, steadily, her face showing nothing. At last she asked: "And how did you plan to introduce this?"

He had meant to spring that on her as a surprise, something like: Miss Coles, a surprisingly young woman for what she has accomplished (she was thirty? thirty-two?) and a very attractive one. . . . "Perhaps I can give you an idea of what she's like if I say she could be taken for the film star Marie Carletta. . . ." The Carletta was a strong earthy blonde, known to be intellectual. He now saw he could not possibly say this: he could imagine her cool look if he did. She said: "Do you mind if we get away from all that—my manifold talents, et cetera. . . ." He felt himself stiffen with annoyance; particularly beause this was not an accusation, he saw she did not think him worth one. She had assessed him: This is the kind of man who uses this kind of flattery and therefore. . . . It made him angrier that she did not even trouble to say: Why did you do exactly what you promised you wouldn't? She was being invincibly polite, trying to conceal her patience with his stupidity.

"After all," she was saying, "it is a stage designer's job to design what comes up. Would anyone take, let's say Johnnie Cranmore" (another stage designer) "onto the air or television and say: How very versatile you are because you did that musical about Java last month and a modern play about Irish labourers this?"

He battened down his anger. "My dear Barbara, I'm sorry. I didn't realise that what I said would sound just like the mixture as before. So what shall we talk about?"

"What I was saying as we walked to the restaurant: can we get away from the personal stuff?"

Now he almost panicked. Then, thank God, he laughed from nervousness, for she laughed and said: "You didn't hear one word I said."

"No, I didn't. I was frightened you were going to be furious because I made you walk so far when you were tired."

They laughed together, back to where they had been in the theatre. He leaned over, took her hand, kissed it. He said: "Tell me again." He thought: Damn, now she's going to be earnest and intellectual.

But he understood he had been stupid. He had forgotten himself at twenty—or, for that matter, at thirty; forgotten one could live inside an idea, a set of ideas, with enthusiasm. For in talking about her ideas (also the ideas of the people she worked with) for a new theatre, a new style of theatre, she was as she had been with her colleagues over the sketches or the blue material. She was easy, informal, almost chattering. This was how, he remembered, one talked about ideas that were a breath of life. The ideas, he thought, were intelligent enough; and he would agree with them, with her, if he believed it mattered a damn one way or another, if any of these enthusiasms mattered a damn. But at least he now had the key, he knew what to do. At the end of not more than half an hour, they were again two professionals, talking about ideas they shared, for he remembered caring about all this himself once. *When? How many years ago was it that he had been able to care?*

At last he said: "My dear Barbara, do you realise the impossible position you're putting me in? Margaret Ruyen who runs this programme is determined to do you personally, the poor woman hasn't got a serious thought in her head."

Barbara frowned. He put his hand on hers, teasing her for the frown: "No, wait, trust me, we'll circumvent her." She smiled. In fact Margaret Ruyen had left it all to him, had said nothing about Miss Coles.

"They aren't very bright—the brass," he said. "Well, never mind: we'll work out what we want, do it, and it'll be a *fait accompli*."

"Thank you, what a relief. How lucky I was to be given you to interview me." She was relaxed now, because of the whisky, the food, the wine, above all because of this new complicity against Margaret Ruyen. It would all be easy. They worked out five or six questions, over coffee, and took a taxi through rain to the studios. He noted that the cold necessity to have her, to make her, to beat her down, had left him. He was even seeing himself, as the evening ended, kissing her on the cheek and going home to his wife. This comradeship was extraordinarily pleasant. It was balm to the wound he had not known he carried until that evening, when he had had to accept the justice of the word *journalist*. He felt he could talk forever about the state of the theatre, its finances, the stupidity of the government, the philistinism of . . .

At the studios he was careful to make a joke so that they walked in on the laugh. He was careful that the interview began at once, without conversation with Margaret Ruyen; and that from the moment the green light went on, his voice lost its easy familiarity. He made sure that not one personal note was struck during the interview. Afterwards, Margaret Ruyen, who was pleased, came forward to say so; but he took her aside to say that Miss Coles was tired and needed to be taken home at once: for he knew this must look to Barbara as if he were squaring a producer who had been expecting a different interview. He led Barbara off, her hand held tight in his against his side. "Well," he said, "we've done it, and I don't think she knows what hit her."

"Thank you," she said, "it really was pleasant to talk about something sensible for once."

He kissed her lightly on the mouth. She returned it, smiling. By now he felt sure that the mood need not slip again, he could hold it.

"There are two things we can do," he said. "You can come to my club and have a drink. Or I can drive you home and you can give me a drink. I have to go past you."

"Where do you live?"

"Wimbledon." He lived, in fact, at Highgate; but she lived in Fulham. He was taking another chance, but by the time she found out, they would be in a position to laugh over his ruse.

"Good," she said. "You can drop me home then. I have to get up early." He made no comment. In the taxi he took her hand; it was heavy in his, and he asked: "Does James slave-drive you?"

"I didn't realize you knew him—no, he doesn't."

"Well I don't know him intimately. What's he like to work with?"

"Wonderful," she said at once. "There's no one I enjoy working with more."

Jealousy spurted in him. He could not help himself: "Are you having an affair with him?"

She looked: what's it to do with you? but said: "No, I'm not."

"He's very attractive," he said, with a chuckle of worldly complicity. She said nothing, and he insisted: "If I were a woman I'd have an affair with James."

It seemed she might very well say nothing. But she remarked: "He's married."

His spirits rose in a swoop. It was the first stupid remark she had made. It was a remark of such staggering stupidity that . . . he let out a humoring snort of laughter, put his arm around her, kissed her, said: "My dear little Babs."

She said: "Why Babs?"

"Is that the prerogative of James. And of the stagehands?" he could not prevent himself adding.

"I'm only called that at work." She was stiff inside his arm.

"My dear Barbara, then . . ." He waited for her to enlighten and explain but she said nothing. Soon she moved out of his arm, on the pretext of lighting a cigarette. He lit it for her. He noted that his determination to lay her, and at all costs, had come back. They were outside her house. He said quickly: "And now, Barbara, you can make me a cup of coffee and give me a brandy." She hesitated; but he was out of the taxi, paying, opening the door for her. The house had no lights on, he noted. He said: "We'll be very quiet so as not to wake the children."

She turned her head slowly to look at him. She said, flat, replying to his real question: "My husband is away. As for the children, they are visiting friends tonight." She now went ahead of him to the door of the house. It was a small house, in a terrace of small and not very pretty houses. Inside a little, bright, intimate hall, she said: "I'll go and make some coffee. Then, my friend, you must go home because I'm very tired."

The my friend struck him deep, because he had become vulnerable during their comradeship. He said gabbling: "You're annoyed with me—oh, please don't, I'm sorry."

She smiled, from a cool distance. He saw, in the small light from the ceiling, her extraordinary eyes. "Green" eyes are hazel, are brown with green flecks, are even blue. Eyes are chequered, flawed, changing. Hers were solid green, but really, he had never seen anything like them before. They were like very deep water. They were like—well, emeralds; or the absolute clarity of green in the depths of a tree in summer. And now, as she smiled almost perpendicularly up at him, he saw a darkness come over them. Darkness swallowed the clear green. She said: "I'm not in the least annoyed." It was as if she had yawned with boredom. "And now I'll get the things . . . in there." She nodded at a white door and left him. He went into a long, very tidy white room, that had a narrow bed in one corner, a table covered with drawings, sketches, pencils. Tacked to the walls with drawing pins were swatches of coloured stuffs. Two small chairs stood near a low round table: an area of comfort in the working room. He was thinking: I wouldn't like it if my wife had a room like this. I wonder what Barbara's husband . . . ? He had not thought of her till now in relation to her husband, or to her children. Hard to imagine her with a frying pan in her hand, or for that matter, cosy in the double bed.

A noise outside: he hastily arranged himself, leaning with one arm on the mantelpiece. She came in with a small tray that had cups, glasses, brandy, coffeepot. She looked abstracted. Graham was on the whole flattered by this: it probably meant she was at ease in his presence. He realised he was a little tight and rather tired. Of course, she was tired too, that was why she was vague. He remembered that earlier that evening he had lost a chance by not using her tiredness. Well now, if he were intelligent . . . She was about to pour coffee. He firmly took the coffeepot out of her hand, and nodded at a chair. Smiling, she obeyed him. "That's better," he said. He poured coffee, poured brandy, and pulled the table towards her. She watched him. Then he took her hand, kissed it, patted it, laid it down gently. Yes, he thought, I did that well.

Now, a problem. He wanted to be closer to her, but she was fitted into a damned silly little chair that had arms. If he were to sit by her on the floor . . . ? But no, for him, the big bulky reassuring man, there could be no casual gestures, no informal postures. Suppose I scoop her out of the chair onto the bed? He drank his coffee as he plotted. Yes, he'd carry her to the bed, but not yet.

"Graham," she said, setting down her cup. She was, he saw with annoyance, looking tolerant. "Graham, in about half an hour I want to be in bed and asleep."

As she said this, she offered him a smile of amusement at this situation—man and woman maneuvering, the great comic situation. And with part of himself he could have shared it. Almost, he smiled with her, laughed. (Not till days later he exclaimed to himself: Lord what a mistake I made, not to share the joke with her then: that was where I went seriously wrong). But he could not smile. His face was frozen, with a stiff pride. Not because she had been watching him plot; the amusement she now offered him took the sting out of that; but because of his revived determination that he was going to have his own way, he was going to have her. He was not going home. But he felt that he held a bunch of keys, and did not know which one to choose.

He lifted the second small chair opposite to Barbara, moving aside the coffee table for this purpose. He sat in this chair, leaned forward, took her two hands, and said: "My dear, don't make me go home yet, don't, I beg you." The trouble was, nothing had happened all evening that could be felt to lead up to these words and his tone—simple, dignified, human being pleading with human being for surcease. He saw himself leaning forward, his big hands swallowing her small ones; he saw his face, warm with the appeal. And he realised he had meant the words he used. They were nothing more

ADULTHOOD, Women and Work

than what he felt. He wanted to stay with her because she wanted him to, because he was her colleague, a fellow worker in the arts. He needed this desperately. But she was examining him, curious rather than surprised, and from a critical distance. He heard himself saying: "If James were here, I wonder what you'd do?" His voice was aggrieved; he saw the sudden dark descend over her eyes, and she said: "Graham, would you like some more coffee before you go?"

He said: "I've been wanting to meet you for years. I know a good many people who know you."

She leaned forward, poured herself a little more brandy, sat back, holding the glass between her two palms on her chest. An odd gesture: Graham felt that this vessel she was cherishing between her hands was herself. A patient, long-suffering gesture. He thought of various men who had mentioned her. He thought of Jack Kennaway, wavered, panicked, said: "For instance, Jack Kennaway."

And now, at the name, an emotion lit her eyes—what was it? He went on, deliberately testing this emotion, adding to it: "I had dinner with him last week—oh, quite by chance!—and he was talking about you."

"Was he?"

He remembered he had thought her sullen, all those years ago. Now she seemed defensive, and she frowned. He said: "In fact he spent most of the evening talking about you."

She said in short, breathless sentences, which he realised were due to anger: "I can very well imagine what he says. But surely you can't think I enjoy being reminded that . . ." She broke off, resenting him, he saw, because he forced her down onto a level she despised. But it was not his level either: it was all her fault, all hers! He couldn't remember not being in control of a situation with a woman for years. Again he felt like a man teetering on a tightrope. He said, trying to make good use of Jack Kennaway, even at this late hour: "Of course, he's a charming boy, but not a man at all."

She looked at him, silent, guarding her brandy glass against her breasts.

"Unless appearances are totally deceptive, of course." He could not resist probing, even though he knew it was fatal.

She said nothing.

"Do you know you are supposed to have had the great affair with Jack Kennaway?" he exclaimed, making this an amused expostulation against the fools who could believe it.

"So I am told." She set down her glass. "And now," she said, standing up, dismissing him. He lost his head, took a step forward, grabbed her in his arms, and groaned: "Barbara!"

She turned her face this way and that under his kisses. He snatched a diagnostic look at her expression—it was still patient. He placed his lips against her neck, groaned "Barbara" again, and waited. She would have to do something. Fight free, respond, something. She did nothing at all. At last she said: "For the Lord's sake, Graham!" She sounded amused: he was again being offered amusement. But if he shared it with her, it would be the end of this chance to have her. He clamped his mouth over hers, silencing her. She did not fight him off so much as blow him off. Her mouth treated his attacking mouth as a woman blows and laughs in water, puffing off waves or spray with a laugh, turning aside her head. It was a gesture half annoyance, half humour. He continued to kiss her while she moved her head and face about under the kisses as if they were small attacking waves.

And so began what, when he looked back on it afterwards, was the most embarrassing experience of his life. Even at the time he hated her for his ineptitude. For he held her there for what must have been nearly half an hour. She was much shorter than he, he had to bend, and his neck ached. He held her rigid, his thighs on either side of hers, her arms clamped to her side in a bear's hug. She was unable to move, except for her head. When his mouth ground hers open and his tongue moved and writhed inside it, she still remained passive. And he could not stop himself. While with his intelligence he watched this ridiculous scene, he was determined to go on, because sooner or later her body must soften in wanting his. And he could not stop because he could not face the horror of the moment when he set her free and she looked at him. And he hated her more, every moment. Catching glimpses of her great green eyes, open and dismal beneath his, he knew he had never disliked anything more than those "jewelled" eyes. They were repulsive to him. It occurred to him at last that even if by now she wanted him, he wouldn't know it, because she was not able to move at all. He cautiously loosened his hold so that she had an inch or so leeway. She remained quite passive. As if, he thought derisively, she had read or been told that the way to incite men maddened by lust was to fight them. He found he was thinking: Stupid cow, so you imagine I find you attractive, do you? You've got the conceit to think that!

The sheer, raving insanity of this thought hit him, opened his arms, his thighs, and lifted his tongue out of her mouth. She stepped back, wiping her mouth with the back of her hand, and stood dazed with incredulity. The embarrassment that lay in wait for him nearly engulfed him, but he let anger postpone it. She said positively apologetic, even, at this moment, humorous: "You're crazy, Graham. What's the matter, are you drunk? You don't seem drunk. You don't even find me attractive."

The blood of hatred went to his head and he gripped her again. Now she had got her face firmly twisted away so that he could not reach her mouth, and she repeated steadily as he kissed the parts of her cheeks and neck that were available to him: "Graham, let me go, do let me go, Graham." She went on saying this; he went on squeezing, grinding, kissing and licking. It might go on all night: it was a sheer contest of wills, nothing else. He thought: It's only a really masculine woman who wouldn't have given in by now out of sheer decency of the flesh! One thing he knew, however: that she would be in that bed, in his arms, and very soon. He let her go, but said: "I'm going to sleep with you tonight, you know that, don't you?"

She leaned with hand on the mantelpiece to steady herself. Her face was colourless, since he had licked all the makeup off. She seemed quite different: small and defenceless with her large mouth pale now, her smudged green eyes fringed with gold. And now, for the first time, he felt what it might have been supposed (certainly by her) he felt hours ago. Seeing the small damp flesh of her face, he felt kinship, intimacy with her, he felt intimacy of the flesh, the affection and good humour of sensuality. He felt she was flesh of his flesh, his sister in the flesh. He felt desire for her, instead of the will to have her; and because of this, was ashamed of the farce he had been playing. Now he desired simply to take her into bed in the affection of his senses.

She said: "What on earth am I supposed to do? Telephone for the police, or what?" He was hurt that she still addressed the man who had ground her into sulky apathy; she was not addressing *him* at all.

She said: "Or scream for the neighbours, is that what you want?"

The gold-fringed eyes were almost black, because of the depth of the shadow of boredom over them. She was bored and weary to the point of falling to the floor, he could see that.

He said: "I'm going to sleep with you."

"But how can you possibly want to?"—a reasonable, a civilised demand addressed to a man who (he could see) she believed would respond to it. She said: "You know I don't want to, and I know you don't really give a damn one way or the other."

He was stung back into being the boor because she had not the intelligence to see that the boor no longer existed; because she could not see that this was a man who wanted her in a way which she must respond to.

There she stood, supporting herself with one hand, looking small and white and exhausted, and utterly incredulous. She was going to turn and walk off out of simple incredulity, he could see that. "Do you think I don't mean it?" he demanded, grinding this out between his teeth. She made a movement—she was on the point of going away. His hand shot out on its own volition and grasped her wrist. She frowned. His other hand grasped her other wrist. His body hove up against hers to start the pressure of a new embrace. Before it could, she said: "Oh Lord, no, I'm not going through all that again. Right, then."

"What do you mean—right, then?" he demanded.

She said: "You're going to sleep with me. O.K. Anything rather than go through that again. Shall we get it over with?"

He grinned, saying in silence: "No darling, oh no you don't, I don't care what words you use, I'm going to have you now and that's all there is to it."

She shrugged. The contempt, the weariness of it, had no effect on him, because he was now again hating her so much that wanting her was like needing to kill something or someone.

She took her clothes off, as if she were going to bed by herself: her jacket, skirt, petticoat. She stood in white bra and panties, a rather solid girl, brown-skinned still from the summer. He felt a flash of affection for the brown girl with her loose yellow hair as she stood naked. She got into bed and lay there, while the green eyes looked at him in civilised appeal: Are you really going through with this? Do you have to? Yes, his eyes said back: I do have to. She shifted her gaze aside, to the wall, saying silently: Well, if you want to take me without any desire at all on my part, then go ahead, if you're not ashamed. He was not ashamed, because he was maintaining the flame of hate for her which he knew quite well was all that stood between him and shame. He took off his clothes, and got into bed beside her. As he did so, knowing he was putting himself in the position of raping a woman who was making it elaborately clear he bored her, his flesh subsided completely, sad, and full of reproach because a few moments ago it was reaching out for his sister whom he could have made happy. He lay on his side by her, secretly at work on himself, while he supported himself across her body on his elbow, using the free hand to manipulate her breasts. He saw that she gritted her teeth against his touch. At least she could not know that after all this fuss he was not potent.

In order to incite himself, he clasped her again. She felt his smallness, writhed free of him, sat up and said: "Lie down."

While she had been lying there, she had been thinking: The only way to get this over with is to make him big again, otherwise I've got to put up with him all night. His hatred of her was giving him a clairvoyance: he knew very well what went on through her mind. She had switched on, with the determination to *get it all over with*, a sensual good humour, a patience. He lay down. She squatted beside him, the light from the ceiling blooming on her brown shoulders, her flat fair hair falling over her face. But she would not look at his face. Like a bored, skilled wife, she was: or like a prostitute. She administered to him, she was setting herself to please him. Yes, he thought, she's sensual, or she could be. Meanwhile she was succeeding in defeating the reluctance of his flesh, which was the tender token of a possible desire for her, by using a cold skill that was the result of her contempt for him. Just as he decided: Right, it's enough, now I shall have her properly, she made him come. It was not a trick, to hurry or cheat him, what defeated him was her transparent thought: Yes, that's what he's worth.

Then, having succeeded, and waited for a moment or two, she stood up, naked, the fringes of gold at her loins and in her armpits speaking to him a language quite different from that of her green, bored eyes. She looked at him and thought, showing it plainly: What sort of man is it who . . . ? He watched the slight movement of her shoulders: a just-checked shrug. She went out of the room: then the sound of running water. Soon she came back in a white dressing gown, carrying a yellow towel. She handed him the towel, looking away in politeness as he used it. "Are you going home now?" she enquired hopefully, at this point.

"No, I'm not." He believed that now he would have to start fighting her again, but she lay down beside him, not touching him (he could feel the distaste of her flesh for his) and he thought: Very well, my dear, but there's a lot of the night left yet. He said aloud: "I'm going to have you properly tonight." She said nothing, lay silent, yawned. Then she remarked consolingly, and he could have laughed outright from sheer surprise: "Those were hardly conducive circumstances for making love." She was *consoling* him. He hated her for it. A proper little slut: I force her into bed, she doesn't want me, but she still has to make me feel good, like a prostitute. But even while he hated her he responded in kind, from the habit of sexual generosity. "It's because of my admiration for you, because . . . after all, I was holding in my arms one of the thousand women."

A pause. "The thousand?" she enquired, carefully.

"The thousand especial women."

"In Britain or in the world? You choose them for their brains, their beauty—what?"

"Whatever it is that makes them outstanding," he said, offering her a compliment.

"Well," she remarked at last, inciting him to be amused again: "I hope that at least there's a short list you can say I am on, for politeness' sake."

He did not reply for he understood he was sleepy. He was still telling himself that he must stay awake when he was slowly waking and it was morning. It was about eight. Barbara was not there. He thought: My God! What on earth shall I tell my wife? Where was Barbara? He remembered the ridiculous scenes of last night and nearly succumbed to shame. Then he thought, reviving anger: If she didn't sleep beside me here I'll never forgive her. . . . He sat up, quietly, determined to go through the house until he found her and, having found her, to possess her, when the door opened and she came in. She was fully dressed in a green suit, her hair done, her eyes made up. She carried a tray of coffee, which she set down beside the bed. He was conscious of his big loose hairy body, half uncovered. He said to himself that he was not going to lie in bed, naked, while she was dressed. He said: "Have you got a gown of some kind?" She handed him, without speaking, a towel, and said: "The bathroom's second on the left." She went out. He followed, the towel around him. Everything in this house was gay, intimate—not at all like her efficient working room. He wanted to find out where she had slept, and opened the first door. It was the kitchen, and she was in it, putting a brown earthenware dish into the oven. "The next door," said Barbara. He went hastily past the second door, and opened (he hoped quietly) the third. It was a cupboard full of linen. "This door," said Barbara, behind him.

"So all right then, where did you sleep?"

"What's it to do with you? Upstairs, in my own bed. Now, if you have everything, I'll say goodbye, I want to get to the theatre."

"I'll take you," he said at once.

He saw again the movement of her eyes, the dark swallowing the light in deadly boredom. "I'll take you," he insisted.

"I'd prefer to go by myself," she remarked. Then she smiled: "However, you'll take me. Then you'll make a point of coming right in, so that James and everyone can see—that's what you want to take me for, isn't it?"

He hated her, finally, and quite simply, for her intelligence; that not once had he got away with anything, that she had been watching, since they had met yesterday, every movement of his campaign for her. However, some fate or inner urge over which he had no control made him say sentimentally: "My dear, you must see that I'd like at least to take you to your work."

"Not at all, have it on me," she said, giving him the lie direct. She went past him to the room he had slept in. "I shall be leaving in ten minutes," she said.

He took a shower, fast. When he returned, the workroom was already tidied, the bed made, all signs of the night gone. Also, there were no signs of the coffee she had brought in for him. He did not like to ask for it, for fear of an outright refusal. Besides, she was ready, her coat on, her handbag under her arm. He went, without a word, to the front door, and she came after him, silent.

He could see that every fibre of her body signalled a simple message: Oh God, for the moment when I can be rid of this boor! She was nothing but a slut, he thought.

A taxi came. In it she sat as far away from him as she could. He thought of what he should say to his wife.

Outside the theatre she remarked: "You could drop me here, if you liked." It was not a plea, she was too proud for that. "I'll take you in," he said, and saw her thinking: Very well, I'll go through with it to shame him. He was determined to take her in and hand her over to her colleagues, but he was afraid she would give him the slip. But far from playing it down, she seemed determined to play it his way. At the stage door, she said to the doorman: "This is Mr. Spence, Tom—do you remember, Mr. Spence from last night?" "Good morning, Babs," said the man, examining Graham, politely, as he had been ordered to do.

Barbara went to the door to the stage, opened it, held it open for him. He went in first, then held it open for her. Together they walked into the cavernous, littered, badly lit place and she called out: "James, James!" A man's voice called out from the front of the house: "Here, Babs, why are you so late?"

The auditorium opened before them, darkish, silent, save for an early-morning busyness of charwomen. A vacuum cleaner roared, smally, somewhere close. A couple of stagehands stood looking up at a drop which had a design of blue and green spirals. James stood with his back to the auditorium, smoking. "You're late, Babs," he said again. He saw Graham behind her, and nodded. Barbara and James kissed. Barbara said, giving allowance to every syllable: "You remember Mr. Spence from last night?" James nodded: How do you do? Barbara stood beside him, and they looked together up at the blue-and-green backdrop. Then Barbara looked again at Graham, asking silently: All right now, isn't that enough? He could see her eyes, sullen with boredom.

He said: "Bye, Babs. Bye, James. I'll ring you, Babs." No response, she ignored him. He walked off slowly, listening for what might be said. For instance: "Babs, for God's sake, what are you doing with him?" Or she might say: "Are you wondering about Graham Spence? Let me explain."

Graham passed the stagehands who, he could have sworn, didn't recognise him. Then at last he heard James's voice to Barbara: "It's no good, Babs, I know you're enamoured of that particular shade of blue, but do have another look at it, there's a good girl. . . ." Graham left the stage, went past the office where the stage doorman sat reading a newspaper. He looked up, nodded, went back to his paper. Graham went to find a taxi, thinking: I'd better think up something convincing, then I'll telephone my wife.

Luckily he had an excuse not to be at home that day, for this evening he had to interview a young man (for television) about his new novel.

[1958]

For Discussion

1. What makes Graham Spence interested in Barbara Coles? What do we learn of her through his eyes?

2. Why does so much of the story appear to be about Graham Spence rather than Barbara Coles? Instead of first-person narration by either of the characters, what point of view does Lessing use?

3. Describe Spence's "two moments of clarity" and his formula for life. How would you describe the place of women in his life plans?

4. What makes Spence want to sleep with Barbara Coles? Describe his feelings in the pub and at dinner.

5. Explain the significance of Spence's plans for introducing Coles. What does his introduction reveal about his attitude towards women and work?

6. Why does he refer to her as "my dear Barbara" and "my dear little Babs?" Explain how the "complicity against Margaret Ruyen" fits in with Spence's attitude towards women.

7. Describe the power struggle underlying the sex act in the story. Is this "date rape"? What do you think of Spence's actions? of Barbara's?

8. What is the significance of the title of the story?

9. Explain why Barbara introduces Graham again to the men at work, and why this is a final humiliation for Spence.

10. What principles are in opposition throughout the story, and what is Doris Lessing saying about women and work?

For Further Exploration

1. In *Women Have Always Worked: A Historical Overview,* Alice Kessler-Harris mentions the appropriateness in the workplace of

    > one of the most meaningful slogans of the contemporary women's movement, "the personal is political." The slogan embodies a recognition that problems women experienced as individuals often reflected larger social relations. . . . Sexual harassment on the job, for example, reflected the general perception of women as "sex objects" who were not to be taken seriously in the world of ideas or of work.

    Contrast how Barbara Coles in this story is treated by the men at work and by Graham Spence. Then look at the other stories in this section to determine whether or not "the personal is political."

2. Which of the following "Ten Ways to Make a Woman Lose Effectiveness in an Organization," identified by Judith D. Palmer, does Spence use? Use direct quotations from the story to prove your arguments:

    > overprotecting her; excluding, avoiding, ignoring, or forgetting; inappropriate sexualization; male-oriented language structures; drawing her into traditional female roles; staying one up; discounting and discrediting; loyalty tests (joking about another woman); male solidarity; self-protection.

Anzia Yezierska

1885–1970

In this compelling account of an immigrant's attempt to find fulfilling work in the New World, Anzia Yezierska explores what it means to be an American. Do Americans only compete for selfish gain, or is there room for every individual to make a contribution in the workplace? Reminding readers of America's past and present, Yezierska touches the heart as well as the mind.

AMERICA AND I

As one of the dumb, voiceless ones I speak. One of the millions of immigrants beating, beating out their hearts at your gates for a breath of understanding.

Ach! America! From the other end of the earth where I came, America was a land of living hope, woven of dreams, aflame with longing and desire.

Choked for ages in the airless oppression of Russia, the Promised Land rose up—wings for my stifled spirit—sunlight burning through my darkness—freedom singing to me in my prison—deathless songs turning prison-bars into strings of a beautiful violin.

I arrived in America. My young, strong body, my heart and soul pregnant with the unlived lives of generations clamoring for expression.

What my mother and father and their mother and father never had a chance to give out in Russia, I would give out in America. The hidden sap of centuries would find release; colors that never saw light—songs that died unvoiced—romance that never had a chance to blossom in the black life of the Old World.

In the golden land of flowing opportunity I was to find my work that was denied me in the sterile village of my forefathers. Here I was to be free from the dead drudgery for bread that held me down in Russia. For the first time in America, I'd cease to be a slave of the belly. I'd be a creator, a giver, a human being! My work would be the living joy of fullest self-expression.

But from my high visions, my golden hopes, I had to put my feet down on earth. I had to have food and shelter. I had to have the money to pay for it.

I was in America, among the Americans, but not of them. No speech, no common language, no way to win a smile of understanding from them, only my young, strong body and my untried faith. Only my eager, empty hands, and my full heart shining from my eyes!

God from the world! Here I was with so much richness in me but my mind was not wanted without the language. And my body, unskilled, untrained, was not even wanted in the factory. Only one of two chances was left open to me: the kitchen, or minding babies.

My first job was as a servant in an Americanized family. Once, long ago, they came from the same village from where I came. But they were so well-dressed, so well-fed, so successful in America, that they were ashamed to remember their mother tongue.

"What were to be my wages?" I ventured timidly, as I looked up to the well-fed, well-dressed "American" man and woman.

They looked at me with a sudden coldness. What have I said to draw away from me their warmth? Was it so low from me to talk of wages? I shrank back into myself like a low-down bargainer. Maybe they're so high up in well-being they can't any more understand my low thoughts for money.

From his rich height the man preached down to me that I must not be so grabbing for wages. Only just landed from the ship and already thinking about money when I should be thankful to associate with "Americans."

The woman, out of her smooth, smiling fatness assured me that this was my chance for a summer vacation in the country with her two lovely children. My great chance to learn to be a civilized being, to become an American by living with them.

So, made to feel that I was in the hands of American friends, invited to share with them their home, their plenty, their happiness, I pushed out from my head the worry for wages. Here was my first chance to begin my life in the sunshine, after my long darkness. My laugh was all over my face as I said to them: "I'll trust myself to you. What I'm worth you'll give me." And I entered their house like a child by the hand.

The best of me I gave them. Their house cares were my house cares. I got up early. I worked till late. All that my soul hungered to give I put into the passion with which I scrubbed floors, scoured pots, and washed clothes. I was so grateful to mingle with the American people, to hear the music of the American language, that I never knew tiredness.

There was such a freshness in my brains and such a willingness in my heart that I could go on and on—not only with the work of the house, but work with my head—learning new words from the children, the grocer, the butcher, the iceman. I was not even afraid to ask for words from the policeman on the street. And every new word made me see new American things with American eyes. I felt like a Columbus, finding new worlds through every new word.

But words alone were only for the inside of me. The outside of me still branded me for a steerage immigrant. I had to have clothes to forget myself that I'm a stranger yet. And so I had to have money to buy these clothes.

The month was up. I was so happy! Now I'd have money. *My own, earned* money. Money to buy a new shirt on my back—shoes on my feet. Maybe yet an American dress and hat!

Ach! How high rose my dreams! How plainly I saw all that I would do with my visionary wages shining like a light over my head!

In my imagination I already walked in my new American clothes. How beautiful I looked as I saw myself like a picture before my eyes! I saw how I would throw away my immigrant rags tied up in my immigrant shawl. With money to buy—free money in my hands—I'd show them that I could look like an American in a day.

Like a prisoner in his last night in prison, counting the seconds that will free him from his chains, I trembled breathlessly for the minute I'd get the wages in my hand.

Before dawn I rose.

I shined up the house like a jewel-box.

I prepared breakfast and waited with my heart in my mouth for my lady and gentleman to rise. At last I heard them stirring. My eyes were jumping out of my head to them when I saw them coming in and seating themselves by the table.

Like a hungry cat rubbing up to its boss for meat, so I edged and simpered around them as I passed them the food. Without my will, like a beggar, my hand reached out to them.

The breakfast was over. And no word yet from my wages.

"*Gottuniu!*" I thought to myself. Maybe they're so busy with their own things they forgot it's the day for my wages. Could they who have everything know what I was to do with my first American dollars? How could they, soaking in plenty, how could they feel the longing and the fierce hunger in me, pressing up through each visionary dollar? How could they know the gnawing ache of my avid fingers for the feel of my own, earned dollars? *My* dollars that I could spend like a free person. *My* dollars that would make me feel with everybody alike!

Breakfast was long past.

Lunch came. Lunch past.

Oi-i weh! Not a word yet about my money.

It was near dinner. And not a word yet about my wages.

I began to set the table. But my head—it swam away from me. I broke a glass. The silver dropped from my nervous fingers. I couldn't stand it any longer. I dropped everything and rushed over to my American lady and gentleman.

"*Oi weh!* The money—my money—my wages!" I cried breathlessly.

Four cold eyes turned on me.

"Wages? Money?" The four eyes turned into hard stone as they looked me up and down. "Haven't you a comfortable bed to sleep, and three good meals a day? You're only a month here. Just came to America. And you already think about money. Wait till you're worth any money. What use are you without knowing English? You should be glad we keep you here. It's like a vacation for you. Other girls pay money yet to be in the country."

It went black for my eyes. I was so choked no words came to my lips. Even the tears went dry in my throat.

I left. Not a dollar for all my work.

For a long, long time my heart ached and ached like a sore wound. If murderers would have robbed me and killed me it wouldn't have hurt me so much. I couldn't think through my pain. The minute I'd see before me how they looked at me, the words they said to me—then everything began to bleed in me. And I was helpless.

For a long, long time the thought of ever working in an "American" family made me tremble with fear, like the fear of wild wolves. No—never again would I trust myself to an "American" family, no matter how fine their language and how sweet their smile.

It was blotted out in me all trust in friendship from "Americans." But the life in me still burned to live. The hope in me still craved to hope. In darkness, in dirt, in hunger and want, but only to live on!

There had been no end to my day—working for the "American" family.

Now rejecting false friendships from higher-ups in America, I turned back to the Ghetto. I worked on a hard bench with my own kind on either side of me. I knew before I began what my wages were to be. I knew what my hours were to be. And I knew the feeling of the end of the day.

From the outside my second job seemed worse than the first. It was in a sweat-shop of a Delancey Street basement, kept up by an old, wrinkled woman that looked like a black witch of greed. My work was sewing on buttons. While the morning was still dark I walked into a dark basement. And darkness met me when I turned out of the basement.

Day after day, week after week, all the contact I got with America was handling dead buttons. The money I earned was hardly enough to pay for bread and rent. I didn't have a room to myself. I didn't even have a bed. I slept on a mattress on the floor in a rat-hole of a room occupied by a dozen other immigrants. I was always hungry—oh, so hungry! The scant meals I could afford only sharpened my appetite for real food. But I felt myself better off than working in the "American" family, where I had three good meals a day and a bed to myself. With all the hunger and darkness of the sweat-shop, I had at least the evening to myself. And all night was mine. When all were asleep, I used to creep up on the roof of the tenement and talk out my heart in silence to the stars in the sky.

"Who am I? What am I? What do I want with my life? Where is America? Is there an America? What is this wilderness in which I'm lost?"

I'd hurl my questions and then think and think. And I could not tear it out of me, the feeling that America must be somewhere, somehow—only I couldn't find it—*my America*, where I would work for love and not for a living. I was like a thing following blindly after something far off in the dark!

"*Oi weh!*" I'd stretch out my hand up in the air. "My head is so lost in America! What's the use of all my working if I'm not in it? Dead buttons is not me."

Then the busy season started in the shop. The mounds of buttons grew and grew. The long day stretched out longer. I had to begin with the buttons earlier and stay with them till later in the night. The old witch turned into a huge greedy maw for wanting more and more buttons.

For a glass of tea, for a slice of herring over black bread, she would buy us up to stay another and another hour, till there seemed no end to her demands.

One day, the light of self-assertion broke into my cellar darkness.

"I don't want the tea. I don't want your herring," I said with terrible boldness. "I only want to go home. I only want the evening to myself!"

"You fresh mouth, you!" cried the old witch. "You learned already too much in America. I want no clock-watchers in my shop. Out you go!"

I was driven out to cold and hunger. I could no longer pay for my mattress on the floor. I no longer could buy the bite in the mouth. I walked the streets. I knew what it is to be alone in a strange city, among strangers.

But I laughed through my tears. So I learned too much already in America because I wanted the whole evening to myself? Well America has yet to teach me still more: how to get not only the whole evening to myself, but a whole day a week like the American workers.

That sweat-shop was a bitter memory but a good school. It fitted me for a regular factory. I could walk in boldly and say I could work at something, even if it was only sewing on buttons.

Gradually, I became a trained worker. I worked in a light, airy factory, only eight hours a day. My boss was no longer a sweater and a blood-squeezer. The first freshness of the morning was mine. And the whole evening was mine. All day Sunday was mine.

Now I had better food to eat. I slept on a better bed. Now, I even looked dressed up like the American-born. But inside of me I knew that I was not yet an American. I choked with longing when I met an American-born, and I could say nothing.

Something cried dumb in me. I couldn't help it. I didn't know what it was I wanted. I only knew I wanted. I wanted. Like the hunger in the heart that never gets food.

An English class for foreigners started in our factory. The teacher had such a good, friendly face, her eyes looked so understanding, as if she could see right into my heart. So I went to her one day for an advice:

"I don't know what is with me the matter," I began. "I have no rest in me. I never yet done what I want."

"What is it you want to do, child?" she asked me.

"I want to do something with my head, my feelings. All day long, only with my hands I work."

"First you must learn English." She patted me as if I was not yet grown up. "Put your mind on that, and then we'll see."

So for a time I learned the language. I could almost begin to think with English words in my head. But in my heart the emptiness still hurt. I burned to give, to give something, to do something, to be something. The dead work with my hands was killing me. My work left only hard stones on my heart.

Again I went to our factory teacher and cried to her: "I know already to read and write the English language, but I can't put it into words what I want. What is it in me so different that can't come out?"

She smiled at me down from her calmness as if I were a little bit out of my head. "What *do you want* to do?"

"I feel. I see. I hear. And I want to think it out. But I'm like dumb in me. I only feel I'm different—different from everybody."

She looked at me close and said nothing for a minute. "You ought to join one of the social clubs of the Women's Association," she advised.

"What's the Women's Association?" I implored greedily.

"A group of American women who are trying to help the working-girl find herself. They have a special department for immigrant girls like you."

I joined the Women's Association. On my first evening there they announced a lecture: "The Happy Worker and His Work," by the Welfare director of the United Mills Corporation.

"Is there such a thing as a happy worker at his work?" I wondered. Happiness is only by working at what you love. And what poor girl can ever find it to work at what she loves? My old dreams about my America rushed through my mind. Once I thought that in America everybody works for love. Nobody has to worry for a living. Maybe this welfare man came to show me the *real* America that till now I sought in vain.

With a lot of polite words the head lady of the Women's Association introduced a higher-up that looked like the king of kings of business. Never before in my life did I ever see a man with such a sureness in his step, such power in his face, such friendly positiveness in his eye as when he smiled upon us.

"Efficiency is the new religion of business," he began. "In big business houses, even in up-to-date factories, they no longer take the first comer and give him any job that happens to stand empty. Efficiency begins at the employment office. Experts are hired for the one purpose, to find out how best to fit the worker to his work. It's economy for the boss to make the worker happy." And then he talked a lot more on efficiency in educated language that was over my head.

I didn't know exactly what it meant—efficiency—but if it was to make the worker happy at his work, then that's what I had been looking for since I came to America. I only felt from watching him that he was happy by his job. And as I looked on this clean, well-dressed, successful, one, who wasn't ashamed to say he rose from an office-boy, it made me feel that I, too, could lift myself up for a person.

He finished his lecture, telling us about the Vocational-Guidance Center that the Women's Association started.

The very next evening I was at the Vocational-Guidance Center. There I found a young, college-looking woman. Smartness and health shining from her eyes! She, too, looked as if she knew her way in America. I could tell at the first glance: here is a person that is happy by what she does.

"I feel you'll understand me," I said right away.

She leaned over with pleasure in her face: "I hope I can."

"I want to work by what's in me. Only, I don't know what's in me. I only feel I'm different."

She gave me a quick, puzzled look from the corner of her eyes. "What are you doing now?"

"I'm the quickest shirtwaist hand on the floor. But my heart wastes away by such work. I think and think, and my thoughts can't come out."

"Why don't you think out your thoughts in shirtwaists? You could learn to be a designer. Earn more money."

"I don't want to look on waists. If my hands are sick from waists, how could my head learn to put beauty into them?"

"But you must earn your living at what you know, and rise slowly from job to job."

I looked at her office sign: "Vocational Guidance," "What's your vocational guidance?" I asked. "How to rise from job to job—how to earn more money?"

The smile went out from her eyes. But she tried to be kind yet. "What *do* you want?" she asked, with a sigh of last patience.

"I want America to want me."

She fell back in her chair, thunderstruck with my boldness. But yet, in a low voice of educated self-control, she tried to reason with me:

"You have to *show* that you have something special for America before America has need of you."

"But I never had a chance to find out what's in me, because I always had to work for a living. Only, I feel it's efficiency for America to find out what's in me so different, so I could give it out by my work."

Her eyes half closed as they bored through me. Her mouth opened to speak, but no words came from her lips. So I flamed up with all that was choking in me like a house on fire:

"America gives free bread and rent to criminals in prison. They got grand houses with sunshine, fresh air, doctors and teachers, even for the crazy ones. Why don't they have free boarding-schools for immigrants—strong people—willing people? Here you see us burning up with something different, and America turns her head away from us."

Her brows lifted and dropped down. She shrugged her shoulders away from me with the look of pity we give to cripples and hopeless lunatics.

"America is no Utopia. First you must become efficient in earning a living before you can indulge in your poetic dreams."

I went away from the vocational-guidance office with all the air out of my lungs. All the light out of my eyes. My feet dragged after me like dead wood.

Till now there had always lingered a rosy veil of hope over my emptiness, a hope that a miracle would happen. I would open my eyes some day and suddenly find the America of my dreams. As a young girl hungry for love sees always before her eyes the picture of lover's arms around her, so I saw always in my heart the vision of Utopian America.

But now I felt that the America of my dreams never was and never could be. Reality had hit me on the head as with a club. I felt that the America that I sought was nothing but a shadow—an echo—a chimera of lunatics and crazy immigrants.

Stripped of all illusion, I looked about me. The long desert of wasting days of drudgery stared me in the face. The drudgery that I had lived through, and the endless drudgery still ahead of me rose over me like a withering wilderness of sand. In vain were all my cryings, in vain were all frantic efforts of my spirit to find the living waters of understanding for my perishing lips. Sand, sand was everywhere. With every seeking, every reaching out I only lost myself deeper and deeper in a vast sea of sand.

I knew now the American language. And I knew now, if I talked to the Americans from morning till night, they could not understand what the Russian soul of me wanted. They could not understand *me* anymore than if I talked to them in Chinese. Between my soul and the American soul were worlds of difference that no words could bridge over. What was that difference? What made the Americans so far apart from me?

I began to read the American history. I found from the first pages that America started with a band of Courageous Pilgrims. They had left their native country as I had left mine. They had crossed an unknown ocean and landed in an unknown country, as I.

But the great difference between the first Pilgrims and me was that they expected to make America, build America, create their own world of liberty. I wanted to find it ready made.

I read on. I delved deeper down into the American history. I saw how the Pilgrim Fathers came to a rocky desert country, surrounded by Indian savages on all sides. But undaunted, they pressed on—through danger—through famine, pestilence, and want—they pressed on. They did not ask the Indians for sympathy, for understanding. They made no demands on anybody, but on their own indomitable spirit of persistence.

And I—I was forever begging a crumb of sympathy, a gleam of understanding from strangers who could not sympathize, who could not understand.

I, when I encountered a few savage Indian scalpers, like the old witch of the sweat-shop, like my "Americanized" countryman, who cheated me of my wages—I, when I found myself on the lonely, untrodden path through which all seekers of the new world must pass, I lost heart and said: "There is no America!"

Then came a light—a great revelation! I saw America—a big idea—a deathless hope—a world still in the making. I saw that it was the glory of America that it was not yet finished. And I, the last comer, had her share to give, small or great, to the making of America, like those Pilgrims who came in the *Mayflower*.

Fired up by this revealing light, I began to build a bridge of understanding between the American-born and myself. Since their life was shut out from such as me, I began to open up my life and the lives of my people to them. And life draws life. In only writing about the Ghetto I found America.

Great chances have come to me. But in my heart is always a deep sadness. I feel like a man who is sitting down to a secret table of plenty, while his near ones and dear ones are perishing before his eyes. My very joy in doing the work I love hurts me like secret guilt, because all about me I see so many with my longings, my burning eagerness, to do and to be, wasting their days in drudgery they hate, merely to buy bread and pay rent. And America is losing all that richness of the soul.

The Americans of to-morrow, the America that is every day nearer coming to be, will be too wise, too open-hearted, too friendly-handed, to let the least last-comer at their gates knock in vain with his gifts unwanted.

[1923]

For Discussion

1. Explain the significance of the many references to voice, speech, music, and language in the story.

2. Why does the narrator feel set apart from other immigrants as well as from naturalized and natural-born Americans? Explore the sources of alienation in the story.

3. Trace the emotional ups and downs of the narrator, finding examples of figurative language (metaphors, similes) such as "my heart ached and ached like a sore wound" used to intensify each experience.

4. Compare each work experience (domestic, sweatshop, etc.) in order to determine what the narrator achieves with each move.

5. What are the narrator's definitions of "my America," "the real America"?

6. How are the Women's Association and Vocational Guidance portrayed in this narrative?

7. Describe how the narrator's vision of the "America of tomorrow" arises out of the lessons she discovers from American history.

8. Identify the tone of the last paragraph—is it hopeful or despairing, jubilant or wary?

For Further Exploration

1. Compare this brief fictional account to Yezierska's novel *Breadgivers,* the story of a Jewish immigrant's struggle to rise above her ascribed roles as a worker and as a woman. What limitations must each character surmount, both within herself and in society?

2. Select one of the many best-selling books considered "subliterature" (many paperbacks available in grocery stores, for example, and made into TV miniseries) about women—often immigrants—who start out poor but "make it to the top." How do these accounts compare with Yezierska's narrator's experience? What qualities in real life create success for women in the workplace?

Poems About
Women and Work

In these poems, work of all kinds is presented—housework, clerical work, waitressing, business work, and working as a writer. Marge Piercy describes the laudable side of the impulse to "be of use," while other poets satirize the mundane quality of much of the work expected of women.

An interesting dimension of some of the poems is that the adolescent dream of being "special yet accepted" is carried into the adult arena of work. Women's happiness or despair at work seem to be directly related to the extent to which their work is valued by bosses and coworkers. At the same time, some resent being the "token woman," singled out to surpass one's "sisters."

Allusions to Cinderella and other models of "success" contrast with symbols and images of restriction in the workplace, leading to the ironic tone evident in many of these poems. These poets seem to be trying to decide what kind of work is worthwhile, and whether there is the possibility that women's contributions can be accepted and valued.

Alice Dunbar Nelson

1875–1935

I SIT AND SEW

I sit and sew—a useless task it seems,
My hands grown tired, my head weighed down with
    dreams—
The panoply of war, the material tread of men,
Grim-faced, stern-eyed, gazing beyond the ken
Of lesser souls, whose eyes have not seen Death,
Nor learned to hold their lives but as a breath—
But—I must sit and sew.

I sit and sew—my heart aches with desire—
That pageant terrible, that fiercely pouring fire
On wasted fields, and writhing grotesque things
Once men. My soul in pity flings
Appealing cries, yearning only to go
There in that holocaust of hell, those fields of woe—
But—I must sit and sew.

The little useless seam, the idle patch;
Why dream I here beneath my homely thatch,
When there they lie in sodden mud and rain,
Pitifully calling me, the quick ones and the slain!
You need me, Christ! It is no roseate dream
That beckons me—this pretty futile seam,
It stifles me—God, must I sit and sew?

[1920]

Anne Halley

1928–

HOUSEWIFE'S LETTER:
TO MARY

If I could, I'd write
how glad I live and cultivate:
to put tomatoes in and squash,
green salad on a yellow cloth,
how especially the white and blue
plates please me then. Also, I do
ironing mornings, make my list,
go squeeze fruit, open corn husks, watch
the butcher while he cuts our meat
and tote up prices in my head.
Evenings, I shake the cloth and fold
clean sheets away, count socks, and read
desultorily, and then to bed.

All this, could I, I'd write to you
and—doctored—parts are almost true.
But this is so: some days I've seen
my neighbor in her curlers, frowning intently, sweeping hard
her porch, her sidewalk, her paved yard.
Her serious eye, following broom,
penetrates to my scratchpad room
and so—on my good days—I sweep
the front porch hard, and hope to keep
a neighbor image in my eye,
good aproned neighbor, whom I'd try
to emulate, to mimic, be—
translate some certainties to me.

That mothers' meeting, visit, when
Elisabeth first felt her son
leap into life: Mother of God
and Prophet's Mother, forward bowed,
embracing secrets, each in each,
they celebrate each other's fruit—
cylindrical and gravid, plain,
I puzzle over what they mean;
what do they speak of, in what tone,
how calmly stand. If mortal men
could touch them thus—O sacred, grim
they look to me: this year, I'm thin
have cut my washerwoman hair—
yet they persist, so solid, there,
content to carry, bear this weight
and be as vines, initiate.

I have been fruitful, lucky, blessed
more ways than I can count, at rest—
or ought to be—and even thrive
efficiently: yet come alive
odd moments in surprise that I
should still expect, impossibly,
and at the same time wholly hate
my old expectancy. I wait
long past my time, like the old Saint,
but unlike her, I'll make complaint.

For when I stand here on the step
and sigh and nod my housewife's head
and wipe my hands and click my tongue
at dust, or rain, or noise, or sun,
though motion's right, I feel it wrong.
I can remember all my dolls'
tea-sets and washboards, cribs on wheels,
and the whole mess, the miniatures
of pie-tins, babies, plastic meals—
a dustblown attic full of wrapped-
up child's play. How begin, unpack,
through splintery crates and newsprint feel
the living child and make it real.

It's real enough. Inside my house,
uncustomed, unceremonious,
I seem to wade among the shards
proliferating, wrecked discards,
a whole decline of Western Man
in microcosm: who'd begin
to sort it out, make do, decide
to deal with this, to let that ride—
make love, patch plaster, choose your work,
your car, your party, and your church,
keep conscience, throw out sense of sin,
free impulse, but in discipline—
a ruptured rug, a beaten chair
stare at me, stupid as despair.

And I am full of anger, need
not words made flesh, nor wordless act,
nor cycles inarticulate,
have never felt a moral thrill
at choosing good against my will
and no orgasm, man or God's,
delivers long from my black thoughts—
Housewifely Guardians, sweeping yet,
sweep out their graves and ours: O let
those flourish surely on, who know
the laws in which they bear and grow,
let multiply, secure from ill,
vessels wellformed for grace to fill.

[1965]

Judy Grahn

1940–

From THE COMMON WOMEN

II. Ella, in a square apron, along Highway 80

She's a copperheaded waitress,
tired and sharp-worded, she hides
her bad brown tooth behind a wicked
smile, and flicks her ass
out of habit, to fend off the pass
that passes for affection.
She keeps her mind the way men
keep a knife—keen to strip the game
down to her size. She has a thin spine,
swallows her eggs cold, and tells lies.
She slaps a wet rag at the truck drivers
if they should complain. She understands
the necessity for pain, turns away
the smaller tips, out of pride, and
keeps a flask under the counter. Once,
she shot a lover who misused her child.
Before she got out of jail, the courts had pounced
and given the child away. Like some isolated lake,
her flat blue eyes take care of their own stark
bottoms. Her hands are nervous, curled, ready
to scrape.
The common woman is as common
as a rattlesnake.

[1978]

P. K. Page

1916–

TYPISTS

They without message, having read
the running words on their machines,
know every letter as a stamp
cutting the stencils of their ears.
Deep in their hands, like pianists,
all longing gropes and moves, is trapped
behind the tensile gloves of skin.

Or blind, sit with their faces locked
away from work. Their varied eyes
are stiff as everlasting flowers.
While fingers on a different plane
perform the automatic act
as questions grope along the dark
and twisting corridors of brain.

Crowded together typists touch
softly as ducks and seem to sense
each others' anguish with the swift
sympathy of the deaf and dumb.

[1943]

Olga Broumas

1949–

CINDERELLA

. . . the joy that isn't shared
I heard, dies young.
Anne Sexton, 1928–1974

Apart from my sisters, estranged
from my mother, I am a woman alone
in a house of men
who secretly
call themselves princes, alone
with me usually, under cover of dark. I am the one allowed in

to the royal chambers, whose small foot conveniently
fills the slipper of glass. The woman writer, the lady
umpire, the madam chairman, anyone's wife.
I know what I know.
And I once was glad

of the chance to use it, even alone
in a strange castle, doing overtime on my own, cracking
the royal code. The princes spoke
in their fathers' language, were eager to praise me
my nimble tongue. I am a woman in a state of siege, alone

as one piece of laundry, strung on a windy clothesline a
mile long. A woman co-opted by promises: the lure
of a job, the ruse of a choice, a woman forced
to bear witness, falsely
against my kind, as each
other sister was judged inadequate, bitchy, incompetent,
jealous, too thin, too fat. I know what I know.
What sweet bread I make

for myself in this prosperous house
is dirty, what good soup I boil turns
in my mouth to mud. Give
me my ashes. A cold stove, a cinder-block pillow, wet
canvas shoes in my sisters', my sisters' hut. Or I swear

I'll die young
like those favored before me, hand-picked each one
for her joyful heart.

[1977]

ADULTHOOD, Women and Work

Carolyn Kizer
1925–

From PRO FEMINA
Three

I will speak about women of letters, for I'm in the racket.
Our biggest successes to date? Old maids to a woman.
And our saddest conspicuous failures? The married spinsters
On loan to the husbands they treated like surrogate fathers.
Think of that crew of self-pitiers, not-very-distant,
Who carried the torch for themselves and got first-degree
    burns.
Or the sad sonneteers, toast-and-teasdales[1] we loved at
    thirteen;
Middle-aged virgins seducing the puerile anthologists
Through lust-of-the-mind; barbiturate-drenched Camilles[2]
With continuous periods, murmuring softly on sofas
When poetry wasn't a craft but a sickly effluvium,
The air thick with incense, musk, and emotional blackmail.

I suppose they reacted from an earlier womanly modesty
When too many girls were scabs[3] to their stricken
    sisterhood,
Impugning our sex to stay in good with the men,
Commencing their insecure bluster. How they must have
    swaggered
When women themselves indorsed their own inferiority!
Vestals, vassals and vessels, rolled into several,
They took notes in rolling syllabics, in careful journals,
Aiming to please a posterity that despises them.
But we'll always have traitors who swear that a woman
    surrenders
Her Supreme Function, by equating Art with aggression
And failure with Femininity. Still, it's just as unfair
To equate Art with Femininity, like a prettily-packaged
    commodity
When we are the custodians of the world's best-kept
    secret:
Merely the private lives of one-half of humanity.

But even with masculine dominance, we mares and
    mistresses
Produced some sleek saboteuses, making their cracks

---

[1]Poet Sara Teasdale.

[2]Languishing character in literature.

[3]Strike breakers.

Which the porridge-brained males of the day were too
  thick to perceive.
Mistaking young hornets for perfectly harmless
  bumblebees.
Being thought innocuous rouses some women to frenzy;
They try to be ugly by aping the ways of the men
And succeed. Swearing, sucking cigars and scorching the
  bedspread,
Slopping straight shots, eyes blotted, vanity-blown
In the expectation of glory: *she writes like a man!*

This drives other women mad in a mist of chiffon
(one poetess draped her gauze over red flannels, a practical
  feminist).
But we're emerging from all that, more or less,
Except for some lady-like laggards and Quarterly
  priestesses
Who flog men for fun, and kick women to maim
  competition.
Now, if we struggle abnormally, we may almost seem
  normal;
If we submerge our self-pity in disciplined industry;
If we stand up and be hated, and swear not to sleep with
  editors;
If we regard ourselves formally, respecting our true
  limitations
Without making an unseemly show of trying to unfreeze
  our assets;
Keeping our heads and our pride while remaining
  unmarried;
And if wedded, kill guilt in its tracks when we stack up the
  dishes
And defect to the typewriter. And if mothers, believe in the
  luck of our children,
Whom we forbid to devour us, whom we shall not devour,
And the luck of our husbands and lovers, who keep
  free women.

[1963]

Marge Piercy

1936–

TO BE OF USE

The people I love the best
jump into work head first
without dallying in the shallows
and swim off with sure strokes almost out of sight.
They seem to become natives of that element,
the black sleek heads of seals
bouncing like half-submerged balls.

I love people who harness themselves, an ox to a heavy cart,
who pull like water buffalo, with massive patience,
who strain in the mud and the muck to move things forward,
who do what has to be done, again and again.

I want to be with people who submerge
in the task, who go into the fields to harvest
and work in a row and pass the bags along,
who stand in the line and haul in their places,
who are not parlor generals and field deserters
but move in a common rhythm
when the food must come in or the fire be put out.

The work of the world is common as mud.
Botched, it smears the hands, crumbles to dust.
But the thing worth doing well done
has a shape that satisfies, clean and evident.
Greek amphoras for wine or oil,
Hopi vases that held corn, are put in museums
but you know they were made to be used.
The pitcher cries for water to carry
and a person for work that is real.

[1973]

For Discussion

1. In "I Sit and Sew," explain why Dunbar's narrator "aches with desire"
   and counts herself as one of the "lesser souls" whose work is "futile."
   Examine what this means about traditional "women's work."
2. What mixed feelings about housework does Anne Halley's narrator
   present in "Housewife's Letter: To Mary"?
3. How is "Ella" in Judy Grahn's poem similar or different from Page's
   "Typists"?
4. Explain how each stanza of the "Cinderella" poem can be interpreted as
   referring to an issue about women in the workplace.

5. How has the work of being a writer changed for women throughout the years, as indicated in Carolyn Kizer's "Pro Femina"?

6. What are the characteristics of the best workers in Piercy's "To Be Of Use"?

For Further Exploration

1. Identify the negative characteristics of women's roles at work, as described in these poems, then extrapolate what might be more positive roles. What suggestions for change are implied by these poets and who must change—men, women, and/or "the system"?

2. *Daughter of Earth* is a fascinating semi-autobiographical account of writer Agnes Smedley's work life. Describe the many jobs Smedley's narrator has, and compare her attitudes towards work to the attitudes of the women in these poems. Which feelings—energy, lethargy, enjoyment, resignation—does the "daughter of earth" share with these working women?

Drama About Women and Work

Susan Glaspell's famous play, *Trifles,* reveals assumptions and provides sur-prises about the relative importance of "men's" and "women's" work. Society's expectations for a successful housewife are brought to life in Glaspell's dramatization, and the "second-class" nature of a woman's work is magnificently captured by the repeated use of the title word, "trifles."

Central to the enormous ongoing popularity of this 1916 play (and the story version of it) is the notion of solidarity of the sexes. The system of male authority already in place at the beginning of the story is the target of Glaspell's satire and is ripe to be overturned. Along with this challenge to the nature of authority, the notions of "duty" and "law" are redefined, leaving the audience with a number of ethical, moral, and social questions.

Susan Glaspell

1882–1948

TRIFLES

Characters

GEORGE HENDERSON, *County Attorney*   MRS. PETERS

HENRY PETERS, *Sheriff*   MRS. HALE

LEWIS HALE, *A Neighboring Farmer*

Scene

The kitchen in the now abandoned farmhouse of JOHN WRIGHT, *a gloomy kitchen, and left without having been put in order—unwashed pans under the sink, a loaf of bread outside the breadbox, a dish towel on the table—other signs of incompleted work. At the rear the outer door opens and the* SHERIFF *comes in followed by the* COUNTY ATTORNEY *and* HALE. *The* SHERIFF *and* HALE *are men in middle life, the* COUNTY ATTORNEY *is a young man; all are much bundled up and go at once to the stove. They are followed by two women—the* SHERIFF's *wife first; she is a slight wiry woman, a thin nervous face.* MRS. HALE *is larger and would ordinarily be called more comfortable looking, but she is disturbed now and looks fearfully about as she enters. The women have come in slowly, and stand close together near the door.*

COUNTY ATTORNEY   [*Rubbing his hands.*] This feels good. Come up to the fire, ladies.

MRS. PETERS   [*After taking a step forward.*] I'm not—cold.

SHERIFF   [*Unbuttoning his overcoat and stepping away from the stove as if to mark the beginning of official business.*] Now, Mr. Hale, before we move things about, you explain to Mr. Henderson just what you saw when you came here yesterday morning.

COUNTY ATTORNEY   By the way, has anything been moved? Are things just as you left them yesterday?

SHERIFF   [*Looking about.*] It's just the same. When it dropped below zero last night I thought I'd better send Frank out this morning to make a fire for us—no use getting pneumonia with a big case on, but I told him not to touch anything except the stove—and you know Frank.

COUNTY ATTORNEY   Somebody should have been left here yesterday.

SHERIFF   Oh—yesterday. When I had to send Frank to Morris Center for that man who went crazy—I want you to know I had my hands full yesterday, I knew you could get back from Omaha by today and as long as I went over everything here myself—

COUNTY ATTORNEY   Well, Mr. Hale, tell just what happened when you came here yesterday morning.

HALE   Harry and I had started to town with a load of potatoes. We came along the road from my place and as I got here I said, "I'm going to see if I can't get John Wright to go in with me on a party telephone." I spoke to

Wright about it once before and he put me off, saying folks talked too much anyway, and all he asked was peace and quiet—I guess you know about how much he talked himself; but I thought maybe if I went to the house and talked about it before his wife, though I said to Harry that I didn't know as what his wife wanted made much difference to John—

COUNTY ATTORNEY Let's talk about that later, Mr. Hale. I do want to talk about that, but tell now just what happened when you got to the house.

HALE I didn't hear or see anything; I knocked at the door, and still it was all quiet inside. I knew they must be up, it was past eight o'clock. So I knocked again, and I thought I heard somebody say, "Come in." I wasn't sure, I'm not sure yet, but I opened the door—this door [*Indicating the door by which the two women are still standing*] and there in that rocker—[*Pointing to it.*] sat Mrs. Wright.

[*They all look at the rocker.*]

COUNTY ATTORNEY What—was she doing?

HALE She was rockin' back and forth. She had her apron in her hand and was kind of—pleating it.

COUNTY ATTORNEY And how did she—look?

HALE Well, she looked queer.

COUNTY ATTORNEY How do you mean—queer?

HALE Well, as if she didn't know what she was going to do next. And kind of done up.

COUNTY ATTORNEY How did she seem to feel about your coming?

HALE Why, I don't think she minded—one way or other. She didn't pay much attention. I said, "How do, Mrs. Wright, it's cold, ain't it?" And she said, "Is it?"—and went on kind of pleating at her apron. Well, I was surprised; she didn't ask me to come up to the stove, or to set down, but just sat there, not even looking at me, so I said, "I want to see John." And then she—laughed. I guess you would call it a laugh. I thought of Harry and the team outside, so I said a little sharp: "Can't I see John?" "No," she says, kind o' dull like. "Ain't he home?" says I. "Yes," says she, "he's home." "Then why can't I see him?" I asked her, out of patience. " 'Cause he's dead," says she. "*Dead?*" says I. She just nodded her head, not getting a bit excited, but rockin' back and forth. "Why—where is he?" says I, not knowing what to say. She just pointed upstairs—like that [*Himself pointing to the room above*]. I got up, with the idea of going up there. I walked from there to here—then I says, "Why, what did he die of?" "He died of a rope round his neck," says she, and just went on pleatin' at her apron. Well, I went out and called Harry. I thought I might—need help. We went upstairs and there he was lyin'—

COUNTY ATTORNEY I think I'd rather have you go into that upstairs, where you can point it all out. Just go on now with the rest of the story.

HALE Well, my first thought was to get that rope off. It looked . . . [*Stops, his face twitches.*] . . . but Harry, he went up to him, and he said, "No, he's dead all right, and we'd better not touch anything." So we went back down stairs. She was still sitting that same way. "Has anybody been notified?" I asked. "No," says she, unconcerned. "Who did this, Mrs. Wright?" said Harry. He said it businesslike—and she stopped pleatin' of her apron. "I don't know," she says. "You don't *know?*" says Harry. "No," says she. "Weren't you sleepin' in the bed with him?" says Harry. "Yes," says she, "but I was on the inside." "Somebody slipped a rope round his neck and strangled him and you didn't wake up?" says Harry. "I didn't wake up," she said after him. We must 'a looked as if we didn't see how that could be, for after a minute she said, "I sleep sound." Harry was going to ask her more questions but I said maybe we ought to let her tell her story first to the coroner, or the sheriff, so Harry went fast as he could to Rivers' place, where there's a telephone.

COUNTY ATTORNEY   And what did Mrs. Wright do when she knew that you had gone for the coroner?

HALE   She moved from that chair to this one over here [*Pointing to a small chair in the corner.*] and just sat there with her hands held together and looking down. I got a feeling that I ought to make some conversation, so I said I had come in to see if John wanted to put in a telephone, and at that she started to laugh, and then she stopped and looked at me—scared. [*The* COUNTY ATTORNEY, *who has had his notebook out, makes a note.*] I dunno, maybe it wasn't scared. I wouldn't like to say it was. Soon Harry got back, and then Dr. Lloyd came, and you, Mr. Peters, and so I guess that's all I know that you don't.

COUNTY ATTORNEY   [*Looking around.*] I guess we'll go upstairs first—and then out to the barn and around there. [*To the* SHERIFF] You're convinced that there was nothing important here—nothing that would point to any motive.

SHERIFF   Nothing here but kitchen things.

[*The* COUNTY ATTORNEY, *after again looking around the kitchen, opens the door of a cupboard closet. He gets up on a chair and looks on a shelf. Pulls his hand away, sticky.*]

COUNTY ATTORNEY   Here's a nice mess.

[*The women draw nearer.*]

MRS. PETERS   [*To the other woman.*] Oh, her fruit; it did freeze. [*To the* COUNTY ATTORNEY] She worried about that when it turned so cold. She said the fire'd go out and her jars would break.

SHERIFF   Well, can you beat the women! Held for murder and worryin' about her preserves.

COUNTY ATTORNEY   I guess before we're through she may have something more serious than preserves to worry about.

HALE   Well, women are used to worrying over trifles.

[*The two women move a little closer together.*]

COUNTY ATTORNEY   [*With the gallantry of a young politician.*] And yet, for all their worries, what would we do without the ladies? [*The women do not unbend. He goes to the sink, takes a dipperful of water from the pail and pouring it into a basin, washes his hands. Starts to wipe them on the roller towel, turns it for a cleaner place.*] Dirty towels! [*Kicks his foot against the pans under the sink.*] Not much of a housekeeper, would you say, ladies?

MRS. HALE   [*Stiffly.*] There's a great deal of work to be done on a farm.

COUNTY ATTORNEY   To be sure. And yet [*With a little bow to her*] I know there are some Dickson county farmhouses which do not have such roller towels.

[*He gives it a pull to expose its full length again.*]

MRS. HALE   Those towels get dirty awful quick. Men's hands aren't always as clean as they might be.

COUNTY ATTORNEY   Ah, loyal to your sex, I see. But you and Mrs. Wright were neighbors. I suppose you were friends, too.

MRS. HALE   [*Shaking her head.*] I've not seen much of her of late years. I've not been in this house—it's more than a year.

COUNTY ATTORNEY   And why was that? You didn't like her?

MRS. HALE   I liked her all well enough. Farmers' wives have their hands full, Mr. Henderson. And then—

COUNTY ATTORNEY   Yes—?

MRS. HALE   [*Looking about.*] It never seemed a very cheerful place.

COUNTY ATTORNEY   No—it's not cheerful. I shouldn't say she had the home-making instinct.

MRS. HALE   Well, I don't know as Wright had, either.

COUNTY ATTORNEY   You mean that they didn't get on very well?

MRS. HALE   No, I don't mean anything. But I don't think a place'd be any cheerfuller for John Wright's being in it.

COUNTY ATTORNEY   I'd like to talk more of that a little later. I want to get the lay of things upstairs now.

[*He goes to the left, where three steps lead to a stair door.*]

SHERIFF   I suppose anything Mrs. Peters does'll be all right. She was to take in some clothes for her, you know, and a few little things. We left in such a hurry yesterday.

COUNTY ATTORNEY   Yes, but I would like to see what you take, Mrs. Peters, and keep an eye out for anything that might be of use to us.

MRS. PETERS   Yes, Mr. Henderson.

[*The women listen to the men's steps on the stairs, then look about the kitchen.*]

MRS. HALE   I'd hate to have men coming into my kitchen, snooping around and criticising.

[*She arranges the pans under sink which the* COUNTY ATTORNEY *had shoved out of place.*]

MRS. PETERS   Of course it's no more than their duty.

MRS. HALE   Duty's all right, but I guess that deputy sheriff that came out to make the fire might have got a little of this on. [*Gives the roller towel a pull.*] Wish I'd thought of that sooner. Seems mean to talk about her for not having things slicked up when she had to come away in such a hurry.

MRS. PETERS   [*Who has gone to a small table in the left rear corner of the room, and lifted one end of a towel that covers a pan.*] She had bread set.

[*Stands still.*]

MRS. HALE   [*Eyes fixed on a loaf of bread beside the breadbox, which is on a low shelf at the other side of the room. Moves slowly toward it.*] She was going to put this in there. [*Picks up loaf, then abruptly drops it. In a manner of returning to familiar things.*] It's a shame about her fruit. I wonder if it's all gone. [*Gets up on the chair and looks.*] I think there's some here that's all right, Mrs. Peters. Yes—here; [*Holding it toward the window.*] this is cherries, too. [*Looking again.*] I declare I believe that's the only one. [*Gets down, bottle in her hand. Goes to the sink and wipes it off on the outside.*] She'll feel awful bad after all her hard work in the hot weather. I remember the afternoon I put up my cherries last summer.

[*She puts the bottle on the big kitchen table, center of the room. With a sigh, is about to sit down in the rocking-chair. Before she is seated realizes what chair it is; with a slow look at it, steps back. The chair which she has touched rocks back and forth.*]

MRS. PETERS   Well, I must get those things from the front room closet. [*She goes to the door at the right, but after looking into the other room, steps back.*] You coming with me, Mrs. Hale? You could help me carry them.

[*They go in the other room; reappear,* MRS. PETERS *carrying a dress and skirt,* MRS. HALE *following with a pair of shoes.*]

MRS. PETERS My, it's cold in there.

[*She puts the clothes on the big table, and hurries to the stove.*]

MRS. HALE [*Examining her skirt.*] Wright was close. I think maybe that's why she kept so much to herself. She didn't even belong to the Ladies Aid. I suppose she felt she couldn't do her part, and then you don't enjoy things when you feel shabby. She used to wear pretty clothes and be lively, when she was Minnie Foster, one of the town girls singing in the choir. But that—oh, that was thirty years ago. This all you was to take in?

MRS. PETERS She said she wanted an apron. Funny thing to want, for there isn't much to get you dirty in jail, goodness knows. But I suppose just to make her feel more natural. She said they was in the top drawer in this cupboard. Yes, here. And then her little shawl that always hung behind the door. [*Opens stair door and looks.*] Yes, here it is.

[*Quickly shuts door leading upstairs.*]

MRS. HALE [*Abruptly moving toward her.*] Mrs. Peters?

MRS. PETERS Yes, Mrs. Hale?

MRS. HALE Do you think she did it?

MRS. PETERS [*In a frightened voice.*] Oh, I don't know.

MRS. HALE Well, I don't think she did. Asking for an apron and her little shawl. Worrying about her fruit.

MRS. PETERS [*Starts to speak, glances up, where footsteps are heard in the room above. In a low voice.*] Mr. Peters says it looks bad for her. Mr. Henderson is awful sarcastic in a speech and he'll make fun of her sayin' she didn't wake up.

MRS. HALE Well, I guess John Wright didn't wake when they was slipping that rope under his neck.

MRS. PETERS No, it's strange. It must have been done awful crafty and still. They say it was such a—funny way to kill a man, rigging it all up like that.

MRS. HALE That's just what Mr. Hale said. There was a gun in the house. He says that's what he can't understand.

MRS. PETERS Mr. Henderson said coming out that what was needed for the case was a motive; something to show anger, or—sudden feeling.

MRS. HALE [*Who is standing by the table.*] Well, I don't see any signs of anger around here. [*She puts her hand on the dish towel which lies on the table, stands looking down at table, one half of which is clean, the other half messy.*] It's wiped to here. [*Makes a move as if to finish work, then turns and looks at loaf of bread outside the breadbox. Drops towel. In that voice of coming back to familiar things.*] Wonder how they are finding things upstairs. I hope she had it a little more red-up up there. You know, it seems kind of *sneaking.* Locking her up in town and then coming out here and trying to get her own house to turn against her!

MRS. PETERS But Mrs. Hale, the law is the law.

MRS. HALE I s'pose 'tis. [*Unbuttoning her coat.*] Better loosen up your things, Mrs. Peters. You won't feel them when you go out.

[MRS. PETERS *takes off her fur tippet, goes to hang it on hook at back of room, stands looking at the under part of the small corner table.*]

MRS. PETERS   She was piecing a quilt.

[*She brings the large sewing basket and they look at the bright pieces.*]

MRS. HALE   It's log cabin pattern. Pretty, isn't it? I wonder if she was goin' to quilt it or just knot it?

[*Footsteps have been heard coming down the stairs. The* SHERIFF *enters followed by* HALE *and the* COUNTY ATTORNEY.]

SHERIFF   They wonder if she was going to quilt it or just knot it!

[*The men laugh; the women look abashed.*]

COUNTY ATTORNEY   [*Rubbing his hands over the stove.*] Frank's fire didn't do much up there, did it? Well, let's go out to the barn and get that cleared up.

[*The men go outside.*]

MRS. HALE   [*Resentfully.*] I don't know as there's anything so strange, our takin' up our time with little things while we're waiting for them to get the evidence. [*She sits down at the big table smoothing out a block with decision.*] I don't see as it's anything to laugh about.

MRS. PETERS   [*Apologetically.*] Of course they've got awful important things on their minds.

[*Pulls up a chair and joins* MRS. HALE *at the table.*]

MRS. HALE   [*Examining another block.*] Mrs. Peters, look at this one. Here, this is the one she was working on, and look at the sewing! All the rest of it has been so nice and even. And look at this! It's all over the place! Why, it looks as if she didn't know what she was about!

[*After she has said this they look at each other, then start to glance back at the door. After an instant* MRS. HALE *has pulled at a knot and ripped the sewing.*]

MRS. PETERS   Oh, what are you doing, Mrs. Hale?

MRS. HALE   [*Mildly.*] Just pulling out a stitch or two that's not sewed very good. [*Threading a needle.*] Bad sewing always made me fidgety.

MRS. PETERS   [*Nervously.*] I don't think we ought to touch things.

MRS. HALE   I'll just finish up this end. [*Suddenly stopping and leaning forward.*] Mrs. Peters?

MRS. PETERS   Yes, Mrs. Hale?

MRS. HALE   What do you suppose she was so nervous about?

MRS. PETERS   Oh—I don't know. I don't know as she was nervous. I sometimes sew awful queer when I'm just tired. [MRS. HALE *starts to say something, looks at* MRS. PETERS, *then goes on sewing.*] Well, I must get these things wrapped up. They may be through sooner than we think. [*Putting apron and other things together.*] I wonder where I can find a piece of paper, and string.

MRS. HALE   In that cupboard, maybe.

MRS. PETERS   [*Looking in cupboard.*] Why, here's a birdcage. [*Holds it up.*] Did she have a bird, Mrs. Hale?

MRS. HALE   Why, I don't know whether she did or not—I've not been here for so long. There was a man around last year selling canaries cheap, but I don't know as she took one; maybe she did. She used to sing real pretty herself.

MRS. PETERS   [*Glancing around.*] Seems funny to think of a bird here. But she must have had one, or why would she have a cage? I wonder what happened to it.

MRS. HALE   I s'pose maybe the cat got it.

MRS. PETERS   No, she didn't have a cat. She's got that feeling some people have about cats—being afraid of them. My cat got in her room and she was real upset and asked me to take it out.

MRS. HALE   My sister Bessie was like that. Queer, ain't it?

MRS. PETERS   [*Examining the cage.*] Why, look at this door. It's broke. One hinge is pulled apart.

MRS. HALE   [*Looking too.*] Looks as if someone must have been rough with it.

MRS. PETERS   Why, yes.

[*She brings the cage forward and puts it on the table.*]

MRS. HALE   I wish if they're going to find any evidence they'd be about it. I don't like this place.

MRS. PETERS   But I'm awful glad you came with me, Mrs. Hale. It would be lonesome for me sitting here alone.

MRS. HALE   It would, wouldn't it? [*Dropping her sewing.*] But I tell you what I do wish, Mrs. Peters. I wish I had come over sometimes when *she* was here. I—[*Looking around the room.*]—wish I had.

MRS. PETERS   But of course you were awful busy, Mrs. Hale—your house and your children.

MRS. HALE   I could've come. I stayed away because it weren't cheerful—and that's why I ought to have come. I—I've never liked this place. Maybe because it's down in a hollow and you don't see the road. I dunno what it is but it's a lonesome place and always was. I wish I had come over to see Minnie Foster sometimes. I can see now—

[*Shakes her head.*]

MRS. PETERS   Well, you mustn't reproach yourself, Mrs. Hale. Somehow we just don't see how it is with other folks until—something comes up.

MRS. HALE   Not having children makes less work—but it makes a quiet house, and Wright out to work all day, and no company when he did come in. Did you know John Wright, Mrs. Peters?

MRS. PETERS   Not to know him; I've seen him in town. They say he was a good man.

MRS. HALE   Yes—good; he didn't drink, and kept his word as well as most, I guess, and paid his debts. But he was a hard man, Mrs. Peters. Just to pass the time of day with him—[*Shivers.*] Like a raw wind that gets to the bone. [*Pauses, her eye falling on the cage.*] I should think she would 'a wanted a bird. But what do you suppose went with it?

MRS. PETERS   I don't know, unless it got sick and died.

[*She reaches over and swings the broken door, swings it again. Both women watch it.*]

MRS. HALE   You weren't raised round here, were you? [MRS. PETERS *shakes her head.*] You didn't know—her?

MRS. PETERS   Not till they brought her yesterday.

MRS. HALE   She—come to think of it, she was kind of like a bird herself—real sweet and pretty, but kind of timid and—fluttery. How—she—did change. [*Silence; then as if struck by a happy thought and relieved to get back to every day things.*] Tell you what, Mrs. Peters, why don't you take the quilt in with you? It might take up her mind.

MRS. PETERS   Why, I think that's a real nice idea, Mrs. Hale. There couldn't possibly be any objection to it, could there? Now, just what would I take? I wonder if her patches are in here—and her things.

[*They look in the sewing basket.*]

MRS. HALE   Here's some red. I expect this has got sewing things in it. [*Brings *out a fancy box.*] What a pretty box. Looks like something somebody would give you. Maybe her scissors are in here. [*Opens box. Suddenly puts her hand to her nose.*] Why—[MRS. PETERS *bends nearer, then turns her face away.*] There's something wrapped up in this piece of silk.

MRS. PETERS   Why, this isn't her scissors.

MRS. HALE   [*Lifting the silk.*] Oh, Mrs. Peters—it's—
[MRS. PETERS *bends closer.*]

MRS. PETERS   It's the bird.

MRS. HALE   [*Jumping up.*] But, Mrs. Peters—look at it! Its neck! Look at its neck! It's all—other side *to.*

MRS. PETERS   Somebody—wrung—its—neck.
[*Their eyes meet. A look of growing comprehension, of horror. Steps are heard outside.* MRS. HALE *slips box under quilt pieces, and sinks into her chair. Enter* SHERIFF *and* COUNTY ATTORNEY. MRS. PETERS *rises.*]

COUNTY ATTORNEY   [*As one turning from serious things to little pleasantries.*] Well, ladies have you decided whether she was going to quilt it or knot it?

MRS. PETERS   We think she was going to—knot it.

COUNTY ATTORNEY   Well, that's interesting, I'm sure. [*Seeing the birdcage.*] Has the bird flown?

MRS. HALE   [*Putting more quilt pieces over the box.*] We think the—cat got it.

COUNTY ATTORNEY   [*Preoccupied.*] Is there a cat?
[MRS. HALE *glances in a quick covert way at* MRS. PETERS.]

MRS. PETERS.   Well, not *now.* They're superstitious, you know. They leave.

COUNTY ATTORNEY   [*To* SHERIFF PETERS, *continuing an interrupted conversation.*] No sign at all of anyone having come from the outside. Their own rope. Now let's go up again and go over it piece by piece. [*They start upstairs.*] It would have to have been someone who knew just the—
[MRS. PETERS *sits down. The two women sit there not looking at one another, but as if peering into something and at the same time holding back. When they talk now it is in the manner of feeling their way over strange ground, as if afraid of what they are saying, but as if they can not help saying it.*]

MRS. HALE   She liked the bird. She was going to bury it in that pretty box.

MRS. PETERS   [*In a whisper.*] When I was a girl—my kitten—there was a boy took a hatchet, and before my eyes—and before I could get there—[*Covers her face an instant.*] If they hadn't held me back I would have—[*Catches herself, looks upstairs where steps are heard, falters weakly.*]—hurt him.

MRS. HALE   [*With a slow look around her.*] I wonder how it would seem never to have had any children around. [*Pause.*] No, Wright wouldn't like the bird—a thing that sang. She used to sing. He killed that, too.

MRS. PETERS   [*Moving uneasily.*] We don't know who killed the bird.

MRS. HALE   I knew John Wright.

MRS. PETERS   It was an awful thing was done in this house that night, Mrs. Hale. Killing a man while he slept, slipping a rope around his neck that choked the life out of him.

MRS. HALE   His neck. Choked the life out of him.
[*Her hand goes out and rests on the birdcage.*]

MRS. PETERS   [*With rising voice.*] We don't know who killed him. We don't know.

MRS. HALE   [*Her own feeling not interrupted.*] If there'd been years and years of nothing, then a bird to sing to you, it would be awful—still, after the bird was still.

MRS. PETERS [*Something within her speaking.*] I know what stillness is. When we homesteaded in Dakota, and my first baby died—after he was two years old, and me with no other then—

MRS. HALE [*Moving.*] How soon do you suppose they'll be through, looking for the evidence?

MRS. PETERS I know what stillness is. [*Pulling herself back.*] The law has got to punish crime, Mrs. Hale.

MRS. HALE [*Not as if answering that.*] I wish you'd seen Minnie Foster when she wore a white dress with blue ribbons and stood up there in the choir and sang. [*A look around the room.*] Oh, I *wish* I'd come over here once in a while! That was a crime! That was a crime! Who's going to punish that?

MRS. PETERS [*Looking upstairs.*] We mustn't—take on.

MRS. HALE I might have known she needed help! I know how things can be—for women. I tell you, it's queer, Mrs. Peters. We live close together and we live far apart. We all go through the same things—it's all just a different kind of the same thing. [*Brushes her eyes; noticing the bottle of fruit, reaches out for it.*] If I was you I wouldn't tell her her fruit was gone. Tell her it *ain't*. Tell her it's all right. Take this in to prove it to her. She—she may never know whether it was broke or not.

MRS. PETERS [*Takes the bottle, looks about for something to wrap it in; takes petticoat from the clothes brought from the other room, very nervously begins winding this around the bottle. In a false voice.*] My, it's a good thing the men couldn't hear us. Wouldn't they just laugh! Getting all stirred up over a little thing like a—dead canary. As if that could have anything to do with—with—wouldn't they *laugh!*

[*The men are heard coming down stairs.*]

MRS. HALE [*Under her breath.*] Maybe they would—maybe they wouldn't.

COUNTY ATTORNEY No, Peters, it's all perfectly clear except a reason for doing it. But you know juries when it comes to women. If there was some definite thing. Something to show—something to make a story about—a thing that would connect up with this strange way of doing it—

[*The women's eyes meet for an instant. Enter* HALE *from outer door.*]

HALE Well, I've got the team around. Pretty cold out there.

COUNTY ATTORNEY I'm going to stay here a while by myself. [*To the* SHERIFF.] You can send Frank out for me, can't you? I want to go over everything. I'm not satisfied that we can't do better.

SHERIFF Do you want to see what Mrs. Peters is going to take in?

[*The* COUNTY ATTORNEY *goes to the table, picks up the apron, laughs.*]

COUNTY ATTORNEY Oh, I guess they're not very dangerous things the ladies have picked out. [*Moves a few things about, disturbing the quilt pieces which cover the box. Steps back.*] No, Mrs. Peters doesn't need supervising. For that matter, a sheriff's wife is married to the law. Ever think of it that way, Mrs. Peters?

MRS. PETERS Not—just that way.

SHERIFF [*Chuckling.*] Married to the law. [*Moves toward the other room.*] I just want you to come in here a minute, George. We ought to take a look at these windows.

COUNTY ATTORNEY [*Scoffingly.*] Oh, windows!

SHERIFF We'll be right out, Mr. Hale.

[HALE *goes outside. The* SHERIFF *follows the* COUNTY ATTORNEY *into the other room. Then* MRS. HALE *rises, hands tight together, looking intensely at* MRS. PETERS, *whose eyes make a slow turn, finally meeting* MRS. HALE'S. *A moment* MRS. HALE *holds her, then her own eyes point the way to where the box is concealed. Suddenly* MRS. PETERS *throws back quilt pieces and tries to put the box in the bag she is wearing. It is too big. She opens box, starts to take bird out, cannot touch it, goes to pieces, stands there helpless. Sound of a knob turning in the other room.* MRS. HALE *snatches the box and puts it in the pocket of her big coat. Enter* COUNTY ATTORNEY *and* SHERIFF.]

COUNTY ATTORNEY [*Facetiously.*] Well, Henry, at least we found out that she was not going to quilt it. She was going to—what is it you call it, ladies?

MRS. HALE [*Her hand against her pocket.*] We call it—knot it, Mr. Henderson.

CURTAIN

[1916]

For Discussion

1. Find instances of the division of labor into men and women's work. Which specific tasks are referred to as "trifles," and which are considered "important"? Why?

2. Describe what we know of Mrs. Wright's most recent life. Why didn't the home seem "cheerful" to neighbors?

3. What do we learn about Mrs. Wright's life before she was married? In what ways have her personality and activities changed, and to what can the change be attributed?

4. Explain the significance of the telephone incident, perhaps comparing it with the telephone as symbol in "Where Are You Going, Where Have You Been?" (Adolescence section).

5. Reconstructing the incidents leading up to the crime, why are the quilt and the bird appropriate as hidden clues?

6. How do the names of the characters reflect the themes? Why don't the women reveal the probable killer of "John Wright"?

7. What is the real "crime" here, according to the women at the end? Explore the many crimes that make up this story, and the multiple meanings of the words "duty" and "law."

8. Explain the dramatic irony of the last line: what do the women and the audience know that the men don't? How does this play—especially the ending—differ from most murder mysteries?

For Further Exploration

1. The women in this play have a "turnabout" remarkably identical to the reversal of attitudes of the women visitors in "The Town Poor" (Old Age section). What are the regrets that the women in both stories share? How do their attitudes change towards the town officials, and why do the

women gradually "move closer together" as the stage directions to *Trifles* indicate?

2. Compare this vision of women's farm work with the chronicle of farm drudgery in Edith S. Kelley's novel *Weeds*. Or, consider the more positive accounts of women's quiltmaking in "Everyday Use" (Women and Family section) or in Dorothy Canfield Fisher's story "The Bedquilt." What combination of factors makes for satisfying or debilitating work? Examine this related issue: is certain work given to women because it is trivial, or is it considered trivial because women do it?

For Discussion and Writing About This Section

1. What is similar about the situations of the women workers in the poems and in the stories? What could each have done to escape the real or attempted tyranny of others? For example, couldn't Delia or "Tom's Husband" or Mrs. Wright simply have left their husbands, or couldn't Barbara in "One Off the Short List" have gotten rid of Graham earlier?

2. Discuss the ways in which women treat each other in the literature (such as Bertha and Delia, the women in "Cinderella"). What effect does competition among women have on the outcome of each narrative? Is it true that there are few depictions of female friendship in literature about work, or can you find examples to the contrary?

3. Which of the major and minor characters in these stories are happy in their work? What accounts for happiness in each case, and how is inner satisfaction related to external success in work?

4. Examine the positive and negative aspects of male-female relationships in the workplace. For example, how is "Tom's Husband's" relationship with men different from that of the women with male coworkers in the stories?

5. How is work used by these authors as a metaphor for women's place in all of society? Examine several poems and stories to separate their literal and symbolic messages.

6. In a chapter on "Cinderella and Women's Work" in *Kiss Cinderella Goodbye*, Madonna Kolbenschlag says that one of the major obstacles to job satisfaction is that women don't see work as integral to their personal identity and autonomy. Is this true of any of the women depicted in the stories and poems in this section? Why or why not?

7. Each of the main characters in the short stories has to make a decision at the end of the story. How are personal ethics, religious values, social codes, sexual codes, and work codes evident in the women's final decisions?

ADULTHOOD
Women and Family

Interacting with parents; forming and dissolving partnerships; marriage and singlehood; childbirth and motherhood; fidelity and infidelity; dealing with separation

What constitutes a woman's "family"? Women can be daughters, mothers, lovers, sisters, and granddaughters simultaneously. Or, if a woman's parents are not living, she could be none of these things, but still have a "family," self-selected and tightly knit.

The women in these works represent part of the wide spectrum of possibilities for women's family relationships. In addition to the traditional family unit represented here and in the stories in other sections, there are also women raising children alone, mother and adult daughter relationships, women living with men, women living with women, and women dealing with family issues such as sibling rivalry and infidelity.

Whether we consider the women in these stories and poems to be family members, "householders" (a Census term), or even "POSSLQ's" (a silly census acronym for "Persons of the Opposite Sex Sharing Living Quarters"), each one is part of a small interpersonal unit that mirrors the woman's relationship with the world at large. In most cases, the type of person a woman is at home with her husband, lover, or mother is shown by these authors to correspond to how she relates to others at work and in society. By settling a dispute between her two daughters, for example, the mother in "Everyday Use" is making a decision about her own principles in life; and the same is true in many of the stories of women and family.

The poetry in this section shows even more clearly that the family is a microcosm of society. Women languish or luxuriate in love just as they fade or thrive in other situations; the "ordinariness" of daily routine is prized by one wife and despised by another, just as the same is true in work situations. Above all, the power struggle in families is symbolic of larger struggles, and is often related to politics and to national and international issues.

The house or a room as a symbol of the world is often used specifically to mean women's place in the world, as in "Breaking Tradition: For My Daughter," in which the narrator rejects her mother's confined life place for her own open spaces. Associated with the house are domestic images turned by some of the poets into objects of mockery. But despite the satirical tone of many of these works, there is a common strength in the women's desires to create a meaningful "family," of whatever type.

The relationships between the women and their mothers are expressed as especially powerful, whether or not the two adult women "get along" on the surface. In fact, one element that almost all of the stories have in common is a reference to the woman communicating with her mother.

Bonds these women maintain with their mothers are only part of the intricate network of people surrounding the women in the stories about family. Women are truly "connected" to others, which is bane as well as boon to the women described here with their families. Society is repeatedly shown as rewarding and fostering women's connectedness to the family unit. In each case, happy or unhappy, rewarded or unrewarded, the women realize that they are all powerfully linked to a family of one sort or another.

In addition to the power struggles that occur as a result of being "hooked" to other people, several other issues—fidelity and infidelity, having and not having children, and being married or not married—appear frequently as dominant themes. In the play *Breakfast Past Noon,* all of these themes are part of the interaction between a mother and "grown" daughter, and each poem or story deals with one or more of these recurrent issues.

The issue of fidelity and infidelity is also a common topic in literature about adult women. Being "faithful" does not stop some of the women from dreading the possibility that the home they have created might one day be "torn in two, blacked out, dissolved . . ." ("The 5:32") and, for at least one woman in the stories, exactly that occurs because of a husband's infidelity. Regardless of living situations, most of the women seem to value permanence, even while they rail out at the confinement of traditional marriage and family. Fidelity, a form of permanence, seems in these works to be cherished, regardless of the trapped feeling some of the narrators display, even those living together without marriage.

The act of deciding whether or not to have children is not as often a subject for fiction and poetry as is the woman's attitude during pregnancy and after childbirth or abortion. So seldom is "deciding" mentioned in the literature about having children, that it seems as if, in many cases, pregnancy or childlessness or abortions are foregone conclusions, or "just happen."

The theme of reluctance to take responsibility for having or not having children is evident in poems about childbirth and about abortion. Even surrogate children, such as the servant "adopted" in the story "Turned," seem to just appear, rather than resulting from conscious decisions on the part of the parent(s). The children themselves seem equally indecisive; for example, the daughter in "A Basket of Apples" can't decide whether or not to tell the mother that the father is dying.

A similar sense of indecision is evident in stories and poems about women living with another person, rather than being married. "Miss Furr and Miss Skeene" seem perfectly happy together, until one arbitrarily takes off for a new type of family grouping.

Regardless of the seemingly haphazard ways in which many families are formed, they are stuck together by "things." The domestic images of appliances, coffee pots, and milkmen as signs of settled "families" are evident not only in the marriages described, but in literature of "living together" as well. Amidst the clutter of household objects and the clatter of pots and pans, though, the natural beauty of family ties is often revealed. Few scenes can rival the emotional power of the mother's reflections in "I Stand Here Ironing," or the calm peace expressed in "Everyday Use" when the mother and daughter sit together in the night air, relaxing before going in to sleep.

There doesn't seem to be a common denominator in creating happy families—neither amount of education, nor amount of time together, nor degree of wealth or status, nor acceptance or rejection of marriage and children seems to be the answer to satisfaction in a household. But the ties between women and their "others" remain, confirming the fact that forming a family is one of the major events of adult life.

Fiction About Women and Family

The surprising mental image that emerges from these stories is the supremely fragile nature of the family; instead of being strong and permanent, the family unit seems instead to be delicately balanced and dynamic, always on the edge of change. Part of the reasons for the shifting nature of family are those to be expected, such as death or natural separations, as when a child grows up and leaves home. Other reasons families change in composition may be gradual alienation of a family member, or unexpected events that precipitate a change.

Even in the area in which one would expect to find the strongest of ties—the mother-daughter relationship—themes of conflict and alienation often become so strong in these stories that the bond stretches near breaking. Some authors depict both the mother and the daughter as "main characters," enabling the reader to discover that two points of view may be equally valid, depending on one's perspective.

When each family unit experiences a subtle or dramatic shift, how are new bonds created? In these stories, many different life styles are shown, and the pairings and groupings seem to be part practicality in "sticking together," and part self-defense in finding a partner with whom one can be most oneself, with fewer group restrictions. Some of the women who strike a new family bond are of different generations, brought together by death or adversity.

In each case, there is the sense of reaching out to others demonstrated by each of the women. Even in what appear to be antagonistic remarks or divisive situations, love is there, the bonding material of the eternally shifting notion of family.

Alice Walker

1944–

The reunion of a small family of women ends unexpectedly when the mother gains insight into the needs and expectations of her two daughters. Each conflict and choice demonstrates the problems and possibilities of women—both mothers and daughters—in modern society.

EVERYDAY USE

I will wait for her in the yard that Maggie and I made so clean and wavy yesterday afternoon. A yard like this is more comfortable than most people know. It is not just a yard. It is like an extended living room. When the hard clay is swept clean as a floor and the fine sand around the edges lined with tiny, irregular grooves, anyone can come and sit and look up into the elm tree and wait for the breezes that never come inside the house.

Maggie will be nervous until after her sister goes: she will stand hopelessly in corners, homely and ashamed of the burn scars down her arms and legs, eying her sister with a mixture of envy and awe. She thinks her sister has held life always in the palm of one hand, that "no" is a word the world never learned to say to her.

You've no doubt seen those TV shows where the child who has "made it" is confronted, as a surprise, by her own mother and father, tottering in weakly from backstage. (A pleasant surprise, of course: What would they do if parent and child came on the show only to curse out and insult each other?) On TV mother and child embrace and smile into each other's faces. Sometimes the mother and father weep, the child wraps them in her arms and leans across the table to tell how she would not have made it without their help. I have seen these programs.

Sometimes I dream a dream in which Dee and I are suddenly brought together on a TV program of this sort. Out of a dark and soft-seated limousine I am ushered into a bright room filled with many people. There I meet a smiling, gray, sporty man like Johnny Carson who shakes my hand and tells me what a fine girl I have. Then we are on the stage and Dee is embracing me with tears in her eyes. She pins on my dress a large orchid, even though she has told me once that she thinks orchids are tacky flowers.

In real life I am a large, big-boned woman with rough, man-working hands. In the winter I wear flannel nightgowns to bed and overalls during the day. I can kill and clean a hog as mercilessly as a man. My fat keeps me hot in zero weather. I can work outside all day, breaking ice to get water for washing; I can eat pork liver cooked over the open fire minutes after it comes steaming from the hog. One winter I knocked a bull calf straight in the brain between the eyes with a sledge hammer and had the meat hung up to chill before nightfall. But of course all this does not show on television. I am the way my daughter would want me to be: a hundred pounds lighter, my skin like an uncooked barley pancake. My hair glistens in the hot bright lights. Johnny Carson has much to do to keep up with my quick and witty tongue.

But that is a mistake. I know even before I wake up. Who ever knew a Johnson with a quick tongue? Who can even imagine me looking a strange white man in the eye? It seems to me I have talked to them always with one foot raised in flight, with my head turned in whichever way is farthest from them. Dee, though. She would always look anyone in the eye. Hesitation was no part of her nature.

"How do I look, Mama?" Maggie says, showing just enough of her thin body enveloped in pink skirt and red blouse for me to know she's there, almost hidden by the door.

"Come out into the yard," I say.

Have you ever seen a lame animal, perhaps a dog run over by some careless person rich enough to own a car, sidle up to someone who is ignorant enough to be kind to him? That is the way my Maggie walks. She has been like this, chin on chest, eyes on ground, feet in shuffle, ever since the fire that burned the other house to the ground.

Dee is lighter than Maggie, with nicer hair and a fuller figure. She's a woman now, though sometimes I forget. How long ago was it that the other house burned? Ten, twelve years? Sometimes I can still hear the flames and feel Maggie's arms sticking to me, her hair smoking and her dress falling off her in little black papery flakes. Her eyes seemed stretched open, blazed open by the flames reflected in them. And Dee. I see her standing off under the sweet gum tree she used to dig gum out of; a look of concentration on her face as she watched the last dingy gray board of the house fall in toward the red-hot brick chimney. Why don't you do a dance around the ashes? I'd wanted to ask her. She had hated the house that much.

I used to think she hated Maggie, too. But that was before we raised the money, the church and me, to send her to Augusta to school. She used to read to us without pity; forcing words, lies, other folks' habits, whole lives upon us two, sitting trapped and ignorant underneath her voice. She washed us in a river of make-believe, burned us with a lot of knowledge we didn't necessarily need to know. Pressed us to her with the serious way she read, to shove us away at just the moment, like dimwits, we seemed about to understand.

Dee wanted nice things. A yellow organdy dress to wear to her graduation from high school; black pumps to match a green suit she'd made from an old suit somebody gave me. She was determined to stare down any disaster in her efforts. Her eyelids would not flicker for minutes at a time. Often I fought off the temptation to shake her. At sixteen she had a style of her own: and knew what style was.

I never had an education myself. After second grade the school was closed down. Don't ask me why: in 1927 colored asked fewer questions than they do now. Sometimes Maggie reads to me. She stumbles along good-naturedly but can't see well. She knows she is not bright. Like good looks and money, quickness passed her by. She will marry John Thomas (who has mossy teeth in an earnest face) and then I'll be free to sit here and I guess just sing church songs to myself. Although I never was a good singer. Never could carry a tune. I was always better at a man's job. I used to love to milk till I was hooked in the side in '49. Cows are soothing and slow and don't bother you, unless you try to milk them the wrong way.

I have deliberately turned my back on the house. It is three rooms, just like the one that burned, except the roof is tin; they don't make shingle roofs any more. There are no real windows, just some holes cut in the sides, like the portholes in a ship, but not round and not square, with rawhide holding the shutters up on the outside. This house is in a pasture, too, like the other one. No doubt when Dee sees it she will want to tear it down. She wrote me once that no matter where we "choose" to live, she will manage to come see us. But she will never bring her friends. Maggie and I thought about this and Maggie asked me, "Mama, when did Dee ever *have* any friends?"

She had a few. Furtive boys in pink shirts hanging about on washday after school. Nervous girls who never laughed. Impressed with her they worshiped the well-turned phrase, the cute shape, the scalding humor that erupted like bubbles in lye. She read to them.

When she was courting Jimmy T she didn't have much time to pay to us, but turned all her faultfinding power on him. He *flew* to marry a cheap city girl from a family of ignorant flashy people. She hardly had time to recompose herself.

When she comes I will meet—but there they are!

Maggie attempts to make a dash for the house, in her shuffling way, but I stay her with my hand. "Come back here," I say. And she stops and tries to dig a well in the sand with her toe.

It is hard to see them clearly through the strong sun. But even the first glimpse of leg out of the car tells me it is Dee. Her feet were always neat-looking, as if God himself had shaped them with a certain style. From the other side of the car comes a short, stocky man. Hair is all over his head a foot long and hanging from his chin like a kinky mule tail. I hear Maggie suck in her breath. "Uhnnnh," is what it sounds like. Like when you see the wriggling end of a snake just in front of your foot on the road. "Uhnnnh."

Dee next. A dress down to the ground, in this hot weather. A dress so loud it hurts my eyes. There are yellows and oranges enough to throw back the light of the sun. I feel my whole face warming from the heat waves it throws out. Earrings gold, too, and hanging down to her shoulders. Bracelets dangling and making noises when she moves her arm up to shake the folds of the dress out of her armpits. The dress is loose and flows, and as she walks closer, I like it. I hear Maggie go "Uhnnnh" again. It is her sister's hair. It stands straight up like the wool on a sheep. It is black as night and around the edges are two long pigtails that rope about like small lizards disappearing behind her ears.

"Wa-su-zo-Tean-o!" she says, coming on in that gliding way the dress makes her move. The short stocky fellow with the hair to his navel is all grinning and he follows up with "Asalamalakim, my mother and sister!" He moves to hug Maggie but she falls back, right up against the back of my chair. I feel her trembling there and when I look up I see the perspiration falling off her chin.

"Don't get up," says Dee. Since I am stout it takes something of a push. You can see me trying to move a second or two before I make it. She turns, showing white heels through her sandals, and goes back to the car. Out she peeks next with a Polaroid. She stoops down quickly and lines up picture after picture of me sitting there in front of the house with Maggie cowering behind me. She never takes a shot without making sure the house is included. When a cow comes nibbling around the edge of the yard she snaps it and me and Maggie *and* the house. Then she puts the Polaroid in the back seat of the car, and comes up and kisses me on the forehead.

Meanwhile Asalamalakim is going through motions with Maggie's hand. Maggie's hand is as limp as a fish, and probably as cold, despite the sweat, and she keeps trying to pull it back. It looks like Asalamalakim wants to shake hands but wants to do it fancy. Or maybe he don't know how people shake hands. Anyhow, he soon gives up on Maggie.

"Well," I say. "Dee."

"No, Mama," she says. "Not 'Dee,' Wangero Leewanika Kemanjo!"

"What happened to 'Dee'?" I wanted to know.

"She's dead," Wangero said. "I couldn't bear it any longer, being named after the people who oppress me."

"You know as well as me you was named after your aunt Dicie," I said. Dicie is my sister. She named Dee. We called her "Big Dee" after Dee was born.

"But who was *she* named after?" asked Wangero.

"I guess after Grandma Dee," I said.

"And who was she named after?" asked Wangero.

"Her mother," I said, and saw Wangero was getting tired. "That's about as far back as I can trace it," I said. Though, in fact, I probably could have carried it back beyond the Civil War through the branches.

"Well," said Asalamalakim, "there you are."

"Uhnnnh," I heard Maggie say.

"There I was not," I said, "before 'Dicie' cropped up in our family, so why should I try to trace it that far back?"

He just stood there grinning, looking down on me like somebody inspecting a Model A car. Every once in a while he and Wangero sent eye signals over my head.

"How do you pronounce this name?" I asked.

"You don't have to call me by it if you don't want to," said Wangero.

"Why shouldn't I?" I asked. "If that's what you want us to call you, we'll call you."

"I know it might sound awkward at first," said Wangero.

"I'll get used to it," I said. "Ream it out again."

Well, soon we got the name out of the way. Asalamalakim had a name twice as long and three times as hard. After I tripped over it two or three times he told me to just call him Hakim-a-barber. I wanted to ask him was he a barber, but I didn't really think he was, so I didn't ask.

"You must belong to those beef-cattle peoples down the road," I said. They said "Asalamalakim" when they met you, too, but they didn't shake hands. Always too busy: feeding the cattle, fixing the fences, putting up salt-lick shelters, throwing down hay. When the white folks poisoned some of the herd the men stayed up all night with rifles in their hands. I walked a mile and a half just to see the sight.

Hakim-a-barber said, "I accept some of their doctrines, but farming and raising cattle is not my style." (They didn't tell me, and I didn't ask, whether Wangero (Dee) had really gone and married him.)

We sat down to eat and right away he said he didn't eat collards and pork was unclean. Wangero, though, went on through the chitlins and corn bread, the greens and everything else. She talked a blue streak over the sweet potatoes. Everything delighted her. Even the fact that we still used the benches her daddy made for the table when we couldn't afford to buy chairs.

"Oh, Mama!" she cried. Then turned to Hakim-a-barber. "I never knew how lovely these benches are. You can feel the rump prints," she said, running her hands underneath her and along the bench. Then she gave a sigh and her hand closed over Grandma Dee's butter dish. "That's it!" she said. "I knew there was something I wanted to ask you if I could have." She jumped up from the table and went over in the corner where the churn stood, the milk in it clabber by now. She looked at the churn and looked at it.

ADULTHOOD, Women and Family

"This churn top is what I need," she said. "Didn't Uncle Buddy whittle it out of a tree you all used to have?"

"Yes," I said.

"Uh huh," she said happily. "And I want the dasher, too."

"Uncle Buddy whittle that, too?" asked the barber

Dee (Wangero) looked up at me.

"Aunt Dee's first husband whittled the dash," said Maggie so low you almost couldn't hear her. "His name was Henry, but they called him Stash."

"Maggie's brain is like an elephant's," Wangero said, laughing. "I can use the churn top as a centerpiece for the alcove table," she said, sliding a plate over the churn, "and I'll think of something artistic to do with the dasher."

When she finished wrapping the dasher the handle stuck out. I took it for a moment in my hands. You didn't even have to look close to see where hands pushing the dasher up and down to make butter had left a kind of sink in the wood. In fact, there were a lot of small sinks; you could see where thumbs and fingers had sunk into the wood. It was beautiful light yellow wood, from a tree that grew in the yard where Big Dee and Stash had lived.

After dinner Dee (Wangero) went to the trunk at the foot of my bed and started rifling through it. Maggie hung back in the kitchen over the dishpan. Out came Wangero with two quilts. They had been pieced by Grandma Dee and then Big Dee and me had hung them on the quilt frames on the front porch and quilted them. One was in the Lone Star pattern. The other was Walk Around the Mountain. In both of them were scraps of dresses Grandma Dee had worn fifty and more years ago. Bits and pieces of Grandpa Jarrell's Paisley shirts. And one teeny faded blue piece, about the size of a penny matchbox, that was from Great Grandpa Ezra's uniform that he wore in the Civil War.

"Mama," Wangero said sweet as a bird. "Can I have these old quilts?"

I heard something fall in the kitchen, and a minute later the kitchen door slammed.

"Why don't you take one or two of the others?" I asked. "These old things was just done by me and Big Dee from some tops your grandma pieced before she died."

"No," said Wangero. "I don't want those. They are stitched around the borders by machine."

"That'll make them last better," I said.

"That's not the point," said Wangero. "These are all pieces of dresses Grandma used to wear. She did all this stitching by hand. Imagine!" She held the quilts securely in her arms, stroking them.

"Some of the pieces, like those lavender ones, come from old clothes her mother handed down to her," I said, moving up to touch the quilts. Dee (Wangero) moved back just enough so that I couldn't reach the quilts. They already belonged to her.

"Imagine!" she breathed again, clutching them closely to her bosom.

"The truth is," I said, "I promised to give them quilts to Maggie, for when she marries John Thomas."

She gasped like a bee had stung her.

"Maggie can't appreciate these quilts!" she said. "She'd probably be backward enough to put them to everyday use."

"I reckon she would," I said. "God knows I been saving 'em for long enough with nobody using 'em. I hope she will!" I didn't want to bring up how I had offered Dee (Wangero) a quilt when she went away to college. Then she had told me they were old-fashioned, out of style.

"But they're *priceless!*" she was saying now, furiously; for she has a temper. "Maggie would put them on the bed and in five years they'd be in rags. Less than that!"

"She can always make some more," I said. "Maggie knows how to quilt."

Dee (Wangero) looked at me with hatred. "You just will not understand. The point is these quilts, *these* quilts!"

"Well," I said, stumped. "What would *you* do with them?"

"Hang them," she said. As if that was the only thing you *could* do with quilts.

Maggie by now was standing in the door. I could almost hear the sound her feet made as they scraped over each other.

"She can have them, Mama," she said, like somebody used to never winning anything, or having anything reserved for her. "I can 'member Grandma Dee without the quilts."

I looked at her hard. She had filled her bottom lip with checkerberry snuff and it gave her face a kind of dopey, hangdog look. It was Grandma Dee and Big Dee who taught her how to quilt herself. She stood there with her scarred hands hidden in the folds of her skirt. She looked at her sister with something like fear but she wasn't mad at her. This was Maggie's portion. This was the way she knew God to work.

When I looked at her like that something hit me in the top of my head and ran down to the soles of my feet. Just like when I'm in church and the spirit of God touches me and I get happy and shout. I did something I never had done before: hugged Maggie to me, then dragged her on into the room, snatched the quilts out of Miss Wangero's hands and dumped them into Maggie's lap. Maggie just sat there on my bed with her mouth open.

"Take one or two of the others," I said to Dee.

But she turned without a word and went out to Hakim-a-barber.

"You just don't understand," she said, as Maggie and I came out to the car.

"What don't I understand?" I wanted to know.

"Your heritage," she said. And then she turned to Maggie, kissed her, and said, "You ought to try to make something of yourself, too, Maggie. It's really a new day for us. But from the way you and Mama still live you'd never know it."

She put on some sunglasses that hid everything above the tip of her nose and her chin.

Maggie smiled; maybe at the sunglasses. But a real smile, not scared. After we watched the car dust settle I asked Maggie to bring me a dip of snuff. And then the two of us sat there just enjoying, until it was time to go in the house and go to bed.

[1973]

For Discussion

1. What is foreshadowed by the narrator's first description of Maggie and her feelings about her sister?

2. Contrast the narrator's TV dream self with the reality of her life and family relationships.

3. How aware is the narrator of the differences between her two children?

4. What is the narrator's attitude toward reading and education? Is she unlearned?

5. Why is Dee's phrase "no matter where we 'choose' to live" significant?

6. How does Walker create humor in the reunion scene between mother and daughters?

7. What many purposes are served by the different names in the story?

8. Analyze the use of furniture, quilts, and clothing to convey the central themes of the story.

9. How does the image of the burning house fit in with the rest of the story? How does it contrast with the quilt as the central symbol?

10. What does the narrator discover at the end of the story that transcends the simple appearance of favoring one child over another?

For Further Exploration

1. Compare the sibling rivalry in this story with that of sisters in other stories, such as "I Stand Here Ironing" (this section). Or, compare the daughter's condescension toward her mother in "Everyday Use" with the same topic in Toni Cade Bambara's "My Man Bovanne."

2. In *Women: A Feminist Perspective*, Jo Freeman makes several perceptive comments about motherhood, including the statement that

> The role of mother brings with it benefits as well as limitations. Children affect parents in ways that lead to personal growth, enable reworking of childhood conflicts, build flexibility and empathy, and provide intimate, loving human connections.

Which of these four benefits of motherhood does the mother experience in this story?

Tillie Olsen

1912–

Silent love and self-sacrificing work are not always enough for a mother to give a child during the formative years. Internal and external forces can prevent the full demonstration of a mother's affection for her daughter, leading to the parental retrospection described here.

I STAND HERE IRONING

I stand here ironing, and what you asked me moves tormented back and forth with the iron.

"I wish you would manage the time to come in and talk with me about your daughter. I'm sure you can help me understand her. She's a youngster who needs help and whom I'm deeply interested in helping."

"Who needs help." Even if I came, what good would it do? You think because I am her mother I have a key, or that in some way you could use me as a key? She has lived for nineteen years. There is all that life that has happened outside of me, beyond me.

And when is there time to remember, to sift, to weigh, to estimate, to total? I will start and there will be an interruption and I will have to gather it all together again. Or I will become engulfed with all I did or did not do, with what should have been and what cannot be helped.

She was a beautiful baby. The first and only one of our five that was beautiful at birth. You do not guess how new and uneasy her tenancy in her now-loveliness. You did not know her all those years she was thought homely, or see her poring over her baby pictures, making me tell her over and over how beautiful she had been—and would be, I would tell her—and was now, to the seeing eye. But the seeing eyes were few or non-existent. Including mine.

I nursed her. They feel that's important nowadays. I nursed all the children, but with her, with all the fierce rigidity of first motherhood, I did like the books then said. Though her cries battered me to trembling and my breasts ached with swollenness, I waited till the clock decreed.

Why do I put that first? I do not even know if it matters, or if it explains anything.

She was a beautiful baby. She blew shining bubbles of sound. She loved motion, loved light, loved color and music and textures. She would lie on the floor in her blue overalls patting the surface so hard in ecstasy her hands and feet would blur. She was a miracle to me, but when she was eight months old I had to leave her daytimes with the woman downstairs to whom she was no miracle at all, for I worked or looked for work and for Emily's father, who "could no longer endure" [he wrote in his good-bye note] "sharing want with us."

I was nineteen. It was the pre-relief, pre-WPA world of the depression. I would start running as soon as I got off the streetcar, running up the stairs, the place smelling sour, and awake or asleep to startle awake, when she saw me she would break into a clogged weeping that could not be comforted, a weeping I can yet hear.

After a while I found a job hashing at night so I could be with her days, and it was better. But it came to where I had to bring her to his family and leave her.

It took a long time to raise the money for her fare back. Then she got chicken pox and I had to wait longer. When she finally came, I hardly knew her, walking quick and nervous like her father, looking like her father, thin, and dressed in a shoddy red that yellowed her skin and glared at the pock marks. All the baby loveliness gone.

She was two. Old enough for nursery school they said, and I did not know then what I know now—the fatigue of the long day, and the lacerations of group life in the nurseries that are only parking places for children.

Except that it would have made no difference if I had known. It was the only place there was. It was the only way we could be together, the only way I could hold a job.

And even without knowing, I knew. I knew the teacher that was evil because all these years it has curdled into my memory, the little boy hunched in the corner, her rasp, "why aren't you outside, because Alvin hits you? that's no reason, go out, scaredy." I knew Emily hated it even if she did not clutch and implore "don't go Mommy" like the other children, mornings.

She always had a reason why we should stay home. Momma, you look sick, Momma. I feel sick. Momma, the teachers aren't there today, they're sick. Momma, we can't go, there was a fire there last night. Momma, it's a holiday today, no school, they told me.

But never a direct protest, never rebellion. I think of our others in their three-, four-year-oldness—the explosions, the tempers, the denunciations, the demands—and I feel suddenly ill. I put the iron down. What in me demanded that goodness in her? And what was the cost, the cost to her of such goodness?

The old man living in the back once said in his gentle way: "You should smile at Emily more when you look at her." What *was* in my face when I looked at her? I loved her. There were all the acts of love.

It was only with the others I remembered what he said, and it was the face of joy, and not of care or tightness or worry I turned to them—too late for Emily. She does not smile easily, let alone almost always as her brothers and sisters do. Her face is closed and somber, but when she wants, how fluid. You must have seen it in her pantomimes, you spoke of her rare gift for comedy on the stage that rouses a laughter out of the audience so dear they applaud and applaud and do not want to let her go.

Where does it come from, that comedy? There was none of it in her when she came back to me that second time, after I had had to send her away again. She had a new daddy now to learn to love, and I think perhaps it was a better time. Except when we left her alone nights, telling ourselves she was old enough.

"Can't you go some other time, Mommy, like tomorrow?" she would ask. "Will it be just a little while you'll be gone? Do you promise?"

The time we came back, the front door open, the clock on the floor in the hall. She rigid awake. "It wasn't just a little while. I didn't cry. Three times I called you, just three times, and then I ran downstairs to open the door so you could come faster. The clock talked loud. I threw it away, it scared me what it talked."

She said the clock talked loud again that night I went to the hospital to have Susan. She was delirious with the fever that comes before red measles, but she was fully conscious all the week I was gone and the week after we were home when she could not come near the new baby or me.

She did not get well. She stayed skeleton thin, not wanting to eat, and night after night she had nightmares. She would call for me, and I would rouse from exhaustion to sleepily call back: "You're all right, darling, go to sleep, it's just a dream," and if she still called, in a sterner voice, "now go to sleep, Emily, there's nothing to hurt you." Twice, only twice, when I had to get up for Susan anyhow, I went in to sit with her.

Now when it is too late (as if she would let me hold and comfort her like I do the others) I get up and go to her at once at her moan or restless stirring. "Are you awake, Emily? Can I get you something, dear?" And the answer is always the same: "No, I'm all right, go back to sleep, Mother."

They persuaded me at the clinic to send her away to a convalescent home in the country where "she can have the kind of food and care you can't manage for her, and you'll be free to concentrate on the new baby." They still send children to that place. I see pictures on the society page of sleek young women planning affairs to raise money for it, or dancing at the affairs, or decorating Easter eggs or filling Christmas stockings for the children.

They never have a picture of the children so I do not know if the girls still wear those gigantic red bows and the ravaged looks on the every other Sunday when parents can come to visit "unless otherwise notified"—as we were notified the first six weeks.

Oh it is a handsome place, green lawns and tall trees and fluted flower beds. High up on the balconies of each cottage the children stand, the girls in their red bows and white dresses, the boys in white suits and giant red ties. The parents stand below shrieking up to be heard and the children shriek down to be heard, and between them the invisible wall "Not To Be Contaminated by Parental Germs or Physical Affection."

There was a tiny girl who always stood hand in hand with Emily. Her parents never came. One visit she was gone. "They moved her to Rose Cottage," Emily shouted in explanation. "They don't like you to love anybody here."

She wrote once a week, the labored writing of a seven-year-old. "I am fine. How is the baby. If I write my leter nicly I will have a star. Love." There never was a star. We wrote every other day, letters she could never hold or keep but only hear read—once. "We simply do not have room for children to keep any personal possessions," they patiently explained when we pieced one Sunday's shrieking together to plead how much it would mean to Emily, who loved so to keep things, to be allowed to keep her letters and cards.

Each visit she looked frailer. "She isn't eating," they told us.

(They had runny eggs for breakfast or mush with lumps, Emily said later, I'd hold it in my mouth and not swallow. Nothing ever tasted good, just when they had chicken.)

It took us eight months to get her released home, and only the fact that she gained back so little of her seven lost pounds convinced the social worker.

I used to try to hold and love her after she came back, but her body would stay stiff, and after a while she'd push away. She ate little. Food sickened her, and I think much of life too. Oh she had physical lightness and brightness, twinkling by on skates, bouncing like a ball up and down up and

ADULTHOOD, Women and Family

down over the jump rope, skimming over the hill; but these were momentary.

She fretted about her appearance, thin and dark and foreign-looking at a time when every little girl was supposed to look or thought she should look a chubby blonde replica of Shirley Temple. The door-bell sometimes rang for her, but no one seemed to come and play in the house or be a best friend. Maybe because we moved so much.

There was a boy she loved painfully through two school semesters. Months later she told me how she had taken pennies from my purse to buy him candy. "Licorice was his favorite and I brought him some every day, but he still liked Jennifer better'n me. Why, Mommy?" The kind of question for which there is no answer.

School was a worry to her. She was not glib or quick in a world where glibness and quickness were easily confused with ability to learn. To her overworked and exasperated teachers she was an overconscientious "slow learner" who kept trying to catch up and was absent entirely too often.

I let her be absent, though sometimes the illness was imaginary. How different from my now-strictness about attendance with the others. I wasn't working. We had a new baby, I was home anyhow. Sometimes, after Susan grew old enough, I would keep her home from school, too, to have them all together.

Mostly Emily had asthma, and her breathing, harsh and labored, would fill the house with a curiously tranquil sound. I would bring the two old dresser mirrors and her boxes of collections to her bed. She would select beads and single ear-rings, bottle tops and shells, dried flowers and pebbles, old postcards and scraps, all sorts of oddments; then she and Susan would play Kingdom, setting up landscapes and furniture, peopling them with action.

Those were the only times of peaceful companionship between her and Susan. I have edged away from it, that poisonous feeling between them, that terrible balancing of hurts and needs I had to do between the two, and did so badly, those earlier years.

Oh there are conflicts between the others too, each one human, needing, demanding, hurting, taking—but only between Emily and Susan, no Emily toward Susan that corroding resentment. It seems so obvious on the surface, yet it is not obvious. Susan, the second child, Susan, golden- and curly-haired and chubby, quick and articulate and assured, everything in appearance and manner Emily was not; Susan, not able to resist Emily's precious things, losing or sometimes clumsily breaking them; Susan telling jokes and riddles to company for applause while Emily sat silent (to say to me later: that was *my* riddle, Mother, I told it to Susan); Susan, who for all the five years' difference in age was just a year behind Emily in developing physically.

I am glad for that slow physical development that widened the difference between her and her contemporaries, though she suffered over it. She was too vulnerable for that terrible world of youthful competition, of preening and parading, of constant measuring of yourself against every other, of envy, "If I had that copper hair," or "If I had that skin. . . ." She tormented herself enough about not looking like the others, there was enough of the unsureness, the having to be conscious of words before you speak, the constant caring—what are they thinking of me? What kind of an impression am I making?—there was enough without having it all magnified by the merciless physical drives.

Ronnie is calling. He is wet and I change him. It is rare there is such a cry now. That time of motherhood is almost behind me when the ear is not one's own but must always be racked and listening for the child cry, the child call. We sit for a while and I hold him, looking out over the city spread in charcoal with its soft aisles of light. "*Shoogily,*" he breathes and curls closer. I carry him back to bed, asleep. *Shoogily.* A funny word, a family word, inherited from Emily, invented by her to say: *comfort.*

In this and other ways she leaves her seal, I say aloud. And startle at my saying it. What do I mean? What did I start to gather together, to try and make coherent? I was at the terrible, growing years. War years. I do not remember them well. I was working, there were four smaller ones now, there was not time for her. She had to help be a mother, and housekeeper, and shopper. She had to set her seal. Mornings of crisis and near hysteria trying to get lunches packed, hair combed, coats and shoes found, everyone to school or Child Care on time, the baby ready for transportation. And always the paper scribbled on by a smaller one, the book looked at by Susan then mislaid, the homework not done. Running out to that huge school where she was one, she was lost, she was a drop; suffering over the unpreparedness, stammering and unsure in her classes.

There was so little time left at night after the kids were bedded down. She would struggle over books, always eating (it was in those years she developed her enormous appetite that is legendary in our family) and I would be ironing, or preparing food for the next day, or writing V-mail to Bill, or tending the baby. Sometimes, to make me laugh, or out of her despair, she would imitate happenings or types at school.

I think I said once: "Why don't you do something like this in the school amateur show?" One morning she phoned me at work, hardly understandable through the weeping: "Mother, I did it. I won, I won; they gave me first prize; they clapped and clapped and wouldn't let me go."

Now suddenly she was Somebody, and as imprisoned in her difference as she had been in anonymity.

She began to be asked to perform at other high schools, even in colleges, then at city and state-wide affairs. The first one we went to, I only recognized her that first moment when thin, shy, she almost drowned herself into the curtains. Then: Was this Emily? The control, the command, the convulsing and deadly clowning, the spell, then the roaring, stamping audience, unwilling to let this rare and precious laughter out of their lives.

Afterwards: You ought to do something about her with a gift like that—but without money or knowing how, what does one do? We have left it all to her, and the gift has as often eddied inside, clogged and clotted, as been used and growing.

She is coming. She runs up the stairs two at a time with her light graceful step, and I know she is happy tonight. Whatever it was that occasioned your call did not happen today.

"Aren't you ever going to finish the ironing, Mother? Whistler painted his mother in a rocker. I'd have to paint mine standing over an ironing-board." This is one of her communicative nights and she tells me everything and nothing as she fixes herself a plate of food out of the icebox.

She is so lovely. Why did you want me to come in at all? Why were you concerned? She will find her way.

She starts up the stairs to bed. "Don't get me up with the rest in the morning." "But I thought you were having midterms." "Oh, those," she comes back in, kisses me, and says quite lightly, "in a couple of years when we'll all be atom-dead they won't matter a bit."

She has said it before. She *believes* it. But because I have been dredging the past, and all that compounds a human being is so heavy and meaningful in me, I cannot endure it tonight.

I will never total it all. I will never come in to say: She was a child seldom smiled at. Her father left me before she was a year old. I had to work her first six years when there was work, or I sent her home and to his relatives. There were years she had care she hated. She was dark and thin and foreign-looking in a world where the prestige went to blondness and curly hair and dimples, she was slow where glibness was prized. She was a child of anxious, not proud, love. We were poor and could not afford for her the soil of easy growth. I was a young mother, I was a distracted mother. There were the other children pushing up, demanding. Her younger sister seemed all that she was not. There were years she did not want me to touch her. She kept too much in herself, her life was such she had to keep too much in herself. My wisdom came too late. She has much to her and probably little will come of it. She is a child of her age, of depression, of war, of fear.

Let her be. So all that is in her will not bloom—but in how many does it? There is still enough left to live by. Only help her to know—help make it so there is cause for her to know that she is more than this dress on the ironing-board, helpless before the iron.

[1953/1955]

For Discussion

1. Examine the recurrent theme of regrets: what does the mother regret, if she loved Emily all along?

2. Describe Emily's progress from an infant, to a child, to the age of nineteen. How is she the same or different from her mother at nineteen?

3. Analyze the role of work, from the title to the first and last lines of the story. Did work hold the family together or keep them apart?

4. What do we know of Emily's father and the narrator's second husband? What is the role of the men as workers, husbands, and fathers in the story?

5. Suggest why Emily might have become a comedian, why she collects things as a hobby, and why she becomes a big eater like the rest of the family members.

6. What role do society and social institutions play in Emily's life? (Consider the school, social worker, convalescent home, etc.). What effects do each of these entities have on Emily as part of a family?

7. How could you defend or condemn the mother in this narrative? What might Emily herself say, and what does she mean by the comment about the end of the world?

8. Explain the mother's message at the end of the story, and its relationships to the dominant themes throughout.

For Further Exploration

1. Examine the bond between mothers and their daughters, as represented in the other stories and poems in this section and others. How do these bonds compare with those between fathers and daughters? Is there any evidence to suggest that parental sex differentiations are natural or stereotyped, innate or learned?

2. Read other exchanges between mothers and adult daughters, such as the interaction between Lesje and her mother in Margaret Atwood's novel *Life Before Man,* and Janet's discussion with her mother in Margaret Drabble's *The Realms of Gold.* How do the accounts change focus depending on whether the story is told from the mother's, or the daughter's, point of view?

Shirley Faessler
1921–

Matriarchal families are often disguised as strong patriarchies, as in this story of loving parents and children for whom real communication goes on underneath the words. As is often true in life, in "A Basket of Apples" tragedy brings family members together.

A BASKET OF APPLES

This morning Pa had his operation. He said I was not to come for at least two or three days, but I slipped in anyway and took a look at him. He was asleep, and I was there only a minute before I was hustled out by a nurse.

'He looks terrible, nurse. Is he all right?'

She said he was fine. The operation was successful, there were no secondaries, instead of a bowel he would have a colostomy, and with care should last another—

Colostomy. The word had set up such a drumming in my ears that I can't be sure now whether she said another few years or another five years. Let's say she said five years. If I go home and report this to Ma she'll fall down in a dead faint. She doesn't even know he's had an operation. She thinks he's in the hospital for a rest, a check-up. Nor did we know—my brother, my sister, and I—that he'd been having a series of x-rays.

'It looks like an obstruction in the lower bowel,' he told us privately. 'and I'll have to go in the hospital for a few days to find out what it's all about. Don't say anything to Ma.'

'I have to go in the hospital,' he announced to Ma the morning he was going in.

She screamed.

'Just for a little rest, a check-up,' he went on, patient with her for once.

He's always hollering at her. He scolds her for a meal that isn't to his taste, finds fault with her housekeeping, gives her hell because her hair isn't combed in the morning and sends her back to the bedroom to tidy herself.

But Ma loves the old man. 'Sooner a harsh word from Pa than a kind one from anyone else,' she says.

'You're not to come and see me, you hear?' he cautioned her the morning he left for the hospital. 'I'll phone you when I'm coming out.'

I don't want to make out that my pa's a beast. He's not. True, he never speaks an endearing word to her, never praises her. He loses patience with her, flies off the handle and shouts. But Ma's content. Poor man works like a horse, she says, and what pleasures does he have. 'So he hollers at me once in a while, I don't mind. God give him the strength to keep hollering at me, I won't repine.'

Night after night he joins his buddies in the back room of an ice-cream parlour on Augusta Avenue for a glass of wine, a game of klaberjass, pinochle, dominoes: she's happy he's enjoying himself. She blesses him on his way out. 'God keep you in good health and return you in good health.'

But when he is home of an evening reading the newspaper and comes across an item that engages his interest, he lets her in on it too. He shows her a picture of the Dionne quintuplets and explains exactly what happened out there in Callander, Ontario. This is a golden moment for her—she and Pa sitting over a newspaper discussing world events. Another time he shows her a picture of the Irish Sweepstakes winner. He won a hundred and fifty thousand, he tells her. She's entranced. *Mmm-mm-mm!* What she couldn't do with that money. They'd fix up the bathroom, paint the kitchen, clean out the backyard. *Mmm-mm-mm!* Pa says if we had that kind of money we could afford to put a match to a hundred-dollar bill, set fire to the house and buy a new one. She laughs at his wit. He's so clever, Pa. Christmas morning King George VI is speaking on the radio. She's rattling around in the kitchen, Pa calls her to come and hear the King of England. She doesn't understand a word of English, but pulls up a chair and sits listening. 'He stutters,' says Pa. This she won't believe. A king? Stutters? But if Pa says so it must be true. She bends an ear to the radio. Next day she has something to report to Mrs. Oxenberg, our next-door neighbour.

I speak of Pa's impatience with her; I get impatient with her too. I'm always at her about one thing and another, chiefly about the weight she's putting on. Why doesn't she cut down on the bread, does she have to drink twenty glasses of tea a day? No wonder her feet are sore, carrying all that weight. (My ma's a short woman a little over five feet and weighs almost two hundred pounds.) 'Go ahead, keep getting fatter,' I tell her. 'The way you're going you'll never be able to get into a decent dress again.'

But it's Pa who finds a dress to fit her, a Martha Washington Cotton size 52, which but for the length is perfect for her. He finds a shoe she can wear, Romeo Slippers with elasticized sides. And it's Pa who gets her to soak her feet, then sits with them in his lap scraping away with a razor blade at the calluses and corns.

Ma is my father's second wife, and our stepmother. My father, now sixty-three, was widowed thirty years ago. My sister was six at the time, I was five, and my brother four when our mother died giving birth to a fourth child who lived only a few days. We were shunted around from one family to another who took us in out of compassion, till finally my father went to a marriage broker and put his case before him. He wanted a woman to make a home for his three orphans. An honest woman with a good heart, these were the two and only requirements. The marriage broker consulted his lists and said he thought he had two or three people who might fill the bill. Specifically, he had in mind a young woman from Russia, thirty years old, who was working without pay for relatives who had brought her over. She wasn't exactly an educated woman; in fact, she couldn't even read or write. As for honesty and heart, this he could vouch for. She was an orphan herself and as a child had been brought up in servitude.

Of the three women the marriage broker trotted out for him, my father chose Ma, and shortly afterward they were married.

A colostomy. So it is cancer. . . .

As of the second day Pa was in hospital I had taken to dropping in on him on my way home from work. 'Nothing yet,' he kept saying, 'maybe tomorrow they'll find out.'

After each of these visits, four in all, I reported to Ma that I had seen Pa. 'He looks fine. Best thing in the world for him, a rest in the hospital.'

'Pa's not lonesome for me?' she asked me once, and laughing, turned her head aside to hide her foolishness from me.

Yesterday Pa said to me, 'It looks a little more serious than I thought. I have to have an operation tomorrow. Don't say anything to Ma. And don't come here for at least two or three days.'

I take my time getting home. I'm not too anxious to face Ma—grinning like a monkey and lying to her the way I have been doing the last four days. I step into a hospital telephone booth to call my married sister. She moans. 'What are you going to say to Ma?' she asks.

I get home about half past six, and Ma's in the kitchen making a special treat for supper. A recipe given her by a neighbour and which she's recently put in her culinary inventory—pieces of cauliflower dipped in batter and fried in butter.

'I'm not hungry, Ma. I had something in the hospital cafeteria.' (We speak in Yiddish; as I mentioned before, Ma can't speak English.)

She continues scraping away at the cauliflower stuck to the bottom of the pan. (Anything she puts in a pan sticks.) 'You saw Pa?' she asks without looking up. Suddenly she thrusts the pan aside. 'The devil take it, I put in too much flour.' She makes a pot of tea, and we sit at the kitchen table drinking it. To keep from facing her I drink mine leafing through a magazine. I can hear her sipping hers through a cube of sugar in her mouth. I can feel her eyes on me. Why doesn't she ask me, How's Pa? Why doesn't she speak? She never stops questioning me when I come from hospital, drives me crazy with the same questions again and again. I keep turning pages, she's still sucking away at that cube of sugar—a maddening habit of hers. I look up. Of course her eyes are fixed on me, probing, searching.

I lash out at her. 'Why are you looking at me like that!'

Without answer she takes her tea and dashes it in the sink. She spits the cube of sugar from her mouth. (Thank God for that; she generally puts it back in the sugar bowl.) She resumes her place, puts her hands in her lap, and starts twirling her thumbs. No one in the world can twirl his thumbs as fast as Ma. When she gets them going they look like miniature windmills whirring around.

'She asks me why I'm looking at her like that,' she says, addressing herself to the twirling thumbs in her lap. 'I'm looking at her like that because I'm trying to read the expression in her face. She tells me Pa's fine, but my heart tells me different.'

Suddenly she looks up, and thrusting her head forward, splays her hands out flat on the table. She has a dark-complexioned strong face, masculine almost, and eyes so black the pupil is indistinguishable from the iris.

'Do you know who Pa is!' she says. 'Do you know who's lying in the hospital? I'll tell you who. The captain of our ship is lying in the hospital. The emperor of our domain. If the captain goes down, the ship goes with him. If the emperor leaves his throne, we can say good-bye to our domain. That's who's lying in the hospital. Now ask me why do I look at you like that.'

She breaks my heart. I want to put my arms around her, but I can't do it. We're not a demonstrative family, we never kiss, we seldom show affection. We're always hollering at each other. Less than a month ago I hollered at Pa. He had taken to dosing himself. He was forever mixing something in a glass, and I became irritated at the powders, pills, and potions lying around in every corner of the house like mouse droppings.

'You're getting to be a hypochondriac!' I hollered at him, not knowing what trouble he was in.

I reach out and put my hand over hers. 'I wouldn't lie to you, Ma. Pa's fine, honest to God.'

She holds her hand still a few seconds, then eases it from under and puts it over mine. I can feel the weight of her hand pinioning mine to the table, and in an unaccustomed gesture of tenderness we sit a moment with locked hands.

'You know I had a dream about Pa last night?' she says. 'I dreamt he came home with a basket of apples. I think that's a good dream?'

Ma's immigration to Canada had been sponsored by her Uncle Yankev. Yankev at the time he sent for his niece was in his mid-forties and had been settled a number of years in Toronto with his wife, Danyeh, and their six children. They made an odd pair, Yankev and Danyeh. He was a tall two-hundred-and-fifty-pound handsome man, and Danyeh, whom he detested, was a lackluster little woman with a pockmarked face, maybe weighing ninety pounds. Yankev was constantly abusing her. Old Devil, he called her to her face and in the presence of company.

Ma stayed three years with Yankev and his family, working like a skivvy for them and without pay. Why would Yankev pay his niece like a common servant? She was one of the family, she sat at table with them and ate as much as she wanted. She had a bed and even a room to herself, which she'd never had before. When Yankev took his family for a ride in the car to Sunnyside, she was included. When he bought ice-cream cones, he bought for all.

She came to Pa without a dime in her pocket.

Ma has a slew of relatives, most of them émigrés from a remote little village somewhere in the depths of Russia. They're a crude lot, loudmouthed and coarse, and my father (but for a few exceptions) had no use for any of them. The Russian Hordes, he called them. He was never rude; any time they came around to visit he simply made himself scarce.

One night I remember in particular; I must have been about seven. Ma was washing up after supper and Pa was reading a newspaper when Yankev arrived, with Danyeh trailing him. Pa folded his paper, excused himself, and was gone. The minute Pa was gone Yankev went to the stove and lifted the lids from the two pots. Just as he thought—*mamaliga* in one pot, in the other one beans, and in the frying pan a piece of meat their cat would turn its nose up at. He sat himself in the rocking chair he had given Ma as a wedding present, and rocking, proceeded to lecture her. He had warned her against the marriage, but if she was satisfied, he was content. One question and that's all. How had she bettered her lot? True, she was no longer an old maid. True, she was now mistress of her own home. He looked around him and snorted. A hovel. '*And* three snot-nose kids,' he said, pointing to us.

Danyeh, hunched over in a kitchen chair, her feet barely reaching the floor, said something to him in Russian, cautioning him, I think. He told her to shut up, and in Yiddish continued his tirade against Ma. He had one word to say to her. To *watch* herself. Against his advice she had married this no-good Rumanian twister, this murderer. The story of how he had kept his first wife pregnant all the time was now well known. Also well known was the story of how she had died in her ninth month with a fourth child. Over an ironing board. Ironing his shirts while he was out playing cards with his Rumanian cronies and drinking wine. He had buried one wife, and now was after burying a second. So Ma had better *watch* herself, that's all.

Ma left her dishwashing and with dripping wet hands took hold of a chair and seated herself facing Yankev. She begged him not to say another word. 'Not another word, Uncle Yankev, I beg you. Till the day I die I'll be grateful to you for bringing me over. I don't know how much money you laid out for my passage, but I tried my best to make up for it the three years I stayed with you, by helping out in the house. But maybe I'm still in your debt? Is this what gives you the right to talk against my husband?'

Yankev, rocking, turned up his eyes and groaned. '*You* speak to her,' he said to Danyeh. 'It's impossible for a *human being* to get through to her.'

Danyeh knew better than to open her mouth.

'Uncle Yankev,' Ma continued, 'every word you speak against my husband is like a knife stab in my heart.' She leaned forward, thumbs whirring away. '*Mamaliga?* Beans? A piece of meat your cat wouldn't eat? A crust of *bread* at his board, and I will still thank God every day of my life that he chose me from the other two the *shadchan* showed him.'

In the beginning my father gave her a hard time. I remember his bursts of temper at her rough ways in the kitchen. She never opened a kitchen drawer without wrestling it—wrenching it open, slamming it shut. She never put a kettle on the stove without its running over at the boil. A pot never came to stove without its lid being inverted, and this for some reason maddened him. He'd right the lid, sometimes scalding his fingers—and all hell would break loose. We never sat down to a set or laid table. As she had been used to doing, so she continued; slamming a pot down on the table, scattering a handful of cutlery, dealing out assorted-size plates. More than once, with one swipe of his hand my father would send a few plates crashing to the floor, and stalk out. She'd sit a minute looking in our faces, one by one, then start twirling her thumbs and talking to herself. What had she done now?

'Eat!' she'd admonish us, and leaving table would go to the mirror over the kitchen sink and ask herself face to face, 'What did I do now?' She would examine her face profile and front and then sit down to eat. After, she'd gather up the dishes, dump them in the sink, and running the water over them, would study herself in the mirror. 'He'll be better,' she'd tell herself, smiling. 'He'll be soft as butter when he comes home. You'll see,' she'd promise her image in the mirror.

Later in life, mellowed by the years perhaps (or just plain defeated—there was no changing her), he became more tolerant of her ways and was kinder to her. When it became difficult for her to get around because of her poor feet, he did her marketing. He attended to her feet, bought her the Martha Washingtons, the Romeo Slippers, and on a summer's evening on his way home from work, a brick of ice cream. She was very fond of it.

Three years ago he began promoting a plan, a plan to give Ma some pleasure. (This was during Exhibition time.) 'You know,' he said to me, 'it would be very nice if Ma could see the fireworks at the Exhibition. She's never seen anything like that in her life. Why don't you take her?'

The idea of Ma going to the Ex for the fireworks was so preposterous, it made me laugh. She never went anywhere.

'Don't laugh,' he said. 'It wouldn't hurt you to give her a little pleasure once in a while.'

He was quite keen that she should go, and the following year he canvassed the idea again. He put money on the table for taxi and grandstand seats. 'Take her,' he said.

'Why don't you take her?' I said. 'She'll enjoy it more going with you.'

'Me? What will I do at the Exhibition?'

As children, we were terrified of Pa's temper. Once in a while he'd belt us around, and we were scared that he might take the strap to Ma too. But before long we came to know that she was the only one of us not scared of Pa, when he got mad. Not even from the beginning when he used to let fly at her was she intimidated by him, not in the least, and in later years was even capable of getting her own back by taking a little dig at him now and then about the 'aristocracy'—as she called my father's Rumanian connections.

Aside from his buddies in the back room of the ice-cream parlour on Augusta Avenue, my father also kept in touch with his Rumanian compatriots (all of whom had prospered), and would once in a while go to them for an evening. We were never invited, nor did they come to us. This may have been my father's doing, I don't know. I expect he was ashamed of his circumstances, possibly of Ma, and certainly of how we lived.

Once in a blue moon during Rosh Hashanah or Yom Kippur after shul, they would unexpectedly drop in on us. One time a group of four came to the house, and I remember Pa darting around like a gadfly, collecting glasses, wiping them, and pouring a glass of wine he'd made himself. Ma shook hands all around, then went to the kitchen to cut some slices of her honey cake, scraping off the burnt part. I was summoned to take the plate in to 'Pa's gentlefolk'. Pretending to be busy, she rattled around the kitchen a few seconds, then seated herself in the partially open door, inspecting them. Not till they were leaving did she come out again, to wish them a good year.

The minute they were gone, my father turned to her. 'Russian peasant! Tartar savage, you! Sitting there with your eyes popping out. Do you think they couldn't see you?'

'What's the matter? Even a cat may look at a king?' she said blandly.

'Why didn't you come out instead of sitting there like a caged animal?'

'Because I didn't want to shame you,' she said, twirling her thumbs and swaying back and forth in the chair Yankev had given her as a wedding present.

My father busied himself clearing table, and after a while he softened. But she wasn't through yet. 'Which one was Falik's wife?' she asked in seeming innocence. 'The one with the beard?'

This drew his fire again. 'No!' he shouted.

'Oh, the other one. The pale one with the hump on her back,' she said wickedly.

So . . . notwithstanding the good dream Ma had of Pa coming home with a basket of apples, she never saw him again. He died six days after the operation.

It was a harrowing six days, dreadful. As Pa got weaker, the more disputatious we became—my brother, my sister, and I—arguing and snapping at each other outside his door, the point of contention being should Ma be told or not.

Nurse Brown, the special we'd put on duty, came out once to hush us. 'You're not helping him by arguing like this. He can hear you.'

'Is he conscious, nurse?'

'Of course he's conscious.'

'Is there any hope?'

'There's always hope,' she said. 'I've been on cases like this before, and I've seen them rally.'

We went our separate ways, clinging to the thread of hope she'd given us. The fifth day after the operation I had a call from Nurse Brown: 'Your father wants to see you.'

Nurse Brown left the room when I arrived, and my father motioned me to undo the zipper of his oxygen tent. 'Ma's a good woman,' he said, his voice so weak I had to lean close to hear him. 'You'll look after her? Don't put her aside. Don't forget about her—'

'What are you talking about!' I said shrilly, then lowered my voice to a whisper. 'The doctor told me you're getting better. Honest to God, Pa, I wouldn't lie to you,' I whispered.

He went on as if I hadn't spoken. 'Even a servant if you had her for thirty years, you wouldn't put aside because you don't need her any more—'

'Wait a minute,' I said, and went to the corridor to fetch Nurse Brown. 'Nurse Brown, will you tell my father what you told me yesterday. You remember? About being on cases like this before, and you've seen them rally. Will you tell that to my father, please. He talks as if he's—'

I ran from the room and stood outside the door, bawling. Nurse Brown opened the door a crack. 'Ssh! You'd better go now; I'll call you if there's any change.'

At five the next morning, my brother telephoned from hospital. Ma was sound asleep and didn't hear. 'You'd better get down here,' he said. 'I think the old man's checking out. I've already phoned Gertie.'

My sister and I arrived at the hospital within seconds of each other. My brother was just emerging from Pa's room. In the gesture of a baseball umpire he jerked a thumb over his shoulder, signifying OUT.

'Is he dead?' we asked our brother.

'Just this minute,' he replied.

Like three dummies we paced the dimly lit corridor, not speaking to each other. In the end we were obliged to speak; we had to come to a decision about how to proceed next.

We taxied to the synagogue of which Pa was a member, and roused the shamus. 'As soon as it's light I'll get the rabbi,' he said. 'He'll attend to everything. Meantime go home.'

In silence we walked slowly home. Dawn was just breaking, and Ma, a habitually early riser, was bound to be up now and in the kitchen. Quietly we let ourselves in and passed through the hall leading to the kitchen. We were granted an unexpected respite; Ma was not up yet. We waited ten minutes for her, fifteen—an agonizing wait. We decided one of us had better go and wake her; what was the sense of prolonging it? The next minute we changed our minds. To awaken her with such tidings would be inhuman, a brutal thing to do.

'Let's stop whispering,' my sister whispered. 'Let's talk in normal tones, do something, make a noise, she'll hear us and come out.'

In an access of activity we busied ourselves. My sister put the kettle on with a clatter; I took teaspoons from the drawer, clacking them like castanets. She was bound to hear, their bedroom was on the same floor at the front of the house—but five minutes elapsed and not a sound from the room.

'Go and see,' my sister said, and I went and opened the door to that untidy bedroom Pa used to rail against.

Ma, her black eyes circled and her hair in disarray, was sitting up in bed. At sight of me she flopped back and pulled the feather tick over her head. I approached the bed and took the covers from her face. 'Ma—'

She sat up. 'You are guests in my house now?'

For the moment I didn't understand. I didn't know the meaning of her words. But the next minute the meaning of them was clear—with Pa dead, the link was broken. The bond, the tie that held us together. We were no longer her children. We were now guests in her house.

'When did Pa die?' she asked.

'How did you know?'

'My heart told me.'

Barefooted, she followed me to the kitchen. My sister gave her a glass of tea, and we stood like mutes, watching her sipping it through a cube of sugar.

'You were all there when Pa died?'

'Just me, Ma,' my brother said.

She nodded. 'His kaddish. Good.'

I took a chair beside her, and for once without constraint or self-consciousness, put my arm around her and kissed her on the cheek.

'Ma, the last words Pa spoke were about you. He said you were a good woman. "Ma's a good woman," that's what he said to me.'

She put her tea down and looked me in the face.

'Pa said that? He said I was a good woman?' She clasped her hands. 'May the light shine on him in paradise,' she said, and wept silently, putting her head down to hide her tears.

Eight o'clock the rabbi telephoned. Pa was now at the funeral parlour on College near Augusta, and the funeral was to be at eleven o'clock. Ma went to ready herself, and in a few minutes called me to come and zip up her black crepe, the dress Pa had bought her six years ago for the Applebaum wedding.

The Applebaums, neighbours, had invited Ma and Pa to the wedding of their daughter, Lily. Right away Pa had declared he wouldn't go. Ma kept coaxing. How would it look? It would be construed as unfriendly, unneighbourly. A few days before the wedding he gave in, and Ma began scratching through her wardrobe for something suitable to wear. Nothing she exhibited pleased him. He went downtown and came back with the black crepe and an outsize corset.

I dressed her for the wedding, combed her hair, and put some powder on her face. Pa became impatient; he had already called a cab. What was I doing? Getting her ready for a beauty contest? The taxi came, and as Pa held her coat he said to me in English, 'You know, Ma's not a bad-looking woman?'

For weeks she talked about the good time she'd had at the Applebaum wedding, but chiefly about how Pa had attended her. Not for a minute had he left her side. Two hundred people at the wedding and not one woman among them had the attention from her husband that she had had from Pa. 'Pa's a gentleman,' she said to me, proud as proud.

Word of Pa's death got around quickly, and by nine in the morning people began trickling in. First arrivals were Yankev and Danyeh. Yankev, now in his seventies and white-haired, was still straight and handsome. The same Yankev except for the white hair and an asthmatic condition causing him to wheeze and gasp for breath. Danyeh was wizened and bent over, her hands hanging almost to her knees. They approached Ma, Danyeh trailing Yankev. Yankev held out a hand and with the other one thumped his chest, signifying he was too congested to speak. Danyeh gave her bony hand to Ma and muttered a condolence.

From then on there was a steady influx of people. Here was Chaim the schnorrer! We hadn't seen him in years. Chaim the schnorrer, stinking of fish and in leg wrappings as always, instead of socks. Rich as Croesus he was said to be, a fish-peddling miser who lived on soda crackers and milk and kept his money in his leg wrappings. Yankev, a minute ago too congested for speech, found words for Chaim. 'How much money have you got in those *gutkess*? The truth, Chaim!'

Ma shook hands with all, acknowledged their sympathy, and to some

ADULTHOOD, *Women and Family*

she spoke a few words. I observed the Widow Spector, a gossip and trouble-maker, sidling through the crowd and easing her way toward Ma. 'The Post' she was called by people on the street. No one had the time of day for her; even Ma used to hide from her.

I groaned at the sight of her. As if Ma didn't have enough to contend with. But no! here was Ma welcoming the Widow Spector, holding a hand out to her. 'Give me your hand, Mrs. Spector. Shake hands, we're partners now. Now I know the taste, I'm a widow too.' Ma patted the chair beside her. 'Sit down, partner. Sit down.'

At a quarter to eleven the house was clear of people. 'Is is time?' Ma asked, and we answered, Yes, it was time to go. We were afraid this would be the breaking point for her, but she went calmly to the bedroom and took her coat from the peg on the door and came to the kitchen with it, requesting that it be brushed off.

The small funeral parlour was jammed to the doors, every seat taken but for four left vacant for us. On a trestle table directly in front of our seating was the coffin. A pine box draped in a black cloth, and in its center a white Star of David.

Ma left her place, approached the coffin, and as she stood before it with clasped hands I noticed the uneven hemline of her coat, hiked up in back by that mound of flesh on her shoulders. I observed that her lisle stockings were twisted at the ankles, and was embarrassed for her. She stood silently a moment, then began to speak. She called him her dove, her comrade, her friend.

'Life is a dream,' she said. 'You were my treasure. You were the light of my eyes. I thought to live my days out with you—and look what it has come to.' (She swayed slightly, the black shawl slipping from her head—and I observed that could have done with a brushing too.) 'If ever I offended you or caused you even a twinge of discomfort, forgive me for it. As your wife I lived like a queen. Look at me now. I'm nothing. You were my jewel, my crown. With you at its head my house was a palace. I return now to a hovel. Forgive me for everything, my dove. Forgive me.'

('Russian peasant,' Pa used to say to her in anger, 'Tartar savage.' If he could see her now as she stood before his bier mourning him. Mourning him like Hecuba mourning Priam and the fall of Troy. And I a minute ago was ashamed of her hiked-up coat, her twisted stockings and dusty shawl.)

People were weeping; Ma resumed her place dry-eyed, and the rabbi began the service.

It is now a year since Pa died, and as he had enjoined me to do, I am looking after Ma. I have not put her aside. I get cross and holler at her as I always have done, but she allows for my testiness and does not hold it against me. I'm a spinster, an old maid now approaching my thirty-seventh year, and she pities me for it. I get bored telling her again and again that Pa's last words were Ma's a good woman, and sometimes wish I'd never mentioned it. She cries a lot, and I get impatient with her tears. But I'm good to her.

This afternoon I called Moodey's, booked two seats for the grandstand, and tonight I'm taking her to the Ex and she'll see the fireworks.

[1969]

For Discussion

1. Analyze the point of view of the story: what do we learn about the daughter that we wouldn't know if the story were told from a third person or omniscient standpoint?
2. Identify the different time periods of the story. What effects do the flashbacks and time passages have on the story?
3. Explain the qualities of "patience" and "impatience" mentioned several times by the narrator.
4. How is affection shown in the story? Why does Ma put up with Pa's treatment?
5. Explain the background of Ma and Pa's marriage and family. How are the "orphan" and "servant" motifs interwoven in the lives of the various family members?
6. What impression do we get when Ma talks about the father as the "captain of our ship" and the "emperor of our domain"? Is this the author's voice?
7. Examine the interaction between mother and daughter before and after the father's death. Has anything changed?

For Further Exploration

1. Explore the idea of love as it is represented here between mother and father, children and family. Then select passages about love from popular "love psychology" books, such as Robin Norwood's *Women Who Love Too Much* or Erich Fromm's *The Art of Loving*. For what reasons might psychologists consider this family or the family in "I Stand Here Ironing" "dysfunctional," and in what sense might they praise the human interactions?
2. Compare this account of a small town Canadian family with the rural American family represented in Joan Chase's novel, *During the Reign of the Queen of Persia*. What makes a viable family, according to these works?

Gertrude Stein

1874–1946

Although the word "gay" did not have a homosexual connotation when this story was written, Gertrude Stein describes a number of lifestyle possibilities within one lifetime, and uses a dramatically different style to convey the ever-shifting quality of "family."

MISS FURR AND MISS SKEENE

Helen Furr had quite a pleasant home. Mrs. Furr was quite a pleasant woman. Mr. Furr was quite a pleasant man. Helen Furr had quite a pleasant voice quite worth cultivating. She did not mind working. She worked to cultivate her voice. She did not find it gay living in the same place where she had always been living. She went to a place where some were cultivating something, voices and other things needing cultivating. She met Georgine Skeene there who was cultivating her voice which some thought was quite a pleasant one. Helen Furr and Georgine Skeene lived together then. Georgine Skeene liked travelling. Helen Furr did not care about travelling, she liked to stay in one place and be gay there. They were together then and travelled to another place and stayed there and were gay there.

They stayed there and were gay there, not very gay there, just gay there. They were both gay there, they were regularly working there both of them cultivating their voices there, they were both gay there. Georgine Skeene was gay there and she was regular, regular in being gay, regular in not being gay, regular in being a gay one who was not being gay longer than was needed to be one being quite a gay one. They were both gay then there and both working there then.

They were in a way both gay there where there were many cultivating something. They were both regular in being gay there. Helen Furr was gay there, she was gayer and gayer there and really she was just gay there, she was gayer and gayer there, that is to say she found ways of being gay there that she was using in being gay there. She was gay there, not gayer and gayer, just gay there, that is to say she was not gayer by using the things she found there that were gay things, she was gay there.

They were quite regularly gay there, Helen Furr and Georgine Skeene, they were regularly gay there where they were gay. They were very regularly gay.

To be regularly gay was to do every day the gay thing that they did every day. To be regularly gay was to end every day at the same time after they had been regularly gay. They were regularly gay. They were gay every day. They ended every day in the same way, at the same time, and they had been every day regularly gay.

The voice Helen Furr was cultivating was quite a pleasant one. The voice Georgine Skeene was cultivating was, some said, a better one. The voice Helen Furr was cultivating she cultivated and it was quite completely a pleasant enough one then, a cultivated enough one then. The voice Georgine Skeene was cultivating she did not cultivate too much. She cultivated it quite some. She cultivated and she would sometime go on cultivating it and it was not then an unpleasant one, it would not be then an unpleasant one, it would be a quite richly cultivated one, it would be quite richly enough to be a pleasant enough one.

They were gay where there were many cultivating something. The two were gay there, were regularly gay there. Georgine Skeene would have liked to do more travelling. They did some travelling, not very much travelling, Georgine Skeene would have liked to do more travelling, Helen Furr did not care about doing travelling, she liked to stay in a place and be gay there.

They stayed in a place and were gay there, both of them stayed there, they stayed together there, they were gay there, they were regularly gay there.

They went quite often, not very often, but they did go back to where Helen Furr had a pleasant enough home and then Georgine Skeene went to a place where her brother had quite some distinction. They both went, every few years, went visiting to where Helen Furr had quite a pleasant home. Certainly Helen Furr would not find it gay to stay, she did not find it gay, she said she would not stay, she said she did not find it gay, she said she would not stay where she did not find it gay, she said she found it gay where she did stay and she did stay there where very many were cultivating something. She did stay there. She always did find it gay there.

She went to see them where she had always been living and where she did not find it gay. She had a pleasant home there, Mrs. Furr was a pleasant enough woman, Mr. Furr was a pleasant enough man, Helen told them and they were not worrying, that she did not find it gay living where she had always been living.

Georgine Skeene and Helen Furr were living where they were both cultivating their voices and they were gay there. They visited where Helen Furr had come from and then they went to where they were living where they were then regularly living.

There were some dark and heavy men there then. There were some who were not so heavy and some who were not so dark. Helen Furr and Georgine Skeene sat regularly with them. They sat regularly with the ones who were dark and heavy. They sat regularly with the ones who were not so dark. They sat regularly with the ones that were not so heavy. They sat with them regularly, sat with some of them. They went with them regularly went with them. They were regular then, they were gay then, they were where they wanted to be then where it was gay to be then, they were regularly gay then. There were men there then who were dark and heavy and they sat with them with Helen Furr and Georgine Skeene and they went with them with Miss Furr and Miss Skeene, and they went with the heavy and dark men Miss Furr and Miss Skeene went with them, and they sat with them, Miss Furr and Miss Skeene sat with them, and there were other men, some were not heavy men and they sat with Miss Furr and Miss Skeene and Miss Furr and Miss Skeene sat with them, and there were other men who were not dark men and they sat with Miss Furr and Miss Skeene and Miss Furr and Miss Skeene sat with them. Miss Furr and Miss Skeene went with them and they went with Miss Furr and Miss Skeene, some who were not heavy men, some who were not dark men. Miss Furr and Miss Skeene sat regularly, they sat with some men. Miss Furr and Miss Skeene went and there were some men with them. There were men and Miss Furr and Miss Skeene went with them, went somewhere with them, went with some of them.

Helen Furr and Georgine Skeene were regularly living where very many were living and cultivating in themselves something. Helen Furr and

Georgine Skeene were living very regularly then, being very regular then in being gay then. They did then learn many ways to be gay and they were then being gay being quite regular in being gay, being gay and they were learning little things, little things in ways of being gay, they were very regular then, they were learning very many little things in ways of being gay, they were being gay and using these little things they were learning to have to be gay with regularly gay with then and they were gay the same amount they had been gay. They were quite gay, they were quite regular, they were learning little things, gay little things, they were gay inside them the same amount they had been gay, they were gay the same length of time they had been gay every day.

They were regular in being gay, they learned little things that are things in being gay, they learned many little things that are things in being gay, they were gay every day, they were regular, they were gay, they were gay the same length of time every day, they were gay, they were quite regularly gay.

Georgine Skeene went away to stay two months with her brother. Helen Furr did not go then to stay with her father and her mother. Helen Furr stayed there where they had been regularly living the two of them and she would then certainly not be lonesome, she would go on being gay. She did go on being gay. She was not any more gay but she was gay longer every day than they had been being gay when they were together being gay. She was gay then quite exactly the same way. She learned a few more little ways of being gay. She was quite gay and in the same way, the same way she had been gay and she was gay a little longer in the day, more of each day she was gay. She was gay longer every day than when the two of them had been being gay. She was gay quite in the way they had been gay, quite in the same way.

She was not lonesome then, she was not at all feeling any need of having Georgine Skeene. She was not astonished at this thing. She would have been a little astonished by this thing but she knew she was not astonished at anything and so she was not astonished at this thing not astonished at not feeling any need of having Georgine Skeene.

Helen Furr had quite a completely pleasant voice and it was quite well enough cultivated and she could use it and she did use it but then there was not any way of working at cultivating a completely pleasant voice when it has become a quite completely well enough cultivated one, and there was not much use in using it when one was not wanting it to be helping to make one a gay one. Helen Furr was not needing using her voice to be a gay one. She was gay then and sometimes she used her voice and she was not using it very often. It was quite completely enough cultivated and it was quite completely a pleasant one and she did not use it very often. She was then, she was quite exactly as gay as she had been, she was gay a little longer in the day than she had been.

She was gay exactly the same way. She was never tired of being gay that way. She had learned very many little ways to use in being gay. Very many were telling about using other ways in being gay. She was gay enough, she was always gay exactly the same way, she was always learning little things to use in being gay, she was telling about using other ways in being gay, she was telling about learning other ways in being gay, she was learning other ways in being gay, she would be using other ways in being gay, she would always be gay in the same way, when Georgine Skeene was there not so long each day as when Georgine Skeene was away.

She came to using many ways in being gay, she came to use every way in being gay. She went on living where many were cultivating something and she was gay, she had used every way to be gay.

They did not live together then Helen Furr and Georgine Skeene. Helen Furr lived there the longer where they had been living regularly together. Then neither of them were living there any longer. Helen Furr was living somewhere else then and telling some about being gay and she was gay then and she was living quite regularly then. She was regularly gay then. She was quite regular in being gay then. She remembered all the little ways of being gay. She used all the little ways of being gay. She was quite regularly gay. She told many then the way of being gay, she taught very many then little ways they could use in being gay. She was living very well, she was gay then, she went on living then, she was regular in being gay, she always was living very well and was gay very well and was telling about little ways one could be learning to use in being gay, and later was telling them quite often, telling them again and again.

[1922]

For Discussion

1. What key words are repeated in the description of Helen Furr's parents' lives? What image of family do they represent?

2. Explain the dichotomy repeated about "staying there" versus "not staying there." If Helen Furr "did not find it gay living in the same place where she had always been living" (first paragraph), why is it that later she "liked to stay in a place and be gay there"?

3. With the help of dictionaries (preferably the *Oxford English Dictionary* (and others)), explore different possibilities for the meaning of the word "gay." What synonyms could be substituted in interpreting the story?

4. List three or four other words that are repeated and relate them to recurrent motifs in the story.

5. Divide the story into sections that show each chronological change in living arrangements. What types of people are included in each new "family"?

6. Describe the relationship between Miss Furr and Miss Skeene. Identify ways of life they share and ways in which their choices differ.

7. What does the amount of time working on cultivating one's voice have to do with the story? Why is the word "singing" avoided in favor of "using her voice"?

8. What is the last type of family Miss Furr creates? What happened to Miss Skeene?

For Further Exploration

1. Contrast this story of two women living together in a social circle that accepts their definition of family to the story of "The Two" in Gloria Naylor's *The Women of Brewster Place*, in which two lesbians living to-

gether are castigated by society. Or, compare the relationship of these women with the overt sexual relationships between women in novels such as *Rubyfruit Jungle* by Rita Mae Brown.

2. Gertrude Stein's line, "A rose is a rose is a rose" is often quoted to characterize the dramatic repetitions she uses in poetry. Analyze why Stein might use repetition of words and phrases so often in this story, and what effects the technique has on the overall tone and theme.

Charlotte Perkins Gilman

1860–1935

Marriage can turn from sweet to sour in a day, according to this story written in 1911 but still true today. How far can the legal and personal bond between a man and a woman stretch before it breaks, and what new bonds can be formed?

TURNED

In her soft-carpeted, thick-curtained, richly furnished chamber, Mrs. Marroner lay sobbing on the wide, soft bed.

She sobbed bitterly, chokingly, despairingly; her shoulders heaved and shook convulsively; her hands were tight-clenched. She had forgotten her elaborate dress, the more elaborate bedcovers; forgotten her dignity, her self-control, her pride. In her mind was an overwhelming, unbelievable horror, an immeasurable loss, a turbulent, struggling mass of emotion.

In her reserved, superior, Boston-bred life, she had never dreamed that it would be possible for her to feel so many things at once, and with such trampling intensity.

She tried to cool her feelings into thoughts; to stiffen them into words; to control herself—and could not. It brought vaguely to her mind an awful moment in the breakers at York Beach, one summer in girlhood when she had been swimming under water and could not find the top.

In her uncarpeted, thin-curtained, poorly furnished chamber on the top floor, Gerta Petersen lay sobbing on the narrow, hard bed.

She was of larger frame than her mistress, grandly built and strong; but all her proud young womanhood was prostrate now, convulsed with agony, dissolved in tears. She did not try to control herself. She wept for two.

If Mrs. Marroner suffered more from the wreck and ruin of a longer love—perhaps a deeper one; if her tastes were finer, her ideals loftier; if she bore the pangs of bitter jealousy and outraged pride, Gerta had personal shame to meet, a hopeless future, and a looming present which filled her with unreasoning terror.

She had come like a meek young goddess into that perfectly ordered house, strong, beautiful; full of goodwil and eager obedience, but ignorant and childish—a girl of eighteen.

Mr. Marroner had frankly admired her, and so had his wife. They discussed her visible perfections and as visible limitations with that perfect confidence which they had so long enjoyed. Mrs. Marroner was not a jealous woman. She had never been jealous in her life—till now.

Gerta had stayed and learned their ways. They had both been fond of her. Even the cook was fond of her. She was what is called "willing," was unusually teachable and plastic; and Mrs. Marroner, with her early habits of giving instructions, tried to educate her somewhat.

"I never saw anyone so docile," Mrs. Marroner had often commented. "It is perfection in a servant, but almost a defect in character. She is so helpless and confiding."

She was precisely that: a tall, rosy-cheeked baby; rich womanhood without, helpless infancy within. Her braided wealth of dead-gold hair, her grave blue eyes, her mighty shoulders and long, firmly moulded limbs seemed those of a primal earth spirit; but she was only an ignorant child, with a child's weakness.

When Mr. Marroner had to go abroad for his firm, unwillingly, hating to leave his wife, he had told her he felt quite safe to leave her in Gerta's hands— she would take care of her.

"Be good to your mistress, Gerta," he told the girl that last morning at breakfast. "I leave her to you to take care of. I shall be back in a month at latest."

Then he turned, smiling to his wife. "And you must take care of Gerta, too," he said, "I expect you'll have her ready for college when I get back."

This was seven months ago. Business had delayed him from week to week, from month to month. He wrote to his wife, long, loving, frequent letters, deeply regretting the delay, explaining how necessary, how profitable it was, congratulating her on the wide resources she had, her well-filled, well-balanced mind, her many interests.

"If I should be eliminated from your scheme of things, by any of those 'acts of God' mentioned on the tickets, I do not feel that you would be an utter wreck," he said. "That is very comforting to me. Your life is so rich and wide that no one loss, even a great one, would wholly cripple you. But nothing of the sort is likely to happen, and I shall be home again in three weeks—if this thing gets settled. And you will be looking so lovely, with that eager light in your eyes and the changing flush I know so well—and love so well! My dear wife! We shall have to have a new honeymoon—other moons come every month, why shouldn't the mellifluous kind?"

He often asked after "little Gerta," sometimes enclosed a picture post-card to her, joked his wife about her laborious efforts to educate "the child," was so loving and merry and wise—

All this was racing through Mrs. Marroner's mind as she lay there with the broad, hemstitched border of fine linen sheeting crushed and twisted in one hand, and the other holding a sodden handkerchief.

She had tried to teach Gerta, and had grown to love the patient, sweet-natured child, in spite of her dullness. At work with her hands, she was clever, if not quick, and could keep small accounts from week to week. But to the woman who held a Ph.D., who had been on the faculty of a college, it was like baby-tending.

Perhaps having no babies of her own made her love the big child the more, though the years between them were but fifteen.

To the girl she seemed quite old, of course; and her young heart was full of grateful affection for the patient care which made her feel so much at home in this new land.

And then she had noticed a shadow on the girl's bright face. She looked nervous, anxious, worried. When the bell rang, she seemed startled, and would rush hurriedly to the door. Her peals of frank laughter no longer rose from the area gate as she stood talking with the always admiring tradesmen.

Mrs. Marroner had labored long to teach her more reserve with men, and flattered herself that her words were at last effective. She suspected the girl of homesickness, which was denied. She suspected her of illness, which was denied also. At last she suspected her of something which could not be denied.

For a long time she refused to believe it, waiting. Then she had to believe it, but schooled herself to patience and understanding. "The poor child," she said. "She is here without a mother—she is so foolish and yielding—I must not be too stern with her." And she tried to win the girl's confidence with wise, kind words.

But Gerta had literally thrown herself at her feet and begged her with streaming tears not to turn her away. She would admit nothing, explain nothing, but frantically promised to work for Mrs. Marroner as long as she lived—if only she would keep her.

Revolving the problem carefully in her mind, Mrs. Marroner thought she would keep her, at least for the present. She tried to repress her sense of ingratitude in one she had so sincerely tried to help, and the cold, contemptuous anger she had always felt for such weakness.

"The thing to do now," she said to herself, "is to see her through this safely. The child's life should not be hurt any more than is unavoidable. I will ask Dr. Bleet about it—what a comfort a woman doctor is! I'll stand by the poor, foolish thing till it's over, and then get her back to Sweden somehow with her baby. How they do come where they are not wanted—and don't come where they are wanted!" And Mrs. Marroner, sitting alone in the quiet spacious beauty of the house, almost envied Gerta.

Then came the deluge.

She had sent the girl out for needed air toward dark. The late mail came; she took it in herself. One letter for her—her husband's letter. She knew the postmark, the stamp, the kind of typewriting. She impulsively kissed it in the dim hall. No one would suspect Mrs. Marroner of kissing her husband's letters—but she did, often.

She looked over the others. One was for Gerta, and not from Sweden. It looked precisely like her own. This struck her as a little odd, but Mr. Marroner had several times sent messages and cards to the girl. She laid the letter on the hall table and took hers to her room.

"My poor child," it began. What letter of hers had been sad enough to warrant that?

"I am deeply concerned at the news you sent." What news to so concern him had she written? "You must bear it bravely, little girl. I shall be home soon, and will take care of you, of course. I hope there is not immediate anxiety—you do not say. Here is money, in case you need it. I expect to get home in a month at latest. If you have to go, be sure to leave your address at my office. Cheer up—be brave—I will take care of you."

The letter was typewritten, which was not unusual. It was unsigned, which was unusual. It enclosed an American bill—fifty dollars. It did not seem in the least like any letter she had ever had from her husband, or any letter she could imagine him writing. But a strange, cold feeling was creeping over her, like a flood rising around a house.

She utterly refused to admit the ideas which began to bob and push about outside her mind, and to force themselves in. Yet under the pressure of these repudiated thoughts she went downstairs and brought up the other letter—the letter to Gerta. She laid them side by side on a smooth dark space on the table; marched to the piano and played, with stern precision, refusing to think, till the girl came back. When she came in, Mrs. Marroner rose quietly and came to the table. "Here is a letter for you," she said.

The girl stepped forward eagerly, saw the two lying together there, hesitated, and looked at her mistress.

"Take yours, Gerta. Open it, please."

The girl turned frightened eyes upon her.

"I want you to read it, here," said Mrs. Marroner.

"Oh, ma'am—No! Please don't make me!"

"Why not?"

There seemed to be no reason at hand, and Gerta flushed more deeply and opened her letter. It was long; it was evidently puzzling to her; it began "My dear wife." She read it slowly.

"Are you sure it is your letter?" asked Mrs. Marroner. "Is not this one yours? Is not that one—mine?"

She held out the other letter to her.

"It is a mistake," Mrs. Marroner went on, with a hard quietness. She had lost her social bearings somehow, lost her usual keen sense of the proper thing to do. This was not life; this was a nightmare.

"Do you not see? Your letter was put in my envelope and my letter was put in your envelope. Now we understand it."

But poor Gerta had no antechamber to her mind, no trained forces to preserve order while agony entered. The thing swept over her, resistless, overwhelming. She cowered before the outraged wrath she expected; and from some hidden cavern that wrath arose and swept over her in pale flame.

"Go and pack your trunk," said Mrs. Marroner. "You will leave my house tonight. Here is your money."

She laid down the fifty-dollar bill. She put with it a month's wages. She had no shadow of pity for those anguished eyes, those tears which she heard drop on the floor.

"Go to your room and pack," said Mrs. Marroner. And Gerta, always obedient, went.

Then Mrs. Marroner went to hers, and spent a time she never counted, lying on her face on the bed.

But the training of the twenty-eight years which had elapsed before her marriage; the life at college, both as student and teacher; the independent growth which she had made, formed a very different background for grief from that in Gerta's mind.

After a while Mrs. Marroner arose. She administered to herself a hot bath, a cold shower, a vigorous rubbing. "Now I can think," she said.

First she regretted the sentence of instant banishment. She went upstairs to see if it had been carried out. Poor Gerta! The tempest of her agony had worked itself out at last as in a child, and left her sleeping, the pillow wet, the lips still grieving, a big sob shuddering itself off now and then.

Mrs. Marroner stood and watched her, and as she watched she considered the helpless sweetness of the face; the defenseless, unformed character; the docility and habit of obedience which made her so attractive—and so easily a victim. Also she thought of the mighty force which had swept over her; of the great process now working itself out through her; of how pitiful and futile seemed any resistance she might have made.

She softly returned to her own room, made up a little fire, and sat by it, ignoring her feelings now, as she had before ignored her thoughts.

Here were two women and a man. One woman was a wife: loving, trusting, affectionate. One was a servant: loving, trusting, affectionate—a young girl, an exile, a dependent; grateful for any kindness; untrained, uneducated, childish. She ought, of course, to have resisted temptation! but Mrs. Marroner was wise enough to know how difficult temptation is to recognize when it comes in the guise of friendship and from a source one does not suspect.

Gerta might have done better in resisting the grocer's clerk; had, indeed, and with Mrs. Marroner's advice, resisted several. But where respect was due, how could she criticize? Where obedience was due, how could she refuse—with ignorance to hold her blinded—until too late?

As the older, wiser woman forced herself to understand and extenuate the girl's misdeed and foresee her ruined future, a new feeling rose in her heart, strong, clear, and overmastering: a sense of measureless condemnation for the man who had done this thing. He knew. He understood. He could fully foresee and measure the consequences of his act. He appreciated to the full the innocence, the ignorance, the grateful affection, the habitual docility, of which he deliberately took advantage. Mrs. Marroner rose to icy peaks of intellectual apprehension, from which her hours of frantic pain seemed far indeed removed. He had done this thing under the same roof with her—his wife. He had not frankly loved the younger woman, broken with his wife, made a new marriage. That would have been heart-break pure and simple. This was something else.

That letter, that wretched, cold, carefully guarded, unsigned letter, that bill—far safer than a check—these did not speak of affection. Some men can love two women at one time. This was not love.

Mrs. Marroner's sense of pity and outrage for herself, the wife, now spread suddenly into a perception of pity and outrage for the girl. All that splendid, clean young beauty, the hope of a happy life, with marriage and motherhood, honorable independence, even—these were nothing to that man. For his own pleasure he had chosen to rob her of her life's best joys.

He would "take care of her," said the letter. How? In what capacity?

And then, sweeping over both her feelings for herself, the wife, and Gerta, his victim, came a new flood, which literally lifted her to her feet. She rose and walked, her head held high. "This is the sin of man against woman," she said. "The offense is against womanhood. Against motherhood. Against—the child."

She stopped.

The child. His child. That, too, he sacrificed and injured—doomed to degradation.

Mrs. Marroner came of stern New England stock. She was not a Calvinist, hardly even a Unitarian, but the iron of Calvinism was in her soul: of that grim faith which held that most people had to be damned "for the glory of God."

Generations of ancestors who both preached and practiced stood behind her; people whose lives had been sternly moulded to their highest moments of religious conviction. In sweeping bursts of feeling, they achieved "conviction," and afterward they lived and died according to that conviction.

When Mr. Marroner reached home a few weeks later, following his letters too soon to expect an answer to either, he saw no wife upon the pier, though he had cabled, and found the house closed darkly. He let himself in with his latch-key, and stole softly upstairs, to surprise his wife.

No wife was there.

He rang the bell. No servant answered it.

He turned up light after light, searched the house from top to bottom; it was utterly empty. The kitchen wore a clean, bald, unsympathetic aspect. He left it and slowly mounted the stairs, completely dazed. The whole house was clean, in perfect order, wholly vacant.

One thing he felt perfectly sure of—she knew.

Yet was he sure? He must not assume too much. She might have been ill. She might have died. He started to his feet. No, they would have cabled him. He sat down again.

For any such change, if she had wanted him to know, she would have written. Perhaps she had, and he, returning so suddenly, had missed the letter. The thought was some comfort. It must be so. He turned to the telephone and again hesitated. If she had found out—if she had gone—utterly gone, without a word—should he announce it himself to friends and family?

He walked the floor; he searched everywhere for some letter, some word of explanation. Again and again he went to the telephone—and always stopped. He could not bear to ask? "Do you know where my wife is?"

The harmonious, beautiful rooms reminded him in a dumb, helpless way of her—like the remote smile on the face of the dead. He put out the lights, could not bear the darkness, turned them all on again.

It was a long night—

In the morning he went early to the office. In the accumulated mail was no letter from her. No one seemed to know of anything unusual. A friend asked after his wife—"Pretty glad to see you, I guess?" He answered evasively.

About eleven a man came to see him: John Hill, her lawyer. Her cousin, too. Mr. Marroner had never liked him. He liked him less now, for Mr. Hill merely handed him a letter, remarked, "I was requested to deliver this to you personally," and departed, looking like a person who is called on to kill something offensive.

"I have gone. I will care for Gerta. Good-bye, Marion."

That was all. There was no date, no address, no postmark, nothing but that.

In his anxiety and distress, he had fairly forgotten Gerta and all that. Her name aroused in him a sense of rage. She had come between him and his wife. She had taken his wife from him. That was the way he felt.

At first he said nothing, did nothing, lived on alone in his house, taking meals where he chose. When people asked him about his wife, he said she was traveling—for her health. He would not have it in the newspapers. Then, as time passed, as no enlightenment came to him, he resolved not to bear it any longer, and employed detectives. They blamed him for not having put them on the track earlier, but set to work, urged to the utmost secrecy.

What to him had been so blank a wall of mystery seemed not to embarrass them in the least. They made careful inquiries as to her "past," found where she had studied, where taught, and on what lines; that she had some little money of her own, that her doctor was Josephine L. Bleet, M.D., and many other bits of information.

As a result of careful and prolonged work, they finally told him that she had resumed teaching under one of her old professors, lived quietly, and apparently kept boarders; giving him town, street, and number as if it were a matter of no difficulty whatever.

He had returned in early spring. It was autumn before he found her.

A quiet college town in the hills, a broad, shady street, a pleasant house standing in its own lawn, with trees and flowers about it. He had the address in his hand, and the number showed clear on the white gate. He walked up the straight gravel path and rang the bell. An elderly servant opened the door.

"Does Mrs. Marroner live here?"

"No, sir."

"This is number twenty-eight?"

"Yes, sir."

"Who does live here?"

"Miss Wheeling, sir."

Ah! Her maiden name. They had told him, but he had forgotten.

He stepped inside. "I would like to see her," he said.

He was ushered into a still parlor, cool and sweet with the scent of flowers, the flowers she had always loved best. It almost brought tears to his eyes. All their years of happiness rose in his mind again—the exquisite beginnings; the days of eager longing before she was really his; the deep, still beauty of her love.

Surely she would forgive him—she must forgive him. He would humble himself; he would tell her of his honest remorse—his absolute determination to be a different man.

Through the wide doorway there came in to him two women. One like a tall Madonna, bearing a baby in her arms.

Marion, calm, steady, definitely impersonal, nothing but a clear pallor to hint of inner stress.

Gerta, holding the child as a bulwark, with a new intelligence in her face, and her blue, adoring eyes fixed on her friend—not upon him.

He looked from one to the other dumbly.

And the woman who had been his wife asked quietly:

"What have you to say to us?"

[1911]

For Discussion

1. Why does Gilman contrast the two women's settings so blatantly in the opening of the story? List the similarities and differences in the two women's ages, appearances, personalities, mentalities, and situations.

2. What is foreshadowed by Mr. Marroner's letters home? What is ironically foreshadowed by the scene with Gerta begging Mrs. Marroner "not to turn her away"?

3. Why is the device of the "switched letters" appropriate instead of some other method of revealing the truth?

4. Trace Mrs. Marroner's changes in feelings and thoughts. Against what or whom is her final tone of righteous indignation directed?

5. What do Mr. Marroner's thoughts and actions when returning home suggest? Do his thoughts confirm or disprove Mrs. Marroner's judgment of him?

6. Why was it so easy for the detective to find Mrs. Marroner, when Mr. Marroner hadn't been successful?

7. Explain the significance of the new family unit that has evolved—how does it differ from the old triangle?

8. What are the many meanings suggested by the title and by the name "Marroner," or chestnut (look up definition)?

For Further Exploration

1. Compare this story with other stories about marital infidelity, such as Katherine Mansfield's "Bliss," Doris Lessing's "A Man and Two Women," or Joyce Carol Oates' "Unmailed, Unwritten Letters." How do the themes change when the wife rather than the husband is unfaithful?

2. Temporarily disregarding the central theme of infidelity, what else is this story about? Or, how might the infidelity be symptomatic of a larger problem or issue? Compare this story with another by Charlotte Perkins Gilman, "The Yellow Wallpaper," in which a woman's progressive deterioration is indicative of larger problems of family and society.

Poetry About
Women and Family

Freud's much-satirized question, "What do women want?" could be the humorous subtitle of this section of poetry, because many of the poems point to a void unfilled by even the fullest family life. But the better question might be, "What does society want?" because the source of disillusionment seems to be the gap between what was "supposed" to be and what actually is.

Women in the poems who give all to others and nothing to themselves end up even more bereft than they began, and those who give all to society's vision of the Superwoman find out the impossibility of the dream. Yet several poems show that a woman is able to be truly herself while at the same time being a dynamic part of a conventional or unconventional family unit.

Phyllis McGinley

1905–1978

THE 5:32

She said, If tomorrow my world were torn in two,
Blacked out, dissolved, I think I would remember
(As if transfixed in unsurrendering amber)
This hour best of all the hours I knew:
When cars came backing into the shabby station,
Children scuffing the seats, and the women driving
With ribbons around their hair, and the trains arriving,
And the men getting off with tired but practiced motion.

Yes, I would remember my life like this, she said:
Autumn, the platform red with Virginia creeper,
And a man coming toward me, smiling, the evening paper
Under his arm, and his hat pushed back on his head;
And wood smoke lying like haze on the quiet town,
And dinner waiting, and the sun not yet gone down.

[1932]

Dorothy Parker

1893–1967

INDIAN SUMMER

In youth, it was a way I had
    To do my best to please,
And change, with every passing lad,
    To suit his theories.

But now I know the things I know,
    And do the things I do;
And if you do not like me so,
    To hell, my love, with you!

[1926]

Gwendolyn Brooks

1917–

THE MOTHER

Abortions will not let you forget.
You remember the children you got that you did not get,
The damp small pulps with a little or with no hair,
The singers and workers that never handled the air.
You will never neglect or beat
Them, or silence or buy with a sweet.
You will never wind up the sucking-thumb
Or scuttle off ghosts that come.
You will never leave them, controlling your luscious sigh,
Return for a snack of them, with gobbling mother-eye.

I have heard in the voices of the wind the voices of my dim killed
        children.
I have contracted. I have eased
My dim dears at the breasts they could never suck.
I have said, Sweets, if I sinned, if I seized
Your luck
And your lives from your unfinished reach,
If I stole your births and your names,
Your straight baby tears and your games,
Your stilted or lovely loves, your tumults, your marriages, aches, and
        your deaths,
If I poisoned the beginnings of your breaths,
Believe that even in my deliberateness I was not deliberate.
Though why should I whine,
Whine that the crime was other than mine?—
Since anyhow you are dead.
Or rather, or instead,
You were never made.
But that too, I am afraid,
Is faulty: oh, what shall I say, how is the truth to be said?

You were born, you had body, you died.
It is just that you never giggled or planned or cried.

Believe me, I loved you all.
Believe me, I knew you, though faintly, and I loved, I loved you
All.

[1944]

Sherley Williams

1944–

SAY HELLO TO JOHN

I swear I ain't done what Richard
told me bout jumpin round and stuff.
And he knew I wouldn't do nothin to make the baby
come, just joke, say I'mo cough

this child up one day.
So in the night when I felt the water tween
my legs, I thought it was pee and I laid
there wonderin if maybe I was in a dream.

Then it come to me that my water broke and I went
in to tell Ru-ise. *You been havin pains?*
she ask. I hear her fumblin for the light.
Naw, I say. Don't think so. The veins

stand out along her temples. *What time
is it?* Goin on toward four o'clock.
*Nigga, I told you:
You ain't havin no babies, not*

*in the middle of the night.
Get yo ass back to bed.
That ain't nothin but pee.* And what
I know bout havin kids cept what she said?

Second time it happen, even she
got to admit this mo'n pee.
And the pain when it come, wa'n't bad
least no mo'n I eva expect to see

again. I remember the doctor smilin,
sayin, Shel, you got a son.
His bright black face above me
sayin, Say hello to John.

[1975]

Sylvia Plath

1932–1963

THE APPLICANT

First, are you our sort of a person?
Do you wear
A glass eye, false teeth or a crutch,
A brace or a hook,
Rubber breasts or a rubber crotch,

Stitches to show something's missing? No, no? Then
How can we give you a thing?
Stop crying.
Open your hand.
Empty? Empty. Here is a hand

To fill it and willing
To bring teacups and roll away headaches
And do whatever you tell it.
Will you marry it?
It is guaranteed

To thumb shut your eyes at the end
And dissolve of sorrow.
We make new stock from the salt.
I notice you are stark naked.
How about this suit—

Black and stiff, but not a bad fit.
Will you marry it?
It is waterproof, shatterproof, proof
Against fire and bombs through the roof.
Believe me, they'll bury you in it.

Now your head, excuse me, is empty.
I have the ticket for that.
Come here, sweetie, out of the closet.
Well, what do you think of *that*?
Naked as paper to start

But in twenty-five years she'll be silver,
In fifty, gold.
A living doll, everywhere you look.
It can sew, it can cook,
It can talk, talk, talk.

It works, there is nothing wrong with it.
You have a cold, it's a poultice.

You have an eye, it's an image.
My boy, it's your last resort
Will you marry it, marry it, marry it.

[1963]

Poetry About Women and Family

Denise Levertov

1923–

ABOUT MARRIAGE

Don't lock me in wedlock, I want
marriage, an
encounter—

I told you about the
green light of
May

        (a veil of quiet befallen
        the downtown park,
        late

        Saturday after
        noon, long
        shadows and cool.

        air, scent of
        new grass,
        fresh leaves,

        blossom on the threshold of
        abundance—

        and the birds I met there,
        birds of passage breaking their journey,
        three birds each of a different species:

        the azalea-breasted with round poll, dark,
        the brindled, merry, mousegliding one,
        and the smallest, golden as gorse and wearing
        a black Venetian mask

        and with them the three douce hen-birds
        feathered in tender, lively brown—
        I stood

        a half-hour under the enchantment,
        no-one passed near,
        the birds saw me and

        let me be
        near them.)

It's not
irrelevant:
I would be
met

and meet you
so,
in a green

airy space, not
locked in.

[1963]

Adrienne Rich

1929–

LIVING IN SIN

She had thought the studio would keep itself;
no dust upon the furniture of love.
Half heresy, to wish the taps less vocal,
the panes relieved of grime. A plate of pears,
a piano with a Persian shawl, a cat
stalking the picturesque amusing mouse
had risen at his urging.
Not that at five each separate stair would writhe
under the milkman's tramp; that morning light
so coldly would delineate the scraps
of last night's cheese and three sepulchral bottles;
that on the kitchen shelf among the saucers
a pair of beetle-eyes would fix her own—
Envoy from some village in the moldings . . .
Meanwhile, he, with a yawn,
sounded a dozen notes upon the keyboard,
declared it out of tune, shrugged at the mirror,
rubbed at his beard, went out for cigarettes;
while she, jeered by the minor demons,
pulled back the sheets and made the bed and found
a towel to dust the table-top,
and let the coffee-pot boil over on the stove.
By evening she was back in love again,
though not so wholly but throughout the night
she woke sometimes to feel the daylight coming
like a relentless milkman up the stairs.

[1955]

Janice Mirikitani

1942–

BREAKING TRADITION: FOR MY DAUGHTER

My daughter denies she is like me,
Her secretive eyes avoid mine.
    She reveals the hatreds of womanhood
    already veiled behind music and smoke and telephones.
I want to tell her about the empty room
    of myself.
    This room we lock ourselves in
    where whispers live like fungus,
    giggles about small breasts and cellulite,
    where we confine ourselves to jealousies,
    bedridden by menstruation.
    This waiting room where we feel our hands
    are useless, dead speechless clamps
    that need hospitals and forceps and kitchens
    and plugs and ironing boards to make them useful.
I deny I am like my mother. I remember why:
    She kept her room neat with silence,
    defiance smothered in requirements to be otonashii,[1]
    passion and loudness wrapped in an obi,[2]
    her steps confined to ceremony,
    the weight of her sacrifice she carried like
    a foetus. Guilt passed on in our bones.
I want to break tradition—unlock this room
    where women dress in the dark.
    Discover the lies my mother told me.
    The lies that we are small and powerless
    that our possibilities must be compressed
    to the size of pearls, displayed only as
    passive chokers, charms around our neck.
Break Tradition.
    I want to tell my daughter of this room
    of myself
    filled with tears of violins,
    the light in my hands,
    poems about madness,
    the music of yellow guitars—
    sounds shaken from barbed wire and
    goodbyes and miracles of survival.
    This room of open window where daring ones escape.
My daughter denies she is like me
    her secretive eyes are walls of smoke

---

[1]Nice.

[2]Binding sash around a kimono.

and music and telephones,
her pouting ruby lips, her skirts
swaying to salsa, teena marie and the stones,
her thighs displayed in carnavals of color.
I do not know the contents of her room.
She mirrors my aging.
She is breaking tradition.

[1981]

For Discussion

1. What combination of domestic and natural images does the woman in "The 5:32" select to vivify a traditional family scene?

2. What stylistic devices does Dorothy Parker use to create humor out of the power struggle between men and women?

3. How could Gwendolyn Brooks' famous poem "The Mother" be used as an argument by either pro-life or pro-choice groups?

4. What attitude toward childbirth does Sherley Williams describe in "Say Hello to John"?

5. What comparisons are there between marriage and job hunting that enable Plath to create the "conceit" (extended metaphor) in "The Applicant"?

6. How does Levertov use natural images to reinforce her distinction between marriage and wedlock?

7. What similarities are there between the poem "Living in Sin" and poems about marriage (for example, "Housewife's Letter: To Mary" in the Women and Work section)?

8. How does the poem "Breaking Tradition" summarize the many roles of women in families?

For Further Exploration

1. Examine other poems for the same themes about women and family, such as Emily Dickinson's "She Rose to His Requirement," Denise Levertov's "The Ache of Marriage," and Anne Sexton's, "The Abortion."

2. In *The Feminine Irony*, Lynne Agress has studied the paradoxical behavior of writers who describe traditional family roles for women in their novels, but in their own lives are women leading highly unconventional lives. Examine biographical summaries of women whose poetry you admire to determine what their own family situations were as contrasted with their writings. Also refer to Carolyn Kizer on poets' lives in "Pro Femina" (Women and Work section).

Drama About
Women and Family

In the following one-act play, Ursule Molinaro has combined almost every common source of contention between mothers and daughters, including cigarettes, food, alcohol, coffee, music, dating, race, sex, marriage, fidelity and infidelity, childrearing, work, getting up, and staying out. Although the daughter is forty-three and the mother is sixty-eight, they could easily be teen-aged and forty, for they represent mothers and daughters of all ages.

As a compendium of elements of the generation gap, the play serves at the same time to affirm the unavoidable link created by biology, asserted by the mother when she says "Whether she liked it or not. I was her *mother.*" Much is made of the fact that one woman "created" the other, that "she herself had come from me." The women themselves have sympathies for each other in their thoughts that never surface into speech or action. The paradox of loving and hating is dramatized in the climactic ending of *Breakfast Past Noon.*

243

Ursule Molinaro

BREAKFAST PAST NOON

Characters

THE MOTHER   sixty-eight, neat dress

THE DAUGHTER   forty-three, terry robe

The Set

> Two giant harp cases, side by side. MOTHER's harp case lid opens stage left, DAUGHTER's stage right.
> All objects—telephone beside DAUGHTER's harp case, magazine, glasses and case, coffeepot, cup, saucer, ashtray, etc., which MOTHER or DAUGHTER take out of or put into harp cases— might be blatant outsized papier-mâché imitations of the real things.
> Radio: Rock and roll (Good Guys or similar station) as background throughout. Turned up and down by DAUGHTER.
> A beautiful day . . . any season.

MOTHER   *(Sitting on rim of her wide-open harp case, reading a magazine, twisting her wedding ring—which she twists throughout the play— almost to the end. She looks up. Looks expectantly at DAUGHTER's closed harp case. Reads some more)*
(Noon siren, long and loud)
(Puts both hands—one holding magazine, the other glasses case—to her ears to blot out siren. Looks expectantly at DAUGHTER's closed harp case. Pushes glasses far down on nose. Looks at DAUGHTER's harp case over top of glasses. Pushes glasses back up. Continues to read magazine, twisting her wedding ring)

DAUGHTER   *(Lid of harp case slowly rises. A wedding-ringed hand appears, pushes lid all the way back. A tousled head yawns out)*

MOTHER   *(Watches DAUGHTER over top of glasses)*
(Radio starts blaring inside DAUGHTER's harp case)

MOTHER   *(Puts hands—holding objects—to her ears)*
(Radio is adjusted inside DAUGHTER's harp case: first still louder, then somewhat toned down)

DAUGHTER   *(Yawns. Swings legs out. Stands up. Stretches. Bends into harp case. Takes out cup and saucer. Sits down on rim of harp case, her back turned on MOTHER)*

MOTHER   *(Twists wedding ring; watches DAUGHTER over top of glasses)*

DAUGHTER   *(Reaches into harp case. Takes out coffeepot. Pours coffee into cup. Massages her forehead. Lifts cup to her lips)*

MOTHER   *(Closes magazine. Carefully places it inside her harp case. Looks at DAUGHTER's back over top of glasses. Removes glasses while looking at DAUGHTER's back. Carefully fits glasses into case. Places case inside harp case. Looks at DAUGHTER's back. Gets up. Walks around own harp case, around top of DAUGHTER's harp case. Stands in front of DAUGHTER, looking down at DAUGHTER)*

DAUGHTER *(Drinking coffee)* Good morning: I said to her. As she had taught me to say to her when she made me get out of bed in the mornings when I was little.

Good morning: I said. Because she had come over to the table at which I had just sat down. She was standing in front of me . . . Over me . . . Her eyes watching. Watching me drink my coffee. *(She drinks)*

MOTHER *(Sitting down on rim of* DAUGHTER's *harp case, knee by knee with* DAUGHTER, *twisting wedding ring)* And I said: good afternoon. Because it *was after* noon. I had heard the noon siren scream a few minutes before she turned that radio on . . . to that awful music . . . That was no *music* . . . Much too loud . . . before she came out of her bedroom. And made coffee for herself. While I sat reading a magazine by the window. Waiting for her to get up.

I stopped reading and walked over to sit with her. To keep her company. As I used to do when she was still a little girl. When I used to sit with her and keep her company while she ate her breakfast before running off to school.

I said the siren sounded terribly loud. And asked if they had known it would be right on top of them when they rented their apartment. And remarked that landlords rarely mentioned those inconveniences to a prospective tenant. And that one ought to make sure for oneself before one rented an apartment.

I couldn't stand that screaming every noon, I said to her.

DAUGHTER *(Wriggles behind along harp-case rim to sit less close to* MOTHER*)* I told her she didn't have to stand it every noon. *(She drinks)*

MOTHER She'd had such sensitive ears as a little girl, I said. The smallest noise would bother her . . . *(She twists wedding ring)* Like that radio, I said. Wouldn't she like me to turn it down a bit? *(She stands up to go and turn radio down)*

DAUGHTER *(Holding cup to her chin . . . with slightly shaking hand)* I told her not to bother. That it was my wake-up music.

MOTHER *(Standing over* DAUGHTER*)* I didn't ask her how she could call that noise music . . . I didn't want to irritate her. She was holding the cup to her chin. Her hand was shaking. And I told her so. *(She twists wedding ring)*

DAUGHTER *(Drinks)* I nodded: yes. So it was.

MOTHER *(Sitting down again on rim of* DAUGHTER's *harp case, closer to* DAUGHTER*)* I asked her how that could be! She was only forty-two!

DAUGHTER *(Pulling herself away from* MOTHER*)* I was forty-three. I said I was forty-three.

MOTHER *(Leaning toward* DAUGHTER*)* But I was seventy! I said. And *my* hands didn't shake. *(She twists wedding ring)*

DAUGHTER *(Wriggling away from* MOTHER*)* I said I thought she was sixty-eight.

MOTHER *(Leaning toward* DAUGHTER*)* I was sure drinking coal-black coffee every morning . . . every afternoon . . . probably didn't help, I said. *(She twists wedding ring)*

DAUGHTER *(Wriggling away from* MOTHER*)* I said it probably didn't. *(She drinks)*

MOTHER *(Wriggling after* DAUGHTER*)* I asked her why she kept drinking it then? *(She twists wedding ring)*

(Throughout the dialogue preceding DAUGHTER's bath, MOTHER continues to wriggle after DAUGHTER on harp-case rim; DAUGHTER continues to wriggle away . . . Until she finds herself sitting at foot of harp case on one buttock with no space left to withdraw to)

DAUGHTER   I said it helped me think.

MOTHER   I said she only *thought* it did. That it only made her nervous. How could she think when she was nervous.

DAUGHTER   I said: I seemed to manage somehow . . . *(She pours another cup)*

MOTHER   Another cup! I said. Why didn't she drink Sanka? *I* drank Sanka, I said. It tasted just as good.

DAUGHTER   It didn't to me, I said. *(She drinks)*

MOTHER   How did she know? I asked her. Had she tried it? It tasted just like *real* coffee . . . With a little milk and sugar, I said. I offered to fix her some—the way I fixed it for myself—the next morning . . . uhh . . . afternoon . . . She wouldn't be able to tell the difference, I told her.

DAUGHTER   I said I hated milk and sugar. That I'd rather drink hot water. *(She drinks)*

MOTHER   She used to *love* milk and sugar as a little girl, I reminded her. Why did she always have to be so *radical*? Did she think I was planning to poison her?

DAUGHTER   I said I hadn't been a little girl in years . . . *(She takes a pack of cigarettes from harp case; lights one . . . with slightly shaking hand)*

MOTHER   She would always be *my* little girl: I said. A boy was a son till he married a wife; a girl stayed a daughter for all of her life . . . I was looking at her shaking hand that was lighting a cigarette. Smoking probably didn't help. Either . . . I said.

DAUGHTER   I said it probably didn't. But that it helped other things. *(She inhales deeply)*

MOTHER   Like "thinking"? I asked. I was teasing her gently.

DAUGHTER   Yes: I said. And like leaving people alone.

MOTHER   I said that wasn't nice.

DAUGHTER   *(Inhaling)* Oh, I didn't know, I said. Leaving people alone could be *very* nice . . . For *them* . . .

MOTHER   I repeated: that she was *not* nice. That I didn't see her that often.

DAUGHTER   *(Smokes; drinks coffee)*

MOTHER   She didn't answer me. Or look at me. She sat drinking her coal-black coffee, puffing away at that cigarette. Visibly ruining the good health I had borne her with. Vice always found excuses, I said.

DAUGHTER   *(Smokes; drinks coffee; strokes her forehead)*

MOTHER   She didn't answer me. Or look at me. I couldn't help looking at her trembling hand which was holding the cigarette. I asked her to look at that poor hand.

DAUGHTER   *(Smokes; drinks coffee; strokes her forehead)*

MOTHER   She did *not* look at her hand. Or at me. She sat staring at something . . . at nothing . . . behind/above my head. With narrowed eyes. Like a sphinx. As though I weren't there. I couldn't just sit by and watch her ruin the good health God had been kind enough to let me bear her with, I said. *(She fishes for ashtray in DAUGHTER's harp case)* I held the ashtray out to her. *(She does)* Here, I said. Put it out.

DAUGHTER   *(Recoils)*

MOTHER   She recoiled. From the ashtray. From her mother's hand. That was only trying to help her. That was *not* trembling at seventy . . . At sixty-eight . . . As though my hand were a poisonous snake . . . A wave of pity flooded my heart. I was only trying to *help* her, I said.

DAUGHTER *(Smokes; drinks coffee; strokes her forehead)*

MOTHER She didn't answer me. Or look at me. She just sat. Smoking. Drinking her wicked coffee. Staring beyond me. A narrow-eyed sphinx. I held out my hand across the breakfast table. *(She holds out hand)* Give *me* that cigarette, I said. *I'll* put it out.

DAUGHTER *(Gestures with cigarette as though to burn* MOTHER's *held-out hand. But doesn't)*

MOTHER For a moment I thought she was going to burn my hand. I pulled it back. *(She does)* Perhaps I should *not* have pulled it back . . . I implored her: WHY—DON'T YOU—STOP—SMOKING!

DAUGHTER I was trying not to see her concerned face. Not to hear her pleading tone. To "keep my cool," as Johnny would have said. *(She smiles a smile of reminiscence: Johnny)* But her persistence won . . . As it always had . . . Why don't *you start!* I said.

MOTHER She was being deliberately unreasonable. I should not have answered. I should have changed the subject. To the weather. Which was beautiful. Perhaps I should have asked what she was planning to do with this beautiful day. Perhaps I should have suggested something she and I might have enjoyed doing together . . . In the sunshine. A leisurely walk. A bit of window-shopping. I refused to believe that she seriously wanted me to start smoking. She was only trying to distract me . . . by shocking me. Because she knew that I was right . . . It had already been one of her tricks, when she was still a little girl . . . When she had been a *bad* little girl. When she would try to distract me by shocking me . . . by trying to hurt me . . . from whatever reason I had for scolding her . . . Or for spanking her. Sometimes . . . Like the time she tried to stop me from hanging the cowbell around her little neck. When she was not quite five. When she couldn't be stopped from wandering off by herself . . . Out of earshot . . . Into the wheat field . . . That stood higher than she did. At not quite five . . . Where I might never have been able to find her again . . . Ever . . . Wandering through the wheat field all the way down to the creek . . . In which she might easily have drowned . . . When she upset me . . . succeeded in upsetting me . . . when she asked . . . at not quite five! . . . why I hadn't hung a cowbell around her daddy's neck? . . . Because her daddy had "wandered off" . . . She had succeeded in making me cry while I hung the cowbell around her little neck . . . Still, I didn't change the subject. I felt I couldn't afford to, if I wanted to help her stop smoking. I didn't see her that often. I pretended to take her seriously. I! Start smoking! I cried. At *my* age! What ever for! Did she want *my* hands to shake too!

DAUGHTER I knew I should have "kept my cool" . . . as Johnny *(smile of reminiscence)* would have said. I should have changed the subject. To the weather. Which was harmless. Which was beautiful. I should have asked her if she didn't want to go for a walk for an hour or so . . . while I took my bath and got dressed . . . *(While Johnny called?)* But I was no longer used to words coming at me in the morning. Or afternoon . . . Whenever it was that I was getting up . . . I had grown used to approaching a new day quietly. On tiptoe. Over a slow cup of coffee. And a couple of cigarettes. To a rock'n'roll undertone . . . Before the world came in . . . Over the telephone . . . Her well-washed well-meaning face was blocking the sunshine beyond the window bars. The flowers I had planted. Our landlord's ivy. I tried not to see her neat sparing hair . . . *(She brushes hair out of forehead)* . . . Which I had inherited. Which was not neat. Still uncombed . . . Which was not yet quite so sparing. Not yet a greyish white. But would become just as sparing greyish white sooner or later . . . I wondered what Johnny *(smile of reminiscence)* thought about my hair. *If* he thought about it. I knew he thought about my painted toenails. He had told me he had thought about them . . . Did he see my hair for what it was: teased and color-rinsed and not very thick. An elaborate time-consuming cheat . . . Or was it just "white folks" hair to him? That could never be as *bad* as his own? I thought of Johnny's mother. Whom I had met. Once. At Johnny's insistence . . . With a permanent bandana around her head . . . Who refused to let him talk to me on the telephone after she'd met me . . . Told me he was out . . . Or asleep . . . when I called him at home . . . Mothers! I thought. I wished her hands *would* start to shake . . . Might shake some of her convictions as well, I said. Here! I said, holding out my pack of cigarettes. *(She holds out pack . . . with slightly shaking hand)* Have one! I said.

MOTHER   I said I didn't think she was glad to see me.

DAUGHTER   *(Chain-lights another cigarette)*

MOTHER   She didn't even protest. Her mouth looked like the rear end of a chicken, puckered around another cigarette she was pulling from the pack with her lips. Another one! I said. And on an empty stomach! Why didn't she *eat* something instead! I offered to fry her an egg or two. The way she'd used to like me to fry her eggs . . . turned over ever so lightly . . . before she'd run off to school in the mornings. When she was still a little girl . . . I thought the memory of the taste might give her an appetite. Distract her from her smoking.

DAUGHTER   I didn't remember having liked *my* eggs "turned over ever so lightly." I remembered only how *fat* her food had made me. At fourteen. Or at fifteen. A fat, undesirable teenager. Whose ego-image it had taken me years to outgrow . . . To shrink . . . I felt like throwing all those dieting, self-remodeling years in the well-meaning well-washed face across the table from me. But I didn't. I thought of Johnny *(smile of reminiscence).* Keep your cool, man . . . Baby . . . Wondering when . . . *if* . . . he would call . . . No, thank you, I said politely. It was too early in the day for me to eat.

MOTHER   Too *early!* I said. It was *past noon!* Normal people were eating *lunch* at this hour.

DAUGHTER   That was nice of the normal people, I said. *(She smokes intently)*

MOTHER   She was turning into a regular chimney. Hiding from me behind a screen of smoke. I asked her to think of her poor lungs. That were probably soot-black by now. The only deep breath I'd seen her take since my arrival at six the previous evening had been at the end of a cigarette.

DAUGHTER   *(Smokes)*

MOTHER   She didn't answer me. Or look at me. She was rejecting my help. But I was her *mother!* And I didn't see her that often. Might not see her again for a long time. Might *die* without *ever* seeing her again. And *who* would have a mother's loving patience to help her then? She'd have to go looking for *professional* help . . . I decided to broach the subject from a different angle. Did she *always* get up this late? I asked.

DAUGHTER   When I had worked late the night before: I said. Keeping my cool . . . *(Smile of reminiscence)*
MOTHER   But she *hadn't* worked the night before, I said. They'd gone out for dinner . . . Without me . . . Not quite two hours after my arrival. I had broiled a lamb chop for myself. And read a bit before going to bed. Since they had no television. She'd probably drunk too much, too, I said.
DAUGHTER   Eating and drinking . . . with people you worked with . . . was part of working sometimes, I said.
MOTHER   Vice always found excuses, I said. How could drinking be part of working! *I'd* never seen anybody do any work when he was drunk.
DAUGHTER   *(Holds out pack of cigarettes . . . with slightly shaking hand)* Have a cigarette! I said.
MOTHER   *(Ignores offered pack)* I said I wasn't as stupid as she thought. Even if *I* was not "creative."
DAUGHTER   *(Smokes; drinks coffee; strokes forehead)*
MOTHER   I had merely created *her*, I said.
DAUGHTER   Without any assistance from my departed father? I asked.
MOTHER   She was trying to shock me. Again. To distract me from trying to help her. But I remembered a lecture I had heard on the radio some time before . . . by that famous psychiatrist . . . whatever his name was . . . Haddad or something . . . Who helped mentally disturbed people . . . And drug addicts . . . And he'd said that in order to win your patient's permission to let you help him you had to pretend that everything he did . . . or said . . . was perfectly normal. That you couldn't afford to be shocked by anything. So I merely asked: Did she always have to reduce everything to the animal level? She didn't have to tell me . . . *me, a mother!* . . . how babies came into this world. I had done my share. And I knew that the man . . . uh . . . inspired life. Still . . . the woman . . .
DAUGHTER   . . . *per*spired? I laughed. Cutting her off. She looked hurt. I didn't want to be mean to her. I got up. *(She does)* Finished my coffee. *(She does)* Stubbed out my cigarette. *(She does)* I was going to take a bath, I said. *(She disappears into harp case, closing the lid)*
MOTHER   I said that was a good idea. But warned her not to let the water run so hot. That that didn't help either . . . I was warning a closed door. She had closed . . . and *locked!* . . . the bathroom door behind her. As though I were a stranger. As though I'd never seen her naked . . . She was opening it again . . . Realizing how absurd she'd been, I thought.
DAUGHTER   *(Opens lid of harp case wide enough to stick head out)* I asked her to call me . . . Please! . . . if anyone called. *(She withdraws head; closes lid of harp case)*
MOTHER   She was locking the door *again* . . . I knew who "anyone" was. He'd waked me up three times the night before. While they were out. Every time I'd try to doze off, the phone would start ringing. With that voice at the other end . . . It was ringing again . . .
     (The telephone rings beside DAUGHTER's harp case)
   I picked it up. Hello? I said. It *was* that voice again. No, I said. She still hadn't come home.
DAUGHTER   *(Opens lid wide enough to stick head out)* I'd heard the phone ring. I saw her hang up.
MOTHER   *(Hangs up)*
DAUGHTER   I asked her who had called.

MOTHER I said whoever it was hadn't told me who he was.

DAUGHTER Had she asked? I asked her.

MOTHER I told her I hadn't had to. That it was the same voice that had waked me up three times the night before.

DAUGHTER Johnny *had* called then. Several times. And she had not let him through to me. Self-righteously. The same way *his* mother refused to let *me* through to *him*. Why hadn't she told me someone—he—had called the night before? I asked her.

MOTHER Because I'd finally fallen asleep by the time they'd come home, I said.

DAUGHTER She might have told me in the morning . . . or afternoon . . . after I got up, I said. She'd had plenty of time to tell me then. And WHY!?! hadn't she called me a moment ago? When I had specifically asked her to call me if anyone—he—called . . .

MOTHER Because *I* had more consideration for her bath than she had for her mother's sleep, apparently, I said. I hadn't wanted her to get out of the tub and catch cold just to talk to that kind of voice on the telephone. I would have called her if it had sounded important, I said.

DAUGHTER I hadn't even climbed into the tub yet, I said. I'd been brushing my teeth. And didn't she think she might have left the decision of who was and who was not important up to me? I was, after all, forty-three. And it so happened that I'd been *waiting* for that particular call.

MOTHER I said that she ought to be ashamed of herself. That I recognized a black man. Even over the telephone. And I wasn't going to be the go-between for that kind of business. She didn't expect me just to sit by and watch her wreck her marriage, did she? The same way she was wrecking her health. With alcohol. And coal-black coffee. And cigarettes!

DAUGHTER What had she said to him? I asked.

MOTHER I was her *mother!* I said. And I was determined to protect her. As long as God allowed me to live. Since her husband wasn't able to protect her, apparently. Or didn't care enough . . . Why hadn't she told me her husband had been unfaithful?

DAUGHTER What had she said? On the telephone? I asked.

MOTHER I wasn't going to sit by and watch while she disgraced herself, I said. That kind of business was bad enough with a white man. Did she want the entire neighborhood . . . all her friends . . . to point a finger at her? That black man himself was probably laughing at her . . . behind her back . . . Telling dirty jokes about her . . .

DAUGHTER What had she said to him? I asked.

MOTHER Perhaps I'd been *fortunate* to lose her father when I did. So young, I said. Before it occurred to him to become unfaithful. Although I doubted very much that that *would* have occurred to her father. Ever. Her father's and my relationship had transcended the animal level . . .

Still, it was different for a man to do that sort of thing. A woman's reputation was her most precious possession, I said. I wasn't just going to sit by and watch her ruin the good reputation I had started her out with. There had to be better ways to get even with an unfaithful husband than ruining that reputation with a black man, I said.

DAUGHTER I asked her never to mind my husband. What he had or had not done. To mind her own business . . . To have a cigarette . . . And to tell me . . . PLEASE! . . . what she had said on the phone!

(The telephone rings)

MOTHER *(Reaching for receiver)* The telephone was ringing again. I reached to pick it up. I was standing right beside it. But she *was* my business, I said. Whether she liked it or not. I was her *mother*. She came charging over like a wild animal and wrestled the receiver out of my hand.

DAUGHTER *(Has run over; tries to take phone from* MOTHER. *They struggle)*

MOTHER I told her she was hurting my hand.

(The ringing stops; the struggle breaks the connection)

DAUGHTER *(Takes phone into arm, climbs back into harp case; forcefully closing lid behind her)*

MOTHER *(Stands in front of* DAUGHTER's *closing harp case; shakes her head; looks at her hand; strokes it gently; flexing fingers)* She was taking the telephone into the bathroom with her. I warned her: to be careful. Not to electrocute herself . . . Through the bathroom door. Which she was locking behind her as before . . . After slamming it in my face . . . My hand was hurting. I walked over to sit by the window again. *(She walks over to own harp case; sits down)* I felt too sad to read. I'd been looking forward to spending a little time with my daughter . . . I looked at the sunshine outside and asked God for help. For her. What could I do to help her? What should I say to her . . . that would not irritate her . . . After she'd come out of the bathroom . . . In which she seemed to be staying forever . . . It began to worry me. Perhaps she *had* electrocuted herself with the telephone . . . I wondered if it were better to go upstairs and ask the landlord for help? Or to find a street telephone booth and call a locksmith? Since she had locked herself in . . . I prayed to God to guard her against electrocuting herself. Even if He thought that she deserved it, maybe . . . Finally I hit on an idea: I would offer to cook dinner for them that night. I thanked God for the inspiration, and started composing a menu in my head to distract me from worrying . . . Until she came out of the bathroom . . .

DAUGHTER *(Lifts harp-case lid with wedding-ringed hand; climbs out, visibly bathed and elaborately combed; still in bathrobe. She sits down on rim of harp case. Starts filing her toenails)*

MOTHER *(Gets up; walks around own harp case. Toward seated* DAUGHTER) I didn't ask if she always spent so much time in the bathroom? Even when her mother was *not* visiting? . . . When she did all that work she told me she was doing? Nor did I mention how worried I'd been, since I couldn't have come to her rescue without breaking down the locked bathroom door . . . *(Standing in front of—over—seated daughter)* I forced my voice to sound casual. Light-hearted. When was her husband coming home? I asked.

DAUGHTER *(Continues to file toenails without looking up)* What was she driving at now? I wondered. With the obstinacy I remembered her for. Her mind running like an El, down the same old high-principled track . . . Johnny had *not* called back. What had she said to him? The night before? That morning . . . or afternoon? It was useless trying to call him at home. Even if he *was* at home . . . I didn't know when my husband was coming home, I said.

MOTHER *(Sitting down on rim of* DAUGHTER's *harp case; twisting wedding ring)* She was rejecting my offer before I'd even made it. As though nothing good could come from me. For her. When she herself had come from me . . . As though there were nothing good about her life . . . But I didn't permit my voice to sound discouraged. That was strange, I said.

After eighteen years of marriage she still didn't know when her husband came home from work?

DAUGHTER *(Filing toenails without looking up) Sixteen* years. We had lived together for two years before we got legalized, I said. Hoping to shock her off the subject of my husband. Which was nothing but a detour. To get back onto the subject of Johnny, I thought. She was obviously trying to pry some kind of confession out of me. To find out if my husband *had* been unfaithful. And with whom? Which would lead into a good long heart-to-heart talk between mother and daughter. With a few hot tears spilled on mother's advice-dispensing shoulder. When she *had* no advice to give. At least not to me. At least not on that subject. Because she'd had little experience with marriage. Because my father had been away . . . traveling . . . most of the not quite six years during which he had been her husband. On paper, mostly. In letters. Before he died. When the El-car in which he was riding . . . in Chicago . . . jumped the track and plunged to the street . . . And she had not risked any new relationship after that. Out of commitment to me, supposedly . . . Like most people, she was offering what she did not have to give. No, I said. After sixteen years of marriage I still didn't know when my husband came home from work. Not any more than she had known when my father came back from his travels. My husband didn't know himself, most of the time. He didn't have a nine-to-five job, I said.

MOTHER *(Twisting wedding ring)* I hadn't known about her living with her husband for two years before she got married. She had never told me before. It grieved me. For her sake. No wonder her husband was having affairs. If she herself had been an "affair" to him to begin with. But I didn't say anything. I merely asked: How she managed to cook dinner for him then? Wondering to myself—worrying a bit—how I'd manage to roast the duck I had planned on. For them. If I had no way of knowing what time to plan it for. I didn't want to serve it half-burned. Or half-raw. I was no French chef, after all . . .

DAUGHTER *(Starts painting toenails; bits of cotton between toes)* Had I been too self-centered, thinking that she was thinking about me? I wondered. About my marriage. And Johnny . . . Not that I wanted her to think about it. Or me. In her proprietary way of thinking about me. As though I were an investment she had made. Worrying that it might not pay off . . . Perhaps her selfishness was more primitive—much more immediate—than I was giving her credit for. In my selfishness. Perhaps she was merely trying to pin me down about dinner. To pressure me into not letting her eat alone. Again. As she had the night before. To make me feel good and guilty, at least, if the pressure did not succeed. I said: we didn't eat at home every night. But when we did I either made a stew. Which kept stewing until my spouse entered the house. Or else I fried a steak. Which I dropped into the pan when I heard his key in the door.

MOTHER Didn't alternating between stews and steaks get a bit tiresome? I asked. Wouldn't they both enjoy a change of menu . . . A roast duck, for instance?

DAUGHTER *(Intent on painting her toenails)* She had lost me. I couldn't imagine what she was after now. Not cooking dinner for us? She'd never been particularly keen on cooking. Nor particularly good at it. The entire conversation proved only one thing: that we had nothing to say to each other. I also made hamburger sometimes, I said. Or chops . . . and we often ate out . . .

MOTHER Restaurant food wasn't the healthiest, I said.

DAUGHTER *(Fanning her toenails)* Oh, I didn't know, I said. We went to pretty good places.

MOTHER But didn't that cost a fortune? Nowadays? I asked. She'd spend two-thirds less cooking the same dishes at home.

DAUGHTER *(Fanning toenails)* I said that was undoubtedly true. But then, in a restaurant, *I* didn't have to do the cooking . . . She forgot: I was a working woman, I said.

MOTHER *(Twisting wedding ring)* Well, that evening she wouldn't have to do the cooking. *Or* go to an expensive restaurant, I said. In a gay voice. *I* was going to make dinner, I said. I'd roast them a duck, I'd thought . . .

DAUGHTER *(Fanning toenails)* I could just picture my husband's gourmet face, biting into a soggy half-raw drumstick. Politely saying what an unusual cook she was. I said nothing. Hoping she would not insist.

MOTHER *(Twisting wedding ring)* For a moment I thought she was going to accept my offer. And panicked a bit. At the thought of roasting a duck in a kitchen with which I was not familiar. And getting it just right in time for a time I didn't know. Seven? Seven-thirty? Eight o'clock? But I told myself that I'd manage. Somehow. With God's help. All she had to do was tell me where to shop for the duck, I said . . . Unless she preferred to come *with* me. It was such a beautiful day. Her lungs would enjoy a breath of fresh air.

DAUGHTER *(Pulls cigarette from pack with lips; lights it)* I said fresh air wasn't one of New York's best features. And thanked her for her kind offer . . . And did not ask: why was she forever offering what she didn't have to give . . . And told her not to bother. That it was not necessary.

MOTHER *(Twisting wedding ring)* I asked myself if my reference to lungs and fresh air had prompted her to smoke another cigarette. And was sorry *if* it had. How careful one had to be with these addicts . . . I pretended not to notice. I was a better cook than she gave me credit for, I said gaily. Why didn't she let me prove it? . . . Or did she think I was planning to poison her? and her husband?

DAUGHTER *(Smoking; blowing smoke on drying toenails)* My husband and I were going out for dinner, I said.

MOTHER *(Twisting wedding ring)* Again! I said. But they'd been out the night before! Were they going to let me eat alone? Again?

DAUGHTER *(Smokes; begins to file fingernails)* Aha! I thought. Bracing myself for a list of guilt-inspiring examples from the past. When *she* had turned down the most enticing invitations. To stay home with *me*. When I was "still a little girl" . . . I was afraid she'd have to eat alone again. Yes, I said.

MOTHER *(Twisting wedding ring)* All their hard-earned money washed down their throats, I said. I was sure they could have bought a house with the money they had carried to restaurants in all those eighteen . . . sorry: sixteen . . . years. A big house. With a garden. In the country, I said.

DAUGHTER *(Begins to paint fingernails)* I said she was undoubtedly right. But that I wasn't interested in a big house in the country . . . That I couldn't afford to be interested. Because of my work. That I couldn't afford not to live in the city. That I had to be within ready reach. By telephone. *(She stubs out cigarette)*

MOTHER *(Twisting wedding ring)* I did *not* ask: Had she to be within ready reach in the middle of the night? For black men to call her in the middle of the night? I merely said: that lots of people commuted. And that, if *she* wasn't interested in a house . . . in the country . . . I was sure her husband was.

DAUGHTER *(Painting fingernails)* I assured her that he was not.

MOTHER *(Twisting wedding ring)* I said: and *I* was sure that her husband would have remained more interested in *her*, if she were interested in making a pleasant home for him. All husbands were interested in a pleasant home. And a pleasant dinner. I was sure her husband would become interested in her again, if she started making a pleasant home for him.

DAUGHTER *(Blowing on painted fingernails)* She kept forgetting that I was a professional woman, I said. That I worked. Even if I did my work at home. And that, even if I *were* interested, I didn't have the time to take care of a house. Besides, what made her so sure my husband had lost interest in me? He was extremely interested. In my work, I said. We even collaborated on things, occasionally . . . *(She blows on painted fingernails)*

MOTHER I said she knew very well that "interest in her work" was not what I'd had in mind. And that she didn't have to take from her working time to give a little more thought to making her husband a pleasant home . . . All she had to do was think a little less about black men . . . Who thought nothing of telephoning her in the middle of the night. Who shouldn't feel free to telephone her in the first place. Who only kept her from working . . . only interrupted her work . . . by telephoning morning noon and night . . . No husband could be expected to put up with that sort of thing forever, I said.

DAUGHTER Oh, have a cigarette, I said. *(She holds pack out to* MOTHER, *careful not to spoil her still-wet nails)*

MOTHER *(Ignores offered pack)* Maybe her husband didn't care . . . Enough . . . Any more . . . I said. But I cared. She couldn't expect me just to sit by and watch her wreck her life! She was flesh of *my* flesh, I said. Blood of *my* blood . . .

DAUGHTER I said: every time I heard the word *blood*, all I could think was *spill* . . . *(She pulls cigarette from pack with her lips; lights it; inhales deeply)*

MOTHER Did she really *have* to smoke that cigarette? I asked. Just to spite me? Still? At her age? . . . She'd just put one out.

DAUGHTER *(Smoke-sigh)* I said I'd be perfectly happy to let her smoke it in my stead. *(She holds cigarette to* MOTHER'*s face)*

MOTHER *(Averts her face)* I said: Didn't she know I only meant well. That I only wanted to help her?

DAUGHTER I couldn't help myself. *(She stuffs cigarette into* MOTHER'*s mouth)* My hands were stuffing the burning cigarette into her mouth. Deep down into her throat. My nail polish hadn't dried. It smeared on her cheek and chin. She bit my fingers . . .

MOTHER *(Speaks with increasing difficulty)* I couldn't believe that she would really hurt me. Physically. That my own flesh would turn against me in bodily earnest. *(Her hands flail out; find* DAUGHTER'*s throat)* My hands found her throat . . . In self-defense . . . and tried to push her away from me . . . and pressed . . .

DAUGHTER   *(Speaks with increasing difficulty)* Her hands were around my
      throat. I could feel the hardness of her wedding ring. That used to hurt
      my cheek when she'd slap me when I was a little girl. When I had been
      "bad" . . . When she used to tell me that slapping me . . . with her hard
      wedding ring . . . hurt her more than it hurt my cheek . . . I couldn't
      believe that she was strangling me in earnest . . .
MOTHER and DAUGHTER   *(Choke and strangle each other. Push each other.*
      Fall into open harp cases)

[1968]

For Discussion

1. What might the stage setting—women in harp cases—suggest, when the
   other props are just common objects such as a coffeepot and telephone?
2. Are the women talking to each other, to themselves, or to the audience?
   What does the unusual point of view allow that regular dialogue might
   not?
3. According to the mother, what had she given her daughter? What does
   the daughter mean by "She was offering what she did not have to give"?
4. How do the two women's versions of the daughter's childhood differ?
   Why is the reminiscence about the cow bell significant?
5. What do we learn about the father? the husband? Johnny?
6. What is the tone of the play? Is there any humor in the comments or
   thoughts of the characters?
7. What is the mother's definition of "vice" and how might the daughter de-
   fine it?
8. What does the mother want from the daughter, and vice versa? Why is
   Johnny's mother included?
9. Analyze the ending, and what it might mean about women and family.
   Are we prepared in any way for what happens?

For Further Exploration

1. Marsha Norman's Pulitzer Prize winning play *'Night, Mother* is another
   dialogue between a mother and her adult daughter. How is the ending of
   'Night, Mother as shocking as the ending to this play, and what themes
   about women and family do the plays have in common?
2. Examine the function of violent acts and images in this play and in stories
   and poems. How is violence used as a symbol, and when is it intended to
   be a realistic reaction to people and events? Or, contrast the hostility between generations with the benevolent feelings expressed in novels such
   as Mary Gordon's *Men and Angels* or Anne Tyler's *Earthly Possessions.*

For Discussion and Writing About This Section

1. Compare the mother-daughter relationships in the stories, poems, and play. Which works continue into three generations, and what qualities are evident in each that are handed down?

2. Examine the women's "significant others" in the stories and poems. What is the definition of "family" in each story? How clear a picture of the "mate" do we get in these works?

3. Find interpersonal triangles in the stories and poems. In which cases does the triangle function well, and in which is it destructive?

4. What is similar about the relationships between family members in other stories and poems and the relationship between Miss Furr and Miss Skeene in Stein's story?

5. Which women have personal power in these poems and stories, and what kinds of power are there?

6. Determine which works are humorous and which are satirical. On a continuum from serious to satirical to humorous, place each poem, story, and play according to tone. What can you find in the most humorous piece that makes it differ from the most serious one?

7. Compare the tone and point of view of the poem "Breaking Tradition: For My Daughter" with that of *Breakfast Past Noon.*

ADULTHOOD
Women and Society

Experiencing satisfaction or dissatisfaction; accepting or combating social codes; dealing with individual differences; race, religion, and sexuality; repeating patterns or seeking awareness

One of the many important contributions of literature by and about women is that it creates an artistic vision of the strong union between public and private worlds. That is, women's literature, rooted as it often is in domestic detail and introspection, nevertheless looks outward as well, and has much to say about society as a whole. This section of stories and poems in particular reveals the constant attempt to relate the life of the individual—the insistent exploration of what constitutes "self"—with the life of "society" as a whole.

Each author creates a small world, with an adult woman at its center. Most of the representation of "society" is achieved by characterizing a variety of people in a small town, in a restricted geographical area, or in a group meeting place. Two stories are set in small country towns whose inhabitants are strikingly similar despite being on different continents; and the other settings—a beach resort, a lunch room, and a party—all show that people who gather together can become a formidable social entity for an individual to confront.

Each individual's reactions to society are presented to us in the form of recorded thoughts often clashing directly with spoken words or with the reality of the situation. For example, a woman planning a seduction is herself seduced and, in another story, while two women are talking, one is carrying on a separate sarcastic commentary in her mind. These separations of "inner" and "outer" reality, public and private selves, are externalized in the play *Overtones,* in which each woman's real thoughts are spoken by a "second self" standing behind her.

The ironies of these situations are compounded by the authors' uses of tableaus, often at the ends of the stories, symbolic poses in which several characters are left standing in spots showing their relative positions in society. Most of the tableaus involve the alienation of the main character from the rest of society—the "one among the many" motif. For example, Mabel in "The New Dress" at first tries to see herself and others as flies caught in a saucer of milk, but finds that the only one she can envision there is herself, increasingly engulfed and entrapped. The reader can identify with one person's plight, especially when the individual is in the eye of the public, or on "the horns of a dilemma," as in the story "Guidance."

The poems about women and society also speak to the theme of the individual's opposition to society, and appeal directly to readers as collective individuals. As a group of individuals we can reject traditional "society," as do the women in many of the poems. Yet to what extent are we a willing part of the society we castigate? "A Happening in Barbados" confronts the issue directly when the narrator realizes that she has inflicted her own misery on another woman. In *Overtones,* the women accuse each other of hypocrisy while each is a hypocrite herself.

These stories and poems go beyond the expected role of women's literature to abjure traditional social mores. They examine real moral issues: who is narrow-minded and restrictive—self, or society? In view of the answer to that question, does the woman in each work change herself or does she rebel against prevailing social codes? In some cases, the author herself has given intrinsic clues: one woman begins with an artificial limb and perhaps is "saved" by losing it. Changing oneself—despite the artificiality and restrictiveness of society—is seen as important for women's survival and growth.

Yet the barriers constructed by "society" are not above notice, and accepted social institutions are scrutinized via personal accounts in poetry and prose. Religion and morality are examined for their applications to women's lives: How should one live? How will one die? For some authors, the struggle is between God and the Devil, whereas for others the conflict is simply between the "divine moments" and "flat moments" of life. For several of the women, such as the main character in "Good Country People," the dichotomy is between the "head" and the "heart," a conflict common in literature about women in society.

Society's woes are well defined by these authors. Not only are the moral and ethical questions delineated, but the gamut of social problems is presented as well. The authors explore interracial relationships, violent acts, and sexual issues such as selecting a partner, jealousy, competition, sexual power, and rape. Power itself is again a factor in most of the interactions among women or between women and men. In fact, the amount of power experienced by each of the women often determines the degree of acceptance or hostility toward each situation and its outcome.

Although many different time periods are represented, the one most evident motif is curiously modern: the theme of reality versus illusion, in which the protagonist tries to discover the meaning of her own and others' existence. In these works, things are not often as they seem, or the "seeming" reality is false. Whether or not the private or the public self is the "real" one is the question asked by a number of the authors. But the overview of different types of women's lives in society reminds us that we are a part of all of society, whether we like it or not.

Part of the human connectedness message is that we must learn not to judge or stereotype others, lest we be judged or typed ourselves. While this lesson is often one of the hardest to learn, in doing so the women gain tremendous insight. Like tragic heroes of classical literature, the bigger these women are in society, the harder they fall; women priding themselves on their personal superiority are too likely to prejudge and end by doing themselves harm. In many of the stories, women's initial pride leads to the final recognition that they have created their own downfalls. By seeing themselves on top of the social hierarchy, they have cast themselves to the bottom. True dignity is achieved by recognizing and accepting the personal worth of others, and the women who seek social equality in the stories must first grant it to others.

Poetry affords less opportunity to explore the main character's learning experience; as fiction provides the space for the main character to change, poetry provides the concentrated statement of one point of view. Women in the poems are rebellious, angry, or sad, but are often also inquiring: Why are women in society separated from each other? What defines a woman if not biological roles, social mores, caring for others, and enduring suffering?

In short, the poetry, fiction, and drama represented here attempt to challenge the frequent assumption that women cannot change themselves or society. By asking questions or by holding mirrors to reality, literature about women in society promotes change, rather than reinforcing the impulse to continue in given patterns of thought and behavior.

Fiction About
Women and Society

One of the most striking qualities of the fiction about adult women and society is the frequency with which reversals occur in each account—reversals of expectations, of status, and of situations. These reversals are almost invariably accompanied by personal insights, suggesting that strong shifts in points of view can result from subtle reversals of fortune.

Many of the reversals appear to result in defeat for the major character; yet these authors assert that out of defeat can come not only insight, but triumph as well. Like the tragic heroes of literature throughout the ages, these women confront their destinies and learn to be better human beings in the process.

In discovering her own humanity, the protagonist sees herself in true relation to the rest of society, instead of remaining removed and falsely superior to the common lot. This new awareness of the uniqueness of others forms the basis for many related themes—such as race, class, and age—all tied closely to struggles between the sexes. There are strong parallels among the situations of oppressed groups, of which the protagonist is often unaware until her final discovery of self and others.

An important underlying reason for the overt struggles between individuals and groups in these stories is power, and the symbol of power used again and again is the sex act. As the focal point of power struggles, sex is used to demonstrate "who is on top" of racial, gender, and class issues; ironically, the supposed victor is often the long-term loser when the victim gains insight leading to more lasting power.

Flannery O'Connor

1925-1964

Thirty-two year old Joy Hopewell, Ph.D., has little real knowledge or experience to help her deal with the microcosm of society represented by the "good country people" in this story. The arrival of a stranger overturns Joy's small world and challenges her avowed world view.

GOOD COUNTRY PEOPLE

Besides the neutral expression that she wore when she was alone, Mrs. Freeman had two others, forward and reverse, that she used for all her human dealings. Her forward expression was steady and driving like the advance of a heavy truck. Her eyes never swerved to left or right but turned as the story turned as if they followed a yellow line down the center of it. She seldom used the other expression because it was not often necessary for her to retract a statement, but when she did, her face came to a complete stop, there was an almost imperceptible movement of her black eyes, during which they seemed to be receding, and then the observer would see that Mrs. Freeman, though she might stand there as real as several grain sacks thrown on top of each other, was no longer there in spirit. As for getting anything across to her when this was the case, Mrs. Hopewell had given it up. She might talk her head off. Mrs. Freeman could never be brought to admit herself wrong on any point. She would stand there and if she could be brought to say anything, it was something like, "Well, I wouldn't of said it was and I wouldn't of said it wasn't" or letting her gaze range over the top kitchen shelf where there was an assortment of dusty bottles, she might remark, "I see you ain't ate many of them figs you put up last summer."

They carried on their most important business in the kitchen at breakfast. Every morning Mrs. Hopewell got up at seven o'clock and lit her gas heater and Joy's. Joy was her daughter, a large blonde girl who had an artificial leg. Mrs. Hopewell thought of her as a child though she was thirty-two years old and highly educated. Joy would get up while her mother was eating and lumber into the bathroom and slam the door, and before long, Mrs. Freeman would arrive at the back door. Joy would hear her mother call, "Come on in," and then they would talk for a while in low voices that were indistinguishable in the bathroom. By the time Joy came in, they had usually finished the weather report and were on one or the other of Mrs. Freeman's daughters, Glynese or Carramae. Joy called them Glycerin and Caramel. Glynese, a redhead, was eighteen and had many admirers; Carramae, a blonde, was only fifteen but already married and pregnant. She could not keep anything on her stomach. Every morning Mrs. Freeman told Mrs. Hopewell how many times she had vomited since the last report.

Mrs. Hopewell liked to tell people that Glynese and Carramae were two of the finest girls she knew and that Mrs. Freeman was a *lady* and that she was never ashamed to take her anywhere or introduce her to anybody they might meet. Then she would tell how she had happened to hire the Freemans in the first place and how they were a godsend to her and how she had had them four years. The reason for her keeping them so long was that they were not trash. They were good country people. She had telephoned the man whose name they had given as reference and he had told her that Mr. Freeman was a good farmer but that his wife was the nosiest woman ever to walk the earth. "She's got to be into everything," the man said. "If she don't get there before the dust settles, you can bet she's dead, that's all. She'll want to know all your business. I can stand him real good," he had said, "but me nor my wife neither could have stood that woman one more minute on this place." That had put Mrs. Hopewell off for a few days.

She had hired them in the end because there were no other applicants but she had made up her mind beforehand exactly how she would handle the woman. Since she was the type who had to be into everything, then, Mrs. Hopewell had decided, she would not only let her be into everything, she would *see to it* that she was into everything—she would give her the responsibility of everything, she would put her in charge. Mrs. Hopewell had no bad qualities of her own but she was able to use other people's in such a constructive way that she had kept them four years.

Nothing is perfect. This was one of Mrs. Hopewell's favorite sayings. Another was: that is life! And still another, the most important, was: well, other people have their opinions too. She would make these statements, usually at the table, in a tone of gentle insistence as if no one held them but her, and the large hulking Joy, whose constant outrage had obliterated every expression from her face, would stare just a little to the side of her, her eyes icy blue, with the look of someone who has achieved blindness by an act of will and means to keep it.

When Mrs. Hopewell said to Mrs. Freeman that life was like that, Mrs. Freeman would say, "I always said so myself." Nothing had been arrived at by anyone that had not first been arrived at by her. She was quicker than Mr. Freeman. When Mrs. Hopewell said to her after they had been on the place a while, "You know, you're the wheel behind the wheel," and winked, Mrs. Freeman had said, "I know it. I've always been quick. It's some that are quicker than others."

"Everybody is different," Mrs. Hopewell said.

"Yes, most people is," Mrs. Freeman said.

"It takes all kinds to make the world."

"I always said it did myself."

The girl was used to this kind of dialogue for breakfast and more of it for dinner; sometimes they had it for supper too. When they had no guest they ate in the kitchen because that was easier. Mrs. Freeman always managed to arrive at some point during the meal and to watch them finish it. She would stand in the doorway if it were summer but in the winter she would stand with one elbow on top of the refrigerator and look down on them, or she would stand by the gas heater, lifting the back of her skirt slightly. Occasionally she would stand against the wall and roll her head from side to side. At no time was she in any hurry to leave. All this was very trying on Mrs. Hopewell but she was a woman of great patience. She realized that nothing is perfect and that in the Freemans she had good country people and that if, in this day and age, you get good country people, you had better hang onto them.

She had had plenty of experience with trash. Before the Freemans she had averaged one tenant family a year. The wives of these farmers were not the kind you would want to be around you for very long. Mrs. Hopewell, who had divorced her husband long ago, needed someone to walk over the fields with her; and when Joy had to be impressed for these services, her remarks were usually so ugly and her face so glum that Mrs. Hopewell would say, "If you can't come pleasantly, I don't want you at all," to which the girl, standing square and rigid-shouldered with her neck thrust slightly forward, would reply, "If you want me, here I am—LIKE I AM."

Mrs. Hopewell excused this attitude because of the leg (which had been shot off in a hunting accident when Joy was ten). It was hard for Mrs. Hopewell to realize that her child was thirty-two now and that for more than twenty years she had had only one leg. She thought of her still as a child because it tore her heart to think instead of the poor stout girl in her thirties who had never danced a step or had any *normal* good times. Her name was really Joy but as soon as she was twenty-one and away from home, she had had it legally changed. Mrs. Hopewell was certain that she had thought and thought until she had hit upon the ugliest name in any language. Then she had gone and had the beautiful name, Joy, changed without telling her mother until after she had done it. Her legal name was Hulga.

When Mrs. Hopewell thought the name, Hulga, she thought of the broad blank hull of a battleship. She would not use it. She continued to call her Joy to which the girl responded but in a purely mechanical way.

Hulga had learned to tolerate Mrs. Freeman who saved her from taking walks with her mother. Even Glynese and Carramae were useful when they occupied attention that might otherwise have been directed at her. At first she had thought she could not stand Mrs. Freeman for she had found that it was not possible to be rude to her. Mrs. Freeman would take on strange resentments and for days together she would be sullen but the source of her displeasure was always obscure; a direct attack, a positive leer, blatant ugliness to her face—these never touched her. And without warning one day, she began calling her Hulga.

She did not call her that in front of Mrs. Hopewell who would have been incensed but when she and the girl happened to be out of the house together, she would say something and add the name Hulga to the end of it, and the big spectacled Joy-Hulga would scowl and redden as if her privacy had been intruded upon. She considered the name her personal affair. She had arrived at it first purely on the basis of its ugly sound and then the full genius of its fitness had struck her. She had a vision of the name working like the ugly sweating Vulcan who stayed in the furnace and to whom, presumably, the goddess had to come when called. She saw it as the name of her highest creative act. One of her major triumphs was that her mother had not been able to turn her dust into Joy, but the greater one was that she had been able to turn it herself into Hulga. However, Mrs. Freeman's relish for using the name only irritated her. It was as if Mrs. Freeman's beady steel-pointed eyes had penetrated far enough behind her face to reach some secret fact. Something about her seemed to fascinate Mrs. Freeman and then one day Hulga realized that it was the artificial leg. Mrs. Freeman had a special fondness for the details of secret infections, hidden deformities, assaults upon children. Of diseases, she preferred the lingering or incurable. Hulga had heard Mrs. Hopewell give her the details of the hunting accident, how the leg had been literally blasted off, how she had never lost consciousness. Mrs. Freeman could listen to it any time as if it had happened an hour ago.

When Hulga stumped into the kitchen in the morning (she could walk without making the awful noise but she made it—Mrs. Hopewell was certain—because it was ugly-sounding), she glanced at them and did not speak. Mrs. Hopewell would be in her red kimono with her hair tied around her head in rags. She would be sitting at the table, finishing her breakfast and Mrs. Freeman would be hanging by her elbow outward from the refrigerator, looking down at the table. Hulga always put her eggs on the stove to boil and then stood over them with her arms folded, and Mrs. Hopewell would look at her—a kind of indirect gaze divided between her and Mrs. Freeman—and would think that if she would only keep herself up a little, she wouldn't be so bad looking. There was nothing wrong with her face that a pleasant expression wouldn't help. Mrs. Hopewell said that people who looked on the bright side of things would be beautiful even if they were not.

Whenever she looked at Joy this way, she could not help but feel that it would have been better if the child had not taken the Ph.D. It had certainly not brought her out any and now that she had it, there was no more excuse for her to go to school again. Mrs. Hopewell thought it was nice for girls to go to school to have a good time but Joy had "gone through." Anyhow, she would not have been strong enough to go again. The doctors had told Mrs. Hopewell that with the best of care, Joy might see forty-five. She had a weak heart. Joy had made it plain that if it had not been for this condition, she would be far from these red hills and good country people. She would be in a university lecturing to people who knew what she was talking about. And Mrs. Hopewell could very well picture her there, looking like a scarecrow and lecturing to more of the same. Here she went about all day in a six-year-old skirt and a yellow sweat shirt with a faded cowboy on a horse embossed on it. She thought this was funny; Mrs. Hopewell thought it was idiotic and showed simply that she was still a child. She was brilliant but she didn't have a grain of sense. It seemed to Mrs. Hopewell that every year she grew less like other people and more like herself—bloated, rude, and squint-eyed. And she said such strange things! To her own mother she had said—without warning, without excuse, standing up in the middle of a meal with her face purple and her mouth half full—"Woman! do you ever look inside? Do you ever look inside and see what you are *not*? God!" she had cried sinking down again and staring at her plate, "Malebranche was right: we are not our own light. We are not our own light!" Mrs. Hopewell had no idea to this day what brought that on. She had only made the remark, hoping Joy would take it in, that a smile never hurt anyone.

The girl had taken the Ph.D. in philosophy and this left Mrs. Hopewell at a complete loss. You could say, "My daughter is a nurse," or "My daughter is a school teacher," or even, "My daughter is a chemical engineer." You could not say, "My daughter is a philosopher." That was something that had ended with the Greeks and Romans. All day Joy sat on her neck in a deep chair, reading. Sometimes she went for walks but she didn't like dogs or cats or birds or flowers or nature or nice young men. She looked at nice young men as if she could smell their stupidity.

One day Mrs. Hopewell had picked up one of the books the girl had just put down and opening it at random, she read, "Science, on the other hand, has to assert its soberness and seriousness afresh and declare that it is concerned solely with what-is. Nothing—how can it be for science anything but a horror and a phantasm? If science is right, then one thing stands firm: science wishes to know nothing of nothing. Such is after all the strictly scientific approach to Nothing. We know it by wishing to know nothing of Nothing." These words had been underlined with a blue pencil and they worked on Mrs. Hopewell like some evil incantation in gibberish. She shut the book quickly and went out of the room as if she were having a chill.

This morning when the girl came in, Mrs. Freeman was on Carramae. "She thrown up four times after supper," she said, "and was up twict in the night after three o'clock. Yesterday she didn't do nothing but ramble in the bureau drawer. All she did. Stand up there and see what she could run up on."

"She's got to eat," Mrs. Hopewell muttered, sipping her coffee, while she watched Joy's back at the stove. She was wondering what the child had said to the Bible salesman. She could not imagine what kind of a conversation she could possibly have had with him.

He was a tall gaunt hatless youth who had called yesterday to sell them a Bible. He had appeared at the door, carrying a large black suitcase that weighted him so heavily on one side that he had to brace himself against the door facing. He seemed on the point of collapse but he said in a cheerful voice, "Good morning, Mrs. Cedars!" and set the suitcase down on the mat. He was not a bad-looking young man though he had on a bright blue suit and yellow socks that were not pulled up far enough. He had prominent face bones and a streak of sticky-looking brown hair falling across his forehead.

"I'm Mrs. Hopewell," she said.

"Oh!" he said, pretending to look puzzled but with his eyes sparkling, "I saw it said 'The Cedars,' on the mailbox so I thought you was Mrs. Cedars!" and he burst out in a pleasant laugh. He picked up the satchel and under cover of a pant, he fell forward into her hall. It was rather as if the suitcase had moved first, jerking him after it. "Mrs. Hopewell!" he said and grabbed her hand. "I hope you are well!" and he laughed again and then all at once his face sobered completely. He paused and gave her a straight earnest look and said, "Lady, I've come to speak of serious things."

"Well, come in," she muttered, none too pleased because her dinner was almost ready. He came into the parlor and sat down on the edge of a straight chair and put the suitcase between his feet and glanced around the room as if he were sizing her up by it. Her silver gleamed on the two sideboards; she decided he had never been in a room as elegant as this.

"Mrs. Hopewell," he began, using her name in a way that sounded almost intimate, "I know you believe in Chrustian service."

"Well yes," she murmured.

"I know," he said and paused, looking very wise with his head cocked on one side, "that you're a good woman. Friends have told me."

Mrs. Hopewell never liked to be taken for a fool. "What are you selling?" she asked.

"Bibles," the young man said and his eye raced around the room before he added, "I see you have no family Bible in your parlor, I see that is the one lack you got!"

Mrs. Hopewell could not say, "My daughter is an atheist and won't let me keep the Bible in the parlor." She said, stiffening slightly, "I keep my Bible by my bedside." This was not the truth. It was in the attic somewhere.

"Lady," he said, "the word of God ought to be in the parlor."

"Well, I think that's a matter of taste," she began. "I think . . ."

"Lady," he said, "for a Chrustian, the word of God ought to be in every room in the house besides in his heart. I know you're a Chrustian because I can see it in every line of your face."

She stood up and said, "Well, young man, I don't want to buy a Bible and I smell my dinner burning."

He didn't get up. He began to twist his hands and looking down at them, he said softly, "Well lady, I'll tell you the truth—not many people want to buy one nowadays and besides, I know I'm real simple. I don't know how to say a thing but to say it. I'm just a country boy." He glanced up into her unfriendly face. "People like you don't like to fool with country people like me!"

"Why!" she cried, "good country people are the salt of the earth! Besides, we all have different ways of doing, it takes all kinds to make the world go 'round. That's life!"

"You said a mouthful," he said.

"Why, I think there aren't enough good country people in the world!" she said, stirred. "I think that's what's wrong with it!"

His face had brightened. "I didn't inraduce myself," he said. "I'm Manley Pointer from out in the country around Willohobie, not even from a place, just from near a place."

"You wait a minute," she said. "I have to see about my dinner." She went out to the kitchen and found Joy standing near the door where she had been listening.

"Get rid of the salt of the earth," she said, "and let's eat."

Mrs. Hopewell gave her a pained look and turned the heat down under the vegetables. "*I* can't be rude to anybody," she murmured and went back into the parlor.

He had opened the suitcase and was sitting with a Bible on each knee.

"You might as well put those up," she told him. "I don't want one."

"I appreciate your honesty," he said. "You don't see any more real honest people unless you go way out in the country."

"I know," she said, "real genuine folks!" Through the crack in the door she heard a groan.

"I guess a lot of boys come telling you they're working their way through college," he said, "but I'm not going to tell you that. Somehow," he said, "I don't want to go to college. I want to devote my life to Chrustian service. See," he said, lowering his voice, "I got this heart condition. I may not live long. When you know it's something wrong with you and you may not live long, well then, lady . . ." He paused, with his mouth open, and stared at her.

He and Joy had the same condition! She knew that her eyes were filling with tears but she collected herself quickly and murmured, "Won't you stay for dinner? We'd love to have you!" and was sorry the instant she heard herself say it.

"Yes mam," he said in an abashed voice, "I would sher love to do that!"

Joy had given him one look on being introduced to him and then throughout the meal had not glanced at him again. He had addressed several remarks to her, which she had pretended not to hear. Mrs. Hopewell could not understand deliberate rudeness, although she lived with it, and she felt she had always to overflow with hospitality to make up for Joy's lack of courtesy. She urged him to talk about himself and he did. He said he was the seventh child of twelve and that his father had been crushed under a tree when he himself was eight years old. He had been crushed very badly, in fact, almost cut in two and was practically not recognizable. His mother had got along the best she could by hard working and she had always seen that her children went to Sunday School and that they read the Bible every evening. He was now nineteen years old and he had been selling Bibles for four months. In that time he had sold seventy-seven Bibles and had the promise of two more sales. He wanted to become a missionary because he thought that was the way you could do most for people. "He who losest his life shall find it," he said simply and he was so sincere, so genuine and earnest that Mrs. Hopewell would not for the world have smiled. He prevented his peas from sliding onto the table by blocking them with a piece of bread which he later cleaned his plate with. She could see Joy observing sidewise how he handled his knife and fork and she saw too that every few minutes, the boy would dart a keen appraising glance at the girl as if he were trying to attract her attention.

After dinner Joy cleared the dishes off the table and disappeared and Mrs. Hopewell was left to talk with him. He told her again about his childhood and his father's accident and about various things that had happened to him. Every five minutes or so she would stifle a yawn. He sat for two hours until finally she told him she must go because she had an appointment in town. He packed his Bibles and thanked her and prepared to leave, but in the doorway he stopped and wrung her hand and said that not on any of his trips had he met a lady as nice as her and he asked if he could come again. She had said she would always be happy to see him.

Joy had been standing in the road, apparently looking at something in the distance, when he came down the steps toward her, bent to the side with his heavy valise. He stopped where she was standing and confronted her directly. Mrs. Hopewell could not hear what he said but she trembled to think what Joy would say to him. She could see that after a minute Joy said something and that then the boy began to speak again, making an excited gesture with his free hand. After a minute Joy said something else at which the boy began to speak once more. Then to her amazement, Mrs. Hopewell saw the two of them walk off together, toward the gate. Joy had walked all the way to the gate with him and Mrs. Hopewell could not imagine what they had said to each other, and she had not yet dared to ask.

Mrs. Freeman was insisting upon her attention. She had moved from the refrigerator to the heater so that Mrs. Hopewell had to turn and face her in order to seem to be listening. "Glynese gone out with Harvey Hill again last night," she said. "She had this sty."

"Hill," Mrs. Hopewell said absently, "is that the one who works in the garage?"

"Nome, he's the one that goes to chiropracter school," Mrs. Freeman said. "She had this sty. Been had it two days. So she says when he brought her in the other night he says, 'Lemme get rid of that sty for you', and she says, 'How?' and he says, 'You just lay yourself down acrost the seat of that car and I'll show you.' So she done it and he popped her neck. Kept on a-popping it several times until she made him quit. This morning," Mrs. Freeman said, "she ain't got no sty. She ain't got no traces of a sty."

"I never heard of that before," Mrs. Hopewell said.

"He ast her to marry him before the Ordinary." Mrs. Freeman went on, "and she told him she wasn't going to be married in no *office*."

"Well, Glynese is a fine girl," Mrs. Hopewell said. "Glynese and Carramae are both fine girls."

"Carramae said when her and Lyman was married Lyman said it sure felt sacred to him. She said he said he wouldn't take five hundred dollars for being married by a preacher."

"How much would he take?" the girl asked from the stove.

"He said he wouldn't take five hundred dollars," Mrs. Freeman repeated.

"Well we all have work to do," Mrs. Hopewell said.

"Lyman said it just felt more sacred to him," Mrs. Freeman said. "The doctor wants Carramae to eat prunes. Says instead of medicine. Says them cramps is coming from pressure. You know where I think it is?"

"She'll be better in a few weeks," Mrs. Hopewell said.

"In the tube," Mrs. Freeman said. "Else she wouldn't be as sick as she is."

Hulga had cracked her two eggs into a saucer and was bringing them to the table along with a cup of coffee that she had filled too full. She sat down carefully and began to eat, meaning to keep Mrs. Freeman there by questions if for any reason she showed an inclination to leave. She could perceive her mother's eye on her. The first round-about question would be about the Bible salesman and she did not wish to bring it on. "How did he pop her neck?" she asked.

Mrs. Freeman went into a description of how he had popped her neck. She said he owned a '55 Mercury but that Glynese said she would rather marry a man with only a '36 Plymouth who would be married by a preacher. The girl asked what if he had a '32 Plymouth and Mrs. Freeman said what Glynese had said was a '36 Plymouth.

Mrs. Hopewell said there were not many girls with Glynese's common sense. She said what she admired in those girls was their common sense. She said that reminded her that they had had a nice visitor yesterday, a young man selling Bibles. "Lord," she said, "he bored me to death but he was so sincere and genuine I couldn't be rude to him. He was just good country people, you know," she said, "—just the salt of the earth."

"I seen him walk up," Mrs. Freeman said, "and then later—I seen him walk off," and Hulga could feel the slight shift in her voice, the slight insinuation, that he had not walked off alone, had he? Her face remained expressionless but the color rose into her neck and she seemed to swallow it down with the next spoonful of egg. Mrs. Freeman was looking at her as if they had a secret together.

"Well, it takes all kinds of people to make the world go 'round," Mrs. Hopewell said, "It's very good we aren't all alike."

"Some people are more alike than others," Mrs. Freeman said.

Hulga got up and stumped, with about twice the noise that was necessary, into her room and locked the door. She was to meet the Bible salesman at ten o'clock at the gate. She had thought about it half the night. She had started thinking of it as a great joke and then she had begun to see profound implications in it. She had lain in bed imagining dialogues for them that were insane on the surface but that reached below to depths that no Bible salesman would be aware of. Their conversation yesterday had been of this kind.

He had stopped in front of her and had simply stood there. His face was bony and sweaty and bright, with a little pointed nose in the center of it, and his look was different from what it had been at the dinner table. He was gazing at her with open curiosity, with fascination, like a child watching a new fantastic animal at the zoo, and he was breathing as if he had run a great distance to reach her. His gaze seemed somehow familiar but she could not think where she had been regarded with it before. For almost a minute he didn't say anything. Then on what seemed an insuck of breath, he whispered, "You ever ate a chicken that was two days old?"

The girl looked at him stonily. He might have just put this question up for consideration at the meeting of a philosophical association. "Yes," she presently replied as if she had considered it from all angles.

"It must have been mighty small!" he said triumphantly and shook all over with little nervous giggles, getting very red in the face, and subsiding finally into his gaze of complete admiration, while the girl's expression remained exactly the same.

"How old are you?" he asked softly.

She waited some time before she answered. Then in a flat voice she said, "Seventeen."

His smiles came in succession like waves breaking on the surface of a little lake. "I see you got a wooden leg," he said. "I think you're real brave. I think you're real sweet."

The girl stood blank and solid and silent.

"Walk to the gate with me," he said. "You're a brave sweet little thing and I liked you the minute I seen you walk in the door."

Hulga began to move forward.

"What's your name?" he asked, smiling down on the top of her head.

"Hulga," she said.

"Hulga," he murmured, "Hulga. Hulga. I never heard of anybody name Hulga before. You're shy, aren't you, Hulga?" he asked.

She nodded, watching his large red hand on the handle of the giant valise.

"I like girls that wear glasses," he said. "I think a lot. I'm not like these people that a serious thought don't ever enter their heads. It's because I may die."

"I may die too," she said suddenly and looked up at him. His eyes were very small and brown, glittering feverishly.

"Listen," he said, "don't you think some people was meant to meet on account of what all they got in common and all? Like they both think serious thoughts and all?" He shifted the valise to his other hand so that the hand nearest her was free. He caught hold of her elbow and shook it a little. "I don't work on Saturday," he said. "I like to walk in the woods and see what Mother Nature is wearing. O'er the hills and far away. Picnics and things. Couldn't we go on a picnic tomorrow? Say yes, Hulga," he said and gave her a dying look as if he felt his insides about to drop out of him. He had even seemed to sway slightly toward her.

During the night she had imagined that she seduced him. She imagined that the two of them walked on the place until they came to the storage barn beyond the two back fields and there, she imagined, that things came to such a pass that she very easily seduced him and that then, of course, she had to reckon with his remorse. True genius can get an idea across even to an inferior mind. She imagined that she took his remorse in hand and changed it into a deeper understanding of life. She took all his shame away and turned it into something useful.

She set off for the gate at exactly ten o'clock, escaping without drawing Mrs. Hopewell's attention. She didn't take anything to eat, forgetting that food is usually taken on a picnic. She wore a pair of slacks and a dirty white shirt, and as an afterthought, she had put some Vapex on the collar of it since she did not own any perfume. When she reached the gate no one was there.

She looked up and down the empty highway and had the furious feeling that she had been tricked, that he had only meant to make her walk to the gate after the idea of him. Then suddenly he stood up, very tall, from behind a bush on the opposite embankment. Smiling, he lifted his hat which was new and wide-brimmed. He had not worn it yesterday and she wondered if he had bought it for the occasion. It was toast-colored with a red and white band around it and was slightly too large for him. He stepped from behind the bush carrying the black valise. He had on the same suit and the same yellow socks sucked down in his shoes from walking. He crossed the highway and said, "I knew you'd come!"

The girl wondered acidly how he had known this. She pointed to the valise and asked, "Why did you bring your Bibles?"

He took her elbow, smiling down on her as if he could not stop. "You can never tell when you'll need the word of God, Hulga," he said. She had a moment in which she doubted that this was actually happening and then they began to climb the embankment. They went down into the pasture toward the woods. The boy walked lightly by her side, bouncing on his toes. The valise did not seem to be heavy today; he even swung it. They crossed half the pasture without saying anything and then, putting his hand easily on the small of her back, he asked softly, "Where does your wooden leg join on?"

She turned an ugly red and glared at him and for an instant the boy looked abashed. "I didn't mean you no harm," he said. "I only meant you're so brave and all. I guess God takes care of you."

"No," she said, looking forward and walking fast, "I don't even believe in God."

At this he stopped and whistled. "No!" he exclaimed as if he were too astonished to say anything else.

She walked on and in a second he was bouncing at her side, fanning with his hat. "That's very unusual for a girl," he remarked, watching her out of the corner of his eye. When they reached the edge of the wood, he put his hand on her back again and drew her against him without a word and kissed her heavily.

The kiss, which had more pressure than feeling behind it, produced that extra surge of adrenalin in the girl that enables one to carry a packed trunk out of a burning house, but in her, the power went at once to the brain. Even before he released her, her mind, clear and detached and ironic anyway, was regarding him from a great distance, with amusement but with pity. She had never been kissed before and she was pleased to discover that it was an unexceptional experience and all a matter of the mind's control. Some people might enjoy drain water if they were told it was vodka. When the boy, looking expectant but uncertain, pushed her gently away, she turned and walked on, saying nothing as if such business, for her, were common enough.

He came along panting at her side, trying to help her when he saw a root that she might trip over. He caught and held back the long swaying blades of thorn vine until she had passed beyond them. She led the way and he came breathing heavily behind her. Then they came out on a sunlit hillside, sloping softly into another one a little smaller. Beyond, they could see the rusted top of the old barn where the extra hay was stored.

The hill was sprinkled with small pink weeds. "Then you ain't saved?" he asked suddenly, stopping.

The girl smiled. It was the first time she had smiled at him at all. "In my economy," she said, "I'm saved and you are damned but I told you I didn't believe in God."

Nothing seemed to destroy the boy's look of admiration. He gazed at her now as if the fantastic animal at the zoo had put its paw through the bars and given him a loving poke. She thought he looked as if he wanted to kiss her again and she walked on before he had the chance.

"Ain't there somewheres we can sit down sometime?" he murmured, his voice softening toward the end of the sentence.

"In that barn," she said.

They made for it rapidly as if it might slide away like a train. It was a large two-story barn, cool and dark inside. The boy pointed up the ladder that led into the loft and said, "It's too bad we can't go up there."

"Why can't we?" she asked.

"Yer leg," he said reverently.

The girl gave him a contemptuous look and putting both hands on the ladder, she climbed it while he stood below, apparently awestruck. She pulled herself expertly through the opening and then looked down at him and said, "Well, come on if you're coming," and he began to climb the ladder, awkwardly bringing the suitcase with him.

"We won't need the Bible," she observed.

"You never can tell," he said, panting. After he had got into the loft, he was a few seconds catching his breath. She had sat down in a pile of straw. A wide sheath of sunlight, filled with dust particles, slanted over her. She lay back against a bale, her face turned away, looking out the front opening of the barn where hay was thrown from a wagon into the loft. The two pink-speckled hillsides lay back against a dark ridge of woods. The sky was cloudless and cold blue. The boy dropped down by her side and put one arm under her and the other over her and began methodically kissing her face, making little noises like a fish. He did not remove his hat but it was pushed far enough back not to interfere. When her glasses got in his way, he took them off of her and slipped them into his pocket.

The girl at first did not return any of the kisses but presently she began to and after she had put several on his cheek, she reached his lips and remained there, kissing him again and again as if she were trying to draw all the breath out of him. His breath was clear and sweet like a child's and the kisses were sticky like a child's. He mumbled about loving her and about knowing when he first seen her that he loved her, but the mumbling was like the sleepy fretting of a child being put to sleep by his mother. Her mind, throughout this, never stopped or lost itself for a second to her feelings. "You ain't said you loved me none," he whispered finally, pulling back from her. "You got to say that."

She looked away from him off into the hollow sky and then down at a black ridge and then down farther into what appeared to be two green swelling lakes. She didn't realize he had taken her glasses but this landscape could not seem exceptional to her for she seldom paid any close attention to her surroundings.

"You got to say it," he repeated. "You got to say you love me."

She was always careful how she committed herself. "In a sense," she began, "if you use the word loosely, you might say that. But it's not a word I use. I don't have illusions. I'm one of those people who see *through* to nothing."

The boy was frowning. "You got to say it. I said it and you got to say it," he said.

The girl looked at him almost tenderly. "You poor baby," she murmured. "It's just as well you don't understand," and she pulled him by the neck, face-down, against her. "We are all damned," she said, "but some of us have taken off our blindfolds and see that there's nothing to see. It's a kind of salvation."

The boy's astonished eyes looked blankly through the ends of her hair. "Okay," he almost whined, "but do you love me or don'tcher?"

"Yes," she said and added, "in a sense. But I must tell you something. There mustn't be anything dishonest between us." She lifted his head and looked him in the eye. "I am thirty years old," she said. "I have a number of degrees."

The boy's look was irritated but dogged. "I don't care," he said. "I don't care a thing about what all you done. I just want to know if you love me or don'tcher?" and he caught her to him and wildly planted her face with kisses until she said, "Yes, yes."

"Okay then," he said, letting her go. "Prove it."

She smiled, looking dreamily out on the shifty landscape. She had seduced him without even making up her mind to try. "How?" she asked, feeling that he should be delayed a little.

He leaned over and put his lips to her ear. "Show me where your wooden leg joins on," he whispered.

The girl uttered a sharp little cry and her face instantly drained of color. The obscenity of the suggestion was not what shocked her. As a child she had sometimes been subject to feelings of shame but education had removed the last traces of that as a good surgeon scrapes for cancer; she would no more have felt it over what he was asking than she would have believed in his Bible. But she was as sensitive about the artificial leg as a peacock about his tail. No one ever touched it but her. She took care of it as someone else would his soul, in private and almost with her own eyes turned away. "No," she said.

"I known it," he muttered, sitting up. "You're just playing me for a sucker."

"Oh no no!" she cried. "It joins on at the knee. Only at the knee. Why do you want to see it?"

The boy gave her a long penetrating look. "Because," he said, "it's what makes you different. You ain't like anybody else."

She sat staring at him. There was nothing about her face or her round freezing-blue eyes to indicate that this had moved her; but she felt as if her heart had stopped and left her mind to pump her blood. She decided that for the first time in her life she was face to face with real innocence. This boy, with an instinct that came from beyond wisdom, had touched the truth about her. When after a minute, she said in a hoarse high voice, "All right," it was like surrendering to him completely. It was like losing her own life and finding it again, miraculously, in his.

Very gently he began to roll the slack leg up. The artificial limb, in a white sock and brown flat shoe, was bound in a heavy material like canvas and ended in an ugly jointure where it was attached to the stump. The boy's face and his voice were entirely reverent as he uncovered it and said, "Now show me how to take it off and on."

She took it off for him and put it back on again and then he took it off himself, handling it as tenderly as if it were a real one. "See!" he said with a delighted child's face. "Now I can do it myself!"

"Put it back on," she said. She was thinking that she would run away with him and that every night he would take the leg off and every morning put it back on again. "Put it back on," she said.

"Not yet," he murmured, setting it on its foot out of her reach. "Leave it off for awhile. You got me instead."

She gave a little cry of alarm but he pushed her down and began to kiss her again. Without the leg she felt entirely dependent on him. Her brain seemed to have stopped thinking altogether and to be about some other function that it was not very good at. Different expressions raced back and forth over her face. Every now and then the boy, his eyes like two steel spikes, would glance behind him, where the leg stood. Finally she pushed him off and said, "Put it back on me now."

"Wait," he said. He leaned the other way and pulled the valise toward him and opened it. It had a pale blue spotted lining and there were only two Bibles in it. He took one of these out and opened the cover of it. It was hollow and contained a pocket flask of whiskey, a pack of cards, and a small blue box with printing on it. He laid these out in front of her one at a time in an evenly-spaced row, like one presenting offerings at the shrine of a goddess. He put the blue box in her hand. THIS PRODUCT TO BE USED ONLY FOR THE PREVENTION OF DISEASE, she read, and dropped it. The boy was unscrewing the top of the flask. He stopped and pointed, with a smile, to the deck of cards. It was not an ordinary deck but one with an obscene picture on the back of each card. "Take a swig," he said, offering her the bottle first. He held it in front of her, but like one mesmerized, she did not move.

Her voice when she spoke had an almost pleading sound. "Aren't you," she murmured, "aren't you just good country people?"

The boy cocked his head. He looked as if he were just beginning to understand that she might be trying to insult him. "Yeah," he said, curling his lip slightly, "but it ain't held me back none. I'm as good as you any day in the week."

"Give me my leg," she said.

He pushed it farther away with his foot. "Come on now, let's begin to have us a good time," he said coaxingly. "We ain't got to know one another good yet."

"Give me my leg!" she screamed and tried to lunge for it but he pushed her down easily.

"What's the matter with you all of a sudden?" he asked, frowning as he screwed the top on the flask and put it quickly back inside the Bible. "You just a while ago said you didn't believe in nothing. I thought you was some girl!"

Her face was almost purple. "You're a Christian!" she hissed. "You're a fine Christian! You're just like them all—say one thing and do another. You're a perfect Christian, you're . . ."

The boy's mouth was set angrily. "I hope you don't think," he said in a lofty indignant tone, "that I believe in that crap! I may sell Bibles but I know which end is up and I wasn't born yesterday and I know where I'm going!"

"Give me my leg!" she screeched. He jumped up so quickly that she barely saw him sweep the cards and the blue box back into the Bible and throw the Bible into the valise. She saw him grab the leg and then she saw it for an instant slanted forlornly across the inside of the suitcase with a Bible at either side of its opposite ends. He slammed the lid shut and snatched up the valise and swung it down the hole and then stepped through himself.

When all of him had passed but his head, he turned and regarded her with a look that no longer had any admiration in it. "I've gotten a lot of interesting things," he said. "One time I got a woman's glass eye this way. And you needn't to think you'll catch me because Pointer ain't really my name. I use a different name at every house I call at and don't stay nowhere long. And I'll tell you another thing, Hulga," he said, using the name as if he didn't think much of it, "you ain't so smart. I been believing in nothing ever since I was born!'' and then the toast-colored hat disappeared down the hole and the girl was left, sitting on the straw in the dusty sunlight. When she turned her churning face toward the opening, she saw his blue figure struggling successfully over the green speckled lake.

Mrs. Hopewell and Mrs. Freeman, who were in the back pasture, digging up onions, saw him emerge a little later from the woods and head across the meadow toward the highway. "Why, that looks like that nice dull young man that tried to sell me a Bible yesterday," Mrs. Hopewell said, squinting. "He must have been selling them to the Negroes back in there. He was so simple," she said, "but I guess the world would be better off if we were all that simple."

Mrs. Freeman's gaze drove forward and just touched him before he disappeared under the hill. Then she returned her attention to the evil-smelling onion shoot she was lifting from the ground. "Some can't be that simple," she said. "I know I never could."

[1955]

For Discussion

1. Identify each of the characters at the beginning of the story as representing one philosophy making up part of the microcosm of society described here. In doing so, interpret the "type names" O'Connor uses: what could be meant by "Freeman," "Hopewell," "Glynese and Carramae," and "Joy/Hulga"?

2. Select some of the dialogue between Mrs. Freeman and Mrs. Hopewell and compare it with comments from Joy's philosophy books. Which makes more sense? Which does the author present seriously and which ironically?

3. How does Manley Pointer gain Mrs. Hopewell's confidence? Joy's confidence?

4. How does Hulga's vision of what will happen at the picnic differ from what really happens?

5. Find examples of the "head versus heart" dichotomy, especially in the scene between Manley and Hulga in the barn. What point might the author be making?

6. What is the significance of the objects hidden in the Bible? What do Hulga's shock and her comments reveal about whether or not she believes in "Nothing"?

7. Analyze the double ironies of Manley's Bible quotations, such as "He who loses his life shall find it," and "You can never tell when you'll need the word of God." That is, why does Joy (or the reader) first accept these statements at face value, then mistrust them, then perhaps find that they are true after all?

8. What do "believing," having a "soul," and being "saved" have to do with this story of one woman in a society of "good country people"?

9. Listen to the name "Manley Pointer." Has a man pointed her in a good, or a bad direction? Argue a case for Joy/Hulga as a new type of person—how will she live in society in the future?

10. What is the final irony of Mrs. Hopewell and Mrs. Freeman's comments as Manley leaves?

For Further Exploration

1. Compare the experience that Joy/Hulga has with Manley Pointer to the experience that Connie has with Arnold Friend in "Where Are You Going, Where Have You Been?" Why do both of the men "seem familiar" to the women, then turn out to be other than what they seemed? How are the authors' admonitions to women the same, and how do they differ?
2. Read another story by Flannery O'Connor, such as "Revelation" (another microcosm of society) to determine what she means by "salvation" as it relates to society. What does the theme of human connectedness have to do with personal satisfaction and salvation?

Louise Meriwether

1923–

In this story, each person ostensibly seeking a sexual partner is actually looking for something else not provided by the larger society—power, affection, respect, or a sense of belonging. Is it possible to gain something for oneself without taking it away from others?

A HAPPENING IN BARBADOS

The best way to pick up a Barbadian man, I hoped, was to walk alone down the beach with my tall, brown frame squeezed into a skintight bathing suit. Since my hotel was near the beach, and Dorothy and Alison, my two traveling companions, had gone shopping, I managed this quite well. I had not taken more than a few steps on the glittering, white sand before two black men were on either side of me vying for attention.

I chose the tall, slim-hipped one over the squat, muscle-bound man who was also grinning at me. But apparently they were friends, because Edwin had no sooner settled me under his umbrella than the squat one showed up with a beach chair and two other boys in tow.

Edwin made the introductions. His temporary rival was Gregory, and the other two were Alphonse and Dimitri.

Gregory was ugly. He had thick, rubbery lips, a scarcity of teeth, and a broad nose splattered like a pyramid across his face. He was all massive shoulders and bulging biceps. No doubt he had a certain animal magnetism, but personally I preferred a lean man like Edwin, who was well built but slender, his whole body fitting together like a symphony. Alphonse and Dimitri were clean-cut and pleasant looking.

They were all too young—twenty to twenty-five at the most—and Gregory seemed the oldest. I inwardly mourned their youth and settled down to make the most of my catch.

The crystal-blue sky rivaled the royal blue of the Caribbean for beauty, and our black bodies on the white sand added to the munificence of colors. We ran into the sea like squealing children when the sudden raindrops came, then shivered on the sand under a makeshift tent of umbrellas and damp towels waiting for the sun to reappear while nourishing ourselves with straight Barbados rum.

As with most of the West Indians I had already met on my whirlwind tour of Trinidad and Jamaica, who welcomed American Negroes with open arms, my new friends loved their island home, but work was scarce and they yearned to go to America. They were hungry for news of how Negroes were faring in the States.

Edwin's arm rested casually on my knee in a proprietary manner, and I smiled at him. His thin, serious face was smooth, too young for a razor, and when he smiled back, he looked even younger. He told me he was a waiter at the Hilton, saving his money to make it to the States. I had already learned not to be snobbish with the island's help. Yesterday's waiter may be tomorrow's prime minister.

Dimitri, very black with an infectious grin, was also a waiter, and lanky Alphonse was a tile setter.

Gregory's occupation was apparently women, for that's all he talked about. He was able to launch this subject when a bony white woman—more peeling red than white, really looking like a gaunt cadaver in a loose-fitting bathing suit—came out of the sea and walked up to us. She smiled archly at Gregory.

"Are you going to take me to the Pigeon Club tonight, sugar?"

"No, mon," he said pleasantly, with a toothless grin. "I'm taking a younger pigeon."

The woman turned a deeper red, if that was possible, and, mumbling something incoherent, walked away.

"That one is always after me to take her some place," Gregory said. "She's rich, and she pays the bills but, mon, I don't want an old hag nobody else wants. I like to take my women away from white men and watch them squirm."

"Come down, mon," Dimitri said, grinning. "She look like she's starving for what you got to spare."

We all laughed. The boys exchanged stories about their experiences with predatory white women who came to the islands looking for some black action. But, one and all, they declared they liked dark-skinned meat the best, and I felt like a black queen of the Nile when Gregory winked at me and said, "The blacker the berry, mon, the sweeter the juice."

They had all been pursued and had chased some white tail, too, no doubt, but while the others took it all in good humor, it soon became apparent that Gregory's exploits were exercises in vengeance.

Gregory was saying: "I told that bastard, 'You in my country now, mon, and I'll kick your ass all the way back to Texas. The girl agreed to dance with me, and she don't need your permission.' That white man's face turned purple, but he sat back down, and I dance with his girl. Mon, they hate to see me rubbing bellies with their women because they know once she rub bellies with me she wanna rub something else, too." He laughed, and we all joined in. Serves the white men right, I thought. Let's see how they liked licking *that* end of the stick for a change.

"Mon, you gonna get killed yet," Edwin said, moving closer to me on the towel we shared. "You're crazy. You don't care whose woman you mess with. But it's not gonna be a white man who kill you but some bad Bajan."

Gregory led in the laughter, then held us spellbound for the next hour with intimate details of his affair with Glenda, a young white girl spending the summer with her father on their yacht. Whatever he had, Glenda wanted desperately, or so Gregory told it.

Yeah, I thought to myself, like LSD, a black lover is the thing this year. I had seen the white girls in the Village and at off-Broadway theaters clutching their black men tightly while I, manless, looked on with bitterness. I then vowed I would find me an ofay in self-defense, but I could never bring myself to condone the wholesale rape of my slave ancestors by letting a white man touch me.

We finished the rum, and the three boys stood up to leave, making arrangements to get together later with us and my two girl friends and go clubbing.

Edwin and I were left alone. He stretched out his muscled leg and touched my toes with his. I smiled at him and let our thighs come together.

Why did he have to be so damned young? Then our lips met, his warm and demanding, and I thought, what the hell, maybe I will. I was thirty-nine—good-bye, sweet bird of youth—an angry divorcee, uptight and drinking too much, trying to disown the years which had brought only loneliness and pain. I had clawed my way up from the slums of Harlem via night school and was now a law clerk on Wall Street. But the fight upward had taken its toll. My husband, who couldn't claw as well as I, got lost somewhere in that concrete jungle. The last I saw of him, he was peering under every skirt around, searching for his lost manhood.

I had always felt contempt for women who found their kicks by robbing the cradle. Now here I was on a Barbados beach with an amorous child young enough to be my son. Two sayings flitted unbidden across my mind. "Judge not, that ye be not judged" and "The thing which I feared is come upon me." I thought, ain't it the god-damned truth?

Edwin kissed me again, pressing the length of his body against mine.

"I've got to go," I gasped. "My friends have probably returned and are looking for me. About ten tonight?"

He nodded; I smiled at him and ran all the way to my hotel.

At exactly ten o'clock, the telephone in our room announced we had company downstairs.

"Hot damn," Alison said, putting on her eyebrows in front of the mirror. "We're not going to be stood up."

"Island men," I said loftily, "are dependable, not like the bums you're used to in America."

Alison, freckled and willowy, had been married three times and was looking for her fourth. Her motto was, if at first you don't succeed, find another mother. She was a real estate broker in Los Angeles, and we had been childhood friends in Harlem.

"What I can't stand," Dorothy said from the bathroom, "are those creeps who come to your apartment, drink up your liquor, then dirty up your sheets. You don't even get a dinner out of the deal."

She came out of the bathroom in her slip. Petite and delicate with a pixie grin, at thirty-five Dorothy looked more like one of the high school girls she taught then their teacher. She had never been married. Years before, while she was holding onto her virginity with a miser's grip, her fiancé messed up and knocked up one of her friends.

Since then, all of Dorothy's affairs had been with married men, displaying perhaps a subconscious vendetta against all wives.

By ten-twenty we were downstairs and I was introducing the girls to our four escorts, who eyed us with unconcealed admiration. We were looking good in our Saks Fifth Avenue finery. They were looking good, too, in soft shirts and loose slacks, all except Gregory, whose bulging muscles confined in clothing made him seem more gargantuan.

We took a cab and a few minutes later were squeezing behind a table in a small, smoky room called the Pigeon Club. A Trinidad steel band was blasting out the walls, and a tiny dance area was jammed with wiggling bottoms and shuffling feet. The white tourists trying to do the hip-shaking calypso were having a ball and looking awkward.

I got up to dance with Edwin. He had a natural grace and was easy to follow. Our bodies found the rhythm and became one with it while our eyes locked in silent ancient combat, his pleading, mine teasing.

We returned to our seats and to tall glasses of rum and cola tonic. The party had begun.

I danced every dance with Edwin, his clasp becoming gradually tighter until my face was smothered in his shoulder, my arms locked around his neck. He was adorable. Very good for my ego. The other boys took turns dancing with my friends, but soon preferences were set—Alison with Alphonse and Dorothy with Dimitri. With good humor, Gregory ordered another round and didn't seem to mind being odd man out, but he wasn't alone for long.

During the floor show, featuring the inevitable limbo dancers, a pretty white girl, about twenty-two, with straight, red hair hanging down to her shoulders, appeared at Gregory's elbow. From his wink at me and self-satisfied grin, I knew this was Glenda from the yacht.

"Hello," she said to Gregory. "Can I join you, or do you have a date?"

Well, I thought, that's the direct approach.

"What are you doing here?" Gregory asked.

"Looking for you."

Gregory slid over on the bench, next to the wall, and Glenda sat down as he introduced her to the rest of us. Somehow, her presence spoiled my mood. We had been happy being black, and I resented this intrusion from the white world. But Glenda was happy. She had found the man she'd set out to find and a swing party to boot. She beamed a dazzling smile around the table.

Alphonse led Alison onto the dance floor, and Edwin and I followed. The steel band was playing a wild calypso, and I could feel my hair rising with the heat as I joined in the wildness.

When we returned to the table, Glenda applauded us, then turned to Gregory. "Why don't you teach me to dance like that?"

He answered with his toothless grin and a leer, implying he had better things to teach her.

White women were always snatching our men, I thought, and now they want to dance like us.

I turned my attention back to Edwin and met his full stare.

I teased him with a smile, refusing to commit myself. He had a lusty, healthy appetite, which was natural, I supposed, for a twenty-one-year-old lad. Lord, but why did he have to be that young? I stood up to go to the ladies' room.

"Wait for me," Glenda cried, trailing behind me.

The single toilet stall was occupied, and Glenda leaned against the wall waiting for it while I flipped open my compact and powdered my grimy face.

"You married?" she asked.

"Divorced."

"When I get married, I want to stay hooked forever."

"That's the way I planned it, too," I said dryly.

"What I mean," she rushed on, "is that I've gotta find a cat who wants to groove only with me."

Oh Lord, I thought, don't try to sound like us, too. Use your own, sterile language.

"I really dug this guy I was engaged to," Glenda continued, "but he couldn't function without a harem. I could have stood that, maybe, but when he didn't mind if I made it with some other guy, too, I knew I didn't want that kind of life."

I looked at her in the mirror as I applied my lipstick. She had been hurt, and badly. She shook right down to her naked soul. So she was dropping down a social notch, according to her scale of values, and trying to repair her damaged ego with a black brother.

"You gonna make it with Edwin?" she asked, as if we were college chums comparing dates.

"I'm not a one-night stand." My tone was frigid. That's another thing I can't stand about white people. Too familiar because we're colored.

"I dig Gregory," she said, pushing her hair out of her eyes. "He's kind of rough, but who wouldn't be, the kind of life he's led."

"And what kind of life is that?" I asked.

"Didn't you know? His mother was a whore in an exclusive brothel for white men only. That was before when the British owned the island."

"I take it you like rough men?" I asked.

"There's usually something gentle and lost underneath," she replied.

A white woman came out of the toilet and Glenda went in. Jesus, I thought, Gregory gentle? The woman walked to the basin, flung some water in the general direction of her hands, and left.

"Poor Daddy is having a fit," Glenda volunteered from the john, "but there's not much he can do about it. He's afraid I'll leave him again, and he gets lonely without me, so he just tags along and tries to keep me out of trouble."

"And he pays the bills?"

She answered with a laugh. "Why not? He's loaded."

Why not, I thought with bitterness. You white women have always managed to have your cake and eat it, too. The toilet flushed with a roar like Niagara Falls. I opened the door and went back to our table. Let Glenda find her way back alone.

Edwin pulled my chair out and brushed his lips across the nape of my neck as I sat down. He still had not danced with anyone else, and his apparent desire was flattering. For a moment, I considered it. That's what I really needed, wasn't it? To walk down the moonlit beach wrapped in his arms, making it to some pad to be made? It would be a delightful story to tell at bridge sessions. But I shook my head at him, and this time my smile was more sad than teasing.

Glenda came back and crawled over Gregory's legs to the seat beside him. The bastard. He made no pretense of being a gentleman. Suddenly, I didn't know which of them I disliked the most. Gregory winked at me. I don't know where he got the impression I was his conspirator, but I got up to dance with him.

"That Glenda," he grinned, "she's the one I was on the boat with last night. I banged her plenty, in the room right next to her father. We could hear him coughing to let us know he was awake, but he didn't come in."

He laughed like a naughty schoolboy, and I joined in. He was a nerveless bastard all right, and it served Glenda right that we were laughing at her. Who asked her to crash our party, anyway? That's when I got the idea to take Gregory away from her.

"You gonna bang her again tonight?" I asked, a new, teasing quality in my voice. "Or are you gonna find something better to do?" To help him get the message I rubbed bellies with him.

He couldn't believe this sudden turn of events. I could almost see him thinking. With one stroke he could slap Glenda down a peg and repay Edwin for beating his time with me on the beach that morning.

"You wanna come with me?" he asked, making sure of his quarry.

"What you got to offer?" I peered at him through half-closed lids.

"Big Bamboo," he sang, the title of a popular calypso. We both laughed.

I felt a heady excitement of impending danger as Gregory pulled me back to the table. The men paid the bill, and suddenly we were standing outside the club in the bright moonlight. Gregory deliberately uncurled Glenda's arm from his and took a step toward me. Looking at Edwin and nodding in my direction, he said, "She's coming with me. Any objections?"

Edwin inhaled a mouthful of smoke. His face was inscrutable. "You want to go with him?" he asked me quietly.

I avoided his eyes and nodded. "Yes."

He flipped the cigarette with contempt at my feet and lit another one. "Help yourself to the garbage," he said, and leaned back against the building, one leg braced behind him. The others suddenly stilled their chatter, sensing trouble.

I was holding Gregory's arm now, and I felt his muscle tense. "No," I said as he moved toward Edwin. "You've got what you want. Forget it."

Glenda was ungracious in defeat. "What about me?" she screamed. She stared from one black face to another, her glance lingering on Edwin. But he wasn't about to come to her aid and take Gregory's leavings.

"You can go home in a cab," Gregory said, pushing her ahead of him and pulling me behind him to a taxi waiting at the curb.

Glenda broke from his grasp. "You bastard. Who in the hell do you think you are, King Solomon? You can't dump me like this." She raised her hands as if to strike Gregory on the chest, but he caught them before they landed.

"Careful, white girl," he said. His voice was low but ominous. She froze.

"But why," she whimpered, all hurt child now. "You liked me last night. I know you did. Why are you treating me like this?"

"I didn't bring you here"—his voice was pleasant again—"so don't be trailing me all over town. When I want you, I'll come to that damn boat and get you. Now get in that cab before I throw you in. I'll see you tomorrow night. Maybe."

"You go to hell." She eluded him and turned on me, asking with incredible innocence, "What did I ever do to you?" Then she was running past toward the beach, her sobs drifting back to haunt me like a forlorn melody.

What had she ever done to me? And what had I just done? In order to degrade her for the crime of being white, I had sunk to the gutter. Suddenly Glenda was just another woman, vulnerable and lonely, like me.

We were sick, sick, sick. All fucked up. I had thought only Gregory was hung up in his love-hate black-white syndrome, decades of suppressed hatred having sickened his soul. But I was tainted, too. I had forgotten my own misery long enough to inflict it on another woman who was only trying to ease her loneliness by making it with a soul brother. Was I jealous because she was able to function as a woman when I couldn't, because she realized that a man is a man, color be damned, while I was crucified on my own, anti-white-man cross?

What if she were going black trying to repent for some ancient Nordic sin? How else could she atone except with the gift of herself? And if some black brother wanted to help a chick off her lily-white pedestal, he was entitled to that freedom, and it was none of my damned business anyway.

"Let's go, baby," Gregory said, tucking my arm under his.

The black bastard. I didn't even like the ugly ape. I backed away from him. "Leave me alone," I screamed. "Goddamit, just leave me alone!"

For a moment, we were all frozen into an absurd fresco—Alison, Dorothy, and the two boys looking at me in shocked disbelief, Edwin hiding behind a nonchalant smokescreen, Gregory off balance and confused, reaching out toward me.

I moved first, toward Edwin, but I had slammed the door behind me. He laughed, a mirthless sound in the stillness. He knew. I had forsaken him, but at least not for Gregory.

Then I was running down the beach looking for Glenda, hot tears of shame burning my face. How could I have been such a bitch? But the white beach, shimmering in the moonlight, was empty. And once again, I was alone.

[1968]

For Discussion

1. There are four men and four women in the story. Why might Meriwether have included so many characters, when other authors usually include only character pairs or triangles?
2. Contrast Edwin and Gregory's looks and personalities, as the narrator sees them at the beginning of the story. Does her view change later?
3. Describe the power struggle and shifting balance of power in the story. Who is "dominant" at each point, and why?
4. What impact does each main character's personal history have on how he or she acts and reacts in the present?
5. Find examples of violence (or threats of violence) and references to "vengeance." How is the overtone of sex related to the undertone of violence in the story?
6. Why does Meriwether emphasize descriptions of physical bodies and body parts? How are related details of age and race conveyed?
7. Find examples of the narrator's comments that mock herself and others. In what sense is her world view ironic?
8. Explain the "lesson" the narrator learns about Glenda and about herself.
9. How is the "absurd fresco" at the end of the story a small view of society's attitudes, and what is the meaning of the last line?

For Further Exploration

1. Trace the impact of the following factors in the story—sex, race, age, and social status. How does Meriwether intertwine these themes in the story, and for what purpose?
2. Make a list of your favorite movies or books, especially those in which a woman is the central character. In how many of the works listed does the woman have a female friend, and in how many is the woman alone or in competition with other women? Compare the theme of friendship among women in this story and in another story from your list.

Virginia Woolf

1882-1941

A self-conscious forty-year-old woman tries to create a "divine moment" for herself out of an ordinary, drab existence. Are her dreams of grandeur illusions, or possibilities?

THE NEW DRESS

Mabel had her first serious suspicion that something was wrong as she took her cloak off and Mrs. Barnet, while handing her the mirror and touching the brushes and thus drawing her attention, perhaps rather markedly, to all the appliances for tidying and improving hair, complexion, clothes, which existed on the dressing table, confirmed the suspicion—that it was not right, not quite right, which growing stronger as she went upstairs and springing at her, with conviction as she greeted Clarissa Dalloway, she went straight to the far end of the room, to a shaded corner where a looking-glass hung and looked. No! It was not *right*. And at once the misery which she always tried to hide, the profound dissatisfaction—the sense she had had, ever since she was a child, of being inferior to other people—set upon her, relentlessly, remorselessly, with an intensity which she could not beat off, as she would when she woke at night at home, by reading Borrow or Scott; for oh these men, oh these women, all were thinking—"What's Mabel wearing? What a fright she looks! What a hideous new dress!"—their eyelids flickering as they came up and then their lids shutting rather tight. It was her own appalling inadequacy; her cowardice; her mean, water-sprinkled blood that depressed her. And at once the whole of the room where, for ever so many hours, she had planned with the little dressmaker how it was to go, seemed sordid, repulsive; and her own drawing-room so shabby, and herself, going out, puffed up with vanity as she touched the letters on the hall table and said: "How dull!" to show off—all this now seemed unutterably silly, paltry, and provincial. All this had been absolutely destroyed, shown up, exploded, the moment she came into Mrs. Dalloway's drawing-room.

What she had thought that evening when, sitting over the teacups, Mrs. Dalloway's invitation came, was that, of course, she could not be fashionable. It was absurd to pretend it even—fashion meant cut, meant style, meant thirty guineas at least—but why not be original? Why not be herself, anyhow? And, getting up, she had taken that old fashion book of her mother's, a Paris fashion book of the time of the Empire, and had thought how much prettier, more dignified, and more womanly they were then, and so set herself—oh, it was foolish—trying to be like them, pluming herself in fact, upon being modest and old-fashioned, and very charming, giving herself up, no doubt about it, to an orgy of self-love, which deserved to be chastised, and so rigged herself out like this.

But she dared not look in the glass. She could not face the whole horror—the pale yellow, idiotically old-fashioned silk dress with its long skirt and its high sleeves and its waist and all the things that looked so charming in the fashion book, but not on her, not among all these ordinary people. She felt like a dressmaker's dummy standing there, for young people to stick pins into.

"But, my dear, it's perfectly charming!" Rose Shaw said, looking her up and down with that little satirical pucker of the lips which she expected—Rose herself being dressed in the height of fashion, precisely like everybody else, always.

We are all like flies trying to crawl over the edge of the saucer, Mabel thought, and repeated the phrase as if she were crossing herself, as if she were trying to find some spell to annul this pain, to make this agony endurable. Tags of Shakespeare, lines from books she had read ages ago, suddenly came to her when she was in agony, and she repeated them over and over again. "Flies trying to crawl," she repeated. If she could say that over often enough and make herself see the flies, she would become numb, chill, frozen, dumb. Now she could see flies crawling slowly out of a saucer of milk with their wings stuck together; and she strained and strained (standing in front of the looking-glass, listening to Rose Shaw) to make herself see Rose Shaw and all the other people as flies, trying to hoist themselves out of something, or into something, meagre, insignificant, toiling flies. But she could not see them like that, not other people. She saw herself like that—she was a fly, but the others were dragonflies, butterflies, beautiful insects, dancing, fluttering, skimming, while she alone dragged herself up out of the saucer. (Envy and spite, the most detestable of the vices, were her chief faults.)

"I feel like some dowdy, decrepit, horribly dingy old fly," she said, making Robert Haydon stop just to hear her say that, just to reassure herself by furbishing up a poor weak-kneed phrase and so showing how detached she was, how witty, that she did not feel in the least out of anything. And, of course, Robert Haydon answered something, quite polite, quite insincere, which she saw through instantly, and said to herself, directly he went (again from some book), "Lies, lies, lies!" For a party makes things either much more real, or much less real, she thought; she saw in a flash to the bottom of Robert Haydon's heart; she saw through everything. She saw the truth. *This* was true, this drawing-room, this self, and the other false. Miss Milan's little workroom was really terribly hot, stuffy, sordid. It smelt of clothes and cabbage cooking; and yet, when Miss Milan put the glass in her hand, and she looked at herself with the dress on, finished, an extraordinary bliss shot through her heart. Suffused with light, she sprang into existence. Rid of cares and wrinkles, what she had dreamed of herself was there—a beautiful woman. Just for a second (she had not dared look longer, Miss Milan wanted to know about the length of the skirt), there looked at her, framed in the scrolloping mahogany, a grey-white, mysteriously smiling, charming girl, the core of herself, the soul of herself; and it was not vanity only, not only self-love that made her think it good, tender, and true. Miss Milan said that the skirt could not well be longer; if anything the skirt, said Miss Milan, puckering her forehead, considering with all her wits about her, must be shorter; and she felt, suddenly, honestly, full of love for Miss Milan, much, much fonder of Miss Milan than of any one in the whole world, and could have cried for pity that she should be crawling on the floor with her mouth full of pins, and her face red and her eyes bulging—that one human being should be doing this for another, and she saw them all as human beings merely, and herself going off to her party, and Miss Milan pulling the cover over the canary's cage, or letting him pick a hempseed from between her lips, and the thought of it, of this side of human nature and its patience and its endurance and its being content with such miserable, scanty, sordid, little pleasures filled her eyes with tears.

And now the whole thing had vanished. The dress, the room, the love, the pity, the scrolloping looking-glass, and the canary's cage—all had vanished, and here she was in a corner of Mrs. Dalloway's drawing-room, suffering tortures, woken wide awake to reality.

But it was all so paltry, weak-blooded, and petty-minded to care so much at her age with two children, to be still so utterly dependent on people's opinions and not have principles or convictions, not to be able to say as other people did, "There's Shakespeare! There's death! We're all weevils in a captain's biscuit"—or whatever it was that people did say.

She faced herself straight in the glass; she pecked at her left shoulder; she issued out into the room, as if spears were thrown at her yellow dress from all sides. But instead of looking fierce or tragic, as Rose Shaw would have done—Rose would have looked like Boadicea—she looked foolish and self-conscious, and simpered like a schoolgirl and slouched across the room, positively slinking, as if she were a beaten mongrel, and looked at a picture, an engraving. As if one went to a party to look at a picture! Everybody knew why she did it—it was from shame, from humiliation.

"Now the fly's in the saucer," she said to herself, "right in the middle, and can't get out, and the milk," she thought, rigidly staring at the picture, "is sticking its wings together."

"It's so old-fashioned," she said to Charles Burt, making him stop (which by itself he hated) on his way to talk to some one else.

She meant, or she tried to make herself think that she meant, that it was the picture and not her dress, that was old-fashioned. And one word of praise, one word of affection from Charles would have made all the difference to her at the moment. If he had only said, "Mabel, you're looking charming tonight!" it would have changed her life. But then she ought to have been truthful and direct. Charles said nothing of the kind, of course. He was malice itself. He always saw through one, especially if one were feeling particularly mean, paltry, or feeble-minded.

"Mabel's got a new dress!" he said, and the poor fly was absolutely shoved into the middle of the saucer. Really, he would like her to drown, she believed. He had no heart, no fundamental kindness, only a veneer of friendliness. Miss Milan was much more real, much kinder. If only one could feel that and stick to it, always. "Why," she asked herself—replying to Charles much too pertly, letting him see that she was out of temper, or "ruffled" as he called it. ("Rather ruffled?" he said and went on to laugh at her with some woman over there)—"Why," she asked herself, "can't I feel one thing always, feel quite sure that Miss Milan is right, and Charles wrong and stick to it, feel sure about the canary and pity and love and not be whipped all round in a second by coming into a room full of people?" It was her odious, weak, vacillating character again, always giving at the critical moment and not being seriously interested in conchology, etymology, botany, archaeology, cutting up potatoes and watching them fructify like Mary Dennis, like Violet Searle.

Then Mrs. Holman, seeing her standing there, bore down upon her. Of course a thing like a dress was beneath Mrs. Holman's notice, with her family always tumbling downstairs or having the scarlet fever. Could Mabel tell her if Elmthorpe was ever let for August and September? Oh, it was a conversation that bored her unutterably!—it made her furious to be treated like a house agent or a messenger boy, to be made use of. Not to have value, that was it, she thought, trying to grasp something hard, something real, while she tried to answer sensibly about the bathroom and the south aspect and the hot water to the top of the house; and all the time she could see little bits of her yellow dress in the round looking-glass which made them all the size of boot-buttons or tadpoles; and it was amazing to think how much humiliation and agony and self-loathing and effort and passionate ups and downs of feeling were contained in a thing the size of a threepenny bit. And what was still odder, this thing, this Mabel Waring, was separate, quite disconnected: and though Mrs. Holman (the black button) was leaning forward and telling her how her eldest boy had strained his heart running, she could see her, too, quite detached in the looking-glass, and it was impossible that the black dot, leaning forward, gesticulating, should make the yellow dot, sitting solitary, self-centered, feel what the black dot was feeling, yet they pretended.

"So impossible to keep boys quiet"—that was the kind of thing one said.

And Mrs. Holman, who could never get enough sympathy and snatched what little there was greedily, as if it were her right (but she deserved much more for, there was her little girl who had come down this morning with a swollen knee-joint), took this miserable offering and looked at it suspiciously, grudgingly, as if it were a half-penny when it ought to have been a pound and put it away in her purse, must put up with it, mean and miserly though it was, times being hard, so very hard; and on she went, creaking, injured Mrs. Holman, about the girl with the swollen joints. Ah, it was tragic, this greed, this clamour of human beings, like a row of cormorants, barking and flapping their wings for sympathy—it was tragic, could one have felt it and not merely pretended to feel it!

But in her yellow dress to-night she could not wring out one drop more; she wanted it all, all for herself. She knew (she kept on looking into the glass, dipping into that dreadfully showing-up blue pool) that she was condemned, despised, left like this in a backwater, because of her being like this a feeble, vacillating creature; and it seemed to her that the yellow dress was a penance which she had deserved, and if she had been dressed like Rose Shaw, in lovely, clinging green with a ruffle of swansdown, she would have deserved that; and she thought that there was no escape for her—none whatever. But it was not her fault altogether, after all. It was being one of a family of ten; never having money enough; always skimping and paring; and her mother carrying great cans, and the linoleum worn on the stair edges, and one sordid little domestic tragedy after another—nothing catastrophic, the sheep farm failing, but not utterly; her eldest brother marrying beneath him but not very much—there was no romance, nothing extreme about them all. They petered out respectably in seaside resorts; every watering-place had one of her aunts even now asleep in some lodging with the front windows not quite facing the sea. That was so like them—they had to squint at things always. And she had done the same—she was just like her aunts. For all her dreams of living in India, married to some hero like Sir Henry Lawrence, some empire builder (still the sight of a native in a turban filled her with romance), she had failed utterly. She had married Hubert, with his safe, permanent underling's job in the Law Courts, and they managed tolerably in a smallish house, without proper maids, and hash when she was alone or just bread and butter, but now and then—Mrs. Holman was off, thinking her the most dried-up, unsympathetic twig she had ever met, absurdly dressed, too, and would tell every one about Mabel's fantastic appearance—now and then, thought

Mabel Waring, left alone on the blue sofa, punching the cushion in order to look occupied, for she would not join Charles Burt and Rose Shaw, chattering like magpies and perhaps laughing at her by the fireplace—now and then, there did come to her delicious moments, reading the other night in bed, for instance, or down by the sea on the sand in the sun, at Easter—let her recall it—a great tuft of pale sand-grass standing all twisted like a shock of spears against the sky, which was blue like a smooth china egg, so firm, so hard, and then the melody of the waves—"Hush, hush," they said, and the children's shouts paddling—yes, it was a divine moment, and there she lay, she felt, in the hand of the Goddess who was the world; rather a hard-hearted, but very beautiful Goddess, a little lamb laid on the altar (one did think these silly things, and it didn't matter so long as one never said them). And also with Hubert sometimes she had quite unexpectedly—carving the mutton for Sunday lunch, for no reason, opening a letter, coming into a room—divine moments, when she said to herself (for she would never say this to anybody else), "This is it. This has happened. This is it!" And the other way about it was equally surprising—that is, when everything was arranged—music, weather, holidays, every reason for happiness was there—then nothing happened at all. One wasn't happy. It was flat, just flat, that was all.

Her wretched self again, no doubt! She had always been a fretful, weak, unsatisfactory mother, a wobbly wife, lolling about in a kind of twilight existence with nothing very clear or very bold, or more one thing than another, like all her brothers and sisters, except perhaps Herbert—they were all the same poor water-veined creatures who did nothing. Then in the midst of this creeping, crawling life, suddenly she was on the crest of a wave. That wretched fly—where had she read the story that kept coming into her mind about the fly and the saucer?—struggled out. Yes, she had those moments. But now that she was forty, they might come more and more seldom. By degrees she would cease to struggle any more. But that was deplorable! That was not to be endured! That made her feel ashamed of herself!

She would go to the London Library tomorrow. She would find some wonderful, helpful, astonishing book, quite by chance, a book by a clergyman, by an American no one had ever heard of; or she would walk down the Strand and drop, accidentally, into a hall where a miner was telling about the life in the pit, and suddenly she would become a new person. She would be absolutely transformed. She would wear a uniform; she would be called Sister Somebody; she would never give a thought to clothes again. And for ever after she would be perfectly clear about Charles Burt and Miss Milan and this room and that room; and it would be always, day after day, as if she were lying in the sun or carving the mutton. It would be it!

So she got up from the blue sofa, and the yellow button in the looking-glass got up too, and she waved her hand to Charles and Rose to show them she did not depend on them one scrap, and the yellow button moved out of the looking-glass, and all the spears were gathered into her breast as she walked towards Mrs. Dalloway and said, "Good night."

"But it's too early to go," said Mrs. Dalloway, who was always so charming.

"I'm afraid I must," said Mabel Waring. "But," she added in her weak, wobbly voice which only sounded ridiculous when she tried to strengthen it, "I have enjoyed myself enormously."

"I have enjoyed myself," she said to Mr. Dalloway, whom she met on the stairs.

"Lies, lies, lies!" she said to herself, going downstairs, and "Right in the saucer!'' she said to herself as she thanked Mrs. Barnet for helping her and wrapped herself, round and round and round, in the Chinese cloak she had worn these twenty years.

[1927]

For Discussion

1. What fears underlie Mabel's concern over her appearance?
2. Why is a new dress an appropriate symbol for the story's themes?
3. Identify the fluctuations in Mabel's moods. Why does she think that her "orgy of self love . . . deserved to be chastised''? List the other faults with which she chastises herself throughout the story.
4. Explain the role of books in Mabel's life, examining each mention of her reading.
5. What is Mabel's attitude toward others and toward books, and what does her attitude reveal about the way "plain" women function in society?
6. Trace how the images of insects and animals are developed throughout the story.
7. List and explain contrasting images and themes on which the story is built, such as elation and depression, dreams and reality, yellow and black, etc.
8. What does Mabel wish that she could do or be at the end of the story, and how does her dilemma mirror feelings many women have?

For Further Exploration

1. Virginia Woolf is noted for her descriptions of "epiphanies," the "divine moments" of life mentioned in this story. Compare the woman's experiences in "The New Dress" with the moments of joy and despair of characters in novels by Jean Rhys (such as *After Leaving Mr. Mackenzie*) or Margaret Drabble (such as *The Needle's Eye*). How does each woman attempt to elevate an ordinary life into something special? What attitude does society take towards their efforts?
2. Mabel would like to have the courage to "break out" of her confining social role. Compare her inner turmoil with that of Edna Pontelier in Kate Chopin's famous novel of women and society, *The Awakening*. What effect do the other women in the novel and this story have on the plight of the main characters?

Margaret Atwood

1939–

Beneath the light and flippant tone of Atwood's narrator is a down-to-earth interior monologue about one of society's biggest problems—rape. Are the narrator's thoughts any more enlightened than those of the other women at work?

RAPE FANTASIES

The way they're going on about it in the magazines you'd think it was just invented, and not only that but it's something terrific, like a vaccine for cancer. They put it in capital letters on the front cover, and inside they have these questionnaires like the ones they used to have about whether you were a good enough wife or an endomorph or an ectomorph, remember that? with the scoring upside down on page 73, and then these numbered do-it-yourself dealies, you know? RAPE, TEN THINGS TO DO ABOUT IT, like it was ten new hairdos or something. I mean, what's so new about it?

So at work they all have to talk about it because no matter what magazine you open, there it is, staring you right between the eyes, and they're beginning to have it on the television, too. Personally I'd prefer a June Allyson movie anytime but they don't make them any more and they don't even have them that much on the Late Show. For instance, day before yesterday, that would be Wednesday, thank god it's Friday as they say, we were sitting around in the women's lunch room—the *lunch* room, I mean you'd think you could get some peace and quiet in there—and Chrissy closes up the magazine she's been reading and says, "How about it girls, do you have rape fantasies?"

The four of us were having our game of bridge the way we always do, and I had a bare twelve points counting the singleton with not that much of a bid in anything. So I said one club, hoping Sondra would remember about the one club convention, because the time before when I used that she thought I really meant clubs and she bid us up to three, and all I had was four little ones with nothing higher than a six, and we went down two and on top of that we were vulnerable. She is not the world's best bridge player. I mean, neither am I but there's a limit.

Darlene passed but the damage was done, Sondra's head went round like it was on ball bearings and she said, "*What* fantasies?"

"Rape fantasies," Chrissy said. She's a receptionist and she looks like one; she's pretty but cool as a cucumber, like she's been painted all over with nail polish, if you know what I mean. Varnished. "It says here all women have rape fantasies."

"For Chrissake, I'm eating an egg sandwich," I said, "and I bid one club and Darlene passed."

"You mean, like some guy jumping you in an alley or something," Sondra said. She was eating her lunch, we all eat our lunches during the game, and she bit into a piece of that celery she always brings and started to chew away on it with this thoughtful expression in her eyes and I knew we might as well pack it in as far as the game was concerned.

"Yeah, sort of like that," Chrissy said. She was blushing a little, you could see it even under her makeup.

"I don't think you should go out alone at night," Darlene said, "you put yourself in a position," and I may have been mistaken but she was looking at me. She's the oldest, she's forty-one though you wouldn't know it and neither does she, but I looked it up in the employees' file. I like to guess a person's age and then look it up to see if I'm right. I let myself have an extra pack of cigarettes if I am, though I'm trying to cut down. I figure it's harmless as long as you don't tell. I mean, not everyone has access to that file, it's more or less confidential. But it's all right if I tell you, I don't expect you'll ever meet her, though you never know, it's a small world. Anyway.

"For *heaven's* sake, it's only *Toronto*," Greta said. She worked in Detroit for three years and she never lets you forget it, it's like she thinks she's a war hero or something, we should all admire her just for the fact that she's still walking this earth, though she was really living in Windsor the whole time, she just worked in Detroit. Which for me doesn't really count. It's where you sleep, right?

"Well, do you?" Chrissy said. She was obviously trying to tell us about hers but she wasn't about to go first, she's cautious, that one.

"I certainly don't," Darlene said, and she wrinkled up her nose, like this, and I had to laugh. "I think it's disgusting." She's divorced, I read that in the file too, she never talks about it. It must've been years ago anyway. She got up and went over to the coffee machine and turned her back on us as though she wasn't going to have anything more to do with it.

"Well," Greta said. I could see it was going to be between her and Chrissy. They're both blondes, I don't mean that in a bitchy way but they do try to outdress each other. Greta would like to get out of Filing, she'd like to be a receptionist too so she could meet more people. You don't meet much of anyone in Filing except other people in Filing. Me, I don't mind it so much, I have outside interests.

"Well," Greta said, "I sometimes think about, you know my apartment? It's got this little balcony, I like to sit out there in the summer and I have a few plants out there. I never bother that much about locking the door to the balcony, it's one of those sliding glass ones, I'm on the eighteenth floor for heaven's sake, I've got a good view of the lake and the CN Tower and all. But I'm sitting around one night in my housecoat, watching TV with my shoes off, you know how you do, and I see this guy's feet, coming down past the window, and the next thing you know he's standing on the balcony, he's let himself down by a rope with a hook on the end of it from the floor above, that's the nineteenth, and before I can even get up off the chesterfield he's inside the apartment. He's all dressed in black with black gloves on"—I knew right away what show she got the black gloves off because I saw the same one—"and then he, well, you know."

"You know what?" Chrissy said, but Greta said, "And afterwards he tells me that he goes all over the outside of the apartment building like that, from one floor to another, with his rope and his hook . . . and then he goes out to the balcony and tosses his rope, and he climbs up it and disappears."

"Just like Tarzan," I said, but nobody laughed.

"Is that all?" Chrissy said. "Don't you ever think about, well, I think about being in the bathtub, with no clothes on . . ."

"So who takes a bath in their clothes?" I said, you have to admit it's stupid when you come to think of it, but she just went on, ". . . with lots of bubbles, what I use is Vitabath, it's more expensive but it's so relaxing, and my hair pinned up, and the door opens and this fellow's standing there. . . ."

"How'd he get in?" Greta said.

"Oh, I don't know, through a window or something. Well, I can't very well get out of the bathtub, the bathroom's too small and besides he's blocking the doorway, so I just *lie* there, and he starts to very slowly take his own clothes off, and then he gets into the bathtub with me."

"Don't you scream or anything?" said Darlene. She'd come back with her cup of coffee, she was getting really interested. "I'd scream like bloody murder."

"Who'd hear me?" Chrissy said. "Besides, all the articles say it's better not to resist, that way you don't get hurt."

"Anyway you might get bubbles up your nose," I said, "from the deep breathing," and I swear all four of them looked at me like I was in bad taste, like I'd insulted the Virgin Mary or something. I mean, I don't see what's wrong with a little joke now and then. Life's too short, right?

"Listen," I said, "those aren't *rape* fantasies. I mean, you aren't getting *raped*, it's just some guy you haven't met formally who happens to be more attractive than Derek Cummins"—he's the Assistant Manager, he wears elevator shoes or at any rate they have these thick soles and he has this funny way of talking, we call him Derek Duck—"and you have a good time. Rape is when they've got a knife or something and you don't want to."

"So what about you, Estelle," Chrissy said, she was miffed because I laughed at her fantasy, she thought I was putting her down. Sondra was miffed too, by this time she'd finished her celery and she wanted to tell about hers, but she hadn't got in fast enough.

"All right, let me tell you one," I said. "I'm walking down this dark street at night and this fellow comes up and grabs my arm. Now it so happens that I have a plastic lemon in my purse, you know how it always says you should carry a plastic lemon in your purse? I don't really do it, I tried it once but the darn thing leaked all over my checkbook, but in this fantasy I have one, and I say to him, 'You're intending to rape me, right?' and he nods, so I open my purse to get the plastic lemon, and I can't find it! My purse is full of all this junk, Kleenex and cigarettes and my change purse and my lipstick and my driver's license, you know the kind of stuff; so I ask him to hold out his hands, like this, and I pile all this junk into them and down at the bottom there's the plastic lemon, and I can't get the top off. So I hand it to him and he's very obliging, he twists the top off and hands it back to me, and I squirt him in the eye."

I hope you don't think that's too vicious. Come to think of it, it is a bit mean, especially when he was so polite and all.

"*That's* your rape fantasy?" Chrissy says. "I don't believe it."

"She's a card," Darlene says, she and I are the ones that've been here the longest and she never will forget the time I got drunk at the office party and insisted I was going to dance under the table instead of on top of it, I did a sort of Cossack number but then I hit my head on the bottom of the table— actually it was a desk—when I went to get up, and I knocked myself out cold. She's decided that's the mark of an original mind and she tells everyone new about it and I'm not sure that's fair. Though I did do it.

"I'm being totally honest," I say. I always am and they know it. There's no point in being anything else, is the way I look at it, and sooner or later the truth will out so you might as well not waste the time, right? "You should hear the one about the Easy-Off Oven Cleaner."

But that was the end of the lunch hour, with one bridge game shot to hell, and the next day we spent most of the time arguing over whether to start a new game or play out the hands we had left over from the day before, so Sondra never did get a chance to tell about her rape fantasy.

It started me thinking though, about my own rape fantasies. Maybe I'm abnormal or something, I mean I have fantasies about handsome strangers coming in through the window too, like Mr. Clean, I wish one would, please god somebody without flat feet and big sweat marks on his shirt, and over five feet five, believe me being tall is a handicap though it's getting better, tall guys are starting to like someone whose nose reaches higher than their belly button. But if you're being totally honest you can't count those as rape fantasies. In a real rape fantasy, what you should feel is this anxiety, like when you think about your apartment building catching on fire and whether you should use the elevator or the stairs or maybe just stick your head under a wet towel, and you try to remember everything you've read about what to do but you can't decide.

For instance, I'm walking along this dark street at night and this short, ugly fellow comes up and grabs my arm, and not only is he ugly, you know, with a sort of puffy nothing face, like those fellows you have to talk to in the bank when your account's overdrawn—of course I don't mean they're all like that—but he's absolutely covered in pimples. So he gets me pinned against the wall, he's short but he's heavy, and he starts to undo himself and the zipper gets stuck. I mean, one of the most significant moments in a girl's life, it's almost like getting married or having a baby or something, and he sticks the zipper.

So I say, kind of disgusted, "Oh for Chrissake," and he starts to cry. He tells me he's never been able to get anything right in his entire life, and this is the last straw, he's going to go jump off a bridge.

"Look," I say, I feel so sorry for him, in my rape fantasies I always end up feeling sorry for the guy, I mean there has to be something *wrong* with them, if it was Clint Eastwood it'd be different but worse luck it never is. I was the kind of little girl who buried dead robins, know what I mean? It used to drive my mother nuts, she didn't like me touching them, because of the germs I guess. So I say, "Listen, I know how you feel. You really should do something about those pimples, if you got rid of them you'd be quite good looking, honest; then you wouldn't have to go around doing stuff like this. I had them myself once," I say, to comfort him, but in fact I did, and it ends up I give him the name of my old dermatologist, the one I had in high school, that was back in Leamington, except I used to go to St. Catharines for the dermatologist. I'm telling you, I was really lonely when I first came here; I thought it was going to be such a big adventure and all, but it's a lot harder to meet people in a city. But I guess it's different for a guy.

Or I'm lying in bed with this terrible cold, my face is all swollen up, my eyes are red and my nose is dripping like a leaky tap, and this fellow comes in through the window and *he* has a terrible cold too, it's a new kind of flu that's been going around. So he says, "I'b goig do rabe you"—I hope you don't mind me holding my nose like this but that's the way I imagine it—and he lets out this terrific sneeze, which slows him down a bit, also I'm no object of beauty myself, you'd have to be some kind of pervert to want to rape someone with a cold like mine, it'd be like raping a bottle of LePages mucilage the way my nose is running. He's looking wildly around the room, and I realize it's because he doesn't have a piece of Kleenex! "Id's ride here," I say, and I pass him the Kleenex, god knows why he even bothered to get out of bed, you'd think if you were going to go around climbing in windows you'd wait till you were healthier, right? I mean, that takes a certain amount of energy. So I ask him why doesn't he let me fix him a Neo-Citran and scotch, that's what I always take, you still have the cold but you don't feel it, so I do and we end up watching the Late Show together. I mean, they aren't all sex maniacs, the rest of the time they must lead a normal life. I figure they enjoy watching the Late Show just like anybody else.

I do have a scarier one though . . . where the fellow says he's hearing angel voices that're telling him he's got to kill me, you know, you read about things like that all the time in the papers. In this one I'm not in the apartment where I live now, I'm back in my mother's house in Leamington and the fellow's been hiding in the cellar, he grabs my arm when I go downstairs to get a jar of jam and he's got hold of the axe too, out of the garage, that one is really scary. I mean, what do you say to a nut like that?

So I start to shake but after a minute I get control of myself and I say, is he sure the angel voices have got the right person, because I hear the same angel voices and they've been telling me for some time that I'm going to give birth to the reincarnation of St. Anne who in turn has the Virgin Mary and right after that comes Jesus Christ and the end of the world, and he wouldn't want to interfere with that, would he? So he gets confused and listens some more, and then he asks for a sign and I show him my vaccination mark, you can see it's sort of an odd-shaped one, it got infected because I scratched the top off, and that does it, he apologizes and climbs out the coal chute again, which is how he got in in the first place, and I say to myself there's some advantage in having been brought up a Catholic even though I haven't been to church since they changed the service into English, it just isn't the same, you might as well be a Protestant. I must write to Mother and tell her to nail up that coal chute, it always has bothered me. Funny, I couldn't tell you at all what this man looks like but I know exactly what kind of shoes he's wearing, because that's the last I see of him, his shoes going up the coal chute, and they're the old-fashioned kind that lace up the ankles, even though he's a young fellow. That's strange, isn't it?

Let me tell you though I really sweat until I see him safely out of there and I go upstairs right away and make myself a cup of tea. I don't think about that one much. My mother always said you shouldn't dwell on unpleasant things and I generally agree with that, I mean, dwelling on them doesn't make them go away. Though not dwelling on them doesn't make them go away either, when you come to think of it.

Sometimes I have these short ones where the fellow grabs my arm but I'm really a Kung-Fu expert, can you believe it, in real life I'm sure it would just be a conk on the head and that's that, like getting your tonsils out, you'd wake up and it would be all over except for the sore places, and you'd be lucky if your neck wasn't broken or something, I could never even hit the volleyball in gym and a volleyball is fairly large, you know?—and I just go *zap* with my fingers into his eyes and that's it, he falls over, or I flip him against a wall or something. But I could never really stick my fingers in anyone's eyes, could you? It would feel like hot jello and I don't even like cold jello, just thinking about it gives me the creeps. I feel a bit guilty about that one, I mean how would you like walking around knowing someone's been blinded for life because of you?

But maybe it's different for a guy.

The most touching one I have is when the fellow grabs my arm and I say, sad and kind of dignified, "You'd be raping a corpse." That pulls him up short and I explain that I've just found out I have leukemia and the doctors have only given me a few months to live. That's why I'm out pacing the streets alone at night, I need to think, you know, come to terms with myself. I don't really have leukemia but in the fantasy I do, I guess I chose that particular disease because a girl in my grade four class died of it, the whole class sent her flowers when she was in the hospital. I didn't understand then that she was going to die and I wanted to have leukemia too so I could get flowers. Kids are funny, aren't they? Well, it turns out that he has leukemia himself, and *he* only has a few months to live, that's why he's going around raping people, he's very bitter because he's so young and his life is being taken from him before he's really lived it. So we walk along gently under the street lights, it's spring and sort of misty, and we end up going for coffee, we're happy we've found the only other person in the world who can understand what we're going through, it's almost like fate, and after a while we just sort of look at each other and our hands touch, and he comes back with me and moves into my apartment and we spend our last months together before we die, we just sort of don't wake up in the morning, though I've never decided which one of us gets to die first. If it's him I have to go on and fantasize about the funeral, if it's me I don't have to worry about that, so it just about depends on how tired I am at the time. You may not believe this but sometimes I even start crying. I cry at the ends of movies, even the ones that aren't all that sad, so I guess it's the same thing. My mother's like that too.

The funny thing about these fantasies is that the man is always someone I don't know, and the statistics in the magazines, well, most of them anyway, they say it's often someone you do know, at least a little bit, like your boss or something—I mean, it wouldn't be *my* boss, he's over sixty and I'm sure he couldn't rape his way out of a paper bag, poor old thing, but it might be someone like Derek Duck, in his elevator shoes, perish the thought—or someone you just met, who invites you up for a drink, it's getting so you can hardly be sociable any more, and how are you supposed to meet people if you can't trust them even that basic amount? You can't spend your whole life in the Filing Department or cooped up in your own apartment with all the doors and windows locked and the shades down. I'm not what you would call a drinker but I like to go out now and then for a drink or two in a nice place, even if I am by myself, I'm with Women's Lib on that even though I can't agree with a lot of other things they say. Like here for instance, the waiters all know me and if anyone, you know, bothers me. . . . I don't know why I'm telling you all this, except I think it helps you get to know a person, especially at first, hearing some of the things they think about. At work they call me the office worry wart, but it isn't so much like worrying, it's more like figuring out what you should do in an emergency, like I said before.

Anyway, another thing about it is that there's a lot of conversation, in fact I spend most of my time, in the fantasy that is, wondering what I'm going to say and what he's going to say, I think it would be better if you could get a conversation going. Like, how could a fellow do that to a person he's just had a long conversation with, once you let them know you're human, you have a life too, I don't see how they could go ahead with it, right? I mean, I know it happens but I just don't understand it, that's the part I really don't understand.

[1971]

For Discussion

1. How does diction (word choice) help to create the tone of the story?
2. What techniques does Atwood use to involve the reader in the thought process?
3. Is the treatment of the subject witty, or offensive? Does the story trivialize a serious issue?
4. Examine each incident in which the narrator says, "But maybe it's different for a guy." Specifically, what can men do that women cannot, according to Atwood's narrator?
5. What effect does the point of view have on the story, and what do we find out about the narrator's personality through her monologue?
6. Contrast the narrator's world view with that of the Mabel in "The New Dress." What thoughts and actions characterize each? Conjecture about what influences could have formed two such different characters, had they been real people.
7. How much "aesthetic distance" is there; that is, to what extent does the narrator seem to represent the author, and to what extent is the narrator a "persona" or mask?
8. Is there any serious message to this narrative?

For Further Exploration

1. Almost all of Atwood's fiction deals with one or more crises in an adult woman's life, such as marriage or living together, childbirth or abortion, mastectomy, infidelity, and rape. Compare the tone and theme of "Rape Fantasies" with a chapter from another Atwood work, such as *Surfacing, The Edible Woman,* or *Life Before Man.*
2. In Atwood's novel *Surfacing,* communication is not only a theme but is one of the most important forms of salvation for the narrator. Compare this line from the novel with the communication theme in "Rape Fantasies": "For us it's necessary, the intercession of words; and we will probably fail, sooner or later, more or less painfully."

Dinah Silveira de Queiroz
1911–

*The Brazilian town in this story is typical of society everywhere in the
expectations it has for its leaders. Mama is called to the task of "exerting
a moral influence," only to find that society's definition of "moral" might
not correspond with her own sense of right and wrong.*

GUIDANCE

When people talk to me about virtue, about morality and immorality, about
deportment, about anything, in short, that has to do with right and wrong, I
see Mama in my mind's eye. Not exactly Mama. Just Mama's neck, her
white, tremulous throat, as she was enjoying one of her giggles. They
sounded like someone delicately sipping coffee from a saucer. She used to
laugh this way chiefly at night when, with just the three of us in the house,
she would come to the dinner table in one of her gay, loose, low-necked
gowns as if she were going to a ball. She would be so perfumed that the
objects around her developed a little atmosphere of their own and became
lighter and more delicate. She never used rouge or lipstick, but she must
have done something to her skin to get that smoothness of freshly washed
china. On her, even perspiration was lovely, like moisture on clear glass.
Before such beauty, my face was a miserable and busy topography, where I
would explore furiously, and with physical enjoyment, little underground
caves in the deep, dark pores, or tiny volcanoes which, to my pleasure, would
burst between my nails. Mama's laugh was a "thank you so much" to my
father, who used to flatter her as if his life depended on her good will. He
tried, however, to conceal this adulation by joking and by treating her
eternally as a child. A long time before, a woman spiritualist had said
something that certainly must have provoked her very best and special
giggle:

"Why don't you try to exert a moral influence on people? You don't realize it, but you have an extraordinary power over others. You should go in
for counselling. People sense your authority as soon as they meet you. Give
guidance. Your advice will never fail. It comes from your mediumistic
power. . . ."

Mama repeated this four or five times among her lady friends and the
idea caught on, in our town of Laterra.

If someone was contemplating a business transaction, you can be sure
he'd show up at our house to get advice. On these occasions Mama, who was
blonde and petite, seemed to grow taller and very erect, with her little head
high and her chubby fingers upraised. They used to consult Mama about politics and about marriages. Because everything she said was sensible and
turned out to be correct, they began also to send wayward persons to her.
Once a certain rich lady brought her son, an incorrigible drunkard. I remember Mama said the most beautiful things about the reality of the Devil and

Translated by William L. Grossman

about having to side with either the Beast or the Angel. She explained the misery in which the young man was foundering and scolded him with tremendous words. Her fat little finger was poised threateningly and her whole body trembled in righteous anger, although her voice was not raised above its natural tone. The young man and the lady wept together.

Papa was enchanted with the prestige which, as her husband, he enjoyed.

Quarrels between employer and employee, between husband and wife, between parents and children, all found their way to our house.

Mama would hear both sides, would advise, would moralize. And Papa, in his little shop, felt the influx of confidence spreading to his dominion.

It was at this time that Laterra found itself without a priest, for the vicar had died and the bishop had not yet sent a replacement. The townspeople had to go to San Antonio to get married or to baptize their children. But, for their novenas and their beads, they relied on my mother. Suddenly everyone became more religious. She would go to evening prayer in a lace veil, so fragrant and smooth of skin, so pure of face, that everybody said she looked like, and indeed was, a real saint. Untrue: a saint would not have emitted those little giggles, a saint would not have had so much fun. Fun is a sort of insult to the unhappy, and that is why Mama laughed and enjoyed herself only when we were alone.

One day, at the market fair in Laterra, a yokel asked:

"They say you got a lady priest here. Where does she live?"

Mama was told about it. She did not laugh.

"I don't like that." And she added: "I never was a religious fanatic. I'm just a normal person who wants to help her neighbour. If they go on with that kind of talk, I'll never take out my beads again."

But that very night, I saw her throat tremble with delight:

"Now they're calling me a lady priest. . . . Imagine!"

She had found her vocation. And she continued to give advice, to say fine things, to console those who had lost their loved ones. Once, on the birthday of a man whose child she had godmothered, Mama said such beautiful words about old age, about the flight of time, about the good we should do before night falls, that the man asked:

"Why don't you give a talk like this every Sunday? We have no vicar and the young people need guidance. . . ."

Everyone thought it an excellent idea. A society was founded, the Laterra Parents' Circle, which had its meetings at the city hall. People came from far away to hear Mama speak. Everybody said that she did an enormous amount of good to people's souls, that the sweetness of her words comforted those who were suffering. A number of individuals were converted by her. I think my father believed in her more than anyone else did. But I couldn't think of my mother as a predestined being, come to the world just to do good. It seemed to me that she was playacting and I felt a little ashamed. But at the same time I asked myself:

"Why should you feel this way? Doesn't she reconcile couples who have separated, doesn't she console widows, doesn't she even correct the incorrigible?"

One day, at lunchtime, Mama said to my father:

"Today they brought me a difficult case. . . . A strange young man. You're going to give him work. Just for the love of God. He came asking for help . . . and I must not turn him away. The poor boy cried so, he implored me . . . telling about his terrible problem. He's wretched!"

A dream of glory enticed her:

"Do you know that the doctors in San Antonio could do nothing for him? I want you to help me. I think it's important for him to work . . . here. It will cost you nothing. He says he wants to work for us free because he knows that I don't accept payment for my work either and do everything just out of kindness."

The new employee looked like a pretty girl. He was rosy-cheeked, had dark eyes with long lashes, moved about without making the least noise. He knew some poetry by heart and sometimes recited it in a soft voice while cleaning the counter in the store. When people learned that he was employed by us, they advised my father:

"This isn't the kind of person to work in a respectable house!"

"She wanted it," replied my father. "She always knows what she's doing."

The new employee worked with a will, but he had crises of anxiety. Although it was agreed that he would dine with us, on certain nights he did not do so. And he would appear later with his eyes red.

Many times, Mama shut herself in the living room with him and her quiet voice scolded and wounded him. She would also correct him before my father and even before me, but smiling with kindness:

"Take your hand away from your waist. You look like a girl, and if you act this way, then . . ."

But she knew how to say things that he surely wanted to hear:

"There is no one better than you on this earth! Why are you afraid of other people? Come on, lift up your head!"

Stimulated by this, my father guaranteed:

"In my house no one will ever insult you. I'd just like to see someone try!"

No one ever did. Even the boys in the street, who used to point at him and talk loudly and laugh, became serious and fled as soon as my father appeared at the door.

And for a long time the young man was never absent from dinner. In his leisure hours he made pretty things for Mama. He painted a fan for her and made a jar in the form of a swan, out of old, wet paper, glue, and heaven knows what. He became my friend. He knew about clothes and styles as nobody else did. He would express opinions about my dresses. At the hour of prayer he, who had been so humiliated, whose look had been that of a beaten creature, now would come and take a place next to Mama, with a chaplet in his hand. If visitors called while he was with us, he did not scurry away as he had previously done. He remained in a corner, looking at everyone calmly and amicably. I watched his gradual metamorphosis. Less timid, he had become less effeminate. His movements were more confident, his physical attitudes less ridiculous.

Mama, who had carefully watched her conversation when he was present, now virtually forgot that he was not one of us. She would laugh freely, with her delightful, tremulous giggles. She seemed to have stopped teaching him how to behave, for it was no longer necessary. And he, when not at the counter, began to follow her about. He helped her in the house, he went shopping with her. Mama had reproved certain young women for their love intrigues; seeing her pass by they would say, hidden behind their windows:

"Don't you think maybe she's cured him . . . too much?"

Laterra took pride in Mama, the most important person in the community. It pained many persons to observe that almost comical affection. They would see her walk by quickly, erect, with firm step, and the young man behind, carrying her packages, or at her side, holding her parasol with a certain fervour as if it had been a pallium[1] in a religious procession. An obvious restlessness pervaded the city. It reached such a point that one Sunday, when Mama was talking on conjugal happiness and the duties of marriage, some heads turned toward the young man, almost imperceptibly but enough for me to perceive their thought. And an absurd feeling of forboding oppressed my heart.

Mama was the last to become aware of the passion she had aroused.

"Look," she said, "I only tried to build up his morale. . . . His own mother gave him up as lost—she even wished him dead! And today he's a fine young man! I'm only saying what everybody knows."

Papa was becoming despondent. One day he got it off his chest:

"I think it's better if he leaves. Obviously, you've succeeded in what you were trying to do. You've made him decent and hard-working, like anybody else. Let's thank God and send him back home. You did a wonderful job!"

"But," said Mama in amazement, "don't you see that more time is needed . . . so they'll forget about him? To send this boy back now would be a sin! A sin that I don't want on my conscience."

There was one night when the young man told a story at dinner about a hillbilly. Mama laughed as she had never laughed before, throwing back her petite head, showing her most disturbing nudity—her neck—with that tremulous chirp of hers. I saw his face become red and his eyes shine at the sight of her white splendour. Papa did not laugh. I felt unhappy and frightened. Three days later the young man fell ill with a grippe. It was while Mama was visiting him in his room that he said something to her. I'll never know what it was. For the first time, we heard Mama raise her voice. It was loud, strident, furious. A week later he was well and resumed work. She said to my father:

"You're right. It's time for him to go back home."

At dinner hour Mama told the maidservant:

"We'll be the only ones tonight. Just set three places. . . ."

The next day, at the hour of prayer, the young man arrived in a state of fear, but he came along and took his usual place next to Mama.

"Go away!" she said in a low voice before beginning the prayer. He obeyed, not even pleading with his eyes.

Every head slowly followed him. I watched him, with his unobtrusive, school-girl walk, going out into the night.

In a few moments Mama's voice, slightly tremulous, was praying:

"Our Father who art in heaven, hallowed be Thy name. . . ."

The voices that accompanied hers were stronger than they had been in many days.

He did not return to his own town, where he had been the accepted object of ridicule. That very night a farmer, on leaving Laterra, saw a long shape swinging from a tree. He thought it might be an assailant, but he courageously approached the figure. He discovered the young man. We were called. I saw him. Mama didn't. By the light of the lantern he seemed more ridiculous than tragic . . . so frail, hanging there like a Judas with a face of purple cloth. An enormous crowd soon encircled the mango tree. I was con-

---

[1]Cloak or vestment.

vinced that all of Laterra was breathing easier. Now it had proof! Its lady had not transgressed, its moralist had not failed it.

For several months Mama, perfect and perfumed as always, uttered none of her giggles, although she continued, now without great conviction (I could tell), to give guidance. Even at dinner she wore dark dresses, closed at the neck.

[1957]

For Discussion

1. Analyze the social and moral codes of the town of Laterra.

2. Explain how the motifs of "virtue" and "morality and immorality" are associated with manners or "deportment" in the story.

3. What does laughter have to do with the story, and why does Mama hide her giggles?

4. Reread the advice Mama gives, especially about the "reality of the Devil and about having to side with either the Beast or the Angel." How could her own words be used against her at the end?

5. Identify examples of "moral inversion" (bad represented as good, and vice versa) in the story. Which acts are bad or good, contrary to society's views?

6. What are the attitudes of Papa and the narrator toward Mama's counseling?

7. What is considered "wrong" with the "strange young man," and is he "cured" by Mama's help?

8. After the lengthy exposition (rising action), why are the climax (high point), and denouement (falling action) so abrupt?

For Further Exploration

1. How does the climax of the story involve religion and sex in much the same way as does the climactic scene in "Good Country People"? Examine how religion and sex are related to the individual's interaction with other people in society.

2. Apply several criteria for classical tragic heroes to Mama's character in this story: a tragic hero is of high rank in society, but because of a tragic flaw—often overweening pride—he or she has a downfall. The hero recognizes his or her own part in this reversal of fortunes, which was predicted by a prophet, and followed by a chanting chorus. How does the story fit or fall short of being "tragic" in the classical sense? You might compare this story with Sophocles' *Antigone* or Anouilh's modern version of the same tragedy (both filmed).

Poetry About
Women and Society

Adult women must come to terms with the complexity of society—including money, status, work, politics, home, religion, sexuality, friendship, love, marriage, motherhood, sisterhood, widowhood, and death—all mentioned in these poems.

There is a great deal of sympathy exhibited for women struggling to survive, or challenging society's codes. In response to these women's struggles, many of the poets create mental pictures of energy and action; not one of the poems advocates passivity. One persona goes on a dangerous journey of discovery, while another is about to "bust out of girlscout camp." But the destructive image of being a "handgrenade set to explode" is juxtaposed with the generative image of a woman being "like goldenrod ready to bloom." Bursting out of the old self is seen as necessary to allow the new self to emerge.

Above all, these poets exhort women to reach out to other women, regardless of social class, status, race, or point of view, embracing whatever is good in themselves and others in order to combat the many problems of women and society.

Genny Lim

1946–

WONDER WOMAN

Sometimes I see reflections on bits of glass on sidewalks
I catch the glimmer of empty bottles floating out to sea
Sometimes I stretch my arms way above my head and wonder if
There are women along the Mekong doing the same

Sometimes I stare longingly at women who I will never know
Generous, laughing women with wrinkled cheeks and white teeth
Dragging along chubby, rosy-cheeked babies on fat, wobbly legs
Sometimes I stare at Chinese grandmothers
Getting on the 30 Stockton with shopping bags
Japanese women tourists in European hats
Middle-aged mothers with laundry carts
Young wives holding hands with their husbands
Lesbian women holding hands in coffee-houses
Smiling debutantes with bouquets of yellow daffodils
Silver-haired matrons with silver rhinestoned poodles
Painted prostitutes posing along MacArthur Boulevard
Giddy teenage girls snapping gum in fast cars
Widows clutching bibles, crucifixes

I look at them and wonder if
They are a part of me
I look in their eyes and wonder if
They share my dreams

I wonder if the woman in mink is content
if the stockbroker's wife is afraid of growing old
If the professor's wife is an alcoholic
If the woman in prison is me

There are copper-tanned women in Hyannis Port playing tennis
Women who eat with finger bowls
There are women in factories punching time clocks
Women tired every waking hour of the day

I wonder why there are women born with silver spoons
        in their mouths
Women who have never known a day of hunger
Women who have never changed their own bed linen
And I wonder why there are women who must work
Women who must clean other women's houses
Women who must shell shrimps for pennies a day
Women who must sew other women's clothes
Who must cook
Who must die

In childbirth
In dreams

Why must a woman stand divided?
Building the walls that tear them down?
Jill-of-all-trades
Lover, mother, housewife, friend, breadwinner
Heart and spade
A woman is a ritual
A house that must accommodate
A house that must endure
Generation after generation
Of wind and torment, of fire and rain
A house with echoing rooms
Closets with hidden cries
Walls with stretchmarks
Windows with eyes

Short, tall, skinny, fat
Pregnant, married, white, yellow, black, brown, red
Professional, working-class, aristocrat
Women cooking over coals in sampans
Women shining tiffany spoons in glass houses
Women stretching their arms way above the clouds
In Samarkand, in San Francisco
Along the Mekong

[1981]

Marge Piercy

1936–

THE WOMAN IN THE ORDINARY

The woman in the
ordinary pudgy graduate student girl
is crouching with eyes and muscles clenched.
Round and smooth as a pebble
you efface yourself
under ripples of conversation and debate.
The woman in the block of ivory soap
has massive thighs that neigh
and great breasts and strong arms that blare and trumpet.
The woman of the golden fleece
laughs from the belly uproariously
inside the girl who imitates
a Christmas card virgin with glued hands.
It is time to bust out of girlscout camp.
It is time to stop running
for most popular sweetheart of Campbell Soup.
You are still searching for yourself in others' eyes
and creeping so you wont be punished.
In you bottled up is a woman peppery as curry,
a yam of a woman of butter and brass,
compounded of acid and sweet like a pineapple,
like a handgrenade set to explode,
like goldenrod ready to bloom.

[1971]

Audre Lorde

1934–

THE WOMAN THING

The hunters are back
From beating the winter's face
In search of a challenge or task
In search of food
Making fresh tracks for their children's hunger
They do not watch the sun
They cannot wear its heat for a sign
Of triumph or freedom
The hunters are treading heavily homeward
Through snow that is marked
With their own footprints
Emptyhanded the hunters return
Snow-maddened, sustained by their rages.

In the night, after food
They will seek
Young girls for their amusement.
Now the hunters are coming
And the unbaked girls flee from their angers.
All this day I have craved
Food for my child's hunger.
Emptyhanded the hunters come shouting
Injustices drip from their mouths
Like stale snow melted in sunlight.

And this womanthing my mother taught me
Bakes off its covering of snow
Like a rising blackening sun.

[1970]

Leonora Speyer

1872–1956

THE LADDER

I had a sudden vision in the night,
I did not sleep, I dare not say I dreamed,
Beside my bed a curious ladder gleamed
And lifted upward toward the sky's dim height;
And every rung shone luminous and white,
And every rung a woman's body seemed
Out-stretched, and down the sides her long hair
   streamed:
And you, you climbed that ladder of delight.

You climbed sure-footed, naked rung by rung,
Clasped them and trod them, called them by their name,
And my name too, I heard you speak at last;
You stood upon my breast the while and flung
A hand up to the next—and then, oh shame,
I kissed the foot that bruised me as it passed.

[1931]

Lucille Clifton

1936–

THE THIRTY EIGHTH YEAR OF MY LIFE

the thirty eighth year
of my life,
plain as bread
round as a cake
an ordinary woman.

an ordinary woman.

i had expected to be
smaller than this,
more beautiful,
wiser in Afrikan ways,
more confident,
i had expected
more than this.

i will be forty soon.
my mother once was forty.

my mother died at forty four,
a woman of sad countenance
leaving behind a girl
awkward as a stork.
my mother was thick,
her hair was a jungle and
she was very wise
and beautiful
and sad.

i have dreamed dreams
for you mama
more than once.
i have wrapped me
in your skin
and made you live again
more than once.
i have taken the bones you hardened
and built daughters
and they blossom and promise fruit
like Afrikan trees.
i am a woman now.
an ordinary woman.

in the thirty eighth
year of my life,
surrounded by life,
a perfect picture of
blackness blessed,
i had not expected this
loneliness.

if it is western,
if it is the final
Europe in my mind,
if in the middle of my life
i am turning the final turn
into the shining dark
let me come to it whole
and holy
not afraid
not lonely

out of my mother's life
into my own.
into my own.

i had expected more than this.
i had not expected to be
an ordinary woman.

[1974]

Maya Angelou

1928–

WOMAN ME

Your smile, delicate
rumor of peace.
Deafening revolutions nestle in the
cleavage of
your breasts
Beggar-Kings and red-ringed Priests
seek glory at the meeting
of your thighs
A grasp of Lions, A lap of Lambs.

    Your tears, jeweled
    strewn a diadem
    caused Pharaohs to ride
    deep in the bosom of the
    Nile. Southern spas lash fast
    their doors upon the night when
    winds of death blow down your name
    A bride of hurricanes, A swarm of summer wind

Your laughter, pealing tall
above the bells of ruined cathedrals.
Children reach between your teeth
for charts to live their lives.
A stomp of feet, A bevy of swift hands.

[1975]

Marianne Moore

1887–1972

NEVERTHELESS

you've seen a strawberry
    that's had a struggle; yet
    was, where the fragments met,

a hedgehog or a star-
    fish for the multitude
    of seeds. What better food

than apple seeds—the fruit
    within the fruit—locked in
    like counter-curved twin

hazelnuts? Frost that kills
    the little rubber-plant-
    leaves of *kok-saghyz*-stalks, can't

harm the roots; they still grow
    in frozen ground. Once where
    there was a prickly-pear-

leaf clinging to barbed wire,
    a root shot down to grow
    in earth two feet below;

as carrots form mandrakes
    or a ram's-horn root some-
    times. Victory won't come

to me unless I go
    to it; a grape tendril
    ties a knot in knots till

knotted thirty times—so
    the bound twig that's under-
    gone and over-gone, can't stir.

The weak overcomes its
    menace, the strong over-
    comes itself. What is there

like fortitude! What sap
    went through that little thread
    to make the cherry red!

[1935]

[1]Dandelion.

For Discussion

1. Summarize Genny Lim's central question in "Wonder Woman." What is the pun in the title?

2. Analyze the effectiveness of the repeated image of a woman inside of something else in the poem "The Woman in the Ordinary."

3. Why is the oxymoron "blackening sun" (opposite words juxtaposed) appropriate for the "womanthing" Audre Lorde describes?

4. How could the narrator's night vision in "The Ladder" be interpreted as an allegory of women's role in society?

5. What does Clifton's narrator mean by comparing her personal feelings of ordinariness and loneliness with being "Western," the "final Europe in my mind"?

6. Explain how the personal is made universal in "Woman Me" as it is in "The Thirty Eighth Year of My Life."

7. What lesson for the individual in society is presented for the reader of Moore's "Nevertheless"?

For Further Exploration

1. The first half of "Wonder Woman" is strikingly similar in style and theme to Walt Whitman's "Song of Myself," part of *Leaves of Grass.* How does the final message of the poem differ from Whitman's celebration of himself as a part of all of the society around him?

2. Analyze the poems "Wonder Woman," "The Woman Thing," and "The Woman in the Ordinary" to find the authors' answers to the question, "What is a woman's place in society?"

Drama About
Women and Society

Overtones, a play written in 1913 by Alice Gerstenberg, seems at first to be a light satire of the superficiality of the roles women play in society. "Twin" actresses are used to represent the "head" and the "heart" of each of the main characters, and to exaggerate the contrast between what each says and what she really thinks. Competition over wealth and status overlaps with sexual jealousy to expose a picture of the shallowness of social interchange.

Yet is there a "double exposure"? Critics Sullivan and Hatch mention in their introduction to *Plays By and About Women* that the women in *Overtones* are depicted only as they relate to the men in both of their lives—an observation that cannot be denied. The remark leads readers to wonder whether Gerstenberg is criticizing the women themselves for being self-centered and male-dominated, or society for promoting those attributes. The same issue has been raised in different ways by the authors of poems and stories about women and society—who has to change first, women or society?

Alice Gerstenberg

1893–

OVERTONES

TIME: *The present.*

SCENE: HARRIET'S *fashionable living room. The door at the back leads to the hall. In the center a tea table with a high-backed chair at each side.*

HARRIET'S *gown is a light, "jealous" green. Her counterpart,* HETTY, *wears a gown of the same design but in a darker shade.* MARGARET *wears a gown of lavender chiffon while her counterpart,* MAGGIE, *wears a gown of the same design in purple, a purple scarf veiling her face. Chiffon is used to give a sheer effect, suggesting a possibility of primitive and cultured selves merging into one woman. The primitive and cultured selves never come into actual physical contact but try to sustain the impression of mental conflict.* HARRIET *never sees* HETTY, *never talks to her but rather thinks aloud looking into space.* HETTY, *however, looks at* HARRIET, *talks intently and shadows her continually. The same is true of* MARGARET *and* MAGGIE. *The voices of the cultured women are affected and lingering, the voices of the primitive impulsive and more or less staccato.*

When the curtain rises HARRIET *is seated right of tea table, busying herself with the tea things.*

HETTY   Harriet. *(There is no answer)* Harriet, my other self. *(There is no answer)* My trained self.

HARRIET   *(Listens intently)* Yes?

(From behind HARRIET'S *chair* HETTY *rises slowly)*

HETTY   I want to talk to you.

HARRIET   Well?

HETTY   *(Looking at* HARRIET *admiringly)* Oh, Harriet, you are beautiful to-day.

HARRIET   Am I presentable, Hetty?

HETTY   Suits me.

HARRIET   I've tried to make the best of the good points.

HETTY   My passions are deeper than yours. I can't keep on the mask as you do. I'm crude and real, you are my appearance in the world.

HARRIET   I am what you wish the world to believe you are.

HETTY   You are the part of me that has been trained.

HARRIET   I am your educated self.

HETTY   I am the rushing river; you are the ice over the current.

HARRIET   I am your subtle overtones.

HETTY   But together we are one woman, the wife of Charles Goodrich.

HARRIET   There I disagree with you, Hetty, I alone am his wife.

HETTY   *(Indignantly)* Harriet, how can you say such a thing!

HARRIET   Certainly. I am the one who flatters him. I have to be the one who talks to him. If I gave you a chance you would tell him at once that you dislike him.

HETTY   (*Moving away*) I don't love him, that's certain.

HARRIET   You leave all the fibbing to me. He doesn't suspect that my calm, suave manner hides your hatred. Considering the amount of scheming it causes me it can safely be said that he is my husband.

HETTY   Oh, if you love him—

HARRIET   I? I haven't any feelings. It isn't my business to love anybody.

HETTY   Then why need you object to calling him my husband?

HARRIET   I resent your appropriation of a man who is managed only through the cleverness of my artifice.

HETTY   You may be clever enough to deceive him, Harriet, but I am still the one who suffers. I can't forget he is my husband. I can't forget that I might have married John Caldwell.

HARRIET   How foolish of you to remember John, just because we met his wife by chance.

HETTY   That's what I want to talk to you about. She may be here at any moment. I want to advise you about what to say to her this afternoon.

HARRIET   By all means tell me now and don't interrupt while she is here. You have a most annoying habit of talking to me when people are present. Sometimes it is all I can do to keep my poise and appear *not* to be listening to you.

HETTY   Impress her.

HARRIET   Hetty, dear, is it not my custom to impress people?

HETTY   I hate her.

HARRIET   I can't let her see that.

HETTY   I hate her because she married John.

HARRIET   Only after you had refused him.

HETTY   (*Turning to* HARRIET) Was it my fault that I refused him?

HARRIET   That's right, blame me.

HETTY   It was your fault. You told me he was too poor and never would be able to do anything in painting. Look at him now, known in Europe, just returned from eight years in Paris, famous.

HARRIET   It was too poor a gamble at the time. It was much safer to accept Charles's money and position.

HETTY   And then John married Margaret within the year.

HARRIET   Out of spite.

HETTY   Freckled, gauky-looking thing she was, too.

HARRIET   (*A little sadly*) Europe improved her. She was stunning the other morning.

HETTY   Make her jealous today.

HARRIET   Shall I be haughty or cordial or caustic or—

HETTY   Above all else you must let her know that we are rich.

HARRIET   Oh, yes, I do that quite easily now.

HETTY   You must put it on a bit.

HARRIET   Never fear.

HETTY   Tell her I love my husband.

HARRIET   My husband—

HETTY   Are you going to quarrel with me?

HARRIET   (*Moves away*) No, I have no desire to quarrel with you. It is quite too uncomfortable. I couldn't get away from you if I tried.

HETTY   (*Stamping her foot and following* HARRIET) You were a stupid fool to make me refuse John, I'll never forgive you—never—

HARRIET   (*Stopping and holding up her hand*) Don't get me all excited. I'll be in no condition to meet her properly this afternoon.

HETTY   *(Passionately)* I could choke you for robbing me of John.

HARRIET   *(Retreating)* Don't muss me!

HETTY   You don't know how you have made me suffer.

HARRIET   *(Beginning to feel the strength of* HETTY'S *emotion surge through her and trying to conquer it)* It is not my business to have heartaches.

HETTY   You're bloodless. Nothing but sham—sham—while I—

HARRIET   *(Emotionally)* Be quiet! I can't let her see that I have been fighting with my inner self.

HETTY   And now after all my suffering you say it has cost you more than it has cost me to be married to Charles. But it's the pain here in my heart—I've paid the price—I've paid—Charles is not your husband!

HARRIET   *(Trying to conquer emotion)* He is.

HETTY   *(Follows* HARRIET*)* He isn't.

HARRIET   *(Weakly)* He is.

HETTY   *(Towering over* HARRIET*)* He isn't! I'll kill you!

HARRIET   *(Overpowered, sinks into a chair)* Don't—don't you're stronger than I—you're—

HETTY   Say he's mine.

HARRIET   He's ours.

HETTY   *(The telephone rings)* There she is now.

    (HETTY *hurries to 'phone but* HARRIET *regains her supremacy)*

HARRIET   *(Authoritatively)* Wait! I can't let the telephone girl down there hear my real self. It isn't proper. *(At phone)* Show Mrs. Caldwell up.

HETTY   I'm so excited, my heart's in my mouth.

HARRIET   *(At the mirror)* A nice state you've put my nerves into.

HETTY   Don't let her see you're nervous.

HARRIET   Quick, put the veil on, or she'll see *you* shining through me.

    (HARRIET *takes a scarf of chiffon that has been lying over the back of a chair and drapes it on* HETTY, *covering her face. The chiffon is the same color of their gowns but paler in shade so that it pales* HETTY'S *darker gown to match* HARRIET'S *lighter one. As* HETTY *moves in the following scene the chiffon falls away revealing now and then the gown of deeper dye underneath.)*

HETTY   Tell her Charles is rich and fascinating—boast of our friends, make her feel she needs us.

HARRIET   I'll make her ask John to paint us.

HETTY   That's just my thought—if John paints our portrait—

HARRIET   We can wear an exquisite gown—

HETTY   And make him fall in love again and—

HARRIET   *(Schemingly)* Yes. (MARGARET *parts the portières back center and extends her hand.* MARGARET *is followed by her counterpart* MAGGIE) Oh, Margaret, I'm so glad to see you!

HETTY   *(To* MAGGIE*)* That's a lie.

MARGARET   *(In superficial voice throughout)* It's enchanting to see you, Harriet.

MAGGIE   *(In emotional voice throughout)* I'd bite you, if I dared.

HARRIET   *(To* MARGARET*)* Wasn't our meeting a stroke of luck?

MARGARET   *(Coming down left of table)* I've thought of you so often, Harriet; and to come back and find you living in New York.

HARRIET   *(Coming down right of table)* Mr. Goodrich has many interests here.

MAGGIE   *(To* MARGARET*)* Flatter her.

MARGARET   I know, Mr. Goodrich is so successful.

HETTY *(To* HARRIET*)* Tell her we´re ricn.

HARRIET *(To* MARGARET*)* Won't you sit down?

MARGARET *(Takes a chair)* What a beautiful cabinet!

HARRIET Do you like it? I'm afraid Charles paid an extravagant price.

MAGGIE *(To* HETTY*)* I don't believe it.

MARGARET *(Sitting down. To* HARRIET*)* I am sure he must have.

HARRIET *(Sitting down)* How well you are looking, Margaret.

HETTY Yes, you are not. There are circles under your eyes.

MAGGIE *(To* HETTY*)* I haven't eaten since breakfast and I'm hungry.

MARGARET *(To* HARRIET*)* How well you are looking, too.

MAGGIE *(To* HETTY*)* You have hard lines about your lips, are you happy?

HETTY *(To* HARRIET*)* Don't let her know that I'm unhappy.

HARRIET *(To* MARGARET*)* Why shouldn't I look well? My life is full, happy, complete—

MAGGIE I wonder.

HETTY *(In* HARRIET'S *ear)* Tell her we have an automobile.

MARGARET *(To* HARRIET*)* My life is complete, too.

MAGGIE My heart is torn with sorrow; my husband cannot make a living. He will kill himself if he does not get an order for a painting.

MARGARET *(Laughs)* You must come and see us in our studio. John has been doing some excellent portraits. He cannot begin to fill his orders.

HETTY *(To* HARRIET*)* Tell her we have an automobile.

HARRIET *(To* MARGARET*)* Do you take lemon in your tea?

MAGGIE Take cream. It's more filling.

MARGARET *(Looking nonchalantly at tea things)* No, cream, if you please. How cozy!

MAGGIE *(Glaring at tea things)* Only cakes! I could eat them all!

HARRIET *(To* MARGARET*)* How many lumps?

MAGGIE *(To* MARGARET*)* Sugar is nourishing.

MARGARET *(To* HARRIET*)* Three, please. I used to drink very sweet coffee in Turkey and ever since I've—

HETTY I don't believe you were ever in Turkey.

MAGGIE I wasn't, but it is none of your business.

HARRIET *(Pouring tea)* Have you been in Turkey? Do tell me about it.

MAGGIE *(To* MARGARET*)* Change the subject.

MARGARET *(To* HARRIET*)* You must go there. You have so much taste in dress you would enjoy seeing their costumes.

MAGGIE Isn't she going to pass the cake?

MARGARET *(To* HARRIET*)* John painted several portraits there.

HETTY *(To* HARRIET*)* Why don't you stop her bragging and tell her we have an automobile?

HARRIET *(Offers cake across the table to* MARGARET*)* Cake?

MAGGIE *(Stands back of* MARGARET, *shadowing her as* HETTY *shadows* HARRIET. MAGGIE *reaches claws out for the cake and groans with joy)* At last!

   (But her claws do not touch the cake.)

MARGARET *(With a graceful, nonchalant hand places cake upon her plate and bites at it slowly and delicately)* Thank you.

HETTY *(To* HARRIET*)* Automobile!

MAGGIE *(To* MARGARET*)* Follow up the costumes with the suggestion that she would make a good model for John. It isn't too early to begin getting what you came for.

MARGARET *(Ignoring* MAGGIE*)* What delicious cake.

HETTY *(Excitedly to* HARRIET*)* There's your chance for the auto.

HARRIET *(Nonchalantly to* MARGARET*)* Yes, it is good cake, isn't it? There are always a great many people buying it at Harper's. I sat in my automobile fifteen minutes this morning waiting for my chauffeur to get it.

MAGGIE *(To* MARGARET*)* Make her order a portrait.

MARGARET *(To* HARRIET*)* If you stopped at Harper's you must have noticed the new gowns at Henderson's. Aren't the shop windows alluring these days?

HARRIET Even my chauffeur notices them.

MAGGIE I know you have an automobile, I heard you the first time.

MARGARET I notice gowns now with an artist's eye as John does. The one you have on, my dear, is very paintable.

HETTY Don't let her see you're anxious to be painted.

HARRIET *(Nonchalantly)* Oh, it's just a little model.

MAGGIE *(To* MARGARET*)* Don't seem anxious to get the order.

MARGARET *(Nonchalantly)* Perhaps it isn't the gown itself but the way you wear it that pleases the eye. Some people can wear anything with grace.

HETTY Yes, I'm very graceful.

HARRIET *(To* MARGARET*)* You flatter me, my dear.

MARGARET On the contrary, Harriet, I have an intense admiration for you. I remember how beautiful you were—as a girl. In fact, I was quite jealous when John was paying you so much attention.

HETTY She is gloating because I lost him.

HARRIET Those were childhood days in a country town.

MAGGIE *(To* MARGARET*)* She's trying to make you feel that John was only a country boy.

MARGARET Most great men have come from the country. There is a fair chance that John will be added to the list.

HETTY I know it and I am bitterly jealous of you.

HARRIET Undoubtedly he owes much of his success to you, Margaret, your experience in economy and your ability to endure hardship. Those first few years in Paris must have been a struggle.

MAGGIE She is sneering at your poverty.

MARGARET Yes, we did find life difficult at first, not the luxurious start a girl has who marries wealth.

HETTY *(To* HARRIET*)* Deny that you married Charles for his money.

(HARRIET *deems it wise to ignore* HETTY'S *advice)*

MARGARET But John and I are so congenial in our tastes, that we were impervious to hardship or unhappiness.

HETTY *(In anguish)* Do you love each other? Is it really true?

HARRIET *(Sweetly)* Did you have all the romance of starving for his art?

MAGGIE *(To* MARGARET*)* She's taunting you. Get even with her.

MARGARET Not for long. Prince Rier soon discovered John's genius, and introduced him royally to wealthy Parisians who gave him many orders.

HETTY *(To* MAGGIE*)* Are you telling the truth or are you lying?

HARRIET If he had so many opportunities there, you must have had great inducements to come back to the States.

MAGGIE *(To* HETTY*)* We did, but not the kind you think.

MARGARET John became the rage among Americans traveling in France, too, and they simply insisted upon his coming here.

HARRIET Whom is he going to paint here?

MAGGIE *(Frightened)* What names dare I make up?

MARGARET *(Calmly)* Just at present Miss Dorothy Ainsworth of Oregon is posing. You may not know the name, but she is the daughter of a wealthy miner who found gold in Alaska.

HARRIET   I dare say there are many Western people we have never heard of.

MARGARET   You must have found social life in New York very interesting, Harriet, after the simplicity of our home town.

HETTY   *(To MAGGIE)* There's no need to remind us that our beginnings were the same.

HARRIET   Of course Charles's family made everything delightful for me. They are so well connected.

MAGGIE   *(To MARGARET)* Flatter her.

MARGARET   I heard it mentioned yesterday that you had made yourself very popular. Some one said you were very clever!

HARRIET   *(Pleased)* Who told you that?

MAGGIE   Nobody!

MARGARET   *(Pleasantly)* Oh, confidences should be suspected—respected, I mean. They said, too, that you are gaining some reputation as a critic of art.

HARRIET   I make no pretences.

MARGARET   Are you and Mr. Goodrich interested in the same things, too?

HETTY   No!

HARRIET   Yes, indeed, Charles and I are inseparable.

MAGGIE   I wonder.

HARRIET   Do have another cake.

MAGGIE   *(In relief)* Oh, yes.

   (Again her claws extend but do not touch the cake)

MARGARET   *(Takes cake delicately)* I really shouldn't—after my big luncheon. John took me to the Ritz and we are invited to the Bedfords' for dinner—they have such a magnificent house near the drive—I really shouldn't, but the cakes are so good.

MAGGIE   Starving!

HARRIET   *(To MARGARET)* More tea?

MAGGIE   Yes!

MARGARET   No, thank you. How wonderfully life has arranged itself for you. Wealth, position, a happy marriage, every opportunity to enjoy all pleasures; beauty, art—how happy you must be.

HETTY   *(In anguish)* Don't call me happy. I've never been happy since I gave up John. All these years without him—a future without him—no—no—I shall win him back—away from you—away from you—

HARRIET   *(Does not see MAGGIE pointing to cream and MARGARET stealing some)* I sometimes think it is unfair for anyone to be as happy as I am. Charles and I are just as much in love now as when we married. To me he is just the dearest man in the world.

MAGGIE   *(Passionately)* My John is. I love him so much I could die for him. I'm going through hunger and want to make him great and he loves me. He worships me!

MARGARET   *(Leisurely to HARRIET)* I should like to meet Mr. Goodrich. Bring him to our studio. John has some sketches to show. Not many, because all the portraits have been purchased by the subjects. He gets as much as four thousand dollars now.

HETTY   *(To HARRIET)* Don't pay that much.

HARRIET   *(To MARGARET)* As much as that?

MARGARET   It is not really too much when one considers that John is in the foremost ranks of artists today. A picture painted by him now will double and treble in value.

MAGGIE   It's a lie. He is growing weak with despair.

HARRIET   Does he paint all day long?

MAGGIE   No, he draws advertisements for our bread.

MARGARET   *(To* HARRIET*)* When you and your husband come to see us, telephone first—

MAGGIE   Yes, so he can get the advertisements out of the way.

MARGARET   Otherwise you might arrive while he has a sitter, and John refuses to let me disturb him then.

HETTY   Make her ask for an order.

HARRIET   *(To* MARGARET*)* Le Grange offered to paint me for a thousand.

MARGARET   Louis Le Grange's reputation isn't worth more than that.

HARRIET   Well, I've heard his work well mentioned.

MAGGIE   Yes, he is doing splendid work.

MARGARET   Oh, dear me, no. He is only praised by the masses. He is accepted not at all by artists themselves.

HETTY   *(Anxiously)* Must I really pay the full price?

HARRIET   Le Grange thought I would make a good subject.

MAGGIE   *(To* MARGARET*)* Let her fish for it.

MARGARET   Of course you would. Why don't you let Le Grange paint you, if you *trust* him?

HETTY   She doesn't seem anxious to have John do it.

HARRIET   But if Le Grange isn't accepted by artists, it would be a waste of time to pose for him, wouldn't it?

MARGARET   Yes, I think it would.

MAGGIE   *(Passionately to* HETTY *across back of table)* Give us the order. John is so despondent he can't endure much longer. Help us! Help me! Save us!

HETTY   *(To* HARRIET*)* Don't seem too eager.

HARRIET   And yet if he charges only a thousand one might consider it.

MARGARET   If you really wish to be painted, why don't you give a little more and have a portrait really worth while? John might be induced to do you for a little below his usual price considering that you used to be such good friends.

HETTY   *(In glee)* Hurrah!

HARRIET   *(Quietly to* MARGARET*)* That's very nice of you to suggest—of course I don't know—

MAGGIE   *(In fear)* For God's sake, say yes.

MARGARET   *(Quietly to* HARRIET*)* Of course, I don't know whether John would. He is very peculiar in these matters. He sets his value on his work and thinks it beneath him to discuss price.

HETTY   *(To* MAGGIE*)* You needn't try to make us feel small.

MARGARET   Still, I might quite delicately mention to him that inasmuch as you have many influential friends you would be very glad to—to—

MAGGIE   *(To* HETTY*)* Finish what I don't want to say.

HETTY   *(To* HARRIET*)* Help her out.

HARRIET   Oh, yes, introductions will follow the exhibition of my portrait. No doubt I—

HETTY   *(To* HARRIET*)* Be patronizing.

HARRIET   No doubt I shall be able to introduce your husband to his advantage.

MAGGIE   *(Relieved)* Saved.

MARGARET   If I find John in a propitious mood I shall take pleasure, for your sake, in telling him about your beauty. Just as you are sitting now would be a lovely pose.

MAGGIE   *(To* MARGARET*)* We can go now.

HETTY   *(To* HARRIET*)* Don't let her think she is doing us a favor.

HARRIET   It will give me pleasure to add my name to your husband's list of patronesses.

MAGGIE   *(Excitedly to* MARGARET*)* Run home and tell John the good news.

MARGARET   *(Leisurely to* HARRIET*)* I little guessed when I came for a pleasant chat about old times that it would develop into business arrangements. I had no idea, Harriet, that you had any intention of being painted. By Le Grange, too. Well, I came just in time to rescue you.

MAGGIE   *(To* MARGARET*)* Run home and tell John. Hurry, hurry!

HETTY   *(To* HARRIET*)* You managed the order very neatly. She doesn't suspect that you wanted it.

HARRIET   Now if I am not satisfied with my portrait I shall blame you, Margaret, dear. I am relying upon your opinion of John's talent.

MAGGIE   *(To* MARGARET*)* She doesn't suspect what you came for. Run home and tell John!

HARRIET   You always had a brilliant mind, Margaret.

MARGARET   Ah, it is you who flatter, now.

MAGGIE   *(To* MARGARET*)* You don't have to stay so long. Hurry home!

HARRIET   Ah, one does not flatter when one tells the truth.

MARGARET   *(Smiles)* I must be going or you will have me completely under your spell.

HETTY   *(Looks at clock)* Yes, do go. I have to dress for dinner.

HARRIET   *(To* MARGARET*)* Oh, don't hurry.

MAGGIE   *(To* HETTY*)* I hate you!

MARGARET   *(To* HARRIET*)* No, really I must, but I hope we shall see each other often at the studio. I find you so stimulating.

HETTY   *(To* MAGGIE*)* I hate you!

HARRIET   *(To* MARGARET*)* It is indeed gratifying to find a kindred spirit.

MAGGIE   *(To* HETTY*)* I came for your gold.

MARGARET   *(To* HARRIET*)* How delightful it is to know you again.

HETTY   *(To* MAGGIE*)* I am going to make you and your husband suffer.

HARRIET   My kind regards to John.

MAGGIE   *(To* HETTY*)* He has forgotten all about you.

MARGARET   *(Rises)* He will be so happy to receive them.

HETTY   *(To* MAGGIE*)* I can hardly wait to talk to him again.

HARRIET   I shall wait, then, until you send me word?

MARGARET   *(Offering her hand)* I'll speak to John about it as soon as I can and tell you when to come.

> (HARRIET *takes* MARGARET'S *hand affectionately.* HETTY *and* MAGGIE *rush at each other, throw back their veils, and fling their speeches fiercely at each other.)*

HETTY   I love him—I love him—

MAGGIE   He's starving—I'm starving—

HETTY   I'm going to take him away from you—

MAGGIE   I want your money—and your influence.

HETTY and MAGGIE   I'm going to rob you—rob you.

> (There is a cymbal crash, the lights go out and come up again slowly, leaving only MARGARET and HARRIET visible.)

MARGARET *(Quietly to* HARRIET*)* I've had such a delightful afternoon.
HARRIET *(Offering her hand)* It has been a joy to see you.
MARGARET *(Sweetly to* HARRIET*)* Good-bye.
HARRIET *(Sweetly to* MARGARET *as she kisses her)* Good-bye, my dear.

CURTAIN

[1913]

For Discussion

1. How does the statement "I am your subtle overtones" near the beginning of the play help to clarify the title?

2. Discuss the theme of appearance versus reality as it is suggested in the line, "I am crude and real, you are my appearance in the world." Which selves are the "real" ones?

3. Analyze the diction used by Hetty and Maggie. What words do they use that are unacceptable in polite society?

4. Contrast the images used for the dual selves, such as the "rushing river" versus "ice over the current."

5. Whose "side" are we on—Harriet's or Margaret's, Hetty or Maggie's, the public selves or the private selves?

6. What role do men play? Examine each reference to the husbands to discover their personalities and functions in the play.

7. Discuss the questions posed at the end of the introduction to *Overtones.* Who or what is Gerstenberg satirizing?

For Further Exploration

1. Read or watch a classic play in which a woman rebels against becoming a social stereotype, such as William Luce's *The Belle of Amherst* (the life of Emily Dickinson), any version of *Antigone,* Henrik Ibsen's *A Doll's House* or *Hedda Gabbler* (all filmed). Which women could be considered "successful" at the ends of the plays?

2. Note that the plays mentioned above are all written by men. To further examine women's roles in society as represented in drama, quickly list as many plays as you can think of. How many are written by women? How many are about women, or have a woman as a main character? How often is the woman as a secondary character seen only in her relation to a man? If you can think of few women-centered plays, conduct research to find collections such as *New Plays by Women, Plays By and About Women,* and *The New Women's Theatre.*

For Discussion and Writing About This Section

1. Compare the attitude of townspeople in the story "Guidance" with society's attitudes in the poem "In the Counselor's Waiting Room" (Adolescence section).

2. Compare the women's attitudes toward other women in "A Happening in Barbados" with stories from other sections (Women and Work, Family, Old Age).

3. Why are Joy/Hulga in "Good Country People" and Mabel in "The New Dress" similar to "The Woman in the Ordinary"?

4. Examine the relationship of tone to theme in the stories and poems. Which stories treat frivolous topics seriously, and vice versa? What different effects are produced?

5. The women in several poems and stories sound angry or bitter. List the sources of their discontent, and identify satire where it is used for effective criticism.

6. Several of the narrators sound unsure of themselves. Which stories and poems deal with a woman trying to distinguish reality from illusion (or personal reality from society's expectations)?

7. What do these works have to say about men's roles in society?

8. What qualities would an ideal adult woman have, according to these authors? What type of a society would be ideal?

9. What might the poets of women in society say to the women in *Overtones?*

OLD AGE

Experiencing loss and alienation; dealing with generational differences; approaching sagacity or senility; enlarging the world view; reevaluation and renewal

Growing old is by no means new; every young and adult woman has seen older relatives, friends, and acquaintances affected by the benefits and detriments of age. Yet few are ready to be beset by problems of declining health, voluntary or involuntary retirement, death of a partner, dependency, financial insecurity, lack of mobility, and loneliness.

These physical and mental hardships on women, as well as the societal codes that confine women as they grow old, are presented for our attention in the works that follow. The stories, poems, and play also show the differing ways in which women deal with the problems associated with aging. Some despair, and for them the remaining years are bitter torture; however, there are those for whom aging brings enlightenment and renewed vigor.

Indeed, the women in these stories and poems each grow old differently. Some seem to have died already, while others are enlivening to themselves and others. All, however, are confronted with gradual physical changes that often seem a betrayal of the spirit by the body. Which self—the remembered image in one's prime, or the current face in the mirror—is the "real" one? Is the present bodily shell the essence of a person, or is identity made up of the past as well as the present? These are questions asked by aging women characters from Hilary Stevens in the first story to Jill Jeffers in the play at the end of this section.

Memory and dreams combine to become the woman's "other half," an omnipresent refuge from the current reality. Writers often objectify this ego struggle by creating an "alter ego" or subconscious "double," a fantasized version of the character's self. The desire to discard the present, unwanted self, in place of one's image of past reality, is embodied by some writers in the "doppelganger" theme—a character split in two. This recurrent motif of twin personalities is used as a means of externalizing conflicts which are, in actuality, internal. It is not a coincidence that women characters are paired in several works about old age, such as "Island" and "The Town Poor." In its most extreme form, the woman with a subconscious "double" in real life is the aged person drifting in and out of the present, seeming to be two persons existing in the same body.

Women's internal conflicts between differing views of "self" too often result in the isolation evident in many of these stories. Without a clear notion of self, without acceptance of the changing nature of personality, the characters have little basis for human interaction beyond social convention. Women such as "Miss Brill" and the performer in *Not Waving* can maintain only impersonal connections, even with members of their own families.

Images of imprisonment—self-imposed, or imposed by society—pervade literature about aging women. Seeing one's aging self as "other" further alienates the women characters for whom the circle of personal contacts has already been dwindling. Dreams—not only of the past, but of a fantasy life of freedom and independence—threaten to replace reality.

Yet women's struggles and conflicts are not always portrayed negatively, just as women's aging is often, in reality, an enlightening and fulfilling process, if not a joy. How do women who survive the process manage to prevail, as does Hilary in *Mrs. Stevens Hears the Mermaids Singing?* The stories and poems about aging concur on at least one element in a successful woman's life: the desire for human connectedness which leads the woman out of herself and the beloved dream world to acts of human caring and sharing. The overwhelming image of woman (especially aging woman) going "beyond herself" to care for others is clearly the stereotype of a successful aging female in literature.

Extending herself to at least one other person (usually on a humane rather than a friendly or sexual basis), the aging woman is redeemed; she achieves the salvation of belonging to the world, even if on a superficial level she is no longer a part of society. She is less concerned than other women about acceptance or rejection by society, because in embracing another person she has forged a link to humanity.

The redemptive strength of what seems to be a predominantly female concern for involvement with other people appears many times in these stories. Women who relate to others are saved, and those who deny their humanity are frustrated and lonely. Altruism is personal salvation at the same time as it is society's imposed stereotype of women in literature, especially aging women. While the model of woman as caretaker ties in to sexist assumptions that nurturing is a woman's reason for being, one could argue that all humans should become more humane and caring.

Women's active roles in "human charity" are viewed as especially positive when they are depicted in contrast with group charity or social institutions' collective handouts. The theme of money—having it, giving it, wanting it, or taking it—appears so often in literature about aging women that one begins to wonder if having financial security isn't even more satisfying to a woman than having established interpersonal relationships.

In old age, does money buy happiness, while poverty ensures despair? It is not surprising that money assumes such importance in literature about aging women, since the largest percentage of the poor senior population, at least in the United States, is made up of women. Several of the stories grapple with this issue, dealing with the positive and negative correlations between money and power which affect women in their later life stages. Some works present aging women with money as able to survive because they can keep up the appearances of the past, whereas others show that the meek and the poor do indeed inherit the earth.

If wealth is one form of power in these stories, certainly marriage or being part of a "couple" is status. When a woman has outlived her husband, as many do, she often acquiesces to a lesser social standing than the older married woman; in the same manner, the never-married older woman ("Miss

Brill" or the "Misses Bray") is often denigrated by society, and in earlier literature was more often the recipient than the giver of human charity.

"Giving," whether money or kindness, with hidden selfish motives or altruistic devotion, is seen in these stories as a recurrent concern. The process, not the product, is important for women's selfhood, and is portrayed in several of the stories as a literal and symbolic journey, in which the purpose is the mission itself, not the achievement of the goal. Aging women are often depicted as martyrs; unlike men, women such as Phoenix Jackson in "A Worn Path" are not necessarily wise, but are long-suffering. Better than dreams and other escapes, alleviating another human's suffering mitigates the pain of old age for these women.

The poetry about aging women in this section reinforces many of the above themes and adds some other concerns. Physical frailty is linked with age, and in some poems is attributed to women's biological burden of childbearing. But a paradoxical strength emerges as women such as "Grandmother" and Sappho's narrator face their burdens, and aging is depicted in some poems as a time much superior to ignorant youth.

The isolation of old age is described in these poems and stories as a cyclical casting off which is as much a part of nature as the seasons. Some women are "captives" of the young, others are merely "displaced" by impersonal life changes, but many are lauded for their contributions to the generations of women to follow.

Fiction About Old Age

What is a meaningful life? The women in these stories of aging are concerned with preserving their self-identities and maintaining the personal dignity that gives life meaning. They are unwilling to sacrifice their security for the often well-meaning but uncaring society that seeks, in many cases, to isolate the aged in one way or another.

Health, human interactions, and financial status are the indicators of power or powerlessness in old age. The women seek to be independent at the same time as they retain strong connections with others. Several of the women in these stories fail to achieve the desired balance, but those who do discover the joy of finally being both alone and together with others achieve satisfaction.

In the process of maintaining a whole and healthy attitude toward herself and others, the woman has an old enemy to confront directly—submissive self-sacrifice. Whether the conflict has to do with being sent off to a nursing home against her will or ostracized from all activities except those that serve others, the women in these stories must learn to fight rather than fold.

For this reason, the stories in this section represent the culmination of the issue of women as nurturers: Has the stereotypical caretaking function been women's strength or weakness? How does a woman who has served the needs of others all of her life begin to accept less than secondary status? Where is the joy that existed in giving to others when one now gets so little in return? Aging women ask these questions not only of each other, but of God—questions that are even more evident in the next section on women and death.

May Sarton
1912–

The following selection describes a poet in her seventies whose isolation may be viewed on several levels. Her inner dialogue reveals the conflict between different views of "self," but ultimately shows the desire for personal interaction which makes Hilary ageless rather than aged, and humane beyond the vulnerability of being simply human.

an excerpt from the novel
MRS. STEVENS HEARS THE
MERMAIDS SINGING

Part I: Hilary

Hilary Stevens half opened her eyes, then closed them again. There was some reason to dread this day, although she had taken in that the sun was shining. The soft green silk curtains pulled across the windows created an aqueous light and added to the illusion that she was swimming up into consciousness from deep water: she had had such dreams! Too many people . . . landscapes . . . fading in and out of each other.

"The thing is," she told herself, "that I am badgered by something."

Perhaps if she turned over it would go away.

Instead she was forced awake by the twice-repeated piercing notes of an oriole in the flowering plum just outside her windows. At the same moment the French clock cut through this spontaneous song with its rigid intervals. Six o'clock.

"Old thing, it's high time you pulled yourself together!"

But the other party of the dialogue rebelled, wanted to stay comfortably in bed, wanted to ward off whatever was to be demanded, wanted to be left in peace. Lately Hilary had observed that she seemed to be two distinct entities, at war. There was a hortatory and impatient person who was irritated by her lethargic twin, that one who had to be prodded awake and commanded like a doddering servant and who was getting old, seventy as one counted years.

First things first. The mind must be summoned back, then one might manage to lift oneself out of bed. Hilary closed her eyes and set herself to cope with consciousness. But oh to slip back into that other world, where in her dreams she flew, covered immense distances with ease, and so often came to such beautiful understanding and peace with those ghosts who in reality had represented chiefly anguish. The past had been extraordinarily present all night . . . , she was preparing herself.

"For what?" the doddering servant wished to know.

"The interviewers, you old fool. They are coming this afternoon!"

This realization acted like a pail of water flung in her face, and Hilary found herself cold-awake, standing rather shakily, supporting herself with one hand on the night table. The room around her was in unusual disorder, open cardboard boxes of files standing about and, on the night table, photographs and old letters. Oh dear! She took refuge in the usual actions, those which began every day. She went first to the window and drew back the curtains. There in the distance, seen across granite boulders and an assortment of wild cherry and locust, lay the great quivering expanse of ocean, blue, blue to the slightly paler line at the horizon. There it was, the old sea, the restorer! Hilary drank it down in one swift glance, and then walked over to the bureau and, over the inexorable minute hand of the French clock, looked into her own eyes, shallow and pale in the morning light.

"God, you look awful," she told herself. "Old crone, with hardly a wisp of hair left, and those dewlaps, and those wrinkles." Merciless she was. But there was also the pleasure of recognition. In the mirror she recognized her *self,* her life companion, for better or worse. She looked at this self with compassion this morning, unmercifully prodded and driven as she had been for just under seventy years. The sense of who she was and what she meant about her own personage began to flow back as she ran a comb through the fine childlike hair, hardly gray, and brushed her teeth—her own, and those the dentists had had to provide over the years.

"Damn it!" she said aloud. It meant, in spite of it all, false teeth, falling hair, wrinkles, I am still myself. They haven't got me yet.

They, . . . the enemies. Who were "they" exactly, she asked herself while she put the kettle on, and admired the breakfast tray as she did each morning, resting her eyes on the red cocks painted on the white cup and saucer, the red linen cloth, the Quimper jam jar with a strawberry for a knob, rejoicing in order and beauty, as if she had not herself arranged it all the night before.

There were moments when Hilary saw life as tending always toward chaos, when it seemed that all one could be asked was just to keep the ashtrays clean, the bed made, the wastebaskets emptied, as if one never got to the real things because of the constant exhausting battle to keep ordinary life from falling apart. She gave orders to the doddering servant about all this, but the old thing was getting slow. . . .

Now, for instance, she had almost forgotten Sirenica in the cellar! Released, the white cat wound herself round Hilary's legs and purred ecstatically, lifting first one paw and then another and stretching it out into the air, giving a single high-pitched mew when she heard the frigidaire door slam and saw her plate being lifted down.

"Who are 'they,' Sirenica?" Hilary asked aloud, but there was no time to make an answer, for it was necessary while the eggs boiled to put the two little turtles into warm water to wake them up; they looked up at her with eyes as cold as her own, then swam wildly about waiting for their disgusting breakfast of mealy worms. Hilary had bought them on an impulse in the five-and-ten. Their coldness was restful; and she delighted in their beauty, like animated pieces of jade. Also it had been rather comforting to read in a turtle book that they might live to be forty, that the absurd creatures would outlive her. Still, any life is in constant peril, and before she knew it, she had taken on another anxiety, worried when they did not eat for a day, found herself involved, trying to imagine what they might enjoy, an hour outdoors in the sun, or a little piece of fish for a change. She gazed down into the bowl intently, now, studying the delicate webbed feet and tiny tails, often kept wound in under the shell. She forgot about her toast. It was cold when she finally buttered it and took the tray upstairs.

Heaven, to get back into bed for this best hour of the day!—the hour when the door between sleep and waking, between conscious and unconscious, was still ajar and Hilary could consider the strange things that welled up through the night, could lie there looking out to sea, and feel energy flow back while she drank two or three strong cups of tea. With the first, she found herself observing Sirenica, who had jumped up on the bed (hoping no doubt there might be bacon this morning), and had settled down to wash her face. It was a long, intricate process; it began with the long rose-petal tongue lapping all around her mouth and chin, up and down and around, at least fifty times. When every taste of fish and every drop of oiliness had been savored, a wash-cloth paw lifted, to be licked in its turn, then rubbed back of the ears, round the nose, past the strong whiskers. Hilary watched it all as intently as a cat watches a bird: this was something she had never managed to "get down" in a satisfactory form, but she still had hopes.

With her second cup of tea the unfinished dialogue about "they" was resumed, and she lay back on the pillows ruminating. Of course "they" varied a good deal. At one time in her life, "they" had certainly been the critics. Even the accolade on her last book of poems had left a slightly sour taste. She could not help suspecting that it might be a consolation prize, given rather for endurance than achievement. Her distinguished contemporaries had been dying lately, one by one, so it was all very well to be praised for her vitality and intensity, but . . . , anyway Hilary felt it degrading even to consider the critics. "Old fool, *they* are your own demons," she adjured herself, "the never-conquered demons with whom you carry on the struggle for survival against laziness, depression, guilt, and fatigue." She had hit on the only possible answer to the question. It was completely fruitless to quarrel with the world, whereas the quarrel with oneself was occasionally fruitful, and always, she had to admit, interesting. What sort of questions were those interviewers going to ask? It would be exhilarating to be set what Hilary called "real" questions . . . in fact she had agreed to this visitation because it appeared to be a challenge. Hopefully, she might be forced to confront certain things in her own life and in her work that seemed unresolved, and she was just about to consider these prickly matters when she heard a familiar whistle under the window.

"Drat the boy! What does he want?"

She nearly tipped the whole tray over getting out of bed, and of course Sirenica jumped down at once in a huff. Hilary threw an old Japanese kimono over her shoulders and went to the window, peering down into the strong sunlight. The boy teetered there on the stone wall, head bent, his whole figure betraying unease. She could guess, though she could not see it, that the face under the shock of tow hair, was frowning.

"What is it?" Hilary shouted. "It's the day, you know. You might have let me have my breakfast in peace!"

"What day?"

"The day the interviewers are coming!"

"That's not till four." Now he looked straight up, and she saw something in that face she thought she knew by heart, something she had never seen before.

"Up all night, I suppose." What was it? She asked herself, trying to probe the sullen shadowed eyes looking up at her.

"I've got to see you, Hilary. Just a half hour!"

"Oh all right, come back in an hour or so. Give me time to pull myself together."

He was gone before she closed the window, off and away, while Hilary stood there wondering what sort of night he had spent? Curiously enough she sensed some affinity with her own night of troubled dreams after her long vigil raking up the past—the effect, at least, was the same, for Mar looked exactly as she felt, dissipated, ruffled, a seabird who has been battered by wind, whose wings are stuck with flotsam and jetsam, oil, tar, God knows what.

"Trapped by life," Hilary muttered. She almost fell on one of the cardboard boxes. Oh dear, the morning which had begun rather well, all things considered, was already disintegrating into confusion. Back in bed, she leaned her head against the pillows so she could look at the appeasing ocean and forget all that stuff on the floor . . . , but she could not really rest. She must hurry up if she was to be ready for Mar. Trapped by life. There was, even at seventy, no escape. One did one's work against a steady barrage of demands, of people . . . and the garden too! (It was high time she thought about sowing seeds.) It was all very well to insist that art was art and had no sex, but the fact was that the days of men were not in the same way fragmented, atomized by indefinite small tasks. There was such a thing as woman's work and it consisted chiefly, Hilary sometimes thought, in being able to stand constant interruption and keep your temper. Each single day she fought a war to get to her desk before her little bundle of energy had been dissipated, to push aside or cut through an intricate web of slight threads pulling her in a thousand directions—that unanswered letter, that telephone call, or Mar. It really was not fair of Mar to come this morning with his load of intensity, his deep-set blue eyes, his grief. Oh, she had recognized him all right, the very first day when he turned up to ask if he could moor his boat off her dock!

"In exchange for what?" she had asked, testing him. She was sick and tired of the expectations of the young, that they had rights and all must be done for them, with no return.

Mar had half shut his eyes, ducked his head, and made no answer.

"I need someone to dig up flower beds, spread manure, bring in wood," she said sharply as if it made her cross. "I used to do those things myself, but lately I have found it cuts into my work, don't you know? I get tired. So?"

"I don't like doing any of those things," he had said, "but if you need someone, I guess I'll have to!" He had looked down at her from his spindling height in a rather fatherly way, and Hilary felt herself being tamed.

"Who are you, anyway?"

"Mar. Mar Hemmer." He kicked a pebble with one sneakered foot, no longer fatherly, troubled by her probing gaze. Now she remembered. Why, she knew the boy! "Old Mar Hemmer's grandson, of course!"

Cape Ann used to be full of these tow-headed Finns who came over in the days when the big stone piers berthed sailing ships that carried granite round the world; now the place was a honeycomb of abandoned quarries, many of them deep lakes, taken over by summer people for swimming naked in. The Finns had gone into factories. Yes, it appeared that Mar was living with his grandfather; that was all she learned that day. The facts came later; she had recognized at once her own kind, conflicted, nervous, driven, violent, affectionate. . . . Hilary had read all this in his shy glance and guessed at some trouble. Well, she could use a boy round the place, and she knew herself well enough to accept that anyone she took in would have to be taken into her heart, sooner or later.

[1965]

For Discussion

1. What internal and external conflicts does Hilary Stevens encounter, and how does she deal with them?

2. What effect does the impending approach of "the interviewers" have on Mrs. Stevens?

3. Who are "they . . . the enemies" against Mrs. Stevens? How might the "doppelganger" or "dual self" motif relate to this story?

4. Which elements of old age are positive for Hilary, and which are negative? What tone does the author use to describe Hilary's attitudes?

5. Give examples of how Mrs. Stevens interacts with animals and other natural objects. What importance do these interactions have in her life?

6. What are Mrs. Stevens' feelings about the young man introduced at the end of the excerpt, and what might his name signify?

7. Hilary refers several times to being "trapped by life," and at other times decries "women's work," the "barrage of demands, of people . . . and the garden too!" which limit her. What does she mean, and how are her internal and external conflicts related to these issues of age and sex?

For Further Exploration

1. The title of Sarton's novel is an allusion to a line near the end of T. S. Eliot's poem, "The Love Song of J. Alfred Prufrock": "And I have heard the mermaids singing, each to each. . . . I do not think that they will sing to me." Read Eliot's poem (also mentioned in connection with "The New Dress" in the Women and Society section) and determine the ways in which Mrs. Stevens' situation is the same or different from Prufrock's. For example, do the mermaids sing to Mrs. Stevens? Does Hilary Stevens face the "overwhelming question" Prufrock faces?

2. Read the rest of the novel, *Mrs. Stevens Hears the Mermaids Singing.* What is Sarton's viewpoint about old age as expressed through the character of Hilary Stevens? Or, analyze how Sarton's character fares in comparison with the retired women in Barbara Pym's *Quartet in Autumn.*

Shirley Jackson
1919–1965

In this account of an invalid and her caretaker hired by an attentive son, we see that wealth has little control over the ravages of old age. Mrs. Montague's conflicts result in an exaggerated form of Hilary Stevens' dreaming in the previous story, becoming an escape from the demands of others and from the recognition of her own frailty.

ISLAND

Mrs. Montague's son had been very good to her, with the kind affection and attention to her well-being that is seldom found toward mothers in sons with busy wives and growing families of their own; when Mrs. Montague lost her mind, her son came into his natural role of guardian. There had always been a great deal of warm feeling between Mrs. Montague and her son, and although they lived nearly a thousand miles apart by now, Henry Paul Montague was careful to see that his mother was well taken care of; he ascertained, minutely, that the monthly bills for her apartment, her food, her clothes, and her companion were large enough to ensure that Mrs. Montague was getting the best of everything; he wrote to her weekly, tender letters in longhand inquiring about her health; when he came to New York he visited her promptly, and always left an extra check for the companion, to make sure that any small things Mrs. Montague lacked would be given her. The companion, Miss Oakes, had been with Mrs. Montague for six years, and in that time their invariable quiet routine had been broken only by the regular visits from Mrs. Montague's son, and by Miss Oakes's annual six-weeks' leave, during which Mrs. Montague was cared for no less scrupulously by a carefully chosen substitute.

Between such disturbing occasions, Mrs. Montague lived quietly and expensively in her handsome apartment, following with Miss Oakes a life of placid regularity, which it required all of Miss Oakes's competence to engineer, and duly reported on to Mrs. Montague's son. "I *do* think we're very lucky, dear," was Miss Oakes's frequent comment, "to have a good son like Mr. Montague to take care of us so well."

To which Mrs. Montague's usual answer was, "Henry Paul was a good boy."

Mrs. Montague usually spent the morning in bed, and got up for lunch; after the effort of bathing and dressing and eating she was ready for another rest and then her walk, which occurred regularly at four o'clock, and which was followed by dinner sent up from the restaurant downstairs, and, shortly after, by Mrs. Montague's bedtime. Although Miss Oakes did not leave the apartment except in an emergency, she had a great deal of time to herself and her regular duties were not harsh, although Mrs. Montague was not the best company in the world. Frequently Miss Oakes would look up from her magazine to find Mrs. Montague watching her curiously; sometimes Mrs. Montague, in a spirit of petulant stubbornness, would decline all food under any persuasion until it was necessary for Miss Oakes to call in Mrs. Montague's doctor for Mrs. Montague to hear a firm lecture on her duties as a patient. Once Mrs. Montague had tried to run away, and had been recaptured by Miss Oakes in the street in front of the apartment house, going vaguely through the traffic; and always, constantly, Mrs. Montague was trying to give things to Miss Oakes, many of which, in absolute frankness, it cost Miss Oakes a pang to refuse.

Miss Oakes had not been born to the luxury which Mrs. Montague had known all her life; Miss Oakes had worked hard and never had a fur coat; no matter how much she tried Miss Oakes could not disguise the fact that she relished the food sent up from the restaurant downstairs, delicately cooked and prettily served; Miss Oakes was persuaded that she disdained jewelry, and she chose her clothes hurriedly and inexpensively, under the eye of an impatient, badly dressed salesgirl in a department store. No matter how agonizingly Miss Oakes debated under the insinuating lights of the budget dress department, the clothes she carried home with her turned out to be garish reds and yellows in the daylight, inexactly striped or dotted, badly cut. Miss Oakes sometimes thought longingly of the security of her white uniforms, neatly stacked in her dresser drawer, but Mrs. Montague was apt to go into a tantrum at any outward show of Miss Oakes's professional competence, and Miss Oakes dined nightly on the agreeable food from the restaurant downstairs in her red and yellow dresses, with her colorless hair drawn ungracefully to a bun in back, her ringless hands moving appreciatively among the plates. Mrs. Montague, who ordinarily spilled food all over herself, chose her dresses from a selection sent every three or four months from an exclusive dress shop near by; all information as to size and color was predigested in the shop, and the soft-voiced saleslady brought only dresses absolutely right for Mrs. Montague. Mrs. Montague usually chose two dresses each time, and they went, neatly hung on sacheted hangers, to live softly in Mrs. Montague's closet along with other dresses just like them, all in soft blues and grays and mauves.

"We *must* try to be more careful of our pretty clothes," Miss Oakes would say, looking up from her dinner to find Mrs. Montague, almost deliberately, it seemed sometimes, emptying her spoonful of oatmeal down the front of her dress. "Dear, we really *must* try to be more careful; remember what our nice son has to pay for those dresses."

Mrs. Montague stared vaguely sometimes, holding her spoon; sometimes she said, "I want my pudding now; I'll be careful with my pudding." Now and then, usually when the day had gone badly and Mrs. Montague was overtired, or cross for one reason or another, she might turn the dish of oatmeal over onto the tablecloth, and then, frequently, Miss Oakes was angry, and Mrs. Montague was deprived of her pudding and sat blankly while Miss Oakes moved her own dishes to a coffee table and called the waiter to remove the dinner table with its mess of oatmeal.

It was in the late spring that Mrs. Montague was usually at her worst; then, for some reason, it seemed that the stirring of green life, even under the dirty city traffic, communicated a restlessness and longing to her that she felt only spasmodically the rest of the year; around April or May, Miss Oakes began to prepare for trouble, for runnings-away and supreme oatmeal overturnings. In summer, Mrs. Montague seemed happier, because it was possible to walk in the park and feed the squirrels; in the fall, she quieted, in preparation for the long winter when she was almost dormant, like an animal, rarely speaking, and suffering herself to be dressed and undressed without rebellion; it was the winter that Miss Oakes most appreciated, although as the months moved on into spring Miss Oakes began to think more often of giving up her position, her pleasant salary, the odorous meals from the restaurant downstairs.

It was in the spring that Mrs. Montague so often tried to give things to Miss Oakes; one afternoon when their walk was dubious because of the rain, Mrs. Montague had gone as of habit to the hall closet and taken out her coat, and now sat in her armchair with the rich dark mink heaped in her lap, smoothing the fur as though she held a cat. "Pretty," Mrs. Montague was saying, "pretty, pretty."

"We're very lucky to have such lovely things," Miss Oakes said. Because it was her practice to keep busy always, never to let her knowledgeable fingers rest so long as they might be doing something useful, she was knitting a scarf. It was only half-finished, but already Miss Oakes was beginning to despair of it; the yarn, in the store and in the roll, seemed a soft tender green, but knit up into the scarf it assumed a gaudy chartreuse character that made its original purpose—to embrace the firm fleshy neck of Henry Paul Montague—seem faintly improper; when Miss Oakes looked at the scarf impartially it irritated her, as did almost everything she created.

"Think of the money," Miss Oakes said, "that goes into all those beautiful things, just because your son is so generous and kind."

"I will give you this fur," Mrs. Montague said suddenly. "Because you have no beautiful things of your own."

"Thank you, dear," Miss Oakes said. She worked busily at her scarf for a minute and then said, "It's not being very grateful for nice things like that, dear, to want to give them away."

"It wouldn't look nice on you," Mrs. Montague said, "it would look awful. You're not very pretty."

Miss Oakes was silent again for a minute, and then she said, "Well, dear, shall we see if it's still raining?" With great deliberation she put down the knitting and walked over to the window. When she pulled back the lace curtain and the heavy dark-red drape she did so carefully, because the curtain and the drape were not precisely her own, but were of service to her, and pleasant to her touch, and expensive. "It's almost stopped," she said brightly. She squinted her eyes and looked up at the sky. "I *do* believe it's going to clear up," she went on, as though her brightness might create a sun of reflected brilliance. "In about fifteen minutes . . ." She let her voice trail off, and smiled at Mrs. Montague with vast anticipation.

"I don't want to go for any walk," Mrs. Montague said sullenly. "Once when we were children we used to take off all our clothes and run out in the rain."

Miss Oakes returned to her chair and took up her knitting. "We can start to get ready in a few minutes," she promised.

"I couldn't do that *now*, of course," Mrs. Montague said. "I want to color."

She slid out of her chair, dropping the mink coat into a heap on the floor, and went slowly, with her faltering walk, across the room to the card table where her coloring book and box of crayons lay. Miss Oakes sighed, set her knitting down, and walked over to pick up the mink coat; she draped it tenderly over the back of the chair, and went back and picked up her knitting again.

"Pretty, pretty," Mrs. Montague crooned over her coloring, "Pretty blue, pretty water, pretty, pretty."

Miss Oakes allowed a small smile to touch her face as she regarded the scarf; it was a bright color, perhaps too bright for a man no longer very young, but it was gay and not really *unusually* green. His birthday was three weeks off; the card in the box would say "To remind you of your loyal friend and admirer, Polly Oakes." Miss Oakes sighed quickly.

"I want to go for a *walk*," Mrs. Montague said abruptly.

"Just a minute, dear," Miss Oakes said. She put the knitting down again and smiled at Mrs. Montague. "I'll help you," Miss Oakes said, and went over to assist Mrs. Montague in the slow task that getting out of a straight chair always entailed. "Why, look at you," Miss Oakes said, regarding the coloring book over Mrs. Montague's head. She laughed, "You've gone and made the whole thing blue, you silly child." She turned back a page. "And here," she said, and laughed again. "Why does the man have a blue face? And the little girl in the picture—she mustn't be blue, dear, her face should be pink and her hair should be—oh, yellow, for instance. Not *blue*."

Mrs. Montague put her hands violently over the picture. "Mine," she said. "Get away, this is mine."

"I'm sorry," Miss Oakes said smoothly, "I wasn't laughing at you, dear. It was just funny to see a man with a blue face." She helped Mrs. Montague out of the chair and escorted her across the room to the mink coat. Mrs. Montague stood stiffly while Miss Oakes put the coat over her shoulders and helped her arms into the sleeves, and when Miss Oakes came around in front of her to button the coat at the neck Mrs. Montague turned down the corners of her mouth and said sullenly into Miss Oakes's face, so close to hers, "You don't know what things *are*, really."

"Perhaps I don't," Miss Oakes said absently. She surveyed Mrs. Montague, neatly buttoned into the mink coat, and then took Mrs. Montague's rose-covered hat from the table in the hall and set it on Mrs. Montague's head, with great regard to the correct angle and the neatness of the roses. "Now we look so pretty," Miss Oakes said. Mrs. Montague stood silently while Miss Oakes went to the hall closet and took out her own serviceable blue coat. She shrugged herself into it, settled it with a brisk tug at the collar, and pulled on her hat with a quick gesture from back to front that landed the hatbrim at exactly the usual angle over her eye. It was not until she was escorting Mrs. Montague to the door that Miss Oakes gave one brief, furtive glance at the hall mirror, as one who does so from a nervous compulsion rather than any real desire for information.

Miss Oakes enjoyed walking down the hall; its carpets were so thick that even the stout shoes of Miss Oakes made no sound. The elevator was self-service, and Miss Oakes, with superhuman control, allowed it to sweep soundlessly down to the main floor, carrying with it Miss Oakes herself, and Mrs. Montague, who sat docilely on the velvet-covered bench and stared at the paneling as though she had never seen it before. When the elevator door opened and they moved out into the lobby Miss Oakes knew that the few people who saw them—the girl at the switchboard, the doorman, another tenant coming to the elevator—recognized Mrs. Montague as the rich old lady who lived high upstairs, and Miss Oakes as the infinitely competent companion, without whose unswerving assistance Mrs. Montague could not live for ten minutes. Miss Oakes walked sturdily and well through the lobby, her firm hand guiding soft little Mrs. Montague; the lobby floor was pale carpeting on which their feet made no sound, and the lobby walls were painted an expensive color so neutral as to be almost invisible; as Miss Oakes went with Mrs. Montague through the lobby it was as though they walked upon clouds, through the noncommittal areas of infinite space. The doorway was their aim, and the doorman, dressed in gray, opened the way for them with a flourish and a "Good afternoon" which began by being directed at Mrs. Montague, as the employer, and ended by addressing Miss Oakes, as the person who would be expected to answer.

"Good afternoon, George," Miss Oakes said, with a stately smile, and passed on through the doorway, leading Mrs. Montague. Once outside on the sidewalk, Miss Oakes steered Mrs. Montague quickly to the left, since, allowed her head, Mrs. Montague might as easily have turned unexpectedly to the right, although they always turned to the left, and so upset Miss Oakes's walk for the day. With slow steps they moved into the current of people walking up the street, Miss Oakes watching ahead to avoid Mrs. Montague's walking into strangers, Mrs. Montague with her face turned up to the gray sky.

"It's a *lovely* day," Miss Oakes said. "Pleasantly cool after the rain."

They had gone perhaps half a block when Mrs. Montague, by a gentle pressure against Miss Oakes's arm, began to direct them toward the inside of the sidewalk and the shop windows; Miss Oakes, resisting at first, at last allowed herself to be reluctantly influenced and they crossed the sidewalk to stand in front of the window to a stationery store.

They stopped here every day, and, as she said every day, Mrs. Montague murmured softly, "*Look* at all the lovely things." She watched with amusement a plastic bird, colored bright red and yellow, which methodically dipped its beak into a glass of water and withdrew it; while they stood watching the bird lowered its head and touched the water, hesitated, and then rose.

"Does it stop when we're not here?" Mrs. Montague asked, and Miss Oakes laughed, and said, "It never stops. It goes on while we're eating and while we're sleeping and all the time."

Mrs. Montague's attention had wandered to the open pages of a diary, spread nakedly to the pages dated June 14–June 15. Mrs. Montague, looking at the smooth unwritten paper, caught her breath. "I'd like to have *that*," she said, and Miss Oakes, as she answered every day, said, "What would you write in it, dear?"

The thing that always caught Mrs. Montague next was a softly curved blue bowl which stood in the center of the window display; Mrs. Montague pored lovingly and speechlessly over this daily, trying to touch it through the glass of the window.

"Come *on*, dear," Miss Oakes said finally, with an almost-impatient tug at Mrs. Montague's arm. "We'll never get our walk finished if you don't come *on*."

Docilely Mrs. Montague followed. "Pretty," she whispered, "pretty, pretty."

She opened her eyes suddenly and was aware that she saw. The sky was unbelievably, steadily blue, and the sand beneath her feet was hot; she could see the water, colored more deeply than the sky, but faintly greener. Far off was the line where the sky and water met, and it was infinitely pure.

"Pretty," she said inadequately, and was aware that she spoke. She was walking on the sand, and with a sudden impatient gesture she stopped and slipped off her shoes, standing first on one foot and then on the other. This encouraged her to look down at herself; she was very tall, high above her shoes on the sand, and when she moved it was freely and easily except for the cumbering clothes, the heavy coat and the hat, which sat on her head with a tangible, oppressive weight. She threw the hat onto the hot lovely sand, and it looked so offensive, lying with its patently unreal roses against the smooth clarity of the sand, that she bent quickly and covered the hat with handfuls of sand; the coat was more difficult to cover, and the sand ran delicately between the hairs of the short dark fur; before she had half covered the coat she decided to put the rest of her clothcs with it, and did so, slipping easily out of the straps and buttons and catches of many garments, which she remembered as difficult to put on. When all her clothes were buried she looked with satisfaction down at her strong white legs, and thought, aware that she was thinking it: they are almost the same color as the sand. She began to run freely, with the blue ocean and the bluer sky on her right, the trees on her left, and the moving sand underfoot; she ran until she came back to the place where a corner of her coat still showed through the sand. When she saw it she stopped again and said, "Pretty, pretty," and leaned over and took a handful of sand and let it run through her fingers.

Far away, somewhere in the grove of trees that centered the island she could hear the parrot calling. "Eat, eat," it shrieked, and then something indistinguishable, and then, "Eat, eat."

An idea came indirectly and subtly to her mind; it was the idea of food, for a minute unpleasant and as though it meant a disagreeable sensation, and then glowingly happy. She turned and ran—it was impossible to move slowly on the island, with the clear hot air all around her, and the ocean stirring constantly, pushing at the island, and the unbelievable blue sky above—and when she came into the sudden warm shade of the trees she ran from one to another, putting her hand for a minute on each.

"Hello," the parrot gabbled, "Hello, who's there, eat?" She could see it flashing among the trees, no more than a saw-toothed voice and a flash of ugly red and yellow.

The grass was green and rich and soft, and she sat down by the little brook where the food was set out. Today there was a great polished wooden bowl, soft to the touch, full of purple grapes; the sun that came unevenly between the trees struck a high shine from the bowl, and lay flatly against the grapes, which were dusty with warmth, and almost black. There was a shimmering glass just full of dark red wine; there was a flat blue plate filled with little cakes; she touched one and it was full of cream, and heavily iced with soft chocolate. There were pomegranates, and cheese, and small, sharp-flavored candies. She lay down beside the food, and closed her eyes against the heavy scent from the grapes.

"Eat, eat," the parrot screamed from somewhere over her head. She opened her eyes lazily and looked up, to see the flash of red and yellow in the trees. "Be still, you noisy beast," she said, and smiled to herself because it was not important, actually, whether the parrot were quiet or not. Later, after she had slept, she ate some of the grapes and the cheese, and several of the rich little cakes. While she ate the parrot came cautiously closer, begging for food, sidling up near to the dish of cakes and then moving quickly away.

"Beast," she said pleasantly to the parrot, "greedy beast."

When she was sure she was quite through with the food, she put one of the cakes on a green leaf and set it a little bit away from her for the parrot. It came up to the cake slowly and fearfully, watching on either side for some sudden prohibitive movement; when it finally reached the cake it hesitated, and then dipped its head down to bury its beak in the soft frosting; it lifted its head, paused to look around, and then lowered its beak to the cake again. The gesture was familiar, and she laughed, not knowing why.

She was faintly aware that she had slept again, and awakened wanting to run, to go out into the hot sand on the beach and run shouting around the island. The parrot was gone, its cake a mess of crumbs and frosting on the ground. She ran out onto the beach, and the water was there, and the sky. For a few minutes she ran, going down to the water and then swiftly back before it could touch her bare feet, and then she dropped luxuriously onto the sand and lay there. After a while she began to draw a picture in the sand; it was a round face with dots for eyes and nose and a line for a mouth. "Henry Paul," she said, touching the face caressingly with her fingers and then, laughing, she leaped to her feet and began to run again, around the island. When she passed the face drawn on the sand she put one bare foot on it and ground it away. "Eat, eat," she could hear the parrot calling from the trees; the parrot was afraid of the hot sand and the water and stayed always in the trees near the food. Far off, across the water, she could see the sweet, the always comforting, line of the horizon.

When she was tired with running she lay down again on the sand. For a little while she played idly, writing words on the sand and then rubbing them out with her hand; once she drew a crude picture of a doorway and punched her fist through it.

Finally she lay down and put her face down to the sand. It was hot, hotter than anything else had ever been, and the soft grits of the sand slipped into her mouth, where she could taste them, deliciously hard and grainy against her teeth; they were in her eyes, rich and warm; the sand was covering her face and the blue sky was gone from above her and the sand was cooler, then grayer, covering her face, and cold.

"*Nearly* home," Miss Oakes said brightly, as they turned the last corner of their block. "It's been a *nice* walk, hasn't it?"

She tried, unsuccessfully, to guide Mrs. Montague quickly past the bakery, but Mrs. Montague's feet, moving against Miss Oakes's pressure from habit, brought them up to stand in front of the bakery window.

"I don't know *why* they leave those fly-specked éclairs out here," Miss Oakes said irritably. "There's nothing *less* appetizing. *Look* at that cake; the cream is positively *curdled.*"

She moved her arm insinuatingly within Mrs. Montague's. "In a few minutes we'll be home," she said softly, "and then we can have our nice cocktail, and rest for a few minutes, and then dinner."

"Pretty," Mrs. Montague said at the cakes. "I want some."

Miss Oakes shuddered violently. "Don't even *say* it," she implored. "Just *look* at that stuff. You'd be sick for a week."

She moved Mrs. Montague along, and they came, moving quicker than they had when they started, back to their own doorway where the doorman in gray waited for them. He opened the door and said, beginning with Mrs. Montague and finishing with Miss Oakes, "Have a nice walk?"

"Very pleasant, thank you," Miss Oakes said agreeably. They passed through the doorway and into the lobby where the open doors of the elevator waited for them. "Dinner soon," Miss Oakes said as they went across the lobby.

Miss Oakes was careful, on their own floor, to see that Mrs. Montague found the right doorway; while Miss Oakes put the key in the door Mrs. Montague stood waiting without expression.

Mrs. Montague moved forward automatically when the door was opened, and Miss Oakes caught her arm, saying shrilly, "Don't *step* on it!" Mrs. Montague stopped, and waited, while Miss Oakes picked up the dinner menu from the floor just inside the door; it had been slipped under the door while they were out.

Once inside, Miss Oakes removed Mrs. Montague's rosy hat and the mink coat, and Mrs. Montague took the mink coat in her arms and sat down in her chair with it, smoothing the fur. Miss Oakes slid out of her own coat and hung it neatly in the closet, and then came into the living room, carrying the dinner menu.

"Chicken liver omelette," Miss Oakes read as she walked. "The last time it was a trifle underdone; I could *mention* it, of course, but they never seem to pay much attention. Roast turkey. Filet mignon. I *really* do think a nice little piece of . . . " she looked up at Mrs. Montague and smiled. "Hungry?" she suggested.

"No," Mrs. Montague said, "I've had enough."

"Nice oatmeal?" Miss Oakes said. "If you're *very* good you can have ice cream tonight."

"Don't want ice cream," Mrs. Montague said.

Miss Oakes sighed, and then said "Well . . . " placatingly. She returned to the menu. "French-fried potatoes," she said. "They're *very* heavy on the stomach, but I do have my heart set on a nice little piece of steak and some french-fried potatoes. It sounds just *right*, tonight."

"Shall I give you this coat?" Mrs. Montague asked suddenly.

Miss Oakes stopped on her way to the phone and patted Mrs. Montague lightly on the shoulder. "You're very generous, dear," she said, "but of course you don't really want to give me your beautiful coat. What would your dear son say?"

Mrs. Montague ran her hand over the fur of the coat affectionately. Then she stood up, slowly, and the coat slid to the floor. "I'm going to color," she announced.

Miss Oakes turned back from the phone to pick up the coat and put it over the back of the chair. "All right," she said. She went to the phone, sat so she could keep an eye on Mrs. Montague while she talked, and said into the phone "Room service."

Mrs. Montague moved across the room and sat down at the card table. Reflectively she turned the pages of the coloring book, found a picture that pleased her, and opened the crayon box. Miss Oakes hummed softly into the phone. "Room service?" she said finally. "I want to order dinner sent up to Mrs. Montague's suite, please." She looked over the phone at Mrs. Montague and said, "You all right, dear?"

Without turning, Mrs. Montague moved her shoulders impatiently, and selected a crayon from the box. She examined the point of it with great care while Miss Oakes said, "I want one very sweet martini, please. And Mrs. Montague's prune juice." She picked up the menu and wet her lips, then said, "One crab-meat cocktail. And tonight will you see that Mrs. Montague has milk with her oatmeal; you sent cream last night. Yes, milk, please. You'd think they'd know by *now*," she added to Mrs. Montague over the top of the phone. "Now let me see," she said, into the phone again, her eyes on the menu.

Disregarding Miss Oakes, Mrs. Montague had begun to color. Her shoulders bent low over the book, a vague smile on her old face, she was devoting herself to a picture of a farmyard; a hen and three chickens strutted across the foreground of the picture, a barn surrounded by trees was the background. Mrs. Montague had laboriously colored the hen and the three chickens, the barn and the trees a rich blue, and now, with alternate touches of the crayons, was engaged in putting a red and yellow blot far up in the blue trees.

[1950]

For Discussion

1. What constitutes Mrs. Montague's "identity"? What do we know about her, and what does she know about herself?

2. What effects do the physical details of the story's setting have on the themes? Discuss, for example, the apartment, clothes, and food in the story.

3. Why isn't Mrs. Montague's first name mentioned? Why isn't her husband mentioned, and why does she seem so indifferent to her son Henry? Discuss the role of males in the story.

4. What kind of interaction is there between Mrs. Montague and Miss Oakes? Which one "gives," and which one "takes"? What do they have in common, and what is different, in terms of their names, social station, marital status, tastes, abilities, and dreams?

5. Examine the details of the "real" experience of Mrs. Montague leaving her apartment, and compare them with the details of the "dream" experience on the island. What dualities are suggested by the experiences?

6. Compare Mrs. Montague's dinner with Miss Oakes' meal at the end of the story. Is Miss Oakes the villain of the story? Is there any other way of viewing her situation?

7. What implications are there about the theme of power and powerlessness in the story, and how is power related to the themes of age, sex, marriage, and money?

8. What is suggested about the images and symbols in the story (such as the parrot), and what is significant about the color imagery throughout?

9. What multiple meanings might the title of the story suggest?

For Further Exploration

1. Read Shirley Jackson's famous story "The Lottery," in which a town tradition becomes an individual's nightmare. What elements are similar in these two stories by Jackson, and what concerns do they reveal? What do the stories have to say about social conventions and about human desires? Who are the victims, and who are the victimizers, and why, according to Jackson?

2. Explore the idea of character pairs in this story and others. When an author creates two parallel characters, what points are being made? Can the two women in this story be considered two mutually dependent halves, or are they meant to be the protagonist and antagonist of the story? Compare or contrast with the "doppleganger" motif mentioned in connection with the preceding story by May Sarton.

Sarah Orne Jewett

1849–1909

"The Town Poor" includes many dominant motifs in fiction about aging women: the conflict between despair and hope, the distinctions between men's and women's roles, the importance of money as power and status, the desire for escape into the past, and the redemptive strength of genuine human involvement.

THE TOWN POOR

Mrs. William Trimble and Miss Rebecca Wright were driving along Hampden east road, one afternoon in early spring. Their progress was slow. Mrs. Trimble's sorrel horse was old and stiff, and the wheels were clogged by clay mud. The frost was not yet out of the ground, although the snow was nearly gone, except in a few places on the north side of the woods, or where it had drifted all winter against a length of fence.

"There must be a good deal o' snow to the nor'ard of us yet," said weather-wise Mrs. Trimble. "I feel it in the air; 't is more than the ground-damp. We ain't goin' to have real nice weather till the up-country snow's all gone."

"I heard say yesterday that there was good sleddin' yet, all up through Parsley," responded Miss Wright. "I shouldn't like to live in them northern places. My cousin Ellen's husband was a Parsley man, an' he was obliged, as you may have heard, to go up north to his father's second wife's funeral; got back day before yesterday. 'T was about twenty-one miles, an' they started on wheels; but when they'd gone nine or ten miles, they found 't was no sort o' use, an' left their wagon an' took a sleigh. The man that owned it charged 'em four an' six, too. I shouldn't have thought he would; they told him they was goin' to a funeral; an' they had their own buffaloes[1] an' everything."

"Well, I expect it's a good deal harder scratchin', up that way; they have to git money where they can; the farms is very poor as you go north," suggested Mrs. Trimble kindly. " 'T ain't none too rich a country where we be, but I've always been grateful I wa'n't born up to Parsley."

The old horse plodded along, and the sun, coming out from the heavy spring clouds, sent a sudden shine of light along the muddy road. Sister Wright drew her large veil forward over the high brim of her bonnet. She was not used to driving, or to being much in the open air; but Mrs. Trimble was an active business woman, and looked after her own affairs herself, in all weathers. The late Mr. Trimble had left her a good farm, but not much ready money, and it was often said that she was better off in the end than if he had lived. She regretted his loss deeply, however; it was impossible for her to speak of him, even to intimate friends, without emotion, and nobody had ever hinted that this emotion was insincere. She was most warm-hearted and generous, and in her limited way played the part of Lady Bountiful in the town of Hampden.

[1]Blankets of buffalo skin.

"Why, there's where the Bray girls lives, ain't it?" she exclaimed, as, beyond a thicket of witch-hazel and scruboak, they came in sight of a weather-beaten, solitary farm-house. The barn was too far away for thrift or comfort, and they could see long lines of light between the shrunken boards as they came nearer. The fields looked both stony and sodden. Somehow, even Parsley itself could be hardly more forlorn.

"Yes'm," said Miss Wright, "that's where they live now, poor things. I know the place, though I ain't been up here for years. You don't suppose, Mis' Trimble—I ain't seen the girls out to meetin' all winter. I've re'lly been covetin' "—

"Why, yes, Rebecca, of course we could stop," answered Mrs. Trimble heartily. "The exercises was over earlier 'n I expected, an' you're goin' to remain over night long o' me, you know. There won't be no tea till we git there, so we can't be late. I'm in the habit o' sendin' a basket to the Bray girls when any o' our folks is comin' this way, but I ain't been to see 'em since they moved up here. Why, it must be a good deal over a year ago. I know 't was in the late winter they had to make the move. 'T was cruel hard, I must say, an' if I hadn't been down with my pleurisy fever I'd have stirred round an' done somethin' about it. There was a good deal o' sickness at the time, an'—well, 't was kind o' rushed through, breakin' of 'em up, an' lots o' folks blamed the selec'*men;* but when 't was done, 't was done, an' nobody took holt to undo it. Ann an' Mandy looked same 's ever when they come to meetin', 'long in the summer,—kind o' wishful, perhaps. They've always sent me word they was gittin' on pretty comfortable."

"That would be their way," said Rebecca Wright. "They never was any hand to complain, though Mandy's less cheerful than Ann. If Mandy'd been spared such poor eyesight, an' Ann hadn't got her lame wrist that wa'n't set right, they'd kep' off the town fast enough. They both shed tears when they talked to me about havin' to break up, when I went to see 'em before I went over to brother Asa's. You see we was brought up neighbors, an' we went to school together, the Brays an' me. 'T was a special Providence brought us home this road, I've been so covetin' a chance to git to see 'em. My lameness hampers me."

"I'm glad we come this way, myself," said Mrs. Trimble.

"I'd like to see just how they fare," Miss Rebecca Wright continued. "They give their consent to goin' on the town because they knew they'd got to be dependent, an' so they felt 't would come easier for all than for a few to help 'em. They acted real dignified an' right-minded, contrary to what most do in such cases, but they was dreadful anxious to see who would bid 'em off, town-meeting day; they did so hope 't would be somebody right in the village. I just sat down an' cried good when I found Abel Janes's folks had got hold of 'em. They always had the name of bein' slack an' poor-spirited, an' they did it just for what they got out o' the town. The selectmen this last year ain't what we have had. I hope they've been considerate about the Bray girls."

"I should have be'n more considerate about fetchin' of you over," apologized Mrs. Trimble. "I've got my horse, an' you're lame-footed; 't is too far for you to come. But time does slip away with busy folks, an' I forgot a good deal I ought to remember."

"There's nobody more considerate than you be," protested Miss Rebecca Wright.

Mrs. Trimble made no answer, but took out her whip and gently touched the sorrel horse, who walked considerably faster, but did not think it worth while to trot. It was a long, round-about way to the house, farther down the road and up a lane.

"I never had any opinion of the Bray girls' father, leavin' 'em as he did," said Mrs. Trimble.

"He was much praised in his time, though there was always some said his early life hadn't been up to the mark," explained her companion. "He was a great favorite of our then preacher, the Reverend Daniel Longbrother. They did a good deal for the parish, but they did it their own way. Deacon Bray was one that did his part in the repairs without urging. You know 't was in his time the first repairs was made, when they got out the old soundin'-board an' them handsome square pews. It cost an awful sight o' money, too. They hadn't done payin' up that debt when they set to alter it again an' git the walls frescoed. My grandmother was one that always spoke her mind right out, an' she was dreadful opposed to breakin' up the square pews where she'd always set. They was countin' up what 't would cost in parish meetin', an' she riz right up an' said 't wouldn't cost nothin' to let 'em stay, an' there wa'n't a house carpenter left in the parish that could do such nice work, an' time would come when the great-grandchildren would give their eye-teeth to have the old meetin'-house look just as it did then. But haul the inside to pieces they would and did."

"There come to be a real fight over it, didn't there?" agreed Mrs. Trimble soothingly. "Well, 't wa'n't good taste. I remember the old house well. I come here as a child to visit a cousin o' mother's, an' Mr. Trimble's folks was neighbors, an' we was drawed to each other then, young 's we was. Mr. Trimble spoke of it many's the time,—that first time he ever see me, in a leghorn hat with a feather; 't was one that mother had, an' pressed over."

"When I think of them old sermons that used to be preached in that old meetin'-house of all, I'm glad it's altered over, so's not to remind folks," said Miss Rebecca Wright, after a suitable pause. "Them old brimstone discourses, you know, Mis' Trimble. Preachers is far more reasonable, nowadays. Why, I set an' thought, last Sabbath, as I listened, that if old Mr. Longbrother an' Deacon Bray could hear the difference they'd crack the ground over 'em like pole beans, an' come right up 'long side their headstones."

Mrs. Trimble laughed heartily, and shook the reins three or four times by way of emphasis. "There's no gitting round you," she said, much pleased. "I should think Deacon Bray would want to rise, any way, if 't was so he could, an' knew how his poor girls was farin'. A man ought to provide for his folks he's got to leave behind him, specially if they're women. To be sure, they had their little home; but we've seen how, with all their industrious ways, they hadn't means to keep it. I s'pose he thought he'd got time enough to lay by, when he give so generous in collections; but he didn't lay by, an' there they be. He might have took lessons from the squirrels: even them little wild creatur's makes them their winter hoards, an' menfolks ought to know enough if squirrels does. 'Be just before you are generous:' that's what was always set for the B's in the copy-books, when I was to school, and it often runs through my mind."

"'As for man, his days are as grass,' that was for A; the two go well together," added Miss Rebecca Wright soberly. "My good gracious, ain't this a starved lookin' place? It makes me ache to think them nice Bray girls has to brook it here."

The sorrel horse, though somewhat puzzled by an unexpected deviation from his homeward way, willingly came to a stand by the gnawed corner of the door-yard fence, which evidently served as hitching-place. Two or three ragged old hens were picking about the yard, and at last a face appeared at the kitchen window, tied up in a handkerchief, as if it were a case of toothache. By the time our friends reached the side door next this window, Mrs. Janes came disconsolately to open it for them, shutting it again as soon as possible, though the air felt more chilly inside the house.

"Take seats," said Mrs. Janes briefly. "You'll have to see me just as I be. I have been suffering these four days with the ague, and everything to do. Mr. Janes is to court, on the jury. 'T was inconvenient to spare him. I should be pleased to have you lay off your things."

Comfortable Mrs. Trimble looked about the cheerless kitchen, and could not think of anything to say; so she smiled blandly and shook her head in answer to the invitation. "We'll just set a few minutes with you, to pass the time o' day, an' then we must go in an' have a word with the Miss Brays, bein' old acquaintance. It ain't been so we could git to call on 'em before. I don't know 's you're acquainted with Miss R'becca Wright. She's been out of town a good deal."

"I heard she was stopping over to Plainfields with her brother's folks," replied Mrs. Janes, rocking herself with irregular motion, as she sat close to the stove. "Got back some time in the fall, I believe?"

"Yes'm," said Miss Rebecca, with an undue sense of guilt and conviction. "We've been to the installation over to the East Parish, an' thought we'd stop in; we took this road home to see if 't was any better. How is the Miss Brays gettin' on?"

"They're well's common," answered Mrs. Janes grudgingly. "I was put out with Mr. Janes for fetchin' of 'em here, with all I've got to do, an' I own I was kind o' surly to 'em 'long to the first of it. He gits the money from the town, an' it helps him out; but he bid 'em off for five dollars a month, an' we can't do much for 'em at no such price as that. I went an' dealt with the selec-'men, an' made 'em promise to find their firewood an' some other things extra. They was glad to get rid o' the matter the fourth time I went, an' would ha' promised 'most anything. But Mr. Janes don't keep me half the time in oven-wood, he's off so much, an' we was cramped o' room, any way. I have to store things up garrit[2] a good deal, an' that keeps me trampin' right through their room. I do the best for 'em I can, Mis' Trimble, but 't ain't so easy for me as 't is for you, with all your means to do with."

The poor woman looked pinched and miserable herself, though it was evident that she had no gift at house or home keeping. Mrs. Trimble's heart was wrung with pain, as she thought of the unwelcome inmates of such a place; but she held her peace bravely, while Miss Rebecca again gave some brief information in regard to the installation.

"You go right up them back stairs," the hostess directed at last. "I'm glad some o' you church folks has seen fit to come an' visit 'em. There ain't been nobody here this long spell, an' they've aged a sight since they come. They always send down a taste out of your baskets, Mis' Trimble, an' I relish it, I tell you. I'll shut the door after you, if you don't object. I feel every draught o' cold air."

"I've always heard she was a great hand to make a poor mouth. Wa'n't she from somewheres up Parsley way?" whispered Miss Rebecca, as they stumbled in the half-light.

[2]Attic.

"Poor meechin' body,[3] wherever she come from," replied Mrs. Trimble, as she knocked at the door.

There was silence for a moment after this unusual sound; then one of the Bray sisters opened the door. The eager guests stared into a small, low room, brown with age, and gray, too, as if former dust and cobwebs could not be made wholly to disappear. The two elderly women who stood there looked like captives. Their withered faces wore a look of apprehension, and the room itself was more bare and plain than was fitting to their evident refinement of character and self-respect. There was an uncovered small table in the middle of the floor, with some crackers on a plate; and, for some reason or other, this added a great deal to the general desolation.

But Miss Ann Bray, the elder sister, who carried her right arm in a sling, with piteously drooping fingers, gazed at the visitors with radiant joy. She had not seen them arrive.

The one window gave only the view at the back of the house, across the fields, and their coming was indeed a surprise. The next minute she was laughing and crying together. "Oh, sister!" she said, "if here ain't our dear Mis' Trimble!—an' my heart o' goodness, 't is 'Becca Wright, too! What dear good creatur's you be! I've felt all day as if something good was goin' to happen, an' was just sayin' to myself 't was most sundown now, but I wouldn't let on to Mandany I'd give up hope quite yet. You see, the scissors stuck in the floor this very mornin' an' it's always a reliable sign. There, I've got to kiss ye both again!"

"I don't know where we can all set," lamented sister Mandana. "There ain't but the one chair an' the bed; t' other chair's too rickety; an' we've been promised another these ten days; but first they've forgot it, an' next Mis' Janes can't spare it,—one excuse an' another. I am goin' to git a stump o' wood an' nail a board on to it, when I can git outdoor again," said Mandana, in a plaintive voice. "There, I ain't goin' to complain o' nothin', now you've come," she added; and the guests sat down, Mrs. Trimble, as was proper, in the one chair.

"We've sat on the bed many's the time with you, 'Becca, an' talked over our girl nonsense, ain't we? You know where 't was—in the little back bedroom we had when we was girls, an' used to peek out at our beaux through the strings o' mornin'-glories," laughed Ann Bray delightedly, her thin face shining more and more with joy. "I brought some o' them mornin'-glory seeds along when we come away, we'd raised 'em so many years; an' we got 'em started all right, but the hens found 'em out. I declare I chased them poor hens, foolish as 't was; but the mornin'-glories I'd counted on a sight to remind me o' home. You see, our debts was so large, after my long sickness an' all, that we didn't feel 't was right to keep back anything we could help from the auction."

It was impossible for any one to speak for a moment or two; the sisters felt their own uprooted condition afresh, and their guests for the first time really comprehended the piteous contrast between that neat little village house, which now seemed a palace of comfort, and this cold, unpainted upper room in the remote Janes farmhouse. It was an unwelcome thought to Mrs. Trimble that the well-to-do town of Hampden could provide no better for its poor than this, and her round face flushed with resentment and the shame of personal responsibility. "The girls shall be well settled in the village before

[3]Skulking person.

another winter, if I pay their board myself," she made an inward resolution, and took another almost tearful look at the broken stove, the miserable bed, and the sisters' one hair-covered trunk, on which Mandana was sitting. But the poor place was filled with a golden spirit of hospitality.

Rebecca was again discoursing eloquently of the installation; it was so much easier to speak of general subjects, and the sisters had evidently been longing to hear some news. Since the late summer they had not been to church, and presently Mrs. Trimble asked the reason.

"Now, don't you go to pouring out our woes, Mandy!" begged little old Ann, looking shy and almost girlish, and as if she insisted upon playing that life was still all before them and all pleasure. "Don't you go to spoilin' their visit with our complaints! They know well's we do that changes must come, an' we'd been so wonted to our home things that this come hard at first; but then they felt for us, I know just as well's can be. 'T will soon be summer again, an' 't is real pleasant right out in the fields here, when there ain't too hot a spell. I've got to know a sight o' singin' birds since we come."

"Give me the folks I've always known," sighed the younger sister, who looked older than Miss Ann, and less even-tempered. "You may have your birds, if you want 'em. I do re'lly long to go to meetin' an' see folks go by up the aisle. Now, I will speak of it, Ann, whatever you say. We need, each of us, a pair o' good stout shoes an' rubbers,—ours are all wore out; an' we've asked an' asked, an' they never think to bring 'em, an' "—

Poor old Mandana, on the trunk, covered her face with her arms and sobbed aloud. The elder sister stood over her, and patted her on the thin shoulder like a child, and tried to comfort her. It crossed Mrs. Trimble's mind that it was not the first time one had wept and the other had comforted. The sad scene must have been repeated many times in that long, drear winter. She would see them forever after in her mind as fixed as a picture, and her own tears fell fast.

"You didn't see Mis' Janes's cunning little boy, the next one to the baby, did you?" asked Ann Bray, turning round quickly at last, and going cheerfully on with the conversation. "Now, hush, Mandy, dear; they'll think you're childish! He's a dear, friendly little creatur', an' likes to stay with us a good deal, though we feel 's if it was too cold for him, now we are waitin' to get us more wood."

"When I think of the acres o' woodland in this town!" groaned Rebecca Wright. "I believe I'm goin' to preach next Sunday, 'stead o' the minister, an' I'll make the sparks fly. I've always heard the saying, 'What's everybody's business is nobody's business,' an' I've come to believe it."

"Now, don't you, 'Becca. You've happened on a kind of a poor time with us, but we've got more belongings than you see here, an' a good large cluset, where we can store those things there ain't room to have about. You an' Mis' Trimble have happened on a kind of poor day, you know. Soon's I git me some stout shoes an' rubbers, as Mandy says, I can fetch home plenty o' little dry boughs o' pine; you remember I was always a great hand to roam in the woods? If we could only have a front room, so 't we could look out on the road an' see passin', an' was shod for meetin', I don' know's we should complain. Now we're just goin' to give you what we've got, an' make out with a good welcome. We make more tea 'n we want in the mornin', an' then let the fire go down, since 't has been so mild. We've got a *good* cluset" (disappearing as she spoke), "an' I know this to be good tea, 'cause it's some o' yourn, Mis' Trimble. An' here's our sprigged chiny cups that R'becca knows by sight, if Mis' Trimble don't. We kep' out four of 'em, an' put the even half dozen with the rest of the auction stuff. I've often wondered who'd got 'em, but I never asked, for fear 't would be somebody that would distress us. They was mother's, you know."

The four cups were poured, and the little table pushed to the bed, where Rebecca Wright still sat, and Mandana, wiping her eyes, came and joined her. Mrs. Trimble sat in her chair at the end, and Ann trotted about the room in pleased content for a while, and in and out of the closet, as if she still had much to do; then she came and stood opposite Mrs. Trimble. She was very short and small, and there was no painful sense of her being obliged to stand. The four cups were not quite full of cold tea, but there was a clean old table-cloth folded double, and a plate with three pairs of crackers neatly piled, and a small—it must be owned, a very small—piece of hard white cheese. Then, for a treat, in a glass dish, there was a little preserved peach, the last—Miss Rebecca knew it instinctively—of the household stores brought from their old home. It was very sugary, this bit of peach; and as she helped her guests and sister Mandy, Miss Ann Bray said, half unconsciously, as she often had said with less reason in the old days, "Our preserves ain't so good as usual this year; this is beginning to candy." Both the guests protested, while Rebecca added that the taste of it carried her back, and made her feel young again. The Brays had always managed to keep one or two peach-trees alive in their corner of a garden. "I've been keeping this preserve for a treat," said her friend. "I'm glad to have you eat some, 'Becca. Last summer I often wished you was home an' could come an' see us, 'stead o' being away off to Plainfields."

The crackers did not taste too dry. Miss Ann took the last of the peach on her own cracker; there could not have been quite a small spoonful, after the others were helped, but she asked them first if they would not have some more. Then there was a silence, and in the silence a wave of tender feeling rose high in the hearts of the four elderly women. At this moment the setting sun flooded the poor plain room with light; the unpainted wood was all of a golden-brown, and Ann Bray, with her gray hair and aged face, stood at the head of the table in a kind of aureole. Mrs. Trimble's face was all aquiver as she looked at her; she thought of the text about two or three being gathered together,[4] and was half afraid.

"I believe we ought to 've asked Mis' Janes if she wouldn't come up," said Ann. "She's real good feelin', but she's had it very hard, an gits discouraged. I can't find that she's ever had anything real pleasant to look back to, as we have. There, next time we'll make a good heartenin' time for her too."

The sorrel horse had taken a long nap by the gnawed fence-rail, and the cool air after sundown made him impatient to be gone. The two friends jolted homeward in the gathering darkness, through the stiffening mud, and neither Mrs. Trimble nor Rebecca Wright said a word until they were out of sight as well as out of sound of the Janes house. Time must elapse before they could reach a more familiar part of the road and resume conversation on its natural level.

"I consider myself to blame," insisted Mrs. Trimble at last. "I haven't no words of accusation for nobody else, an' I ain't one to take comfort in calling names to the board o' selec'men. I make no reproaches, an' I take it all on my own shoulders; but I'm goin' to stir about me, I tell you! I shall begin early to-morrow. They're goin' back to their own house,—it's been standin' empty

---

[4]"For where two or three have gathered together in my name, I am there among them." (Jesus in *The Bible*)

all winter,—an' the town's goin' to give 'em the rent an' what firewood they need; it won't come to more than the board's payin' out now. An' you an' me'll take this same horse an' wagon, an' ride an' go afoot by turns, an' git means enough together to buy back their furniture an' whatever was sold at that plaguey auction; an' then we'll put it all back, an' tell 'em they've got to move to a new place, an' just carry 'em right back again where they come from. An' don't you never tell, R'becca, but here I be a widow woman, layin' up what I make from my farm for nobody knows who, an' I'm goin' to do for them Bray girls all I'm a mind to. I should be sca't to wake up in heaven, an' hear anybody there ask how the Bray girls was. Don't talk to me about the town o' Hampden, an' don't ever let me hear the name o' town poor! I'm ashamed to go home an' see what's set out for supper. I wish I'd brought 'em right along."

"I was goin' to ask if we couldn't git the new doctor to go up an' do somethin' for poor Ann's arm," said Miss Rebecca. "They say he's very smart. If she could get so's to braid straw or hook rugs again, she'd soon be earnin' a little somethin'. An' may be he could do somethin' for Mandy's eyes. They did use to live so neat an' ladylike. Somehow I couldn't speak to tell 'em there that 't was I bought them six best cups an' saucers, time of the auction; they went very low, as everything else did, an' I thought I could save it some other way. They shall have 'em back an' welcome. You're real whole-hearted, Mis' Trimble. I expect Ann'll be sayin' that her father's child'n wa'n't goin' to be left desolate, an' that all the bread he cast on the water's comin' back through you."

"I don't care what she says, dear creatur'!" exclaimed Mrs. Trimble. "I'm full o' regrets I took time for that installation, an' set there seepin' in a lot o' talk this whole day long, except for its kind of bringin' us to the Bray girls. I wish to my heart 't was to-morrow mornin' a'ready, an' I a-startin' for the selec'*men*."

[1890]

For Discussion

1. Compare the different types of "charity" in the story, as expressed or implied by the Selectmen, Deacon Bray, Mrs. Trimble, Miss Wright, and the
   Misses Bray. Are there any differences between male and female views of
   charity presented in the story?

2. Why are the female characters depicted in pairs? Are there any similarities or differences of note between Mrs. Trimble and Miss Wright, or Ann
   and Mandy Bray?

3. Explore the idea of the individual versus the group, as suggested by the
   story's title, the omnipresent image of the "town," and then the banding
   together of the four women. Which side is Jewett on—individual or
   group?

4. What might be meant by Biblical references such as "where two or three
   are gathered together" and the Misses Bray extending love to their "cap-
   tors," and the golden "aureole" over Ann Bray's head?

5. How does the concept of charity relate to the idea of salvation in Jewett's
   story?

6. What ideas does Jewett present about poverty and old age? Do the meek inherit the earth in this story?

7. What is ironic about power and powerlessness as the fate of the Misses Bray changes from the beginning of the story to the end?

For Further Exploration

1. Find the famous "charity/love" and "communion" messages from the New Testament of the Bible. What is Jewett's depiction of "true Christian charity" and how does it compare to Biblical references?

2. Read Virginia Woolf's *A Room of One's Own*, in which she discusses the importance of women's financial and personal independence as embodied in being able to have a personal place in which to live and create. Compare Woolf's tenets in the essay with Jewett's themes in "The Town Poor." How important for each author is money for a "room of one's own"?

Katherine Mansfield

1888–1923

The microcosm created by Katherine Mansfield contains old and young in a number of combinations of happy and sad, wealthy and poor. Miss Brill herself experiences the exhilaration of belonging to the world, and the agony of being ostracized from it, as Mansfield explores what it means to "grow up" when one is already old.

MISS BRILL

Although it was so brilliantly fine—the blue sky powdered with gold and great spots of light like white wine splashed over the Jardins Publiques—Miss Brill was glad that she had decided on her fur. The air was motionless, but when you opened your mouth there was just a faint chill, like a chill from a glass of iced water before you sip, and now and again a leaf came drifting—from nowhere, from the sky. Miss Brill put up her hand and touched her fur. Dear little thing! It was nice to feel it again. She had taken it out of its box that afternoon, shaken out the moth powder, given it a good brush, and rubbed the life back into the dim little eyes. "What has been happening to me?" said the sad little eyes. Oh, how sweet it was to see them snap at her again from the red eiderdown! . . . But the nose, which was of some black composition, wasn't at all firm. It must have had a knock, somehow. Never mind—a little dab of black sealing wax when the time came—when it was absolutely necessary . . . Little rogue! Yes, she really felt like that about it. Little rogue biting its tail just by her left ear. She could have taken it off and laid it on her lap and stroked it. She felt a tingling in her hands and arms, but that came from walking, she supposed. And when she breathed, something light and sad—no, not sad, exactly—something gentle seemed to move in her bosom.

There were a number of people out this afternoon, far more than last Sunday. And the band sounded louder and gayer. That was because the Season had begun. For although the band played all the year round on Sundays, out of season it was never the same. It was like some one playing with only the family to listen; it didn't care how it played if there weren't any strangers present. Wasn't the conductor wearing a new coat, too? She was sure it was new. He scraped with his foot and flapped his arms like a rooster about to crow, and the bandsmen sitting in the green rotunda blew out their cheeks and glared at the music. Now there came a little "flutey" bit—very pretty!—a little chain of bright drops. She was sure it would be repeated. It was; she lifted her head and smiled.

Only two people shared her "special" seat: a fine old man in a velvet coat, his hands clasped over a huge carved walking-stick, and a big old woman, sitting upright, with a roll of knitting on her embroidered apron. They did not speak. This was disappointing, for Miss Brill always looked forward to the conversation. She had become really quite expert, she thought, at listening as though she didn't listen, at sitting in other people's lives just for a minute while they talked round her.

She glanced, sideways, at the old couple. Perhaps they would go soon.

Last Sunday, too, hadn't been as interesting as usual. An Englishman and his wife, he wearing a dreadful Panama hat and she button boots. And she'd gone on the whole time about how she ought to wear spectacles; she knew she needed them; but that it was no good getting any; they'd be sure to break and they'd never keep on. And he'd been so patient. He'd suggested everything—gold rims, the kind that curved round your ears, little pads inside the bridge. No, nothing would please her. "They'll always be sliding down my nose!" Miss Brill had wanted to shake her.

The old people sat on the bench, still as statues. Never mind, there was always the crowd to watch. To and fro, in front of the flower beds and the band rotunda, the couples and groups paraded, stopped to talk, to greet, to buy a handful of flowers from the old beggar who had his tray fixed to the railings. Little children ran among them, swooping and laughing; little boys with big white silk bows under their chins, little girls, little French dolls, dressed up in velvet and lace. And sometimes a tiny staggerer came suddenly rocking into the open from under the trees, stopped, stared, as suddenly sat down "flop," until its small high-stepping mother, like a young hen, rushed scolding to its rescue. Other people sat on the benches and green chairs, but they were nearly always the same, Sunday after Sunday, and—Miss Brill had often noticed—there was something funny about nearly all of them. They were odd, silent, nearly all old, and from the way they stared they looked as though they'd just come from dark little rooms or even—even cupboards!

Behind the rotunda the slender trees with yellow leaves down drooping, and through them just a line of sea, and beyond the blue sky with gold-veined clouds.

Turn tum-tum tiddle-um! tiddle-um! tum tiddley-um tum ta! blew the band.

Two young girls in red came by and two young soldiers in blue met them, and they laughed and paired and went off arm-in-arm. Two peasant women with funny straw hats passed, gravely, leading beautiful smoke-colored donkeys. A cold, pale nun hurried by. A beautiful woman came along and dropped her bunch of violets, and a little boy ran after to hand them to her, and she took them and threw them away as if they'd been poisoned. Dear me! Miss Brill didn't know whether to admire that or not! And now an ermine toque and a gentleman in gray met just in front of her. He was tall, stiff, dignified, and she was wearing the ermine toque she'd bought when her hair was yellow. Now everything, her hair, her face, even her eyes, was the same color as the shabby ermine, and her hand, in its cleaned glove, lifted to dab her lips, was a tiny yellowish paw. Oh, she was so pleased to see him—delighted! She rather thought they were going to meet that afternoon. She described where she'd been—everywhere, here, there, along by the sea. The day was so charming—didn't he agree? And wouldn't he, perhaps? . . . But he shook his head, lighted a cigarette, slowly breathed a great deep puff into her face, and even while she was still talking and laughing, flicked the match away and walked on. The ermine toque was alone; she smiled more brightly than ever. But even the band seemed to know what she was feeling and played more softly, played tenderly, and the drum beat, "The Brute! The Brute!" over and over. What would she do? What was going to happen now? But as Miss Brill wondered, the ermine toque turned, raised her hand as though she'd seen some one else, much nicer, just over there, and pattered away. And the band changed again and played more quickly, more gayly than ever, and the old couple on Miss Brill's seat got up and marched away, and such a funny old man with long whiskers hobbled along in time to the music and was nearly knocked over by four girls walking abreast.

Oh, how fascinating it was! How she enjoyed it! How she loved sitting here, watching it all! It was like a play. It was exactly like a play. Who could believe the sky at the back wasn't painted? But it wasn't till a little brown dog trotted on solemn and then slowly trotted off, like a little "theater" dog, a little dog that had been drugged, that Miss Brill discovered what it was that made it so exciting. They were all on the stage. They weren't only the audience, not only looking on; they were acting. Even she had a part and came every Sunday. No doubt somebody would have noticed if she hadn't been there; she was part of the performance after all. How strange she'd never thought of it like that before! And yet it explained why she made such a point of starting from home at just the same time each week—so as not to be late for the performance—and it also explained why she had quite a queer, shy feeling at telling her English pupils how she spent her Sunday afternoons. No wonder! Miss Brill nearly laughed out loud. She was on the stage. She thought of the old invalid gentleman to whom she read the newspaper four afternoons a week while he slept in the garden. She had got quite used to the frail head on the cotton pillow, the hollowed eyes, the open mouth and the high pinched nose. If he'd been dead she mightn't have noticed for weeks; she wouldn't have minded. But suddenly he knew he was having the paper read to him by an actress! "An actress!" The old head lifted; two points of light quivered in the old eyes. "An actress—are ye?" And Miss Brill smoothed the newspaper as though it were the manuscript of her part and said gently; "Yes, I have been an actress for a long time."

The band had been having a rest. Now they started again. And what they played was warm, sunny, yet there was just a faint chill—a something, what was it?—not sadness—no, not sadness—a something that made you want to sing. The tune lifted, lifted, the light shone; and it seemed to Miss Brill that in another moment all of them, all the whole company, would begin singing. The young ones, the laughing ones who were moving together, they would begin, and the men's voices, very resolute and brave, would join them. And then she too, she too, and the others on the benches—they would come in with a kind of accompaniment—something low, that scarcely rose or fell, something so beautiful—moving . . . And Miss Brill's eyes filled with tears and she looked smiling at all the other members of the company. Yes, we understand, we understand, she thought—though what they understood she didn't know.

Just at that moment a boy and a girl came and sat down where the old couple had been. They were beautifully dressed; they were in love. The hero and heroine, of course, just arrived from his father's yacht. And still soundlessly singing, still with that trembling smile, Miss Brill prepared to listen.

"No, not now," said the girl. "Not here, I can't."

"But why? Because of that stupid old thing at the end there?" asked the boy. "Why does she come here at all—who wants her? Why doesn't she keep her silly old mug at home?"

"It's her fu-fur which is so funny," giggled the girl. "It's exactly like a fried whiting."

"Ah, be off with you!" said the boy in an angry whisper. Then: "Tell me, ma petite chère—"

"No, not here," said the girl. "Not yet."

On her way home she usually bought a slice of honeycake at the baker's. It was her Sunday treat. Sometimes there was an almond in her slice, sometimes not. It made a great difference. If there was an almond it was like carrying home a tiny present—a surprise—something that might very well not have been there. She hurried on the almond Sundays and struck the match for the kettle in quite a dashing way.

But today she passed the baker's by, climbed the stairs, went into the little dark room—her room like a cupboard—and sat down on the red eiderdown. She sat there for a long time. The box that the fur came out of was on the bed. She unclasped the necklet quickly; quickly, without looking, laid it inside. But when she put the lid on she thought she heard something crying.

[1922]

For Discussion

1. Making a list of the old people Miss Brill sees in the park, identify which are wealthy, and which are not. What details help us to draw conclusions about each character's social status? Does there seem to be any correlation between social status and apparent happiness?

2. Which of the old people Miss Brill sees are alone and which are not? Is any connection drawn between being with others and being happy?

3. Examine the descriptions of the young people in the story. Are they wealthy or poor, alone or together, happy or unhappy? What details suggest these qualities?

4. How does Miss Brill fit into the scene (old versus young, rich versus poor, isolated versus together, happy versus unhappy) at the beginning of the story?

5. What is the "epiphany," or exhilarating experience, Miss Brill has when she hears the music? How might her new awareness affect her relationships with other people, such as her English students and the "invalid gentleman"?

6. What is the "climax" or turning point in the story? How does Miss Brill's attitude change, and how might she relate to people (including her students and the invalid gentleman) in the future?

7. What role do the fox fur and the "ermine toque" play in the story? Can you think of more than one explanation for the fact that the fox fur is crying at the end of the story?

For Further Exploration

1. Comparing this story with the previous stories in this section, how might Hilary Stevens, Mrs. Montague, or the Misses Bray have reacted to the social rejection Miss Brill experiences? What different responses are there to being an aging individual in society, and what are the effects of those responses?

2. Katherine Mansfield's story "Bliss" deals with the same sequence of a woman's ecstasy at being a part of the world, only to overhear a comment which destroys her happiness. Comparing the two stories, try to determine what Mansfield is saying about personal identity and the individual's relationships to others.

Eudora Welty

1909–

This tale of a woman on a yearly pilgrimage to save her grandson's life shows the theme of women's altruism at its most dramatic. Phoenix Jackson's human charity assumes mythic proportions as she encounters setbacks both in nature and from humanity; her triumph is the joy of giving shown here in her Christmas-time arrival in an almost celestial city.

A WORN PATH

It was December—a bright frozen day in the early morning. Far out in the country there was an old Negro woman with her head tied in a red rag, coming along a path through the pinewoods. Her name was Phoenix Jackson. She was very old and small and she walked slowly in the dark pine shadows, moving a little from side to side in her steps, with the balanced heaviness and lightness of a pendulum in a grandfather clock. She carried a thin, small cane made from an umbrella, and with this she kept tapping the frozen earth in front of her. This made a grave and persistent noise in the still air, that seemed meditative like the chirping of a solitary little bird.

She wore a dark striped dress reaching down to her shoe tops, and an equally long apron of bleached sugar sacks, with a full pocket: all neat and tidy, but every time she took a step she might have fallen over her shoelaces, which dragged from her unlaced shoes. She looked straight ahead. Her eyes were blue with age. Her skin had a pattern all its own of numberless branching wrinkles and as though a whole little tree stood in the middle of her forehead, but a golden color ran underneath, and the two knobs of her cheeks were illumined by a yellow burning under the dark. Under the red rag her hair came down on her neck in the frailest of ringlets, still black, and with an odor like copper.

Now and then there was a quivering in the thicket. Old Phoenix said, "Out of my way, all you foxes, owls, beetles, jack rabbits, coons and wild animals! . . . Keep out from under these feet, little bob-whites. . . Keep the big wild hogs out of my path. Don't let none of those come running my direction. I got a long way." Under her small black-freckled hand her cane, limber as a buggy whip, would switch at the brush as if to rouse up any hiding things.

On she went. The woods were deep and still. The sun made the pine needles almost too bright to look at, up where the wind rocked. The cones dropped as light as feathers. Down in the hollow was the mourning dove—it was not too late for him.

The path ran up a hill. "Seem like there is chains' about my feet, time I get this far," she said, in the voice of argument old people keep to use with themselves. "Something always take a hold of me on this hill—pleads I should stay."

After she got to the top she turned and gave a full, severe look behind her where she had come. "Up through pines," she said at length. "Now down through oaks."

Her eyes opened their widest, and she started down gently. But before she got to the bottom of the hill a bush caught her dress.

Her fingers were busy and intent, but her skirts were full and long, so that before she could pull them free in one place they were caught in another. It was not possible to allow the dress to tear. "I in the thorny bush," she said. "Thorns, you doing your appointed work. Never want to let folks pass, no sir. Old eyes thought you was a pretty little *green* bush."

Finally, trembling all over, she stood free, and after a moment dared to stoop for her cane.

"Sun so high!" she cried, leaning back and looking, while the thick tears went over her eyes. "The time getting all gone here."

At the foot of this hill was a place where a log was laid across the creek. "Now comes the trial," said Phoenix.

Putting her right foot out, she mounted the log and shut her eyes. Lifting her skirt, leveling her cane fiercely before her, like a festival figure in some parade, she began to march across. Then she opened her eyes and she was safe on the other side.

"I wasn't as old as I thought," she said.

But she sat down to rest. She spread her skirts on the bank around her and folded her hands over her knees. Up above her was a tree in a pearly cloud of mistletoe. She did not dare to close her eyes, and when a little boy brought her a plate with a slice of marble-cake on it she spoke to him. "That would be acceptable," she said. But when she went to take it there was just her own hand in the air.

So she left that tree, and had to go through a barbed-wire fence. There she had to creep and crawl, spreading her knees and stretching her fingers like a baby trying to climb the steps. But she talked loudly to herself: she could not let her dress be torn now, so late in the day, and she could not pay for having her arm or her leg sawed off if she got caught fast where she was.

At last she was safe through the fence and risen up out in the clearing. Big dead trees, like black men with one arm, were standing in the purple stalks of the withered cotton field. There sat a buzzard.

"Who you watching?"

In the furrow she made her way along.

"Glad this not the season for bulls," she said, looking sideways, "and the good Lord made his snakes to curl up and sleep in the winter. A pleasure I don't see no two-headed snake coming around that tree, where it come once. It took a while to get by him, back in the summer."

She passed through the old cotton and went into a field of dead corn. It whispered and shook and was taller than her head. "Through the maze now," she said, for there was no path.

Then there was something tall, black, and skinny there, moving before her.

At first she took it for a man. It could have been a man dancing in the field. But she stood still and listened, and it did not make a sound. It was as silent as a ghost.

"Ghost," she said sharply, "who be you the ghost of? For I have heard of nary death close by."

But there was no answer—only the ragged dancing in the wind.

She shut her eyes, reached out her hand, and touched a sleeve. She found a coat and inside that an emptiness, cold as ice.

"You scarecrow," she said. Her face lighted. "I ought to be shut up for good," she said with laughter. "My senses is gone. I too old. I the oldest people I ever know. Dance, old scarecrow," she said, "while I dancing with you."

She kicked her foot over the furrow, and with mouth drawn down, shook her head once or twice in a little strutting way. Some husks blew down and whirled in streamers about her skirts.

Then she went on, parting her way from side to side with the cane, through the whispering field. At last she came to the end, to a wagon track where the silver grass blew between the red ruts. The quail were walking around like pullets, seeming all dainty and unseen.

"Walk pretty," she said. "This the easy place. This the easy going."

She followed the track, swaying through the quiet bare fields, through the little strings of trees silver in their dead leaves, past cabins silver from weather, with the doors and windows boarded shut, all like old women under a spell sitting there. "I walking in their sleep," she said, nodding her head vigorously.

In a ravine she went where a spring was silently flowing through a hollow log. Old Phoenix bent and drank. "Sweet-gum makes the water sweet," she said, and drank more. "Nobody know who made this well, for it was here when I was born."

The track crossed a swampy part where the moss hung as white as lace from every limb. "Sleep on, alligators, and blow your bubbles." Then the track went into the road.

Deep, deep the road went down between the high green-colored banks. Overhead the live-oaks met, and it was as dark as a cave.

A black dog with a lolling tongue came up out of the weeds by the ditch. She was meditating, and not ready, and when he came at her she only hit him a little with her cane. Over she went in the ditch, like a little puff of milkweed.

Down there, her senses drifted away. A dream visited her, and she reached her hand up, but nothing reached down and gave her a pull. So she lay there and presently went to talking. "Old woman," she said to herself, "that black dog come up out of the weeds to stall you off, and now there he sitting on his fine tail, smiling at you."

A white man finally came along and found her—a hunter, a young man, with his dog on a chain.

"Well, Granny!" he laughed. "What are you doing there?"

"Lying on my back like a June-bug waiting to be turned over, mister," she said, reaching up her hand.

He lifted her up, gave her a swing in the air, and set her down. "Anything broken, Granny?"

"No sir, them old dead weeds is springy enough," said Phoenix, when she had got her breath. "I thank you for your trouble."

"Where do you live, Granny?" he asked, while the two dogs were growling at each other.

"Away back yonder, sir, behind the ridge. You can't even see it from here."

"On your way home?"

"No sir, I going to town."

"Why, that's too far! That's as far as I walk when I come out myself, and I get something for my trouble." He patted the stuffed bag he carried, and there hung down a little closed claw. It was one of the bob-whites, with its beak hooked bitterly to show it was dead. "Now you go on home, Granny!"

"I bound to go to town, mister," said Phoenix. "The time come around."

OLD AGE

He gave another laugh, filling the whole landscape. "I know you old colored people! Wouldn't miss going to town to see Santa Claus!"

But something held old Phoenix very still. The deep lines in her face went into a fierce and different radiation. Without warning, she had seen with her own eyes a flashing nickel fall out of the man's pocket onto the ground.

"How old are you, Granny?" he was saying.

"There is no telling, mister," she said, "no telling."

Then she gave a little cry and clapped her hands and said, "Git on away from here, dog! Look! Look at that dog!" She laughed as if in admiration. "He ain't scared of nobody. He a big black dog." She whispered, "Sic him!"

"Watch me get rid of that cur," said the man. "Sic him, Pete! Sic him!"

Phoenix heard the dogs fighting, and heard the man running and throwing sticks. She even heard a gunshot. But she was slowly bending forward by that time, further and further forward, the lids stretched down over her eyes, as if she were doing this in her sleep. Her chin was lowered almost to her knees. The yellow palm of her hand came out from the fold of her apron. Her fingers slid down and along the ground under the piece of money with the grace and care they would have in lifting an egg from under a setting hen. Then she slowly straightened up, she stood erect, and the nickel was in her apron pocket. A bird flew by. Her lips moved. "God watching me the whole time. I come to stealing."

The man came back, and his own dog panted about them. "Well, I scared him off that time," he said, and then he laughed and lifted his gun and pointed it at Phoenix.

She stood straight and faced him.

"Doesn't the gun scare you?" he said, still pointing it.

"No, sir, I seen plenty go off closer by, in my day, and for less than what I done," she said, holding utterly still.

He smiled, and shouldered the gun. "Well, Granny," he said, "you must be a hundred years old, and scared of nothing. I'd give you a dime if I had any money with me. But you take my advice and stay home, and nothing will happen to you."

"I bound to go on my way, mister," said Phoenix. She inclined her head in the red rag. Then they went in different directions, but she could hear the gun shooting again and again over the hill.

She walked on. The shadows hung from the oak trees to the road like curtains. Then she smelled wood-smoke, and smelled the river, and she saw a steeple and the cabins on their steep steps. Dozens of little black children whirled around her. There ahead was Natchez shining. Bells were ringing. She walked on.

In the paved city it was Christmas time. There were red and green electric lights strung and crisscrossed everywhere, and all turned on in the daytime. Old Phoenix would have been lost if she had not distrusted her eyesight and depended on her feet to know where to take her.

She paused quietly on the sidewalk where people were passing by. A lady came along in the crowd, carrying an armful of red-, green- and silver-wrapped presents; she gave off perfume like the red roses in hot summer, and Phoenix stopped her.

"Please, missy, will you lace up my shoe?" She held up her foot.

"What do you want, Grandma?"

"See my shoe," said Phoenix. "Do all right for out in the country, but wouldn't look right to go in a big building."

"Stand still then, Grandma," said the lady. She put her packages down on the sidewalk beside her and laced and tied both shoes tightly.

"Can't lace 'em with a cane," said Phoenix. "Thank you, missy. I doesn't mind asking a nice lady to tie up my shoe, when I gets out on the street."

Moving slowly and from side to side, she went into the big building, and into a tower of steps, where she walked up and around and around until her feet knew to stop.

She entered a door, and there she saw nailed up on the wall the document that had been stamped with the gold seal and framed in the gold frame, which matched the dream that was hung up in her head.

"Here I be," she said. There was a fixed and ceremonial stiffness over her body.

"A charity case, I suppose," said an attendant who sat at the desk before her.

But Phoenix only looked above her head. There was sweat on her face, the wrinkles in her skin shone like a bright net.

"Speak up, Grandma," the woman said. "What's your name? We must have your history, you know. Have you been here before? What seems to be the trouble with you?"

Old Phoenix only gave a twitch to her face as if a fly were bothering her.

"Are you deaf?" cried the attendant.

But then the nurse came in.

"Oh, that's just old Aunt Phoenix," she said. "She doesn't come for herself—she has a little grandson. She makes these trips just as regular as clockwork. She lives away back off the Old Natchez Trace." She bent down. "Well, Aunt Phoenix, why don't you just take a seat? We won't keep you standing after your long trip." She pointed.

The old woman sat down, bolt upright in the chair.

"Now, how is the boy?" asked the nurse.

Old Phoenix did not speak.

"I said, how is the boy?"

But Phoenix only waited and stared straight ahead, her face very solemn and withdrawn into rigidity.

"Is his throat any better?" asked the nurse. "Aunt Phoenix, don't you hear me? Is your grandson's throat any better since the last time you came for the medicine?"

With her hands on her knees, the old woman waited, silent, erect and motionless, just as if she were in armor.

"You mustn't take up our time this way, Aunt Phoenix," the nurse said. "Tell us quickly about your grandson, and get it over. He isn't dead, is he?"

At last there came a flicker and then a flame of comprehension across her face, and she spoke.

"My grandson. It was my memory had left me. There I sat and forgot why I made my long trip."

"Forgot?" The nurse frowned. "After you came so far?"

Then Phoenix was like an old woman begging a dignified forgiveness for waking up frightened in the night. "I never did go to school, I was too old at the Surrender," she said in a soft voice. "I'm an old woman without an education. It was my memory fail me. My little grandson, he is just the same, and I forgot it in the coming."

"Throat never heals, does it?" said the nurse, speaking in a loud, sure voice to old Phoenix. By now she had a card with something written on it, a little list. "Yes. Swallowed lye. When was it?—January—two–three years ago—"

Phoenix spoke unasked now. "No, missy, he not dead, he just the same. Every little while his throat begin to close up again, and he not able to swallow. He not get his breath. He not able to help himself. So the time come around, and I go on another trip for the soothing medicine."

"All right. The doctor said as long as you came to get it, you could have it," said the nurse. "But it's an obstinate case."

"My little grandson, he sit up there in the house all wrapped up, waiting by himself." Phoenix went on. "We is the only two left in the world. He suffer and it don't seem to put him back at all. He got a sweet look. He going to last. He wear a little patch quilt and peep out holding his mouth open like a little bird. I remembers so plain now. I not going to forget him again, no, the whole enduring time. I could tell him from all the others in creation."

"All right." The nurse was trying to hush her now. She brought her a bottle of medicine. "Charity," she said, making a check mark in a book.

Old Phoenix held the bottle close to her eyes, and then carefully put it into her pocket.

"I thank you," she said.

"It's Christmas time, Grandma," said the attendant. "Could I give you a few pennies out of my purse?"

"Five pennies is a nickel," said Phoenix stiffly.

"Here's a nickel," said the attendant.

Phoenix rose carefully and held out her hand. She received the nickel and then fished the other nickel out of her pocket and laid it beside the new one. She stared at her palm closely, with her head on one side.

Then she gave a tap with her cane on the floor.

"This is what come to me to do," she said. "I going to the store and buy my child a little windmill they sells, made out of paper. He going to find it hard to believe there such a thing in the world. I'll march myself back where he waiting, holding it straight up in this hand."

She lifted her free hand, gave a little nod, turned around, and walked out of the doctor's office. Then her slow step began on the stairs, going down.

[1941]

For Discussion

1. What is the literal nature of Phoenix Jackson's "journey"? What might be the symbolic nature of her journey, and why does she have to repeat it each year?

2. In what ways is the image of the Phoenix—a mythical bird that rises again out of its own ashes—appropriate for this woman? Rereading the examples of "deadness" described in the landscape of this story, in what sense does Phoenix "rise" from them?

3. Find the religious allusions (such as the snake, thorns, etc.) in the story and suggest what Welty might have meant by the destination, "a paved city" in which "it was Christmas time."

4. Why does Phoenix take money as she does twice in the story? What role does money play and what attitude is there toward the poor?

5. What are the various definitions of "charity" in this story?

6. Phoenix is not only poor; she is also old, black, and a woman. Analyze the remarks made about these characteristics. In spite of her status in society, why is she so powerful?

7. What are various meanings of the title?

For Further Exploration

1. In an essay called "Is Phoenix Jackson's grandson really *dead?*" Eudora Welty answers that often-asked question about the story "A Worn Path." Read the essay to find the answer, then relate how Welty herself explains the meaning of the story.

2. Welty says that the idea for this story came from the sight of an old woman trudging across a far-away field. How might Welty have imagined the purpose of the trek differently if the old person she saw had been a man? Read "Mr. Flood's Party" by E. A. Robinson and "Death of a Hired Man" by Robert Frost. In these poems about old men's journeys, how is the motive or purpose for the journey the same or different from Phoenix Jackson's?

Poetry About Old Age

Aging is a time of contrasts and paradoxes, joys and defeats, exemplified in the poetry as well as in the fiction about old age. Physical frailty and loss of attractiveness are recurrent concerns, but there is often an inner strength which belies the bodily weaknesses of these women.

The isolation of old age is sometimes described as a cyclical casting off which is as much a part of nature as the seasons. When a woman's role as lover or nurturer is done, she is often shown as feeling powerless, with no real reason to live. In contrast, strong older women are recognized and lauded in poems such as "In Praise of Old Women" and "Lineage." As these poets make clear, hope and hopelessness, vigor or loss of vitality in old age are not purely personal variables, but are to a large extent results of wealth, health, and other uncontrollable or unpredictable factors.

Sandra Hochman

1936–

POSTSCRIPT

I gave my life to learning how to live.
Now that I have organized it all, now that
I have finally found out how to keep my clothes
In order, when to wash and when to sew, how
To control my glands and sexual impulses,
How to raise a family, which friends to get
Rid of and which to be loyal to, who
Is phony and who is true, how to get rid of
Ambition and how to be thrifty, now that I have
Finally learned how to be closer to the nude
And secret silence, my life
Is just about over.

[1969]

Ambapali

4th century B.C. (?)

BLACK AND GLOSSY AS A BEE

Black and glossy as a bee and curled was my hair;
now in old age it is just like hemp or bark-cloth.
Not otherwise is the word of the truthful. . . .

My hair clustered with flowers was like a box of sweet
    perfume;
now in old age it stinks like a rabbit's pelt.
Not otherwise is the word of the truthful. . . .

Once my eyebrows were lovely, as though drawn by an
    artist;
now in old age they are overhung with wrinkles.
Not otherwise is the word of the truthful. . . .

Dark and long-lidded, my eyes were bright and flashing
    as jewels;
now in old age they are dulled and dim.
Not otherwise is the word of the truthful. . . .

My voice was as sweet as the cuckoo's, who flies in the
    woodland thickets;
now in old age it is broken and stammering.
Not otherwise is the word of the truthful. . . .

Once my hands were smooth and soft, and bright with
    jewels and gold;
now in old age they twist like roots.
Not otherwise is the word of the truthful. . . .

Once my body was lovely as polished gold;
now in old age it is covered all over with tiny wrinkles.
Not otherwise is the word of the truthful. . . .

Once my two feet were soft, as though filled with down;
now in old age they are cracked and wizened.
Not otherwise is the word of the truthful. . . .

Such was my body once. Now it is weary and tottering,
the home of many ills, an old house with flaking plaster.
Not otherwise is the word of the truthful.

Translated from the Pali by A. L. Basham

[4th century B.C.?]

Larin Paraske

(1833–1904)

A WOMAN SOON GROWS OLD

Fair is not my face
Cherry-red are not my cheeks
White is not my weary skin;
Age has reached me early
Youth has left me soon.
Once a year I have a lamb
Once a month a calf.
   Did the great God make me
Did the Lord create me
Once a year to have a lamb
Once a month to have a calf.
Often am I by my husband
Always in the arms of man.

Translated from Finnish by Jaakko A. Ahokas

[about 1890]

Marya Fiamengo

1926–

IN PRAISE OF OLD WOMEN

Yes, Tadeusz Rozewicz,[1] I too
prefer old women.
They bend over graves
with flowers,
they wash the limbs of the dead,
they count the beads of their rosaries,
they commit no murders
they give advice
or tell fortunes,
they endure.

In Poland, in Russia,
in Asia, in the Balkans,
I see them shawled, kerchiefed,
bent-backed, work-wrinkled.

But Tadeusz,
have you been to America?

Where we have no old women.
No Stara Babas,[2]
no haggard Madonnas.

Everyone, Tadeusz, is young in America.
Especially the women
with coifed blue hair
which gleams like the steel
of jets in the daytime sky.
Smooth-skinned at sixty,
second debuts at fifty
renascent
they never grow old in America.

And we have in America
literate, sexually liberated women
who wouldn't touch a corpse
who confuse lechery with love,
not out of viciousness
but boringly
out of confusion, neurosis, identity crises.

[1]Contemporary Polish poet.
[2]Old women.

Tadeusz,
I go to the cemetery
with my mother
one of us stoically old,
the other aging,
and I tell you, Tadeusz,
I will grow old in America.
I will have no second debut.
I will raise my son on old battles,
Kossovo, Neretva, Thermopylae,
Stalingrad and Britain
and I will wrinkle adamantly in America.

I will put salt in the soup
and I will offer bread and wine
to my friends,
and I will stubbornly praise old women
until their thin taut skins
glow like Ikons ascending on escalators
like Buddhas descending in subways,
and I will liberate all women
to be old in America
because the highest manifestation of
Hagia Sophia[3]
is old and a woman.

[1976]

[3]Holy Wisdom.

Paula Gunn Allen

1939–

GRANDMOTHER

Out of her own body she pushed
silver thread, light, air
and carried it carefully on the dark, flying
where nothing moved.

Out of her body she extruded
shining wire, life, and wove the light
on the void.

From beyond time,
beyond oak[1] trees and bright clear water flow,
she was given the work of weaving the strands
of her body, her pain, her vision
into creation, and the gift of having created,
to disappear.

After her,
the women and the men weave blankets into tales of life,
memories of light and ladders,
infinity-eyes, and rain.
After her I sit on my laddered rain-bearing rug
and mend the tear with string.

[1975]

[1] I am a member of Oak Clan.

Margaret Walker Alexander
1915—

LINEAGE

My grandmothers were strong.
They followed plows and bent to toil.
They moved through fields sowing seed.
They touched earth and grain grew.
They were full of sturdiness and singing.
My grandmothers were strong.

My grandmothers are full of memories
Smelling of soap and onions and wet clay
With veins rolling roughly over quick hands
They have many clean words to say.
My grandmothers were strong.
Why am I not as they?

[1942]

Sappho

6th century B.C.

HERE ARE FINE GIFTS, CHILDREN

Here are fine gifts, children,
O friend, singer on the clear tortoise lyre,

all my flesh is wrinkled with age,
my black hair has faded to white,

my legs can no longer carry me,
once nimble like a fawn's,

but what can I do?
It cannot be undone,

no more than can pink-armed Dawn
not end in darkness on earth,

or keep her love for Tithonos,
who must waste away;

yet I love refinement, and beauty and light
are for me the same as desire for the sun.

[6th century B.C.]

For Discussion

1. Although Sandra Hochman was relatively young when she wrote "Post-script," how does the persona she creates reveal the thoughts of many aging women?

2. In Ambapali's poem beginning "Black and glossy as a bee . . . ," what are several meanings of the refrain, "Not otherwise is the word of the truthful"? What are the "truths" of old age?

3. To what does Paraske's narrator in "A Woman Soon Grows Old" attribute her physical deterioration?

4. Why is America the place to grow old selected by Marya Fiamengo in "In Praise of Old Women," and what does she praise about old women?

5. What attitude toward the generations is shown in the poem "Grand-mother"? Explain how the images of weaving threads, wires, and blankets are used to convey the messages of the poem.

6. Compare "Lineage" with "Grandmother." What different images are used to convey the themes?

7. What is ironic about the "fine gifts" Sappho describes?

1. Read poems about aging men (such as Robert Frost's "An Old Man's Winter Night" and E. A. Robinson's "Isaac and Archibald"). Examine the similarities and differences between these works and the poems about women aging.

2. What characteristics of old age are exhibited in these poems, aside from physical changes? Compare or contrast these characteristics with the qualities identified in poems of childhood, adolescence, and adulthood. With which other life stage does aging have the most in common?

Drama About Old Age

Old age is any age at which your audience starts to walk out, according to the play *Not Waving* by British dramatist Catherine Hayes. The self-deprecating humor of a fifty-two year old comedian turns to pathos on her last night of a stage contract.

In the first act, the audience meets Jill Jeffers, who has been told by her manager that the club owners are displeased with her act, and has been told by her daughter that Raymond, a man they both had loved, has committed suicide. Despite pleas for her to allow a younger woman to take over, Jeffers goes into her act with a fervor that dwindles to false enthusiasm and insecurity. The jokes she makes about aging, marriage, children, work, and social outcasts show the powerlessness she feels as an individual who has outlived her place in society.

Like many other women in literature about aging, Jill Jeffers is afraid— of losing her health, physical attractiveness, job, and most recent lover. In desperation she tries in Act I to re-establish contact with her neglected children—now grown—but in the face of rejection returns to using her children as material for her jokes. Regardless of her sometimes cruel and often stereotyped jokes, there is much about Jill Jeffers to applaud.

Catherine Hayes
1949–

NOT WAVING

Act Two

Musical introduction.

VOICE   And now, ladies and gentlemen, put your hands together for the star of our show, Miss Jill Jeffers. *(Applause. Enter* JILL, *dressed for the stage. When she's doing her 'legitimate' act, she can use a more common accent, 'old-fashioned'.)*

JILL   Thank you, thank you, thank you. Good evening, ladies and gentlemen. My name is Jill Jeffers and I've come here tonight to entertain you.
(More applause. The above speech is a kind of signature tune which the audience has been expecting.)
I hope you're ready for a laugh. You are? Well, I know a little place around the corner, you've still got time to get to . . . no, I'm only joking. Stay where you are. You know me, Jill Jeffers—the biggest thing about her is her smile. That's what they used to say. Wouldn't say it now, though. The biggest thing about her is her hip measurement. A hundred and one. Metric, that is. Everything sounds bigger in French, doesn't it?
   Are any of you a hundred and one round here? *(She demonstrates her hips)* . . . No? . . . You're trying to make out that I'm the fattest person in the room. Well, me and that woman stuck in the doorway . . . It's a hard life, isn't it? I tried everything when I was young to get rid of some weight. Did no good—all I ever lost was my virginity. I think I left it on the top deck of a bus one time. It was either that or my plastic mac. You forget the details as you grow older . . . I missed it, though. You know what the British summers are like.
   Look at these legs. They're like a pair of Californian redwoods. I found a squirrel storing nuts in them once. I won't say where.
   Oh God, have you seen my overhanging ankles? I haven't got a spare tyre: it's an inflatable life-raft . . . and my double chin . . . It's not fat, you know . . . It's water . . . If you put your hand on my stomach *(She demonstrates)* there, just there—press it in a bit, and swivel it around—oh, I'll give you a go later—you know what it feels like? One of those plastic bags you win at the fair with a goldfish in. It does, you know. You'd think that was what it was. Mind you, you could get more than a goldfish in there these days. The size of it now, it'd take a couple of fresh salmon. Half a dozen trout.
   Listen, there's that much water in my body I'm thinking of fitting flippers on my vitals. I believe a lot of fellers go for that nowadays. It turns them on . . . There's no accounting for taste, like, as the man said when he kissed the cow.
   Your body lets you down though, doesn't it? If my gums recede

any further, my eyes'll drop out. Ooooooh, the things I regret doing with my body! . . . Like smoking. Smoking's knocked years off my life. I'm fifty-two. If I hadn't smoked, I'd be sixty-six. You've got to laugh.

I've just come out of hospital actually. I had a certain operation. Quite unusual in a woman of my age. I bet some of you've had it, though. It's fairly common in young people apparently, although they don't always do what I did because attitudes are changing. Every case is assessed on its merits. So they say. But I got mine done quick enough. No messing. You're only in a day. I said to the surgeon afterwards, 'How long before I can have sexual relations?' He said, 'I've got no idea, love. You're the first patient who's asked me that after a tonsillectomy.'

Ah, but you can't trust doctors nowadays, can you? They do what they like with you. There was a nice young feller on the ward I was on, though. He said to me one morning, 'I've just brought in two cases of dysentery.' I said to him, 'Well, that's very kind of you, darling, but I'll stick to the Lucozade if it's all the same to you.' You've got to laugh.

What I don't like about doctors is the way they start writing the prescription as you walk through the door. I know a woman went to the doctor to get a coil fitted. Came out with a hearing-aid . . . they'll put anything anywhere. They don't care.

(Short pause. JILL says the next lines as if pretending to the audience that they are jokes a comedian has to tell, by virtue of being a comedian, even though they're not very funny.)

Oh, God! What's green and pear-shaped? . . . A pear.

What's green and pear-shaped and splattered on the floor? . . . A peardrop.

I thought that one up myself. I didn't pinch it off any other comic. Well, you wouldn't would you? If any other comic had that joke, I'd be quite happy to leave it with him.

What d'ye call a septic cat? . . . Puss.

A Greek washing-up liquid? . . . Plato.

How about an Englishman, a Frenchman and a Yank in the middle of the ocean? . . . Nato.

It's a gift being able to think of these. It is, you know. I got it free in a packet of Sugar Puffs.

Did I ever tell you about my Uncle Henry? . . . Sad story. He was only a young man. Died of asbestosis. Took us six months to cremate the body. You've got to laugh.

You can get a laugh out of death, can't you? You know what they say about old fisherman? They never die: they always smell like that.

Oh God, I suppose I've insulted some fisherman in the audience. I'm not kidding, you've got to be so careful these days. You can't tell Irish jokes, you can't tell Asian jokes, you can't tell spastic, mongol, cross-eyed, hunchback, one leg longer than the other jokes. Who's left? Personally, I can't see anything wrong with having one leg longer than the other. It's better than having one leg shorter than the other.

Men have always been good for a laugh, though, haven't they? I must've thought so once or I wouldn't've kept marrying them. Mind you, as it turned out, the only thing I ever had in common with most of my husbands was the cake and the photograph album . . . Well, how would you feel on your wedding night? You're all propped up in bed— see-through nightie, no rollers, you've had a wash down—and there he is getting undressed—this happened to me, it really did—when out from under his shirt falls a piece of paper: batteries not included. Jees.

And they think they're God's gift, don't they? Women are much better. Friend of mine went on a day trip to heaven once. *(As if contradicting)* She did, you know. Booked it with the LRT. Anyway, when she got there, God was sorting out the new intake. 'All the men who've been henpecked by their wives,' he said, 'queue up on the left. And all the men who haven't been henpecked, queue up on the right.' About three hundred big, burly men went and stood on the left, and one little feller, six stone, pigeon-chest, knock-knees—this isn't ethnic, honest—stood on the right. So God went over to him. 'Pull the other one,' he said. 'This is the queue for the men who haven't been henpecked. Why are you standing here?' 'My wife told me to,' he said.

And that's typical of them, isn't it? Do as they're told so long as it suits them. My first husband was like that . . . Oh, when I think of it. I was a sweet, young thing then. I was a child bride. So was he . . . it was a white wedding: we were both terrified. The first night was a disaster. He told me what he knew, and I told him what I knew. I'll never forget the look on his face. 'You've just made that up,' he said. 'Haven't you?'

Of course, the whole bloody relationship was a failure. I don't know why I did it. He used to lie in bed at night and kiss me. It was very dull. And very wet and slobbery. It gave me bad skin here round my mouth. I used to have to stop and wipe it off on the sheet. Best bit of the whole thing. I haven't seen him, now, for years. Donkeys years. I wouldn't know him any more. Well, I presume I wouldn't, though I might if he kissed me. Funny thing life, isn't it?

His name was Bill, or Will, or Phil, or Ill, I don't know. Something like that. It rhymed, anyway. Will Hill, or Phil Mill, or Bill Lill, or something. I've got no memory for detail. But he was no thrill. I don't know that they ever are. I mean, one of the others, God, d'ye know what he did? You wouldn't believe it. He bought me a set of saucepans. I don't mean he bought a set of saucepans. I mean he bought me a set of saucepans. For my birthday. I didn't know what to do with them. I thought it was . . . like . . . sports equipment. I thought you had to hit something with them. I kept looking for the ball. And he didn't seem to crack on, that was the thing.

All my husbands've been like that. A bit of a disappointment. There was the one who died. Of all the days he could've snuffed it, he had to choose one the week before my Royal Command Performance. I suppose ultimately it was of no real consequence. I didn't have a ticket for him anyway. And the publicity was good. Put me centre stage so to speak. I closed the first half of the show. The Queen admired my professionalism. And I admired hers . . . Mind you, I almost didn't make it. He was being buried that same afternoon. I had to go. Put in an appearance . . . and someone had had the bright idea of bringing the body home. A little romantic touch. First time we'd been under the same roof together for months. Of course, the undertakers arsed around. You'd've thought I had all the time in the world. I kept saying to him, 'Will you put a move on? I'm in a hurry.' But he just supped his whisky and said 'There's still a few minutes.' Well, there was, but I didn't want him hanging around. I mean, they didn't freeze the bodies in those days. The bloody man was still fresh.

And then one of his relatives barged in. 'Oh my God!' she said. 'He looks as healthy now as when he was alive.' 'Is that a fact?' I said. 'Well let me say one thing: I no longer care what he looks like. All I know is, dead or alive, he goes out of here at three o'clock.'

Life's a joke, isn't it? And someone's laughing. It's a pity he hasn't come tonight. Whoever he is.

(Short pause.)

It's not as difficult as it seems, this, you know. Lots of people can stand up on stage and tell jokes. They kid you up it's hard but it's not so bad. Particularly if you can't do anything else. And let's face it, you've got to do something to pass the time if it's only sit in a chair and breathe. This is all I can do. I can't dance. I'm not artistic. I can barely sing. I'm not musical at all . . . Did you hear the one about Beethoven? . . . No, neither did he. Beethoven was so deaf he thought he was a mime artist. A feller told me once he was a government artist—drew the dole. I said to him, 'Oh really. I thought you had something wrong with your bladder.'

But it's a good job we're not all the same, isn't it? You're not even like the other members of your family, are you? I'll be glad when this genetic engineering comes in. I'm putting myself down for two robots and a clockwork mouse. Less trouble all round.

Actually, I've got two robots already. Have I told you about them? They're the reason I'm the way I am today. Insanity's hereditary. You get it off your kids. Well, you do if they're anything like mine. They're twins. One's identical, one isn't. But they're the same sex—a boy and a girl. Well, a man and a woman really. I can't tell them apart. I never could. He's the one who used to have 'David' on a piece of sellotape around his wrist. But they don't make sellotape like they used to. After a couple of years it was anybody's guess.

I gave him everything he ever wanted. When he was a boy he had dinky cars. And Meccano. He sailed boats in the bath. He liked six-guns and penknives and pea-shooters. He was a macho-baby: he smashed up his sister's dolls. It was through him I learned the value of unbreakable toys. You use them for breaking up breakable toys. He was a vicious little sod. And that's a mother talking.

(Pause. JILL *is thinking about* DAVID *but rouses herself to launch into* MIRIAM.*)*

The other one was as bad. Miriam. Miriam's a girl's name in case you didn't know. Some people've never heard of it. It's a derivative of Mary, meaning 'wished-for child.' I didn't know that when I had her. David means 'beloved.'

Actually, I called her Miriam in the hope that she might think her father was Jewish. He wasn't. But I thought she'd be more likely to develop some business sense with a name like that. In the event, however, she's finished up with nothing but a distaste for sausages and the Jewish ability to look a gift-horse in the mouth. That's a reference to the history of Revelation in case there are any pagans here tonight. It comes to something when you have to explain your jokes.

Not that I was ever any good at explaining. Not to Miriam anyway. She always wanted to know where I was. Why I wasn't there. 'Jesus,' I'd say. 'I can't be in two places at once. I'm a comedian not a bloody magician. A bloody illusionist. If I'm making people laugh, I haven't got time for pushing you and your pram along the road. Why didn't you want a bicycle like David? David's independent. You can't even steer the pram properly. Your dolls keep falling out of it. Can't you strap the damn things in? Oh, they're a bloody nuisance, these bloody dolls. Miriam, for God's sake, watch the kerb. You're walking right off the goddam kerb. I'm not shouting at you. Why can't you be like David? Why can't you ride a bike? . . . Stop crying, for God's sake. I'm not shouting at you. I'm not. God, you're enough to make anybody shout. Look at David. He's alright. What's the matter with you? Will you stop crying? Will you stop that bloody crying? For God's sake, Miriam, will you shut up? You're driving me mad. I'm insane with the noise. Stop it. Stop it! I'm warning you. This is your last chance, or I'll . . . '

Oh, that kid! David could ride a bike. She wouldn't even try. 'I want my dolls. I want my dolls.' She was always standing against the wall clutching a doll to her breast. Chest. Silly cow. 'It's bloody plastic,' I'd say. 'Look, you can put your fingers in its eyes. You can pull its arms off. I'll show you . . . Yes, I know it wets itself, but you can pull its arms off. What sort of a love-object is that? For Christ's sake, Miriam, stick this jelly baby in your mouth and shut up . . . I've got a joke about jelly babies, Miriam. D'ye want to hear it? How d'ye tell the legitimate jelly babies from the illegitimate jelly babies? Hey, Miriam, how d'ye do that? . . . You turn the bag upside down and the bastards fall out.'
(Pause.)
D'ye know what she did to spite me? She learned to play the piano. Classical pieces. She got her grade eight. She was always on about her grade eight. And later it was her advanced driving. Mind you, I wouldn't go in a car with her. Bloody woman couldn't manoeuvre a pram. What's she going to be like in a car?
(Short pause.)
When I think of what he got off with, that man. When I think of what I went through and he didn't. It's not the giving birth. You can get over that. It's being expected to care tuppence afterwards.

I entered Miriam for a charming child contest once. There were only eight kids in it. She came ninth. I know that isn't true. But it's how I feel.

Oh God, somebody, give us a song. Stick 10 pence in Maurice's navel and let's have a bit of music.
(JILL sings loudly and brashly.)

    Oh, the sun was shining on the old pretty wall,
    When the muck man fell in a fit.
    And he cried, 'Hey, Mother, will you come and
    pull me out
    Cause I'm up to my eyes in shit.'

(JILL speaks again.)
Oh, shit. That's all you get out of kids, isn't it? Mind you, you didn't get it out of Miriam. She was forever constipated. She found it very difficult to let go of anything once she had it in her grasp. As I know to my cost.
(JILL makes a deliberate effort to change the mood.)
Have I introduced you to Maurice, ladies and gentlemen? He's the musical director around here. He's the God figure if you like. We don't see him but we know he's there. He's not very active in our affairs and occasionally we even doubt his existence. But we'll hear an uncalled-for trumpet blast now and then, or a waltz in march time. Some minor disaster. Our creator saying hello.

He's a very talented man of course. Not musically, although I don't suppose you need me to tell you that. His wife's just left him, apparently. He says he can't understand why: he's got fitted carpet everywhere . . . But we all have our cross to bear.

Maurice and I have been having a little contretemps during the week, haven't we, darling? *(To the audience)* A contretemps? Don't you know what that is? It's a difference of opinion. A tiff. A disagreement. A bloody great row. Maurice has been a pain in the arse since the day I got here. No wonder your wife left you, Maurice. No wonder she went off with the binman, or the coalman, or whoever it was. No wonder she got out from under before you bored her to death. Living with Maurice, audience, must be about as exciting as watching an iceberg melt . . . No, well, maybe not as exciting as that. But similar.

I'm not joking, audience. I caught rigor mortis off Maurice earlier in the week. Well, that was what the doctor said it was . . . I was surprised too. Because I thought that was a sexually-transmitted disease. I mean, I got it off each of my husbands, not to mention one or two others. But there you go. We live and learn.

I doubt if you could get anything transmitted off Maurice. Not even if you plugged him into the mains and threw a bucket of water over him. Some people are simply inert. They don't actually do anything. I've been waiting for Maurice to show himself all week. I've been at this club six nights now, during which time he's had ample opportunity to take hold of his baton and demonstrate his prowess. Or, alternatively, he could've conducted the band. I'd've enjoyed either. Up to fairly recently I'd've enjoyed both. But I'm at a difficult age now. Aren't we all?

You come to a point in life where people don't look at you the same way any more. Men digging ditches don't whistle. A wolf cub offered to carry my bag the other day. I nearly hit him . . . I tell jokes about the war, but sometimes I wonder if people know which war I'm talking about. I thought there was only one, really. And it was a good laugh, wasn't it? I could tell you a joke about the war if it's not too old-fashioned. If it's not beneath you. Takes place in the middle of the blitz. Shells exploding all over. One old man was very slow to get out of the house and into the air raid shelter—Oh, you could change that to nuclear shelter and tell this joke in thirty years time. 'Come on, Grandad,' someone shouted. 'Hurry up.' 'I can't,' he yelled. 'I can't find my teeth.' 'Oh, bugger your teeth,' the other feller shouted back. 'They're dropping bombs, not sandwiches.'

I know it's not hysterical, but it's OK. It's the sort of thing they laughed at years ago. And there's nothing wrong with that. We all stand on the shoulders of previous generations. I know that's been said before, as well, but that doesn't make it untrue. Far from it. I can't go on writing new jokes. I could do it once. I did it for years. All that must count for something. For God's sake, I am fifty-two. I'm not exactly a babe in arms. Can't you give my past some credit? I was slim once. I had a good figure. A figure like a nigger, only bigger. But you can't say that any more. A figure like Trigger only bigger . . . Trigger's a horse. A bloody horse. You remember Roy Rogers, don't you? And Gene Autrey? She had a nice voice . . . Well, I know they're all past it now, but what difference does that make? Some people never get up to it.

If you don't want to laugh, don't. I can take it. I've had knocks before. Life hasn't been that easy. What d'ye think it was like when I had those babies? David was first. Out like a shot. And then the after-birth. No problem. It's fashionable to eat that nowadays, you know. Placenta and chips. Very tasty. They do it at the Chinese up the road. Ask for number 36 . . . I thought that was it. I thought it was over. 'And again,' they said. 'What?' I said. 'There's more?' 'Oh, yes,' they said. 'There's another.' 'Oh, God,' I said. 'Isn't one enough? Can't you just plaster over the crack?' . . . But out she came, fists clenched, screaming and crying, bringing God knows what with her. What a performance. What a performance. . . .

(JILL *now makes an attempt to fight off the mood she has got herself into.*)

Oh, God, Maurice, do something, will you? Play me that song. *(To the audience)* It's one about bananas. It seems appropriate somehow, I don't know. I used to sing it years ago. Come on, Maurice, it's in 4/4 time. One, two, three—

(JILL *sings, with music:*)[1]

    Standing by the fruit stall on the corner
    Once I heard a customer complain
    You never seem to show
    The fruit we all love so
    That's why business hasn't been the same.

    I don't like your peaches
    They are full of stones
    I like bananas
    Because they have no bones.

    Don't give me tomatoes
    Can't stand ice cream cones
    I like bananas
    Because they have no bones.

    No matter where I go
    With Susie, May or Anna,
    I want the world to know
    I must have my banana.

    Cabbages and onions
    Hurt my singing tones
    I like bananas
    Because they have no bones.
    I like bananas because they have no bones.

(JILL *speaks again*)

Great wasn't it . . . I know I got a bit over-emotional before, ladies and gentlemen. You'll have to forgive me. It's been that sort of a day. One thing after another.

But it's all good experience. You can't be up if you're never down. D'ye know the one thing in the world I wouldn't do? Ever. No matter what. Cycle round Holland. . . . The rest of Europe's OK. In fact we've got family connections there through my Father. His legs are in France.

---

[1]'I Like Bananas (Because They Have No Bones)' is published by Chappell Music Ltd.

                                               OLD AGE

Just his legs. The rest of him's over here . . . He lost his legs in the war. . . . I know a joke about losing your legs. It's very funny. An Irish feller—well, he mightn't've been Irish—stepped on a bomb. 'Paddy, Paddy,' he shouted to his mate, 'I've lost my legs.' 'No you haven't,' he said, 'they're over there.' Anyway, my old feller lost his. They were blown off. It was the First World War. Lots of people had legs blown off. The best you can say about it is no one lost more than two.

It made a difference, though. But not to me because I never knew him any other way. He was three feet two inches tall. Except one day when he fell out of his wheelchair. Then he was three feet two inches long. You've got to laugh, haven't you?

People used to talk to him in a loud voice as if he was deaf. As though when his legs had come away from his body, they'd stuffed themselves down his ears. For some reason. I drew a picture of him once like that, with big legs sticking out the sides of his head. My mother went mad, but he saw the joke. He was a comic . . . I used to lie awake at night and wonder where his legs had gone. I used to visualize them stuck in a tree, or maybe one fell down somebody's chimney. I could conceive of a *fermier*[2] in northern France coming across them one day in a field of turnips. As they must.

(She acts out picking up a leg.)

Oh, mais, qu'est-ce que c'est? . . . It's amazing the things you leave behind you. They'll be dug up eventually by archaeologists. He'll probably be pieced together in millenniums to come. Or is it millennia?

(Pause.)

Oh, God, this is depressing, isn't it? . . . I'm sorry, ladies and gentlemen. I don't know what's the matter with me tonight. . . . Maurice, have you got that other song? The one Vera used to sing? . . . Yes, Vera. Vera Lynn.

(JILL sings without waiting for the music.)

> Send for the midwife, Mary,
> Something in my belly's gone pop.

(JILL speaks again.)

Yes, Vera sang that. Don't you remember? Only she used to sing it and bang a big bass drum at the same time.

(JILL sings again and bangs a bass drum.)

> Send for the midwife, bang
> Something in my belly's gone bang.

(JILL speaks.)

She won't crack on about it now, but that's what she did. And what's wrong with it? If that's what you have to do to get yourself noticed, then that's what you have to do . . . It's nothing compared with what I've done . . . What did you do in the war, Mummy? Well, I wasn't in the Resistance. I'll tell you that for nothing.

I thought men grew on trees. I really did. There's never been a time in my life when I couldn't pluck someone off at will. Never. Till now. Till just recently . . . ah, sod the lot of them. They're not worth it.

(Pause.)

You know when people hang themselves, what do they do first? Do they put the rope around their neck, or do they attach it to the hook, or what-

---

[2]Farmer.

ever, that's going to take their weight? And then put it around? They've got to secure it to something as well, haven't they? . . . They must put it round their neck last—next to last—because otherwise they'd have too much. They'd just stand there looking foolish.

(Pause.)

I watched a peasant woman skin a rabbit once. It was hanging upside down in her farmyard. She scooped its eyes out first. Kind of scraped them out with a knife. Then she skinned it. Very clean. Not a drop of blood. A kind of quiet dignity. A skilful art. It's amazing how small a rabbit's head looks with its fur off and no ears. It was a fascinating performance. It was dextrous, and solemn. Almost hypnotic. Of course, she must've got it in the jugular first.

I think it's better if you don't remember it, that blow. That one that really hurts. Just get over it quick and go on to something else. Another town. Another audience . . . What d'ye think they give you anaesthetics for in hospital? If they wanted you to enjoy pain, they'd never put you to sleep. You come out of your operation and it's gone, whatever it was that was bothering you. They've cut it out. It's in the bin. They'll burn it for you. You don't even have to do it yourself. They'll take it away and you'll forget about it. Nothing'll ever be that bad again. The worst they can do to you is over. You can't lose three legs. You can't . . . Not unless you're Manx.

(Pause.)

There was a man once called Raymond. That's not much of a name. This man used to tell me things and quite honestly, although I don't like to admit it, I believed him. I bloody well believed him. This man told me things that I wanted to hear. I used to think about this man while I was doing other, and as it turned out, more useful things. Like blowing my nose. I thought about Raymond for a whole afternoon once while I grouted some tiles in the bathroom. These were tiles behind the bath that reached up to the ceiling. I could've paid someone to do them, but I was feeling creative and it allowed me to indulge my mind with dreams of him. I was not a young woman at the time. I can never look at bathroom fitments now without thinking of him. He's wash-basins, he's plugs, he's bidets. He's wormed his way into every item of sanitary ware that I can conceive of. I see him in bathcubes and tooth mugs and loofahs. He hangs over my towel rail and dangles on a chain between my taps. When I pull back the curtain of my shower I will find him there, waiting, lurking, ready to surprise me. About to pounce. To deal me a death blow.

If I let him. If I don't deal him one first. Of course, in reality, I can't deal him one now because . . . well, because . . .

There was always something strange about Raymond. He smiled involuntarily. He had a nervous tic. It endeared him to me. He wasn't all there. I mean he had doubts . . . I've been doing this for thirty-five years . . .

I think the whole of existence is an accessory. There's something else that we all clip on to. But try as I might I can't figure out what it is. Or where it is. Or who's got it. Or what they're doing with it. Or why . . . I never could.

(Pause. JILL looks around the stage, confused. As an elderly person might.)

I don't know where to go. I want to get off the stage now, Maurice. I want to go home. Can you show me the way, please? . . . Maurice . . .

(JILL *remembers where she is but is still not in full control.*)

I'm sorry, ladies and gentlemen . . . this isn't typical . . . it's not normal . . . I can always ad lib. I've never forgotten my lines before. I've always had a joke ready. Anyone'll tell you that.

Oh God. My father used to tell a joke about the docks. It was the new bloke on the docks asking the foreman where the urinal was. 'I don't know,' he said. 'How many funnels has she got?'

You need to understand that that joke's years old because they don't have funnels any more. Not like they used to. And the docks are closing down. But it was a good joke once, wasn't it? You can appreciate that, even now . . . it was a good joke for a man with no legs. If he'd lost anything else he might've been wittier. I don't know . . . you never know.

Oh God. He took out his knife and cut up a back street . . . We used to have one but the wheel fell off . . . A woman went into a shop and asked the feller, 'Do you have asparagus tips?' 'No, we don't,' he said, 'Only Woodbines and Embassy Regal' . . . 'May I join you?' a man asked me one time. 'Why?' I said. 'Am I coming apart?' . . . Halitosis is better than no breath at all . . . Just because you're paranoid, it doesn't mean everyone isn't out to get you . . . Some people still understand all this. God be with the days when the boys went in one door and the girls went in the other.

I was brought up by people years older than me. My roots are in the nineteenth century.

Oh God . . . I want a song, Maurice. You've been a wonderful audience, audience. You really have. I won't forget you . . . and I had nothing else planned for tonight. Did you? . . .

Come on, Maurice. All comedians finish on a song. They should finish on a joke, but they don't. That's why they're comedians. They've got things arseways. They're in the wrong setting . . . Oh God.

(*Pause.* MAURICE *starts the music to get* JILL *off.* JILL *sings, but shakily at first:*)[3]

Though plans may often go wrong
Let'em hear your voice.
You'll find that rhythm and song
Make the world rejoice.
Make life go with a swing.
Laugh at trouble and sing.
Tra la la la la la la lal
Count your blessings and smile.

While you're playing your part
Keep a song in your heart
Tra la la la la la la lal
Count your blessings and smile.

Sing low, sing high
Isn't it grand, beating the band?
Who wants to die?

---

[3]'Count Your Blessings and Smile' is published by Campbell Connelly and Co. Ltd.

Oh what a happy land, hie!
Show them what you can do
Make a hullabaloo
Tra la la la la la la lal
Count your blessings and smile.

You've got to get together, swing it around.
Get together swing it around.

Make life go with a swing and a smile
Laugh at trouble and sing all the while
Now count your blessings and smile.
While you're playing your own little part
You've got to keep a song in your heart
Now count your blessings and smile.

(JILL *has difficulty here.*)

Sing low, sing high
Isn't it grand, beating the band?
Who wants to die?
Oh what a happy land, hie!
Show them what you can do
Make a hullabaloo
Hoo hoo hoo hoo ha ha ha ha
Count your blessings one two three
Count your blessings four five six
Count your blessings and smile.

(JILL *speaks.*)
Goodnight, ladies and gentlemen. Goodnight.
(JILL *bows and makes a theatrical exit but with a lack of confidence remaining.*)

THE END

[1984]

For Discussion

1. How much of Jeffers' monologue is taken up with making fun of herself? What do people find laughable about growing old? Can we laugh and still be sympathetic?

2. How much of the monologue makes fun of others? What people or groups does she satirize? Discuss which type of humor is most effective—self-mockery or lampooning others.

3. Analyze the comments about parts of a woman's body and why female parts are often "butts" of humor. What stereotypes about women are evident?

4. What do we find out about Jeffers' husbands? How does the joke about the "henpecked husband" continue the stereotyping?

5. Examine the comments about Jill's children. Does she love them or is she a "bad mother"?

6. Before her act, Jeffers' daughter Miriam had told her that Raymond (loved first by the mother, then by the daughter) had committed suicide. What might this have to do with the comments about Raymond in Act II and the overall tone?

7. Explain the function of the little "ditties" Jeffers sings, and how the words to the songs apply to the rest of the act.

8. What can you extrapolate from the ending about Jeffers' future?

For Further Exploration

1. In the section on Death, Mary Wilkins Freeman's "A Village Singer" describes a woman's last musical performances after her church members try to force her to retire. What many traits do these women have in common that we should applaud?

2. Tina Howe's play *Painting Churches* also deals with an artist's relationship with her family. Compare how humor is used in the two plays to cope with issues of work, family, and the woman's stage in life.

For Discussion or Writing About This Section

1. How important are physical qualities mentioned about women in this section, and how do the comments compare with physical descriptions of women in the adolescent and adulthood sections?

2. What are the various types of escape in these works on aging, and how are they the same or different from escapism in earlier life stages?

3. Which of the characters could be described as tragic heroines? Which authors infuse comedy or satire into literature about aging?

4. What does each character's relationship to men, children, and other women show about her personality? Are these attitudes stereotyped or realistic?

5. Miss Brill was contented until her rude awakening, and Mrs. Montague enjoys her fantasy "Island." Is ignorance bliss or do the stories advocate awareness for women?

6. Which of these women are one-dimensional portraits, and which have multifaceted personalities? Is it possible, in a short poem or story, to create depth of character?

7. What effect does the stylistic point of view (first person, third person, or omniscient) have on each story or poem? How would the impact of the work change with a change in point of view?

8. Are religious images and themes used more extensively in literature about aging and death than in works about earlier life stages? Is the connection often drawn between female characters and religion also drawn in works about male characters?

9. How is the archetypal motif of seasonal change used in these stories and poems? Do any of the authors simply repeat a hackneyed image, or are the seasons integral to the action and meaning of all of the works?

10. How does Act II of *Not Waving* repeat the major concerns of women considered old?

DEATH

Fear and denial; the life review; resolving old conflicts; attention to "self"; rejection or acceptance of society; religious faith and doubt; final acts

Death is an act—more often a process—one can only complete alone. Perhaps the most pervasive feeling conveyed in literature about death is the overwhelming sense of isolation of the protagonist, whether she has family or friends around her, and whether she sees death as friend or foe. The surprising magnitude of the atmosphere of isolation is evident in stories such as these, in which women spend their last days supposedly surrounded by loved ones, but actually feeling alienated from other living beings.

The private act of dying becomes even lonelier because most of the living people surrounding the main character are denying death—saying "it can't be happening to you" when they really mean "it is not going to happen to me." Even those who recognize their own mortality in the deaths of others can only state the universal truth as a kind of philosophical exercise. There is the sense that belief in our own mortality is a perfunctory admission from which our natural inclination is to escape. When a dying woman in one story finds something she has in common with a young woman, she realizes that "that's the wrong thing to say. So much distance lies between us, she doesn't want any such similarity."

In "So Many Have Died," the ninety-one year old woman talking on the telephone to her relatives is thinking that the significant people in her life are now dead and that she is alone. Even more bereft is the well-known "Granny Weatherall" in Katherine Anne Porter's story, who despairs of finding ultimate meaning in life, despite the fact that she has survived a number of life stages on her own.

While some of the secondary characters admit—however grudgingly—the ever-present certainty of death, others are indifferent to the plight of old women dying, and some give in to the feeling that the death of another is for the most part an inconvenience to oneself. In each of the stories about death, there is at least one person who seems callous to the needs of the dying woman. One character, Alma Way, says that she can't help feeling guilty that she is taking the older woman's place at work. Is she embarrassed to be young and alive while others are old and dying, or is she afraid to follow in the woman's footsteps? Like Alma Way, we are all "on our way" to taking the places of the old and dying, and we do so with regret.

385

The natural reluctance to face death—our own or another's—is the first step in the five death stages described by researcher Elisabeth Kübler-Ross. The first three steps—denial ("no, not me"), anger ("why me?"), then bargaining ("not yet!")—can be traced in fictional accounts of dying. Denial and anger are evident in all of the stories here, and some of the "bargaining" is actually externalized into a kind of combat between characters. Almost all of the dying characters try to "work a trade." The "Village Singer" is unsatisfied with the bargain foisted on her (a scrapbook in return for her withdrawal from life) and negotiates a better trade (a house for human consideration in the form of a hymn). Granny Weatherall offers up her life of hard work and rejection for a final sign of acceptance, and the aging doctor in "So Many Have Died" gives her life in an attempt to be of further use to someone before she dies.

According to Kübler-Ross' model, after bargaining comes depression, then acceptance. However, these emotions are more evident throughout the stories than at the end. In fact, in fictional accounts the women usually fight death, rather than accepting it. Despite their old age, some of the women seem to be surprised by death and do not reach the final stage of acceptance.

Few stories and poems show death as a peaceful process. The epigraph Margaret Laurence chose for *Stone Angel* (Dylan Thomas' "Do Not Go Gentle into That Good Night") could introduce the entire section, urging us to "Rage, rage against the dying of the light." With the exception of Dickinson's famous portrayal of a carriage ride with death, there is very little acquiescence in these works. For the most part, the poets acknowledge death's power without succumbing to its self-abnegating influence.

While literary versions of the death moment may depart somewhat from true-life accounts, the emotional conflicts described in the stories and poems do parallel psychologists' findings. People dying are often lonely, afraid, sad, and in pain. They suffer not only from bodily ailments, but also from feelings of loss of self-identity. The powerlessness these women feel is evident throughout literature and life. They have little power over their bodies, which often betray them, and little control over their powers of communication, which fade in and out. Memory rather than present reality takes over fitfully, and the women often find themselves to be speaking out inappropriately.

The "life review" process reflected in the shifts between past and present is obviously important to the dying women, and each protagonist reviews her life to some extent. Studies confirm that communication becomes extremely important as death approaches, and that most dying people want to know about and discuss their own impending deaths.

The communication between characters in the stories often takes the form of "speaking one's mind," since there is a tendency among the very old, as among the very young, to disdain hypocrisy. The women are independent of mind and speech even when no longer able to be physically independent. The assertion of selfhood by speaking directly is paradoxically an attempt to finally get close to others, while at the same time effectively breaking away. By breaking down artificial barriers of politeness, the women often alienate family members struggling to maintain the veneer of civility in the face of the frightening reality of death.

Often the image of leaving exemplifies the separation of the dying woman from others. One woman has run away from home, the village singer has "revolted" and sung her own song above the music of an entire chorus, another woman refuses help in drinking her last glass of water, and Dickinson's narrator rides off alone with death, leaving other people behind.

The independence of these women who separate themselves from others is a bane as well as a blessing, and their final acts are studies in how they lived as well as how they die. The process of death can lead to knowledge and peace, or resentment and despair. In either case, our respect for these women grows as we recognize in each the determination to maintain personal identity in the face of old age and death.

Fiction About Death

Old age has been compared with adolescence, and the stage of dying with childhood. While the analogies may seem puerile or even offensive in that they could imply senility rather than sagacity in old age, both a physical and psychological parallel can be drawn between the transitions experienced in old age and those experienced in adolescence. Specifically, the often unwanted dependency of age can be compared with the similar state in adolescence. Further, childhood's assertive honesty may be laudably compared with the forthrightness displayed by dying women in these stories.

Yet, as forceful as many of these women are as they approach death, in each story there seems to be some element missing in the final moments. None appears to be satisfied with either her previous life or with the prospects of life to come. They are "stone angels" in several senses, justifiably unwilling to sprout wings and take off. There is the strong sense throughout that life has denied them an important role and that, in refusing to give up, they have wrenched an additional personal recognition from life.

The archaic question, "What do women want?" is answered by these stories; the women want to be appreciated and loved for themselves, not for the services they have rendered others. They want their voices to be heard until the very last, raised in a song or subdued in a sigh. They want to be seen as unique individuals, not a combination of genetic material that led them through puberty, perhaps pregnancy, menopause, and deteriorating health. In death, we see many regrets; but there is also the final triumph of recognition—whether positive or negative—that these women experience.

Mary Wilkins Freeman

1852–1930

Rebelling against forced retirement, Candace Whitcomb asserts her right to live until she dies. In doing so, she brings to light the hypocrisy of the church and community of which she has been a part. By forgiving them, she can accept death peacefully.

A VILLAGE SINGER

The trees were in full leaf, a heavy south wind was blowing, and there was a loud murmur among the new leaves. The people noticed it, for it was the first time that year that the trees had so murmured in the wind. The spring had come with a rush during the last few days.

The murmur of the trees sounded loud in the village church, where the people sat waiting for the service to begin. The windows were open; it was a very warm Sunday for May.

The church was already filled with this soft sylvan music—the tender harmony of the leaves and the south wind, and the sweet, desultory whistles of birds—when the choir arose and began to sing.

In the centre of the row of women singers stood Alma Way. All the people stared at her, and turned their ears critically. She was the new leading soprano. Candace Whitcomb, the old one, who had sung in the choir for forty years, had lately been given her dismissal. The audience considered that her voice had grown too cracked and uncertain on the upper notes. There had been much complaint, and after long deliberation the church-officers had made known their decision as mildly as possible to the old singer. She had sung for the last time the Sunday before, and Alma Way had been engaged to take her place. With the exception of the organist, the leading soprano was the only paid musician in the large choir. The salary was very modest, still the village people considered it large for a young woman. Alma was from the adjoining village of East Derby; she had quite a local reputation as a singer.

Now she fixed her large solemn blue eyes; her long, delicate face, which had been pretty, turned paler; the blue flowers on her bonnet trembled; her little thin gloved hands, clutching the singing-book, shook perceptibly; but she sang out bravely. That most formidable mountain-height of the world, self-distrust and timidity, arose before her, but her nerves were braced for its ascent. In the midst of the hymn she had a solo; her voice rang out piercingly sweet; the people nodded admiringly at each other; but suddenly there was a stir; all the faces turned toward the windows on the south side of the church. Above the din of the wind and the birds, above Alma Way's sweetly straining tones, arose another female voice, singing another hymn to another tune.

"It's her," the women whispered to each other; they were half aghast, half smiling.

Candace Whitcomb's cottage stood close to the south side of the church. She was playing on her parlor organ, and singing, to drown out the voice of her rival.

Alma caught her breath; she had almost stopped; the hymn-book waved like a fan; then she went on. But the long husky drone of the parlor organ and the shrill clamor of the other voice seemed louder than anything else.

When the hymn was finished, Alma sat down. She felt faint; the woman next to her slipped a peppermint into her hand. "It ain't worth minding," she whispered, vigorously. Alma tried to smile; down in the audience a young man was watching her with a kind of fierce pity.

In the last hymn Alma had another solo. Again the parlor organ droned above the carefully delicate accompaniment of the church organ, and again Candace Whitcomb's voice clamored forth in another tune.

After the benediction, the other singers pressed around Alma. She did not say much in return for their expressions of indignation and sympathy. She wiped her eyes furtively once or twice, and tried to smile. William Emmons, the choir leader, elderly, stout, and smooth-faced, stood over her, and raised his voice. He was the old musical dignitary of the village, the leader of the choral club and the singing-schools. "A most outrageous proceeding," he said. People had coupled his name with Candace Whitcomb's. The old bachelor tenor and old maiden soprano had been wont to walk together to her home next door after the Saturday night rehearsals, and they had sung duets to the parlor organ. People had watched sharply her old face, on which the blushes of youth sat pitifully, when William Emmons entered the singing-seats. They wondered if he would ever ask her to marry him.

And now he said further to Alma Way that Candace Whitcomb's voice had failed utterly of late, that she sang shockingly, and ought to have had sense enough to know it.

When Alma went down into the audience-room, in the midst of the chattering singers, who seemed to have descended, like birds, from song flights to chirps, the minister approached her. He had been waiting to speak to her. He was a steady-faced, fleshy old man, who had preached from that one pulpit over forty years. He told Alma, in his slow way, how much he regretted the annoyance to which she had been subjected, and intimated that he would endeavor to prevent a recurrence of it. "Miss Whitcomb—must be—reasoned with," said he: he had a slight hesitation of speech, not an impediment. It was as if his thoughts did not slide readily into his words, although both were present. He walked down the aisle with Alma, and bade her good-morning when he saw Wilson Ford waiting for her in the doorway. Everybody knew that Wilson Ford and Alma were lovers; they had been for the last ten years.

Alma colored softly, and made a little imperceptible motion with her head; her silk dress and the lace on her mantle fluttered, but she did not speak. Neither did Wilson, although they had not met before that day. They did not look at each other's faces—they seemed to see each other without that—and they walked along side to side.

They reached the gate before Candace Whitcomb's little house. Wilson looked past the front yard, full of pink and white spikes on flowering bushes, at the lace-curtained windows; a thin white profile, stiffly inclined, apparently over a book, was visible at one of them. Wilson gave his head a shake. He was a stout man, with features so strong that they overcame his flesh. "I'm going up home with you, Alma," said he; "and then—I'm coming back, to give Aunt Candace one blowing up."

"Oh, don't, Wilson."

"Yes, I shall. If you want to stand this kind of a thing you may; I sha'n't."

"There's no need of your talking to her. Mr. Pollard's going to."

"Did he say he was?"

"Yes. I think he's going in before the afternoon meeting, from what he said."

"Well, there's one thing about it, if she does that thing again this afternoon, I'll go in there and break that old organ up into kindling-wood." Wilson set his mouth hard, and shook his head again.

Alma gave little side glances up at him, her tone was deprecatory, but her face was full of soft smiles. "I suppose she does feel dreadfully about it," said she. "I can't help feeling kind of guilty, taking her place."

"I don't see how you're to blame. It's outrageous, her acting so."

"The choir gave her a photograph album last week, didn't they?"

"Yes. They went there last Thursday night, and gave her an album and a surprise-party. She ought to behave herself."

"Well, she's sung there so long, I suppose it must be dreadful hard for her to give it up."

Other people going home from church were very near Wilson and Alma. She spoke softly that they might not hear; he did not lower his voice in the least. Presently Alma stopped before a gate.

"What are you stopping here for?" asked Wilson.

"Minnie Lansing wanted me to come and stay with her this noon."

"You're going home with me."

"I'm afraid I'll put your mother out."

"Put mother out! I told her you were coming, this morning. She's got all ready for you. Come along; don't stand here."

He did not tell Alma of the pugnacious spirit with which his mother had received the announcement of her coming, and how she had stayed at home to prepare the dinner, and make a parade of her hard work and her injury.

Wilson's mother was the reason why he did not marry Alma. He would not take his wife home to live with her, and was unable to support separate establishments. Alma was willing enough to be married and put up with Wilson's mother, but she did not complain of his decision. Her delicate blond features grew sharper, and her blue eyes more hollow. She had had a certain fine prettiness, but now she was losing it, and beginning to look old, and there was a prim, angular, old maiden carriage about her narrow shoulders.

Wilson never noticed it, and never thought of Alma as not possessed of eternal youth, or capable of losing or regretting it.

"Come along, Alma," said he; and she followed meekly after him down the street.

Soon after they passed Candace Whitcomb's house, the minister went up the front walk and rang the bell. The pale profile at the window had never stirred as he opened the gate and came up the walk. However, the door was promptly opened, in response to his ring. "Good-morning, Miss Whitcomb," said the minister.

"*Good*-morning." Candace gave a sweeping toss of her head as she spoke. There was a fierce upward curl to her thin nostrils and her lips, as if she scented an adversary. Her black eyes had two tiny cold sparks of fury in them, like an enraged bird's. She did not ask the minister to enter, but he stepped lumberingly into the entry, and she retreated rather than led the way into her little parlor. He settled into the great rocking-chair and wiped his face. Candace sat down again in her old place by the window. She was a tall woman, but very slender and full of pliable motions, like a blade of grass.

"It's a—very pleasant day," said the minister.

Candace made no reply. She sat still, with her head drooping. The wind stirred the looped lace-curtains; a tall rose-tree outside the window waved; soft shadows floated through the room. Candace's parlor organ stood in front of an open window that faced the church; on the corner was a pitcher with a bunch of white lilacs. The whole room was scented with them. Presently the minister looked over at them and sniffed pleasantly.

"You have—some beautiful—lilacs there."

Candace did not speak. Every line of her slender figure looked flexible, but it was a flexibility more resistant than rigor.

The minister looked at her. He filled up the great rocking-chair; his arms in his shiny black coat-sleeves rested squarely and comfortably upon the hair-cloth arms of the chair.

"Well, Miss Whitcomb, I suppose I—may as well come to—the point. There was—a little—matter I wished to speak to you about. I don't suppose you were—at least I can't suppose you were—aware of it, but—this morning, during the singing by the choir, you played and—sung a little too—loud. That is, with—the windows open. It—disturbed us—a little. I hope you won't feel hurt—my dear Miss Candace, but I knew you would rather I would speak of it, for I knew—you would be more disturbed than anybody else at the idea of such a thing."

Candace did not raise her eyes; she looked as if his words might sway her through the window. "I ain't disturbed at it," said she. "I did it on purpose; I meant to."

The minister looked at her.

"You needn't look at me. I know jest what I'm about. I sung the way I did on purpose, an' I'm goin' to do it again, an' I'd like to see you stop me. I guess I've got a right to set down to my own organ, an' sing a psalm tune on a Sabbath day, 'f I want to; an' there ain't no amount of talkin' an' palaverin' a-goin' to stop me. See there!" Candace swung aside her skirts a little. "Look at that!"

The minister looked. Candace's feet were resting on a large red-plush photograph album.

"Makes a nice footstool, don't it?" said she.

The minister looked at the album, then at her; there was a slowly gathering alarm in his face; he began to think she was losing her reason.

Candace had her eyes full upon him now, and her head up. She laughed, and her laugh was almost a snarl. "Yes; I thought it would make a beautiful footstool," said she. "I've been wantin' one for some time." Her tone was full of vicious irony.

"Why, miss—" began the minister; but she interrupted him:

"I know what you're a-goin' to say, Mr. Pollard, an' now I'm goin' to have my say: I'm a-goin' to speak. I want to know what you think of folks that pretend to be Christians treatin' anybody the way they've treated me? Here I've sung in those singin'-seats forty year. I ain't never missed a Sunday, except when I've been sick, an' I've gone an' sung a good many times when I'd better been in bed, an' now I'm turned out without a word of warnin'. My voice is jest as good as ever 'twas: there can't anybody say it ain't. It wa'n't ever quite so high-pitched as that Way girl's, mebbe; but she flats the whole durin' time. My voice is as good an' high today as it was twenty years ago; an' if it wa'n't, I'd like to know where the Christianity comes in. I'd like to know if it wouldn't be more to the credit of folks in a church to keep an old singer an' an old minister, if they didn't sing an' hold forth quite so smart as they used to, ruther than turn 'em off an' hurt their feelin's. I guess it would be full as much to the glory of God. S'pose the singin' an' the preachin' wa'n't quite so

DEATH

good, what difference would it make? Salvation don't hang on anybody's hittin' a high note, that I ever heard of. Folks are gettin' as high-steppin' an' fussy in a meetin'-house as they are in a tavern, nowadays. S'pose they should turn you off, Mr. Pollard, come an' give you a photograph album, an' tell you to clear out, how'd you like it? I ain't findin' any fault with your preachin'; it was always good enough to suit me; but it don't stand to reason folks'll be as took up with your sermons as when you was a young man. You can't expect it. S'pose they should turn you out in your old age, an' call in some young bob squirt, how'd you feel? There's William Emmons, too; he's three years older'n I am, if he does lead the choir an' run all the singin' in town. If my voice has gi'en out, it stan's to reason his has. It ain't, though. William Emmons sings jest as well as he ever did. Why don't they turn him out the way they have me, an' give him a photograph album? I dun know but it would be a good idea to send everybody, as soon as they get a little old an' gone by, an' young folks begin to push, onto some desert island, an' giv 'em each a photograph album. Then they can sit down an' look at pictures the rest of their days. Mebbe government'll take it up.

"There they come here last week Thursday, all the choir, jest about eight o'clock in the evenin', an' pretended they'd come to give me a nice little surprise. Surprise! h'm! Brought cake an' oranges, an' was jest as nice as they could be, an' I was real tickled. I never had a surprise-party before in my life. Jenny Carr she played, an' they wanted me to sing alone, an' I never suspected a thing. I've been mad ever since to think what a fool I was, an' how they must have laughed in their sleeves.

"When they'd gone I found this photograph album on the table, all done up as nice as you please, an' directed to Miss Candace Whitcomb from her many friends, an' I opened it, an' there was the letter inside givin' me notice to quit.

"If they'd gone about it any decent way, told me right out honest that they'd got tired of me, an' wanted Alma Way to sing instead of me, I wouldn't minded so much; I should have been hurt 'nough, for I'd felt as if some that had pretended to be my friends wa'n't; but it wouldn't have been as bad as this. They said in the letter that they'd always set great value on my services, an' it wa'n't from any lack of appreciation that they turned me off, but they thought the duty was gettin' a little too arduous for me. H'm! I hadn't complained. If they'd turned me right out fair an' square, showed me the door, an' said, 'Here, you get out,' but to go an' spill molasses, as it were, all over the threshold, tryin' to make me think it's all nice an' sweet—

"I'd sent that photograph album back quick's I could pack it, but I didn't know who started it, so I've used it for a footstool. It's all it's good for, 'cordin' to my way of thinkin'. An' I ain't been particular to get the dust off my shoes before I used it neither."

Mr. Pollard, the minister, sat staring. He did not look at Candace; his eyes were fastened upon a point straight ahead. He had a look of helpless solidity, like a block of granite. This country minister, with his steady, even temperament, treading with heavy precision his one track for over forty years, having nothing new in his life except the new sameness of the seasons, and desiring nothing new, was incapable of understanding a woman like this, who had lived as quietly as he, and all the time held within herself the elements of revolution. He could not account for such violence, such extremes, except in a loss of reason. He had a conviction that Candace was getting beyond herself. He himself was not a typical New Englander; the national elements of character were not pronounced in him. He was aghast and bewildered at this outbreak, which was tropical, and more than tropical, for a New England nature has a floodgate, and the power which it releases is an accumulation. Candace Whitcomb had been a quiet woman, so delicately resolute that the quality had been scarcely noticed in her, and her ambition had been unsuspected. Now the resolution and the ambition appeared raging over her whole self.

She began to talk again. "I've made up my mind that I'm goin' to sing Sundays the way I did this mornin', an' I don't care what folks say," said she. "I've made up my mind that I'm goin' to take matters into my own hands. I'm goin' to let folks see that I ain't trod down quite flat, that there's a little rise left in me. I ain't goin' to give up beat yet a while; an' I'd like to see anybody stop me. If I ain't got a right to play a psalm tune on my organ an' sing, I'd like to know. If you don't like it, you can move the meetin'-house."

Candace had had an inborn reverence for clergymen. She had always treated Mr. Pollard with the utmost deference. Indeed, her manner toward all men had been marked by a certain delicate stiffness and dignity. Now she was talking to the old minister with the homely freedom with which she might have addressed a female gossip over the back fence. He could not say much in return. He did not feel competent to make headway against any such tide of passion; all he could do was to let it beat against him. He made a few expostulations, which increased Candace's vehemence; he expressed his regret over the whole affair, and suggested that they should kneel and ask the guidance of the Lord in the matter, that she might be led to see it all in a different light.

Candace refused flatly. "I don't see any use prayin' about it," said she. "I don't think the Lord's got much to do with it, anyhow."

It was almost time for the afternoon service when the minister left. He had missed his comfortable noontide rest, through this encounter with his revolutionary parishioner. After the minister had gone, Candace sat by the window and waited. The bell rang, and she watched the people file past. When her nephew Wilson Ford with Alma appeared, she grunted to herself. "She's thin as a rail," said she; "guess there won't be much left of her by the time Wilson gets her. Little softspoken nippin' thing, she wouldn't make him no kind of a wife, anyway. Guess it's jest as well."

When the bell had stopped tolling, and all the people entered the church, Candace went over to her organ and seated herself. She arranged a singing-book before her, and sat still, waiting. Her thin, colorless neck and temples were full of beating pulses; her black eyes were bright and eager; she leaned stiffly over toward the music-rack, to hear better. When the church organ sounded out she straightened herself; her long skinny fingers pressed her own organ-keys with nervous energy. She worked the pedals with all her strength; all her slender body was in motion. When the first notes of Alma's solo began, Candace sang. She had really possessed a fine voice, and it was wonderful how little she had lost it. Straining her throat with jealous fury, her notes were still for the main part true. Her voice filled the whole room; she sang with wonderful fire and expression. That, at least, mild little Alma Way could never emulate. She was full of steadfastness and unquestioning constancy, but there were in her no smouldering fires of ambition and resolution. Music was not to her what it had been to her older rival. To this obscure woman, kept relentlessly by circumstances in a narrow track, singing in the village choir had been as much as Italy was to Napoleon—and now on her island of exile she was still showing fight.

After the church service was done, Candace left the organ and went over to her old chair by the window. Her knees felt weak, and shook under her. She sat down, and leaned back her head. There were red spots on her cheeks. Pretty soon she heard a quick slam of her gate, and an impetuous tread on the gravelwalk. She looked up, and there was her nephew Wilson Ford hurrying up to the door. She cringed a little, then she settled herself more firmly in her chair.

Wilson came into the room with a rush. He left the door open, and the wind slammed it to after him.

"Aunt Candace, where are you?" he called out, in a loud voice.

She made no reply. He looked around fiercely, and his eyes seemed to pounce upon her.

"Look here, Aunt Candace," said he, "are you crazy?" Candace said nothing. "Aunt Candace!" She did not seem to see him. "If you don't answer me," said Wilson, "I'll just go over there and pitch that old organ out of the window!"

"Wilson Ford!" said Candace, in a voice that was almost a scream.

"Well, what say! What have you got to say for yourself, acting the way you have? I tell you what 'tis, Aunt Candace, I won't stand it."

"I'd like to see you help yourself."

"I will help myself. I'll pitch that old organ out of the window, and then I'll board up the window on that side of your house. Then we'll see."

"It ain't your house, and it won't never be."

"Who said it was my house? You're my aunt, and I've got a little look-out for the credit of the family. Aunt Candace, what are you doing this way for?"

"It don't made no odds what I'm doin' so for. I ain't bound to give my reasons to a young fellar like you, if you do act so mighty toppin'. But I'll tell you one thing, Wilson Ford, after the way you've spoke today, you sha'n't never have one cent of my money, an' you can't never marry that Way girl if you don't have it. You can't never take her home to live with your mother, an' this house would have been might nice an' convenient for you some day. Now you won't get it. I'm goin' to make another will. I'd made one, if you did but know it. Now you won't get a cent of my money, you nor your mother neither. An' I ain't goin' to live a dreadful while longer, neither. Now I wish you'd go home; I want to lay down. I'm 'bout sick."

Wilson could not get another word from his aunt. His indignation had not in the least cooled. Her threat of disinheriting him did not cow him at all; he had too much rough independence, and indeed his aunt Candace's house had always been too much of an air-castle for him to contemplate seriously. Wilson, with his burly frame and his headlong common-sense, could have little to do with air-castles, had he been hard enough to build them over graves. Still, he had not admitted that he never could marry Alma. All his hopes were based upon a rise in his own fortunes, not by some sudden convulsion, but by his own long and steady labor. Some time, he thought, he should have saved enough for the two homes.

He went out of his aunt's house still storming. She arose after the door had shut behind him, and got out into the kitchen. She thought that she would start a fire and make a cup of tea. She had not eaten anything all day. She put some kindling-wood into the stove and touched a match to it; then she went back to the sitting-room, and settled down again into the chair by the window. The fire in the kitchen-stove roared, and the light wood was soon burned out. She thought no more about it. She had not put on the tea-kettle. Her head ached, and once in a while she shivered. She sat at the window while the afternoon waned and the dusk came on. At seven o'clock the meeting bell rang again, and the people flocked by. This time she did not stir. She had shut her parlor organ. She did not need to out-sing her rival this evening; there was only congregational singing at the Sunday-night prayer-meeting.

She sat still until it was nearly time for meeting to be done; her head ached harder and harder, and she shivered more. Finally she arose. "Guess I'll go to bed," she muttered. She went about the house, bent over and shaking, to lock the doors. She stood a minute in the back door, looking over the fields to the woods. There was a red light over there. "The woods are on fire," said Candace. She watched with a dull interest the flames roll up, withering and destroying the tender green spring foliage. The air was full of smoke, although the fire was half a mile away.

Candace locked the door and went in. The trees with their delicate garlands of new leaves, with the new nests of song birds, might fall, she was in the roar of an intenser fire; the growths of all her springs and the delicate wontedness of her whole life were going down in it. Candace went to bed in her little room off the parlor, but she could not sleep. She lay awake all night. In the morning she crawled to the door and hailed a little boy who was passing. She bade him go for the doctor as quickly as he could, then to Mrs. Ford's, and ask her to come over. She held on to the door while she was talking. The boy stood staring wonderingly at her. The spring wind fanned her face. She had drawn on a dress skirt and put her shawl over her shoulders, and her gray hair was blowing over her red cheeks.

She shut the door and went back to her bed. She never arose from it again. The doctor and Mrs. Ford came and looked after her, and she lived a week. Nobody but herself thought until the very last that she would die; the doctor called her illness merely a light run of fever; she had her senses fully.

But Candace gave up at the first. "It's my last sickness," she said to Mrs. Ford that morning when she first entered; and Mrs. Ford had laughed at the notion; but the sick woman held to it. She did not seem to suffer much physical pain; she only grew weaker and weaker, but she was distressed mentally. She did not talk much, but her eyes followed everybody with an agonized expression.

On Wednesday William Emmons came to inquire for her. Candace heard him out in the parlor. She tried to raise herself on one elbow that she might listen better to his voice.

"William Emmons come in to ask how you was," Mrs. Ford said, after he was gone.

"I—heard him," replied Candace. Presently she spoke again. "Nancy," said she, "where's that photograph album?"

"On the table," replied her sister, hesitatingly.

"Mebbe—you'd better—brush it up a little."

"Well."

Sunday morning Candace wished that the minister should be asked to come in at the noon intermission. She had refused to see him before. He came and prayed with her, and she asked his forgiveness for the way she had spoken the Sunday before. "I—hadn't ought to—spoke so," said she. "I was—dreadful wrought up."

"Perhaps it was your sickness coming on," said the minister smoothingly.

Candace shook her head. "No—it wa'n't. I hope the Lord will—forgive me."

After the minister had gone, Candace still appeared unhappy. Her pitiful eyes followed her sister everywhere with the mechanical persistency of a portrait.

"What is it you want, Candace?" Mrs. Ford said at last. She had nursed her sister faithfully, but once in a while her impatience showed itself.

"Nancy!"

"What say?"

"I wish—you'd go out when—meetin's done, an'—head off Alma an' Wilson, an'—ask 'em to come in. I feel as if—I'd like to—hear her sing."

Mrs. Ford stared. "Well," said she.

The meeting was now in session. The windows were all open, for it was another warm Sunday. Candace lay listening to the music when it began, and a look of peace came over her face. Her sister had smoothed her hair back, and put on a clean cap. The white curtain in the bedroom window waved in the wind like a white sail. Candace almost felt as if she were better, but the thought of death seemed easy.

Mrs. Ford at the parlor window watched for the meeting to be out. When the people appeared, she ran down the walk and waited for Alma and Wilson. When they came she told them what Candace wanted, and they all went in together.

"Here's Alma an' Wilson, Candace," said Mrs. Ford, leading them to the bedroom door.

Candace smiled. "Come in," she said, feebly. And Alma and Wilson entered and stood beside the bed. Candace continued to look at them, the smile straining her lips.

"Wilson!"

"What is it, Aunt Candace?"

"I ain't altered that—will. You an' Alma can—come here an'—live—when I'm—gone. Your mother won't mind livin' alone. Alma can have—all—my things."

"Don't, Aunt Candace." Tears were running over Wilson's cheeks, and Alma's delicate face was all of a quiver.

"I thought—maybe—Alma 'd be willin' to—sing for me." said Candace.

"What do you want me to sing?" Alma asked, in a trembling voice.

" 'Jesus, lover of my soul.' "

Alma, standing there beside Wilson, began to sing. At first she could hardly control her voice, then she sang sweetly and clearly.

Candace lay and listened. Her face had a holy and radiant expression. When Alma stopped singing it did not disappear, but she looked up and spoke, and it was like a secondary glimpse of the old shape of a forest tree through the smoke and flame of the transfiguring fire the instant before it falls. "You flattened a little on—soul," said Candace.

[1891]

For Discussion

1. What effect does the setting—especially the season—have on the story?

2. Compare and contrast Candace Whitcomb and Alma Way. What dichotomous themes (such as youth versus age) do they represent?

3. Analyze William Emmons' role in the story. How does his relationship with Candace compare with Wilson Ford's relationship with Alma?

4. Which characters dominate others in the story, and what images are used to describe the combatants in the power struggle?

5. Summarize Candace's interpretation of Christianity. Why is her view seen as "revolutionary" to Mr. Pollard?

6. Why is the photograph album mentioned so often? What might it represent?

7. How does Candace's revolutionary act change her relationship to men? What is Wilson Ford's reaction?

8. What does the confrontation show about Wilson Ford and Candace as representative Americans (especially New Englanders, as the author hints)?

9. Why does Candace relent at the end and what do her final acts demonstrate about Christianity?

10. Explain the meaning of the last line in relation to the overall themes and characterization in the story.

For Further Exploration

1. Read another story by Mary Wilkins Freeman, such as "Old Woman Magoun" or "Gentian" to analyze the lessons ordinary townspeople growing old can learn about love and rejection.

2. Compare and contrast a younger generation's view of death with this account, or with the account in *Stone Angel* (this section), by reading Katherine Anne Porter's "The Grave," or the death of Mrs. Taylor in Maya Angelou's *I Know Why the Caged Bird Sings.*

Katherine Anne Porter

1890–1980

Like Phoenix Jackson in the old age story "A Worn Path," Granny Weatherall has worked hard and has suffered much her entire life. Jilted once at the altar, can she "weather" the final journey to the altar of death? Will she be alone again?

THE JILTING OF
GRANNY WEATHERALL

She flicked her wrist neatly out of Doctor Harry's pudgy careful fingers and pulled the sheet up to her chin. The brat ought to be in knee breeches. Doctoring around the country with spectacles on his nose! "Get along now, take your schoolbooks and go. There's nothing wrong with me."

Doctor Harry spread a warm paw like a cushion on her forehead where the forked green vein danced and made her eyelids twitch. "Now, now, be a good girl, and we'll have you up in no time."

"That's no way to speak to a woman nearly eighty years old just because she's down. I'd have you respect your elders, young man."

"Well, Missy, excuse me." Doctor Harry patted her cheek. "But I've got to warn you, haven't I? You're a marvel, but you must be careful or you're going to be good and sorry."

"Don't tell me what I'm going to be. I'm on my feet now, morally speaking. It's Cornelia. I had to go to bed to get rid of her."

Her bones felt loose, and floated around in her skin, and Doctor Harry floated like a balloon around the foot of the bed. He floated and pulled down his waistcoat and swung his glasses on a cord. "Well, stay where you are, it certainly can't hurt you."

"Get along and doctor your sick," said Granny Weatherall. "Leave a well woman alone. I'll call for you when I want you. . . . Where were you forty years ago when I pulled through milk-leg and double pneumonia? You weren't even born. Don't let Cornelia lead you on," she shouted, because Doctor Harry appeared to float up to the ceiling and out. "I pay my own bills, and I don't throw my money away on nonsense!"

She meant to wave good-by, but it was too much trouble. Her eyes closed of themselves, it was like a dark curtain drawn around the bed. The pillow rose and floated under her, pleasant as a hammock in a light wind. She listened to the leaves rustling outside the window. No, somebody was swishing newspapers; no, Cornelia and Doctor Harry were whispering together. She leaped broad awake, thinking they whispered in her ear.

"She was never like this, *never* like this!" "Well, what can we expect?" "Yes, eighty years old. . . ."

Well, and what if she was? She still had ears. It was like Cornelia to whisper around doors. She always kept things secret in such a public way. She was always being tactful and kind. Cornelia was dutiful; that was the trouble with her. Dutiful and good: "So good and dutiful," said Granny, "that I'd like to spank her." She saw herself spanking Cornelia and making a fine job of it.

"What'd you say, Mother?"

Granny felt her face tying up in hard knots.

"Can't a body think, I'd like to know?"

"I thought you might want something."

"I do. I want a lot of things. First off, go away and don't whisper."

She lay and drowsed, hoping in her sleep that the children would keep out and let her rest a minute. It had been a long day. Not that she was tired. It was always pleasant to snatch a minute now and then. There was always so much to be done, let me see: tomorrow.

Tomorrow was far away and there was nothing to trouble about. Things were finished somehow when the time came; thank God there was always a little margin over for peace: Then a person could spread out the plan of life and tuck in the edges orderly. It was good to have everything clean and folded away, with the hair brushes and tonic bottles sitting straight on the white embroidered linen: the day started without fuss and the pantry shelves laid out with rows of jelly glasses and brown jugs and white stone-china jars with blue whirligigs and words painted on them: coffee, tea, sugar, ginger, cinnamon, allspice: and the bronze clock with the lion on top nicely dusted off. The dust that lion could collect in twenty-four hours! The box in the attic with all those letters tied up, well, she'd have to go through that tomorrow. All those letters—George's letters and John's letters and her letters to them both—lying around for the children to find afterwards made her uneasy. Yes, that would be tomorrow's business. No use to let them know how silly she had been once.

While she was rummaging around she found death in her mind and it felt clammy and unfamiliar. She had spent so much time preparing for death there was no need for bringing it up again. Let it take care of itself now. When she was sixty she had felt very old, finished, and went around making farewell trips to see her children and grandchildren, with a secret in her mind. This is the very last of your mother, children! Then she made her will and came down with a long fever. That was all just a notion like a lot of other things, but it was lucky too, for she had once for all got over the idea of dying for a long time. Now she couldn't be worried. She hoped she had better sense now. Her father had lived to be one hundred and two years old and had drunk a noggin of strong hot toddy on his last birthday. He told the reporters it was his daily habit, and he owed his long life to that. He had made quite a scandal and was very pleased about it. She believed she'd just plague Cornelia a little.

"Cornelia! Cornelia!" No footsteps, but a sudden hand on her cheek. "Bless you, where have you been?"

"Here, Mother."

"Well, Cornelia, I want a noggin of hot toddy."

"Are you cold, darling?"

"I'm chilly, Cornelia. Lying in bed stops the circulation. I must have told you that a thousand times."

Well, she could just hear Cornelia telling her husband that Mother was getting a little childish and they'd have to humor her. The thing that most annoyed her was that Cornelia thought she was deaf, dumb, and blind. Little hasty glances and tiny gestures tossed around her and over her head saying, "Don't cross her, let her have her way, she's eighty years old," and she sitting there as if she lived in a thin glass cage. Sometimes Granny almost made up her mind to pack up and move back to her own house where nobody could remind her every minute that she was old. Wait, wait, Cornelia, till your own children whisper behind your back!

In her day she had kept a better house and had got more work done. She wasn't too old yet for Lydia to be driving eighty miles for advice when one of the children jumped the track, and Jimmy still dropped in and talked things over: "Now, Mammy, you've a good business head, I want to know what you think of this? . . . " Old. Cornelia couldn't change the furniture around without asking. Little things, little things! They had been so sweet when they were little. Granny wished the old days were back again with the children young and everything to be done over. It had been a hard pull, but not too much for her. When she thought of all the food she had cooked, and all the clothes she had cut and sewed, and all the gardens she had made— well, the children showed it. There they were, made out of her, and they couldn't get away from that. Sometimes she wanted to see John again and point to them and say, Well, I didn't do so badly, did I? But that would have to wait. That was for tomorrow. She used to think of him as a man, but now all the children were older than their father, and he would be a child beside her if she saw him now. It seemed strange and there was something wrong in the idea. Why, he couldn't possibly recognize her. She had fenced in a hundred acres once, digging the post holes herself and clamping the wires with just a negro boy to help. That changed a woman. John would be looking for a young woman with the peaked Spanish comb in her hair and the painted fan. Digging post holes changed a woman. Riding country roads in the winter when women had their babies was another thing: sitting up nights with sick horses and sick negroes and sick children and hardly ever losing one. John, I hardly ever lost one of them! John would see that in a minute, that would be something he could understand, she wouldn't have to explain anything!

It made her feel like rolling up her sleeves and putting the whole place to rights again. No matter if Cornelia was determined to be everywhere at once, there were a great many things left undone on this place. She would start tomorrow and do them. It was good to be strong enough for everything, even if all you made melted and changed and slipped under your hands, so that by the time you finished you almost forgot what you were working for. What was it I set out to do? she asked herself intently, but she could not remember. A fog rose over the valley, she saw it marching across the creek swallowing the trees and moving up the hill like an army of ghosts. Soon it would be at the near edge of the orchard, and then it was time to go in and light the lamps. Come in, children, don't stay out in the night air.

Lighting the lamps had been beautiful. The children huddled up to her and breathed like little calves waiting at the bars in the twilight. Their eyes followed the match and watched the flame rise and settle in a blue curve, then they moved away from her. The lamp was lit, they didn't have to be scared and hang on to mother any more. Never, never, never more. God, for all my life I thank Thee. Without Thee, my God, I could never have done it. Hail, Mary, full of grace.

I want you to pick all the fruit this year and see that nothing is wasted. There's always someone who can use it. Don't let good things rot for want of using. You waste life when you waste good food. Don't let things get lost. It's bitter to lose things. Now, don't let me get to thinking, not when I am tired and taking a little nap before supper. . . .

The pillow rose about her shoulders and pressed against her heart and the memory was being squeezed out of it: oh, push down the pillow, somebody: it would smother her if she tried to hold it. Such a fresh breeze blowing and such a green day with no threats in it. But he had not come, just the same. What does a woman do when she has put on the white veil and set out the white cake for a man and he doesn't come? She tried to remember. No, I swear he never harmed me but in that. He never harmed me but in that . . . and what if he did? There was the day, the day, but a whirl of dark smoke rose and covered it, crept up and over into the bright field where everything was planted so carefully in orderly rows. That was hell, she knew hell when she saw it. For sixty years she had prayed against remembering him and against losing her soul in the deep pit of hell, and now the two things were mingled in one and the thought of him was a smoky cloud from hell that moved and crept in her head when she had just got rid of Doctor Harry and was trying to rest a minute. Wounded vanity, Ellen, said a sharp voice in the top of her mind. Don't let your wounded vanity get the upper hand of you. Plenty of girls get jilted. You were jilted, weren't you? Then stand up to it. Her eyelids wavered and let in streamers of blue-gray light like tissue paper over her eyes. She must get up and pull the shades down or she'd never sleep. She was in bed again and the shades were not down. How could that happen? Better turn over, hide from the light, sleeping in the light gave you nightmares. "Mother, how do you feel now?" and a stinging wetness on her forehead. But I don't like having my face washed in cold water!

Hapsy? George? Lydia? Jimmy? No, Cornelia, and her features were swollen and full of little puddles. "They're coming, darling, they'll all be here soon." Go wash your face, child, you look funny.

Instead of obeying, Cornelia knelt down and put her head on the pillow. She seemed to be talking but there was no sound. "Well, are you tongue-tied? Whose birthday is it? Are you going to give a party?"

Cornelia's mouth moved urgently in strange shapes. "Don't do that, you bother me, daughter."

"Oh, no, Mother. Oh, no. . . . "

Nonsense. It was strange about children. They disputed your every word. "No what, Cornelia?"

"Here's Doctor Harry."

"I won't see that boy again. He just left five minutes ago."

"That was this morning, Mother. It's night now. Here's the nurse."

"This is Doctor Harry, Mrs. Weatherall. I never saw you look so young and happy!"

"Ah, I'll never be young again—but I'd be happy if they'd let me lie in peace and get rested."

She thought she spoke up loudly, but no one answered. A warm weight on her forehead, a warm bracelet on her wrist, and a breeze went on whispering, trying to tell her something. A shuffle of leaves in the everlasting hand of God. He blew on them and they danced and rattled. "Mother, don't mind, we're going to give you a little hypodermic." "Look here, daughter, how do ants get in this bed? I saw sugar ants yesterday." Did you send for Hapsy too?

It was Hapsy she really wanted. She had to go a long way back through a great many rooms to find Hapsy standing with a baby on her arm. She seemed to herself to be Hapsy also, and the baby on Hapsy's arm was Hapsy and himself and herself, all at once, and there was no surprise in the meeting. Then Hapsy melted from within and turned flimsy as gray gauze and the baby was a gauzy shadow, and Hapsy came up close and said, "I thought you'd never come," and looked at her very searchingly and said, "You haven't changed a bit!" They leaned forward to kiss, when Cornelia began whispering from a long way off, "Oh, is there anything you want to tell me? Is there anything I can do for you?"

Yes, she had changed her mind after sixty years and she would like to see George. I want you to find George. Find him and be sure to tell him I forgot him. I want him to know I had my husband just the same and my children and my house like any other woman. A good house too and a good husband that I loved and fine children out of him. Better than I hoped for even. Tell him I was given back everything he took away and more. Oh, no, oh, God, no, there was something else besides the house and the man and the children. Oh, surely they were not all? What was it? Something not given back. . . . Her breath crowded down under her ribs and grew into a monstrous frightening shape with cutting edges; it bored up into her head, and the agony was unbelievable: Yes, John, get the Doctor now, no more talk, my time has come.

When this one was born it should be the last. The last. It should have been born first, for it was the one she had truly wanted. Everything came in good time. Nothing left out, left over. She was strong, in three days she would be as well as ever. Better. A woman needed milk in her to have her full health.

"Mother, do you hear me?"

"I've been telling you— "

"Mother, Father Connolly's here."

"I went to Holy Communion only last week. Tell him I'm not so sinful as all that."

"Father just wants to speak to you."

He could speak as much as he pleased. It was like him to drop in and inquire about her soul as if it were a teething baby, and then stay on for a cup of tea and a round of cards and gossip. He always had a funny story of some sort, usually about an Irishman who made his little mistakes and confessed them, and the point lay in some absurd thing he would blurt out in the confessional showing his struggles between native piety and original sin. Granny felt easy about her soul. Cornelia, where are your manners? Give Father Connolly a chair. She had her secret comfortable understanding with a few favorite saints who cleared a straight road to God for her. All as surely signed and sealed as the papers for the new Forty Acres. Forever . . . heirs and assigns forever. Since the day the wedding cake was not cut, but thrown out and wasted. The whole bottom dropped out of the world, and there she was blind and sweating with nothing under her feet and the walls falling away. His hand had caught her under the breast, she had not fallen, there was the freshly polished floor with the green rug on it, just as before. He had cursed like a sailor's parrot and said, "I'll kill him for you." Don't lay a hand on him, for my sake leave something to God. "Now, Ellen, you must believe what I tell you. . . . "

So there was nothing, nothing to worry about any more, except sometimes in the night one of the children screamed in a nightmare, and they both hustled out shaking and hunting for the matches and calling, "There, wait a minute, here we are!" John, get the doctor now, Hapsy's time has come. But there was Hapsy standing by the bed in a white cap. "Cornelia, tell Hapsy to take off her cap. I can't see her plain."

Her eyes opened very wide and the room stood out like a picture she had seen somewhere. Dark colors with the shadows rising towards the ceiling in long angles. The tall black dresser gleamed with nothing on it but John's picture, enlarged from a little one, with John's eyes very black when they should have been blue. You never saw him, so how do you know how he looked? But the man insisted the copy was perfect, it was very rich and handsome. For a picture, yes, but it's not my husband. The table by the bed had a linen cover and a candle and a crucifix. The light was blue from Cornelia's silk lampshades. No sort of light at all, just frippery. You had to live forty years with kerosene lamps to appreciate honest electricity. She felt very strong and she saw Doctor Harry with a rosy nimbus around him.

"You look like a saint, Doctor Harry, and I vow that's as near as you'll ever come to it."

"She's saying something."

"I heard you, Cornelia. What's all this carrying-on?"

"Father Connolly's saying— "

Cornelia's voice staggered and bumped like a cart in a bad road. It rounded corners and turned back again and arrived nowhere. Granny stepped up in the cart very lightly and reached for the reins, but a man sat beside her and she knew him by his hands, driving the cart. She did not look in his face, for she knew without seeing, but looked instead down the road where the trees leaned over and bowed to each other and a thousand birds were singing a Mass. She felt like singing too, but she put her hand in the bosom of her dress and pulled out a rosary, and Father Connolly murmured Latin in a very solemn voice and tickled her feet. My God, will you stop that nonsense? I'm a married woman. What if he did run away and leave me to face the priest by myself? I found another a whole world better. I wouldn't have exchanged my husband for anybody except St. Michael himself, and you may tell him that for me with a thank you in the bargain.

Light flashed on her closed eyelids, and a deep roaring shook her. Cornelia, is that lightning? I hear thunder. There's going to be a storm. Close all the windows. Call the children in. . . . "Mother, here we are, all of us." "Is that you, Hapsy?" "Oh, no, I'm Lydia. We drove as fast as we could." Their faces drifted above her, drifted away. The rosary fell out of her hands and Lydia put it back. Jimmy tried to help, their hands fumbled together, and Granny closed two fingers around Jimmy's thumb. Beads wouldn't do, it must be something alive. She was so amazed her thoughts ran round and round. So, my dear Lord, this is my death and I wasn't even thinking about it. My children have come to see me die. But I can't, it's not time. Oh, I always hated surprises. I wanted to give Cornelia the amethyst set—Cornelia, you're to have the amethyst set, but Hapsy's to wear it when she wants, and, Doctor Harry, do shut up. Nobody sent for you. Oh, my dear Lord, do wait a minute. I meant to do something about the Forty Acres, Jimmy doesn't need it and Lydia will later on, with that worthless husband of hers. I meant to finish the altar cloth and send six bottles of wine to Sister Borgia for her dyspepsia. I want to send six bottles of wine to Sister Borgia, Father Connolly, now don't let me forget.

Cornelia's voice made short turns and tilted over and crashed. "Oh, Mother, oh, Mother, oh, Mother. . . . "

"I'm not going, Cornelia. I'm taken by surprise. I can't go."

You'll see Hapsy again. What about her? "I thought you'd never come." Granny made a long journey outward, looking for Hapsy. What if I don't find her? What then? Her heart sank down and down, there was no bottom to death, she couldn't come to the end of it. The blue light from Cornelia's lampshade drew into a tiny point in the center of her brain, it flickered and winked like an eye, quietly it fluttered and dwindled. Granny lay curled down within herself, amazed and watchful, staring at the point of light that was herself; her body was now only a deeper mass of shadow in an endless darkness and this darkness would curl around the light and swallow it up. God, give a sign!

For the second time there was no sign. Again no bridegroom and the priest in the house. She could not remember any other sorrow because this grief wiped them all away. Oh, no, there's nothing more cruel than this—I'll never forgive it. She stretched herself with a deep breath and blew out the light.

[1930]

For Discussion

1. What does Granny find objectionable about Cornelia's personality and behavior?

2. What is Granny proud of in her life? What does her name suggest?

3. Explain the circumstance of Granny's first "jilting" and how she feels about it in retrospect.

4. Explain Granny's preoccupation with Hapsy, and what Hapsy's name might suggest (look up the definition of "hap").

5. Why had Granny been "easy about her soul"? If so, why isn't she ready for death?

6. Describe the scene around Granny's bedside—who is there? Where is Hapsy?

7. What role does Father Connolly play in the story?

8. Why doesn't Granny want to die yet? How does this scene resemble the earlier episode in which Granny was jilted?

9. Explore the religious meaning of Christ as a "bridegroom" and the faithful as "brides of Christ." In what sense is Granny jilted at the end?

10. Analyze the use of light and darkness throughout the story and in the final line.

For Further Exploration

1. Compare this story with the equally famous death account "Tell Me a Riddle" by Tillie Olsen. How do Granny's thoughts correspond with Eva's as each dies? In each story, is the final attitude bitter or peaceful?

2. Compare Katherine Porter's description of death with Willa Cather's short novel, *My Mortal Enemy.* Or, analyze Porter's description of a young girl's coming to terms with death in her short story "The Fig Tree."

Joyce Marshall

1913–

A ninety-one year old retired doctor finds that there are still surprises in store for her as she tries to convey her active, self-assertive philosophy of life to others. While her body has aged, her will has remained strong and she does not give up to death without a struggle.

SO MANY HAVE DIED

On that day, her last, Georgiana Dinsborough was three months into her ninety-first year. She was a marvel. Everyone told her so and, though the reiteration grew tiresome, Georgiana herself acknowledged that in many ways she was. Marvellously lucky, at least, for how much of her reasonably steady health and mental clearness she owed to nature, how much to the habit, so long part of her, of weeding out any hint of frailty or contradiction, she didn't know. (As if it were possible even to think of untangling what you'd brought to life—no doubt squawling from the weight of it in that big farm-bedroom in the Eastern Townships—from what life and you yourself had made of what you'd brought.) She'd continued in practice till she was 80; her patients hadn't wanted her to retire and she had felt loyal to them, the grandchildren in many cases (even the male grandchildren) of those young women who had come timidly or in fierce feminist solidarity to the office she'd opened with her friend Mary Balsam in the livingroom of this very flat. Loyal above all to her profession; anything so strenuously fought for acquired rights, couldn't be put aside the moment you began to feel a little tired. For ten years she'd taken no new patients and might have continued in that way, the attrition of death and dispersal slowly lightening the load, if she hadn't felt that quite new wish to have some time for herself, time to ask questions and find answers, evaluate her life. Wasn't that what you were supposed to do when you were very old? With the honesty she'd always required of herself, she'd wondered whether her decision wasn't a shade suspect, much like her Grandfather Dinsborough's announcement when he was 80 and crippled with arthritis, that deer were too beautiful to kill so he'd never hunt again. But if it was softness to want to go out proud, under her own steam, why not? She might even deserve it. So she booked passage for England and stayed away for six months, looked up old friends and family connections, learned about leisure in new places. When she returned, her office equipment had been sold, files stored in the basement, she was retired. It was as painless as such a thing could ever be.

She found that she rather liked this part of her life, as she'd liked all the other parts. (Liked it at least on her good days. Lying in bed, waiting for the telephone to ring, she was sure this would be one of the best. No aches, not even a twinge in her bad hip, broken in a fall three years ago. Sun washed through the room. Spring, that treacherous season, was coming in cool and bright—and very slow.) Despite urgings to move to a more compact apartment, she'd stayed on in the long duplex flat in Notre Dame de Gráce where her entire adult life had been lived—with Mary Balsam first, then briefly with her mother, for almost 50 years alone. She went to concerts, read, watched television, could count on at least one visit a week with some member of her large family connection. A varied lot, which provided stimulation and just enough irritation to keep her feeling alive. From time to time she considered her life (or, as it sometimes seemed, her life came back to consider her) though more as pure memory, she had to admit, than as material for questions she must answer. Perhaps once you've decided, as she had at eighteen, to be an agnostic, there were no questions, the notions of God and immortality having been packed away, to be taken out if ever only after you've ceased to breathe. She laughed at the thought of breathing her last, with relief if her final illness was painful (and she would fight, she knew that, even unconscious she'd fight) only to be roused at once by a voice—from where?—'Well now, Georgiana Lilian, about that deferred matter of My existence?' Her mind supplied the capital and she laughed again, for God had spoken in Grandfather Dinsborough's voice, coming clear and intimidating across 70 years.

She was still laughing when the phone gave its first warning ding. (Good. Now she'd be able to get up.) Who would it be today? Though she supposed they'd arranged some schedule, she'd never cracked it. Her lying alone all those hours with her hip broken had alarmed them—and God knows it had alarmed her—so she played along with their concern (and with their wariness of her that drove them to subterfuge) by pretending not to notice that, except on Tuesdays and Fridays when her charwoman came, there was always a call at just this time, when she was awake but not yet in her bath.

'Hi, Aunt George.' The tiny voice identified herself as Phyllis, granddaughter of Raymond, her youngest brother, a skinny little creature who'd recently put on the trappings of rebellion—cascades of muffling hair, ragged trousers, a vocabulary her mother found distressing—and though this child wasn't one of the coterie of fussers, Georgiana said exactly what she'd planned when she picked up the phone, 'Your great—no, *great* great grandfather just spoke to me out of a cloud like God.'

'Aunt George, you're kidding.' No humour. That was the real trouble with the young, the thing, at least, that worried her. It made conversation so patchy. The older lot, like Nora, her mother, could share the occasional joke, if you sneaked it in on them, though even they seemed to think your bones had become so brittle real laughter might break them. (Were we the last of the belly-laughers? It seems to me that we were always laughing and I miss it. How Charles and I could laugh. And after all these years, she wanted him. My God, it never ends, she thought, with astonishment, with delight.) 'What did he say, Aunt George?' Phyllis was asking.

'Some rot about my soul. He was a sadly limited old man. Godlike. Ruling unto the third and fourth generation. With some success till he encountered me.' Now why do I tell her this, she wondered and said briskly, 'Well, time's a-wasting. What can I do for you this fine May morning?'

'How's about lunch, Aunt George? I could pick you up, Mother says she'll let me have her car so if you like we can—'

'Out of the question, alas. Unless you want to eat here—no, that won't do either. Place will be a shambles. Got a man coming to take down double windows, put up screens.'

'Oh,' said Phyllis.

'Is it so urgent? Won't some other day do?'

'No you see I'm going to Europe next week and Mother's laid on all sorts of dentists and—' ('Breathe, child,' said Georgiana.) 'Oh sorry, I—I'd like very much to see you, Aunt George I'm proud of you. No-one else in our group has a relative like you. Your generation made a lot of mistakes but *you* didn't chicken out, not about everything. Aunt George I'm going *away,* I want to talk to you, you might even be able to tell me some things.'

Touched by this longest, if rambling, speech she'd ever heard from the child, intrigued too, novelty wasn't all that abundant nowadays, 'Well, come then,' Georgiana said. 'I'm charmed to hear I give you prestige with your group. Come at four. Fellow should be through and I'll be ready for a break.'

'Oh thanks,' said Phyllis. 'I'll turn you over to Mother, she wants to—'

'But hasn't that been settled,' said Georgiana, 'that I'm still breathing and in one piece?' and hung up laughing.

Nora rang back at once. Georgiana had just started the slow vertebra by vertebra stretching that preceded the foot and ankle exercises that enabled her to walk so well. With a cane, of course, but well. (Steve, her doctor-nephew, had feared she'd never walk. 'We'll see about that,' she'd said.)

'Phyllis hung up.' At 55 Nora still had almost the light, breathy voice of her youth. 'I wanted to talk to you too, Aunt George.'

'Then talk,' said Georgiana, 'while I get on with my exercises.' When she'd lain in the dark in frightening pain, she'd sobbed for three people—her mother, Charles and Nora. (Before she'd begun to inch that eternity down the hall to the point, just inside her bedroom door, where she could jiggle the phone from its stand. She'd learned then, she believed, what death would be like—an empty calling and help so far down the hall no inching could reach it.) The choice of names had startled her and she'd felt uneasy with her once-favourite niece since then. That was one of the risks in loving seldom. There was too much space in you, roots grew deep. For a few years she and Nora had seemed equal, almost contemporaries, and she, who confided seldom, had confided fully in Nora; even now the memory was humiliation. Rubbish, she thought, the girl probably doesn't remember. Though it might be amusing to try her out. You know, Nora, she could say, a moment ago I actually felt a stir of sexual longing for Charles.

'Aunt George,' Nora was saying sternly, 'Phyllis tells me you're going to be traipsing around after some man while he puts up screens.'

'Did I say that? I'll only traipse if it seems necessary. Since Antoine died and I've had to rely on agencies—But tell me,' she said, cutting off any impulse Nora might feel to come and supervise, as if even giving instructions was beyond you now. 'This European jaunt of Phyllis's. Isn't it a bit sudden?'

'She just sprang it on us. She's going with one of her girl friends.' And only eighteen, she wailed. And the way they dressed. Like fishermen. 'I want her to look in on my English relatives. Use them as a base. She won't hear of it.'

'Very wise,' said Georgiana. 'In your cousin Isabel's house, as I recall, there were plastic tulips and china dogs. And do you know? Each of those damn dogs had its snout pointing into the street.'

Nora laughed. 'Aunt George, you sure have a gift for putting people down. But when she comes . . . We tend to forget what it's like. How fragile they are. And you grew up in a tough school. She's gone a bit overboard about women's lib,' and before Georgiana could say, 'Well, good for her,' 'Don't try to influence her, Aunt George,' said Nora firmly.

'I couldn't. I didn't succeed with you, did I?'

'Well, in a way you did.' Nora paused, as if startled by her own words. 'You may not believe this but there's always been something whispering in my ear. I may break out yet, Aunt George.'

'No, not you, Nora,' said Georgiana. 'And look here. I believe I apologized at the time for any harm I might have done. I'll do so again if you insist.'

'Aunt George, it's marvellous the way you never change.' Why did she have to say that? What was so marvellous about continuing to be one's self? 'I've often wondered. Have you ever had doubts in your life? About anything?'

'*Doubts?* Oh Nora.'

At one time her life had been all doubt, she thought, after Nora had rung off and, with a final rotation of her ankles, she began to edge out of bed. (Whenever you became absorbed in a single thing, talking in this case, you forgot what a bag of recalcitrant bones you inhabited now. I have never felt more alive and yet it must take me 30 seconds to sit, then pull myself to my feet. Someone—Yeats?—put it well—*this caricature, decrepit age, that has been tied to me as to a dog's tail.* This *thing.* This hindrance. A tin can rattling behind. Never me.) Doubts, Nora? she repeated as she clumped down to the bathroom, the day's first steps so balky, feet like shovels, and set about preparing her bath. Doubt she'd be admitted to medicine at McGill, doubts she'd get through the course—discrimination could go to almost any length; you're damn right I grew up in a tough school—doubts she'd be allowed to intern, that patients would come. Doubt of herself. She might make some early disastrous error in diagnosis; she'd never be permitted another. But the War came—it would always be that to her, 'the War', the word a gong, sounding only once. What a society, she thought with an old, undiminished rage— it had to murder its men before it could value its women. And a few years later she was appointed examining physician to some of the Protestant schools. One of those who read of her death next day remembered her from that time: A stumpy alarming figure who spoke disparagingly of her tonsils and gave her a note to take home, which 'home', being somewhat harum scarum, ignored. She'd been puzzled at the doctor's being a lady, such a comically dressed lady—ankle-length skirt, frogged jacket hugging ample hips. Now she wondered whether the poor dear was impervious to her own appearance or couldn't afford to buy clothes. The suit in question, which gave Georgiana years of wear, had been a hand-me-down from her mother. And people seemed to like women doctors to be dowdy. Though Mary was always elegant, hard not to be with those delicate bones and perfect Grecian head.

Georgiana smiled, remembering the day during their second year when they'd marched down to St James Street and sold their long hair to a wig-maker; the proceeds bought them a skeleton. (A screen lifted to show her the two of them running through a Montreal snowstorm, hats loose on their shorn heads.) What a furor that created, my little Phyllis. Sniggers from the male students, our mothers sobbing, Grandfather Dinsborough quoting St Paul. (She eased onto the little stool in the tub, built by a handyman nephew at just the right, most comfortable height). Imagine that little snip informing me coolly that we made mistakes. As if we had the time or the energy to be perfect. Still it was real rebellion and, if you don't understand, that's because we succeeded. Fun too; such vigour came from being an outsider. Though thank God for Mary, soft and boneless and tiny, but tough as the best steel. (Could she have managed alone? She'd often wondered.) One of the 'mistakes', she supposed, was in not demanding sexual equality. But the child has no idea how vulnerable we were. Morally we had to be impeccable and only odd around the edges. In one of their 'serious talks'—they'd had a great many in their little room at the residence; no chaperoned cocoa-parties or mountain sleigh-rides or dances for them (and don't think we didn't sometimes wish there were; it's part of being human to want everything)—she and Mary had renounced all thought of marriage, superfluously perhaps, since only the rarest of men, they knew, could take both their persons and their professions. And the two were indivisible, no question about that. (Laugh if you like, Phyllis. Call us pathetic, childish. It was so.)

Her graduation picture, when it turned up among her mother's things, had showed a round face, which she remembered as being rosy, good eyes and a cheerful mouth. Perhaps men's eyes had followed her and she hadn't known. Charles had said they must have, that she was one of the sexiest bits of goods he'd ever seen. Charles. Moving slowly, washing her old body, she could see him, though his face slid away in a dark smudge, leaving only his hands, rather small, always slightly cupped. She was 42, a useful and fairly happy woman but dry, she knew, a little too gruff and hearty. (They all read Huxley and Lawrence, knew the signs.) Two days, she thought—meeting at a medical convention, first kiss, first fondling, bedding down. Now, she'd told herself—belatedly, the harm done, looking with some amazement at her undergarments strewn about the hotel-room floor—she could risk this sort of thing. Discretion proved easy, privacy so much a matter of finances; she'd simply bought the building and moved her mother, who'd just come to live with her, into the upper flat. No-one had guessed the connection that had continued so happily for twenty years.

Tamped down so long, she should have been impossible to rouse. But she'd known the ecstasies of any twenty-year-old. (How Charles would laugh at my trying to be poetic. It was wild and vigorous, heady as good wine.) The storms too, passions of jealous weeping when he stayed away too long, humiliation at what seemed to her servitude, less to Charles than to claims unleashed in her own body. This only for the first years till she realized that he was as bound to her as she to him. So that now she chiefly remembered their laughter. And when he died, suddenly of a stroke two days after they'd been together, it hadn't seemed to matter that her grief couldn't be public, that though there was a blackclad widow at the funeral, it wasn't she. (She'd had no wish to be present while Charles's body, washed by those lovely unmeaning words, was committed to the ground. Bad enough to have to see it done to parents, brothers, sister, friends. I am not resigned, she thought. I have never grown used to it. Death is the final obscenity, sooner or later taking almost every one of those I fought to keep. The first time a child she had delivered died under her care—only three years separating the birth-bellow, tiny gasp—she and Mary had got drunk in the kitchen. Or at least Georgiana had got drunk for she had dim recollections of Mary helping her to bed. So only Mary had heard words she'd never repeated to anyone else, only Mary knew the despair that underlay her life. The battle is lost in advance yet I fight. I fight because it's lost.) She'd have shrieked and moaned at Charles's funeral; just as well she could grieve in her own way and in private. Her love hadn't been public either and perhaps the better and stronger for that.

This she'd tried to tell Nora, that it wasn't loss necessarily to be barred from dailiness; it could be gain. If you had enough in yourself, enough to bring and to go back to. And Nora hadn't. Perhaps everyone had a right to one mistake, Nora had certainly been hers. She'd felt so alone with Charles gone and Nora the only child of Raymond, her favourite brother, whom she'd watched for eighteen years as he coughed up lungs that had drunk mustard gas at Ypres. A rangy girl, not pretty but with something open and quirky about her, 27 years old and still fighting to escape from her twittery Limey mother. Georgiana had helped set her up in a studio and, when Jérôme came along, encouraged that. Nora had been almost too apt a pupil; it was her nature to say yes. Georgiana hadn't realized she was saying yes, not to painting as a career (though she had talent), not to Jérôme as a lover (though she'd loved him) but to the admired (blind) aunt who talked to her and listened and made that absurd mistake of thinking she saw her ideas going forward in another. (She was the vanguard; Nora, the inheritor, would go farther, more freely.) And then tearfully, messily (at 35) the girl tossed everything away for a 'normal', very wealthy marriage with a man a little younger than herself, apologizing to Georgiana as if the last years had been a college course and she had failed. It had been the apology Georgiana had found hardest to forgive . . . 'It's your life,' she'd said. 'You must live it. If you want to marry whoever-it-is, go ahead and marry him.' And now there was Phyllis, cosseted child of Nora's middle years, who'd 'gone a bit overboard' about women's lib (as well she might, given the example of her parents, Nora having assumed all her husband's opinions as swiftly as she'd once assumed Georgiana's) and wanted to see her mother's ancient aunt. When was the last time, Georgiana wondered, when anyone wanted to see me in that sense. People share with me now, give generously, kindly. No-one takes.

Well, well, she thought, out of her bath and dressed. She'd trained herself to think along the edge of her mind so she wouldn't have to look too clearly at her body as she prepared it for the day. She'd been stocky, breasts and buttocks like rocks. (Built like a duck, they'd said at home.) Her breasts had emptied, everything else—hips, abdomen, thighs—slipped down till she became pear-shaped, then emptied in their turn. (*This caricature,* she thought. It isn't me but I'm *in* it.) Well, better think of something more cheerful such as what poor little Phyllis wanted. If the child was actually curious about the past—could she be? None of the young were—Georgiana would simply tell her about it. Trying not to sound like a character. She'd slipped rather on the phone. It was so easy; people trapped you with shrieks of 'how marvellous', as if it were a miracle anyone so old could speak, let alone arrange words in sentences that ran coherently. So you performed. It was diverting at the time but shaming later. I didn't live so long just to become a stereotype peppery old lady. I'm very complex. I'm Georgiana.

At nine she was in the kitchen, eating the bowl of hot Roman Meal that had fueled each of her days for 50 years. The man to do the windows was due at 9.30; she'd told the agency she wouldn't let him in if he arrived one minute before. She'd lit her first cigarette and poured coffee when Paul Thomas, her upstairs tenant, knocked and came in to leave his key. On family orders she'd consented to leave the door into the shared back vestibule unlocked; the day she broke her hip, Paul and her nephew Steve had had to smash it down. She'd been semi-delirious by then; the sounds and their faces above her had fitted into some black dream of rending and threatened attack. 'Go away,' she'd screamed. 'I'm not ready for you yet.' Since then, her tenants, a working couple in their thirties, wandered in rather often, always with an excuse, to bring something, ask something. Of the two she preferred Paul. He had more life and, with her, sometimes dropped the over-heartiness she knew was a defence. Not today. He looked tired and agitated.

'Great morning, Dr Din.'

Georgiana agreed that it was, agreed that it would be fine to have the double windows off. She could leave his key on the table, he said, and if he got home before his wife, he'd pop in and get it.

'Is Cynthia quite up to par?' she asked. 'I've wondered.'

'Oh—well—she took a long time getting round after that London flu.' Georgiana nodded. She'd had it too, had fought (successfully) against going to the hospital, had got even with Steve's insistence on a practical nurse by sharing the woman with Cynthia. 'Needs some sun and rest,' Paul said. 'You know Cynthia. She won't ever give in, won't leave the floor without wax or a dish in the sink.'

Georgiana was about to suggest he tell the girl to drop in—just the worried look (so known) on Paul's face. He seemed honestly to love that pinched, terribly house-proud little woman. 'I forgot,' she said, delighted. 'Forgot I wasn't still a practising physician.' She was going to add that she'd never felt more alive but to Paul, looking down at her froglike form and the face, firm and rosy once, now putty-coloured, creased and re-creased as if someone had gone at it too vigorously with a sewing-machine—no, that wouldn't do. No need to make a fool of yourself. So she merely laughed. 'Been laughing like a maniac all morning. Losing my marbles no doubt.'

'Dr Din, you're not losing a thing,' Paul said. 'Not only that. You're a living doll. If I were 60 years older, you'd be afraid to leave your door unlocked.'

'God spare me from a 95-year-old lover,' she said and they parted laughing. (He remembered this later with pleasure and pain, for he'd been fond of the old girl. 'She was so gay this morning,' he kept saying to Phyllis when he came in at five and found her coping so well for such a youngster.)

Georgiana had lit her second cigarette when the phone rang; she reached for it (phones in every room were another concession to the family)— Stella Farnham, not yet 80 but of all the people she knew now the closest in age. (One by one they toppled off the edge and left her the oldest.) Damn, she thought, outraged, barely hearing Stella as she twittered something about thinking of the old days (as if that fluttery idiot had been present in the real old days), sick suddenly, as happened every now and then, from the force of all those steady, single deaths. Her friends. Her kind. The other early graduates in medicine, the pioneers with her in the women's suffrage movement (before they turned it over to the French where it belonged). How good and tolerant they'd been with each other, even those earnest souls who'd muddled prohibition of liquor with women's rights. Well, they'd all been odd in one way or another, but freed and strengthened by that. And every one of them had aged better than poor Stella, keeping enough of themselves to serve as reminders of how they'd once moved and looked. (She'd tell Phyllis this, so someone would know, what friends they'd been, how none of them had become senile; worked hard and widely, their minds had simply given out when the time came. Mary, dying of cancer at 55, had been perfectly intact. Die, Mary, she'd thought, looking down at that bit of bone and waste. Stop fighting, Mary. But Mary couldn't and Georgiana had continued to help for as long as she must. And I still don't know why, why it has to be or what it means. This I was supposed to discover in my last years. This is one of the questions I put off asking.) Thank God, she needn't participate in another death—except one, but then the choice (at what point to withdraw and let the body die) would be Steve's. Thank God, she repeated, listening to Stella's voice, as she was forced to now that it was rising, lamenting that her son had done this and her daughter the other, or rather not done this and the other, for they were neglectful, wouldn't—

'Then tell them so,' said Georgiana, who'd delivered both these children; the boy had been magnificent, lungs like bellows. 'Aren't you a grown woman and their mother?'

'George, if I were only like you,' Stella wailed.

'Well, why aren't you for mercy's sake? Stella, I braced you during your pregnancies. I prevailed on you to nurse when you didn't want to. I tried to put starch into you. I'm an old woman now. I'm retired. You're on your own.'

The doorbell rang. Georgiana excused herself, saying she'd call back. (A lie. She didn't intend to.) She reached for her cane, put her other hand palm-down on the table and pulled herself to her feet, then started the slow journey down the hall of this very stretched-out flat. (The hall she used to take at a run when the ring meant Charles; she could almost feel that other woman rising out of her bones and rushing forward. They're dead, she thought. Everyone who meant anything. There's no-one who remembers what I remember. Damn. I didn't ask to be the survivor. It should have been someone stronger. Mary.)

'You were supposed to come to the back door,' she told the young man from the agency. He muttered something, looking down. 'Français?' He shook his head. 'Too bad. I used to speak it pretty well, with a lousy accent. Like the Spanish cow, as the French say.' He didn't answer. One of those battened-down young people clearly. Just what I need. About 25, she judged, and with the green waxy look of malnutrition. Like so many of the young. Phyllis too. You'd swear Nora had never heard of vitamins. 'Well, don't just stand there,' she said, shooing him towards the kitchen.

'The strange thing about being old,' she told his back as she stumped after him, 'is that though your flesh goes, you don't get lighter. You get heavier. A paradox.'

He was silent, just walked straight through to the kitchen and stood with his back against the farther door.

'See here,' she said. 'I won't have anyone in my house if I can't be human with him. You want your money, I suppose?'

'Yes,' he said and did seem finally to look at her, at least move his eyes in her direction. He was pale in every respect, especially so about the mouth. Even his eyes and wispy hair were pale.

'Very well then,' she said, 'in future speak when you're spoken to,' and told him in what part of the cellar he'd find the screens and the hose, how to line the screens against the fence while he washed them. 'Sort them by rooms. My old valued handyman and friend pencilled it on in French. You can read French?' He said he could.

He was slow, she saw as she watched from the window, smoking another cigarette with some warmed-up coffee, trying to salvage this day that had started so well. Till the dead began to walk. (Be still, be still, she told them. I did what I could.) Look around you, Georgiana. Don't be a damned crybaby. The sky was that high, very dark blue of spring. Soon there'd be crocuses—Paul had moved the patch so she could see them from her window. Later they'd discuss colours and he'd fill the tiny yard with petunias. (Something's eating Paul. I must manage to learn what, must still serve. But I'm fussy and old; I snapped at foolish Stella. But Paul has life. Now watch it, Georgiana. Was it ever your right to decide who was worth your effort and who wasn't?) The young man was spraying the screens, making great pools of slop and walking through them. Naming his actions to himself as she had done during those humiliating months of learning to walk again. Once headed in a particular direction, he continued in that way, no matter how muddy, made no free movements, never improvised. He finished, disconnected the hose and turned back to the house. She heard him scrape each foot on the stoop. Then he came in and stood silent in front of her.

'I'm a retired physician, not a member of the narcotics squad,' she said. 'Are you on drugs?'

He did actually smile then, just a swift tuck of the lips.

'You think that's the first thing we old people think of. Well, not this old person. Call me an interfering old party if you wish but I'm used to taking care of people, sometimes when they'd just as soon I didn't. It's hard to hide things from me. You look what my mother used to call mingy. Never did understand that word. A composite perhaps of miserable and mangy. Have you been ill?'

'No,' he said, 'I haven't,' then, 'Which floor'll I start on?' A shallow breather, the voice using only the upper segment of the lungs.

'Upstairs,' she told him and handed him Paul's key, indicated the pail and cloths, told him where to stack the double windows when he'd scrubbed them. 'Your lunch will be ready on the dot of twelve. Here on this table . . . Did you say something?'

'I go out to lunch.'

'Not from this house you don't. You're going to eat properly for once. No French fries. No Coca Cola.'

'I'd rather you didn't go to too much trouble.' Curiously educated expression.

'I'll go to exactly as much trouble as it requires,' she said, wanting to see that little smile again and thinking that, just briefly, she did so. 'Ha—now I know why the lower part of your face is so white. You used to have a beard.'

'What if I did?' He should have looked at her then but did not.

'Why are you so defensive? I suppose the agency made you shave it. Well, they're damned idiots. I'm accustomed to facial hair. My own father and grandfather had beards—finer and bushier beards than you could grow.'

Her mood lifted. She felt suddenly gay as a girl as she listened to his steps on the stairs and over her head, the pauses. In some ways old age was an adolescence, though a less painful one—hers had been hideous; no other part of her life had touched it for sheer darkness. The feeling of looseness, of belonging nowhere, not even with her own body. (That she might tell Phyllis too; from now on everything has to be better.) The gaieties of old age were like the rare gaieties of adolescence, same sense of spinning off towards some wonderful country that was waiting to receive you if you could only find the way. But now you knew there was no such country and no way, and treasured and drank the joy. There was a dark side too. Like the pubescent you were very conscious of your effect on others. Had to be, knowing they watched you for weakness, ready to take over. Still, life is wonderful, she told Phyllis, told the young man upstairs. If I could just prove it to you. (The dead would say so too. Every one of them. I assure you. There was a young man once who died of what we used to call blood poisoning. With his last bit of strength, he sat bolt upright, staring ahead. His mother thought he'd seen one of God's angels, perhaps the old man himself. But he was looking at me and in the instant before the light went out, there was rage in those eyes— rage and appeal. Having seen that even once, you *know*. It is precious just to be, in a body that will function, and to have senses—even though barely, and with tremendous struggle, as I have them. Don't ask why. It is.)

She'd have to start to fix the young man's lunch—he'd so quickly (though oddly) become an individual that she'd forgotten to ask his name—at half past eleven, was almost late because Nora called again.

'Aunt George, I felt I should warn you. I hope you won't mind. Phyllis has become awfully curious about your sex life.'

'Don't be a solemn ninny, Nora. I'm flattered. It's such ages since anyone's thought I might have had one.'

'She wonders if you were all lesbians. As a defence against chauvinist pigs.' She sighed. 'She's threatening to take that way herself. As a means of consciousness-raising or whatever they call it.'

'Is she indeed? Seems a strange thing to discuss with one's mother. And don't say that you and she discuss everything. I don't believe it. . . . As a matter of fact, several of my friends were—some by nature, others from fear. I think it was the latter with Mary.'

'Aunt Mary Balsam? But she was so—womanly.'

'Your father certainly thought so. I've always believed they'd have married, even though she was a good seven years older, if poor silly Raymond could have brought himself to let her continue in practice. But the War came and, as you know, he met your mother in England.' She became aware of her gabbling voice and Nora's silence. 'You didn't know this?'

'No. No, I never even—So that's why she was always so good to me. . . . Aunt George, are you sure?'

'Oh yes. She told me herself.' She'd gone in to get Mary to fit her for a diaphragm and Mary had made that wry joke about not needing that sort of thing herself. And I was shocked, though I should have seen it in the wind when Mother came to live with me after Father died and Mary moved in with Irene Sanders. But was she happy? How after all these years could it be of any importance or even interest to know whether Mary was happy? She said she was, though all I could think was that it must be sad to turn and find only a similar body, another self. And did I say the right things, so full of myself that day, myself and Charles? A scene in a doctor's examining room, two women talking—neither the room nor the furnishings nor the women (one now only a clumsy bag of bones, the other dust I may have washed from my hand or face) to be found anywhere now—yet I feel I could reach back, change the words. 'What did you say, Nora?'

'That I'd rather you didn't tell Phyllis, Aunt George.'

'Or about Charles? Or,' she couldn't help adding, 'Jérôme?' Silence. That had made the Westmount matron jump. 'He still sends me cards at Christmas. Did you know? Always with a funny note. I do like a man with humour.' Whoever-it-is had none.

'No, you never mentioned—it's not that I'm ashamed—but her own mother—'

'Really, Nora. I'm surprised at your thinking I'd give you away. But as for my life and my friends' lives, if the child asks, I'll tell her. No-one knows, you see. I thought of writing a book, even made a great many notes. But I couldn't. It seemed so—with none of them here to—'

'Yes—I see.' Abruptly, in a softened voice, she asked whether the man had come about the windows and was he doing a satisfactory—?

'Yes, he's a pretty good worker,' Georgiana said. 'And a bit of a challenge besides . . . Oh why should I have to explain?' for Nora was trying to get her to do just that. 'Really you're the world's most exasperating—a different sort of life . . . society. Have you any idea how unusual that is at my—'

'Aunt George, come and have dinner with us next week.' ('Thank God,' she kept saying later to Phyllis and Paul, 'it was the last thing I said to her. She'd been baiting me, as she could, cruel almost, and then, I don't know, being *old*. Thank God I didn't lose my temper.' They had a hard time silencing her. She kept thrusting Phyllis away, almost with hatred, and talking about people they didn't know.) 'I'll call,' she said now, 'and make it more— I'm going to be miserably lonely without Phyllis, Aunt George.'

Damn, Georgiana thought, rubbing angry tears from her eyes, trying to remember what it was she—Oh yes, casserole, put it in the oven. She'd slipped. With Nora of all people. Awkward having to sift each word. Out of character. Why shouldn't she be allowed to say that it was interesting, fun even, to have someone new about the house? Or mourn her friends? Without being found pitiable. Think of something else. So Phyllis was interested in her sexual habits. Well, well. Where had she put those notes? Several bulky folders. The child might like to see them. Georgiana, you old fool, don't go thinking you've found your inheritor so late in the day. Though wouldn't it be a wonderful revenge on whoever-it-is if Phyllis should turn out to be the woman Nora had only played at being? My heir straight from darling Raymond. The baby she'd held in her arms in the big farm kitchen, only hours after his birth. God, she was slow. Slower than a month ago? Washing and tearing greens for salad took so long, even putting bread and knife on the board and groping in the fridge for butter. She set a place and was about to fetch the tea-cart, which she'd ask the lad to wheel into the living-room, when impulsively she put a second set of cutlery on the table for herself.

At five past twelve he came downstairs—a spot of independence in this that she approved of—walked into the kitchen and stood with his back to her, washing his hands at the sink.

'Clean towel to your right,' she told him. 'I forgot to mention another rule of this house. I eat with the help.'

He stiffened. She saw it in his back under the thin t-shirt. This was wrong. An intrusion. Unfortunately phrased too. But she'd have to go through with it now, could scarcely let him put her out of her own kitchen.

'I must ask you to humour me,' she said. 'I enjoy company.'

'You're the boss.' He dried his hands and came to sit in the chair she indicated, sat rather far back from the table, arms hanging at his sides. That nothing face, merely young, but with three tension-cracks across the forehead. Georgiana served him, hands slow but steady, planning what she would say.

'You a native Montrealer?' she asked finally.

'Yes.' She waited, looking at him. 'Yes, I am.'

'I was born on a farm near Compton. In the Townships, as you may have noticed from my speech—if you're familiar with that twangy drawl we have. It was wholly English in those days. And now it's all—or almost all— French. Our farm and most of the neighbouring farms.'

'Anything wrong with that?'

'Wrong? Of course not. Mercy, you *are* defensive.' This was the way with the untalkative. Chatter on with seeming lack of aim while they listened or not, to give yourself space to make certain observations. 'But it was a rather special society. Loyalists. In our case from Massachusetts. My grandfather's grandfather, who was what the French would call our first ancestor, had been a whaling captain sailing out of New Bedford. So, even landlocked, we were always within sight of the sea.' She belched loudly. 'Damn,' she said and continued. 'I wasn't impressed when I was young, all that leaning on the past. It was so hard to escape from, young ladies from such families just didn't become doctors. And now it's gone, something unique. Everything is unique though, wouldn't you agree? And every ending sad. I haven't been back since my father died. The younger of my brothers was to be the farmer but he was a casualty of the War, barely alive for eighteen years. So we sold the place. I've seen people change but I haven't wanted to see the house and the land changed, above all not the land. Is that strange, do you think?'

He didn't reply though she was sure he'd been listening, even that at one point—when?—she'd touched him. Her antenna still served. She felt exhilarated.

'Damned casserole needs salt,' she said. 'Here. It's sea-salt. I remember how mad I felt when I learned that even though I was the eldest I couldn't inherit the farm. I told my brother, the older of the two, a male chauvinist aged six, that I'd be a vet then, look after other people's stock. He said girls couldn't do that either so I said—I was eight years old and chewing a stalk of timothy, funny to remember that—"Very well, I'll be a people's doctor." And so it all began. And you cannot imagine the furor—'But this the young man didn't like to hear, that there was anything their imagination couldn't compass. 'I am garrulous,' she said.

He mumbled.

'What was that?'

He spoke for the first time clearly. 'I said I wouldn't know. Not knowing you and how much you usually run on.'

She laughed. 'As a matter of fact, I don't, as a rule. But you've hardly eaten.' He took up a forkful and she waited for him to swallow, take up a second. 'Why are you doing this kind of work? Don't say it's for the money—or bread as you undoubtedly call it. Surprised I know the term?'

She saw him trying to think of an answer, some sarcasm. He was in a mean mood but didn't know how to let it out. He shrugged finally as if the problem defeated him.

'You speak well,' she said, 'when you speak. Have good table manners. Are you educated?'

'Depends.'

'On what I mean by educated? Good answer.' She shot in a key question. 'Are you married?'

'No.' A lie, she suspected, the word spoken so much too swiftly, less tonelessly.

Ah, she thought, I can still do it, and asked him to fill the kettle for their tea.

'Unless you'd prefer coffee?'

'Tea's fine,' he said and she told him where to find the canister, how much to measure into the pot.

'Can't help giving directions,' she said. 'Been doing it all my life.'

'Guess I'm in no position to complain.'

'I'd find you insolent,' Georgiana said, 'if I didn't know you were unhappy. And now you'll think that's none of my business.' No answer, though she thought again, that his back tightened. 'Well, you may be right. Or so I'd have thought once, since you haven't come to me for help. But I haven't time any more for fine distinctions and niceties. And maybe you haven't either.'

He took the cups and saucers from the counter and put them with the tea-pot beside her. He was sweating, she saw, just a few drops along his upper lip. 'Got any honey?'

'Any—? Oh, honey. For our tea. Excellent idea. Should be a jar towards the back of that second shelf. Good strong buckwheat honey with a bite to it, kind I grew up on.'

He brought it to the table and she spooned some into their cups.

'Like it?'

'It's okay.'

She provided another space by telling him of the wide fields of buckwheat, deep coral and scented—vigorous and coarse and beautiful as the strong things always are; perhaps she'd never had a taste for delicacy (Charles had not been a delicate lover)—and found that the memory and the link with Charles gave her immense pleasure. She longed to see buckwheat in flower again. In fact, must see it. She'd ask someone—Nora—no, one of the others, so the excursion wouldn't involve the presence of whoever-it-is.

'You have a strange effect on me,' she told the young man. 'Or I'm having it on myself. I keep going back. Like thinking about chewing timothy a moment ago. Be telling you next what I was wearing.' And wondered whether she should just continue to go where her mind took her. He so clearly didn't want to open out to some ancient stranger. (Remember what he sees when he looks at you. Something held together with sticks.) No-one had said she need do anything about him. Why not just go on rambling, silly old bag of bones, till the meal was over?

'Got a great-niece coming in later,' she said. 'Wants to quiz me about sex. How's that for irony, eh? What should I tell her?' He said nothing, gulped his tea, no doubt relieved that her attention had wandered. 'Come, you must have some suggestions. Take this. Her mother's afraid she'll become a lesbian to—what was the phrase?—raise her consciousness. How could two young women bouncing awkwardly about in bed raise one another's consciousness? What does that mean even?' It was no use. She saw him trying to deal with this, face working, but, poor young devil, he was too barricaded within himself to come out and consider other people. (I owe him more than this. Owe it to him and to my life. This *will* be a good day. I'll make it so. I'll be useful. I'm not pitiable, damn you, Nora. I'm Georgiana. A very good doctor.) 'Look here, let's be done with this,' she said in the gruff offhand voice she'd always used for such matters. 'You've come to the end of something, haven't you? That's where I reached you before. Endings. And it's chewing at your gut. Admit it. It's not shameful.'

He breathed sawingly. 'Suppose I have. Suppose it is. Isn't it my gut?'

'Not entirely,' said Georgiana. 'When you walked into my house and my life, I think it became partly my gut. Talk. It will be a release. You don't know me. I'll never confront you with it. And I'm not a psychiatrist, except of a rough and ready sort. There can be only one kind of ending at your age. Which of you broke it off? She? Or you?'

He gave that little tuck of the lip that with him might pass for a smile—or was perhaps only a tic, defensive.

'*She* did, eh?' she hazarded.

'What if she did?' Sweat formed again on his upper lip. 'She had good reason to perhaps.'

'She had good reason to perhaps. What sort of answer is that?'

'It's her life,' he said, 'and if she wants to—'

'Are you telling me you didn't fight? Not at all?' He looked at her, emptily but from somewhere very deep inside. 'Obviously she means a lot to you or you wouldn't be walking around like a zombie without her. It's got into your muscles, every movement you make. Aren't you going to fight even now? It may not be too late. Women like strength. They always have and I don't fancy that just because they want to be more independent means they've changed all that—'

'I don't want to talk about it,' he said. 'I came here to do the windows. I'm the help. You said that. I don't have to—' Trembling, he laid his saucer on the plate, then the cup. They clattered.

'Oh leave those, for God's sake. I'll take care of them. Go on about your windows, you poor foolish—'

She snatched the dishes and started to the sink, so swiftly and impetuously that she forgot to hoist herself, forgot her cane, took an unassisted step or two. 'Don't you know that nothing on God's green earth has been got without fighting? Do you imagine for an instant that I didn't fight? I fought all the way for every inch. I'm an old woman and I still know more about fighting— fighting for breath, fighting for strength—' (My God, here I go being a character again. As if life were ever that simple. This particular fighter feared death as few can have feared it. Fighting when you know you're going to lose, especially when, that's what I must tell them, Phyllis too. But is it enough? Enough to give from a long life?)

She had started to speak again when something exploded in her head. She fell, heavily on all fours, as horses do. Good God, it's a stroke, she thought, so that's how, like a blow—'Thank God, you're here. My hand's cut from the—but don't worry about—just help me turn so I can—'

She had half turned on her own when her eyes looked into his. He was stooping over her with the cane. 'You hit me,' she said. 'Oh you silly, silly. Well, just give me a hand and—'

'Let's see you fight now, old know-it-all. Just like her. Just like all of—' He struck again.

'No,' she said. 'No. You don't want to—you can't possibly—' She had averted her face but now, dangerous as she knew this was, she looked back, trying to catch his eye, hold him. 'Your whole life—think of that—your whole life, you foolish, foolish—' The cane whistled down, found its mark, she couldn't move quickly enough. Blood spurted from her cheek. 'But I'll be responsible.' Did she say or only think these words? 'And I'm not supposed to—not me—not destroy—'

'Why did you keep bugging me? Why did you? I didn't ask for your damn—' He was crying now, sobbing aloud. 'Oh I didn't want to. You're not a bad old—Fuck you, I didn't want to.'

The blows came down and down, rhythmically. Georgiana could no longer speak but even in her mind she did not call on any of the names of her life. She fought as she must, would continue to do till pain wiped out her world. Her nose was broken. She was blind. She had never felt more alive.

[1964]

For Discussion

1. Georgiana attributes her long life, in part, to "the habit, so long part of her, of weeding out any hint of frailty or contradiction." How does this habit also lead to her death?

2. What does Georgiana's profession have to do with the story?

3. Find references to "fighting" and explain what is meant by the theme of struggle in the story.

4. What are Georgiana's religious views?

5. Why are Phyllis and Nora in the story, since they don't actually appear? Why are three generations represented, rather than just two?

6. Georgiana's expectations about the day are not fulfilled. What does the element of surprise or the unexpected have to do with the concept of death in the story?

7. What do the ideas of "doubts" and "mistakes" suggest as themes in the story?

8. Analyze the interaction between the young man and Georgiana that leads to the ending.

9. Explain the significance of Georgiana's last words and thoughts.

For Further Exploration

1. Georgiana says that "In some ways old age was an adolescence, though a less painful one." Compare the degrees of pain involved in the stories of adolescence and those of old age and death. What causes the discomfort in these life stages?

2. Compare Georgiana's day with that of Hilary Stevens in *Mrs. Stevens Hears the Mermaids Singing* (Old Age section). How is the quality of life similar for these women and how is the conversation each has with a young man different? What factors allow a woman to age with dignity?

Margaret Laurence

1926–

In this final chapter of the novel Stone Angel, *a ninety-year-old Canadian woman has been returned after running away from her family to avoid being put in a nursing home. Should she relinquish her lifelong independence and pride as she approaches death?*

STONE ANGEL

The world is even smaller now. It's shrinking so quickly. The next room will be the smallest of all.

"The next room will be the smallest of the lot."

"What?" the nurse says absent-mindedly, plumping my pillow.

"Just enough space for me."

She looks shocked. "That's no way to talk."

How right she is. An embarrassing subject, better not mentioned. The way we used to feel, when I was a girl, about undergarments or the two-backed beast of love. But I want to take hold of her arm, force her attention. *Listen. You must listen. It's important. It's—quite an event.*

Only to me. Not to her. I don't touch her arm, nor speak. It would only upset her. She wouldn't know what to say.

This room is light and airy. The walls are primrose, and there's a private bathroom. The curtains are printed with delphiniums on a pale yellow background. I always have liked flowered material, provided it wasn't gaudy. But such a room must cost a lot. And now that I've thought of it, it worries me terribly. Goodness knows what it costs. Marvin never said. I must ask him. I mustn't forget. What if I haven't enough money? I can't ask Marvin and Doris to pay for it. Marvin would do it—that I do know. But I wouldn't ask. They'll have to move me again. That's all there is to it.

There's another bed, but it's empty. I'm alone. A nurse comes in again, not the same nurse. This one can't be a day over twenty, and she's so slight you'd wonder how such an insubstantial frame could support life at all. Her stomach is concave, and her breasts are no bigger than two damson plums. Fashionable, I suppose. Quite likely she's pleased to look that way. Her hips are so narrow, I wonder what she'll ever do if she has children? Or even when she marries. She can't be any wider than a pea-shooter inside.

"You girls are so slim these days."

She smiles. She's used to the inane remarks of old women.

"I'll bet you were just as slim, when you were young, Mrs. Shipley."

"Oh—you know my name." Then I remember it's on a card at the foot of my bed, and I feel a fool. "Yes, I was quite slender at your age. I had black hair, long, halfway down my back. Some people thought me quite pretty. You'd never think so to look at me now."

"Yes, you would," she says, standing back a little and regarding me. "I wouldn't say you'd been exactly *pretty*—handsome is what I'd say. You've got such strong features. Good bones don't change. You're still handsome."

I'm quite well aware that she's flattering me, but I'm pleased all the same. She's a friendly girl. She seems to do it out of friendliness, not pity.

"That's kind of you. You're a nice girl. You're lucky, to be young."

I wish I hadn't added that. I never used to say whatever popped into my head. How slipshod I'm growing.

"I guess so." She smiles, but differently, aloofly. "Maybe you're the lucky one."

"How so, for mercy's sake?"

"Oh well—" she says evasively, "you've had those years. Nothing can take them away."

"That's a mixed blessing, surely," I say dryly, but of course she doesn't see what I mean. We were talking so nicely, and now it's gone. Something lurks behind her eyes, but I don't know what it is. What troubles her? What could possibly trouble anyone as young and attractive as she is, with her health, and with training so she need never worry about getting a job? Yet, even as I think this, I know it's daft. The plagues go on from generation to generation.

"You settle down now," she says. "I'll drop by in a little while to see if you're all right."

But when the long night is upon me, she doesn't come. There are no voices. I cannot hear a living soul. I sleep and waken, sleep and waken, until I no longer know whether I'm asleep and dreaming I'm awake, or wakeful and imagining that I sleep.

The floor is cold, and I don't know where my slippers have got to. Thank heavens at least Doris has moved the mat beside my bed. It was a real hazard, that mat. A person couldn't help but slip on it. Breathing seems so slow, and each breath hurts. How peculiar. It used to be so easy one never considered it at all. The light is on beyond that open door. If I reach it, someone will speak. Will the voice be the one I have been listening for?

What keeps him? He could surely say something. It wouldn't hurt him, just to say a word. *Hagar.* He was the only one who ever called me by my name. It wouldn't hurt him to speak. It's not so much to ask.

"Mrs. Shipley—"

A high alarmed voice, a girl's. And I, a sleepwalker wakened, can only stand stiffly, paralyzed with the impact of her cry. Then a hand grasps my arm.

"It's all right, Mrs. Shipley. Everything's all right. You just come along with me."

Oh. I'm here, am I? And I've been wandering around, and the girl is frightened, for she's responsible. She leads me back to bed. Then she does something else, and at first I don't understand.

"It's like a little bed-jacket, really. It's nothing. It's just to keep you from harm. It's for your own protection."

Coarse linen, it feels like. She slides my arms in, and ties the harness firmly to the bed. I pull, and find I'm knotted and held like a trussed fowl.

"I won't have this. I won't stand for it. It's not right. Oh, it's mean—"

The nurse's voice is low, as though she were half ashamed of what she'd done. "I'm sorry. But you might fall, you see, and—"

"Do you think I'm crazy, that I have to be put into this rig?"

"Of course not. You might hurt yourself, that's all. Please—"

I hear the desperation in her voice. Now that I think of it, what else can she do? She can't sit here by my bed all night.

"I have to do it," she says. "Don't be angry."

She has to do it. Quite right. It's not her fault. Even I can see that.

"All right." I can barely hear my own voice, but I hear her slight answering sigh.

"I'm sorry," she says helplessly, apologizing needlessly, perhaps on behalf of God, who never apologizes. Then I'm the one who's sorry.

"I've caused you so much trouble—"

"No, you haven't. I'm going to give you a hypo now. Then you'll be more comfortable, and probably you'll sleep."

And incredibly, despite my canvas cage, I do.

When I waken, the other bed has an inhabitant. She is sitting up in bed, reading a magazine, or pretending to. Sometimes she cries a little, putting a hand to her abdomen. She is about sixteen, I'd say, and her face is delicately boned, olive-skinned. Her eyes, as she glances hesitantly at me, are dark and only slightly slanted. Her hair is thick and black and straight, and it shines. She's a celestial, as we used to call them.

"Good morning." I don't know if I should speak or not, but she doesn't take it amiss. She lays the magazine down and smiles at me. Grins, rather— it's the bold half-hoydenish smile the youngsters all seem to wear these days.

"Hi," she says. "You're Mrs. Shipley. I saw it on your card. I'm Sandra Wong."

She speaks just like Tina. Obviously she was born in this country.

"How do you do?"

My absurd formality with this child is caused by my sudden certainty that she is the granddaughter of one of the small foot-bound women whom Mr. Oatley smuggled in, when Oriental wives were frowned upon, in the hazardous hold of his false-bottomed boats. Maybe I owe my house to her grandmother's passage money. There's a thought. Mr. Oatley showed me one of their shoes once. It was no bigger than a child's, although it had belonged to a full-grown woman. A silk embroidered case, emerald and gold, where the foot fitted, and beneath, a crescent platform of rope and plaster, so they must have walked as though upon two miniature rockers. I don't say any of this. To her, it would be ancient history.

"I have to have my appendix out," she says. "They're going to get me ready soon. It's an emergency. I was really bad last night. I was real scared and so was my mom. Have you ever had your appendix out? Is it bad?"

"I had mine out years ago," I say, although in fact I've never even had my tonsils out. "It's not a serious operation."

"Yeh?" she says. "Is that right? I've never had an operation before. You don't know what to expect, if it's your first time."

"Well, you needn't worry," I say. "It's just routine these days. You'll be up before you know it."

"Do you really think so? Gee, I don't know. I was pretty scared last night. I don't like the thought of the anesthetic."

"Bosh. That's nothing. You'll feel a bit uncomfortable afterward, but that's all."

"Is that right? You really think so?"

"Of course."

"Well, you oughta know," she says. "I guess you've had lots of operations, eh?"

I can hardly keep from laughing aloud. But she'd be offended, so I restrain myself.

"What makes you think so?"

"Oh well—I just meant, a person who's—you know—not so young—"

"Yes. Of course. Well, I've not had all that many operations. Perhaps I've been lucky."

"I guess so. My mom had a hysterectomy year before last."

At her age I wouldn't have known what a hysterectomy was.

"Dear me. That's too bad."

"Yeh. That's a tough one, all right. It's not so much the operation, you know—it's the emotional upheaval afterward."

"Really?"

"Yeh," she says knowledgeably. "My mom was all on edge for months. It got her down, you know, that she couldn't have any more kids. I don't know why she wanted any more. She's got five already counting me. I'm the second oldest."

"That's a good-sized family, all right. What does your father do?"

"He has a store."

"Well, well. So did mine."

But that's the wrong thing to say. So much distance lies between us, she doesn't want any such similarity.

"Oh?" she says, uninterested. She looks at her watch. "They said they'd be along in a minute. I wonder what's holding them up? A person could get forgotten in a big place like this, I bet."

"They'll be here soon."

"Gee, not too soon, I hope," she says.

Her eyes change, widen, spread until they're shaped like two peach stones. The amber centers glisten.

"They wouldn't let my mom stay." Then, defiantly, "Not that I need her. But it would've been company."

A nurse trots briskly in, pulls the curtains around her bed.

"Oh—is it time?" Her voice is querulous, uncertain. "Will it hurt?"

"You won't feel a thing," the nurse says.

"Will it take long? Will my mom be able to come in afterward? Where do you have to take me? Oh—what're you going to do? You're not going to shave me *there*?"

What a lot of questions, and how appalled she sounds. Fancy being alarmed at such a trifling thing. I lie here smug and fat, thinking—*She'll learn.*

They don't bring her back for hours, and when they do, she's very quiet. The curtains are drawn around her bed. Sometimes she moans a little in the half sleep of the receding anesthetic. The day goes slowly. Trays are brought me, and I make some effort to eat, but I seem to have lost interest in my meals. I look at the ceiling, where the sun patterns it with slivers of light. Someone puts a needle in my flesh. Have I cried out, then? What does it matter if I did? But I'd rather not.

I liked that forest. I recall the ferns, cool and lacy. But I was thirsty, so I had to come here. The man's name was Ferney, and he spoke about his wife. She was never the same. That wasn't fair to him. She just didn't know. But he didn't know, either. He never said how she took the child's death. I drift like kelp. Nothing seems to be around me at all.

"Mother—"

I drag myself to the surface. "What is it? What's the matter?"

"It's me. Doris. How are you? Marv didn't come tonight. He had to see a client. But I've brought Mr. Troy to see you. You remember Mr. Troy, don't you? Our clergyman?"

Oh Lord, what next? Never a minute's peace. I remember him all right. His face beams down at me, round and crimson as a harvest moon.

"How are you, Mrs. Shipley?"

Is that the only phrase that ever comes to anyone's mind in such a place? With a great effort, as though my veins might split, I open my eyes wide and glare at him.

"Dandy. Just dandy. Can't you see?"

"Now, Mother—" Doris cautions. "Now, please—"

Very well. I'll behave myself. I'll be what they desire. Oh, but if Doris doesn't wipe that sanctimonious anguish off her face, I'll dig up one of Bram's epithets and fling it at her. That would do the trick.

"I have to see the nurse a minute," she says with leaden tact. "Maybe you'd like to talk a while with Mr. Troy."

She tiptoes out. We remain in heavy silence, Mr. Troy and I. I glance at him and see he's struggling to speak and finding it impossibly difficult. He thinks me formidable. What a joke. I could feel almost sorry for him, he's perspiring so. Stonily, I wait. Why should I assist him? The drug is wearing off. My bones are sore, and the soreness is spreading like fire over dry grass, quickly, licking its way along. All at once, an eruption of speech, Mr. Troy bursts out.

"Would you—care to pray?"

As though he were asking me for the next dance.

"I've held out this long," I reply. "I may as well hold out a while longer."

"You don't mean that, I'm sure. If you would try—"

He looks at me with such an eagerness that now I'm rendered helpless. It's his calling. He offers what he can. It's not his fault.

"I can't," I say. "I never could get the hang of it. But—you go ahead if you like, Mr. Troy."

His face relaxes. How relieved he is. He prays in a monotone, as though God had ears for one note only. I scarcely listen to the droning words. Then something occurs to me.

"There's one—" I say, on impulse. "That starts out *All people that on earth do dwell*—do you know it?"

"Certainly I know it. You want to hear that? Now?" He sounds taken aback, as though it were completely unsuitable.

"Unless you'd rather not."

"Oh no, it's quite all right. It's usually sung, that's all."

"Well, sing it, then."

"What? Here?" He's stunned. I have no patience with this young man. "Why not?"

"All right, then." He clasps and unclasps his hands. He flushes warmly, and peeks around to see if anyone might be listening, as though he'd pass out if they were. But I perceive now that there's some fibre in him. He'll do it, even if it kills him. Good for him. I can admire that.

Then he opens his mouth and sings, and I'm the one who's taken aback now. He should sing always, and never speak. He should chant his sermons. The fumbling of his speech is gone. His voice is firm and sure.

> "All people that on earth do dwell,
> Sing to the Lord with joyful voice.
> Him serve with mirth, His praise forth tell;
> Come ye before Him and rejoice.

Fiction About Death

I would have wished it. This knowing comes upon me so forcefully, so shatteringly, and with such a bitterness as I have never felt before. I must always, always, have wanted that—simply to rejoice. How is it I never could? I know, I know. How long have I known? Or have I always known, in some far crevice of my heart, some cave too deeply buried, too concealed? Every good joy I might have held, in my man or any child of mine or even the plain light of morning, of walking the earth, all were forced to a standstill by some brake of proper appearances—oh, proper to whom? When did I ever speak the heart's truth?

Pride was my wilderness, and the demon that led me there was fear. I was alone, never anything else, and never free, for I carried my chains within me, and they spread out from me and shackled all I touched. Oh, my two, my dead. Dead by your own hands or by mine? Nothing can take away those years.

Mr. Troy has stopped singing.

"I've upset you," he says uncertainly. "I'm sorry."

"No, you haven't." My voice is muffled and I have my hands over my eyes so he won't see. He must think I've taken leave of my senses. "I've not heard that for a long time, that's all."

I can face him now. I remove my hands and look at him. He's puzzled and worried.

"Are you sure you're all right?"

"Quite sure. Thank you. That wasn't easy—to sing aloud alone."

"If it wasn't," he says morosely, "it's my own fault."

He thinks he's failed, and I can't muster words to reassure him, so he must go uncomforted.

Doris returns. She fusses over me, fixes my pillows, rearranges my flowers, does my hair. How I wish she wouldn't fuss so. She jangles my nerves with her incessant fussing. Mr. Troy has left and is waiting outside in the hall.

"Did you have a nice chat?" she says wistfully.

If only she'd stop prodding at me about it.

"We didn't have a single solitary thing to say to one another," I reply.

She bites her lip and looks away. I'm ashamed. But I won't take back the words. What business is it of hers, anyway?

Oh, I am unchangeable, unregenerate. I go on speaking in the same way, always, and the same touchiness rises within me at the slightest thing.

"Doris—I didn't speak the truth. He sang for me, and it did me good."

She gives me a sideways and suspicious glance. She doesn't believe me.

"Well, no one could say I haven't tried," she remarks edgily.

"No, no one could say that."

I sigh and turn away from her. Who will she have to wreak salvation upon when I'm gone? How she'll miss me.

Later, when she and Mr. Troy have gone, I have another visitor. At first, I can't place him, although he is so familiar in appearance. He grins and bends over me.

"Hi, Gran. Don't you know me? Steven."

I'm flustered, pleased to see him, mortified at not having recognized him immediately.

"Steven. Well, well. Of course. How are you? I haven't seen you for quite some time. You're looking very smart."

"New suit. Glad you like it. Have to look successful, you know."

"You don't only look. You are. Aren't you?"

"I can't complain," he says.

He's an architect, a very clever boy. Goodness knows where he gets his brains from. Not from either parent, I'd say. But Marvin and Doris certainly saved and did without, to get that boy through university, I'll give them that.

"Did your mother tell you to come and see me?"

"Of course not," he says. "I just thought I'd drop in and see how you were."

He sounds annoyed, so I know he's lying. What does it matter? But it would have been nice if it had been his own idea.

"Tina's getting married," I say, conversationally.

I'm tired. I'm not feeling up to much. But I hope he'll stay for a few minutes all the same. I like to look at him. He's a fine-looking boy. Boy, indeed—he must be close to thirty.

"So I hear," he says. "About time, too. Mom wants her to be married here, but Tina says she can't spare the time and neither can August—that's the guy she's marrying. So Mom's going to fly down East for the wedding, she thinks."

I never realized until this moment how cut off I am. I've always been so fond of Tina. Doris might have told me. It's the least she could have done.

"She didn't tell me. She didn't say a word."

"Maybe I shouldn't have said—"

"It's a good job somebody tells me these things. She never bothers, your mother. It never occurs to her."

"Well, maybe she forgot. She's been—"

"I'll bet she forgot. I'll just bet a cookie she did. When is she going, Steven?"

A long pause. My grandson reddens and gazes at my roses, his face averted from mine.

"I don't think it's quite settled yet," he says finally.

Then all at once I understand, and know, too, why Doris never mentioned it. They have to wait and see what happens here. How inconvenient I am proving for them. *Will it be soon?* That's what they're asking themselves. I'm upsetting all their plans. That's what it is to them—an inconvenience.

Steven leans toward me again. "Anything you want, Gran? Anything I could bring you?"

"No. Nothing. There's nothing I want."

"Sure?"

"You might just leave me your packet of cigarettes, Steven. Would you?"

"Oh sure, of course. Here—have one now."

"Thank you."

He lights it for me, and places an ash tray, rather nervously, close by my wrist, as though certain I'm a fire hazard. Then he looks at me and smiles, and I'm struck again with the resemblance.

"You're very like your grandfather, Steven. Except that he wore a beard, you could almost be Brampton Shipley as a young man."

"Oh?" He's only mildly interested. He searches for a comment. "Should I be pleased?"

"He was a fine-looking man, your grandfather."

"Mom always says I look like Uncle Ned."

"What? Doris's brother? Nonsense. You don't take after him a scrap. You're a Shipley through and through."

He laughs. "You're a great old girl, you know that?"

His tone has affection in it, and I would be pleased if it weren't condescending as well, in the same way that gushing matrons will coo over a carriage—*What a cute baby, how adorable.*

"You needn't be impertinent, Steven. You know I don't care for it."

"I didn't mean it like that. Never mind. You should be glad I appreciate you."

"Do you?"

"Sure I do," he says jovially. "I always have. Don't you remember how you used to give me pennies to buy jaw-breakers, when I was a kid? Mom used to be livid, thinking of the dentist's bills."

I'd forgotten. I have to smile, even as my mouth is filled once more with bile. That's what I am to him—a grandmother who gave him money for candy. What does he know of me? Not a blessed thing. I'm choked with it now, the incommunicable years, everything that happened and was spoken or not spoken. I want to tell him. Someone should know. This is what I think. *Someone really ought to know these things.*

But where would I begin, and what does it matter to him, anyway? It might be worse. At least he recalls a pleasant thing.

"I remember," I say. "You were a little monkey, always snooping in my purse."

"I had an eye to the main chance," he says, "even then."

I look at him sharply, hearing in his voice some mocking echo of John's.

"Steven—are you all right, really? Are you—content?"

He is taken by surprise. "Content? I don't know. I'm as well off as the next guy, I suppose. What a question."

And now I see that he is troubled by things I know nothing of, and don't even care to know. I can't take on anything new at this point. It's too much. I have to let it go. Even if I presumed so far, and questioned him, he'd never say. Why should he? It's his life, not mine.

"Thanks for the cigarettes," I say, "and for coming to see me."

"That's okay," he says.

We have nothing more to say to one another. He bends and places a quick and token kiss on my face, and then he goes. I would have liked to tell him he is dear to me, and would be so, no matter what he's like or what he does with his life. But he'd only have been embarrassed and so would I.

My discomfort asserts itself, until the only thing that matters to me in this world is that I'm nauseated and I hurt. The sheets bind me like bandages. It's such a warm evening, not a breath of air.

"Nurse—"

Again the needle, and I'm greedy for it now, and thrust out my arm before she's even ready. *Hurry, hurry, I can't wait.* It's accomplished, and before it has had time to take effect, I'm relieved, knowing the stuff is inside me and at work.

The curtains are pulled aside from the girl's bed, and she's awake. She looks disheveled, puffy-eyed. She's been crying. And now I notice that her mother, a short dark woman with short dark hair and an apologetic smile, is leaving, waving as she walks out, a hopeful helpless flickering of the hands. The woman steps out the door. The girl watches for a moment, then turns her head away.

"How are you feeling?" I ask.

"Awful," she says. "I feel just perfectly awful. You said it wouldn't be bad."

She sounds reproachful. First I'm full of regrets, thinking I've deceived her. Then I feel only annoyance.

"If that's the worst you ever have, my girl, you'll be lucky, I can tell you that."

"Oh—" she cries, outraged, and then subsides into a sulky silence. She won't say a word, nor even look at me. The nurse arrives and the girl whispers. I can hear.

"Do I have to stay here—with her?"

Furious and affronted, I turn over in my bed and reach for Steven's cigarettes. Then I hear the nurse's reply.

"Try to be patient. She's—"

I can't catch the last low murmur. Then the girl's voice, clear and loud.

"Oh, gee, I didn't know. But what if—? Oh, please move me, please."

Am I a burden to her as well? What if anything happens in the night? That's what she's wondering.

"You rest now, Sandra," the nurse says. "We'll see what we can do."

The room at night is deep and dark, like a coal scuttle, and I'm lying like a lump at the bottom of it. I've been wakened by the girl's voice, and now I can't get back to sleep again. How I hate the sound of a person crying. She moans, snuffles wetly, moans again. She won't stop. She'll go on all night like this, more than likely. It's insufferable. I wish she'd make some effort to be quiet. She has no self-control, that creature, none. I could almost wish she'd die, or at least faint, so I wouldn't have to lie here hour after hour and hear this caterwauling.

I can't recall her name. Wong. That's her last name. If I could think of her first name, I could call out to her. How else can I address her? "Miss Wong" sounds foolish, coming from someone my age. I can't say "my dear"—too obviously false. Young lady? Girl? You? *Hey, you*—how rude. Sandra. Her name is Sandra.

"Sandra—"

"Yes?" Her voice is thin, fearful. "What is it?"

"What's the matter?"

"I need to go to the bathroom," she says. "I've called the nurse, but she doesn't hear me."

"Have you put your light on? The little light above your bed. That's how you're supposed to call the nurse."

"I can't reach it. I can't move up by myself. It hurts."

"I'll put my light on, then."

"Oh, would you? Gee, thanks a million."

The faint glow appears, and we wait. No one comes.

"They must be busy tonight," I say, to calm her. "Sometimes it takes a while."

"What'll I do if I can't hold on?" She laughs, a strained and breathless laugh, and I sense her anguish and her terrible embarrassment. To her, it's unthinkable.

"Never you mind," I reply. "That's their look-out."

"Yeh, maybe so," she says. "But I'd feel so awful—"

"Wretched nurse," I said peevishly, feeling now only sympathy for the girl, none for the eternally frantic staff. "Why doesn't she get here?"

The girl cries again. "I can't stand it. And my side hurts so much—"

She's never before been at the dubious mercy of her organs. Pain and humiliation have been only words to her. Suddenly I'm incensed at it, the unfairness. She shouldn't have to find out these things at her age.

"I'm going to get you a bedpan."

"No—" she says, alarmed. "I'm okay, really. You mustn't, Mrs. Shipley."

"I will so. I won't stand for this sort of thing another minute. They keep them in the bathroom, right here. It's only a step."

"Do you think you oughta?"

"Certainly. You just wait. I'll get it for you, you'll see."

Heaving, I pull myself up. As I slide my legs out of bed, one foot cramps and I'm helpless for a second. I grasp the bed, put my toes on the icy floor, work the cramp out, and then I'm standing, the weight of my flesh heavy and ponderous, my hair undone now and slithering lengthily around my bare and chilly shoulders, like snakes on a Gorgon's head. My satin nightgown, rumpled and twisted, hampers and hobbles me. I seem to be rather shaky. The idiotic quivering of my flesh won't stop. My separate muscles prance and jerk. I'm cold. It's unusually cold tonight, it seems to me. I'll wait a moment. There. I'm better now. It's only a few steps, that I do know.

I shuffle slowly, thinking how peculiar it is to walk like this, not to be able to command my legs to pace and stride. One foot and then another. Only a little way now, Hagar. Come on.

There now. I've reached the bathroom and gained the shiny steel grail. That wasn't so difficult after all. But the way back is longer. I miss my footing, lurch, almost topple. I snatch for something, and my hand finds a window sill. It steadies me. I go on.

"You okay, Mrs. Shipley?"

"Quite—okay."

I have to smile at myself. I've never used that word before in my life. *Okay—guy*—such slangy words. I used to tell John. They mark a person.

All at once I have to stop and try to catch the breath that seems to have escaped me. My ribs are hot with pain. Then it ebbs, but I'm left reeling with weakness. I'll reach my destination, though. Easy does it. Come along, now.

There. I'm there. I knew I could. And now I wonder if I've done it for her or for myself. No matter. I'm here, and carrying what she needs.

"Oh, thanks," she says. "Am I ever glad—"

At that moment the ceiling light is switched peremptorily on, and a nurse is standing there in the doorway, a plump and middle-aged nurse, looking horrified.

"Mrs. Shipley! What on earth are you doing out of bed? Didn't you have the restraint put on tonight?"

"They forgot it," I say, "and a good job they did, too."

"My heavens," the nurse says. "What if you'd fallen?"

"What if I had?" I retort. "What if I had?"

She doesn't reply. She leads me back to bed. When she has settled us both, she goes and we're alone, the girl and I. Then I hear a sound in the dark room. The girl is laughing.

"Mrs. Shipley—"

"Yes?"

She stifles her laughter, but it breaks out again.

"Oh, I can't laugh. I mustn't. It pulls my stitches. But did you ever see anything like the look on her face?"

I have to snort, recalling it.

"She was stunned, all right, wasn't she, seeing me standing there? I thought she'd pass out."

My own spasm of laughter catches me like a blow. I can't stave it off. Crazy. I must be crazy. I'll do myself some injury.

"Oh—oh—" the girl gasps. "She looked at you as though you'd just done a crime."

"Yes—that was exactly how she looked. Poor soul. Oh, the poor soul. We really worried her."

"That's for sure. We sure did."

Convulsed with our paining laughter, we bellow and wheeze. And then we peacefully sleep.

It must be some days now, since the girl had her operation. She's up and about, and can walk almost straight now, without bending double and clutching her side. She comes over to my bed often, and hands me my glass of water or pulls my curtains if I want to drowse. She's a slender girl, green and slender, a sapling of a girl. Her face is boned so finely. She wears a blue brocade housecoat—from her father's shop, she tells me. They gave it to her for her last birthday, when she was seventeen. I felt the material—she held a sleeve out, so I could see how it felt. Pure silk, it is. The embroidery on it is red and gold, chrysanthemums and intricate temples. Reminds me of the paper lanterns we used to hang on the porches. That would be a long time ago, I suppose.

The pain thickens, and then the nurse comes and the needle slips into me like a swimmer sliding silently into a lake.

Rest. And swing, swayed and swirled hither and yon. I remember the Ferris wheel at the fairgrounds once a year. *Swoop!* That's how it went. Swooping round and round, and we laughed sickly and prayed for it to stop.

"My mom brought me this cologne. It's called *Ravishing*. Want a dab?"

"Why—all right. Can you spare it?"

"Oh sure. It's a big bottle—see?"

"Oh yes." But I see only a distant glistening of glass.

"There. On each wrist. Now you smell like a garden."

"Well, that's a change."

My ribs hurt. No one knows.

"Hello, Mother."

Marvin. He's alone. My mind surfaces. Up from the sea comes the fish. A little further—try. There.

"Hello, Marvin."

"How are you?"

"I'm—"

I can't say it. Now, at last, it becomes impossible for me to mouth the words—*I'm fine.* I won't say anything. It's about time I learned to keep my mouth shut. But I don't. I can hear my voice saying something, and it astounds me.

"I'm—frightened. Marvin, I'm so frightened—"

Then my eyes focus with a terrifying clarity on him. He's sitting by my bed. He is putting one of his big hands up to his forehead and passing it slowly across his eyes. He bends his head. What possessed me? I think it's the first time in my life I've ever said such a thing. Shameful. Yet somehow it is a relief to speak it. What can he say, though?

Fiction About Death

"If I've been crabby with you, sometimes, these past years," he says in a low voice, "I didn't mean it."

I stare at him. Then, quite unexpectedly, he reaches for my hand and holds it tightly.

Now it seems to me he is truly Jacob, gripping with all his strength, and bargaining. *I will not let thee go, except thou bless me.* And I see I am thus strangely cast, and perhaps have been so from the beginning, and can only release myself by releasing him.

It's in my mind to ask his pardon, but that's not what he wants from me.

"You've not been cranky, Marvin. You've been good to me, always. A better son than John."

The dead don't bear a grudge nor seek a blessing. The dead don't rest uneasy. Only the living. Marvin, looking at me from anxious elderly eyes, believes me. It doesn't occur to him that a person in my place would ever lie.

He lets go my hand, then, and draws away his own.

"You got everything you want, here?" he says gruffly. "Anything you want me to bring you?"

"No, nothing, thanks."

"Well, so long," Marvin says. "I'll be seeing you."

I nod and close my eyes.

As he goes out, I hear the nurse speaking to him in the corridor.

"She's got an amazing constitution, your mother. One of those hearts that just keeps on working, whatever else is gone."

A pause, and then Marvin replies.

"She's a holy terror," he says.

Listening, I feel like it is more than I could now reasonably have expected out of life, for he has spoken with such anger and such tenderness.

I recall the last time I was ever in Manawaka. Marvin and Doris were motoring east that summer, for their holidays, and I accompanied them. We went through Manawaka on the way. We drove out to the old Shipley place. I wouldn't have known it. A new house stood there, a new split-level house painted green. The barn was new, and the fences, and no weeds grew around the gate.

"Look at that," Marvin whistled. "Get a load of the Pontiac, this year's. That guy must be doing well."

"Let's go on," I said. "No use stopping here."

"It's quite an improvement," Marvin said, "if you ask me."

"Oh, I don't dispute that. No sense in parking here, though, and gawking at a strange house."

We drove out to the cemetery. Doris didn't get out of the car. Marvin and I walked over to the family plot. The angel was still standing there, but winters or lack of care had altered her. The earth had heaved with frost around her, and she stood askew and tilted. Her mouth was white. We didn't touch her. We only looked. Someday she'll topple entirely, and no one will bother to set her upright again.

A young caretaker was there, a man who limped, and he came up and spoke to us. He was no one we knew, and he didn't know us or think we were anything but curious tourists.

"Just passing through, are you?" he said, and then, as I nodded, "We got quite a nice cemetery here, a real old one, one of the oldest in the entire province. We got a stone dates back to 1870. Fact. Real interesting, some of the stones here. Take this one—bet you never seen a stone before with two family names, eh? Unusual. This here's the Currie-Shipley stone. The two families was connected by marriage. Pioneering families, the both of them, two of the earliest in the district, so Mayor Telford Simmons told me, and he's quite an old-timer himself. I never knew them, of course. It was before my day. I was raised in South Wachakwa, myself.''

The both of them. Both the same. Nothing to pick and choose between them now. That was as it should be. But all the same, I didn't want to stay any longer. I turned and walked back to the car. Marvin stood talking to the man for a while, and then he came back, too, and we drove on.

I lie in my cocoon. I'm woven around with threads, held tightly, and youngsters come and jab their pins into me. Then the tight threads loosen. There. That's better. Now I can breathe.

If I could, I'd like to have a piper play a pibroch[1] over my grave. *Flowers of the Forest*—is that a pibroch? How would I know? I've never even set foot in the Highlands. My heart's not there. And yet—I'd wish it, as I'm gathered to my fathers. How could anyone explain such an absurdity?

The pattering halts quite close to me. She bends. Her face is heart-shaped, like a lilac leaf. Her face hovers leaf-like, very delicately, nearby.

"The doctor told me I only gotta stay another two or three days. Gee, will I ever be glad to be home. Isn't that swell?"

"Yes. Swell."

"I hope you're outa here soon, too," she says. Then, perceiving her blunder, "I mean—"

"I know. Thanks, child."

She goes away. I lie here and try to recall something truly free that I've done in ninety years. I can think of only two acts that might be so, both recent. One was a joke—yet a joke only as all victories are, the paraphernalia being unequal to the event's reach. The other was a lie—yet not a lie, for it was spoken at least and at last with what may perhaps be a kind of love.

When my second son was born, he found it difficult to breathe at first. He gasped a little, coming into the unfamiliar air. He couldn't have known before or suspected at all that breathing would be what was done by creatures here. Perhaps the same occurs elsewhere, an element so unknown you'd never suspect it at all, until— Wishful thinking. If it happened that way, I'd pass out with amazement. Can angels faint?

Ought I to appeal? It's the done thing. *Our Father*—no. I want no part of that. All I can think is—*Bless me or not, Lord, just as You please, for I'll not beg.*

Pain swells and fills me. I'm distended with it, bloated and swollen like soft flesh held under by the sea. Disgusting. I hate this. I like things to be tidy. But even disgust won't last. It has to be relinquished, too. Only urgency remains. The world is a needle.

"Hurry, please—I can't wait—"

"Just a minute, Mrs. Shipley. I'll be right with you."

Where's she got to, stupid woman?

"Doris! Doris! I need you!"

She's beside me.

"You took your time in coming, I must say. Hurry up, now—"

[1]Mournful bagpipe song.

I must get back, back to my sleek cocoon, where I'm almost comfortable, lulled by potions. I can collect my thoughts there. That's what I need to do, collect my thoughts.

"You're so slow—"

"Sorry. That better?"

"Yes. No. I'm—thirsty. Can't you even—"

"Here. Here you are. Can you?"

"Of course. What do you think I am? What do you take me for? Here, give it to me. Oh, for mercy's sake let me hold it myself!"

I only defeat myself by not accepting her. I know this—I know it very well. But I can't help it—it's my nature. I'll drink from this glass, or spill it, just as I choose. I'll not countenance anyone else's holding it for me. And yet—if she were in my place, I'd think her daft, and push her hands away, certain I could hold it for her better.

I wrest from her the glass, full of water to be had for the taking. I hold it in my own hands. There. There.

And then—

[1964]

For Discussion

1. Analyze Hagar Shipley's interactions with the nurses and patient representing the younger generation.

2. What topics does Mrs. Shipley think about as she lives her last day? How are her concerns the same or different from women's thoughts in earlier life stages?

3. Explain the significance of the restraints used to keep Mrs. Shipley in bed. What types of restraints, if any, were used in other life stages?

4. Examine the lies Hagar tells in this chapter, and the reasons that she lies to Sandra Wong and to Marvin. Hasn't she always prided herself on being forthright?

5. Describe Hagar's moment of insight when Mr. Troy sings "All Creatures That On Earth Do Dwell." What does she suddenly realize?

6. Find instances in which Hagar's behavior fluctuates between irascibility and compassion. To what extent does her behavior seem to be part of her personality, and to what extent is she erratic because of her situation?

7. How does Steven relate to Hagar's age and situation? Why does Sandra Wong's attitude change?

8. In what ways is death an inconvenience to others in the story, or is Hagar being oversensitive?

9. How do Hagar's thoughts and actions in the final episode reaffirm the principles by which she lived?

For Further Exploration

1. Compare this death-bed account with that of Tillie Olsen's "Tell Me a Riddle" or Katherine Anne Porter's "The Jilting of Granny Weatherall" (this section). In particular, how are the women's relationships with their fami-

lies and religious leaders the same or different, and how do they deal with death when it comes?

2. Show how the remaining lines of Dylan Thomas' poem "Do Not Go Gentle into That Good Night" relate to Hagar Shipley's death in *Stone Angel.* Why might Laurence have selected the first two lines of the poem for the epigraph to the novel?

Dorothy Richardson

1873–1957

This brief but powerful story of a woman's final thoughts before dying presents us with insights about how to live as well as how to die. Beyond the physical pain and feelings of regret the narrator experiences are perceptive comments about what is—or should be—important once each individual accepts the fact of human mortality.

DEATH

This was death this time, no mistake. Her cheeks flushed at the indecency of being seen, dying and then dead. If only she could get it over and lay herself out decent before anyone came in to see and meddle. Mrs. Gworsh winning, left out there in the easy world, coming in to see her dead and lay her out and talk about her. . . . While there's life there's hope. Perhaps she wasn't dying. Only afraid. People can be so mighty bad and get better. But no. Not after that feeling rolling up within, telling her in words, her whom it knew, that this time she was going to be overwhelmed. That was the beginning, the warning and the certainty. To be more and more next time, any minute, increasing till her life flowed out for all to see. Her heart thumped. The rush of life beating against the walls of her body, making her head spin, numbed the pain and brought a mist before her eyes. Death. What she'd always feared so shocking, and put away. But no one knows what it is, how awful beyond everything, till they're in for it. Nobody knows death is this rush of life in all your parts.

The mist cleared. Her face was damp. The spinning in her head had ceased. She drew a careful breath. Without pain. Some of the pain had driven through her without feeling. But she was heavier. It wasn't gone either. Only waiting. She saw the doctor on his way. Scorn twisted her lips against her empty gums. Scores of times she'd waited for him. Felt him drive fear away. Joked. This time he'd say nothing. Watch, for her secret life to come up and out. When his turn came he'd know what it was like letting your life out; and all of them out there. No good telling. You can't know till you're in for it. They're all in for it, rich and poor alike. No help. The great enormous creature driving your innards up, what nobody knows. What *you* don't know. . . . Life ain't worth death.

It's got to be stuck, shame or no . . . but how do you do it?

She lay still and listened for footsteps. They knew next door by now. That piece would never milk Snowdrop dry. Less cream, less butter. Everything going back. Slip-slop, go as you please, and never done. Where'd us be to now if I hadn't? That's it. What they don't think of. Slip-slop. Grinning and singing enough to turn the milk. I've got a tongue. I know it. You've got to keep on and keep on at them. Or nothing done. I been young, but never them silly ways. Snowdrop'll go back; for certain. . . .

But I shan't ever *see* it no more . . . the thought flew lifting through her mind. See no more. Work no more. Worry no more. Then what had been the good of it? Why had she gone on year in year out since Tom died and she began ailing, tramping all weathers up to the field, toiling and aching, and black as thunder most times. What was the good? Nobody knew her. Tom never had. And now there was only that piece downstairs, and what she did didn't matter any more. Except to herself, and she'd go on being slip-slop; not knowing she was in for death that makes it all one whatever you do. Good and bad they're all dying and don't know it's the most they've got to do.

Her mind looked back up and down her life. Tom. What a fool she'd been to think him any different. Then when he died she'd thought him the same as at first, and cried because she'd let it all slip in the worries. Little Joe. Tearing her open, then snuggled in her arms, sucking. And all outside bright and peaceful; better than the beginning with Tom. But they'd all stop if they knew where it led. Joe, and his wife, and his little ones, in for all of it, getting the hard of it now, and death waiting for them. She could tell them all now what it was like, all of them, the squire, all the same. All going the same way, rich and poor.

The Bible was right, "Remember now thy Creator in the days of thy youth." What she had always wanted. She had always wanted to be good. Now it was too late. Nothing mattering, having it all lifted away, made the inside of you come back as it was at the first, ready to begin. Too late. Shocking she had thought it when parson said prepare for death, live as if you were going to die tonight. But it's true. If every moment was your last on earth you could be yourself. You'd dare. Everybody would dare. People is themselves when they are children, and not again till they know they'm dying. But conscience knows all the time. I've a heavy bill for all my tempers. God forgive me. But why should He? He was having his turn now, anyhow, with all this dying to do. Death must be got through as life had been, just somehow. But how?

When the doctor had gone she knew she was left to do it alone. While there's life there's hope. But the life in her was too much smaller than the great weight and pain. He made her easier, numb. Trying to think and not thinking. Everything unreal. The piece coming up and downstairs like something in another world. Perhaps God would let her go easy. Then it was all over? Just fading to nothing with everything still to do. . . .

The struggle came unexpectedly. She heard her cries, and then the world leapt upon her and grappled, and even in the midst of the agony of pain was the surprise of her immense strength. The strength that struggled against the huge stifling, the body that leapt and twisted against the heavy darkness, a shape within her shape, that she had not known. Her unknown self rushing forward through all her limbs to fight. Leaping out and curving in a great sweep away from where she lay to the open sill, yet pinned back, unwrenchable from the bed. Back and back she slid, down a long tunnel at terrific speed, cool, her brow cool and wet, with wind blowing upon it. Darkness in front. Back and back into her own young body, alone. In front on the darkness came the garden, the old garden in April, the crab-apple blossom, all as it was before she began, but brighter. . . .

[1924]

For Discussion

1. What does the narrator mean by "this time" in the first sentence? What is the dividing line between old age and death?

2. List the narrator's major concerns. Which have to do with other people? things? herself?

3. Examine the narrator's memories. What topics do they include, and how does she feel about each reminiscence?

4. Analyze the many references to "life" and "her secret life." How are life and death related in the narrator's view?

5. What conclusions does the woman draw about her life's work? What does she mean by, "they'd all stop if they knew where it led"?

6. What advice is the narrator giving about how to live and how to die?

7. How are pain and other extremes of feelings conveyed in the story, and what effects does the style have on the themes?

For Further Exploration

1. Examine this fictional version of death in the light of Elisabeth Kübler-Ross' research in works such as *On Death and Dying, Questions and Answers on Death and Dying,* or *Death: The Final Stage of Growth.* In what ways is Richardson's story similar or different from real death accounts?

2. Compare the use of the stream-of-consciousness style in this death account with the style of Doris Betts' noted childbirth story, "Still Life with Fruit." What does the associational technique provide in these stories that is appropriate for the subject matter in each case?

Poetry About Death

Aging is seen as an alien "thing" in both the Old Age section and in the stories about death. But death itself is represented in these poems as a person—a symbolic device that would be difficult to sustain in realistic fiction. The technique not only is useful for poetry, but is also appropriate for the recurrent motif that we can reject or embrace death, but that we must leave others in order to meet death alone.

In addition to the most familiar personification of death in poetry, the carriage companion in Dickinson's poem beginning "Because I could not stop for death/ He kindly stopped for me," there is also the description of death as an old friend in another poem, and a more inimical figure on horseback in another.

Related to this anthropomorphic presentation of death is the use of animal metaphors, such as a dead body as having snakelike "Castoff Skin." Ironically, making death into a person or dead bodies into animal skins seems to make aging seem more natural and therefore more "human."

Shirley Kaufman

1923–

APPLES

No use waiting for it to stop
raining in my face like a wet towel,
having to catch a plane,
to pick the apples from her tree
and bring them home.

The safest place to be
is under the branches. She
in her bed and her mouth
dry in the dry room.
Don't go out in the rain.

I stretch my arms for apples
anyway, feel how the ripe ones
slide in my hands like cups
that want to be perfect. Juices
locked up in the skin.

She used to slice them in quarters,
cut through the core,
open the inside out. Fingers
steady on the knife, expert
at stripping things.

Sometimes she split them sideways
into halves to let a star break
from the center with tight seeds,
because I wanted that,
six petals in the flesh.

Flavor of apples inhaled as flowers,
not even biting them.
Apples at lunch or after school
like soup, a fragrance rising
in the steam, eat and be well.

I bring the peeled fruit to her
where she lies, carve it
in narrow sections, celery white,
place them between her fingers,
Mother, eat. And be well.

Sit where her brown eyes
empty out the light, watching
her mind slip backwards

on the pillow, swallowing
apples, swallowing her life.

[1970]

Emily Dickinson

1830–1886

BECAUSE I COULD NOT STOP FOR DEATH

Because I could not stop for Death—
He kindly stopped for me—
The Carriage held but just Ourselves—
And Immortality.

We slowly drove—He knew no haste
And I had put away
My labor and my leisure too,
For His Civility—

We passed the School, where Children strove
At Recess—in the Ring—
We passed the Fields of Gazing Grain—
We passed the Setting Sun—

Or rather—He passed Us—
The Dews drew quivering and chill—
For only Gossamer, my Gown—
My Tippet—only Tulle—

We paused before a House that seemed
A Swelling of the Ground—
The Roof was scarcely visible—
The Cornice—in the Ground—

Since then—'tis Centuries—and yet
Feels shorter than the Day
I first surmised the Horses' Heads
Were toward Eternity—

[1890]

Edna St. Vincent Millay

1892–1950

CONSCIENTIOUS OBJECTOR

I shall die, but that is all that I shall do for Death.

I hear him leading his horse out of the stall; I hear the
    clatter on the barn-floor.
He is in haste; he has business in Cuba, business in the
    Balkans, many calls to make this morning.
But I will not hold the bridle while he cinches the girth.
And he may mount by himself: I will not give him a
    leg up.

Though he flick my shoulders with his whip, I will not
    tell him which way the fox ran.
With his hoof on my breast, I will not tell him where the
    black boy hides in the swamp.
I shall die, but that is all that I shall do for Death; I am
    not on his pay-roll.

I will not tell him the whereabouts of my friends nor of
    my enemies either.
Though he promise me much, I will not map him the
    route to any man's door.
Am I a spy in the land of the living, that I should deliver
    men to Death?
Brother, the password and the plans of our city are safe
    with me; never through me
Shall you be overcome.

[1923]

Jane Cooper

1924–

IN THE HOUSE OF THE DYING

So once again, hearing the tired aunts
whisper together under the kitchen globe,
I turn away; I am not one of them.

At the sink I watch the water cover my hands
in a sheath of light. Upstairs she lies alone
dreaming of autumn nights when her children were born.

On the steps between us grows in a hush of waiting
the impossible silence between two generations.
The aunts buzz on like flies around a bulb.

I am dressed like them. Standing with my back turned
I wash the dishes in the same easy way.
Only at birth and death do I utterly fail.

For death is my old friend who waits on the stairs.
Whenever I pass I nod to him like the newsman
who is there every day; for them he is the priest.

While the birth of love is so terrible to me
I feel unworthy of the commonest marriage.
Upstairs she lies, washed through by the two miracles.

[1962]

Honor Moore

From the play
MOURNING PICTURES

Ladies and gentlemen, my mother is
dying. You say "Everyone's mother dies."
I bow to you, smile. Ladies, gentlemen,
my mother is dying. She has cancer.
You say "Many people die of cancer."
I scratch my head. Gentle ladies, gentle
men, my mother has cancer, and, short of
some miracle, will die. You say "This has
happened many times before." You say "Death
is something which repeats itself." I bow.
Ladies and gentlemen, my mother has cancer
all through her. She will die unless there's a
miracle. You shrug. You gave up religion
years ago. Marxism too. You don't believe
in anything. I step forward. My mother
is dying. I don't believe in miracles.
Ladies and gentlemen, one last time: My
mother's dying. I haven't got another.

[1977]

Ruth Whitman

1922–

CASTOFF SKIN

She lay in her girlish sleep at ninety-six,
small as a twig.
Pretty good figure.

for an old lady, she said to me once.
Then she crawled away, leaving
a tiny stretched transparence

behind her. When I kissed her paper cheek
I thought of the snake,
of his quick motion.

[1973]

Christina Rossetti

1830–1894

from
MONNA INNOMINATA[1]

10

'Con miglior corso e con migliore stella.'—DANTE[2]
'La vita fugge e non s'arresta un' ora.'—PETRARCA[3]

Time flies, hope flags, life plies a wearied wing;
   Death following hard on life gains ground apace;
   Faith runs with each and rears an eager face,
Outruns the rest, makes light of everything,
Spurns earth, and still finds breath to pray and sing;
   While love ahead of all uplifts his praise,
   Still asks for grace and still gives thanks for grace,
Content with all day brings and night will bring.

Life wanes; and when love folds his wings above
   Tired hope, and less we feel his conscious pulse,
     Let us go fall asleep, dear friend, in peace:
     A little while, and age and sorrow cease;
     A little while, life reborn annuls
Loss and decay and death, and all is love.

[before 1882]

[1]My Nameless Lady.
[2]Come after me and let the people talk.
[3]Relating the casualties of our life.

For Discussion

1. How are apple images used to draw the generations together in Kaufman's poem about a woman whose mother is dying?

2. The journey Emily Dickinson describes in "Because I Could Not Stop for Death" has often been interpreted as progressive steps from childhood to death. What life stages does she describe?

3. Compare Millay's attitude toward the personification of death with the attitude expressed in Dickinson's poem.

4. What are the "two miracles" Cooper describes in "In the House of the Dying"? Why is the narrator "not one of [the other women]"?

5. How does the technique of poetic repetition, the "refrain" of "Mourning Pictures," make the reader realize the immediacy of death?

6. In what ways is the image of a snake's "Castoff Skin" an appropriate metaphor for dying? What is the possible religious symbolism or how else might you interpret the poem?

7. Explain how Rossetti uses images of running a race to enliven the acceptance of death.

For Further Exploration

1. Compare the poems in this section with other poems about death, such as Christina Rossetti's "Introspective" or 'Is This the End?" or Emily Dickinson's "I've Ceded—I've Stopped Being Theirs." What can keep a woman from being surprised by death?

2. Read the play *Mourning Pictures*, by Honor Moore, from which the last poem in the section is taken. How are the many conflicting emotions of the dying woman and her children brought together?

For Discussion and Writing About This Section

1. Compare the surprise "party" given Candace Whitcomb in "A Village Singer" with the surprise meeting of Granny's children around her bedside in "The Jilting of Granny Weatherall." What is significant about each gathering?

2. Georgiana in "So Many Have Died" considers old age to be an alien "thing" restricting an active mind and willing spirit. Which stories and poems in the Old Age and Death sections express the same view, and which assert the vitality possible despite age?

3. Examine the different attitudes toward religion exhibited in fiction, poetry, and plays about death. What do each of the women say about God as they are dying?

4. Compare the death scenes in the stories. Which women withdraw (turn inward) and which attempt to communicate (turn outward)?

5. In *Stone Angel* and "So Many Have Died," do we have the sense that the women would have been better off if they had not fought death? To what extent does accepting death require one to relinquish self-reliance?

6. Examine the poems and stories for Kübler-Ross' five stages of death (listed in the introduction to this section).

7. What relationships exist among the generations in these stories? Explore which is more likely to be helpful in the woman's death crisis—the second or the third generation.

8. Analyze the images of "casting-off," leaving, or separating from others; then find images of connection and bonding. Is there any relationship between the degree of solitude and the final impact of death?

9. Which of the relatives and minor characters in the stories and poems "really care" about the woman dying? How do we know? Can we trust the perceptions of each protagonist, or do some authors find other ways of conveying the sincerity or lack of it?

10. In the "life reviews" of each dying woman, what is each person proud or ashamed of in her life? How do these feelings influence each character's death?

WORKS CITED

Agress, Lynne. *The Feminine Irony: Women on Women in Early Nineteenth Century English Literature.* Lanham, MD: UP of America, 1984.

Beecher, Catharine Esther. "An Address to the Christian Women of America." *Woman Suffrage and Women's Professions.* 1871. Rpt. in *The Quotable Woman: 1800–1981.* Ed. Elaine Partnow. New York: Facts on File, 1977, 3.

Chapman, Maria Weston. "Address to the Boston Female Anti-Slavery Society." *Liberator.* 1836. Rpt. in *The Quotable Woman: 1800–1981.* Ed. Elaine Partnow. New York: Facts on File, 1977, 16.

Daniels, Pamela, and Kathy Weingarten. *Sooner or Later: The Timing of Parenthood in Adult Lives.* New York: Norton, 1982.

Erikson, Erik. *Childhood and Society.* New York: Norton, 1950.

Freeman, Jo. *Women: A Feminist Perspective.* Palo Alto, CA: Mayfield, 1984.

Fromm, Erich. *The Art of Loving.* New York: Harper, 1974.

Gilligan, Carol. *In A Different Voice.* Cambridge, MA: Harvard UP, 1982.

Goodman, Ellen. *Close to Home.* New York: Fawcett, 1981.

Horner, Matina S. "Women's Need to Fail." *Psychology Today,* Nov. 1969:36–38, 62.

Kessler-Harris, Alice. *Women Have Always Worked: A Historical Overview.* Old Westbury, NY: Feminist, 1981.

Kolbenschlag, Madonna. *Kiss Sleeping Beauty Goodbye: Breaking the Spell of Feminine Myths and Models.* New York: Bantam, 1979.

Kübler-Ross, Elisabeth. *Death: The Final Stage of Growth.* New York: Macmillan, 1969.

Levinson, Daniel J. *The Seasons of a Man's Life.* New York: Ballantine, 1978.

Lewes, George Henry. "The Lady Novelists." *Women's Liberation and Literature.* Ed. Elaine Showalter. New York: Harcourt, 1971, 171–183.

Lifton, Robert J. *The Life of the Self: Toward a New Psychology.* New York: Basic, 1983.

Miller, Jean Baker. *Toward a New Psychology of Women.* Boston: Beacon, 1976.

Morgan, Marabel. *The Total Woman.* Old Tappan, NJ: Revell, 1975.

Norwood, Robin. *Women Who Love Too Much: When You Keep Wishing & Hoping He'll Change.* Los Angeles: JP Tarcher, 1985.

Oakley, Ann. *The Sociology of Housework.* New York: Pantheon, 1975.

Pearson, Carol, and Katherine Pope. *The Female Hero in American and British Literature.* Ed. Joanne O'Hare. New York: Bowker, 1981.

Rich, Adrienne. Introduction. *Working It Out.* By Sara Ruddick and Pamela Daniels. New York: Pantheon, 1977.

Sheehy, Gail. *Passages: Predictable Crises of Adult Life.* New York: Bantam, 1977.

Shroder, Maurice. "The Novel as a Genre." *The Theory of the Novel.* Ed. Philip Stevick. New York: Free, 1967, 13–29.

Washbourn, Penelope. *Becoming Woman: The Quest for Wholeness in Female Experience.* San Francisco: Harper, 1977.

Welty, Eudora. "Artists on Criticism of Their Act: 'Is Phoenix Jackson's Grandson Really Dead?' " *Critical Inquiry,* 1(1974):219–221.

BIOGRAPHICAL
SKETCHES

Adams, Alice (Boyd)   1926–

Born in Fredericksburg, Virginia, Alice Adams held a series of secretarial and bookkeeping jobs before she went on to write *Families and Survivors* (1975) and other novels. She has contributed short stories to periodicals such as *The Atlantic Monthly, The New Yorker,* and *Paris Review.*

Allen, Paula Gunn   1939–

This Laguna Pueblo poet's collected works include *The Blind Lion* (1975), *Coyote's Daylight Trip* (1978), and *A Cannon Between My Knees* (1978). Allen also edited *Studies in American Indian Literature: Critical Essays and Course Designs* (1983).

Ambapali   4th Century B.C.

Ambapali, an historic figure in the poetry of India centuries before the birth of Christ, is unusually compelling even in modern times. Her poems were translated from the Pali by A. L. Basham of Calcutta, who has recently died.

Angelou, Maya   1928–

Maya Angelou held a number of unusual jobs (including streetcar conductor), had a short but versatile theatrical career, and has been celebrated for her series of autobiographical novels, beginning with *I Know Why the Caged Bird Sings* (1970), *Gather Together in My Name* (1974), and *Singin' and Swingin' and Gettin' Merry Like Christmas* (1976). A St. Louis native, Angelou has written several screenplays and books of poetry, and has lectured at numerous universities.

Atwood, Margaret (Eleanor)   1939–

A former waitress and film script writer, this Canadian self-labeled "pessimistic pantheist" writes about such life crises as marriage, childbirth, infidelity, and rape. She is master of two genres, fiction and poetry, and has been included in more than a hundred anthologies. Some works include *The Circle Game* (1966), *The Edible Woman* (1969), *Surfacing* (1972), and *Life Before Man* (1979).

Bambara, Toni Cade   1939–

Bambara studied at Queens College of the City University of New York and at Ecole de Mime Etienne Decroux in Paris, among other places, and served as visiting professor of African American studies at Duke University in 1974. Some of her works include *Tales and Stories for Black Folks* (1971), *Gorilla, My Love* (1972), and *The Sea Birds Are Still Alive: Collected Stories* (1977).

Beauchamp, Kathleen Mansfield   1888–1923
(Katherine Mansfield)

Mansfield was born in New Zealand and wrote about her homeland in *Bliss* (1920) and *The Garden Party* (1922). She later moved to London and established her reputation as a writer of careful observation and distinctive style. Although she suffered through her last years with tuberculosis, Mansfield continued to write works later compiled in *Collected Short Stories* (1945) and *Letters to J. Middleton Murry* (1951).

Breyner, Sophia de Mello   1919–

Contemporary Portuguese poet Sophia de Mello Breyner has published more than a dozen volumes of poetry, several critical studies, a book of short stories, some well-known children's books, and translations of Dante and Shakespeare into Portuguese. In 1987 she published a new version in Portuguese of Shakespeare's *Hamlet*.

Brooks, Gwendolyn   1917–

In 1950, Brooks became the first black author to win the Pulitzer Prize (for her poetry in *Annie Allen*). This Kansas born author has written a novel (*Maud Martha*, 1953) and an autobiography (*Report from Part One*, 1972), along with her numerous collections of poetry—*A Street in Bronzeville* (1945), *The Wall* (1964), *We Real Cool* (1964). Brooks has been awarded more than thirty-eight honorary degrees from colleges and universities.

Broumas, Olga   1949–

Broumas, the daughter of a Greek Army soldier, maintains interests that range from architecture to linguistics. She speaks French and modern Greek and can read five other languages. Aside from contributing to various literary journals, Broumas has written *Caritas* (1976) and *Beginning with O* (1977).

Carrier, Constance   1908–

This former high school Latin teacher's collection of poems, *The Middle Voice*, was the Lamont Poetry Selection of the American Academy of Poets in 1954. She was the translator of *The Poems of Propertius* (1963) and *The Poems of Tibullus* (1968). Carrier's other collection of original poetry is *The Angled Road* (1973).

Clifton, Lucille   1936–

Lucille Clifton has published her poetry in the *Negro Digest* and the *Massachusetts Review*. Born in Depew, New York, Clifton attended both Howard

University and Fredonia State Teachers College before publishing her first book of poetry, *Good Times.*

Colette (Sidonie-Gabrielle)   1873–1954
(Colette Willy)

The premiere French woman novelist and journalist of the early twentieth century, Colette began writing stories of her girlhood under her husband's pen name, Willy. Colette divorced her husband, worked on the stage, and during her second and third marriages became a journalist and celebrated author of *Mitsou; or, How Girls Grow Wise* (1919), *Cheri* (1920), *Gigi* (1944), and other novels.

Cooper, Jane (Marvel)   1924–

A graduate of the University of Wisconsin and the University of Iowa, this Atlantic City native's books include *The Weather of Six Mornings* (1969), *Maps and Windows* (1974), and the most recent *Scaffolding: New and Selected Poems* (1984). Cooper received a Guggenheim fellowship in poetry for 1960–61.

Dickinson, Emily   1830–1886

This Massachusetts poet wrote more than 1500 poems, over half copied and recopied to near perfection. Although Dickinson saw only seven of these published in her lifetime, she is now revered for her perceptive insight, subtle wit, and unconventional style—all evident in the three volumes of *The Poems of Emily Dickinson*, edited by Thomas H. Johnson. Dickinson's brief schooling included six years at Amherst Academy and one shortened year at Mount Holyoke; her distinctive lifestyle is often noted, in that she spent the last seventeen years of her life within the confines of her family home.

Dunbar Nelson, Alice   1875–1935

Born Alice Ruth Moore in New Orleans, this short story writer, poet, teacher, editor, and black activist had her first book, *Violets and Other Tales*, privately printed in 1895. Nelson went on to write *The Goodness of St. Rocque and Other Stories* (1899), as well as teach high school English, write a column for the *Washington Eagle*, and remain active in politics.

Eliot, George   1819–1880

Some of this English novelist's many celebrated works include *Adam Bede* (1859), *The Mill on the Floss* (1860), *Middlemarch* (1871–1872), and *Daniel Deronda* (1887). Her many names include Mary Anne, Mary Ann, and Marian Evans, although her reading public knew her as "George Eliot." Her use of this pseudonym paid tribute to the man who nurtured her writings and with whom she lived for twenty-four years, George Henry Lewes.

Faessler, Shirley   1921(?)–

Faessler's first novel, *Everything in the Window* (1979) is based on the author's background and tells the story of a Rumanian Jewish family in Toronto, Canada, whose daughter marries a gentile. She has also contributed short stories to the *Atlantic Monthly* and *Tamarack Review.*

Fiamengo, Marya   1926–

Long time resident of Vancouver, Canada, Marya Fiamengo has published volumes of poetry since 1958, including *In Praise of Old Women* (1977) and *North of the Cold Star* (1978). Her works have also been widely anthologized and she has acquired both a national and international reputation.

Fraser, Kathleen   1937–

This poet attended Occidental College and was represented in the anthology *Young American Poets* (1968). Her works include *Change of Address and Other Poems* (1966), *Little Notes to You, From Lucas Street* (1972), and the juvenile fiction work *Adam's World: San Francisco* (1971).

Freeman, Mary Eleanor Wilkins   1852–1930
(Mary Wilkins)

Born in Randolph, Massachusetts, Mary Wilkins Freeman is noted for her writings about small town New England, including popular short stories of *A Humble Romance* (1887) and *A New England Nun and Other Stories* (1891). Her novels include *Jane Field* (1893) and *Pembroke* (1894).

Gerstenberg, Alice   1885–1972

One of the first expressionistic playwrights in America, Alice Gerstenberg published her first novel, *Unquenchable Fire* (1913), and the play *Overtones* when she was only in her twenties. She was the founder and director of the Playwrights Theatre in Chicago, and wrote a successful adaptation of *Alice in Wonderland* (1915), among other plays.

Gilman, Charlotte (Anna) Perkins (Stetson)   1860–1935

This cofounder of the Women's Peace Party established herself as an important early American feminist with her first major work, *Women and Economics* (1898), a call for women's financial independence. Gilman also wrote *Man-Made World* (1911), *Human Work* (1904), and *Herland* (1915), published in 1979 as "A Lost Feminist Utopian Novel."

Giovanni, Nikki   1943–

Born Yolande Cornelia, Jr., this former Woman of the Year (Youth Leadership Award, *Ladies Home Journal,* 1972) and student activist is an important figure within the black oral poetry movement. Giovanni has read her poems on television, at the Lincoln Center for the Performing Arts, and on record. Her works include *Black Feeling, Black Talk, Black Judgement* (1970), *My House* (1972), *The Women and the Men* (1975), *Truth Is on Its Way* (record, 1971), and *Like a Ripple on a Pond* (record, 1973).

Glaspell, Susan   1882–1948

Born in Davenport, Iowa, this cofounder of the Provincetown Playhouse won the Pulitzer Prize for drama with *Alison's House* (1930). Other plays she has written include *The Verge* (1921) and *Trifles* (1916). Glaspell also published ten novels and over forty short stories.

Grahn, Judy   1940–

Grahn's poetry deals with the many issues facing working-class and lesbian women today. Raised in New Mexico, this former waitress, meat wrapper, maid, and secretary has had a number of her works published by independent women's presses. Among these, two noted chapbooks—*She Who* and *A Woman Is Talking to Death*—are among those collected in Grahn's *The Work of a Common Woman* (1978).

Hahn, Kimiko   1955–

This Japanese American poet has served on the editorial board of *Bridge: Asian American Perspectives,* and has organized and moderated a panel of Asian American writers at the October, 1981, American Writers' Congress. Hahn's first book, *As the Dolls Grow Older the Girls Change,* is forthcoming from Hanging Loose Press. She has been the recipient of NEA and NYFA Fellowships and is currently coordinating a reading series in New York City's Chinatown.

Halley, Anne   1928–

Born in Germany and educated in the United States, Anne Halley has translated German works and has published both poetry and fiction in various journals. *Between Wars and Other Poems* (1965) was England's Poetry Society's Summer Recommendation.

Hayes, Catherine   1949–

Catherine Hayes was born in Liverpool, England, where she still lives and works as a teacher. Her full-length plays performed include *Jason, Gin and Southport* (1978), *Little Sandra* (1980), and *Skirmishes* (1981). She was Resident Writer at the Liverpool Playhouse in 1980/81, and has also written a radio play, *Rising Dead* (1979), and some short sketches.

Hochman, Sandra   1936–

This author of *Manhattan Pastures, Love Letters from Asia, The Vaudeville Marriage,* and *Voyage Home* has been an actress and teacher after receiving a B.A. from Bennington College.

Hull, Helen (Rose)   1888(?)–1971

After two years as an instructor at Wellesley College, Hull moved on to Columbia University in 1914 where she taught and wrote about writing until her death in 1971. Her writings include *Creative Writing: The Story Form,* with Mabel Robinson (1932), *Uncommon People* (1936), and *Experiment: Four Short Novels* (1940).

Hunter, Kristin (Eggleston)   1931–

This Philadelphia-born author of *The Soul Brothers and Sister Lou* (1968) and *Guests in the Promised Land: Stories* (1973) has also written a television documentary *(Minority of One)* and had her novel *The Landlord* (1966) filmed by United Artists. Hunter's *God Bless the Child* (1964) has been translated into German.

Hurston, Zora Neale   1903–1960

Born in the first incorporated all-black town in America (Eatonville, Florida), Hurston was taken out of school at thirteen yet later went on to graduate from Barnard College in anthropology. Her novels and books of folklore are prime sources of black myth and legend. Some works include *Mules and Men* (1935), *Their Eyes Were Watching God* (1937), and the autobiography *Dust Tracks on a Road* (1939). Zora Neale Hurston has also been represented in numerous anthologies, including *Black Writers in America* and *American Negro Short Stories*.

Jackson, Shirley   1919–1965

"The Lottery," Jackson's most famous short story, established her talents as a writer of the Gothic horror tale. However, this Edgar Allan Poe Award winner could write just as easily about the humor of family life as about magic and witchcraft. Among her many works are *The Witchcraft of Salem Village* (1956), *The Haunting of Hill House* (1959), and *We Have Always Lived in the Castle* (1962).

Jewett, Sarah Orne   1849–1909

This regional novelist, short story writer, essayist, and poet was born in Maine and sold her first story at the age of nineteen. Beginning with *Deephaven* (1877), a collection of her short stories, Jewett proceeded to write about her native state as she watched it grow into the twentieth century. *The Country of the Pointed Firs* (1896) is regarded as her best work; others include *Old Friends and New* (1879) and *A Country Doctor* (1884).

Kaufman, Shirley   1923–

Currently residing in Israel, Shirley Kaufman was born in Seattle and won the Academy of American Poets prize while getting her M.A. at San Francisco State. She has published in numerous journals, including *The Atlantic Monthly*, *Harper's*, *The New Yorker*, and *Poetry*; and she has translated Israeli poetry into English.

Kizer, Carolyn   1925–

Born in Spokane, Washington, and educated in the east, Kizer founded *Poetry Northwest* in Seattle, serving as editor for seven years. Her volumes include *The Ungrateful Garden*, *Knock Upon Silence*, and *Midnight Was My Cry*.

Laurence, Margaret Wemyss   1926–

Only a few of this Canadian-born author's works are set in her Manitoba homeland. One such work, *A Jest of God* (1966) was filmed in 1968 as *Rachel, Rachel*. *The Tomorrow Tamer, and Other Stories* (1964) is set in West Africa while *The Prophet's Camel Bell* (1963) is set in the Haud desert of Somaliland, East Africa.

Lessing, Doris (May)   1919–

A left-wing English novelist born in Persia, Lessing was educated in Roman Catholic schools in Salisbury, Southern Rhodesia. Although her mother wanted her to be a pianist. Lessing left school at fourteen and began writing at eighteen. In addition to the much-lauded novel, *The Golden Notebook* (1962), Lessing also wrote works such as *The Grass Is Singing* (1950), *Mr. Dollinger* (a play, 1958), *Fourteen Poems* (1959), and *A Man and Two Women* (1963).

Levertov, Denise   1923–

This privately educated poet born in England became an American citizen in 1955. She has contributed work to numerous periodicals as well as publishing many influential works such as *The Double Image* (1946), *The Jacob's Ladder* (1961), *O Taste and See* (1964), and *Candles in Babylon* (1982).

Lim, Genny   1946–

This Asian American writer is a native of San Francisco and is co-author of *Island: Poetry and History of Chinese Immigrants on Angel Island, 1910–1940* (1980), which won the American Book Award in 1982. She dealt with this same subject in her play *Paper Angels,* which received numerous awards and was aired on PBS in 1985. Her current award-winning play is entitled *XX.*

Lorde, Audre   1934–

Once the Poet-in-Residence at Tougaloo College in Jackson, Mississippi, Lorde has a Master's degree from Columbia University. She was born in Manhattan and attended Hunter College. Some works include *The First Cities* (1968), *Cables to Rage* (1970), *Coal* (1978), *The Black Unicorn* (1978), and an article to *The Black Scholar.*

Marshall, Joyce   1913–

A Canadian author educated at McGill University, Marshall has written *Presently Tomorrow* (1946), *Love and Strangers* (1957), and *A Private Place* (1975). She also translated Gabrielle Roy's *Enchanted Summer,* from French.

McCullers, (Lula) Carson   1917–1967

Born in Georgia, Carson McCullers had musical talents which led her to study at the Juilliard School of Music in New York City. She later attended writing classes at Columbia University and wrote well-known works such as *The Heart Is a Lonely Hunter* (1940), *The Member of the Wedding* (1946), and *The Ballad of the Sad Cafe* (1951), many of which were filmed.

McElroy, Colleen J(ohnson)   1935–

This versatile member of the United Black Artists Guild and winner of the Best of Small Presses award for poetry in 1976, has served as a speech clinician in Kansas City and has worked as an associate professor of English at the University of Washington. Her writings include *Music From Home: Selected Poems* (1976) and *Winters Without Snow* (1980).

McGinley, Phyllis   1905–

Upon moving to New York in 1928, McGinley worked as English teacher, copy writer, and poetry editor before her successful writing career took hold.

She has written books of verse (*On the Contrary*, 1934; *The Love Letters of Phyllis McGinley*, 1954) and numerous children's books. Among her many awards are a Pulitzer Prize for poetry for *Times Three: Selected Verse From Three Decades* (1961).

Meriwether, Louise   1923–

Once a story analyst for Universal Studios, this member of the Harlem Writers Guild has written for both adults and young adults. *Daddy Was a Numbers Runner* (1970), Meriwether's first novel, was followed by three biographies.

Millay, Edna St. Vincent   1892–1950
(Nancy Boyd)

Born in Maine, this writer of modern sonnets achieved her greatest success during the 1920s and 1930s while residing in Greenwich Village. Millay's *Ballad of the Harp-Weaver* (1922) won the 1923 Pulitzer Prize. *Fatal Interview* (1931), *Wine From These Grapes* (1934), and *Distressing Dialogues* (1924) were some of her other works, the latter written under the pseudonym "Nancy Boyd."

Mirikitani, Janice   1942–

Janice Mirikitani is a Japanese American poet and anthologist. She also has directed arts programs in an Urban Center in San Francisco, and has edited *Third World Women*, *Aion* magazine, and *Ayumi, a Japanese American Anthology*. *Awake in the River* is her collection of poetry and short fiction.

Molinaro, Ursule

Ursule Molinaro is a novelist, playwright, painter, and translator. Some of her more recent novels include *Encores of a Dilettante*, *The Borrower*, and *Positions with White Roses*. She has taught at the Virginia Polytechnic Institute and in Hawaii, and currently is living in New York City.

Moore, Honor   1945–

Honor Moore has read her poems and given lectures throughout the United States. A founder of the Poetry Series at the Manhattan Theater Club, this Radcliffe College graduate's play *Mourning Pictures* was produced on Broadway in 1974. Her published work includes *Leaving and Coming Back* (1979), as well as poems in the anthologies *We Become New* (1975) and *The New Woman's Survival Sourcebook* (1975).

Moore, Marianne   1887–1972

In 1951, Moore won the Pulitzer Prize, the Bollingen Prize, and the National Book Award for her poetry. Once a teacher of stenography to American Indians, this St. Louis, Missouri, native has written *The Pangolin and Other Verse*, *What Are Years?*, *O To Be a Dragon*, and *Observations*, among others.

Murray, Pauli   1910–

Active in the civil rights and women's movements, this poet and lawyer has degrees from Hunter College, Harvard University, the University of California, and Yale University. Included in her writings are *Proud Shoes, States' Laws on Race and Color,* and *Dark Testament.*

Oates, Joyce Carol   1938–

Oates had her first collection of short stories, *By the North Gate* (1963) published at the age of twenty-five while she taught at the University of Detroit. Since then, her work has been frequently anthologized in both scholarly and popular collections including *Best American Short Stories, O. Henry Awards Anthology, Southwest Review, Literary Review,* and *Virginia Quarterly Review.* Some works are *A Garden of Earthly Delights* (1967), *The Sweet Enemy* (a play, 1965), and *Anonymous Sins and Other Poems* (1969).

O'Connor, (Mary) Flannery   1925–1964

A religious writer and winner of three O. Henry Memorial Awards, O'Connor wrote of the Georgia south where her Catholic family has lived since before the Civil War. This author of works such as *Wise Blood* (1952), *A Good Man Is Hard to Find* (1955), and *Everything that Rises Must Converge* (1965) has been translated into seven languages. Her early death cut short a meaningful career.

Olsen, Tillie   1913–

A high school dropout, Olsen was active in the labor movements in Omaha, Kansas City, and San Francisco. This product of the Depression generation spent eight years writing the four stories of *Tell Me a Riddle* (1961), which won the O. Henry Award. Olsen has taught at several colleges and universities on the east and west coasts, and won both Guggenheim and NEH fellowships.

Page, P. K.   1916–

After publishing her first two volumes of poetry, *As Ten as Twenty* (1946) and *The Metal and the Flower* (1954), this former scriptwriter traveled extensively through Australia, Brazil, and Mexico. Upon her return she wrote *Cry Ararat! Poems New and Selected* (1967), *The Sun and the Moon and Other Fictions* (1973), *Poems Selected and New* (1974), and *Evening Dance of the Grey Flies* (1981).

Paley, Grace   1922–

A self-described anarchist, writer Grace Paley was a frequent antiwar activist. Her two major works, *The Little Disturbances of Man* (1959) and *Enormous Changes at the Last Minute* (1974), were separated by fifteen years of contributing stories to numerous periodicals. She received a Guggenheim fellowship in fiction (1961) and the National Institute of Arts and Letters Award for short story writing (1970).

Paraske, Larin   1833–1904

Born in Russia, Larin Paraske was a simple country woman discovered by Finnish folklorists to whom she recited and sang thousands of lyrical poems, magic formulas, and proverbs. Her texts were published in *The Old Poems of Finnish People* (1908–48), thirty-three volumes, of which they make up one.

Parker, Dorothy (Rothschild)   1893–1967

This former drama critic for *Vanity Fair* lived in Hollywood with her actor husband Alan Campbell during the 1930s. Together they wrote screenplays for twenty-two films including *Big Broadcast of 1936* and *A Star Is Born* (1937). Parker's published work includes *Laments for the Living* (1930), *Collected Poems: Not so Deep as a Well* (1936), and the play *Ladies of the Corridor* (1954).

Piercy, Marge   1936–

Marge Piercy has written poetry included in more than thirty anthologies such as *Best Poems of 1967* and *New Women. To Be of Use* (1973) and *Hard Loving* (1969) are but two of her many collections of poetry, in addition to eight novels (e.g., *Going Down Fast, Small Changes, and Fly Away Home*). Her essays have been collected as part of the University of Michigan's series *Parti-Colored Blocks for a Quilt,* and she has co-authored a play, *The Last White Class.*

Plath, Sylvia   1932–1963

The daughter of German immigrants, Plath began writing early and had published some of her work in *Seventeen* and other periodicals by the time she won a scholarship to Smith College in 1950. Plath later studied at Cambridge University before marrying the poet Ted Hughes and returning to teach at Smith. In addition to her well-known novel, *The Bell Jar* (1963), some of Plath's other works include *Daddy* (1963) and *Ariel* (1965), published after Plath committed suicide.

Porter, Katherine Anne   1890–1980

Born in Texas and educated in Southern girls' schools, Porter wrote copiously before she began to publish stories and essays at the age of thirty. Personal experiences and travel provided material for her numerous works, many of which received awards (Pulitzer Prize and National Book Award for *The Collected Stories of Katherine Anne Porter,* Society of the Libraries of New York University medal for *Pale Horse, Pale Rider.) Ship of Fools, Noon Wine,* and other works have been filmed.

Rich, Adrienne Cecile   1929–

Having graduated from Radcliffe College, Adrienne Rich began to write volumes of poetry and literary criticism, plus translations of Russian and Yiddish poetry. Among her much-lauded works are *A Change of World* (1951) and *Diving into the Wreck* (1973). Rich has contributed reviews and critical articles to *Poetry, New York Review of Books,* and *Paris Review.*

Richardson, Dorothy (Miller)   1873–1957

English writer Dorothy Richardson's eleven-volume work, *Pilgrimage,* was begun around 1912 and took three decades to complete. The first volume, *Pointed Roofs,* was published in 1917. Although she was one of the originators of stream-of-consciousness style, Richardson received little tangible recognition in her lifetime.

Rossetti, Christina   1830–1894

One of the "Pre-Raphaelite" poets in late nineteenth-century England,
Christina Rossetti wrote her first book of poetry, *Verses*, followed by the
more popular *Goblin Market and Other Poems* (1862). The sister of painter
and poet Dante Gabriel Rossetti, Christina wrote deeply religious and philosophical poetry.

Saffarzadeh, Tahereh   1939–

Contemporary Iranian poet Tahereh Saffarzadeh has published volumes of
work including *Reverberations in the Delta* (1973) and *The Red Umbrella*.
She has taught at the National University of Iran, and participated in the
Writing Institute at the University of Iowa in the late 1960's.

Sappho   6th–7th Century B.C. (?)

Although little is confirmed about this Greek poet's life, she was part of a
noble family and must have been born about 630 B.C. or earlier. Sappho's
poetic prime came around the 42nd Olympiad (612–608 B.C.) and she lived
at least until 572 B.C. After Sappho's husband Cercylas died, she sought love
and companionship among the women of her salon whom she taught to
chant and sing for marriage ceremonies and the like.

Sarton, (Eleanor) May   1912–

Born in Belgium, Sarton was brought to the United States at the age of four
and became a naturalized citizen eight years later. She founded and served
as director of the Associated Actors Theater in New York City from 1934 to
1937. A former script writer, Sarton has published numerous books of poetry, fiction, nonfiction, and two screenplays. Some works are *Encounter in
April* (1937), *The Small Room* (1961), *Kinds of Love* (1970), *Journal of a
Solitude* (1973), and *The House by the Sea* (1977).

Sellers, Bettie M(ixon)   1926–

This Florida-born poet received her Masters degree from the University of
Georgia, becoming an instructor of English at Young Harris College in North-
ern Georgia. Her works include the privately printed *Westward from Bald
Mountain* (1974) and *Spring Onions and Cornbread* (1977).

Sexton, Anne (Harvey)   1928–1974

Sexton's often-classified "confessional poetry" grew from a form of psychological therapy into an acclaimed body of work. *To Bedlam and Part Way
Back* (1960) was the poetic account of her psychiatric struggles. In 1967,
Sexton won a Pulitzer Prize for *Live or Die*. *The Awful Rowing Toward God*
(1975), *The Wizard's Tears* (1975), and *45 Mercy Street* (1976) were published after her suicide.

Silveira de Queiroz, Dinah   1911–

The first woman to be awarded the Machado de Assis Prize given by the Brazilian Academy of Letters, this author of *Comba Malina* (1939) and *As
Noites do Morro do Encanto* (1957) has also written children's books and
plays.

Speyer, Leonora   **1872–1956**

After a career as a concert violinist, Speyer lived abroad before returning to America and beginning to write poetry and winning the Pulitzer Prize for the collection *Fiddler's Farewell* (1927). During the twenties, she associated with Amy Lowell and the *Poetry Magazine* group.

Stein, Gertrude   **1874–1946**

After abandoning her studies at both Radcliffe College and Johns Hopkins Medical School, the independently wealthy Stein moved to Paris in 1903. She was a patron to such artists and writers as Picasso, Matisse, Hemingway, and Fitzgerald. Her primarily abstract writings include *Three Lives* (1909), *The Making of Americans* (1925), and *Autobiography of Alice B. Toklas* (1933).

Swenson, May   **1919–**

Once a reporter for the *Salt Lake City Desert News*, Swenson moved to New York City and became editor for the publisher of *New Directions* in 1959. She published a number of books of verse including *Another Animal* (1954) and *To Mix with Time: New and Selected Poems* (1963). Among her awards are a Robert Frost fellowship and a Guggenheim fellowship. She has been Poet-in-Residence at Purdue University.

Tepperman, Jean   **1945–**

As a student activist and part of a socialist women's liberation movement, Tepperman worked for SDS and for an underground newspaper. She has published poems in numerous periodicals and in the anthologies *Sisterhood Is Powerful* and *No More Masks! An Anthology of Poems by Women*.

Walker, Alice   **1944–**

This former voter registration worker and New York City welfare department worker was born in Georgia. Her well-known books include *In Love and Trouble: Stories of Black Women* (1973) and *The Color Purple* (1982), for which she won both the Pulitzer Prize and the American Book Award. Walker's work has been widely anthologized and one of her recent works is *In Search of Our Mothers' Gardens: A Collection of Womanist Prose.*

Walker, Margaret Abigail   **1915–**

Winner of the Yale Younger Poets Prize in 1942, Walker holds a Master's degree from the School of Letters of the University of Iowa. A Birmingham, Alabama, native, Margaret Walker has written a novel, *Jubilee* (1965) and a volume of poetry entitled *Prophets for a New Day* (1970). She has been Director of the Institute for the Study of the History, Life, and Culture of Black Peoples. Other poetry collections include *For My People* (1942), *Ballad of the Free* (1966), and *October Journey* (1973).

Welty, Eudora   **1909–**

This regional but universally appealing writer from Mississippi once used the pseudonym Michael Ravenna while writing reviews of World War II battlefield reports for the *New York Times Book Review*. Winner of the 1973 Pulitzer Prize for fiction (*The Optimist's Daughter*, 1969), Welty has written *A Curtain of Green* (1941), *The Ponder Heart* (1954), *And a Sweet Devouring* (1969), among others.

West, Jessamyn   1907–

This Quaker, born in Indiana, has written everything from an opera libretto (*A Mirror for the Sky*, 1948) to collections of short stories (*Love, Death and the Ladies Drill Team*, 1955) to movie scripts (*Friendly Persuasion* and *The Big Country*). West has also contributed to various periodicals and collections.

Whitman, Ruth (Bashein)   1922–

A former freelance editor for the Harvard University Press, this poet and translator received a National Foundation for Jewish Culture grant in 1968. She has cotranslated *Blood and Milk Poems* (1963) and *Selected Poems of Alain Bosquet* (1963). Whitman has also translated modern French and Greek poetry. In 1968, she published *The Marriage Wig and Other Poems* and, in 1973, *The Passion of Lizzie Borden: New and Selected Poems*.

Williams, Sherley Anne   1944–
(Shirley Williams)

In the same year that she received her Master of Arts degree from Brown University (1972), Williams published her first collection of poetry, *Give Birth to Brightness. The Peacock Poems* (1975) was her second collection; she has written *Ours to Make* for television and the play *Traveling Sunshine Show*, as well.

Woolf, (Adeline) Virginia   1882–1941

Born in London to the biographer and critic Sir Leslie Stephen, Woolf and her sister Vanessa were members of the "Bloomsbury" circle, a famous group of intellectuals. Later, in 1917, she formed the Hogarth Press which published the works of Gertrude Stein, T. S. Eliot, and Katherine Mansfield. Her own writings include *To the Lighthouse* (1927), *Night and Day* (1919), *A Room of One's Own* (1929), and *The Waves* (1931).

Yezierska, Anzia   1885–1970

This Polish immigrant left home at the age of seventeen to earn money for an education. She attended college and then published her well-received first collection of ghetto stories, *Hungry Hearts* (1920). After this came *Bread Givers* (1925), *Children of Loneliness* (1923), and *All That I Could Never Be* (1932).

ACKNOWLEDGMENTS

ADAMS, ALICE "By the Sea." From TO SEE YOU AGAIN, by Alice Adams. Copyright © 1982 by Alice Adams. Reprinted by permission of Alfred A. Knopf, Inc.

ALLEN, PAULA GUNN "Grandmother." Published in THE THIRD WOMAN: MINORITY WOMEN WRITERS OF THE UNITED STATES, Dexter Fisher, editor. Boston: Houghton Mifflin, 1980. Copyright © 1977 by Paula Gunn Allen. Reprinted by permission of the author.

ALEXANDER, MARGARET WALKER "Lineage" from FOR MY PEOPLE by Margaret Walker. New Haven: Yale University Press, 1942. Copyright © 1942 by Margaret Walker. Reprinted by permission of the author.

AMBAPALI "Black and Glossy as a Bee. . . ." From THE WONDER THAT WAS INDIA, A.L. Basham, editor. London: Sidgwick & Jackson, Ltd. Reprinted by permission of the publisher.

ANGELOU, MAYA "Woman Me." From OH PRAY MY WINGS ARE GONNA FIT ME WELL by Maya Angelou. Copyright © 1975 by Maya Angelou. Reprinted by permission of Random House, Inc.

ATWOOD, MARGARET "Rape Fantasies." Reprinted by permission of Margaret Atwood from DANCING GIRLS published by McClelland and Stewart, © 1977.

BAMBARA, TONI CADE "The Lesson." From GORILLA, MY LOVE by Toni Cade Bambara. Copyright © 1972 by Toni Cada Bambara. Reprinted by permission of Random House, Inc.

BREYNER, SOPHIA DE MELLO "The Young Girl and the Beach." First published in DUAL, Lisbon: Moraes Editores, 1977. Translated from the Portuguese by Alexis Levitin. Reprinted from WOMEN POETS OF THE WORLD, Joanna Bankier and Dierdre Lashgari, editors. New York: Macmillan, 1983. Reprinted by permission of Alexis Levitin.

BROOKS, GWENDOLYN "The Mother." Reprinted by permission of Gwendolyn Brooks (The David Company, Chicago).

BROUMAS, OLGA "Cinderella." From BEGINNING WITH O by Olga Broumas. New Haven: Yale University Press, 1977. Copyright © 1977 by Yale University Press. Reprinted by permission.

CARRIER, CONSTANCE "Lisa." From THE MIDDLE VOICE by Constance Carrier. Athens, Ohio: The Swallow Press, 1955. Reprinted with the permission of The Ohio University Press, Athens.

CLIFTON, LUCILLE "The Thirty Eighth Year of My Life." From AN ORDINARY WOMAN by Lucille Clifton. New York: Random House, 1974. Copyright © 1974 by Lucille Clifton. Reprinted by permission of Curtis Brown, Ltd.

COLETTE "My Goddaughter." From THE COLLECTED STORIES OF COLETTE. English translation copyright © 1957, 1966, 1983 by Farrar, Straus, and Giroux, Inc. Reprinted by permission of Farrar, Straus, and Giroux, Inc.

COOPER, JANE "In the House of the Dying." Reprinted with permission of Macmillan Publishing Company from THE WEATHER OF SIX MORNINGS by Jane Cooper. Copyright © 1968 by Jane Cooper.

DICKINSON, EMILY   "Because I Could Not Stop for Death." Reprinted by permission of the publishers and the Trustees of Amherst College from THE POEMS OF EMILY DICKINSON, edited by Thomas H. Johnson, Cambridge, Mass.: The Belknap Press of Harvard University Press, Copyright 1951, © 1955, 1979, 1983 by the President and Fellows of Harvard College.

ELIOT, GEORGE   "Brother and Sister." From THE LEGEND OF JUBAL AND OTHER POEMS. Boston: Osgood, 1874.

FAESSLER, SHIRLEY   "A Basket of Apples" by Shirley Faessler. From STORIES BY CA-NADIAN WOMEN, Rosemary Sullivan, editor. Toronto: Oxford University Press, 1984. Copyright © 1969 by Shirley Faessler. Reprinted by permission of McIntosh and Otis, Inc.

FIAMENGO, MARYA   "In Praise of Old Women." From IN PRAISE OF OLD WOMEN by Marya Fiamengo. Copyright © 1976 by Marya Fiamengo, Mosaic Press, P.O. Box 1032, Oakville, Ontario, Canada L6J 5E9.

FRASER, KATHLEEN   "Poem in Which My Legs Are Accepted." From WHAT I WANT, New York: Harper & Row, 1966. Reprinted by permission of Kathleen Fraser.

FREEMAN, MARY WILKINS   "A Village Singer." From GREAT AMERICAN SHORT STO-RIES, Wallace and Mary Stegner, editors. New York: Dell Publishing Company, Inc.

GERSTENBERG, ALICE   OVERTONES Copyright © 1941 by Alice Gerstenberg. Copyright renewed 1941 by Alice Gerstenberg. CAUTION: Professionals and amateurs are hereby warned that OVERTONES is fully protected by the laws of copyright. All rights, including professional, amateur, motion picture, recitation, public reading, radio, cable, video, and television are strictly reserved; for all rights contact Baker's Plays, 100 Chauncy Street, Boston MA 02111.

GILMAN, CHARLOTTE PERKINS   "Turned." First published in THE FORERUNNER, 1911. Also published in THE OTHER WOMAN: STORIES OF TWO WOMEN AND A MAN, Susan Koppelman, editor. Old Westbury NY: The Feminist Press, 1981.

GIOVANNI, NIKKI   "Nikki-Rosa." From BLACK FEELING BLACK TALK BLACK JUDGE-MENT. Detroit MI: Broadside Press, 1973. Reprinted by permission of Broadside Press.

GLASPELL, SUSAN   "Trifles." From PLAYS by Susan Glaspell. New York: Dodd, Mead, & Company, 1920.

GRAHN, JUDY   "II. Ella." Copyright © by Judy Grahn from THE WORK OF A COMMON WOMAN, 1985, The Crossing Press, Freedom, California 95019.

HAHN, KIMIKO   "Dance Instructions for a Young Girl." From COLUMBIA: A MAGAZINE OF POETRY AND PROSE and published in BREAKING SILENCE: AN ANTHOL-OGY OF CONTEMPORARY ASIAN AMERICAN POETS. Reprinted by permission of Kimiko Hahn.

HALLEY, ANNE   "Housewife's Letter: To Mary." Reprinted from BETWEEN WARS AND OTHER POEMS by Anne Halley (Amherst: University of Massachusetts Press, 1968), Copyright © 1968 by Anne Halley. Reprinted by permission.

HAYES, CATHERINE   Act II, "Not Waving." Reprinted by permission of Faber and Faber Ltd. from NOT WAVING by Catherine Hayes.

HOCHMAN, SANDRA   "Postscript." From EARTHWORKS by Sandra Hochman. Copyright © 1969 by Sandra Hochman. Reprinted by permission of Viking Penguin Inc.

HULL, HELEN ROSE   "The Fire." First published in CENTURY, 1917. Reprinted in THE LADDER and LESBIANS HOME JOURNAL: STORIES FROM THE LADDER, B. Grier and C. Rief, editors. Diana Press, 1976.

HUNTER, KRISTIN   "Debut." From Negro Digest, June 1968. Copyright © 1968 by Kristin Hunter. Reprinted by permission of Don Congdon Associates, Inc.

HURSTON, ZORA NEALE   "Sweat" is in the public domain.

JACKSON, SHIRLEY   "Island." From COME ALONG WITH ME by Shirley Jackson. Copyright © 1960 by Shirley Jackson. Reprinted by permission of Viking Penguin Inc.

JEWETT, SARAH ORNE   "Tom's Husband." First published in THE MATE OF THE DAY-LIGHT, AND FRIENDS ASHORE, 1884. Reprinted in WOMEN WORKING: AN ANTHOLOGY OF STORIES AND POEMS, Nancy Hoffman and Florence Howe, editors. Old Westbury NY: The Feminist Press, 1979.

JEWETT, SARAH ORNE   "The Town Poor." First published in STRANGERS AND WAY-
FARERS. New York: Houghton, 1980.

KAUFMAN, SHIRLEY   "Apples." From GOLD COUNTRY by Shirley Kaufman. Pittsburgh:
University of Pittsburgh Press, 1973. Copyright © 1973 by Shirley Kaufman.
Reprinted by permission of the University of Pittsburgh Press.

KIZER, CAROLYN   "Pro Femina" Part III. From MERMAIDS IN THE BASEMENT by Carolyn Kizer. Port Townsend WA: Copper Canyon Press, 1963. Copyright © 1963
by Copper Canyon Press. Reprinted by permission.

LAURENCE, MARGARET   From THE STONE ANGEL (Chapter 10, pp. 282–308) by Margaret Laurence. Reprinted by permission of Alfred A. Knopf, Inc.

LESSING, DORIS   "One Off the Short List." From A MAN AND TWO WOMEN by Doris
Lessing. Copyright © 1958, 1962, 1963 by Doris Lessing. Reprinted by permission of SIMON & SCHUSTER, INC.

LEVERTOV, DENISE   "About Marriage." Denise Levertov, O TASTE AND SEE. Copyright
© 1963 by Denise Goodman. First published in *Poetry*. Reprinted by permission
of New Directions Publishing Corporation.

LIM, GENNY   "Wonder Woman." From THIS BRIDGE CALLED MY BACK, Persephone,
1981.

LORDE, AUDRE   "The Woman Thing" is reprinted from CHOSEN POEMS, OLD AND
NEW, by Audre Lorde, by permission of W.W. Norton & Company, Inc. Copyright © 1982, 1976, 1974, 1973, 1970, 1968 by Audre Lorde.

MANSFIELD, KATHERINE   "Miss Brill." Copyright © 1922 by Alfred A. Knopf, Inc. and renewed 1950 by John Middleton Murry. Reprinted from THE SHORT STORIES
OF KATHERINE MANSFIELD by permission of Alfred A. Knopf, Inc.

MARSHALL, JOYCE   "So Many Have Died." First published in TAMARACK REVIEW,
1974. Reprinted in A PRIVATE PLACE, Oberon Press, 1975. Reprinted by permission of Joyce Marshall.

McCULLERS, CARSON   Wunderkind." From THE BALLAD OF THE SAD CAFE AND COL-
LECTED SHORT STORIES by Carson McCullers. Copyright © 1936, 1941,
1942, 1950, 1955 by Carson McCullers. Copyright © renewed by Floria V.
Lasky. Reprinted by permission of Houghton Mifflin Company.

McELROY, COLLEEN J.   "Defining It for Vanessa." From WINTERS WITHOUT SNOW by
Colleen J. McElroy. Berkeley CA: I. Reed Books, Co., 1979. Reprinted by permission of Colleen J. McElroy.

McGINLEY, PHYLLIS   "The 5:32." From TIMES THREE by Phyllis McGinley. Copyright
© 1969 by Julie Elizabeth Hayden and Phyllis Hayden Blake. Originally published in *The New Yorker*. Reprinted by permission of Viking Penguin Inc.

MERIWETHER, LOUISE   "A Happening in Barbados." From THE ANTIOCH REVIEW,
1968. Reprinted in THE OTHER WOMAN: STORIES OF TWO WOMEN AND A
MAN, Susan Koppelman, editor. Old Westbury NY: The Feminist Press, 1981.
Reprinted by permission of the author.

MILLAY, EDNA ST. VINCENT   "Conscientious Objector." From COLLECTED POEMS,
Harper & Row. Copyright © 1923, 1934, 1951, 1962 by Edna St. Vincent Millay
and Norma Millay Ellis. Reprinted by permission.

MIRIKITANI, JANICE   "Breaking Tradition" © copyright by Janice Mirikitani. Reprinted
by permission of the author.

MOLINARO, URSULE   "Breakfast Past Noon" by Ursule Molinaro from NEW WOMAN'S
THEATER, Vintage, May 1977. Copyright © 1968 by AMS Press, Inc. Reprinted
by permission of the author.

MOORE, HONOR   Margaret's last speech from *Mourning Pictures* by Honor Moore, from
THE NEW WOMEN'S THEATER, New York: Vintage Books, a division of Random House, 1977. Copyright © 1975 by Honor Moore. Reprinted by permission
of The Julian Bach Literary Agency, Inc.

MOORE, MARIANNE   "Nevertheless." Reprinted with permission of Macmillan Publishing
Company from COLLECTED POEMS by Marianne Moore. Copyright © 1944 and
1972 by Marianne Moore.

MURRAY, PAULI   "Ruth." Reprinted from DARK TESTAMENT AND OTHER POEMS.
Norwalk CT: Silvermine Publishers, 1970.

NELSON, ALICE DUNBAR   "I Sit and Sew" is in the public domain.

OATES, JOYCE CAROL   "Where Are You Going, Where Have You Been?" Reprinted from THE WHEEL OF LOVE by Joyce Carol Oates by permission of the publisher, Vanguard Press, Inc. Copyright © 1970, 1969, 1968, 1967, 1966, 1965 by Joyce Carol Oates.

O'CONNOR, FLANNERY   "Good Country People." From A GOOD MAN IS HARD TO FIND AND OTHER STORIES, copyright © 1955 by Flannery O'Connor; renewed 1983 by Regina O'Connor. Reprinted by permission of Harcourt Brace Jovanovich, Inc.

OLSEN, TILLIE   "I Stand Here Ironing" excerpted from the book TELL ME A RIDDLE by Tillie Olsen. Copyright © 1956 by Tillie Olsen. Reprinted by permission of DELACORTE PRESS/SEYMOUR LAWRENCE.

PAGE, P.K.   "Typists." Copyright © 1943, P.K. Page. Reprinted by permission of the author.

PALEY, GRACE   "The Loudest Voice." From THE LITTLE DISTURBANCES OF MAN. Garden City NY: Doubleday, 1959. Reprinted by permission of the Elaine Markson Literary Agency, Inc.

PARASKE, LARIN   "A Woman Soon Grows Old." From THE PENGUIN BOOK OF WOMEN POETS, Carol Cosman, Joan Keefe, and Kathleen Weaver, editors. New York: Penguin Books, 1979. English translation reprinted by permission of Jaakko A. Ahokas.

PARKER, DOROTHY   "Indian Summer." From THE PORTABLE DOROTHY PARKER. Copyright 1926, renewed by Dorothy Parker. Reprinted by permission of Viking Penguin Inc.

PIERCY, MARGE   "The Woman in the Ordinary." From CIRCLES ON THE WATER by Marge Piercy. Copyright © 1969, 1971, 1973 by Marge Piercy. Reprinted by permission of Alfred A. Knopf, Inc.

PIERCY, MARGE   "To Be of Use." Copyright © 1972 by Marge Piercy. Reprinted from CIRCLES ON THE WATER by Marge Piercy, by permission of Alfred A. Knopf, Inc.

PLATH, SYLVIA   "The Applicant" from THE COLLECTED POEMS OF SYLVIA PLATH, edited by Ted Hughes. Copyright © 1963 by Ted Hughes. Reprinted by permission of Harper & Row, Publishers, Inc.

PORTER, KATHERINE ANNE   "The Jilting of Granny Weatherall." From FLOWERING JUDAS AND OTHER STORIES, copyright 1930, 1958 by Katherine Anne Porter. Reprinted by permission of Harcourt Brace Jovanovich, Inc.

RICH, ADRIENNE   "Living in Sin" is reprinted from THE FACT OF A DOORFRAME, POEMS SELECTED AND NEW, 1950–1984, by Adrienne Rich, by permission of W.W. Norton & Company, Inc. Copyright © 1984 by Adrienne Rich. Copyright © 1975, 1978 by W.W. Norton & Company, Inc. Copyright © 1981 by Adrienne Rich.

RICHARDSON, DOROTHY   "Death." From PILGRIMAGE (1915–1938). Reprinted by Virago Press, 1979, with an introduction by Gillian E. Hanscombe.

ROSSETTI, CHRISTINA   "Monna Innominata" reprinted from THE POETICAL WORKS OF CHRISTINA ROSSETTI, William Michael Rossetti, editor, 1904.

SAFFARAZADEH, TAHEREH   "Birthplace." First published in REVERBERATIONS IN THE DELTA about 1973. From WOMEN POETS OF THE WORLD, Joanna Bankier and Dierdre Lashgari, editors. New York: Macmillan, 1983. Translated from the Farsi by Dierdre Lashgari. Reprinted by permission from Dierdre Lashgari.

SAPPHO   "Here Are Fine Gifts, Children. . . ." Reprinted by permission of Schocken Books, Inc. from GREEK LYRIC POETRY, translated by Willis Barnstone. Copyright © 1962, 1967 by Willis Barnstone.

SARTON, MAY   Excerpt from "Mrs. Stevens Hears the Mermaids Singing." Reprinted from MRS. STEVENS HEARS THE MERMAIDS SINGING by May Sarton, by permission of W.W. Norton, Inc. Copyright © 1965 by May Sarton.

SELLERS, BETTIE   "In the Counselor's Waiting Room." From MORNING OF THE RED-TAILED HAWK, Green River Press, December 1981. Reprinted with permission from Bettie M. Sellers and Green River Press.

SEXTON, ANNE "Young." From ALL MY PRETTY ONES by Anne Sexton. Copyright © 1962 by Anne Sexton. Reprinted by permission of Houghton Mifflin Company.

SILVIERA DE QUEIROZ, DINAH "Guidance." From MODERN BRAZILIAN SHORT STORIES, William Grossman, translator, pp. 100–106. Copyright © 1967 by The Regents of the University of California. Reprinted by permission.

SPEYER, LEONORA "The Ladder." From NAKED HEEL by Leonora Speyer. Copyright © 1931 by Leonora Speyer and renewed 1959 by Countess Daniela Moy and Mrs. Leonora Speyer, Jr. Reprinted by permission of Alfred A. Knopf, Inc.

STEIN, GERTRUDE "Miss Furr and Miss Skeene." Copyright 1922 by The Four Seasons Co., Boston. Reprinted from SELECTED WRITINGS OF GERTRUDE STEIN, by permission of Random House, Inc.

SWENSON, MAY THE CENTAUR by May Swenson is reprinted by permission of the author. Copyright © 1956, renewed copyright 1985 by May Swenson.

TEPPERMAN, JEAN "Witch." From WOMEN: A JOURNAL OF LIBERATION, 1969. Reprinted by permission of the author.

WALKER, ALICE "Everyday Use." Copyright © 1973 by Alice Walker. Reprinted from her volume IN LOVE & TROUBLE by permission of Harcourt Brace Jovanovich, Inc.

WELTY, EUDORA "A Worn Path." From A CURTAIN OF GREEN AND OTHER STORIES, copyright 1941, 1969 by Eudora Welty. Reprinted by permission of Harcourt Brace Jovanovich, Inc.

WEST, JESSAMYN "I Twelve: Fall" ("A Child's Day"). From CRESS DELAHANTY, copyright © 1953 by Jessamyn West. Reprinted by permission of Harcourt Brace Jovanovich, Inc.

WHITMAN, RUTH "Castoff Skin" by Ruth Whitman from THE PASSION OF LIZZIE BORDEN. Copyright © 1973 by Ruth Whitman. Reprinted by permission of October House, Stonington, Connecticut.

WILLIAMS, SHERLEY "Say Hello to John." Copyright © 1975 by Sherley Williams. Reprinted from THE PEACOCK POEMS by permission of Wesleyan University Press.

WOOLF, VIRGINIA "The New Dress." From A HAUNTED HOUSE AND OTHER SHORT STORIES by Virginia Woolf, copyright 1944, 1972 by Harcourt Brace Jovanovich, Inc. Reprinted by permission of the publisher.

YEZIERSKA, ANZIA "America and I." From CHILDREN OF LONELINESS, 1923. Reprinted in WOMEN WORKING: AN ANTHOLOGY OF STORIES AND POEMS, Nancy Hoffman and Florence Howe, editors. Old Westbury NY: The Feminist Press, 1979. Reprinted here by permission of Louise Levitas Henricksen.

INDEXES

Author Index

Title Index

Indexes